Oana Maria Popescu

INTEGRATIVE STRATEGIC PSYCHOTHERAPY

VOLUME 1

THEORETICAL FOUNDATIONS

LETRAS
Promovăm autorii români

CIP description of the National Library of Romania
POPESCU, OANA MARIA
Integrative strategic psychotherapy /
Oana Maria Popescu – Otopeni: Letras, 2026
6 vol.
ISBN 978-630-312-631-9
Vol. 1: Theoretical foundations - 2026 -
ISBN 978-630-312-632-6

159.9
615

Print on Demand Edition, Amazon

ISBN eBook ePUB: 978-630-312-596-1

Book distributed by www.piatadecarte.net
email: office@piatadecarte.com.ro
Orders by phone: 0748 126 309 // 0787 708 844

For publication requests, you can contact the publishing house
by email: edituraletras@piatadecarte.com.ro

Letras Publishing House / www.letras.ro
contact@letras.ro

Contents

PREFACE

The *Integrative Strategic Psychotherapy* series was conceived as both a comprehensive training manual and a continuing professional resource for psychotherapists at all stages of development. Across its six volumes, the series aims to accompany the reader through the evolving landscape of integrative and evidence-informed psychotherapy, blending theoretical depth with clinical practicality.

The series provides a structured and coherent learning path for students and supervisees who wish to understand and apply the Integrative Strategic Psychotherapy (ISP) model in their practice. At the same time, it serves as a reference and reflective resource for experienced psychotherapists seeking to deepen their understanding of integration, refine their technique, and ground their clinical decisions in a theoretically unified framework.

Each volume addresses a distinct aspect of the model—from its theoretical and philosophical foundations, to assessment, formulation, and intervention strategies, to its application in specific clinical areas. Together, the volumes form a cohesive body of knowledge that bridges neuroscience, developmental psychology, and the relational traditions of psychotherapy.

The ISP model integrates multiple dimensions of human functioning: biological, psychological, and relational levels intersect with cognitive, emotional, and psychodynamic axes. At its centre lies the conception of the self as a dynamic and evolving structure, encompassing the proto, core, plastic, and external domains. This framework allows for a flexible yet disciplined approach to therapeutic understanding and intervention—one that honours both the complexity of the human psyche and the uniqueness of each client's story.

The intention is not only to teach a model, but to cultivate an integrative mindset—one that values creativity, critical thinking, and relational authenticity as much as technical skill. Whether used as a training manual, a supervision companion, or a source of inspiration for ongoing clinical reflection, the *Integrative Strategic Psychotherapy* series invites psychotherapists to engage in a process of lifelong integration: between theory and practice, self and other, science and art.

– The Author

CHAPTER 1

HISTORY OF INTEGRATIVE PSYCHOTHERAPY

1.1 What Is Psychotherapy

As a young university student, I vividly remember persistently asking my psychiatry professor, “But what do I actually say to a person with schizophrenia?” At the time, I didn’t yet realise that what I was really asking was a much deeper and broader question: *What is psychotherapy?* Although I never received a particularly satisfying answer, something inside me remained convinced that my path lay in working with people through words.

When I shared my career intentions with my father, he reacted with caution, even fear. He warned me of the dangers of entering the psychotherapy profession, describing it as a risky field in which therapists might be psychologically overwhelmed—or even harmed—by their patients. At the time, the media was abuzz with a macabre story of a cannibalistic psychiatric patient who had literally eaten his psychiatrist. While this may seem extreme, it symbolised a deeper concern: that psychotherapy is not merely a job, but a profound and at times perilous encounter with human suffering.

Despite those warnings, I have spent decades working with patients, sitting with their pain, listening to their stories, and continuously returning to that same question: *What is psychotherapy, really?* Even now, after more than thirty years of clinical experience, I still find myself pausing when my aunt casually asks, “What do you actually do in your office?” I sometimes struggle to give a clear answer. What *do* I say to my patients?

I’ve discovered that this question isn’t unique to relatives at family dinners. It often comes from psychotherapy trainees, clients, and curious friends alike. And rightly so—psychotherapy is difficult to define in a few simple words. It is, at once, a science and an art, a discipline and a mystery. It is a learned craft, yet often feels like something that can only be "stolen" by observing, by being present, by absorbing through intuition rather than manuals.

Over the years, psychotherapy has been described in countless ways. Some see it as a scientifically based professional activity (Senf & Broda, 2005), others as a unique relational encounter between two human beings (Hough, 2010). It has also been defined as an interdisciplinary domain that bridges medicine and psychology (European Association of Psychotherapy, 2011), and as a structured process for resolving emotional or psychological difficulties (Sutton & Stewart, 2008). But perhaps the most meaningful definition I've heard came from a student, who once said: *"Psychotherapy is a way of talking where you use logic, empathy, and every skill you've developed—after understanding how the human mind works—to help your client see the world differently."*

Another student, attending his very first psychotherapy workshop, likened it to science fiction. He observed a psychotherapist working with a client and said, *"It was like the psychotherapist had telepathic powers. They just knew what was going on inside the client—how is that even possible?"* Months later, that same student would chuckle and admit, *"Back then, I didn't understand a thing about psychotherapy."*

Many beginner psychotherapists yearn for structure—for a set of universal techniques they can apply to specific symptoms. I am often asked questions such as: *"If my client has depression and their partner doesn't support them, what should I do?"* My honest answer—one that always surprises them—is: *"I have no idea."* But this is not helplessness; it is truth. I do not know what to do until I understand *everything*—the details, the unspoken meanings, the emotional logic, the relational history. That's what psychotherapy is: a process of *knowing* through listening.

But listening is harder than it seems. Active listening is not merely nodding along or remembering what the client said. It means listening with all your attention—while silencing your own internal dialogue. It requires holding space without mentally drafting your next intervention. It demands that you follow the client's logic rather than your own assumptions. For many trainees, this is a difficult skill to master. In their eagerness to "help," they often focus too much on what to *do* next, and not enough on what to *understand* in the moment.

Psychotherapy is, in many ways, like mathematics. There is a logic to it—an internal coherence in the client's narrative that reveals itself when you listen carefully. I often find that when I am truly attuned to what a client says (and doesn't say), I can identify contradictions, distortions, or unexamined beliefs that shape their suffering. From these patterns, questions arise—precise, strategic, and sometimes transformative. But this process depends on having a conceptual framework, a map of the human psyche that can hold the complexity of emotions, cognition, and relational dynamics.

Yet even the most brilliant framework will fail if it is not grounded in a solid therapeutic relationship. No technique or intervention can compensate for a broken alliance. Psychotherapy is not a one-way application of tools—it is a shared journey that only works when the client feels supported, understood, and never abandoned. This alliance is essential regardless of modality—whether one practices psychodynamic therapy, CBT, humanistic therapy, or integrative psychotherapy.

In fact, one of the biggest mistakes beginner psychotherapists make is rushing the change process. Once they grasp the structure of the client's difficulties, they often feel compelled to start "fixing." But in psychotherapy, the pace is not ours to set. The client determines the rhythm of change. And often, problems persist for good reason. If someone is unable to move forward, it's usually not because they are stubborn or lazy—it's because there are unconscious blocks, unresolved pain, or core beliefs that are so deeply rooted they feel like absolute truths.

So—what is psychotherapy?

According to the Romanian Federation of Psychotherapy (2019), psychotherapy is *"a comprehensive, intentional, and systematic approach to addressing behavioural, emotional, cognitive, psychosomatic, and psychosocial issues, or states of psychological distress, using scientific therapeutic methods. This process involves interaction between one or more clients and one or more psychotherapists, with the aim of alleviating disruptive patterns and fostering psychological change, growth, development, and well-being."*

The European Association for Psychotherapy (EAP, 2003) goes further, defining psychotherapy as *"an interdisciplinary field that bridges medicine and psychology. It is a deliberate, structured, and holistic treatment method based on scientific methodologies, supported by a theoretical and clinical foundation, aimed at alleviating symptoms, mental disorders, psychosocial and/or psychosomatic suffering, and maladaptive behaviours."*

The International Association for Integrative Psychotherapy views the psychotherapist as *"a professional providing psychotherapy and mental health services, including the application of integrative psychotherapy theories and techniques to prevent and alleviate mental and emotional disorders and psychopathology, while promoting optimal mental health, rehabilitation, and growth."*

In simpler terms, a psychotherapist is someone who knows how to listen—not just with their ears, but with their mind and heart. They must understand at least one psychotherapeutic model deeply enough to help clients explore what lies beneath the surface. Because most of the time, the true problem is not immediately visible. It lives in the unconscious. Clients do not understand why they keep sabotaging themselves, why they procrastinate, or why they choose partners who hurt them. If they *could* understand—and change—on their own, they would. No one chooses to suffer.

But suffering often serves a hidden purpose. It may protect against unbearable feelings, reinforce a familiar identity, or preserve a connection to someone long gone. Our job as psychotherapists is to carefully uncover these unconscious mechanisms, bring them into awareness, and help the client find new, healthier ways of being.

Psychotherapy can be individual, couple, family, or group-based. It can be offered to children, adolescents, adults, and the elderly. And while theoretical approaches vary—psychodynamic, cognitive-behavioural, existential, systemic—the common goal remains: to help people live more conscious, coherent, and fulfilling lives. Psychotherapy helps clients understand what they value, harness their inner strengths, explore their feelings, reflect on past experiences, and face life's difficulties with greater clarity and resilience (Sutton & Stewart, 2008).

And sometimes, the most powerful change comes simply from being heard. Words—when chosen with care—can change lives. The human brain is shaped by language. The stories we tell ourselves, the names we give to our emotions, the interpretations we adopt—all these become neural pathways. For example, if as a child I was told repeatedly that I am "too sensitive," my brain would build that story into its architecture. When faced with criticism, I might cry—not because I'm weak, but because that's the most deeply ingrained response.

In psychotherapy, we use language to build new neural maps. We help clients see things differently, respond differently, and ultimately *feel* differently. This is not metaphorical—it is biological. Psychotherapy, then, is not only a conversation. It is a relational, cognitive, and emotional experience that rewires the brain.

It is also, still, a mystery. A place where science meets soul, and logic meets empathy. Where we don't always have answers, but we sit with the questions—together.

1.2. Approaches and Models in Psychotherapy

Modern psychotherapy, as we know it today, traces its roots back to Sigmund Freud (1856–1939), the founder of psychoanalysis and the pioneer of the first structured psychotherapeutic movement (Erskine & Moursund, 2011). In collaboration with Joseph Breuer on the treatment of hysteria, Freud developed a novel clinical approach that one of their patients famously termed the *"talking cure"* (Freud, 1910). This simple yet profound phrase captured a revolutionary idea: that healing could be achieved through conversation—through words rather than physical intervention.

Central to Freud's legacy is the concept of the unconscious mind, a notion that remains one of the most influential and enduring in the field of psychotherapy (Hamlyn, 2007). Freud's ideas gave rise to a multitude of theoretical evolutions. Carl Jung, Alfred Adler, Otto Rank, Wilhelm Reich, and Sándor Ferenczi each took psychoanalysis in new directions, developing their own psychodynamic models and laying the foundation for the diverse schools of depth psychology that followed.

Psychodynamic therapy remains focused on uncovering unconscious conflicts and working through them in the therapeutic relationship. Techniques such as free association, dream analysis, exploration of resistance, transference and countertransference, and the processing of painful memories continue to define this orientation. The emphasis is placed not just on what is said, but on how, when, and why it is said—and what remains unspoken.

Though many of Freud's original concepts have been critiqued or evolved significantly, it's important to recognise the revolutionary nature of his ideas at the time. In the 19th and early 20th centuries, the suggestion that psychological distress could be alleviated through speech was nothing short of radical. Today, research in neuroscience and affective science continues to validate Freud's central intuition: that much of mental life occurs outside of conscious awareness, and that emotions play a foundational role in structuring thought and behaviour (Fonagy, 2017). In fact, a 2011 review by the American Psychological Association confirmed that psychodynamic therapy is an empirically supported treatment, comparable in efficacy to more structured approaches.

By the mid-20th century, however, a number of psychotherapists working within the psychodynamic tradition began to grow dissatisfied with the limitations of classical psychoanalysis. Out of this dissatisfaction, new schools emerged—most notably, behaviourism. Though it remains uncertain whether Hans Eysenck or Arnold Lazarus first coined the term *"behaviour therapy"* (Hamlyn, 2007), what is clear is that behaviourism rose rapidly to prominence in the 1960s. It positioned itself as a more empirically verifiable and efficient alternative to psychoanalysis (Hawkins & Nestoros, 1997), with an emphasis on observable behaviours and measurable outcomes.

Soon, behaviourism gave rise to cognitive-behavioural therapy (CBT), a framework that maintained the empirical rigour of behaviourism while introducing the concept of cognition. Unlike traditional behaviourism, which rejected the study of mental processes as speculative, CBT accepted that beliefs, interpretations, and internal narratives play a crucial role in human experience. Aaron T. Beck, often regarded as the "father" of CBT, showed that many psychological difficulties are rooted not in unconscious forces, but in *automatic thoughts*—beliefs and assumptions that are often just beneath awareness but still accessible (Popescu, 2021; Popescu & Vîșcu, 2016).

Over time, CBT evolved to incorporate a rich array of techniques and sub-approaches. Rational-emotive behaviour therapy (REBT), acceptance and commitment therapy (ACT), dialectical behaviour therapy (DBT), EMDR, cognitive processing therapy, multimodal therapy, and reality therapy are just a few examples of how the cognitive-behavioural tradition has expanded and diversified.

The rapid expansion of CBT sparked a parallel reaction from other psychotherapists—one that led to the rise of the third major orientation in psychotherapy: the humanistic-existential approach. Emerging strongly in the 1940s and 1950s, this movement prioritised the whole person over symptoms or diagnoses. Carl Rogers' person-centred therapy, Fritz Perls' gestalt therapy, Eric Berne's transactional analysis, Viktor Frankl's logotherapy, and J. L. Moreno's psychodrama all emerged from this fertile intellectual soil.

What these approaches share is a commitment to the autonomy, dignity, and potential of the individual. Humanistic approaches aim to free people from limiting beliefs and internalised conditions of worth, using primarily conscious processes. Existential approaches, on the other hand, delve into questions of meaning, mortality, freedom, and isolation. They seek to help individuals confront the existential givens of human life and to create meaningful lives despite uncertainty.

Thus, by the latter half of the 20th century, three primary paradigms had come to dominate psychotherapy: 1. Psychodynamic approaches, which explored unconscious conflicts and symbolic meanings; 2. Behavioural and cognitive-behavioural approaches, which focused on learned responses and thought patterns; and 3. Humanistic-existential approaches, which emphasized agency, presence, and meaning-making (Hawkins & Nestoros, 1997).

But as these paradigms matured, something curious happened. None of them proved sufficient on their own to explain the full complexity of the human psyche. Each offered valuable insights, yet each was also partial. As Fall, Holden, and Marquis (2010) aptly noted, no single model has succeeded in capturing the full breadth of human psychological functioning.

I sometimes compare psychotherapy to a scene from a science fiction novel I read as a teenager. In the book, aliens leave behind a collection of highly sophisticated devices on Earth. Humans, unable to understand their true function, repurpose them for mundane uses. Someone picks up a microscope and uses it to hammer in nails. It works—but it's not what the tool was designed for. Sometimes, I wonder if we're doing the same with psychotherapy: using brilliant tools in ways that only vaguely resemble their intended purpose. Are we truly understanding the human mind—or are we wielding microscopes as hammers? (Popescu & Vîşcu, 2016).

One of the core challenges in our field is the lack of a unified theory. Years ago, I wrote that in 1991, the United States alone had 25,000 psychiatrists, 50,000 psychologists, and countless social workers engaged in psychotherapeutic work (Frank & Frank, 1991). By 2012, Wikipedia listed 167 different psychotherapeutic approaches. By the end of 2020, that number had risen to 182 (Popescu, 2021; Popescu & Vîşcu, 2016).

Some of these approaches are widely known; others are obscure, strange, or even controversial. "Attack therapy," a derivative of "ventilation therapy," involves group confrontation and verbal humiliation. "Chess therapy" uses the game of chess as a relational and projective tool. The "counting method," used in PTSD treatment, involves the therapist counting aloud while the client recalls traumatic memories. "Immobilisation therapy," based on attachment theory and used mainly with children, involves physically restraining the client to provoke catharsis—an approach now linked to several malpractice lawsuits and even fatalities (Gravelles, 2003).

This staggering diversity reflects both the richness of our field and the limits of our knowledge. Even now, potential clients frequently ask me whether I am a cognitive-behavioural psychotherapist or a psychoanalyst—believing that one method is inherently more effective. They've read articles online, perhaps watched a YouTube video, and developed strong opinions without understanding the techniques themselves. Ironically, most people—psychotherapists included—are unaware that specific techniques contribute less than 7% to the success of psychotherapy. It is the therapeutic relationship, the client's engagement, and the shared meaning-making process that matter most.

Despite this, many schools of psychotherapy continue to promote the illusion that they hold the "one true method." Techniques are taught as miracles; rival approaches are dismissed as superficial or pseudoscientific, depending on who's doing the judging.

Years ago (I'll let you guess how many...), I decided to train extensively across a variety of therapeutic orientations: integrative psychotherapy, clinical hypnosis, psychoanalysis, CBT, systemic therapy, gestalt therapy, psychodrama—you name it. I gained something valuable from each. But what saddened me was the hostility I witnessed between schools. In training groups, it was not uncommon to hear one method discredited, even ridiculed, by adherents of another. To avoid conflict, I learned not to mention that I had trained "across enemy lines."

Unfortunately, this tribalism hasn't disappeared. As recently as 2024, I've had workshop participants from other modalities arrive with the intention of correcting or confronting integrative models. Yet, by the end of the workshop, they often realise they already use elements of CBT, psychodynamic thinking, or systemic theory—just under different names. That's the beauty of integration: it honours complexity and welcomes plurality.

As Fall, Holden, and Marquis (2010) asked in their book "*Theoretical Models of Counselling and Psychotherapy*": *"Why isn't there one counselling theory that everyone agrees on?"* Their answer is elegant: psychotherapy is like a hologram. Each theoretical model reflects a different angle of the same whole. Each is true, and yet incomplete—because each captures only a fragment of the human experience.

It is important therefore not be a fanatic of certain techniques or ideas, which could lead to serious mistakes. Sometimes clients arrive at therapy after multiple previous attempts that left them feeling disillusioned or unsupported. However, the story of Miss D stands out (Popescu & Vîșcu, 2016). She had been struggling with recurring panic attacks and was actively seeking a solution. Following a psychiatric consultation, she was prescribed medication and advised to begin psychotherapy. Motivated and hopeful, she scheduled her first session with a cognitive-behavioural therapist—having read that CBT was considered the gold standard for treating panic attacks.

At her initial session, she carefully described her symptoms. The psychotherapist listened attentively, then explained the cognitive model of panic: the cycle of catastrophic thoughts, bodily sensations, and behavioural avoidance. He encouraged her to confront her fears at home, reminding her that *"it's all in your head."* Though Miss D intellectually understood this—she had read about it before—she felt overwhelmed and incapable of implementing the advice alone. Disheartened, she decided to try another psychotherapist.

Her second therapist practised transactional analysis. After listening to her story, this psychotherapist informed her that understanding the model would be essential for therapy. She began introducing the basic concepts of ego states, transactions, and life scripts—explaining that the next four sessions would be devoted to teaching the theoretical framework. Once again, Miss D found herself overwhelmed—not by the content this time, but by the cognitive load and lack of immediate emotional connection. She moved on, still believing psychotherapy could help, and considered trying psychoanalysis.

The psychoanalyst was kind and present, and Miss D felt heard in a different way. After several sessions, she asked, *"How long do you think this therapy will take?"* The psychotherapist peered over his glasses and replied, *"At least two years, of course."* The certainty with which this was stated—along with the long timeline—felt too daunting. She quietly withdrew once again.

Still determined, she gave cognitive therapy another try. But this time, the psychotherapist explained that the first three sessions would be spent conducting a structured clinical interview. Exhausted from repeatedly narrating her story to strangers, she left after just 15 minutes.

Yet Miss D still wasn't ready to give up. A friend recommended experiential therapy. She agreed to try again. After retelling her experience once more, the experiential therapist asked her to stand on a large white sheet of paper and inquired, *"How do you feel right now?" "Terrible,"* she replied honestly. The psychotherapist then invited her to stand on a yellow sheet and asked again, *"And now?" "Still terrible,"* she said. The psychotherapist nodded and reassured her, *"With repetition, you'll begin to feel differently."* She didn't return.

She tried one more experiential therapist. After her story, the psychotherapist posed a rather unusual question: *"If you were a fern, how would you feel?"* At that moment, overwhelmed and tearful, Miss D stood up and left.

Three weeks later, she returned to her psychiatrist, who referred her to our practice. Upon entering the room, her first words were filled with both desperation and humour: *"Please don't turn me into a fern!"*

(While this story is true, some identifying details have been altered to protect the client's confidentiality.)

1.3. Why Is Psychotherapy Effective

Over the past fifty years, psychotherapy research has increasingly pointed to the conclusion that psychotherapy is best understood as a clinical craft—one that includes elements that can be scientifically examined, but which also relies heavily on the psychotherapist's creativity, presence, and responsiveness (Joyce, Wolfaardt et al., 2006). Despite the emergence of over 400 distinct schools of psychotherapy throughout its evolution (Prochaska & Norcross, 1999), the mechanisms of therapeutic change appear to transcend rigid theoretical boundaries.

Historically, debates surrounding the effectiveness of psychotherapy have been both intense and polarizing. Hans Eysenck famously argued that, absent pharmacological intervention, psychotherapy was no more effective than the passage of time. However, meta-analyses conducted in subsequent decades have consistently shown that psychotherapy yields positive outcomes in approximately 80% of cases (Joyce, Wolfaardt et al., 2006).

Still, psychotherapy's legitimacy is sometimes questioned. As Nassralach (2013, p.18) notes, *"Despite its well-documented effectiveness for a multitude of neuropsychiatric disorders, psychotherapy has never managed to shake off the unwanted aura of being a medically illegitimate intervention."* For many, it remains a "talking cure"—a phrase that can elicit scepticism and ironic smiles, particularly when contrasted with biomedical treatments like medication or surgery.

This scepticism has real-world consequences. In many healthcare systems, psychotherapy is underfunded or insufficiently reimbursed, often being deprioritized in favour of pharmacological treatments. Yet neuroimaging studies provide compelling evidence for psychotherapy's efficacy: positron emission tomography has shown that psychotherapy induces measurable changes in brain function, often targeting the same regions affected by medication (Nassralach, 2013). The underlying processes—verbal and non-verbal communication, memory recall, emotional processing, insight, empathy, and catharsis—activate neuroplastic mechanisms, facilitating structural and functional changes in neural networks associated with thought, emotion, and behaviour.

The human brain is in a constant state of flux, creating new dendritic connections in response to lived experience. In this context, psychotherapy might be more accurately termed "neuro-psychotherapy," a process that reshapes the architecture of the brain through language and relational engagement.

Yet a persistent challenge remains: the fragmentation of the field. In 1980, there were roughly 250 psychotherapeutic approaches. By 1996, this had grown to 450, and by 2016, the number exceeded 200 regularly practiced modalities worldwide. This proliferation risks undermining psychotherapy's credibility, particularly when rivalries between orientations persist in the 21st century.

In 2013, Ofovwe posed a poignant question: *"Is it possible to reach a state of harmony, unity, or the 'I'm OK, You're OK' position proposed by transactional analysis? Can psychoanalysis, cognitive-behavioural therapy, client-centred therapy, psychodrama, logotherapy, etc., recognise their shared foundations despite their theoretical and methodological differences?"* (Ofovwe, 2013, p.137). The answer increasingly appears to be yes.

Blagys and Hilsenroth (2000) conducted a comparative study of psychodynamic and cognitive-behavioural psychotherapists and discovered that, while theoretical emphases differ, commonalities exist in clinical practice: 1. Psychodynamic psychotherapists focus on emotional exploration, interpersonal dynamics, transference and countertransference, historical patterns, and the therapeutic relationship itself; 2. CBT therapists emphasize skills acquisition, behavioural interventions, psychoeducation, and future-oriented thinking, often providing structured exercises between sessions; and 3. Both approaches, however, involve supportive engagement, goal setting, and encouragement—highlighting the overlapping behaviours of effective psychotherapists, regardless of orientation (Brown, 2015).

Indeed, successful psychotherapy seems less determined by the model used and more by the psychotherapist's capacity to engage and retain the client in the process of change (Sexton, Whiston, Bleuer, & Walz, 1997). Therapeutic transformation arises from a dynamic blend of relationship, method, expectancy, and ritual (Lin, 2016).

In 2009, Kazdin underscored the field's epistemological gap: *"After decades of research in psychotherapy, we still do not have an evidence-based explanation for how and why psychotherapeutic interventions lead to change"* (Kazdin, 2009, p. 426). While some modalities, particularly CBT, enjoy greater empirical support (largely due to the volume and structure of research), there is little robust evidence to suggest that one approach is universally superior to another (Wampold, 2001). Indeed, research by Luborsky et al. (2002) and Lundh (2014) has led to the formulation of the *"Dodo bird verdict":* all bona fide psychotherapies are roughly equivalent in outcome.

This has shifted attention toward common or non-specific factors as the active ingredients of effective psychotherapy. Some scholars argue that change mechanisms lie within these shared elements—such as therapeutic alliance, empathic atonement, and expectancy—while others propose that the methods themselves matter, but overlap in practice more than in theory (Lundh, 2014).

For example, the principle of exposure—commonly associated with behavioural therapies—also appears in paradoxical interventions, emotion-focused methods, and psychodynamic confrontation. Similarly, the processing of emotion, including identification, differentiation, and regulation, is now recognised as a core change mechanism across modalities (Hayes et al., 2005; Leahy, 2007).

As early as 1980, Goldfried observed that despite their theoretical distinctions, most psychotherapies share foundational mechanisms such as corrective emotional experiences and heightened awareness through feedback. Barlow (2004) later added that empirically supported treatments combine these common factors with disorder-specific interventions grounded in theory. For example, prolonged exposure for PTSD is based on emotional processing theory (Foa, Hembree, & Rothbaum, 2007), interpersonal therapy stems from attachment and interpersonal theory (Markowitz et al., 2009), and ACT and CBT are rooted in distinct philosophical traditions (Hayes, Strosahl, & Wilson, 2012).

Recent developments in transdiagnostic protocols further support this integrative view. Common symptoms across disorders have led to unified treatment models that often mirror the structure and content of common factors (Laska, Gurman, & Wampold, 2014).

According to Wampold (2001), the common factors model views psychotherapy as a socially constructed healing practice. Laska, Gurman, and Wampold (2014, p. 469) identify five key ingredients in all effective psychotherapies: 1. An emotionally attuned, collaborative bond between client and psychotherapist; 2. A healing context or ritualised setting; 3. A culturally valid explanatory model of distress; 4. An adaptive narrative accepted by the client; and 5. A set of structured, participatory procedures aimed at promoting change.

From this perspective, the psychotherapist's theoretical allegiance is but one contributor to outcome. More critical are the conditions for change, which transcend schools of thought. Furthermore, several core predictions of the common factors model have been empirically validated (Laska et al., 2014, p. 469): 1. Any therapy containing these five elements will likely be effective (Lambert, 2013); 2. Relational qualities such as empathy, collaboration, and acceptance are powerful predictors of outcome; 3. Therapist variability significantly influences success; and 4. Psychotherapy consistently outperforms placebo and supportive interventions.

In conclusion, while theoretical diversity in psychotherapy reflects the complexity of human suffering, the path to effective change may lie less in exclusive technique and more in shared humanity, clinical presence, and the artful application of science.

1.4. Common Factors in Psychotherapy

As early as 1936, Saul Rosenzweig observed that all forms of psychotherapy seemed to produce beneficial outcomes, coining the term "Dodo bird verdict" from *Alice in Wonderland*: *"Everyone has won, and all must have prizes"* (Greencavage & Norcross, 1990). This insight suggests that, despite their theoretical differences, psychotherapeutic approaches may not be as distinct in effectiveness as they appear. In 1980, Goldfried echoed this sentiment, stating, *"Given that practitioners from various orientations arrive at common psychotherapeutic strategies, it is likely that important phenomena are occurring—phenomena that have managed to survive the distortions caused by therapists' theoretical biases"* (p. 996).

Rosenzweig's 1936 article, *Some implicit common factors in diverse methods of psychotherapy*, laid the foundation for the common factors approach as we know it today. He highlighted the importance of instilling hope, offering a new interpretive framework, and providing meaningful therapeutic engagement. His ideas were further disseminated at the 1940 American Orthopsychiatric Association conference, where Carl Rogers also introduced key elements for child psychotherapy, emphasizing relational and humanistic components (Sparks, Duncan, & Miller, 2006). In the following years, other theorists expanded the concept: Alexander and French (1946) underscored the "corrective emotional experience," while Fiedler (1950) focused on the therapeutic relationship.

By 1953, Heine formally proposed that all psychotherapeutic methods likely shared fundamental elements. In 1957, both Sol Garfield and Carl Rogers advanced this line of thinking. Garfield identified empathy, a strong therapeutic relationship, and client insight as core elements, while Rogers posited that the effectiveness of therapy lies less in techniques and more in the presence of empathy, congruence, and unconditional positive regard (Rogers, 2008).

Jerome Frank's *Persuasion and Healing* (1961) became the first major work dedicated to the common factors model. He identified core mechanisms of change across psychotherapies—placebo, hope, ritual, new perspectives on the self, and extra-therapeutic activities—as central to all psychotherapeutic success.

In the 1970s and 1980s, researchers like Truax, Mitchell, Shapiro, Garfield, Strupp, and Luborsky continued refining the common factors model. Appelbaum (1982) identified six necessary conditions for change: therapeutic explanation, relationship, client expectations, corrective experience, and altered states. By the 1990s, scholars began developing more formal frameworks for integrating these factors across modalities, culminating in Norcross and Goldfried's *Handbook of Psychotherapy Integration* (1992).

Three primary directions emerged for psychotherapy integration: the development of comprehensive theories, eclectic approaches, and the refinement of common factors (Arkowitz, 1989). Researchers sought to uncover mechanisms of change that transcend orientation-specific techniques. This led to a questioning of whether psychotherapists genuinely adhere to their schools' theoretical principles in practice (Locke, 1971; Castonguay & Goldfried, 1994).

Jorgensen (2004) identified four core questions that most psychotherapeutic models seek to answer: 1. What is the nature ofpsychopathology?; 2. What techniques are central to psychotherapy?; 3. How is therapeutic change defined and measured?; and 4. What are the active ingredients in psychotherapy?

Different schools offer distinct answers. Psychoanalysis views pathology as the result of intrapsychic conflict, emphasizing insight and ego strengthening. Cognitive approaches focus on core beliefs and schemas, aiming to change distorted thinking patterns. Yet these frameworks are themselves social constructs (Jorgensen, 2004).

Research shows considerable overlap among therapeutic orientations, particularly regarding the working alliance, client expectations, and corrective experiences (Castonguay, 2000). Although techniques may vary, outcomes tend to be similar across modalities (Assay & Lambert, 1999). Still, no single approach is effective for all problems, and combining common factors with modality-specific techniques often produces the best results (Garfield, 1992; Castonguay, 2000).

Goldfried (1980) outlined three meta-levels of psychotherapy: the theory of human functioning, the model of change, and the interventions. Agreement is rare at the theoretical level, but techniques and change processes share much in common. Both cognitive-behavioural and psychodynamic psychotherapists, for instance, aim to shift clients' self-perceptions (Castonguay et al., 1996).

It is important to note that a strong therapeutic alliance, while predictive of success, is not sufficient on its own. According to the APA (2013), outcomes often depend on relational and contextual variables rather than technique-specific differences. The Tolin (2010) meta-analysis found CBT marginally superior for depression and anxiety, but the majority of meta-analyses point to equivalence among psychotherapies (Laska, Gurman, & Wampold, 2014).

Specific interventions remain essential in certain cases—such as exposure for phobias—but the modality through which this occurs may vary (Antony & Roemer, 2011). Still, psychotherapist skill is a stronger predictor of outcomes than the therapeutic model itself (Zuroff et al., 2010). Around 5% of outcome variance is attributed to the psychotherapist, compared to just 1% from specific techniques (Baldwin & Imel, 2013).

In sum, the rise of common factors reflects a shift from allegiance to specific schools toward a broader understanding of what makes psychotherapy work. Research suggests that shared processes—relationship, empathy, belief change, emotional processing, and client engagement—account for most of psychotherapy's success (Lambert & Ogles, 2004; Lin, 2016). As early as the 1990s, scholars acknowledged the declining relevance of rigid school-based theories (Bergin & Garfield, 1994). Today, integrative and common factor models offer a more inclusive, client-centred framework for psychotherapy.

1.5. Models of Common Psychotherapeutic Factors

Lundh (2014) identifies two prevailing conceptual models that explain common factors in psychotherapy: the Relational–Procedural–Persuasion (RPP) model and the Methodological Principles and Skills (MPS) model.

The RPP model posits that psychotherapy rests on three foundational pillars: (1) establishing a strong therapeutic relationship—not as an end in itself, but as a necessary condition for change; (2) engaging the client in a structured psychotherapeutic procedure; and (3) persuading the client to adopt a new explanatory framework that fosters meaning and life reorientation. In this model, psychotherapeutic procedures are not assumed to be effective due to intrinsic qualities but rather because they provide the client with a "successful experience." The psychotherapist's task includes offering a compelling rationale that motivates the client to adopt this new framework and engage in the corresponding process (Lundh, 2014). In essence, this model emphasises the *form* of psychotherapy over its *content*, suggesting that outcomes depend more on procedural structure and therapeutic credibility than on any specific technique.

In contrast, the MPS model asserts that effective psychotherapy depends on core methodological principles, which are shared across psychotherapeutic orientations, even if they manifest differently. Moreover, competent psychotherapists are those who can flexibly apply these principles across various clinical scenarios (Lundh, 2014).

The conceptual foundation of the MPS model can be traced back to Goldfried (1980), who proposed a three-tiered hierarchy of psychotherapy comparison: 1. Theoretical models (high abstraction) – the frameworks used to conceptualize human functioning and change; 2. Methodological principles (intermediate abstraction) – foundational mechanisms such as establishing the working alliance or creating a corrective emotional experience; and 3. Specific techniques (low abstraction) – particular interventions aimed at implementing these principles in clinical practice.

According to Lundh (2014), virtually every psychotherapeutic approach involves three shared components, each rooted in a different tradition: 1. The provision of *new learning experiences* (central to psychodynamic approaches); 2. The *exposure principle* (derived from cognitive-behavioural therapy); and 3. An attitude of *empathic validation* (fundamental to humanistic and experiential approaches).

These elements represent integrative, trans-theoretical mechanisms that contribute to change across diverse psychotherapeutic frameworks.

1.6. The History of Integrative Psychotherapy

The emergence of integrative psychotherapy can be seen as a natural evolution in response to the proliferation and limitations of individual psychotherapeutic schools. Psychoanalysis arose as a humane alternative to the harsh psychiatric interventions of its time. Cognitive-behavioural therapy (CBT) followed with a focus on measurable mental processes and behaviour change. Humanistic-existential therapy sought to reconcile the introspective depth of psychoanalysis with the pragmatic structure of CBT. Amid this growing diversity, integrative psychotherapy was born—an approach designed to bring together the strengths of multiple modalities.

The earliest recorded attempt at integration is attributed to Thomas French in 1932, who explored connections between psychoanalysis and Pavlovian conditioning (Newman & Goldfried, 1996). Since then, integration has moved from being a speculative endeavour to a serious and evidence-informed practice.

One of the most compelling aspects of psychotherapy is that it appears to work across a wide array of theoretical orientations. Whether it's psychodynamic therapy, CBT, humanistic-existential methods, or family therapy, all seem to demonstrate clinical effectiveness. If a single theory offered a complete explanation for psychological change, this wouldn't be the case. This paradox has prompted many researchers to investigate what elements are shared across psychotherapeutic approaches.

In 1936, Saul Rosenzweig proposed that three common elements contribute to therapeutic success: the personality of the psychotherapist, the provision of an alternative perspective to the client, and the observation that transformation in one area of life often leads to change in others (Gilbert & Orlans, 2011). Using the now-famous metaphor from *Alice in Wonderland*, Rosenzweig likened the phenomenon to the "Dodo bird verdict": *"Everybody has won, and all must have prizes"* (Greencavage & Norcross, 1990). His landmark article, *Some Implicit Factors in Diverse Methods of Psychotherapy* (Rosenzweig, 1936), marked the beginning of the common factors paradigm.

Subsequent studies, especially those in the 1950s, reinforced the idea that psychotherapy's success relies more on shared mechanisms than on theoretical distinctions (Hawkins & Nestoros, 1997). By the late 20th century, the integrative movement had gained considerable traction. A pivotal moment came in 1992 when Norcross and Goldfried published a comprehensive model of integrative psychotherapy. Since then, the integrative framework has expanded along three key trajectories: developing unified theories, employing eclectic strategies, and investigating the common factors that underlie all effective psychotherapy (Arkowitz, 1989).

Importantly, integrative psychotherapy does not seek to replace existing models with a new, all-encompassing theory. Instead, it encourages a flexible, pluralistic stance—one that draws from various schools and techniques to best meet the needs of each individual client (Hawkins & Nestoros, 1997).

Over time, integrative psychotherapy has branched into several sub-approaches:

- Technical Eclecticism: This strategy involves selecting techniques based on their clinical utility, without necessarily subscribing to the theoretical assumptions behind them. While pragmatic, this approach may lack coherence between theory and practice (Norcross & Goldfried, 2005);
- Theoretical Integration: Here, different theories and methods are merged into a cohesive conceptual framework. The aim is to preserve the integrity of each component while generating a richer understanding of change mechanisms (Dafinoiu, 2000);
- The Common Factors Approach: This orientation focuses on identifying core elements—such as the therapeutic alliance, empathy, and client expectations—that are shared across modalities and appear crucial to successful outcomes; and
- Assimilative Integration: Practitioners grounded in one primary theory selectively incorporate methods and ideas from other orientations to enrich their work, all while maintaining theoretical consistency.

As a result of this evolution, integrative psychotherapy has become a recognised school of thought, spawning a range of distinct models. Among these are the assimilative model (e.g., Stricker & Gold, Castonguay, Newman), the common factors model (e.g., Frank & Frank; Wampold; Miller, Duncan, & Hubble; Gilbert & Orlans; Erskine & Moursund), the eclectic model (e.g., Lazarus; Beutler; Consoli & Lane; Norcross & Goldfried) and the theoretical integration model (e.g., Wachtel; Ryle; Prochaska & DiClemente).

Despite this rich development, integrative psychotherapy has not yet produced a single, unified theory capable of fully capturing the complexity of the human psyche. As Fall, Holden, and Marquis (2010) suggest, we may still be working with fragmented pieces of a much larger "hologram" of the human mind. Thus, while the first great debate in psychotherapy was about whether integration is possible, the next may well be about how best to conceptualise integration itself—not as a compromise, but as a rigorous, inclusive, and dynamic model of human change.

1.7. Contemporary Integrative Psychotherapy

In today's clinical landscape, most psychotherapeutic models—regardless of their theoretical lineage—share a number of foundational assumptions, albeit expressed in varied conceptual languages (Popescu, 2021; Popescu & Drobot, 2012; Popescu & Vîşcu, 2016). Among the most widely accepted are the following:

1. The human brain is a dynamic, self-organising system. At its core lies the "self," an integrative structure that offers continuity, self-reflection, and relational agency;
2. Present psychological functioning is shaped by past experiences, with both biological predispositions and environmental conditions playing pivotal roles;
3. Psychotherapy works because the brain is plastic. Neural pathways can be reshaped through experience, insight, and intentional effort;
4. Reality is not perceived directly but interpreted through individual mental frameworks;
5. Psychological challenges emerge and evolve within relational contexts—be it interpersonal, familial, or socio-cultural;
6. The therapeutic alliance is a central curative factor; and
7. People are meaning-making beings; psychotherapy is often a quest for narrative coherence and existential clarity.

Contemporary integrative psychotherapy seeks to synthesise these principles into a coherent and responsive framework. It is not about allegiance to a singular theory or technique but about weaving together elements from multiple approaches to best serve the client's unique psychological makeup. While clients rarely concern themselves with theoretical nuance, psychotherapists must rely on a structured internal map to inform their clinical decisions. Just as a physician cannot treat an illness without understanding its aetiology, a psychotherapist needs a conceptual framework to understand and intervene effectively.

Today, integrative psychotherapy is best understood as a meta-model—a flexible system that combines theoretical paradigms, clinical strategies, and therapeutic techniques across formats (individual, couple, family, group). The psychotherapist's personal history, worldview, training, and mentorship experiences inevitably shape how this integration unfolds (Halgin, 2006).

According to Norcross and Goldfried (2005), the evolution of a psychotherapist's integrative thinking typically follows three phases: a holistic perception of experience, deconstruction into components (which may temporarily fragment the whole), and eventual re-organisation into a higher-order synthesis. In other words, integration is not only theoretical—it is a developmental journey.

At present, no universally accepted unified theory exists that fully encompasses the entire spectrum of psychotherapeutic knowledge. Yet, given the 21st century's status as the "century of biology," significant advances in neuroscience and epigenetics are likely to reshape the field's foundational assumptions.

But despite the growing interest in integration, the psychotherapy field remains heavily fragmented, with over 400 recognised modalities. Some authors view integrative psychotherapy as a corrective to this fragmentation (O'Brien & Houston, 2009), yet others raise concerns about whether integration simply adds another layer of complexity. These tensions reflect ongoing debates about the nature of evidence, expertise, and the very definition of "effective" psychotherapy.

From the perspective of the author (Popescu, 2021; Popescu & Vîșcu, 2016), integrative psychotherapy is best described as a meta-theoretical and clinical model that encompasses a coherent theory of human functioning, a strategic clinical roadmap, and a diverse but principled set of interventions. It aims to transcend the limitations of any single school of thought and offers a flexible, multi-level understanding of therapeutic processes.

The International Association for Integrative Psychotherapy (2012) defines integrative psychotherapy as the dynamic integration of emotional, cognitive, behavioural, and physiological systems within a relational and transpersonal context. Similarly, Palmer and Wolfe (1999) describe it as a synthesis of theory and technique across modalities, aiming to provide holistic and client-centred care.

Building an integrative identity also involves a reflective and developmental process. Halgin (2006) identifies seven key elements in the construction of an integrative psychotherapist: 1. Personal history and life experience; 2. Influence of mentors; 3. Development of one's own therapeutic model; 4. Understanding of the main factors in therapeutic change; 5. Capacity to bridge research and clinical practice; 6. Ongoing professional development and supervision; and 7. Connection to professional communities and integrative associations

As O'Brien and Houston (2009) note, integrative psychotherapy must also involve clear assessment procedures, contracting, alliance-building, appropriate intervention, reflective practice, and ethical decision-making. These elements are not simply technical; they represent the values of the profession itself.

In conclusion, contemporary integrative psychotherapy is more than a method—it is a mindset. It embraces pluralism without losing coherence and seeks to address each client's individuality within a scientifically informed, relationally attuned, and ethically grounded practice. Drawing from psychodynamic, cognitive-behavioural, humanistic-existential, and neurobiological traditions, integrative psychotherapy represents a hopeful synthesis in an era of increasing complexity.

REFERENCES

American Psychological Association. (2013). *Recognition of psychotherapy effectiveness*. Resolution adopted by the APA Council of Representatives.

Anderson, T., Ogles, B. M., Patterson, C. L., Lambert, M. J., & Verweersch, L. (2009). Therapist effects: Facilitative interpersonal skills as a predictor of therapist success. *Journal of Clinical Psychology, 65*(7), 755–768.

Antony, M. M., & Roemer, L. (2011). *Behavioral and cognitive-behavioral approaches to anxiety disorders: Empirically supported interventions for panic disorder and phobias*. In S. G. Hofmann & D. J. A. Dozois (Eds.), *Cognitive behavioral therapy: Science and practice* (pp. 137–170). Routledge.

Antony, M. M., & Roemer, L. (2011). *Practitioner's guide to empirically based measures of anxiety*. Springer.

Appelbaum, S. A. (1982). Six conditions that facilitate a corrective emotional experience. *Contemporary Psychoanalysis, 18*, 295–312.

Arkowitz, H. (1989). Integrative theories of therapy. In J. Norcross & H. Goldfried (Eds.), *Handbook of psychotherapy integration* (pp. 279–296). Basic Books.

Arkowitz, H. (1989). Integration, eclecticism, and the future of psychotherapy. *Journal of Integrative and Eclectic Psychotherapy*, 8(1), 1–10.

Assay, T. P., & Lambert, M. J. (1999). The empirical case for the common factors in therapy: Quantitative findings. In M. A. Hubble, B. L. Duncan, & S. D. Miller (Eds.), *The heart and soul of change: What works in therapy* (pp. 33–56). APA Books.

Baldwin, S. A., & Imel, Z. E. (2013). Therapist effects: Findings and methods. In M. J. Lambert (Ed.), *Bergin and Garfield's Handbook of Psychotherapy and Behavior Change* (6th ed., pp. 258–297). Wiley.

Baker, T. B., McFall, R. M., & Shoham, V. (2008). *Current status and future prospects of clinical psychology: Toward a scientifically principled approach to mental and behavioral health care.* Psychological Science in the Public Interest, 9(2), 67–103.

Barlow, D. H. (2004). *Psychological treatments*. American Psychologist, 59(9), 869–878.

Bergin, A. E., & Garfield, S. L. (Eds.). (1994). *Handbook of psychotherapy and behavior change* (4th ed.). Wiley.

Blagys, M. D., & Hilsenroth, M. J. (2000). Distinctive features of short-term psychodynamic-interpersonal psychotherapy: A review of the comparative psychotherapy process literature. *Clinical Psychology: Science and Practice, 7*(2), 167–188.

Brown, J. (2015). *The psychotherapist's own story: Empathy, interpretation, and shared humanity*. Routledge.

Castonguay, L. G. (2000). Common factors and the future of psychotherapy integration. *Journal of Psychotherapy Integration, 10*(4), 354–362.

Castonguay, L. G. (2000). Common factors and therapeutic change: Past, present, and future directions. *Psychotherapy Research*, 10(4), 353–366.

Castonguay, L. G., & Goldfried, M. R. (1994). *Psychotherapy integration: An idea whose time has come.* Applied and Preventive Psychology, 3(3), 159–172.

Castonguay, L. G., Goldfried, M. R., Wiser, S., Raue, P. J., & Hayes, A. M. (1996). Predicting the effect of cognitive therapy for depression: A study of unique and common factors. *Journal of Consulting and Clinical Psychology, 64*(3), 497–504.

Dafinoiu, I. (2000). *Psihoterapii contemporane. Teorii şi practici.* Polirom.

DeRubies, R. J., Brotman, M. A., & Gibbons, C. J. (2005). A conceptual and methodological analysis of the nonspecifics argument. *Clinical Psychology: Science and Practice, 12*(2), 174–183.

Erskine, R. G., & Moursund, J. P. (2011). *Integrative psychotherapy in action*. Wadsworth Publishing.

Fall, K. A., Holden, J. M., & Marquis, A. (2010). *Theoretical models of counseling and psychotherapy* (2nd ed.). Routledge.

Fiedler, F. E. (1950). A comparison of therapeutic relationships in psychoanalytic, non-directive, and Adlerian therapy. *Journal of Consulting Psychology, 14*, 436–445.

Foa, E. B., Hembree, E. A., & Rothbaum, B. O. (2007). *Prolonged exposure therapy for PTSD: Emotional processing of traumatic experiences*. Oxford University Press.

Fonagy, P. (2017). *The development of reflective function: Implications for psychotherapy*. Psychoanalytic Inquiry, 37(4), 286–293.

Frank, J. D. (1961). *Persuasion and healing: A comparative study of psychotherapy*. Johns Hopkins University Press.

Frank, J. D., & Frank, J. B. (1991). *Persuasion and healing: A comparative study of psychotherapy*. Johns Hopkins University Press.

Garfield, S. L. (1982). Eclectic psychotherapy: A common factors approach. *Psychotherapy: Theory, Research and Practice, 19*(1), 1–8.

Garfield, S. L. (1992). Eclectic psychotherapy: A common factors approach. *In J. C. Norcross & M. R. Goldfried (Eds.), Handbook of psychotherapy integration* (pp. 169–197). Basic Books.

Gilbert, M., & Orlans, V. (2011). *Integrative therapy: 100 key points and techniques*. Routledge.

Goldfried, M. R. (1980). Toward the delineation of therapeutic change principles. *American Psychologist*, 35(11), 991–999. https://doi.org/10.1037/0003-066X.35.11.991

Greencavange, L. M., & Norcross, J. C. (1990). Where are the commonalities among the therapeutic common factors? *Professional Psychology: Research and Practice, 21*(5), 372–378.

Halgin, R. P. (2006). The development of a psychotherapist: Integrating personal, professional, and theoretical perspectives. In Norcross, J. C., & Goldfried, M. R. (Eds.), *Handbook of psychotherapy integration* (2nd ed., pp. 169–192). Oxford University Press.

Hamlyn, W. (2007). *A history of psychology: From the Greeks to contemporary therapy*. Routledge.

Hawkins, P. J., & Nestoros, J. (1997). Psychotherapy integration and eclecticism: Historical development and current trends. *Journal of Psychotherapy Integration*, 7(1), 1–20.

Hayes, A. M., Beevers, C. G., Feldman, G. C., Laurenceau, J. P., & Perlman, C. A. (2005). Avoidance and processing as predictors of symptom change and positive growth in an integrative psychotherapy for depression. *International Journal of Behavioral Medicine, 12*(2), 111–122.

Hayes, S. C., Strosahl, K. D., & Wilson, K. G. (2012). *Acceptance and commitment therapy: The process and practice of mindful change* (2nd ed.). Guilford Press.

Heine, R. W. (1953). Common therapeutic factors in different methods. *American Journal of Psychotherapy, 7*, 277–284.

Hofmann, S. G., & Asmundson, G. J. G. (2008). Acceptance and mindfulness-based therapy: New wave or old hat? *Clinical Psychology Review, 28*(1), 1–16.

Hough, M. (2010). *Counselling skills and theory*. Hodder Education.

Jorgensen, C. R. (2004). Active ingredients in psychodynamic psychotherapy. *Psychotherapy: Theory, Research, Practice, Training, 41*(4), 516–530.

Joyce, A. S., Wolfaardt, U., & colleagues. (2006). *Effectiveness of psychotherapy: An integrative literature review*. Canadian Journal of Psychiatry, 51(6), 321–329.

Kazdin, A. E. (2009). Understanding how and why psychotherapy leads to change. *Psychotherapy Research, 19*(4–5), 418–428.

Lambert, M. J. (2013). *Bergin and Garfield's Handbook of Psychotherapy and Behavior Change* (6th ed.). Wiley.

Lambert, M. J., & Cattani-Thompson, K. (1996). Current findings regarding the effectiveness of counseling: Implications for practice. *Journal of Counseling & Development, 74*(6), 601–608.

Lambert, M. J., & Ogles, B. M. (2004). The efficacy and effectiveness of psychotherapy. In M. J. Lambert (Ed.), *Bergin and Garfield's Handbook of Psychotherapy and Behavior Change* (5th ed., pp. 139–193). Wiley.

Laska, K. M., Gurman, A. S., & Wampold, B. E. (2014). Expanding the lens of evidence-based practice in psychotherapy: A common factors perspective. *Psychotherapy, 51*(4), 467–481.

Leahy, R. L. (2007). *Emotional schemas and resistance to change in psychotherapy*. Cognitive and Behavioral Practice, 14(3), 258–266.

Lin, L. (2016). Common factors in psychotherapy: Evidence-based practice. *Psychotherapy Bulletin, 51*(1), 6–14.

Locke, D. C. (1971). Cognitive-behavioral versus cognitive versus behavioral therapy: Are distinctions important? *The Counseling Psychologist, 2*(3), 1–7.

Luborsky, L., Rosenthal, R., Diguer, L., Andrusyna, T. P., Berman, J. S., Levitt, J. T., ... & Krause, E. D. (2002). The Dodo bird verdict is alive and well—mostly. *Clinical Psychology: Science and Practice, 9*(1), 2–12.

Lundh, L. G. (2014). The search for common factors in psychotherapy: Two theoretical models with different empirical implications. *Journal of Psychotherapy Integration, 24*(3), 190–206.

Markowitz, J. C., Milrod, B., Bleiberg, K., & Marshall, R. D. (2009). Interpersonal factors in the pathogenesis and treatment of PTSD. *Journal of Affective Disorders, 116*(3), 144–150.

Messer, S. B. (1992). A critical examination of belief structures in integrative and eclectic psychotherapy. *Psychotherapy: Theory, Research, Practice, Training*, 29(1), 41–51.

Miller, S. D., Duncan, B. L., & Hubble, M. A. (1997). *Escape from Babel: Toward a unifying language for psychotherapy practice*. Norton.

Nassralach, T. (2013). *Neuropsychotherapy: How the talking cure changes the brain.* Karnac Books.

Newman, C. F., & Goldfried, M. R. (1996). Cognitive-behavioral therapy for the 21st century: Integrating the best from the past and present. In Norcross, J. C. (Ed.), *Handbook of eclectic psychotherapy* (pp. 155–168). Brunner/Mazel.

Norcross, J. C., & Goldfried, M. R. (Eds.). (1992). *Handbook of psychotherapy integration.* Basic Books.

Norcross, J. C., & Goldfried, M. R. (2005). *Handbook of psychotherapy integration* (2nd ed.). Oxford University Press.

Norcross, J. C., & Newman, C. F. (1992). Psychotherapy integration: Setting the context. In J. C. Norcross & M. R. Goldfried (Eds.), *Handbook of psychotherapy integration* (pp. 3–45). Basic Books.

O'Brien, M., & Houston, G. (2009). *Integrative therapy: A practitioner's guide.* Sage Publications.

Ofovwe, C. (2013). Towards integrative psychotherapy: Can we agree to agree? *Journal of Contemporary Psychotherapy, 43*(3), 135–142.

Palmer, S., & Woolfe, R. (1999). *Integrative and eclectic counselling and psychotherapy.* Sage.

Patterson, C. H. (1989). Foundations for a systematic eclectic psychotherapy. *Journal of Integrative and Eclectic Psychotherapy, 8*(1), 1–13.

Popescu, O.M. (2021). *Psihoterapie integrativă strategică. Vol.1. Teorie și aplicații practice*. București: Letras.

Popescu, O. M., & Vîșcu, L. (2016). *Fundamentele psihoterapiei integrative: Teorie, metode și aplicații*. Timișoara: Eurostampa.

Prochaska, J. O., & Norcross, J. C. (1999). *Systems of psychotherapy: A transtheoretical analysis* (4th ed.). Brooks/Cole.

Rogers, C. R. (2008). The necessary and sufficient conditions of therapeutic personality change. *Psychotherapy: Theory, Research, Practice, Training, 44*(3), 240–248. (Original work published 1957)

Rosenzweig, S. (1936). Some implicit common factors in diverse methods of psychotherapy. *American Journal of Orthopsychiatry, 6*, 412–415.

Sexton, T. L., Whiston, S. C., Bleuer, J. C., & Walz, G. R. (1997). *Integrating outcome research into clinical practice*. American Counseling Association.

Sparks, J. A., Duncan, B. L., & Miller, S. D. (2006). *Common factors in psychotherapy*. In J. C. Norcross, L. E. Beutler, & R. F. Levant (Eds.), *Evidence-based practices in mental health: Debate and dialogue on the fundamental questions* (pp. 259–268). APA Books.

Stiles, W. B., Barkham, M., Mellor-Clark, J., & Connell, J. (2008). Effectiveness of cognitive-behavioral, person-centered, and psychodynamic therapies in UK primary-care routine practice: Replication in a larger sample. *Psychological Medicine, 38*(5), 677–688.

Stricker, G. (2010). Psychotherapy integration: A postmodern critique. *Journal of Psychotherapy Integration*, 20(2), 118–123.

Sutton, J., & Stewart, W. (2008). *Learning to counsel*. Oxford: How To Books.

Tolin, D. F. (2010). Is cognitive-behavioral therapy more effective than other therapies? A meta-analytic review. *Clinical Psychology Review, 30*(6), 710–720.

Truax, C. B., & Mitchell, K. M. (1971). *Research on certain therapist interpersonal skills in relation to process and outcome*. In A. E. Bergin & S. L. Garfield (Eds.), *Handbook of psychotherapy and behavior change*. Wiley.

Wampold, B. E. (2001). *The great psychotherapy debate: Models, methods, and findings*. Lawrence Erlbaum Associates.

Weinberger, J. (1993). Common factors aren't so common: The common factors dilemma. *Clinical Psychology: Science and Practice, 3*(1), 45–47.

Westen, D., Novotny, C. M., & Thompson-Brenner, H. (2004). The empirical status of empirically supported psychotherapies: Assumptions, findings, and reporting in controlled clinical trials. *Psychological Bulletin, 130*(4), 631–663.

Zuroff, D. C., Kelly, A. C., Leybman, M. J., Blatt, S. J., & Wampold, B. E. (2010). Between-therapist and within-therapist differences in the quality of the therapeutic alliance: Effects on maladaptive interpersonal patterns and depressive symptoms. *Journal of Clinical Psychology, 66*(7), 681–697.

CHAPTER 2

CONTEMPORARY APPROACHES IN INTEGRATIVE PSYCHOTHERAPY

2.1. Multimodal Psychotherapy

Multimodal psychotherapy, developed by Arnold Lazarus (1981, 1997), is an integrative therapeutic approach that views human functioning as inherently multifaceted. Rather than subscribing to a singular theoretical model or technique, multimodal therapy proposes that psychological well-being—and its disturbances—arise from the complex interaction of several discrete yet interrelated dimensions. These dimensions, known collectively as BASIC I.D., include: Behaviour, Affect, Sensation, Imagery, Cognition, Interpersonal relationships, and biological/Drug-related factors.

The origins of multimodal therapy are rooted in behaviourism and social learning theory, yet the model expands to incorporate insights from psychodynamic, cognitive, and experiential theories. Lazarus (2006) asserted that no single modality can capture the richness of the human psyche or the full range of client difficulties. Consequently, effective psychotherapy must assess and intervene across all BASIC I.D. components, identifying which are most salient and tailoring interventions accordingly.

Basic principles of multimodal psychotherapy

One of the fundamental tenets of multimodal psychotherapy is that learning can occur implicitly and unconsciously. Individuals often internalise beliefs without explicit awareness. For instance, someone might not consciously recall being told they were incompetent during childhood, yet still develop a pervasive self-schema such as *"I'm not good enough."* This implicit learning, often based on subtle or repeated cues (e.g., tone of voice, facial expressions, comparisons with siblings), can shape one's core beliefs and behavioural patterns over time (Beck, 2011). Lazarus emphasized that such unconscious learning can have long-term consequences unless brought into awareness and challenged through a multimodal lens.

Another core idea is that psychological issues are often entangled with relational dynamics. Multimodal therapy, while primarily focused on the individual, recognises the systemic and interpersonal origins of distress. For example, family systems theory suggests that an adolescent's substance use may function as a symptom that stabilises dysfunctional family dynamics—by focusing attention on one member's behaviour, underlying conflicts between other family members may be temporarily obscured (Minuchin, 1974; Lazarus, 2006). In multimodal therapy, the interpersonal dimension becomes crucial for understanding such cases.

The model also recognises that communication is inevitable—even silence conveys meaning. From a multimodal perspective, non-responses or bodily expressions (sighs, shrugs, posture) can be just as telling as verbal statements. Every act of omission or commission can be interpreted across different modalities. For example, if a client fails to answer a partner's question about weekend plans, that silence may signal avoidance, ambivalence, resentment, or even a plea for closeness—depending on the wider behavioural and emotional context (Lazarus, 1997).

Multimodal therapy is also aligned with social learning theory, asserting that maladaptive beliefs are often socially transmitted. Children absorb implicit messages from parents, teachers, media, and peers. A mother's chronic warnings about external threats may cultivate a child's worldview of danger, unpredictability, or helplessness. As Bandura (1977) argued, much of human behaviour is shaped through observation and modelling—mechanisms that multimodal therapists are trained to uncover and reframe.

A fifth foundational principle is that biological vulnerabilities interact with psychological states. Lazarus integrated this biopsychosocial view into the "D" component of BASIC I.D.—referring to drugs, diet, disease, and biological aspects. A lack of sleep, chronic pain, poor nutrition, or hormonal fluctuations can exacerbate anxiety, irritability, or low mood (Sapolsky, 2004). As such, multimodal therapists are encouraged to evaluate the physical health and lifestyle of clients as part of a comprehensive assessment.

Multimodal therapy also emphasises the role of developmental gaps, which can manifest as deficits in emotional regulation, relational capacities, or problem-solving abilities. A client who lacked a secure attachment figure may struggle to form trusting relationships or manage separation anxiety. These gaps often reveal themselves through a multimodal analysis—where affective dysregulation, maladaptive imagery, and interpersonal avoidance converge (Siegel, 2012).

Another essential aspect of multimodal therapy lies in the recognition that defensive reactions serve to protect the self from pain. Individuals often employ psychological defences—such as denial, rationalisation, repression, or projection—to cope with overwhelming internal experiences (Freud, 1936; Vaillant, 1992). Lazarus (2006) acknowledged that while these defences may be adaptive in the short term, they often become maladaptive when they prevent emotional processing or disrupt relationships. For instance, during the COVID-19 pandemic, some individuals denied the virus's severity as a way to manage anxiety and maintain psychological equilibrium. A multimodal therapist would not necessarily confront this belief head-on but would explore the emotional, cognitive, and interpersonal patterns that support such a defence.

Moreover, multimodal therapy points out that maladaptive habits often emerge without conscious intention. Just as brushing one's teeth or making morning coffee becomes automatic through repetition, dysfunctional behaviours such as nail biting, emotional eating, or avoidance of social interaction can become ingrained patterns that no longer serve the client. These habits are often formed as coping strategies in earlier life stages and persist into adulthood, long after their usefulness has expired. Behavioural interventions, such as habit reversal training or behaviour chaining, can help clients become more aware of these automatisms and implement alternative behaviours (Lazarus, 1997).

The model also recognises that the impact of trauma is highly individualised. Two people may experience the same external event, yet their psychological responses can differ dramatically based on prior experiences, genetic predispositions, attachment histories, and coping mechanisms (van der Kolk, 2015). For one person, a car accident may lead to long-term post-traumatic stress symptoms, while for another, the event might result in a temporary period of heightened vigilance or sleep disturbance. Multimodal assessment helps clarify which component(s) of the BASIC I.D. system have been most affected by trauma—be it sensation (e.g., flashbacks), affect (e.g., chronic fear), cognition (e.g., catastrophising), or interpersonal functioning (e.g., withdrawal).

One of the most poignant contributions of Lazarus's work is the acknowledgment that a lack of self-acceptance is a core source of distress. Clients who struggle with perfectionism, excessive guilt, or chronic self-criticism often exhibit deep-rooted problems in the affective and cognitive domains. According to Lazarus (2006), effective therapy in such cases should not only challenge irrational beliefs but also strengthen self-compassion and emotional resilience. This aligns with later developments in compassion-focused therapy (Gilbert, 2009), which also recognise the importance of building a more accepting relationship with the self.

Additionally, interpersonal resistance to change is a phenomenon that multimodal therapists must be prepared to address. Clients may return to environments where others—partners, family members, colleagues—unconsciously or consciously undermine their progress. For example, a woman who learns to assert herself in therapy may encounter increased conflict at home if her partner is accustomed to compliance. Lazarus (1997) emphasised that treatment plans must consider systemic dynamics and prepare clients for possible relational pushback.

Finally, and most distinctively, multimodal therapy asserts that lasting psychological change requires working across all seven modalities. The BASIC I.D. system is not a checklist but a comprehensive framework for assessment and intervention. Each individual will have one or more "dominant modalities"—areas where issues are most salient or where therapeutic entry points are most effective. However, all seven areas interact, and therapeutic change is most stable when interventions address these interactions (Lazarus, 1997). For example, a client presenting with social anxiety might initially identify problematic behaviours (avoidance of social gatherings), cognitions (fear of negative evaluation), and sensations (blushing, sweating). But deeper exploration may also uncover vivid imagery (imagining humiliation), interpersonal beliefs ("people will reject me if I'm nervous"), and unresolved physiological issues (hyperthyroidism). A multimodal formulation would weave these elements together and sequence interventions to address the most accessible or motivating areas first.

The BASIC.ID model

A defining strength of multimodal psychotherapy is its flexibility in assessment and treatment planning, made possible by the BASIC I.D. model. This model does not treat symptoms in isolation but offers a multidimensional framework where interventions are tailored across seven interdependent domains. This approach addresses a crucial critique of many uni-modal therapies: they often overlook the complexity of human functioning by focusing exclusively on cognition, behaviour, or emotion (Norcross & Goldfried, 2005). Multimodal therapy, by contrast, accommodates the diversity of client presentations and developmental histories.

Let us now explore the BASIC I.D. components more systematically.

B – Behaviour: Behavioural interventions are often the starting point for clients presenting with overt difficulties such as procrastination, compulsive checking, or social withdrawal. Techniques like behavioural activation (Jacobson et al., 2001), self-monitoring, and contingency management are frequently employed. Importantly, behavioural change is seen not as the endpoint of therapy but as a lever for modifying affective, cognitive, and interpersonal domains.

A – Affect: Clients often struggle with identifying, expressing, or tolerating emotional states. In multimodal therapy, this is addressed through emotion-focused techniques such as affect labelling, guided affective imagery, and affect tolerance training. The therapist helps clients recognise emotional triggers, understand emotional schemas, and differentiate primary from secondary emotions (Greenberg, 2011). This emotional literacy is essential for long-term regulation and psychological resilience.

S – Sensation: Bodily sensations—tightness in the chest, stomach tension, headaches—are crucial indicators of affective distress and often provide the earliest signs of dysregulation. Mindfulness-based techniques (Kabat-Zinn, 1990), progressive muscle relaxation, and somatic tracking are often used to restore body awareness and reduce physiological arousal. Sensations are frequently linked to trauma, anxiety disorders, or dissociative symptoms, making their integration vital in treatment planning.

I – Imagery: Mental imagery is a powerful yet underused therapeutic tool. Distorted or intrusive imagery (e.g., catastrophic visualisations in panic disorder) can be processed using rescripting, narrative therapy, or trauma-informed imagery techniques such as EMDR (Shapiro, 2001). Positive imagery exercises—like visualising success, resilience, or safety—can also enhance motivation and counter negative schemas.

C – Cognition: Dysfunctional beliefs and cognitive distortions are common transdiagnostic factors in psychological distress (Beck, 1976). Cognitive restructuring, schema therapy, and metacognitive interventions are integrated based on the client's level of insight and readiness for reflection. Automatic thoughts, intermediate beliefs, and core schemas are all explored within the client's lived context rather than as abstract targets.

I – Interpersonal: Multimodal therapy stresses the centrality of relational functioning. Clients are encouraged to explore attachment patterns, assertiveness skills, communication styles, and relational expectations. Interpersonal role-plays, genograms, and systemic interventions may be used. In many cases, interpersonal dynamics mirror therapeutic alliance patterns, offering valuable material for in-session work (Safran & Muran, 2000).

D – Drugs/Biology: Finally, multimodal assessment includes biological and medical variables—nutrition, sleep hygiene, hormonal changes, medication effects, and substance use. For example, if insomnia exacerbates anxiety, then behavioural sleep interventions may precede cognitive or emotional work. Collaborating with medical professionals is often necessary to address underlying physical health issues that may amplify psychological symptoms.

This expansive view allows the multimodal therapist to consider the interdependence among modalities. For instance, a thought (C) may evoke a negative image (I), trigger a somatic sensation (S), and result in avoidance behaviour (B). The therapist might choose to intervene cognitively (challenging the thought), interpersonally (exploring communication patterns), or behaviourally (through exposure).

Bridging and tracking

Multimodal therapy is not eclecticism without structure. Its principle is systematic assessment, targeted planning, and flexible implementation—not the indiscriminate combination of techniques. As Lazarus (2006) emphasised, it is the methodical analysis of modality interactions that guides which techniques are employed and in what sequence.

One of the most innovative aspects of multimodal therapy is its use of bridging techniques—interventions designed to move fluidly between modalities, especially when a direct approach is blocked by the client's resistance or preference. Lazarus (1997) emphasized that each client has a "modality profile"—a unique configuration of dominant and auxiliary channels of psychological functioning. Therapy becomes most effective when it respects this profile, initially engaging the client through their preferred modality and then "bridging" toward less developed or more conflicted areas.

For example, when a client intellectualises emotions and resists affective processing, directly probing emotional content may be counterproductive. Instead, the psychotherapist might begin with cognitive reframing or behavioural analysis—modalities where the client feels safer. Once rapport is established, the psychotherapist can guide the client gently into the affective domain by introducing sensation-based or imagery-based interventions. This progression—from cognition to sensation to affect—offers a less threatening route into vulnerable emotional material (Lazarus, 2006; Drobot & Popescu, 2013)

Bridging also plays a vital role in addressing modality mismatches—when a client's presenting problem lies in one domain, but their expressive strength or therapeutic openness lies in another. For instance, a client may present with interpersonal difficulties (I), but have limited self-awareness in that area. If their imagery (I) is more accessible, the psychotherapist might use guided imagery to recreate relational scenes, then discuss the interpersonal implications. This layered approach respects the client's natural access points while still targeting core concerns.

Another key component of multimodal therapy is trigger tracking—a technique used to map the sequence in which symptoms unfold across modalities. In the case of a panic attack, the client might report feeling tightness in the chest (Sensation), visualising a hospital emergency room (Imagery), thinking *"I'm going to die"* (Cognition), and then fleeing the situation (Behaviour). Understanding this sequence—S → I → C → B—allows the psychotherapist to choose the most strategic entry point for intervention. For a client whose panic begins with imagery, imagery rescripting or desensitisation through visual exposure may be most effective (Hackmann, Bennett-Levy, & Holmes, 2011).

Importantly, multimodal therapists do not assume that the same sequence applies universally. Some clients may begin with cognitive distortions, others with bodily sensations, or even interpersonal cues. This flexibility requires the psychotherapist to be observant, adaptable, and well-versed in diverse interventions. In this sense, multimodal therapy reflects what Beutler (2002) called a "prescriptive match" model of psychotherapy—one that aligns interventions with client characteristics and symptom presentation.

The modality grid

Therapists trained in multimodal thinking are encouraged to create a "modality grid" during case formulation. This grid charts the client's functioning across each of the BASIC I.D. components, listing both strengths and deficits. For example, a client may show: 1. Strong cognitive insight but poor emotional awareness; 2. High somatic reactivity but low body literacy; 3. Rich imagery but intrusive, trauma-related scenes; and 4. Relational longing but avoidant attachment patterns.

This grid guides the selection of interventions, the sequence of therapeutic work, and the language used to communicate with the client. As such, multimodal therapy is deeply collaborative, respecting not only what the client brings but how they process and express it.

Furthermore, the therapist maintains a stance of technical neutrality: there is no ideological allegiance to a single method. If exposure works best in one case and expressive writing in another, both are legitimate. This eclecticism is not random but principled—each intervention is chosen based on careful multimodal analysis and the client's evolving process (Lazarus, 2006; Norcross & Goldfried, 2005).

To aid this process, Lazarus (1997) introduced the Multimodal Life History Inventory (MMI), a comprehensive questionnaire that evaluates a client's current functioning, stressors, beliefs, habits, interpersonal patterns, and personal history across all seven modalities. This inventory is not meant to be rigidly applied, but rather used as a heuristic tool to deepen clinical understanding. By beginning psychotherapy with a multimodal assessment, the therapist avoids the trap of reductionism—where, for example, cognitive distortions are targeted in isolation while neglecting unresolved trauma stored in the body or toxic relationship dynamics at home.

2.2. Systematic Treatment Selection

In the contemporary landscape of psychotherapy, the abundance of therapeutic approaches presents both an opportunity and a challenge. While the proliferation of modalities offers clinicians a rich toolbox, it also raises a critical question: how do we choose the most appropriate intervention for a particular client? Systematic Treatment Selection (STS), developed by Beutler, Consoli, and Lane (2005), emerged as a comprehensive integrative framework that addresses this very challenge. The model is rooted in empirical research and clinical pragmatism, aiming to enhance the precision and efficacy of psychotherapy by adapting treatment to the unique characteristics of each client.

Systematic Treatment Selection did not arise in a theoretical vacuum. It was shaped in part as a response to two significant developments in the field: first, the exponential growth of psychotherapeutic methods throughout the 20th century; and second, the persistent discrepancy between what psychotherapists believe fosters change and what is typically measured in psychotherapy research. A growing body of evidence—starting from the landmark findings of Luborsky et al. (2002) and echoed by Norcross and Goldfried (2005)—shows that most mainstream psychotherapies produce comparable outcomes. This equivalence has prompted researchers to look beyond technique-specific factors and investigate more universal elements, such as the psychotherapist-client relationship, motivation, and individual client traits.

Beutler and colleagues (2005) argue that therapeutic change is rarely the result of techniques alone. Instead, it stems from a complex interplay of common factors, client variables, and psychotherapist responsiveness. The STS model posits that psychotherapists should make treatment decisions based not on allegiance to a particular theory, but on how well specific interventions align with the client's personal profile and contextual demands. This marks a shift from theory-driven to client-driven therapy.

The model critiques a major flaw in much of psychotherapy research: the tendency to isolate one treatment and compare it with another, often overlooking the nuanced roles of psychotherapist, client, and their evolving relationship. As Norcross (2011) emphasised, effective psychotherapy is not about finding the "right school" of thought, but about tailoring methods to the client's complexity, readiness, and interpersonal dynamics. Thus, STS provides a framework for selecting, combining, or adapting treatments according to the characteristics that research shows are most predictive of success.

One of the central tenets of STS is that the same treatment may produce different results depending on the client's coping style, resistance level, or degree of distress. For example, a client with high psychological reactance may resist direct suggestions and instead benefit from paradoxical or non-directive interventions. Conversely, a client with low resistance may respond positively to structured, directive guidance. Rather than applying a one-size-fits-all approach, STS invites the psychotherapist to assess key client variables and adjust their interventions accordingly (Beutler & Harwood, 2000).

Key Dimensions in Systematic Treatment Selection

Beutler, Consoli, and Lane (2005) identified six core dimensions that significantly influence the outcome of psychotherapy. These dimensions offer a clinical roadmap for adapting treatment strategies to client-specific factors. Each one reflects an intersection of symptomatology, personality, behavioural tendencies, and environmental context.

1. *Problem Complexity.* Problem complexity refers to the number and severity of psychological issues a client presents, as well as how these issues interact with underlying personality traits. Clients with high complexity—such as those with co-occurring disorders, personality pathology, or extensive trauma histories—often require more flexible, depth-oriented interventions than those with isolated or symptom-specific complaints (Beutler & Clarkin, 1990).

For instance, a client with a single, circumscribed phobia (e.g., fear of dogs) and otherwise stable functioning may benefit from exposure therapy alone. In contrast, a client with multiple anxiety disorders, attachment-related difficulties, and a trauma history may require a layered approach that addresses underlying relational patterns, maladaptive beliefs, and self-regulation capacities. As complexity increases, so too does the need for personalized, integrative formulations (Norcross & Goldfried, 2005).

2. Chronicity of the Problem. Chronicity distinguishes between acute and long-standing problems. It considers how long the symptoms have persisted and whether they have become embedded in the client's identity or relational patterns. Research consistently shows that acute issues—such as a recent grief reaction or adjustment to a life event—are more responsive to brief, solution-focused therapies. Chronic problems, however, often require more sustained, multifaceted interventions that combine behavioural, cognitive, and interpersonal strategies (Beutler et al., 2005).

For example, a recent onset of depressive symptoms following job loss may be addressed with behavioural activation and supportive therapy. By contrast, dysthymia or treatment-resistant depression often reflects ingrained emotional schemas and requires longer-term, insight-oriented work (Cuijpers et al., 2010).

3. Functional Impairment. This dimension evaluates the degree to which a client's symptoms interfere with everyday life—social functioning, occupational performance, family life, and self-care. It also serves as a prognostic indicator: lower levels of impairment typically predict faster improvement, while high levels often necessitate broader systemic or environmental interventions.

A client with social anxiety who maintains employment and friendships, albeit with discomfort, may have a more favourable prognosis than someone whose panic disorder confines them to their home. The psychotherapist must consider the interaction between symptom severity and social support, access to resources, and cognitive flexibility (Wampold & Imel, 2015).

4. Coping Style. A client's coping style refers to their habitual pattern of internalising or externalising psychological distress. Internalisers tend to blame themselves, suppress affect, and engage in rigid self-monitoring. They may present with high levels of anxiety, self-criticism, or perfectionism. Externalisers, in contrast, project blame outward, act impulsively, and may exhibit aggression or entitlement. These patterns loosely correspond to certain personality traits: internalisers resemble avoidant or obsessive-compulsive tendencies, while externalisers may reflect narcissistic, antisocial, or borderline traits (Beutler & Harwood, 2000).

This distinction has direct implications for treatment planning. Internalisers benefit from emotion-focused, insight-oriented interventions—such as psychodynamic, humanistic, or emotion-focused therapy—that facilitate emotional expression and self-understanding. Externalisers, by contrast, respond better to structured, behaviourally focused approaches, such as CBT or contingency management, which encourage accountability and promote concrete behavioural change (Castonguay & Beutler, 2006).

5. Resistance or Reactance. Resistance—or psychological reactance—reflects a client's sensitivity to external control. High-resistance clients tend to reject suggestions, challenge authority, and may experience therapeutic guidance as intrusive. These individuals often engage in passive-aggressive behaviours, therapy-interfering attitudes, or paradoxical life patterns. Beutler et al. (2005) suggest that resistance is not merely a defence mechanism but a trait-like factor that can be reliably assessed and used to tailor interventions.

Low-resistance clients, on the other hand, are open to guidance and eager to follow recommendations. High-resistance clients benefit more from non-directive or paradoxical techniques, such as motivational interviewing or narrative therapy. Low-resistance clients are well suited for directive strategies, including psychoeducation, structured cognitive interventions, and behavioural assignments (Safran & Muran, 2000).

6. Level of Subjective Distress. This final dimension reflects the intensity of emotional discomfort. Low levels of distress may correspond to low motivation, while excessive distress may impair concentration, overwhelm coping mechanisms, and disrupt the therapeutic process. Psychotherapists must navigate the "Goldilocks zone" of distress—where the discomfort is sufficient to motivate change but not so overwhelming as to paralyse the client (Norcross, 2011).

Clients with mild distress may require activation through evocative techniques (e.g., guided imagery or emotion-focused processing). Those with severe distress often benefit from containment-focused interventions, such as breathing exercises, grounding techniques, or cognitive reframing.

Clinical Decision-Making in Systematic Treatment Selection

Systematic Treatment Selection (STS) is not simply a theoretical model—it is a structured clinical methodology that helps psychotherapists make decisions tailored to individual client profiles. Rather than prescribing a fixed treatment path, it offers a decision matrix to guide the clinician through four iterative phases:

1. Assessment of Client Problems and Prognostic Indicators. The STS model begins with a comprehensive, multifactorial assessment. This includes: 1. DSM-based diagnosis (to identify symptom clusters)ş 2. Personality traits and structure (using tools like the MMPI or clinical interviews); 3. Functional status (daily living, work, social relationships); 4. Contextual factors (e.g., socioeconomic status, family dynamics); and 5. Prognostic dimensions, such as: problem complexity, chronicity, functional impairment, coping style, resistance/reactance, and level of distress.

The goal of this stage is not just to assign labels but to understand the client as a dynamic, interactive system, influenced by internal and external variables (Beutler et al., 2005). This biopsychosocial overview allows psychotherapists to move from simplistic diagnosis to personalised psychological formulation.

For example, a client diagnosed with generalized anxiety disorder, scoring high on internalising traits and low on functional impairment, may present with a chronic but mild problem, low resistance, and moderate distress. Such a profile suggests the appropriateness of insight-oriented therapy with gradual emotion-focused interventions.

2. Evaluation of the Treatment Context. Once the client is assessed, the psychotherapist evaluates the treatment format and setting variables, including: 1. Intensity: Weekly vs. biweekly sessions; short-term vs. long-term work; 2. Modality: Individual, couple, family, or group psychotherapy; 3. Therapist resources: Time, expertise, and access to multidisciplinary collaboration; and 4. Client's practical limitations: Financial means, transportation, child care, etc.

The STS model recommends choosing a treatment modality and frequency that align with the client's severity and complexity, their coping resources, and the psychotherapist's capacity to provide sustained support. For instance, a client with high distress and limited access to psychotherapy may benefit more from brief, skills-focused sessions (e.g., behavioural activation, emotion regulation skills), supplemented with self-help tools or digital interventions.

3. Building and Aligning the Therapeutic Relationship. In STS, the therapeutic alliance is not a generic prerequisite, but a dynamic, adjustable tool. The psychotherapist must flex their relational stance based on the client's personality and resistance level. High-resistance clients benefit from collaborative, non-directive interactions, where the psychotherapist supports autonomy and avoids premature interpretations. Low-resistance clients can tolerate directive approaches, including goal-setting, therapist-led problem-solving, and structured homework.

The alliance is also the arena where initial expectations and goals are negotiated. Clients often enter psychotherapy with externalised goals (e.g., "fix my partner," "make my child behave"). STS encourages psychotherapists to gently renegotiate goals that foster personal responsibility and therapeutic engagement.

4. Tailoring Interventions to Client Variables. This final phase is where the six predictive dimensions guide treatment customisation. This tailored strategy stands in contrast to "manualised" or "one-size-fits-all" treatments. It recognises that psychotherapy is not a series of fixed steps, but a responsive and interactive dance between therapist, client, and context.

For example, a high-reactance client with chronic interpersonal trauma may resist standard CBT protocols. However, a non-directive stance that includes narrative reframing and paradoxical interventions (e.g., prescribing the symptom, reframing avoidance as safety-seeking) might gradually reduce avoidance and open the door to emotional processing.

2.3. Beitman's Future Predictions Model

The human mind is not only a repository of past experiences—it is an architect of imagined futures. In his seminal work, psychiatrist Bernard Beitman introduced the Future Prediction Model, a theory situated at the intersection of psychotherapeutic integration, cognitive-emotional processing, and meaning-making (Beitman & Yue, 2004). This model asserts that our actions are not only influenced by our memories, but also—and perhaps more profoundly—by the mental images we construct about the future. These future-oriented simulations function as cognitive-emotional blueprints, shaping expectations, behaviour, and affective reactions. In essence, the future, as imagined, begins to function as if it were a recollected past.

For example, an individual anticipating a social event might imagine meeting an ideal romantic partner, feeling excited and connected. When this ideal does not manifest, the emotional response is not neutral disappointment but a sense of loss, as though the imagined event had truly occurred and then failed. The brain, as Beitman notes, reacts to imagined futures as if they were remembered experiences, creating a neurocognitive conflation between anticipation and memory. This phenomenon is supported by contemporary neuroscience research, which shows that the same neural networks involved in remembering the past are also activated when imagining the future (Schacter et al., 2007; Addis et al., 2009).

Theoretical Foundations of the Model

Beitman and Yue (2004) delineated the core principle of the Future Prediction Model as follows: *"People's actions are guided by their mental images of the future, causing the future to resemble memories of past images."* This proposition is not merely metaphorical but grounded in clinical reality. In therapy, clients often behave in ways that enact the future they fear or expect—be it failure, rejection, or success. This process has profound implications for case formulation, treatment planning, and therapeutic change.

Principles of The Future Predictions Model

1. The Therapeutic Relationship as a Scaffold for Future Scripts. Beitman situates integration in psychotherapy within the framework of relationship development, highlighting three successive stages: 1. Recognition of Patterns; 2. Initiation of Change (letting go of old scripts, testing new ones); and

3. Conclusion (closure, consolidation, and symbolic integration). The therapeutic relationship becomes a corrective emotional and cognitive environment in which the client can revise not only their past-based beliefs but also their future-oriented scenarios. A practical example may involve a client who repeatedly feels abandoned in friendships. Rather than merely exploring childhood abandonment, the future predictions model investigates the anticipatory template—the future image—projected onto new relationships. If the client envisions inevitable rejection, their behaviour may unconsciously elicit that very outcome. Psychotherapy, then, involves both affective repair and expectation recalibration.

2. Discrepancies Between Expectations and Reality. A central insight in Beitman's theory is that psychological suffering often arises from misalignments between internal expectations and external realities. These discrepancies can be classified into five primary domains: 1. Limited Future Vision – The individual cannot imagine multiple possible futures or pathways, resulting in hopelessness or paralysis (often seen in depressive cognition); 2. Catastrophic Future – Persistent belief in imminent disaster, frequently accompanying anxiety disorders; 3. Interpersonal Mismatch – Anticipations of being dominated, abandoned, or rejected in social settings; 4. Conflicting Relational Expectations – Simultaneous, contradictory anticipations within a single relationship (e.g., the wish for closeness alongside fear of engulfment); and 5. Developmental Mismatches – Internalized future scripts about normative milestones (e.g., "I should be married by 30") which create distress when unmet. Beitman's framework encourages psychotherapists to identify these mismatches and examine how they originate and are maintained.

3. The Role of Self-Observation in Future Re-Scripting. The capacity for self-observation, or what we might call meta-awareness or reflexivity, determines a client's ability to change maladaptive future images. Beitman emphasizes that the more a person can observe, reflect upon, and analyse their thought-emotion-action cycles, the more they can disrupt automatic future enactments. This links closely with mentalisation and decentration techniques, which allow clients to become aware of the symbolic material they project into the future. The psychotherapist acts as a co-narrator in this reflective process, guiding the client to identify the hidden assumptions embedded in their predictive scripts.

4. Formulation and Intervention Strategies. Building on Norcross and Goldfried (2005), Beitman outlines the following steps in case formulation within the future prediction model: 1. Define the problem in change-oriented terms, e.g., rather than *"I'm stuck,"* reframe as *"I'm facing a decision that requires specific steps"*; and 2. Develop change strategies, e.g., break large tasks (like changing jobs) into manageable actions, thus creating a sense of agency and timeline.

Beitman further identifies six domains critical to therapy planning: 1. Triggering Events – Why is the client seeking therapy now?; 2. Developmental Challenges – What life-stage tasks are being disrupted?; 3. Reframing Client Statements – What assumptions and predictions underlie their narrative?; 4. Diagnostic Clarity – How does the diagnosis inform their predictive errors (e.g., depression leading to hopeless future images)?; 5. Stages of Change – Identifying, observing, recalibrating, and adjusting expectations or contexts; and 6. Therapeutic Fit and Contextual Factors – This includes evaluating the client's ability for introspection, environmental support systems, therapist-client compatibility, and predictors of success.

2.4. Informed Clinical Strategy

Empirical research consistently demonstrates that the majority of symptom improvement in psychotherapy occurs early in the treatment process. According to Norcross and Goldfried (2005), approximately 60% to 65% of clients report significant symptom relief within the first 1 to 7 sessions. This initial phase serves as a powerful prognostic window: the client's early experience of psychotherapy—whether it includes emotional relief, insight, behavioural change, or enhanced hope—is one of the most reliable indicators of long-term success.

Conversely, the absence of any observable progress during the first two months of psychotherapy may suggest that the current therapeutic approach is ineffective for that client. In such cases, clinicians are advised to critically reassess and adjust their methods, rather than persist with a strategy that is not yielding movement. This reinforces the need for ongoing evaluation, flexibility, and a willingness to co-construct the therapeutic process in alignment with client responsiveness.

While theoretical orientation has traditionally been viewed as central to the therapeutic process, accumulating evidence indicates that the specific modality (e.g., cognitive-behavioural, psychodynamic, systemic) plays a comparatively minor role in determining outcome. As Miller, Duncan, and Hubble (1995) argue, a strong therapeutic alliance and a collaborative strategy consistently predict success—regardless of the techniques employed.

According to their model of informed clinical strategy, four key domains account for most of the variance in treatment outcome:

1. Client factors (40%): These include the client's personal resilience, motivation, relational context, and the resources they bring into the therapy room;
2. The therapeutic relationship (30%): The quality of the alliance—emotional attunement, trust, collaboration, and mutual understanding—emerges as a cornerstone of change;
3. Techniques and methods (15%): The chosen psychotherapeutic modality contributes a relatively small proportion to the final outcome; and
4. Expectancy/placebo and hope (15%): The client's belief in the process and hope for improvement also play a non-negligible role.

The implication for clinical practice is clear: psychotherapy must be adapted to the client, not the other way around. Rigid adherence to protocol without attention to the client's unique worldview, values, and needs is unlikely to yield significant transformation.

It is also essential to contextualise psychotherapy within the broader framework of a client's life. A standard psychotherapy session lasts about one hour per week—a tiny fraction of the 168 hours that make up the rest of the client's lived experience. Therefore, what occurs outside the session—in relationships, workplaces, families, and inner self-talk—plays a far more substantial role in driving or undermining change.

This perspective further supports the client-centred approach, which views the client not as a passive recipient of expertise but as an active partner in the therapeutic process. As such, therapeutic interventions should aim to mobilise internal resources, encourage self-reflection, and promote generalisation of learning and change into the client's broader life context.

Miller, Duncan, and Hubble (2005) offer a compelling metaphor to illustrate the essential components of successful psychotherapy: the "three-legged stool." The legs of the stool represent: (1) Agreement on goals – What are we working toward?, (2) Agreement on methods – How will we work together to achieve these goals? and (3) Emotional bond – Do the client and psychotherapist feel safe, heard, and respected in the relationship? The "seat" that binds these legs together is the client's perspective on change. Without this stabilising seat, even well-structured therapy can collapse. When clients believe that psychotherapy is relevant, supportive, and tailored to their needs, the alliance deepens, and the likelihood of improvement increases substantially.

Furthermore, regularly seeking client feedback throughout the therapeutic process—particularly on the perceived helpfulness of sessions and the quality of the alliance—has been shown to enhance outcomes and reduce dropout rates. In this sense, feedback becomes a mechanism of accountability that redistributes power in the therapeutic dyad and honours the client's voice as central to the process.

To operationalise this client-responsive philosophy, Miller, Duncan, and Hubble (2005) recommend the use of two brief, validated instruments:

1. The Session Rating Scale (SRS 3.0): A 4-item tool that invites clients to rate the quality of the therapeutic alliance at the end of each session; and
2. The Outcome Rating Scale (ORS): A measure of client well-being across personal, interpersonal, social, and overall domains—administered at the beginning of each session to track change over time.

These tools offer a simple yet powerful way to stay attuned to the client's evolving needs, increase collaboration, and course-correct as needed.

2.5. The Transtheoretical Model

The Transtheoretical Model (TTM), developed by James Prochaska and Carlo DiClemente in the late 1970s and expanded in the decades since, remains one of the most influential and integrative frameworks for conceptualising behaviour change across a wide spectrum of clinical presentations (Prochaska & DiClemente, 2005). Rather than aligning with one school of thought, TTM draws upon cognitive, behavioural, psychodynamic, and systemic principles, positioning itself as a meta-theoretical model that can inform a wide range of psychotherapeutic approaches.

The Transtheoretical Model (TTM) emerged from Prochaska and DiClemente's comparative analysis of over 300 psychotherapy theories, aiming to identify common patterns across diverse therapeutic modalities. Their conclusion: the most central and unifying dimension was not a particular technique or theory, but the concept of "change" itself—how it is initiated, resisted, and sustained over time.

At its core, the Transtheoretical Model articulates that psychological change is not an event, but a process. This process unfolds over time and involves distinct yet overlapping stages of readiness and engagement. Through decades of research, Prochaska and DiClemente identified three central components of change: (1) Stages of Change – the temporal dimension (readiness); (2) Processes of Change – the mechanisms of transition; and (3) Levels of Change – the content dimension (targets). This dynamic triad offers clinicians a structured yet flexible lens through which to understand where the client is in their journey, what interventions are most suitable, and how progress can be supported without forcing premature action.

By focusing on strategic timing and therapeutic flexibility, the TTM offers a map of the client's psychological terrain, allowing the psychotherapist to adjust their interventions based on where the client is, rather than where the psychotherapist wishes them to be.

The Stages of Change represent the readiness dimension of the Transtheoretical Model. Each stage reflects a different level of intention and engagement with the change process. Movement between stages is often non-linear, with relapses and regressions being a natural part of growth:

- *Precontemplation.* The individual does not intend to change behaviour in the near future (typically within six months). They may be unaware of the problem, denying its significance, feeling hopeless due to previous failed attempts, or minimising the impact of the behaviour. From a psychotherapeutic perspective, clients in this stage often resist interpretation, challenge motivation, and externalise blame. Interventions at this stage are most effective when focused on enhancing awareness, exploring ambivalence and reducing defensiveness through empathic confrontation. For example, a client in an emotionally abusive relationship may describe distressing incidents but insist *"it's not that bad"* or *"I'm used to it."* Gentle reflection and reframing may help them begin to perceive the incongruence between their values and current situation.

– *Contemplation.* The individual is ambivalent. They are aware of the problem and weighing the pros and cons of change, but are not yet committed. This stage may last months or even years, particularly in relational or identity-based issues. Clinically, clients in this stage benefit from: validating their inner conflict, highlighting cognitive dissonance, supporting decisional balance exercises, and fostering hope and self-efficacy. The psychotherapist's role is not to push, but to support the client's meaning-making process, helping them envision a future without the problematic behaviour or situation.

– *Preparation.* Here, the client intends to act soon (within a month) and may already be taking small steps. However, their plan may lack structure or emotional support. Key therapeutic tasks in this stage include: helping the client clarify goals, developing a realistic action plan, anticipating emotional resistance or sabotage, and strengthening the client's sense of agency. In relational therapy, this may involve discussing how to set boundaries, role-playing difficult conversations, or identifying potential sources of support.

– *Action.* The client is actively modifying their behaviour, environment, or relationships. This phase involves sustained effort, vulnerability, and accountability. It is the most visible phase of change and often includes terminating harmful behaviours, establishing new habits, seeking external feedback, and experiencing both support and resistance. This stage is deceptively complex: external change does not always equal internal transformation. A client may leave a toxic relationship but still struggle with internalised guilt or self-blame. Thus, the psychotherapist must continue to attend to core beliefs, identity shifts, and emotional repair, even when behaviours improve.

– *Maintenance.* The focus here is on sustaining gains and preventing relapse. The individual feels more confident in their new identity and is developing strategies for long-term resilience. Common therapeutic goals include: normalising setbacks, reinforcing adaptive coping, strengthening self-narratives, and deepening insight into the transformation that has occurred. This phase is not the end, but a consolidation of psychological growth. For many clients, long-standing issues resurface in different forms, and the therapist's job is to support ongoing integration and emotional autonomy.

Relapse refers to the return to a previous problematic behaviour after a period of change or progress. Importantly, TTM does not treat relapse as failure, but as a recycling process—an opportunity to reassess triggers and vulnerabilities, re-engage appropriate processes of change, deepen self-awareness and self-compassion and strengthen the maintenance phase in future cycles. In this sense, relapse is best understood as a temporary return to an earlier stage, most often contemplation or preparation, rather than a complete loss of progress. It may occur multiple times before lasting change is achieved.

Beyond the five stages, the Transtheoretical Model (TTM) proposes ten essential processes of change—cognitive, emotional, behavioural, and relational mechanisms that enable individuals to move through the stages toward sustainable change. These processes are not tied to any one stage; rather, they are strategically applied based on the client's current position in the change cycle.

Each process offers a therapeutic leverage point—a way of activating movement from one stage to another, or of deepening and stabilising change already underway:

– *Consciousness-Raising.* This refers to increasing awareness about the causes, consequences, and potential solutions related to the problematic behaviour. It often involves psychoeducation, Socratic questioning, feedback from assessments, and naming patterns. The psychotherapist functions as an informational mirror, helping the client see what has previously remained unconscious or minimised. For instance, a client who repeatedly self-sabotages in relationships may begin to recognise the influence of childhood neglect once they are guided to explore attachment patterns. Consciousness-raising is most critical in the precontemplation and contemplation stages, where insight is still emerging;

– *Dramatic Relief.* This process involves emotional arousal and catharsis—experiencing and expressing feelings connected to the problem. It helps the client move from cognitive insight to emotional engagement, experience a "wake-up call" or emotional turning point and access grief, anger, shame, or fear that has been suppressed;

– *Self-Re-evaluation.* This is a reflective process in which clients assess how their current behaviour aligns—or conflicts—with their self-image and values. It integrates cognitive and emotional dimensions, often producing guilt or sadness about the status quo, a clearer vision of the "ideal self" and motivation for congruence. Self-re-evaluation becomes central in the transition from contemplation to preparation. The psychotherapist may ask, *"How does staying in this behaviour affect how you see yourself as a parent/partner/professional?"*;

– *Environmental Re-evaluation.* Here, the client explores how their behaviour affects others—family, colleagues, community. This process encourages empathy, social responsibility and recognition of relational consequences. This re-evaluation is particularly powerful when working on relational axis material—such as passive aggression, avoidance, or controlling behaviours. It promotes a shift from self-focused thinking to an awareness of interconnected impact. For example, a father realises how his emotional withdrawal influences his child's anxiety and begins to work on emotional availability;

– *Self-Liberation.* This process involves belief in one's ability to change (self-efficacy) and commitment to act based on that belief. Techniques include affirmations, decision-making rituals, and cognitive restructuring. A key question is: *"What would it mean to trust yourself to follow through?"*;

– *Social Liberation.* This reflects increased access to social opportunities, norms, or roles that support the new behaviour. In psychotherapy, it may include community resources, support groups, exposure to empowering role models and reduction in systemic barriers (especially for marginalised identities). It ties to the relational and systemic level in integrative therapy. Psychotherapists can advocate, inform, or empower clients to access liberating contexts that reinforce their evolving identity. For instance, a client exploring gender transition may begin to engage with LGBTQ+ affirming spaces that validate their experience and reduce shame;

– *Counterconditioning.* This is the process of substituting healthy behaviours in place of maladaptive ones. It reflects a behavioural learning model: one cannot simply "stop" a behaviour; it must be replaced. Common strategies include mindfulness in place of avoidance, assertiveness instead of passive aggression, and physical activity instead of rumination. Counterconditioning is central during the action and maintenance stages, helping to reinforce neural pathways for new habits;

– *Stimulus Control.* Stimulus control involves managing environmental cues and triggers that prompt problematic behaviours. The psychotherapist may work with the client to identify triggers (people, places, internal states), remove or reduce them and introduce reminders of the desired behaviour. For example, a client struggling with binge eating deletes food delivery apps and places affirming messages on the fridge. This is also essential in trauma treatment, where internal cues (body sensations, memories) act as emotional triggers;

– *Contingency Management (Reinforcement).* This behavioural strategy includes: introducing rewards for positive behaviours, withdrawing reinforcement from negative ones and tracking progress through tangible means. In psychotherapy, this may take the form of self-monitoring journals, celebrating milestones and token economies (in adolescent or group work); and

– *Helping Relationships.* Finally, effective change is seldom a solo journey. Clients need trusting, affirming, and consistent relationships to support change—both within and beyond the therapy room. The therapeutic alliance itself is a model of secure attachment, offering a corrective relational experience. But psychotherapists may also encourage clients to build external support, reassure them that they are not alone and model attuned listening and emotional presence.

In addition to the stages and processes of change, the Transtheoretical Model (TTM) introduces the concept of "Levels of Change," a framework for differentiating the complexity, depth, and psychological focus of the issues addressed in psychotherapy. This hierarchy recognises that not all problems are equal in scope, origin, or therapeutic difficulty.

Prochaska and DiClemente (2005) categorise five levels of change:

– *Situational or Symptomatic Problems.* These involve behaviours or symptoms that are relatively superficial or context-specific—such as smoking, excessive screen time, or avoiding difficult conversations. These issues are often observable, conscious, more responsive to behavioural interventions and easier to change with minimal resistance. Clients at this level may benefit from brief strategic interventions focused on problem-solving, goal-setting and accountability structures. However, symptom relief does not always equate to deeper change. The integrative psychotherapist must assess whether the symptom is the problem itself or a symbol of a deeper conflict;

– *Maladaptive Cognitions.* At this level, the focus shifts to rigid thought patterns, core beliefs, and dysfunctional schemas. These include catastrophic thinking, self-sabotaging internal dialogues, cognitive distortions and core limiting beliefs (e.g., *"I am unworthy," "People can't be trusted"*). These beliefs often stem from earlier developmental experiences and are maintained by selective attention and emotional confirmation. Interventions might include cognitive restructuring, Socratic dialogue and imagery rescripting;

– *Current Interpersonal Conflicts.* These are relationship-based issues in the client's present life, such as boundary violations, emotional dependency, conflict avoidance and repetition of dysfunctional relational patterns. Often, these conflicts mirror unresolved issues from the past but are now re-enacted in current partnerships, family systems, or work contexts. Therapeutic work at this level involves mapping relational dynamics, developing communication skills, addressing attachment-based patterns and navigating forgiveness or rupture;

– *Family/Systemic Conflicts.* Here, the focus extends to multi-generational patterns, role entanglements, and internalised family myths. Common examples include parentification, sibling rivalry, enmeshment or cut-off and cultural/familial roles that restrict individuation. Psychotherapy at this level may involve genogram exploration, identifying systemic roles, working with transgenerational narratives and externalising internalised family voices; and

– Intrapersonal or Intrapyschic Conflicts. This deepest level involves internal divisions within the self—often rooted in unresolved trauma, shame, guilt, or disavowed aspects of identity. These conflicts may manifest as inner critic vs inner child, ego fragmentation, dissociative parts and unconscious self-sabotage Therapy at this level is typically long-term and emotionally intense, requiring the integration of parts work (e.g., ego states, IFS), inner child healing, compassionate inquiry and reparation of core shame.

The Transtheoretical Model (TTM) has earned widespread respect across psychotherapy, public health, addiction treatment, and behavioural medicine due to its comprehensive, developmental, and flexible nature. TTM does not claim allegiance to any single psychotherapeutic school. Instead, it synthesises cognitive, behavioural, psychodynamic, and systemic perspectives. Originally designed for health behaviours like smoking cessation, it has been successfully adapted to a wide range of clinical presentations: depression, substance abuse, anxiety disorders, relationship difficulties, eating disorders and trauma recovery. Its versatility makes it a useful "map" for clinicians, particularly when clients appear ambivalent, stuck, or resistant.

Rather than pathologising hesitation, TTM normalises ambivalence as a natural part of change. This is a particularly helpful stance when working with clients in precontemplation or contemplation, who may feel shamed or misunderstood in more directive or insight-oriented therapies. The model allows clinicians to match strategies to the client's stage, thereby avoiding premature action or inappropriate confrontation. For instance, consciousness-raising fits precontemplation, self-re-evaluation fits contemplation, counterconditioning fits action and helping relationships support maintenance.

Numerous longitudinal studies support the model's core principles (Prochaska & Velicer, 1997; Norcross et al., 2011), and tools such as the University of Rhode Island Change Assessment Scale (URICA) and the Stages of Change Readiness and Treatment Eagerness Scale (SOCRATES) offer validated ways to assess client readiness.

2.6. Cyclical Relational Psychodynamics

Cyclical Relational Psychodynamics (CRP) is an integrative model of psychotherapy developed by Paul Wachtel. It offers a sophisticated synthesis of psychodynamic, behavioural, and systemic perspectives, united around the central idea that problematic behavioural and relational patterns are maintained through circular, self-reinforcing interpersonal processes. The model moves beyond traditional intra-psychic formulations to examine how current interactions perpetuate and validate earlier relational experiences, often without the client's conscious awareness.

At the heart of CRP lies the recognition that relational patterns developed in early life tend to be repeated in the present. These patterns are not simply passive repetitions but are often active attempts to resolve earlier pain or unmet needs. However, in trying to repair the past through the present, clients often elicit responses from others that reinforce their original fears and confirm their internal working models. This process creates a cyclical dynamic in which early experiences and current behaviours are linked through ongoing interpersonal feedback loops.

The defining feature of CRP is its model of circular causality. The client behaves in a manner shaped by past experiences, often unconsciously attempting to prevent further harm or rejection. These behaviours then elicit predictable responses from others, which in turn reinforce the client's pre-existing beliefs about the self and others. These beliefs become more entrenched with each cycle, sustaining the client's difficulties. For example, a client who expects rejection may behave in ways that create distance in relationships, thereby increasing the likelihood of the rejection they fear. The therapeutic task becomes not only to interpret these patterns but to engage the client in new relational experiences that disrupt the cycle.

Cyclical Relational Psychodynamics is a model of theoretical integration in the truest sense. From psychodynamic theory, it draws on the importance of early attachment experiences, unconscious processes, defensive mechanisms, and internalised object relations. From behavioural theory, it incorporates the principles of reinforcement, learning, and behavioural outcomes. Systemic and interpersonal theories contribute the understanding of reciprocal influence and feedback processes within relational systems. This integration avoids the reductionism often present in single-school approaches, allowing the psychotherapist to conceptualise the client in a holistic, context-sensitive way.

Central to the CRP approach is the role of the therapeutic relationship. This is not merely a neutral or interpretive space, but the primary vehicle for psychological change. The psychotherapist seeks to provide a relational experience that is sufficiently new and emotionally meaningful to challenge the client's entrenched expectations. Within this relationship, the client may begin to experiment with behaviours, affective expressions, and relational positions that would previously have felt too threatening. The goal is not just insight, but transformation through experience.

According to Wachtel, change occurs through a new kind of interaction between therapist and client—one that does not replicate the client's problematic cycles. The psychotherapist actively contributes to this by behaving in ways that contradict the client's expectations, offering a space in which old patterns are not confirmed but gradually dissolved. When the client's usual relational strategies do not result in the anticipated rejection, criticism, or abandonment, they begin to re-evaluate their assumptions. Through this process, the therapeutic relationship becomes a platform for reconfiguring the client's internal models.

The core theoretical assumptions of CRP have been articulated in a number of key texts. Wachtel, Kruk, and McKinney (2005) outline several guiding principles. First, both early life experiences and current relationships are seen as contributing to psychological distress. The model rejects any exclusive focus on the past or the present; rather, it is their interaction that sustains the client's difficulties. Second, while insight is valuable, it is not sufficient for lasting change. Emotional safety and the opportunity to enact new behaviours within the therapeutic relationship are essential. Third, change requires the reduction of anxiety. When clients feel threatened, they are likely to revert to familiar defences. Only when safety is established can new experiences be tolerated and integrated.

CRP also places significant emphasis on social learning. Clients must acquire new relational and emotional skills, not simply uncover unconscious meanings. In this regard, the model affirms the importance of behavioural rehearsal, modelling, and experimentation. It holds that the individual's environment and behaviour are reciprocally influential: behaviour shapes context, and context shapes behaviour. Thus, CRP draws upon the systemic concept of circular causality to describe how symptoms are maintained not just internally, but within the client's broader relational ecology.

A further principle is that psychological problems are sustained by cyclical interpersonal patterns. Clients often act in ways that unknowingly elicit the very responses they fear, thereby confirming and reinforcing their existing self-image. These patterns are frequently unconscious and stem from repressed or dissociated parts of the self. CRP encourages clients to reconnect with these disowned aspects, reintegrating them into their conscious sense of self. The therapeutic process involves gently uncovering and affirming these parts, allowing the client to reclaim agency over their internal world.

Another important idea in CRP is the concept of self-fulfilling prophecies. Individuals develop expectations based on previous experiences, especially those formed in significant early relationships. These expectations influence behaviour in the present, which then shapes outcomes in ways that confirm the original belief. For instance, a client who fears being a burden may withhold needs or desires, which can result in others viewing them as emotionally distant. This then confirms the client's belief that closeness leads to rejection. The therapeutic relationship provides an opportunity to interrupt this cycle by allowing clients to test new ways of relating and to experience different responses.

The process of change in CRP requires disconfirmation of these negative expectations through lived relational experience. Clients must encounter consistent, emotionally authentic responses that challenge their assumptions. This process is not purely cognitive; it unfolds through affective engagement and relational depth. As clients begin to internalise new experiences of safety and acceptance, their motivation and belief in change increase. The model holds that motivation is not static but is influenced by the relational and behavioural context. Thus, rather than waiting for clients to be "ready" for change, the therapist seeks to co-create conditions in which motivation can emerge and strengthen.

A client's presenting issues, from the CRP perspective, are shaped by developmental experiences but maintained and perpetuated by present relational dynamics. Anxiety, shame, and avoidance behaviours are often functional adaptations to earlier environments. These adaptations become problematic when they continue to be employed in contexts where they are no longer necessary or are misapplied. Unlike traditional psychoanalytic theories, which may view motivations and conflicts as fixed, CRP views them as flexible and subject to revision. Early experiences are not deterministic but contribute to an evolving narrative that can be reshaped through new relational encounters.

For example, a client who experienced emotional invalidation in childhood may develop a pattern of minimising their own needs and avoiding vulnerability. In adult relationships, this may lead to feelings of isolation and unmet needs. In therapy, the client may initially enact this same minimisation. However, if the therapist consistently responds with validation and encouragement, without overwhelming or pressuring the client, a new experience becomes possible. Over time, the client may begin to express more of their emotional reality, both in therapy and in life, breaking the cycle that had previously governed their relationships.

Cyclical Relational Psychodynamics offers a compelling, integrative vision of how change occurs in psychotherapy. It retains the emotional depth and developmental sensitivity of psychodynamic therapy while incorporating the practical, action-oriented tools of behavioural and systemic models. By focusing on the dynamic interplay between past and present, internal and external, thought and action, CRP offers a rich framework for understanding and intervening in the patterns that maintain human suffering. Its emphasis on the therapeutic relationship as the crucible of transformation makes it not only a theory of change, but a deeply humane approach to healing.

2.7. Assimilative Psychodynamic Psychotherapy

Assimilative psychodynamic psychotherapy is a contemporary integrative model that combines the depth and insight of psychoanalytic approaches with the pragmatic and structured techniques of cognitive-behavioural, experiential, and systemic therapies. Developed by George Stricker and Jerry Gold, this model falls under the broader category of relational psychodynamic psychotherapies and represents a form of theoretical and technical assimilation. Rather than opposing other modalities, assimilative psychodynamic psychotherapy adopts the view that diverse techniques can be meaningfully incorporated into a psychoanalytic framework, provided they are used within a coherent and consistent conceptual structure.

The foundational idea of this model is that an individual's psychological organisation—how they think, remember, feel, act, and relate to others—is significantly shaped by internalised representations of important early relationships. Memories, self-concepts, and interpersonal schemas are encoded within the mind in a manner that reflects early interactions with caregivers and other significant figures.

These internal structures guide the way a person interprets experiences, regulates affect, and engages in relationships. When early experiences are painful or inconsistent with the child's need for safety, predictability, or love, aspects of those experiences may be excluded from conscious awareness. However, despite being repressed or dissociated, they continue to influence emotional states, behavioural responses, and expectations in later relationships.

Stricker and Gold argue that these internalised relational patterns not only shape the content of memory but also structure the way memory itself operates. In this sense, the mind does not simply store experiences passively but actively encodes them according to relational templates. Consequently, psychotherapy must not only uncover hidden memories or interpretations, but also offer a new interpersonal context in which such memories and representations can be restructured. The therapeutic relationship becomes the medium through which old templates are re-examined and revised, allowing for psychological integration and emotional change.

Central to assimilative psychodynamic psychotherapy is a model of psychological functioning that encompasses three interrelated domains. First, the domain of behaviour and interpersonal relationships involves the ways in which individuals enact patterns in their interactions and how these patterns reflect both conscious and unconscious motivations. Second, the domain of cognition, perception, and emotion focuses on the internal processes through which individuals make sense of the world, regulate affect, and interpret others' behaviours. Third, the psychodynamic domain addresses unconscious conflicts, internalised self- and object-representations, and the symbolic and affective dimensions of psychological life. Together, these three levels provide a comprehensive framework for both case formulation and intervention.

Insight is considered the central mechanism of therapeutic change in this model. Through a process of guided exploration, the therapist helps the client become aware of unconscious aspects of their inner life, including hidden meanings, conflicting desires, unresolved attachment needs, and the projection of past relational figures onto present-day people. The therapist assists the client in recognising how past patterns are re-enacted in present relationships, how fears and desires are expressed through indirect or symbolic means, and how unconscious defences shape emotional experience. Interpretation, when appropriately timed and collaboratively explored, becomes a tool not only for understanding but for change. It links the client's narrative across time and experience, revealing coherence beneath confusion.

The therapeutic process in assimilative psychodynamic psychotherapy may shift in emphasis depending on the client's developmental needs, personality style, and goals. At times, it may focus more intensively on the past—exploring childhood experiences, unconscious fantasy, and the formation of internal working models. At other times, the emphasis may rest more firmly on the present—examining ongoing relationships, current sources of emotional pain, or interpersonal dynamics in the therapeutic dyad itself.

An important strength of this model is its flexibility. It recognises that different clients require different approaches and that no single intervention style is universally effective. For clients who are introspective, emotionally attuned, and interested in exploring the origins of their difficulties, the psychotherapist may prioritise psychodynamic and person-centred techniques such as empathic atonement, reflective listening, and the exploration of unconscious material through dreams, free associations, or transference interpretations. These clients often benefit from a psychotherapy process that helps them make sense of internal conflict and develop a more integrated self-narrative.

For clients who are more action-oriented, concrete, or pragmatically focused, the therapist may integrate interventions from cognitive-behavioural therapy, systemic family therapy, or experiential methods. These may include cognitive restructuring to challenge maladaptive beliefs, social skills training to enhance interpersonal effectiveness, systematic desensitisation to reduce anxiety responses, or experiential techniques such as the empty-chair dialogue from Gestalt therapy. The psychotherapist's task is to select and adapt these techniques within a psychoanalytic understanding of the client's internal world and relational needs, ensuring that they are used not simply as tools for symptom relief but as components of deeper change.

Assimilative psychodynamic psychotherapy thus avoids the pitfalls of both theoretical rigidity and unstructured eclecticism. It maintains a coherent conceptual centre—rooted in relational psychoanalysis and object relations theory—while allowing for the inclusion of interventions from other modalities when they are developmentally appropriate and therapeutically congruent. In doing so, it provides a model of psychotherapy that is simultaneously deep and flexible, insight-oriented and skill-based, interpretive and experiential.

This model is particularly suited to clinicians who value the richness of psychodynamic formulations but also seek to respond effectively to the diverse needs of contemporary clients. By integrating structured techniques into a relational and dynamic framework, assimilative psychodynamic psychotherapy offers a way to bridge the gap between understanding and change, between historical narrative and current functioning. It recognises that clients come to therapy not only to explore their inner world but also to develop new capacities for living, relating, and growing.

As such, assimilative psychodynamic psychotherapy represents an important contribution to the field of integrative psychotherapy, demonstrating that the depth of psychoanalysis and the pragmatism of other modalities can be meaningfully combined within a unified, relationally grounded model.

2.8. Cognitive-Behavioural Assimilative Integration

Cognitive-behavioural assimilative integration is a contemporary development in psychotherapy that emerges from the recognition that the effectiveness of treatment does not depend solely on techniques unique to a single orientation, but rather on a set of common factors that operate across diverse approaches. Pioneered and developed by researchers such as Louis Castonguay and his colleagues, this model seeks to broaden the scope of cognitive-behavioural therapy (CBT) by integrating essential elements from psychodynamic and interpersonal perspectives, all while retaining a coherent cognitive-behavioural framework.

The foundational premise of this model is that many therapeutic techniques, although originally associated with particular schools of thought, are in fact specific expressions of broader and universal principles of human change. These common factors include the development of a strong therapeutic alliance, the experience of emotional insight and corrective relational experiences, the acquisition of a new perspective on the self, and the transfer of therapeutic learning into the client's everyday life. In this view, the success of psychotherapy is not determined solely by adherence to a specific set of technical procedures, but by the therapist's ability to address key mechanisms of change that are present in all effective therapies.

Cognitive-behavioural assimilative integration rests on the understanding that CBT, while traditionally focused on structured interventions aimed at challenging distorted cognitions and modifying maladaptive behaviours, can be significantly enriched by incorporating dimensions typically emphasized in other therapeutic modalities. In particular, research has shown that CBT outcomes improve when psychotherapists attend to interpersonal dynamics, address relational schemas, and work within the emotional and attachment-based context of the client's experience. This perspective represents a shift from a strictly technique-oriented approach to one that recognises the importance of integrating deeper levels of experience within the cognitive-behavioural framework.

Castonguay and colleagues argue that psychotherapists working within CBT can increase their effectiveness by expanding the therapeutic process beyond traditional cognitive restructuring to include explorations of emotion, self-other representations, and relational expectations. The client is encouraged not only to identify and challenge maladaptive beliefs but also to explore the emotional underpinnings of those beliefs, including the desires, fears, and relational patterns that shape them. The therapeutic dialogue thus becomes a space not just for rational analysis but for affective engagement and reflective interpersonal understanding.

Psychotherapists operating within this model place a strong emphasis on fostering positive expectations for change. This includes building and maintaining a collaborative therapeutic alliance, clarifying goals, and helping the client believe in their capacity to make meaningful changes. Hope and expectancy are not regarded as peripheral or placebo-like effects, but as active ingredients in the therapeutic process that influence motivation, resilience, and engagement. In this sense, the therapeutic relationship is not merely a context for applying techniques but becomes a mechanism of change in its own right.

A second central element in cognitive-behavioural assimilative integration is the facilitation of a new perspective. This involves not only the traditional CBT task of identifying cognitive distortions, irrational beliefs, and maladaptive attributions, but also the deeper exploration of self-perception, relational history, and emotional learning. Clients are invited to experience and express their emotions, to identify patterns of attachment and interpersonal functioning, and to become aware of the ways in which their past relational experiences have shaped their current schemas. In this way, therapeutic interventions can address not only the surface-level cognitive content but also the internalised narratives and emotional structures that give those cognitions their enduring power.

Finally, the model highlights the critical importance of the therapeutic alliance. Research has consistently shown that the quality of the therapeutic relationship is one of the most robust predictors of outcome across all modalities. Within assimilative CBT, the alliance is seen as an opportunity to provide a new relational experience—one that is safe, validating, and responsive to the client's emotional needs. It serves as a corrective experience that can disconfirm the client's dysfunctional relational expectations and contribute to the reorganisation of internal schemas. This aspect of the model reflects the integration of relational psychodynamic principles into the CBT framework, without abandoning its cognitive-behavioural foundations.

Cognitive-behavioural assimilative integration thus represents a response to the limitations of both rigid adherence to technique and unstructured eclecticism. It provides a coherent and flexible model that maintains fidelity to the cognitive-behavioural tradition while embracing the emotional depth and interpersonal complexity highlighted in other approaches. The model reflects a growing consensus in the field of psychotherapy that integrative approaches, when theoretically sound and clinically coherent, can offer more comprehensive and effective treatment.

In practice, this model is particularly useful when working with clients whose difficulties are rooted not only in distorted cognitions but also in unresolved emotional conflicts and relational injuries. For example, a client presenting with social anxiety may initially focus on cognitive distortions about being judged or rejected. As therapy progresses, the exploration of early attachment experiences and chronic patterns of self-protection may reveal deeper fears of abandonment and shame. By integrating techniques such as interpersonal role-play, experiential processing of emotion, and schema-based work, the therapist can help the client address both the cognitive and emotional dimensions of their difficulties.

Importantly, this model preserves the spirit of scientific accountability that characterises CBT, while expanding its scope to include factors that were previously underemphasised. It encourages psychotherapists to adopt a nuanced, responsive, and empirically informed stance—one that acknowledges the complexity of human experience and the multiplicity of pathways to change.

Cognitive-behavioural assimilative integration therefore represents an important evolution in psychotherapy: an approach that draws on the strengths of multiple traditions, prioritises the therapeutic alliance, engages the whole person, and remains grounded in the evidence base. It invites clinicians to think integratively while working within a structured and coherent framework, ultimately enhancing both the depth and effectiveness of their practice.

2.9. The Relational Gilbert-Orlans Model

The relational model developed by Maria Gilbert and Ken Evans, and further elaborated by Gilbert and Orlans, represents a significant contribution to the field of integrative psychotherapy. This approach places the therapeutic relationship at the very centre of psychological healing, asserting that both the process and outcome of psychotherapy are deeply influenced by the unique qualities, behaviours, and presence of the psychotherapist, as well as by the client's subjective experience, preferences, and inner capacities.

At the heart of this model lies the conviction that the therapeutic relationship is not a fixed, neutral context in which therapeutic techniques are applied, but a co-constructed, dynamic field in which meaning is made, emotions are experienced, and patterns of relating are enacted and potentially transformed. The psychotherapist does not stand outside the therapeutic process as an objective observer, but is always part of what emerges in the therapeutic encounter. Their attitudes, responses, personality, and even their presence in the room all contribute to what is seen, felt, and expressed by the client. The clinical material, therefore, is not purely objective; it is always shaped by the interaction between therapist and client.

In this relational framework, integrative psychotherapy takes seriously the multiple dimensions of the self and of human experience. According to Gilbert and Orlans (2011), the therapeutic relationship must attend to the self in its various relational expressions: the client's relationship with their own self, including intrapsychic dynamics and embodiment; the relationship with others, both in explicit interpersonal interactions and implicit relational patterns; the relationship with context, including historical, cultural, political, and social influences; and the relationship with the spiritual or transpersonal dimension of experience. This broad understanding of relationality forms the foundation for a psychotherapy that is not only integrative in method, but also holistic in orientation.

The Gilbert-Orlans model rests on several key assumptions about the nature of change in psychotherapy. First, it assumes that individuals are intrinsically motivated toward growth and healing, and that the role of the psychotherapist is to create the relational conditions in which this motivation can be activated and sustained. Second, it views early relational experiences, particularly those occurring in the context of attachment relationships, as formative in the development of the self, shaping patterns of emotional regulation, interpersonal trust, and internalised expectations of self and other. These early experiences are encoded not only in explicit memory but also in the body, in affective responses, and in implicit relational knowing.

The model recognises that early relational trauma can have profound effects on the developing nervous system, stress regulation mechanisms, and coping strategies. Experiences of neglect, misattunement, or relational rupture in childhood can lead to the development of fragmented or defensive self-states, impaired affect regulation, and difficulties with intimacy and trust. These patterns, though often unconscious, continue to operate in adult life and are frequently enacted in the therapeutic relationship itself. For this reason, the therapeutic encounter is seen as a potential site of both re-enactment and repair.

One of the central contributions of this model is its emphasis on the co-created nature of the therapeutic relationship. Healing is not something the therapist does to the client; it is something that emerges between them. The relationship is not merely the context for change, but the process through which change happens. Within this co-created relational field, the psychotherapist offers empathic atonement, emotional responsiveness, and ethical presence. These qualities are not techniques but ways of being that support the client in exploring their inner world, revisiting past relational wounds, and experimenting with new ways of being and relating.

The Gilbert-Orlans model also places a strong emphasis on ethical relatedness. It posits that the therapeutic relationship must be grounded in mutual respect, emotional honesty, and awareness of power dynamics. The psychotherapist's responsibility is not only to facilitate insight or symptom relief, but to model and embody a different kind of relationship—one that is trustworthy, consistent, and attuned. This ethical stance is not an abstract ideal but a lived reality that manifests in the micro-processes of therapy: in how the psychotherapist listens, responds, repairs ruptures, and holds the client's vulnerability.

Another defining feature of this model is its focus on the client's self-healing capacities. Rather than assuming that the psychotherapist is the expert who imparts knowledge or solutions, this approach views the client as inherently capable of healing, given the right relational conditions. The psychotherapist's task is to help the client access and strengthen these capacities by fostering safety, trust, self-awareness, and integration. This perspective reflects a deep respect for the client's autonomy and inner wisdom, even when that wisdom is obscured by pain or fragmentation.

In this view, the client brings into therapy not only their narrative but also their embodied experience, their affective patterns, and their implicit relational style. The psychotherapist, in turn, brings their own presence, history, and relational stance. Through their interaction, a new relational space is created—one in which past patterns may be re-enacted, but also recognised, made conscious, and transformed. This relational matrix is not static; it evolves throughout the therapeutic process, reflecting the deepening trust and mutual engagement between client and therapist.

Relational work in this model involves both explicit and implicit dimensions. Explicit relational work may include reflecting on transference and countertransference, exploring interpersonal dynamics, and discussing the therapeutic relationship directly. Implicit relational work, on the other hand, unfolds through the quality of atonement, the therapist's responsiveness, and the client's experience of being met and understood. Both forms of relational engagement are essential and must be navigated with sensitivity and reflexivity.

The relational model articulated by Gilbert and Orlans thus offers a deeply humanistic and integrative vision of psychotherapy. It brings together developmental psychology, attachment theory, neurobiology, relational psychoanalysis, and existential philosophy into a coherent framework that honours the complexity of the therapeutic relationship. At its core is a belief in the transformative potential of authentic, ethical, and emotionally attuned human connection.

By foregrounding the relational context of psychological development and healing, this model challenges reductionist or technique-driven approaches to psychotherapy. It reminds us that what heals is not only what we say or do, but how we are with the other. It invites psychotherapists to cultivate presence, humility, and relational courage, and to remain open to being changed by the therapeutic encounter just as they facilitate change in the client.

2.10. The Contact-in-Relationship Model

The Contact-in-Relationship Model, developed by Richard Erskine, Janet Moursund, and Rebecca Trautmann, is a relational and integrative approach to psychotherapy that places the concept of "contact" at the centre of psychological development, relational functioning, and therapeutic change. This model proposes that all forms of psychotherapy are grounded in relationship—both the interpersonal relationship between therapist and client and the client's relationship with themselves. Human beings are inherently relational, and our capacity for meaningful contact—with others, with our bodies, with our emotions, and with our inner world—is essential to psychological well-being.

According to Erskine, Moursund, and Trautmann (1999), the central theme of effective psychotherapy lies in the psychotherapist's ability to establish and sustain meaningful contact with the client. This contact must be responsive, attuned, and developmentally appropriate, based on the client's unique relational needs. The authors describe four dimensions of atonement: emotional, rhythmic, cognitive, and developmental. Emotional atonement refers to the psychotherapist's ability to resonate with the client's affective state, to feel with rather than for the client. Rhythmic atonement involves synchronising with the client's timing, pace, and bodily rhythms. Cognitive atonement refers to aligning with the client's way of thinking, meaning-making, and internal logic. Developmental atonement acknowledges that a client's current struggles may reflect earlier unmet needs and requires responses that address those developmental deficits.

From this perspective, psychological distress arises from what the authors term "interruptions of contact." These are internal disruptions in the client's capacity to remain in meaningful, present-moment connection with themselves or with others. Contact interruptions may have originated as protective adaptations to early relational injuries, including misattunement, neglect, abuse, or abandonment. Over time, these adaptations become ingrained defensive patterns that interfere with self-awareness, emotional regulation, and relational intimacy. They not only represent the effects of psychological pain but also perpetuate it.

Erskine and Moursund (2011) conceptualise these interruptions of contact as both a result of unmet relational needs and a continuing source of distress. They describe a range of defensive strategies that clients employ to manage psychological pain, many of which involve varying degrees of dissociation from the self or others. Denial involves the suppression of troubling memories or feelings and is often accompanied by a lack of initiative in addressing life challenges. Disengagement reflects an inability to remain present with one's own emotional states, particularly painful ones, and can manifest as emotional numbness or withdrawal. Desensitisation indicates a loss of bodily awareness or responsiveness, often seen in individuals who have survived overwhelming experiences. Depersonalisation involves a sense of being psychologically detached from the self or body, while dissociation reflects a fragmentation of consciousness in which parts of the self operate independently of one another, sometimes taking the form of distinct identities or ego states.

The therapeutic goal in this model is not merely the resolution of symptoms, but the re-establishment of authentic contact—internally, interpersonally, and existentially. Psychotherapy becomes a process of slowly and respectfully reversing the layers of defensive organisation that have developed over time. This reversal requires attuned relational presence, the creation of emotional safety, and the capacity to explore and integrate the parts of the self that have been excluded from awareness. In this sense, psychotherapy is not just about insight or behavioural change, but about relational healing through presence, validation, and connection.

Erskine, Moursund, and Trautmann (1999) identify four progressive levels of contact interruption, which reflect the deepening layers of disconnection a person may experience in relation to a psychological problem. The first level involves a restriction of problem awareness, where the individual keeps the issue out of conscious awareness entirely. This may take the form of repression, avoidance, or intellectualisation. The second level is characterised by the denial of the problem's significance, in which the individual may acknowledge the issue but minimises its impact or importance. The third level involves the denial of problem-solving potential, where the client feels helpless or incapable of initiating change. At this stage, the person may believe that the problem is permanent or that they lack the resources to address it. The fourth and deepest level is the denial of self-worth, in which the individual not only feels unable to solve the problem but believes they are fundamentally inadequate or undeserving of healing.

These levels of interruption are not rigidly distinct, nor are they necessarily experienced sequentially. Rather, they represent different degrees and manifestations of relational disconnection, each of which requires a specific kind of attuned response from the psychotherapist. At each level, the therapeutic task involves supporting the client to gradually re-establish contact—first with the awareness of the problem, then with its emotional and relational meaning, then with their capacity to address it, and finally with their intrinsic worth and potential for growth.

The Contact-in-Relationship Model is grounded in a deeply humanistic and relational view of psychotherapy. It recognises that change cannot be imposed from the outside or achieved through technical interventions alone. Rather, transformation emerges through the relational field co-created by psychotherapist and client. The psychotherapist's presence is not a neutral container but an active, responsive force that facilitates the reorganisation of the client's internal world. Healing requires a relationship in which the client can feel emotionally held, intellectually understood, and developmentally supported.

Importantly, this model also incorporates an embodied dimension of psychotherapy. Contact is not only emotional or cognitive—it is also somatic. The body holds the memory of relational injury, and the therapeutic process must include bodily awareness and integration. Rhythmic and physical atonement help the client feel safe enough to reconnect with bodily sensations and restore a sense of vitality and grounding.

2.11. The Developmental Needs Meeting Strategy – DNMS

In the landscape of trauma-informed integrative psychotherapy, the Developmental Needs Meeting Strategy (DNMS), developed by Shirley Jean Schmidt (2006), emerges as a structured, compassionate, and neurobiologically grounded method for healing wounded parts of the self. Rooted in ego state theory and informed by attachment science, DNMS is a non-pathologising approach designed to help clients with complex developmental trauma repair internalised relational injuries by activating healthy internal resources and fostering internal reparenting.

The DNMS model assumes that psychopathology often stems from unmet developmental needs and relational trauma experienced in early life. When caregivers are abusive, neglectful, rejecting, over-involved, or inconsistent, the developing child internalises these interactions as wounded parts of the self—ego states that carry unprocessed affect, dysfunctional beliefs, and maladaptive coping strategies. In contrast, when the child encounters consistent, loving, and attuned caregiving, they form healthy parts of the self that serve as lifelong internal resources.

This duality—between resourceful and wounded internal parts—forms the foundation of the DNMS process. The therapeutic goal is not to eliminate wounded parts, but to meet their unmet needs, soothe their pain, and reintegrate them into the self-system. The process involves a form of "internal family therapy," where resourceful ego states reparent wounded or reactive parts and disempower maladaptive introjects. These internal dialogues are both emotionally reparative and neurologically rewiring.

As an integrative model, DNMS synthesises insights from Ego State Therapy (Watkins & Watkins, 1997), Attachment Theory (Bowlby, 1969/1982), Internal Family Systems (Schwartz, 1995), and neuroscience of mirror neurons (Gallese et al., 2004).

The conceptual foundation of DNMS draws from multiple integrative traditions:

- Attachment theory proposes that the quality of early caregiver relationships significantly shapes internal working models of self and other (Bowlby, 1969/1982). DNMS takes this further by operationalising how unmet needs in these early attachments result in dissociated ego states or wounded parts;
- Ego State Therapy provides a framework for understanding the multiplicity of the self—not as pathology (e.g., DID), but as a normative response to developmental challenges and trauma (Watkins & Watkins, 1997). DNMS builds on this model by distinguishing between "healthy parts," "reactive parts," and "maladaptive introjects";
- Neuroscientific research on mirror neurons provides an explanatory mechanism for how maladaptive introjects are encoded. Mirror neurons fire in response to observed actions, intentions, and emotions of others, creating internalised representations of significant figures—especially when experiences are emotionally intense (Gallese et al., 2004; Frederick, 2005); and
- Parts-based psychotherapy models, such as Internal Family Systems (Schwartz, 1995), also inform DNMS. However, DNMS distinguishes itself through its specific protocols, developmental lens, and focus on reparenting wounded parts via resourced ego states.

The healthy parts of the self are those formed in the presence of nurturing, consistent, and emotionally attuned caregivers. According to Emmerson (2007), these parts are capable of: living in the present moment, accessing and regulating a full range of emotions, holding adaptive, compassionate beliefs about the self and others, engaging in effective and relationally sensitive behaviours and making grounded decisions based on the present, not the past. Some healthy parts may take the form of adaptive introjects—internalised images or voices of loving caregivers, teachers, mentors, or even spiritual figures. These serve as powerful inner resources when activated in psychotherapy.

In DNMS, these healthy parts are intentionally recruited, activated, and strengthened in order to facilitate healing. They become the "reparenting team"—a concept central to the DNMS process. Their job is to meet the unmet developmental needs of wounded parts, not merely to observe or offer insight, but to provide internalised nurturing, protection, and guidance.

On the other hand, reactive parts are ego states that form as direct psychological responses to relational trauma, neglect, rejection, or developmental overwhelm. These parts hold the raw emotional residue of early painful experiences and are often cut off from present-moment awareness, existing in a kind of internal emotional time capsule. Though they are no longer developmentally appropriate, their coping strategies persist, often surfacing in adult life as symptoms of emotional dysregulation, maladaptive behaviours, or relational conflict (Frederick, 2005; Schmidt, 2009). Reactive parts have certain characteristics:

- They live in the past, emotionally speaking—anchored in the age or stage of the original trauma;
- They hold primary emotional pain, such as terror, shame, despair, abandonment, or helplessness;
- They are often highly polarised in their beliefs: e.g., "I am unlovable," "I am bad," "No one can be trusted"; and
- They express themselves through maladaptive or impulsive behaviours that were once adaptive survival strategies.

Clients are usually consciously aware of their reactive parts, even if they do not conceptualise them as parts per se. These parts may surface during emotional flashbacks, inner criticism, interpersonal triggers, or moments of self-sabotage. DNMS therapy provides a framework to work with them compassionately, not confrontationally—building bridges between them and the healthy parts of the self.

These reactive parts have different sub-types:

- Emotion-holding parts: anxiety, sadness, rage, terror, shame, helplessness;
- Behavioural parts: self-harm, addiction, withdrawal, avoidance, eating disorders;
- Protector parts: aggression, hyper-vigilance, people-pleasing, control, perfectionism; and
- Internal critics: punitive, scolding, or shaming voices—often shaped in response to social or familial rejection.

Each of these reactive parts carries a developmental wound and an unmet need: for safety, love, atonement, autonomy, or recognition. Left unaddressed, they drive repetitive cycles of suffering. DNMS invites not just understanding, but internal relational repair.

While reactive parts represent the injured child's responses to trauma, maladaptive introjects represent the internalised voices of the trauma perpetrator or emotionally unavailable caregiver. These parts are not inherently "bad" or pathological; rather, they are internal ego states shaped by mirror neuron activity—a kind of neurobiological recording of how significant others treated the child during emotionally charged moments (Frederick, 2005).

These introjects are, in essence, parts of the self, wearing the mask of an internalised other—often a parent, teacher, sibling, or authority figure—who consistently conveyed harmful messages. They play back those messages in the form of scolding, shaming, dismissing, rejecting, threatening or controlling. When activated, maladaptive introjects re-trigger the reactive parts, creating an internal dynamic where one part wounds another—a tragic reenactment of early relational trauma. Maladaptive introjects form during emotionally intense interactions, mirror neurons in the child's brain fire in synchrony with the behaviour and affect of the caregiver. These recordings are stored as internal templates: "*This is how people treat me*," or worse, "*This is how I deserve to be treated*." The result is an internal critic, controller, or attacker who may sound or feel like the original perpetrator.

Frederick (2005) emphasises that maladaptive introjects are not malevolent; they are parts of the self that unwillingly carry toxic messages. When treated with compassion and separated from the "mask" they wear, these parts can shed their harmful roles and re-integrate into the broader personality system.

DNMS offers a structured process by which the psychotherapist helps the client engage resourceful parts of the self to reparent wounded ones and disempower harmful introjects. The process unfolds in several phases:

- *Resource Activation.* The client activates healthy ego states that embody nurturing, protective, and spiritual qualities. These are often visualised as inner guides, wise figures, or loving parts of the self;
- *Establishing Internal Safety.* Using visualisation and somatic awareness, the therapist ensures that reactive parts feel safe and contained before reparenting begins;
- *Dialoguing with Wounded Parts.* The reparenting team engages in compassionate internal dialogue with reactive parts: listening, soothing, validating, and meeting developmental needs;
- *Disempowering Maladaptive Introjects.* The client is guided to recognise the "mask" worn by introjects, separating the harmful message from the inherently good nature of the part. The reparenting team intervenes to challenge and neutralise these messages; and
- *Reintegration and Resolution.* Once the reactive part's needs have been consistently met, it is invited to integrate with the self-system—often symbolised by visualisation, naming, or creative expression.

This structured, compassionate process allows for corrective emotional experiences within the self, ultimately rewiring internal dynamics through repeated empathic engagement.

The DNMS model was developed specifically to address complex developmental trauma—including attachment injuries, neglect, emotional abuse, and early relational ruptures. It is particularly effective with clients whose adult functioning is impaired by persistent internal conflicts, self-criticism, and maladaptive relational patterns rooted in the past. In such cases, traditional insight-based approaches or purely behavioural techniques may fail to reach the subcortical emotional imprints that maintain suffering.

Importantly, DNMS is not intended for dissociative identity disorder (DID) or clients who experience uncontrollable switching between states. It requires a certain degree of internal coherence, present-moment orientation, and emotional stability to safely activate and work with internal parts. However, in clients with mild dissociative symptoms or fragmented self-structures, DNMS can gently promote internal dialogue and self-acceptance, preparing the ground for deeper integrative work.

2.12. The Internal Family Systems Model

The Internal Family Systems (IFS) model is an innovative and increasingly influential integrative approach in individual psychotherapy. Developed by Richard Schwartz in the 1980s, it draws upon systemic thinking and the understanding that the human psyche is not monolithic but composed of multiple distinct sub-personalities, or "parts," each with its own intentions, emotions, and history. These parts function much like members of an internal family system, interacting with one another and influencing the individual's behaviour, beliefs, and emotional life. IFS proposes that all parts, regardless of how extreme or dysfunctional they may appear, serve a protective function and possess a positive intent.

The central tenet of the IFS model is that the human mind is inherently multiple. Each person has within them a constellation of parts—sub-personalities with distinct thoughts, feelings, memories, and relational styles. These parts are not merely metaphorical; they are treated as discrete aspects of the self that can be dialogued with, understood, and transformed. Importantly, IFS holds that these parts are not pathological in and of themselves. Even when their behaviour appears self-destructive, they are attempting to serve a protective or adaptive function, typically shaped by earlier life experiences, especially unresolved trauma or unmet developmental needs.

IFS differentiates between healthy and extreme roles taken on by these parts. While healthy parts support daily functioning, creativity, and relational engagement, extreme parts often develop as protective responses to overwhelming emotional pain or trauma. The model organises these extreme roles into three primary categories: managers, exiles, and firefighters.

Managers are proactive, controlling parts that work to maintain the individual's social and emotional functioning by preventing pain from emerging into awareness. They often manifest as perfectionism, people-pleasing, inner criticism, or emotional detachment. Their purpose is to avoid triggering emotional wounds, especially those carried by more vulnerable parts.

Exiles are the most wounded parts of the internal system. They are usually formed in response to early relational trauma, neglect, or emotional injury, and they carry intense feelings of shame, fear, sadness, and unworthiness. Because their emotional intensity is often overwhelming, the internal system learns to banish or "exile" them from conscious awareness. However, these parts do not disappear; they continue to influence the individual's inner life and may erupt into consciousness when the system is under stress.

Firefighters are reactive parts that intervene when exiles begin to surface. Their role is to extinguish the emotional distress associated with exiles by any means necessary, often through impulsive or avoidant behaviours. Firefighters may drive behaviours such as substance abuse, binge eating, dissociation, rage, or compulsive work—all intended to protect the system from being overwhelmed by painful emotional content.

The IFS model does not seek to eliminate or suppress these parts. On the contrary, it views them as valuable elements of the psyche that have become overburdened or stuck in roles they were never meant to occupy indefinitely. The goal of therapy is to help each part return to its natural, healthy function within the internal system.

IFS also introduces the concept of the Self, a core of compassionate, wise, and grounded awareness that exists in every person, beneath the layers of protective and wounded parts. The Self is not a part, but the central organising force of the psyche. It possesses inherent healing qualities, including calmness, curiosity, compassion, clarity, courage, confidence, creativity, and connectedness. The therapeutic process involves helping the client access the Self and engage with their parts from this centred and resourceful place. The Self becomes the internal leader, capable of healing wounded parts and restoring balance to the system.

Healing in IFS occurs through a specific process. First, the therapist helps the client make contact with a protective part, such as a manager or firefighter. Through dialogue, the client begins to understand the protective intent of the part and to develop a relationship of curiosity and respect. The therapist supports the client in suspending judgment and approaching the part with openness and appreciation for its service, however misguided or extreme its strategies may have become.

Once a relationship of trust is established, the therapist guides the client to ask the protector whether it would be willing to allow the client to access the exile that the protector has been guarding. This step is crucial and reflects one of the model's key safety principles: work with exiles is never undertaken without the consent of the protectors. This ensures that the client's internal system remains stable and that re-traumatisation is avoided.

If permission is granted, the client then turns toward the exile with the support of the Self. The exile is gently invited to share its story, reveal the pain it carries, and identify the memories or experiences that gave rise to its burden. The exile's burden typically includes negative core beliefs or overwhelming emotions absorbed during distressing events, often in early childhood. These burdens are not intrinsic to the part but are carried as a result of unhealed trauma. Once the burden has been witnessed, validated, and held in the compassionate presence of the Self, the part is helped to release it.

This release is often experienced as a profound shift—clients may feel lighter, clearer, or more connected. Following the unburdening, the protector that previously guarded the exile may also be willing to relinquish its extreme role. It may transform into a supportive, flexible, and adaptive part of the internal system, no longer needing to over-function or suppress the pain of the exile. Through this process, the internal system becomes less conflicted, more harmonious, and better integrated.

In IFS, relationships between parts are also key to understanding the internal dynamics of the client. Three primary forms of relationship between parts have been identified: protection, polarisation, and alliance. Protection refers to the way managers and firefighters work to shield exiles from emotional pain. Polarisation occurs when two parts are in conflict with each other—one may push for control while another demands spontaneity, for example. Each part believes it must counterbalance the other to preserve the system's stability. Alliance describes the situation where two or more parts cooperate toward a shared goal, often to preserve functioning or manage external relationships.

The IFS model is governed by several fundamental principles. First, all parts are valuable and serve a protective function. Even the most extreme behaviours are rooted in a part's attempt to protect the individual from pain. Second, the Self is the innate healer and is always accessible, even in individuals who feel fragmented or overwhelmed. Third, protectors cannot relax or change until the pain carried by the exiles has been acknowledged and released. Fourth, therapeutic work must proceed with the cooperation of the protectors, never bypassing their protective stance. This ensures a respectful and trauma-sensitive approach. Finally, the ultimate goal of therapy is for protectors to come to trust the Self as the internal leader, allowing the Self to guide the system toward healing and integration.

The steps of IFS therapy follow a structured but flexible sequence. The psychotherapist supports the client in identifying and connecting with a protector part. Once the client understands the protector's intent and has built a respectful relationship with it, the therapist helps the client request permission to engage with the exile that the protector is guarding. If permission is granted, the exile is invited to share its experience, and the client, from the perspective of the Self, listens and offers compassion. The exile is then supported in releasing its burdens, and the system is reorganised so that protectors can adopt healthier, more appropriate roles.

While initially developed for individual psychotherapy, the IFS model has been adapted for a variety of clinical contexts. In trauma therapy, it offers a gentle, non-pathologizing approach that honours the protective function of dissociation and internal fragmentation. In couples psychotherapy, IFS can be used to explore how each partner's parts interact, trigger one another, or replicate earlier attachment wounds. The model is also used in personal development and coaching contexts, offering a structured yet deeply personal pathway to self-awareness and emotional resilience.

2.13. Multi-Theoretical Psychotherapy

Multi-theoretical psychotherapy (MTP), as proposed by Jeffrey E. Brooks-Harris (2008), is a deliberately integrative, multidimensional, and pragmatic model of psychotherapy. It reflects a growing consensus in the field that no single theory or technique is sufficient to address the full complexity of human experience, particularly when working with clients from diverse backgrounds and with multifaceted presenting concerns. Instead, MTP encourages clinicians to think in terms of dynamic systems, interrelated domains of functioning, and context-sensitive strategies.

At the heart of this model is the premise that psychotherapy is most effective when it is both intentional and strategic, guided by a multi-dimensional understanding of the person. The model encourages psychotherapists to select, combine, and adapt interventions based on an integrated case formulation, derived from multiple theoretical orientations and focused on the client's unique psychological structure, lived experience, and therapeutic goals.

Brooks-Harris identifies seven foundational theoretical approaches that contribute to the multi-theoretical model: cognitive, behavioural, experiential, biopsychosocial, psychodynamic, systemic, and multicultural. Each of these perspectives offers a distinct lens for understanding human functioning and psychological distress, as well as a repertoire of interventions that can be used selectively or in combination depending on the client's needs.

From the cognitive perspective, psychotherapy focuses on identifying and modifying maladaptive beliefs, automatic thoughts, and cognitive distortions. The behavioural perspective addresses learned behaviours and reinforcement patterns, emphasising the role of conditioning and behavioural activation. The experiential perspective draws on the client's emotional expression, inner awareness, and phenomenological experience, emphasising authenticity, presence, and the processing of affect. The biopsychosocial approach brings attention to the physical body, neurobiology, health conditions, and the interaction between biological vulnerabilities and psychological stressors. The psychodynamic dimension focuses on unconscious processes, developmental history, defence mechanisms, and internalised object relations. The systemic perspective looks at relational patterns, family dynamics, and interactional roles within social systems. Lastly, the multicultural dimension examines the impact of cultural identity, oppression, privilege, societal norms, and the intersectionality of the client's sociocultural context.

Rather than attempting to address all these dimensions simultaneously, MTP encourages therapists to prioritise two or three dimensions that are most salient for a given client at a particular time. For instance, in working with a client suffering from anxiety, the psychotherapist might focus on the cognitive (e.g., catastrophic thoughts), behavioural (e.g., avoidance patterns), and biological (e.g., physiological arousal) dimensions. For another client presenting with relational distress, the therapist might attend to systemic (e.g., family roles), psychodynamic (e.g., transference), and experiential (e.g., unexpressed emotions) aspects.

This emphasis on dimension-based formulation allows for a flexible, client-centred process that avoids the rigidity of manualised or school-specific approaches. The psychotherapist is encouraged to conduct a multidimensional assessment early in the therapeutic process to identify which dimensions are contributing most significantly to the client's presenting difficulties. This assessment informs a multi-theoretical case formulation, which in turn guides the selection of specific interventions. This process is both structured and dynamic, enabling the clinician to shift focus over time as the client's needs evolve.

Brooks-Harris offers a comprehensive framework of clinical "markers" to assist psychotherapists in identifying which dimensions are most relevant at a given time. These markers include observable patterns in the client's language, posture, affect, relational style, cultural references, and symptom presentation. For example, clients who focus on problem-solving and exhibit structured thinking may respond well to cognitive strategies, while those who express emotion somatically or struggle to verbalise their experience may benefit more from experiential or body-based approaches.

The model also recognises the relational dimension of psychotherapy. While not identified as a separate theoretical perspective in Brooks-Harris's original schema, the therapeutic relationship is seen as an essential context through which interventions from all dimensions are delivered. The psychotherapist's atonement, cultural humility, and responsiveness to the client's interpersonal and identity-based experiences are integral to successful outcomes, regardless of the techniques used.

Multi-theoretical psychotherapy further distinguishes itself through its commitment to cultural responsiveness. The model does not treat multiculturalism as an adjunct but as an essential dimension of formulation and intervention. Cultural identity, values, and sociopolitical context are regarded not only as influences on the client's psychological presentation but also as variables that shape the meaning, relevance, and impact of therapeutic interventions. This emphasis is particularly important in diverse clinical settings, where clients may present with worldviews, communication styles, and healing traditions that differ significantly from those assumed in dominant therapeutic paradigms.

By grounding itself in a multidimensional framework, MTP avoids the pitfalls of uncritical eclecticism while maintaining the openness and flexibility needed for responsive and effective therapy. Interventions are not selected at random or based on therapist preference alone but are chosen through a structured process of assessment, formulation, and strategic planning. The model encourages psychotherapists to continually reflect on their theoretical assumptions, evaluate outcomes, and adjust their strategies in collaboration with the client.

Ultimately, multi-theoretical psychotherapy represents a pragmatic, inclusive, and intellectually coherent approach to integrative psychotherapy. It reflects an understanding of the client as a whole person, situated within multiple layers of experience—cognitive, emotional, behavioural, biological, interpersonal, social, and cultural. The psychotherapist, in turn, is invited to draw upon the richness of multiple theoretical traditions, not in competition but in complementarity, guided by clinical judgment, ethical responsibility, and a commitment to the client's growth and well-being.

2.14. Multicultural Integrative Psychotherapy

Multicultural integrative psychotherapy is a contemporary approach that places cultural context at the core of psychological understanding and psychotherapeutic intervention. This model recognises that every individual exists within a complex web of cultural, social, political, and relational systems, and that these systems fundamentally shape identity, meaning-making, behaviour, and emotional expression. It is not simply an add-on to traditional psychotherapy but a foundational lens through which all therapeutic work must be viewed.

The core premise of this approach is that the human self cannot be understood in isolation from its cultural context. Culture is not merely an external variable or demographic descriptor—it is an internalised, lived reality that informs how people see themselves, relate to others, and navigate the world. Identity is formed and re-formed within this cultural matrix, and psychological distress often arises from dissonance, oppression, or marginalisation within one or more of these systems.

Drawing on the work of Brooks-Harris and Ivey (2005), multicultural integrative psychotherapy proposes a multidimensional model of human functioning. In this model, social systems—shaped by macrosocial structures such as political institutions, historical narratives, geographic regions, economic systems, and educational access—exert influence on interpersonal dynamics. These dynamics, in turn, shape psychological experience, including thoughts, emotions, somatic states, and behaviours. Biological aspects of functioning are thus not seen as isolated or deterministic but as deeply influenced by lived experience and systemic factors.

The model conceptualises culture at different levels of systemic organisation. Macrosystems refer to large-scale cultural structures, such as nationality, ethnicity, language, religion, and historical trauma. These systems shape societal norms, collective narratives, and access to power. Microsystems, on the other hand, include the more immediate environments of the individual, such as family, school, peer groups, neighbourhoods, and local community. These smaller systems carry and reproduce cultural messages, often transmitting values and beliefs intergenerationally.

The therapeutic process within this model is fundamentally relational, collaborative, and awareness-based. The psychotherapist and client work together to uncover how cultural systems—both macro and micro—have shaped the client's identity, worldviews, and coping strategies. Particular attention is given to the ways in which power, privilege, and oppression operate within these systems. For clients from historically marginalised groups, therapy may include recognising the internalisation of oppressive narratives, validating resistance, and supporting the reclamation of identity and voice.

One of the central mechanisms of change in multicultural integrative psychotherapy is the development of awareness across multiple domains. Brooks-Harris and Ivey (2005) propose a developmental model of awareness that unfolds in four levels, each representing a different stage in the client's capacity to process and integrate experience.

The first level, sensorimotor awareness, is grounded in immediate, bodily, and emotional experience. At this level, the client is immersed in direct sensation and affect but may have difficulty distinguishing emotions from thoughts or making meaning from their experience. This stage is common in early development or in individuals who have been traumatised, and it is characterised by somatic reactivity, confusion, or emotional overwhelm.

The second level, concrete/situational awareness, involves a focus on the external world. Clients operating at this level are often preoccupied with situational stressors, concrete problems, and behavioural outcomes. Emotions and thoughts are recognised as distinct but are not yet integrated into a broader reflective framework. This level is typical in early or symptom-focused stages of psychotherapy.

The third level, formal/reflective awareness, marks the beginning of psychological insight. Clients at this stage are able to step back from their immediate experiences, reflect on emotional patterns, identify core beliefs, and begin to understand the influence of relationships and context on their internal world. This is often the level where meaning-making becomes possible and where therapeutic change accelerates.

The fourth level, dialectical/systemic awareness, represents the most complex and integrated form of self-understanding. Here, clients are able to hold multiple perspectives simultaneously, recognise contradictions and ambiguities within themselves and their environments, and situate their personal narratives within larger cultural and systemic frameworks. This level supports the development of cultural humility, empathy, resilience, and strategic action in the face of ongoing systemic challenges.

Importantly, the process of moving through these levels is not linear. Clients may oscillate between them, regress under stress, or function at different levels across different domains of experience. The psychotherapist's role is to support this developmental progression, tailoring interventions to the client's current level of awareness while gently challenging them to expand their reflective and relational capacities.

Multicultural integrative psychotherapy also draws attention to the shared factors in psychotherapy, such as empathy, trust, atonement, and collaboration. These common factors are seen not as universal absolutes, but as culturally mediated processes. For example, the expression of empathy in therapy may look different across cultural contexts, and the very concept of "authenticity" may be understood differently in collectivist versus individualist cultures. The model therefore emphasises cultural responsiveness, encouraging therapists to examine their own cultural assumptions and to adapt their relational stance to fit the client's cultural framework.

Therapists working within this model are called to cultivate cultural self-awareness, critical consciousness, and ongoing reflexivity. This includes recognising how their own social identities influence the therapeutic encounter, understanding the sociopolitical dimensions of mental health, and being open to learning from the client's lived experience. It also involves acknowledging the limitations of dominant psychological paradigms and making space for indigenous, community-based, and non-Western understandings of healing.

In practice, multicultural integrative psychotherapy may involve a wide range of interventions, drawn from diverse theoretical traditions, but always grounded in a culturally attuned formulation. These may include narrative techniques that explore identity and migration, emotion-focused strategies to process internalised oppression, cognitive restructuring of culturally shaped core beliefs, somatic work to address embodied trauma, and systemic or advocacy-based interventions to address external sources of distress. What unites these interventions is the commitment to seeing the client not just as an individual with symptoms, but as a person embedded within intersecting systems of meaning, power, and belonging.

2.15. Wilkinson's Theory of Meta-Modality of Psychotherapy

One influential meta-theoretical framework is Wilkinson's Theory of Meta-Modality of Psychotherapy, a model that conceptualises psychotherapy not as a fixed set of techniques or theories, but as a fluid interplay of multiple layers of meaning, process, and relational dynamics. Wilkinson proposes that effective psychotherapy transcends singular schools of thought, functioning instead at the meta-level of integration, where modalities are not simply combined, but are organised into a hierarchical and inter-relational system of meaning (Wilkinson, 2017).

At its core, Wilkinson's theory positions the therapeutic encounter within a broader meta-modal context, a term he uses to describe the levels at which psychotherapy operates—ranging from biological responses and somatic atonement, through psychological narratives and relational dynamics, up to symbolic interpretation, existential inquiry, and transpersonal insight. Rather than prioritising one level over another, Wilkinson argues that psychotherapy is most effective when it is responsive across all these levels, recognising that human experience is inherently multi-modal and meaning-rich (Wilkinson, 2020). The psychotherapist's role becomes that of a meaning negotiator, helping clients navigate between biological experience, emotional resonance, relational patterns, and spiritual or philosophical orientation (Cooper & McLeod, 2011; Wilkinson, 2021).

Importantly, Wilkinson challenges the notion that theoretical integration in psychotherapy must occur through assimilation or eclecticism. Instead, he offers the metaphor of "meta-orchestration"—where each modality is like an instrument in an orchestra. The psychotherapist does not merge these into a singular score but rather listens to which instruments are needed at different times, contexts, and developmental moments in the therapy process (Wilkinson, 2019). This orchestration depends not only on the client's presenting issue but on their epistemic readiness—their capacity to function across different levels of complexity, abstraction, and emotional depth.

In clinical terms, Wilkinson delineates five meta-modal layers which may be engaged in psychotherapy:

- The Somatic Layer – encompassing physiological arousal, neuroception, sensory processing, and embodied regulation. This level often resonates with somatic experiencing, sensorimotor therapy, and polyvagal-informed approaches (Porges, 2011);
- The Affective Layer – involving emotional atonement, regulation, and expression. Modalities such as emotion-focused therapy and psychodynamic affect theory typically operate here (Greenberg, 2017);
- The Cognitive-Narrative Layer – dealing with beliefs, schemas, thought processes, and meaning-making. Cognitive behavioural therapy, narrative therapy, and schema therapy are situated at this level (Young, Klosko & Weishaar, 2003);
- The Relational Layer – focusing on interpersonal patterns, attachment models, and the therapeutic alliance. Relational psychoanalysis and attachment-informed approaches are prominent here (Wallin, 2007); and
- The Symbolic-Transpersonal Layer – which engages archetypal, existential, or spiritual dimensions of experience. This may include Jungian therapy, logotherapy, and transpersonal modalities (Cortright, 1997).

Each of these layers can be activated, bypassed, or neglected depending on the therapist's orientation and the client's needs. A central task in meta-modality is assessing which level(s) require engagement at a given therapeutic moment, and flexibly shifting between them.

A central pillar of Wilkinson's theory is the conviction that psychotherapy cannot be confined to fixed categories, be they technical (like behavioural interventions), epistemological (like evidence-based paradigms), or ontological (like the mind-body split). In his view, psychotherapy is an inherently philosophical practice, concerned not only with symptom alleviation or behavioural change but with the human being's capacity to exist meaningfully, to suffer consciously, and to transform symbolically. This orientation places his theory in alignment with existential phenomenology, particularly the works of Heidegger, Merleau-Ponty, and Gadamer, as well as psychoanalytically informed hermeneutics (e.g., Ricoeur). At the core of his meta-modal position, Wilkinson posits that the therapeutic encounter operates across multiple, coexisting layers of meaning: the clinical (e.g., symptom relief, diagnosis, alliance), the intersubjective (e.g., transference, enactments), the existential (e.g., questions of authenticity, mortality, freedom), and the philosophical (e.g., the client's world-view, the metaphors they live by, the unconscious as ontological ground).

This layering does not imply that one level is reducible to another. Rather, each layer is considered valid and irreducible, and psychotherapy becomes the art of holding these levels together in a reflective, attuned way. This is meta-modal functioning: the psychotherapist's ability to navigate among modalities, paradigms, and ontologies without collapsing the richness of the therapeutic moment into any single frame (Wilkinson, 2010). In clinical practice, this means that the psychotherapist must not be enslaved by one modality, but instead attuned to the shifting ontological register of the session. For instance, a client's depression may be treated not merely as a cognitive-affective disturbance (CBT), or a loss of secure attachment (attachment theory), but also as a spiritual desolation, an existential exile, or a rupture in the narrative self — depending on how the client lives and speaks their world.

Wilkinson radically deconstructs modality-based thinking, which he views as potentially reductive. While not dismissing the utility of psychotherapeutic models (e.g., CBT, EMDR, psychodynamic, etc.), he warns against "ontological foreclosure"—the risk that psychotherapists will see clients only through the lens of their preferred theory, thereby closing off other valid registers of meaning. For example, a psychodynamic therapist might overly interpret a client's behaviour as resistance, while overlooking a biological or sociocultural context; conversely, a behavioural therapist might pathologize emotion without recognizing its existential or archetypal significance. Modalities are lenses, not realities. They offer partial truths, contingent on time, context, and therapist-client fit. A truly meta-modal psychotherapist therefore cultivates a fluidity of perspective—not eclecticism in technique, but epistemic humility and ontological hospitality. The therapeutic encounter is not just a clinical transaction but an existential meeting, where two subjectivities co-construct meaning under the conditions of vulnerability. From this perspective, ethics is not simply about codes or procedures, but about presence, transparency, and responsibility.

Wilkinson's meta-modal vision resonates deeply with the field of archetypal psychology. the psyche does not submit to singular interpretation; it reveals itself through polyphony, contradiction, and aesthetic depth. For instance, rather than diagnosing a client's chronic anxiety strictly as a disorder to be eliminated,

Wilkinson might encourage the therapist to engage the anxiety imaginally: What archetype does this anxiety express? Is it the face of the Wounded Child, the Trickster, or the Exile? What symbolic function might it serve in the person's psychic ecology? Here, the therapist becomes a "mythopoetic companion", able to hold symptom and story within the wider field of archetype, imagination, and meaning.

A key aspect of Wilkinson's meta-modal vision is his critique of contemporary psychotherapy culture, which he views as increasingly reductionistic, managerial, and overly psychotechnical. In his writings and public lectures, Wilkinson warns that psychotherapy risks becoming a mental health service stripped of soul, aligned with neoliberal paradigms of efficiency, outcome, and consumer satisfaction.

Meta-modality is not a *modality among others*, but the *precondition* for all modalities.

2.16. The Predictive Processing (3PI) Model

In recent years, the Predictive Processing Model—also referred to in integrative psychotherapy literature as the 3PI Model (Predictive Processing and Psychotherapy Integration)—has emerged as a compelling neurocognitive framework for understanding human perception, emotion regulation, psychopathology, and the mechanisms of change in psychotherapy. Rooted in Bayesian brain theories, the model suggests that the brain is fundamentally a prediction engine: rather than passively registering sensory data, it continuously generates predictions about incoming information and adjusts these based on prediction errors (Friston, 2010; Clark, 2013).

This neurocomputational approach departs from traditional stimulus-response paradigms by proposing that perception, cognition, and emotion are fundamentally inferential processes. The brain constantly forms probabilistic models—priors—about the world, and adjusts these models by comparing predicted and actual sensory input. In this sense, the brain seeks not to mirror reality, but to minimize surprise or *free energy* (Friston, 2009). These foundational assumptions of predictive coding have significant implications for psychotherapy: they suggest that therapeutic change can be understood as the updating of maladaptive priors through the structured creation of novel, prediction-error-rich experiences within a safe relational context (Van de Cruys et al., 2021; Wilkinson, 2023).

From an integrative perspective, the 3PI model offers a unifying lens to explain core mechanisms across diverse modalities—including CBT, psychodynamic, humanistic, and experiential therapies—by grounding them in a shared neuroscientific language. It allows psychotherapists to reframe intrapsychic and interpersonal processes not only in psychological terms (e.g., schemas, transferences, beliefs), but also as deeply embodied patterns of prediction and error correction, shaped by developmental experience and attachment history (Kiverstein, Miller & Rietveld, 2019).

One of the central tenets of the 3PI model is the hierarchical nature of prediction: higher-order priors (e.g., beliefs about the self, attachment templates, existential meanings) shape and constrain lower-order predictions (e.g., sensory, emotional, and interpersonal responses). Therapeutic work thus involves helping clients access, question, and revise rigid high-level priors that generate maladaptive bottom-up interpretations—such as "*I am unsafe,*" "*Others will abandon me*," or "*Emotions are dangerous*"—even in the absence of congruent environmental input (Wilkinson, 2022).

Moreover, the 3PI model accounts for why insight alone is often insufficient for change: unless prediction errors are encountered at the level of felt experience, the brain may resist updating entrenched priors (Seth & Friston, 2016). This provides a neuroscientific rationale for experiential techniques—such as imaginal exposure, guided imagery, chair work, or sensorimotor integration—often employed in integrative psychotherapy. These techniques aim to create novel experiences that challenge and ultimately recalibrate the client's predictive model of the world.

From this viewpoint, psychotherapy becomes a relationally mediated, prediction-error-inducing dialogue, wherein the psychotherapist serves not just as a reflective witness, but as a regulated co-agent helping the client process mismatches between expectations and actual outcomes. This therapeutic mismatch—when safely contained—opens a window for revising the self and world models that govern perception, behaviour, and emotional regulation (Wilkinson, 2023).

At the core of the Predictive Processing (3PI) model lies the assumption that the brain is fundamentally a prediction engine. Rather than passively receiving sensory input and constructing meaning post hoc, the brain is continuously generating predictions about incoming data based on prior experiences (Clark, 2013; Friston, 2010). These predictions are tested against actual sensory inputs, and the brain minimizes the discrepancy—termed "prediction error"—through perceptual, attentional, or behavioural adjustments. This ongoing recursive process allows the brain to anticipate rather than merely react, thereby constructing a coherent and adaptive model of reality.

In psychotherapy, this has profound implications. Psychological suffering can be conceptualized as the result of maladaptive or rigid predictions—priors—that fail to update in light of new experiences. For example, a client who consistently predicts abandonment in relationships will interpret ambiguous relational cues (e.g., a delayed reply to a message) as confirmation of that belief, reinforcing the prediction rather than revising it. This dynamic is no longer limited to cognitive distortions at the conscious level but includes deeply encoded hierarchical predictions operating below the threshold of awareness (Seth, 2015).

Friston's (2010) Bayesian brain hypothesis informs much of this model: the brain weights prediction errors based on precision estimates. That is, when the brain expects input to be reliable (high precision), it will prioritize prediction errors more strongly and revise its model accordingly. Conversely, when predictions are highly confident (or rigid), even large discrepancies may be ignored or rationalized. This explains why some individuals continue maladaptive behaviours despite clear evidence of their dysfunction—they are operating under rigid priors that resist revision.

In this sense, the self is not a static entity but a generative, hierarchical prediction model across cognitive, affective, behavioural, and interpersonal domains. Each level—from bodily interoception to high-level beliefs—interacts with and updates the others.

From the earliest moments of life, the infant brain begins generating predictions about the world based on sensory input and relational experiences. These early predictions—rooted in attachment, affect regulation, and sensory-motor interactions—form the foundational priors for how the self, others, and reality are interpreted (Fotopoulou & Tsakiris, 2017). The repeated co-occurrence of internal sensations (e.g., hunger, discomfort) and external responses (e.g., soothing or neglect) shapes an implicit model of relational safety, self-worth, and emotional regulation capacity.

In the language of predictive processing, secure attachment promotes flexible priors with moderate precision—meaning that the child learns that their predictions can be trusted but are also updateable in light of new evidence. Insecure or disorganized attachment, on the other hand, may lead to overly rigid or overly uncertain priors. A child who consistently experiences unpredictable or emotionally misattuned caregiving might develop high-precision priors that the world is unsafe or that emotional needs will not be met, leading to persistent hypervigilance or emotional suppression.

These early predictive models are encoded not only in cognitive representations but also somatically and interpersonally. The body becomes a predictive map of expected affective and relational states (Schore, 2012). For example, a client with early trauma may predict danger in any context where vulnerability is present. This prediction might not manifest as a thought, but as muscle tension, nausea, or avoidance—reflecting deeply embodied priors that are "felt" rather than "thought."

Crucially, 3PI theory explains both the stability and the potential plasticity of personality and psychopathology. Predictions that are strongly reinforced by repeated emotional or interpersonal feedback become difficult to dislodge—until sufficient prediction error is experienced in a safe therapeutic context. This underscores the importance of a stable therapeutic alliance as a space where the client's predictive system can be gently but consistently challenged and updated.

In the framework of the Predictive Processing model, psychopathology can be conceptualised as the result of maladaptive or overly rigid predictions that fail to update despite contradictory sensory or interpersonal input. These faulty predictions—often rooted in early developmental experiences—generate persistent prediction errors that are either ignored, misinterpreted, or excessively weighted due to the precision of prior beliefs (Friston, 2010; Badcock et al., 2017).

For example, in anxiety disorders, the brain may assign excessive precision to priors that predict threat. Even in objectively safe situations, the brain continues to predict danger, leading to chronic hyperarousal and hypervigilance. These high-precision priors override incoming sensory evidence (e.g., calm environments), generating a persistent mismatch between perception and reality. This mismatch is experienced subjectively as anxiety, dread, or panic, and reinforces the original prediction—creating a feedback loop that maintains the disorder.

In depression, the predictive system may become biased towards negative expectations about the self, others, and the future (Barrett et al., 2016). Prediction errors (such as positive experiences or signs of approval) are given insufficient weight and therefore fail to update the existing model. A depressed client might consistently anticipate rejection or failure, even when evidence suggests otherwise.

This leads to a narrowing of experiential possibilities and a progressive loss of agency.

Similarly, in trauma-related disorders, prediction mechanisms are deeply disrupted. The system becomes over-sensitised to cues of threat and may generalise fear responses to neutral or ambiguous stimuli. The brain prioritises survival-based predictions over context-sensitive updating, often through mechanisms of dissociation, avoidance, or emotional numbing (van der Kolk, 2014). These are attempts to minimise overwhelming prediction error in the face of irreconcilable trauma-related input.

Predictive Processing also provides an elegant account of dissociation. From this perspective, dissociation may occur when the system suppresses prediction error from lower levels (e.g., interoceptive or affective signals) in order to preserve high-level models that are deemed necessary for coherence or survival. This creates a functional split in consciousness—parts of the system operate on one model (e.g., "I am safe now"), while other parts operate on another (e.g., "I am still in danger"), resulting in compartmentalisation, memory gaps, or somatic flashbacks (Holmes et al., 2005).

In each of these examples, psychopathology is not viewed as the result of a "broken" system but rather as the consequence of an overly constrained predictive hierarchy—one that fails to integrate new evidence because prior beliefs are too rigid or threat-laden. This framing not only de-pathologises the client's symptoms but also opens therapeutic space for compassionate, neurobiologically informed exploration of why these predictions once made sense.

Therapeutic change in the Predictive Processing framework is viewed as a process of gently destabilising maladaptive high-level priors and allowing the client to incorporate new, more adaptive experiences that update the predictive hierarchy (Friston et al., 2017; Holmes & Nolte, 2019). In this model, the goal of psychotherapy becomes the facilitation of *precisely calibrated prediction error*—not too overwhelming (which leads to defensiveness or shutdown), but not so subtle as to go unnoticed.

A skilled psychotherapist helps the client modulate the precision of both prior beliefs and incoming sensory or emotional evidence. For example, if a client holds the belief that "*Others will abandon me if I express anger*," the therapist might gradually invite expressions of frustration within the safety of the therapeutic relationship. By receiving empathic atonement rather than rejection, the client experiences a *prediction error*—their brain must reconcile the expectation of abandonment with the actual experience of acceptance. If repeated and integrated, such moments begin to *update the generative model* of relational safety.

This process closely parallels what many psychotherapeutic modalities already emphasise: the corrective emotional experience (Alexander & French, 1946), the co-construction of meaning (Stiles, 2007), and the reparative attachment relationship (Wallin, 2007). What the 3PI model contributes is a unifying neurocomputational account of these processes, one that links the psychological with the biological, the interpersonal with the perceptual, and the cognitive with the affective.

Notably, the success of this updating process depends on the client's ability to remain regulated and engaged while experiencing disconfirming evidence. This is where the concept of *affective precision* becomes central. If the client is overwhelmed by the intensity of emotional arousal (i.e., too much prediction error with insufficient precision control), they may resort to old defensive strategies—such as withdrawal, dissociation, or intellectualisation. Therefore, the psychotherapist must scaffold the experience, pacing interventions to the client's capacity for tolerance, what is often referred to as working within the "window of tolerance" (Siegel, 2010).

Moreover, the Predictive Processing model accounts for the phenomenon of resistance as a natural defensive mechanism of the predictive mind. Resistance, from this view, is not opposition to change per se, but an *attempt to preserve the coherence of the current model of self and world.* It reflects the brain's preference for stability over chaos and its tendency to minimise surprise. Understanding this allows psychotherapists to work with resistance more compassionately—as a sign that the system is doing its job to protect the client from unbearable disorganisation.

The therapeutic relationship becomes the space in which safety, atonement, and gradual exposure to new patterns of interaction allow for the softening of rigid priors and the integration of new relational templates. When the psychotherapist can provide both predictability (to stabilise the system) and novelty (to facilitate learning), a dynamic equilibrium is created—what we might call *optimal prediction error* for transformation.

References

Alexander, F., & French, T. M. (1946). *Psychoanalytic therapy: Principles and application.* Ronald Press.

Allen, M., & Friston, K. J. (2018). From cognitivism to autopoiesis: Towards a computational framework for the embodied mind. *Synthese*, 195(6), 2459–2482.

Alexander, F., & French, T. M. (1946). *Psychoanalytic Therapy: Principles and Application*. Ronald Press.

Addis, D. R., Wong, A. T., & Schacter, D. L. (2009). *Remembering the past and imagining the future: Common and distinct neural substrates during event construction and elaboration*. Neuropsychologia, 45(7), 1363–1377.

Badcock, P. B., Davey, C. G., Whittle, S., Allen, N. B., & Friston, K. J. (2017). The depressed brain: An evolutionary systems theory. *Trends in Cognitive Sciences, 21*(3), 182–194. https://doi.org/10.1016/j.tics.2017.01.005

Bandura, A. (1977). *Social Learning Theory*. Prentice Hall.

Barrett, L. F., Quigley, K. S., & Hamilton, P. (2016). An active inference theory of allostasis and interoception in depression. *Philosophical Transactions of the Royal Society B: Biological Sciences, 371*(1708), 20160011. https://doi.org/10.1098/rstb.2016.0011

Beck, J. S. (2011). *Cognitive Behavior Therapy: Basics and Beyond* (2nd ed.). Guilford Press.

Beutler, L. E., Consoli, A. J., & Lane, G. (2005). Systematic treatment selection and planning. In J. C. Norcross & M. R. Goldfried (Eds.), *Handbook of psychotherapy integration* (2nd ed., pp. 121–143). Oxford University Press.

Beutler, L. E., Clarkin, J. F. (1990). *Systematic treatment selection: Toward targeted therapeutic interventions*. Brunner/Mazel.

Beutler, L. E., Consoli, A. J., & Lane, G. (2005). Systematic treatment selection and prescriptive therapy: Blending art, science, and subjectivity. In J. C. Norcross & M. R. Goldfried (Eds.), *Handbook of psychotherapy integration* (2nd ed., pp. 121–143). Oxford University Press.

Beitman, B. D., & Yue, G. (2004). *Integrating Psychotherapy*. W. W. Norton.

Beitman, B. D., Celebi, E., & Coleman, J. L. (2003). *What prompts patients to enter psychotherapy?*. Journal of Psychotherapy Practice and Research, 12(1), 20–29.

Bowlby, J. (1982). *Attachment and loss: Vol. 1. Attachment* (2nd ed.). Basic Books. (Original work published 1969)

Brooks-Harris, J. E. (2008). *Integrative Multitheoretical Psychotherapy*. Houghton Mifflin Company.

Brooks-Harris, J. E., & Ivey, A. E. (2005). *Multicultural Counseling and Psychotherapy: A Lifespan Perspective*. Houghton Mifflin.

Castonguay, L. G. (2013). Psychotherapy integration: A postmodern critique. In J. C. Norcross & M. R. Goldfried (Eds.), *Handbook of psychotherapy integration* (2nd ed., pp. 222–235). Oxford University Press.

Castonguay, L. G., & Beutler, L. E. (2006). Common and unique principles of therapeutic change: What do we know and what do we need to know? In L. G. Castonguay & L. E. Beutler (Eds.), *Principles of therapeutic change that work* (pp. 353–369). Oxford University Press.

Castonguay, L. G., Constantino, M. J., & Holtforth, M. G. (2005). The working alliance: Where are we and where should we go? *Psychotherapy: Theory, Research, Practice, Training*, 42(3), 306–323.

Castonguay, L. G., Goldfried, M. R., Hayes, A. M., Rane, D. M., Shapiro, D. A., & Wiser, S. (1996). Predicting the effect of cognitive therapy for depression: A study of unique and common factors. *Journal of Consulting and Clinical Psychology, 64*(3), 497–504.

Castonguay, L. G., Goldfried, M. R., Wiser, S., Raue, P. J., & Hayes, A. M. (2003). Predicting the effect of cognitive therapy for depression: A study of unique and common factors. *Journal of Consulting and Clinical Psychology*, 64(3), 497–504.

Clark, A. (2013). Whatever next? Predictive brains, situated agents, and the future of cognitive science. *Behavioral and Brain Sciences, 36*(3), 181–204. https://doi.org/10.1017/S0140525X12000477

Cooper, M., & McLeod, J. (2011). *Pluralistic Counselling and Psychotherapy*. Sage.

Drobot, L., & Popescu, O. M. (2013). *Terapia integrativă strategică. Fundamente şi aplicaţii clinice*. Timişoara: Eurostampa.

Earley, J. (2012). *Self-therapy: A step-by-step guide to creating wholeness and healing your inner child using Internal Family Systems (IFS)*. Pattern System Books.

Emmerson, G. (2007). *Ego State Therapy*. Crown House Publishing.

Erskine, R. G., Moursund, J. P., & Trautmann, R. L. (1999). *Beyond empathy: A therapy of contact-in-relationship*. Brunner-Routledge.

Erskine, R. G., & Moursund, J. P. (2011). *Integrative psychotherapy in action: A relational approach*. W. W. Norton & Company.

Fall, K. A., Holden, J. M., & Marquis, A. (2010). *Theoretical Models of Counseling and Psychotherapy* (2nd ed.). Routledge.

Frank, J. D., & Frank, M. (1991). *Persuasion and Healing: A Comparative Study of Psychotherapy* (3rd ed.). Johns Hopkins University Press.

Frederick, R. J. (2005). *Healing the fragmented selves of trauma survivors: Overcoming internal self-alienation*. Routledge.

Frederick, R. J. (2005). *Living like you mean it: Use the wisdom and power of your emotions to get the life you really want*. Jossey-Bass.

Fotopoulou, A., & Tsakiris, M. (2017). Mentalizing homeostasis: The social origins of interoceptive inference. *Neuropsychoanalysis, 19*(1), 3–28. https://doi.org/10.1080/15294145.2017.1294031

Friston, K. (2009). The free-energy principle: A rough guide to the brain? *Trends in Cognitive Sciences, 13*(7), 293–301. https://doi.org/10.1016/j.tics.2009.04.005

Friston, K. (2010). The free-energy principle: A unified brain theory? *Nature Reviews Neuroscience, 11*(2), 127–138. https://doi.org/10.1038/nrn2787

Friston, K., FitzGerald, T., Rigoli, F., Schwartenbeck, P., & Pezzulo, G. (2017). Active inference: A process theory. *Neural Computation, 29*(1), 1–49. https://doi.org/10.1162/NECO_a_00912

Gallese, V., Keysers, C., & Rizzolatti, G. (2004). A unifying view of the basis of social cognition. *Trends in Cognitive Sciences, 8*(9), 396–403. https://doi.org/10.1016/j.tics.2004.07.002

Gilbert, M. C., & Orlans, V. (2011). *Integrative therapy: A practitioner's guide*. Sage Publications.

Gold, S. H., & Wachtel, P. L. (2006). *Relational theory and the practice of psychotherapy*. Guilford Press.

Halgin, R. P. (2006). *Abnormal Psychology: Clinical Perspectives on Psychological Disorders* (4th ed.). McGraw-Hill.

Holmes, E. A., Brown, R. J., Mansell, W., Fearon, R. P., Hunter, E. C. M., Frasquilho, F., & Oakley, D. A. (2005). Are there two qualitatively distinct forms of dissociation? A review and some clinical implications. *Clinical Psychology Review, 25*(1), 1–23. https://doi.org/10.1016/j.cpr.2004.08.006

Holmes, J., & Nolte, T. (2019). Attachment and the prediction of mental states. *Psychoanalytic Psychotherapy, 33*(1), 98–110. https://doi.org/10.1080/02668734.2019.1600036

Kiverstein, J., Miller, M., & Rietveld, E. (2019). The feeling of grip: Novelty, error dynamics, and the predictive mind. *Synthese, 196*, 2847–2869. https://doi.org/10.1007/s11229-017-1396-y

Lazarus, A. A. (1976). *Multimodal behavior therapy*. Springer Publishing Company.

Lazarus, A. A. (1981). *The Practice of Multimodal Therapy: Systematic, Comprehensive, and Effective Psychotherapy*. McGraw-Hill.

Lazarus, A. A. (1997). *Brief But Comprehensive Psychotherapy: The Multimodal Way*. Springer Publishing.

Lazarus, A. A. (2006). Multimodal Therapy: Technical Eclecticism with Empirical Support. In J. C. Norcross (Ed.), *Psychotherapy Relationships That Work* (pp. 320–335). Oxford University Press.

Lazarus, A. A. (2006). *Multimodal Therapy: A Useful Framework for the Practicing Clinician*. In Norcross, J. C., Beutler, L. E., & Levant, R. F. (Eds.), *Evidence-Based Practices in Mental Health: Debate and Dialogue on the Fundamental Questions* (pp. 105–114). APA.

Lazarus, A. A., & Lazarus, C. N. (1991). *Multimodal Therapy: A Technical Eclectic Approach*. In A. Freeman, K. M. Simon, L. E. Beutler, & H. Arkowitz (Eds.), *Comprehensive Handbook of Cognitive Therapy* (pp. 165–186). Plenum Press.

Miller, S. D., Duncan, B. L., & Hubble, M. A. (1995). *The heart and soul of change: Delivering what works in therapy*. American Psychological Association.

Minuchin, S. (1974). *Families and Family Therapy*. Harvard University Press.

Norcross, J. C., & Goldfried, M. R. (2005). *Handbook of Psychotherapy Integration* (2nd ed.). Oxford University Press.

Norcross, J. C., Krebs, P. M., & Prochaska, J. O. (2011). Stages of change. *Journal of Clinical Psychology, 67*(2), 143–154. https://doi.org/10.1002/jclp.20758

Prochaska, J. O., & DiClemente, C. C. (2005). The transtheoretical approach. In J. C. Norcross & M. R. Goldfried (Eds.), *Handbook of psychotherapy integration* (2nd ed., pp. 147–171). Oxford University Press.

Prochaska, J. O., & Norcross, J. C. (2010). *Systems of Psychotherapy: A Transtheoretical Analysis* (7th ed.). Brooks/Cole.

Prochaska, J. O., & Velicer, W. F. (1997). The transtheoretical model of health behavior change. *American Journal of Health Promotion, 12*(1), 38–48. https://doi.org/10.4278/0890-1171-12.1.38

Sapolsky, R. M. (2004). *Why Zebras Don't Get Ulcers* (3rd ed.). Holt Paperbacks.

Schacter, D. L., Addis, D. R., & Buckner, R. L. (2007). *Remembering the past to imagine the future: The prospective brain*. Nature Reviews Neuroscience, 8(9), 657–661.

Schmidt, S. J. (2009). *The Developmental Needs Meeting Strategy therapist manual* (2nd ed.). DNMS Institute.

Schore, A. N. (2012). *The science of the art of psychotherapy*. W. W. Norton & Company.

Schwartz, R. C. (1995). *Internal family systems therapy*. Guilford Press.

Schwartz, R. C., & Sweezy, M. (2020). *Internal family systems therapy* (2nd ed.). Guilford Press.

Seth, A. K. (2015). The cybernetic Bayesian brain: From interoceptive inference to sensorimotor contingencies. In T. Metzinger & J. M. Windt (Eds.), *Open MIND*. MIND Group.

Seth, A. K., & Friston, K. J. (2016). Active interoceptive inference and the emotional brain. *Philosophical Transactions of the Royal Society B: Biological Sciences, 371*(1708), 20160007. https://doi.org/10.1098/rstb.2016.0007

Siegel, D. J. (2010). *The Mindful Therapist: A Clinician's Guide to Mindsight and Neural Integration*. Norton.

Siegel, D. J. (2010). *The Developing Mind: How Relationships and the Brain Interact to Shape Who We Are* (2nd ed.). Guilford Press.

Siegel, D. J. (2012). *The Developing Mind: How Relationships and the Brain Interact to Shape Who We Are* (2nd ed.). Guilford Press.

Stiles, W. B. (2007). Theory-building case studies of counselling and psychotherapy. *Counselling and Psychotherapy Research, 7*(2), 122–127. https://doi.org/10.1080/14733140701356742

Stricker, G., & Gold, J. R. (2006). *A Casebook of Psychotherapy Integration*. APA Books.

Stricker, G., & Gold, J. R. (2006). *Assimilative psychodynamic psychotherapy*. In J. C. Norcross & M. R. Goldfried (Eds.), *Handbook of psychotherapy integration* (2nd ed., pp. 205–230). Oxford University Press.

Van de Cruys, S., Evers, K., Van der Hallen, R., Van Eylen, L., Boets, B., De-Wit, L., & Wagemans, J. (2021). Precise minds in uncertain worlds: Predictive coding in autism. *Psychological Review, 128*(1), 45–76. https://doi.org/10.1037/rev0000190

Van der Kolk, B. A. (2014). *The body keeps the score: Brain, mind, and body in the healing of trauma*. Viking.

Wachtel, P. L. (2008). *Relational theory and the practice of psychotherapy*. Guilford Press.

Wachtel, P. L., Kruk, A. J., & McKinney, M. K. (2005). *Cyclical psychodynamics and the contextual self: The inner world, the intimate world, and the world of culture and society*. American Psychological Association.

Wachtel, P. L., & Wachtel, E. F. (1986). *Family dynamics in individual psychotherapy: A guide to clinical strategies*. Guilford Press.

Wallin, D. J. (2007). *Attachment in Psychotherapy*. Guilford Press.

Wampold, B. E. (2001). *The great psychotherapy debate: Models, methods, and findings*. Lawrence Erlbaum Associates.

Watkins, J. G., & Watkins, H. H. (1997). *Ego states: Theory and therapy*. W. W. Norton & Company.

Weinberger, J. (1995). Common factors aren't so common: The common factors dilemma. *Clinical Psychology: Science and Practice, 2*(1), 45–69.

Wilkinson, H. (2005). *The Muse, the Mirror, and the Mirror-Image: Imagination in Psychotherapy*. British Journal of Psychotherapy, 21(4), 515–531.

Wilkinson, H. (2006). *Beyond Postmodernism: Towards a Post-Disciplinary Meta-Modality of Psychotherapy*. Self & Society, 34(4), 10–18.

Wilkinson, H. (2010). *Therapists and the Mystery of the Soul: An Existential Post-Secular Perspective*. Journal of Psychotherapy Integration, 20(3), 258–274.

Wilkinson, H. (2023). *Metamodality of Psychotherapy – Draft*. Retrieved from psychotherapy.org.uk

Wilkinson, H. (2024). *A Bit of a Puzzler: Integrative Psychotherapy as Paradigm and as Impasse: The Meta-modality of Integration and Psychotherapy*. *International Journal of Psychotherapy*, 28(1).

Wilkinson, H. (2025). *Towards: Theory of Metamodality of Psychotherapy*. Unpublished manuscript, retrieved from hewardwilkinson.co.uk

Wilkinson, R. (2022). The therapeutic application of predictive processing: Making sense of emotion, interoception and trauma. *Frontiers in Psychology, 13*, 809345. https://doi.org/10.3389/fpsyg.2022.809345

Wilkinson, R. (2023). *The sense of self: Perspectives from predictive processing*. Routledge.

CHAPTER 3

FUNDAMENTALS OF INTEGRATIVE STRATEGIC PSYCHOTHERAPY

3.1. Theoretical Foundations of Integrative Strategic Psychotherapy

Integrative Strategic Psychotherapy (ISP) rests on a rich and interdisciplinary theoretical foundation, uniting insights from relational, cognitive, emotional, neurobiological, psychodynamic, existential, and systemic frameworks. It does not merely juxtapose techniques but integrates principles strategically and developmentally, addressing the individual in their complexity, within a relational, neurobiological, and symbolic field.

At its core, ISP recognises that no single therapeutic modality can account for the multiplicity of human experience. Instead, it strategically draws from evidence-based traditions to create a coherent model of the self and a flexible system of intervention. This model is grounded in contemporary research in psychotherapy, neuroscience, and developmental psychology, as well as longstanding clinical wisdom (Popescu & Drobot, 2012; Popescu & Vîşcu, 2016; Popescu, 2021).

1. Relational Integrative Psychotherapy

A central tenet of ISP is the primacy of the therapeutic relationship. Influenced by Relational Integrative Psychotherapy (Erskine, 2021), the relationship is not simply a medium for intervention—it is itself the intervention. The relational field becomes the container within which developmental repair, emotional atonement, and experiential transformation unfold. Recent research confirms that psychotherapist responsiveness, empathic atonement, and real relationship quality are among the strongest predictors of therapeutic outcome (Norcross & Lambert, 2023).

2. Common Factors and Strategic Integration

ISP incorporates the common factors framework, identifying core elements that cut across therapeutic schools—such as alliance, empathy, expectation, and enactment—as foundational mechanisms of change (Wampold & Imel, 2022). However, ISP goes further: it does not apply interventions randomly but strategically, based on a developmental understanding of the self. Strategic psychotherapy, originally conceptualised by Haley (1973) and refined by modern integrative theorists (Korman et al., 2021), aligns techniques with targeted levels of functioning—whether biological, emotional, symbolic, or relational. In ISP, every intervention is mapped to a specific level and axis of the self (Popescu, 2021).

3. Developmental Neurobiology and Psychotherapy

Neurobiological theory provides the backbone of the ISP model. The human brain is not merely a passive processor but a socially and emotionally shaped organ. As illustrated in Chapter 6, the development of neural maps is influenced by early experiences, attachment relationships, and environmental input, interacting continuously with the genome and epigenome (Meaney, 2010; Klengel & Binder, 2015). ISP integrates findings from interpersonal neurobiology (Siegel, 2021), affective neuroscience (Panksepp & Biven, 2020), and polyvagal theory (Porges, 2022), recognising that psychotherapy can rewire emotional circuitry through relational safety and co-regulation.

4. Cognitive-Behavioural Contributions

Cognitive-behavioural elements within ISP are not limited to classical CBT interventions but extend to the mapping of cognitive schemas, automatic thoughts, and the correction of maladaptive beliefs. ISP uses these as tools for understanding the cognitive axis of the self, particularly at the level of the core and plastic selves. New developments in third-wave CBT approaches, such as metacognitive therapy and schema therapy, are incorporated when addressing rigidity, cognitive rumination, or dysfunctional mentalisation (Wells & Fisher, 2021; Young et al., 2020).

5. Attachment Theory

Attachment theory is foundational to the ISP model, informing how early relational experiences shape the architecture of the self and its regulatory systems (Schore, 2021; Bowlby, 1988). ISP integrates both developmental attachment science and adult attachment dynamics, recognising their relevance not only for understanding pathology but for shaping therapeutic stance. Secure attachment with the psychotherapist acts as a reparative experience that gradually reorganises internal working models at all levels of the self.

6. Psychodynamic Psychotherapy

ISP draws extensively from psychodynamic theory, especially in its treatment of the unconscious, defence mechanisms, transference, countertransference, and internal conflicts. In line with contemporary psychodynamic research, these elements are considered active and dynamic forces in the therapeutic process (Luyten et al., 2020). ISP particularly values psychodynamic contributions to understanding the vertical depth of the self, including repressed experiences, life scripts, and symbolic narratives that shape identity.

7. Person-Centered Psychotherapy

The person-centered perspective contributes the essential role of unconditional positive regard, empathic atonement, and congruence (Rogers, 1957). ISP uses these not merely as ethical values, but as therapeutic strategies to create a relational field in which conditions of worth are dismantled, and authentic self-expression becomes possible. Emotional processing is prioritised within a warm, non-directive frame before strategic interventions are introduced.

8. Existential Psychotherapy

Drawing from the existential tradition, ISP addresses fundamental human concerns—freedom, death, isolation, and meaning (Yalom, 2020)—as core dynamics in many clinical presentations. The perception of time, existential guilt, and the construction of meaning are frequently explored within ISP, especially at the level of the external self, where symbolic identity and cultural scripts are negotiated.

9. Transactional Analysis

The conceptual tools of Transactional Analysis (Berne, 1961), such as life scripts, ego states (Parent–Adult–Child), and psychological games, are used in ISP to understand repetitive relational patterns and intrapsychic dynamics. These constructs allow a structured analysis of the self's developmental trajectory and are particularly helpful in psychoeducation and re-authoring life narratives (Stewart & Joines, 2012).

10. Ericksonian Hypnosis and Mental Imagery

Ericksonian methods enrich ISP through their focus on utilisation, indirect suggestion, metaphorical language, and mental imagery. These techniques access the symbolic and non-verbal layers of the self—especially the proto-self and unconscious dimensions—to generate change when cognitive insight alone is insufficient (Zeig, 2021). Hypnotic language and imagery are also strategically used to foster internal differentiation, emotion regulation, and embodied transformation.

11. Psychodrama and Expressive Techniques

Psychodramatic and experiential group methods contribute to the ISP approach through role-play, externalisation, and symbolic enactment. These are useful for activating the plastic and external self, working with unfinished business, and deepening emotional integration. Psychodrama allows for corrective symbolic experiences and the rehearsal of new relational scripts (Kellermann, 2021).

12. Family Therapy and Systemic Thinking

ISP is informed by systemic principles, recognising that the self is not an isolated entity but part of multigenerational and cultural systems. It incorporates insights from family roles, alliances, rules, and intergenerational patterns, particularly when working with clients in developmental or relational crisis (Carr, 2020). Strategic interventions are often systemic in nature, addressing not only the self but also the external field in which it is embedded.

13. Gestalt Therapy

From Gestalt therapy, ISP adopts, the importance of here-and-now awareness, and the recognition of unfinished gestalt figures. These principles are used to promote embodied presence, authenticity, and integration, particularly when working with fragmented or dissociated states of self (Perls, Hefferline, & Goodman, 1951; Joyce & Sills, 2022).

In sum, the theoretical foundations of ISP are both broad and deeply integrated. Rather than forming a patchwork of techniques, ISP aligns each concept strategically within a coherent developmental model of the self, guided by the axes of cognition, emotion, and psychodynamic processes, and by the four-level structure of the self: proto-, core, plastic, and external. This alignment enables flexible, precise, and deeply personalised psychotherapy.

3.2. Basic Principles of Integrative Strategic Psychotherapy

The fundamental principles of ISP reflect an evolving understanding of psychotherapy as both an art and a science. As an approach, ISP does not reduce the psychotherapeutic process to techniques or schools. Rather, it organises the psychotherapeutic encounter according to strategic principles: these include clarity of intention, precision in case formulation, flexibility in methodology, and deep respect for the client's internal logic. ISP seeks to mobilise change by integrating multiple levels of the self (biological, cognitive, emotional, relational, existential), while adapting to the temporal, cultural, and developmental context of each individual.

The eight core principles of ISP are: Principle 1 (Common Factors) positions the therapeutic relationship as the heart of change; Principle 2 (Therapeutic Myth) emphasises the need for narrative resonance; Principle 3 (Strategic Phases) ensures a coherent, purposeful treatment trajectory; Principle 4 (Therapist Development) highlights the psychotherapist as the instrument of transformation; Principle 5 (Intervention Match) supports nuanced, case-based intervention planning; Principle 6 (Complexity of the Psyche) encourages deep, multidimensional formulation; Principle 7 (Flexibility) empowers psychotherapists to adjust to context, need, and relational rhythm; and Principle 8 (Research-Based Practice) anchors ISP in the evolving science of psychotherapy.

Principle 1: Common therapeutic factors are the main drivers of change

One of the most enduring findings in psychotherapy research is that no single psychotherapeutic model has demonstrated clear superiority over others across diverse populations and issues (Wampold & Imel, 2015). This "Dodo bird verdict," originally proposed by Saul Rosenzweig in 1936, asserts that most psychotherapies are equally effective due to shared therapeutic factors. This assertion is supported by decades of meta-analytic research (Duncan, 2014; Lambert, 2013) and continues to hold relevance in recent literature (Norcross & Lambert, 2023).

Within ISP, the most significant common factor is the therapeutic relationship itself—seen as a co-created relational matrix between the psychotherapist and the client. This echoes findings from Castonguay (2011), Antononoiu & Blom (2006), and Magnavita (2006), but is also reinforced by more recent evidence demonstrating that the quality of the therapeutic alliance consistently predicts outcome, regardless of technique (Flückiger, Del Re, Wampold, & Horvath, 2020).

Importantly, ISP frames the therapeutic relationship not only as a necessary precondition but as an active change agent in itself. The emotional and psychodynamic axes of the self are fundamentally shaped through relational experiences, especially attachment relationships. Modern attachment-based neuroscience confirms that human beings are biologically wired for co-regulation and interpersonal synchrony (Schore, 2021; Siegel, 2023). Dysregulation, pathology, and trauma are not only internal but relationally encoded—and must therefore be relationally repaired.

Thus, the ISP psychotherapist becomes a strategic partner in creating corrective emotional experiences, functioning as both attachment figure and developmental ally. Every intervention is filtered through the relational matrix. As Berenbaum et al. (2003) and Block (2002) noted, the root of psychopathology often lies in failures of early relational atonement, while the potential for healing resides in the psychotherapist's capacity to engage the client in a new relational template.

Emerging research in interpersonal neurobiology shows that such therapeutic resonance is not metaphorical—it involves measurable changes in right-brain-to-right-brain communication, vagal tone, limbic system synchrony, and even gene expression (Schore, 2021; Geller & Porges, 2021).

Principle 2: The therapeutic myth must be flexible and resonant

Every therapeutic system offers the client a conceptual framework—a "therapeutic myth" that explains suffering and frames hope. In ISP, this myth is not seen as a fixed doctrine but as a symbolic tool for meaning-making. The term myth here is not pejorative, but rather Jungian in spirit: a story that carries psychological truth and resonance.

While the psychotherapist holds the ISP framework for case formulation—an internal compass that integrates diagnostic, developmental, relational, neurobiological, and symbolic aspects—this does not need to be directly transmitted to the client in its full complexity. Instead, psychotherapists are encouraged to construct an explanatory model that is attuned to the client's worldview, language, developmental stage, and cognitive-emotional style.

This approach reflects recent work on the role of "mentalising narratives" in psychotherapy: creating stories that help clients make sense of their experience while fostering agency (Fonagy & Luyten, 2020). It is also supported by findings in psychotherapy process research, which show that client-perceived credibility of the therapeutic rationale predicts better engagement and outcomes (Constantino et al., 2021).

In integrative strategic psychotherapy, this means balancing the "inside map" of the clinician with the "outside map" that is offered to the client. Psychoeducation, metaphors, imagery, developmental explanations, or even humour may be used to generate a shared conceptual space that is both accurate and meaningful. When the therapeutic myth resonates, it becomes a container for complexity. When it does not, it risks becoming noise.

Principle 3: Treatment follows a structured, strategic process

The third principle outlines the structured phases of psychotherapy as envisioned within the ISP model, recognising that while each client follows a unique path, the therapeutic process moves through predictable arcs.

The following stages are essential: (1) Establishing the therapeutic alliance and co-creating the relational frame; (2) Maintaining and developing the therapeutic relationship across rupture and repair cycles; (3) Diagnostic process: both categorical (DSM, ICD) and dimensional (attachment, relational patterns, IWM structure, personality); (4) Case formulation grounded in ISP axes and levels of the self; (5) Presentation of a therapeutic myth, co-constructed and culturally sensitive; (6) Strategic treatment planning, adapted to stage of change and relational readiness; (7) Selection of interventions, matched to both deficits and resources; (8) Management of verbal and non-verbal processes: tone, pacing, metaphor, silence; (9) Relearning and re-experiencing, especially in relational, emotional and symbolic domains; and (10) Transfer and generalisation, where internal change becomes externalised in life.

These stages echo classical formulations (e.g., Eells, 2015), but in ISP they are dynamically integrated. The focus is always on intentionality: what do we target, why, and in what sequence? As Popescu & Drobot (2012) have written, ISP is defined by *strategic integration*, where method follows formulation—not theoretical allegiance.

Newer literature supports this structured flexibility. For example, Cuijpers et al. (2021) emphasise that effective psychotherapies typically involve clarity of goals, a credible rationale, phased progression, and outcome monitoring.

Principle 4: The psychotherapist's personal development influences the outcome of psychotherapy

In ISP, the psychotherapist is not a neutral technician but a central instrument of change. This principle recognises that the personal development of the psychotherapist—emotional maturity, relational atonement, capacity for self-reflection, and embodied presence—directly correlates with therapeutic effectiveness.

Research consistently shows that psychotherapist variables account for significant variance in psychotherapy outcomes, sometimes more than specific techniques or diagnoses (Baldwin & Imel, 2013; Wampold & Imel, 2015). Gilbert & Orlans (2011) and Connor (1994) argue that psychotherapists must cultivate not only technical competence but also personal insight, emotional resilience, and relational flexibility.

Recent studies deepen this understanding. Lutz et al. (2021) highlight how psychotherapist interpersonal skills, attachment style, and regulation of countertransference predict the depth and quality of therapeutic engagement. Similarly, Pakenham & Stafford-Brown (2022) found that psychotherapists with higher levels of emotional intelligence and psychological flexibility were better able to adapt interventions and manage therapeutic ruptures.

ISP identifies several key dimensions of therapist development: 1. Understanding and accepting one's own self, including internal contradictions and woundedness; 2. Awareness of strengths, not as achievements but as capacities for presence and service; 3. Recognition of blind spots and unresolved issues, especially those that activate countertransference; 4. Commitment to ongoing personal development, including supervision, therapy, and self-reflection; 5. Embodied understanding of developmental transitions, allowing empathy with client struggles; and 5. Relational sensitivity across contexts, with adaptive boundaries and attuned communication.

From an ISP perspective, the psychotherapist is engaged in a lifelong dialectic between the core self (internal integration), the plastic self (developmental flexibility), and the external self (relational competence). A stagnant psychotherapist cannot foster change. A rigid psychotherapist cannot model flexibility. A defensive psychotherapist cannot support vulnerability.

Neuroscience reinforces this. Therapists' own regulation patterns shape the therapeutic dyad's physiology—heart rate variability, mirror neuron activation, and right-hemisphere atonement (Geller & Porges, 2021; Schore, 2021). In other words, the psychotherapist's nervous system *is* part of the intervention. Thus, ISP frames personal development as a clinical necessity—not an optional luxury.

Principle 5: Interventions must be strategically adapted to the client's profile

Flexibility in intervention is not eclecticism. In ISP, the choice of intervention is neither random nor based on psychotherapist preference. Instead, interventions are selected based on a comprehensive, strategic understanding of the client's deficits, resources, internal logic, developmental stage, and relational matrix.

This principle emerges directly from the ISP approach to case formulation. The psychotherapist analyses the client's structure of the self across multiple axes (cognitive, emotional, psychodynamic) and domains (proto-self, core self, plastic self, external self). From this analysis, a therapeutic strategy is derived that includes: 1. Targeting *deficits* (e.g., emotional dysregulation, cognitive distortions, disorganised attachment); 2. Activating *resources* (e.g., intellectual insight, relational capacities, symbolic thinking); 3. Matching interventions to the *developmental stage* (e.g., early trauma requires different pacing than adolescent anxiety); 4. Adjusting interventions to *psychodynamic readiness* (e.g., defences, transference, ego strength); and 5. Considering *neurobiological patterns* (e.g., dissociation, somatisation, chronotype, arousal level).

For example, a client with unresolved early trauma and disorganised attachment may not benefit initially from purely cognitive interventions. Instead, interventions focusing on regulation, co-regulation, sensory integration, and body-based safety (e.g., guided imagery, rhythmic movement, somatic tracking) may be more effective. Later, cognitive and narrative work can be introduced to integrate insight with embodied experience.

New literature supports this precision. Hayes et al. (2020) emphasise that effective psychotherapy depends on *treatment fit*: the right intervention at the right moment in the right relational context. Similarly, Eubanks et al. (2021) argue that psychotherapist responsiveness—not allegiance to protocol—is the best predictor of client engagement and progress.

In ISP, this principle is not merely pragmatic—it is ethical. To impose one's preferred techniques without adapting to the client's profile risks re-traumatisation, rupture, or therapeutic impasse.

Principle 6: The integrative theoretical framework must account for the full complexity of intrapsychic functioning

Integrative Strategic Psychotherapy is founded on a metamodel that embraces complexity without fragmentation. It integrates theories, but not arbitrarily; the goal is to understand the whole person—not through theoretical synthesis alone, but through lived experience, relational dynamics, and biological processes. This principle asserts that intrapsychic dynamics must be approached from multiple lenses simultaneously: 1. Cognitive: schemas, beliefs, meaning-making, attentional bias; 2. Behavioural: habits, conditioning, avoidance strategies, skill deficits; 3. Psychodynamic: unconscious processes, internal conflicts, transference; 4. Emotional: expression and regulation of emotions, suppression / repression, guilt and shame; 5. Systemic: family dynamics, role expectations, intergenerational scripts; 6. Developmental: attachment history, trauma, resilience across stages; 7. Cultural and multicultural: identity, context, intersectionality, collective narratives; 8. Personality: temperament, traits, characterological patterns; and 9. Motivational: goal orientation, inner drives, avoidance/approach systems.

Importantly, this theoretical integration is not for conceptual display—it must guide clinical choices. ISP therapists are trained to identify which axes are dominant, which levels are active, and which formulations offer the clearest map for therapeutic movement.

Recent scholarship has emphasised the need for such trans-theoretical, multilevel approaches. For instance, Cooper & McLeod (2021) advocate for "pluralistic practice," where the client's unique needs shape the model, not the reverse. Likewise, the APA's 2023 task force on integrative care calls for combining biological, psychological, social, and spiritual dimensions in treatment.

In ISP, integration is grounded in neurobiological coherence. The genome and epigenome influence neural organisation, stress reactivity, temperament, and memory consolidation. Psychotherapeutic work at the psychological level can, over time, influence biology—reshaping patterns of gene expression, hormonal regulation, and neural connectivity (Doidge, 2020; Yehuda et al., 2021). Thus, ISP offers not only conceptual integration but *biological plausibility*—a model in which psyche and soma are not separate, but synergistically intertwined.

Principle 7: The Principle of Flexibility

Flexibility lies at the heart of ISP's clinical philosophy. It is the capacity to shift theoretical lenses, therapeutic stances, and intervention strategies to match the evolving needs of the client within the therapeutic relationship. Flexibility is not the absence of structure, but rather the capacity to strategically *use* structure while staying responsive to the moment-to-moment therapeutic process.

Unlike rigid, one-size-fits-all approaches, ISP embraces the principle that no single model can adequately account for the entire range of human experience.

The psychotherapist is therefore encouraged to be fluent in multiple theoretical languages and clinically adept in selecting, sequencing, and adapting interventions. This requires both theoretical integration and clinical creativity.

Recent psychotherapy literature has strongly endorsed this principle. Messina et al. (2022) argue that treatment responsiveness is a key predictor of outcome and that therapeutic inflexibility correlates with dropout and poor engagement. Meanwhile, Flückiger et al. (2020) highlight the psychotherapist's capacity to modulate technique and pacing in real time as one of the "hidden mechanisms" behind effective psychotherapy.

ISP applies flexibility in three main dimensions:

1. Flexibility across psychopathologies: The psychotherapist adapts strategies based on diagnostic profiles (e.g., ISP for depression integrates existential, attachment-based, and neurobiological interventions tailored to lethargy and loss of meaning; ISP for anxiety emphasises cognitive, regulatory, and exposure-based techniques);
2. Flexibility across relational patterns: Depending on the client's attachment style, defences, and transference dynamics, the psychotherapist may offer more structure or more freedom, more confrontation or more containment, more cognitive clarity or more embodied work; and
3. Flexibility across stages of change: Clients in pre-contemplation require different strategies (motivational, validating, relational containment) than those in action or relapse prevention (behavioural rehearsal, internalisation of insight, and transfer of change to external systems).

In neuropsychological terms, flexibility reflects *executive function*—the capacity to inhibit automatic responses, consider alternatives, and reorient to context. For the psychotherapist, this involves meta-cognition, tolerance of ambiguity, and emotional regulation.

Principle 8: Psychotherapy is Based on Research

A foundational principle of ISP is that integrative strategic psychotherapists must remain grounded in contemporary scientific research—both to enhance treatment outcomes and to uphold ethical standards of care. Psychotherapy is not a purely intuitive or artistic endeavour; it is also a scientifically informed practice that evolves alongside advances in clinical, neuroscientific, and psychological knowledge.

This principle is especially salient in the current era, as psychotherapy undergoes significant transformations informed by interpersonal neurobiology (Schore, 2021; Siegel, 2023), epigenetics and trauma (Yehuda et al., 2021; Klengel & Binder, 2020), cultural neuroscience and identity studies (Kim & Sasaki, 2022), evidence-based practice and practice-based evidence (Norcross & Wampold, 2023), process-based therapy and transtheoretical integration (Hofmann & Hayes, 2021).

ISP is aligned with this evolution. The model incorporates findings from developmental psychology, neuroscience, psychodynamic theory, CBT, trauma studies, systems theory, and psychotherapy process research to create a coherent, layered, and dynamic understanding of the self.

Scientific foundations in ISP include: 1. The neurobiological understanding of attachment, stress regulation, memory, and emotion (Doidge, 2020; Schore, 2021); 2. The role of early relational experiences in shaping brain architecture and epigenetic expression (Meaney & Szyf, 2020); 3. The recursive interaction between behaviour and biology (Howe & Lewis, 2021); 4. Evidence-based recognition of the therapeutic alliance as the most powerful predictor of change (Flückiger et al., 2020); 5. The integrative efficacy of common factors across modalities (Castonguay, 2020; Wampold & Imel, 2015); 6. The impact of transgenerational trauma on biology and behaviour (Yehuda et al., 2021); and 7. The clinical importance of psychotherapist factors such as empathy, regulation, and development (Lutz et al., 2021; Geller & Porges, 2021).

Psychotherapists working within ISP are therefore not only clinicians, but scientist-practitioners, continuously reflecting on their interventions, integrating new knowledge, and tailoring strategies to fit both theory and the lived experience of the client.

3.3. Case Formulation in Integrative Strategic Psychotherapy

Case formulation is a foundational process in Integrative Strategic Psychotherapy (ISP), serving as both a map and compass for therapeutic intervention. It bridges assessment and intervention, guiding clinical reasoning while remaining open to strategic adjustments. Unlike diagnostic classification systems that often reduce the client to a label, ISP's approach to formulation aims to construct a multidimensional, dynamic understanding of the self in context—biological, psychological and relational. Case formulation is not a static assessment but a flexible, evolving narrative that reflects the strategic nature of integrative psychotherapy (Wachtel, 2020).

For beginner psychotherapists, the initial sessions are often perceived as moments of exploration, where clients are encouraged to present their concerns and tell their story (Beck, 2021). However, within ISP, these early encounters are viewed not merely as opportunities for passive listening but as moments of diagnostic precision and therapeutic action. Even in the first session, the psychotherapist engages with the client's verbal and non-verbal cues, relational patterns, and intrapsychic dynamics, beginning the formulation process and potentially offering interventions—ranging from containment and clarification to micro-interpretation or psychoeducation (Hayes et.al., 2020).

One of the central challenges in early formulation is the process of clarification (Kernberg, 2020). While seemingly simple, clarification is often a subtle and complex task that distinguishes clinical listening from conversational understanding. In practice, it demands a disciplined form of presence, where the psychotherapist resists assumptions, projections, or theoretical shortcuts and remains attuned to the actual lived experience of the client (Magnavita, 2006). The Integrative Strategic psychotherapist aims to "clarify to precision," ensuring that each element of the client's problem is well understood before attempting to intervene.

Lack of clarity often arises from specific dynamics within the psychotherapist (Popescu, 2021; van der Kolk, 2021):

- *Accepting vague client formulations:* Beginner psychotherapists may feel uncomfortable asking for specificity, fearing it may appear intrusive or controlling. Yet, vague language often conceals emotional avoidance or confusion and requires gentle but firm deconstruction (Eells, 2022);
- *Countertransference distortions*: Psychotherapists may unknowingly project their own histories onto the client, leading to a premature or distorted formulation. Training in self-awareness and supervision is essential to prevent these enactments from shaping the case (Gelso & Hayes, 2023);
- *Cognitive overload:* In early sessions, novice clinicians may struggle to stay present, as they internally debate which questions to ask, what hypotheses to make, or how to behave "correctly." This performance anxiety can interfere with genuine listening and block accurate clarification;
- *Category-based thinking:* Instead of formulating the client's unique lived experience, the psychotherapist may reduce it to a diagnostic template,

assuming all clients with "anxiety" or "depression" follow the same mechanisms. ISP opposes this reductionism, insisting on tailored formulations rooted in the singularity of the client;

- *Engagement in unconscious psychological games:* The psychotherapist may unconsciously collude with the client's defences, distractions, or passive–aggressive enactments, missing critical cues for understanding (Stewart & Joines, 2012); and
- *Over-eagerness for interpretation:* Some psychotherapists attempt to interpret too soon, assuming insight will create change. However, premature interpretations often bypass the foundational stages of alliance, safety, and emotional atonement (Norcross & Lambert, 2023).

In ISP, the clarified formulation is one in which the psychotherapist arrives at a complete, multidimensional picture of the client's problem, grounded in both observable phenomena and the hypothesised dynamics underlying them. A clarified case allows the psychotherapist to understand: What exactly is the client's presenting concern? How does the concern manifest across the domains of the self (biological, core, plastic, external)? What are the psychological mechanisms that maintain the problem? Which past experiences contribute to the current suffering? What relational, cultural, or existential themes are embedded in the narrative? What are the client's internal resources, capacities, and developmental scaffolds?

Let us consider a simplified example. A client says: "*I'm overwhelmed—I have too much to do and I don't prioritise well.*" A surface-level response might validate the stress and offer basic strategies. However, a strategic integrative formulation would explore: What exactly does the client "have to do"? How does the day unfold? Is there internal fragmentation, avoidance, or perfectionism? What attachment anxieties or guilt may underlie the inability to prioritise? What self-states or unconscious injunctions might be sabotaging efficiency? How does the client experience time and failure existentially?

This deeper exploration creates a fertile ground for strategic interventions. Importantly, clarification is not a one-time event but an ongoing process, evolving alongside the client's capacity for insight and the unfolding of the therapeutic relationship. In Integrative Strategic Psychotherapy (ISP), case formulation represents a dynamic and recursive process that begins in the first session and continues throughout the therapeutic relationship. It is neither a static diagnosis nor a rigid theoretical template, but rather a hypothesis-generating framework that adapts to the complexity of the client's subjective experience, developmental history, and relational context. From the ISP perspective, case formulation is a central clinical act that integrates biological, cognitive, emotional, psychodynamic, systemic, cultural, and existential data into a coherent and strategically useful narrative (Eells, 2022; Popescu, 2021; Norcross & Goldfried, 2021).

Beyond Listening: The Active Role of the First Sessions

Beginner psychotherapists often enter clinical practice with the assumption that the early sessions are devoted exclusively to passive listening, intended only for gathering background information. While empathic listening is indeed fundamental, ISP emphasises that therapeutic intervention begins from the very first moment of contact. Even in the initial phase, interventions such as active clarification, empathic reflection, or supportive restructuring can influence the client's internal narrative and begin the process of change (Gelso & Hayes, 2023; Luyten, Campbell & Fonagy, 2020).

The act of clarification—a deceptively simple task—becomes one of the most powerful tools in early case formulation. Clarification involves more than paraphrasing or mirroring; it demands a strategic, intentional exploration of the client's experience in order to uncover implicit meanings, inconsistencies, and overlooked details. ISP recognises that early formulation is not about constructing a definitive diagnosis but about understanding the problem in its lived context and emotional valence (Castonguay, 2011; Cloitre et al., 2022). The therapeutic task is to co-construct a formulation that is meaningful, accurate, and strategically actionable.

Clarification is the scaffolding on which the entire case formulation is built. In ISP, we do not proceed to hypothesise about mechanisms of change or intervention strategies until we have achieved a working model of the client's experience that includes the following dimensions:

- *Content* — What exactly is the client reporting? What are the events, behaviours, or symptoms?
- *Form* — How does the client express their difficulties? What metaphors, narratives, or affective tones dominate?
- *Context* — When do these difficulties occur? With whom? In what developmental or relational history?

- *Meaning* — What does the client believe the problem signifies? How do they explain it to themselves and others?

Clarification moves the client from a vague, often affect-laden complaint ("*I feel overwhelmed all the time*") to a detailed, contextualised narrative ("*I feel overwhelmed especially when I'm with my partner, because I feel I have to be perfect and anticipate all his needs. This reminds me of how I had to behave with my mother growing up.")*. This shift marks the beginning of psychological insight, which in ISP is the platform for strategic intervention (Korman, Diamond, & Winter, 2021; Eells, 2022).

Clarifying also helps differentiate between the presenting problem and the underlying problem—a distinction fundamental to strategic models. The presenting problem is what the client initially brings to therapy. The underlying problem includes the intrapsychic, interpersonal, and systemic patterns that sustain it. For example, a complaint about poor time management may mask deeper issues of self-worth, perfectionism, or unconscious self-sabotage rooted in early attachment experiences.

In ISP, clarification is always relationally co-constructed. It is not imposed by the psychotherapist but developed through empathic inquiry, Socratic dialogue, and strategic use of questions and metaphors. It requires active engagement and collaboration with the client's cognitive and emotional processing systems (Popescu, 2021; Norcross & Lambert, 2023).

In strategic integrative psychotherapy, case formulation is not a static or one-size-fits-all template, but a dynamic, hypothesis-generating process that evolves through the therapeutic alliance. It requires the psychotherapist to engage in a multidimensional inquiry (Fonagy et.al., 2021): decoding the intrapsychic architecture of the self, recognising relational and environmental influences, and integrating biological and developmental variables. Within the ISP framework, this means constructing a working model of the self that spans all four domains (proto-self, core self, plastic self, and external self) and integrates the three fundamental psychological axes (cognitive, emotional, and psychodynamic).

To begin formulating a case within ISP, one must balance scientific rigour with clinical intuition. This is achieved through strategic clarification, which is not merely an act of information gathering but a therapeutic intervention in itself (Luyten et.al., 2020). Clarification serves both diagnostic and relational purposes: it helps the therapist understand the client's reality, and it communicates attentiveness and respect. As emphasized by Eells (2022), clarification and hypothesis-testing are cornerstones of integrative case formulation and must be revisited continually.

Inexperienced psychotherapists often avoid rigorous clarification out of a misplaced desire to "follow" the client or due to anxieties about being intrusive. Others may prematurely formulate based on their own projections or experiences, falling into the trap of countertransference contamination (Gelso & Hayes, 2023). ISP encourages therapists to develop strategic patience—the capacity to stay with ambiguity while actively structuring the dialogue to bring underlying processes to the surface.

Presenting Problems and Underlying Problems

A foundational step in ISP case formulation is identifying and differentiating between presenting problems and underlying problems. The presenting problem may be overt (e.g., panic attacks, work-related stress), but it often serves as a mask for deeper, unconscious conflicts, unresolved attachment ruptures, or rigid cognitive schemas. This distinction mirrors the structure of the self in ISP: the external self manifests the symptoms, while the core and plastic selves often contain the deeper unresolved dynamics.

Effective Case Formulations

An effective ISP case formulation includes the following elements:

1. Clarified Problem Description (The What)

What precisely is the client struggling with? What is the functional impairment or subjective suffering? How is the problem maintained (e.g., avoidance behaviours, secondary gains)?

This phase requires moving from abstract to concrete language (Safran & Muran, 2022). For instance, *"I'm overwhelmed"* must be broken down into observable behaviours, internal states, and contextual triggers.

2. Multiaxial Analysis (The Why)

The ISP model considers that every clinical presentation emerges from a convergence of the cognitive, emotional, and psychodynamic axes. For each, the psychotherapist investigates:

a. Cognitive Axis

What maladaptive core beliefs and intermediate assumptions are active? Are automatic thoughts distorted or repetitive? Is the client aware of their internal dialogue? What is the level of metacognitive functioning (Wells & Fisher, 2021)?

Example: A client may hold the belief, *"I must be perfect to be loved,"* leading to persistent self-monitoring and anxiety in performance contexts.

b. Emotional Axis

What emotions are expressed, repressed, or denied? What is the client's capacity for emotional regulation and affect labelling (Linehan, 2021)? How secure is the client's attachment history, and are there indicators of relational trauma? Are shame, neurotic guilt, or existential anxiety active (Yalom, 2020)?

Example: A client may suppress anger due to early experiences of rejection when asserting themselves.

c. Psychodynamic Axis

Are there identifiable states of the self or internal parts in conflict (Erskine, 2021)? Are there unconscious motivations or life scripts reinforcing self-sabotaging behaviour (Stewart & Joines, 2012)? What is the nature of transference and countertransference already present in the therapeutic relationship (Hill & Knox, 2020)? Are there enactments or repetitions of early relational patterns occurring in the present (McWilliams, 2022)?

These insights emerge over time but must be hypothesised early in the process.

3. Developmental and Relational History (The When and Where)

What significant developmental ruptures or trauma events are evident (Beutler et.al., 2022)? What caregiving patterns shaped the proto-self and attachment strategies (Siegel, 2021)? Are there moments of relational repair, resilience, or positive scaffolding (Siegel, 2023)? What family myths, roles, or unspoken rules have defined the client's worldview (Carr, 2020)?

ISP case formulation acknowledges that adverse early experiences often become biologically embedded through epigenetic modulation, shaping the client's emotional and behavioural patterns well into adulthood (Klengel & Binder, 2015).

4. Phenotypic and Somatic Indicators (The How)

What is observable in the client's nonverbal communication—body posture, voice tone, eye contact, affective synchrony (Tseliou & Borcsa, 2023)? Are there somatic symptoms or dysregulations suggesting affective fragmentation or trauma (Ogden & Fisher, 2021)? Do body schema disruptions (e.g., disembodiment, posture collapse) provide clues about underlying trauma or dissociation?

The ISP psychotherapist incorporates this embodied data into the formulation, recognising the somatic level as a crucial window into the core self.

5.Systemic and Cultural Factors (The Context)

What macro-level influences shape the client's identity, worldview, and behavioural patterns (Chung & Hunt, 2021)? Are there sociocultural scripts, gender norms, or religious injunctions that reinforce the presenting problem (Kahl et.al., 2022)? How do ethnicity, class, or marginalisation influence the narrative of the self (Casement, 2014)?

These aspects are especially pertinent when working with clients from collectivist cultures or minority backgrounds, where intergenerational transmission of trauma, shame, or silence may prevail (Triandis & Suh, 2002).

6. Functional Diagnosis and Working Hypotheses (The Mechanisms)

Once the elements above are assessed, the psychotherapist can begin to formulate functional hypotheses about the mechanisms maintaining the client's difficulty. These may include (Greenberg & Pascual-Leone, 2020): avoidant coping styles perpetuating anxiety; repetition compulsion rooted in early attachment trauma; dysregulated self-states interacting through enactment; core beliefs reinforced through relational feedback loops; and somatic symptomatology protecting against unbearable affects. Each hypothesis must be testable through intervention, and adjusted if the client's response suggests otherwise (Eells, 2022; Wampold & Imel, 2022).

Strategic Structuring of Treatment Plans Based on Case Formulation

In Integrative Strategic Psychotherapy (ISP), the transition from case formulation to treatment planning is not linear but recursive. The plan must be dynamically adapted as new data emerges from the therapeutic process (Norcross & Goldfried, 2021). However, the initial structure plays a foundational role in setting the therapeutic direction and in creating a sense of safety and containment for the client.

A well-formulated treatment plan should mirror the complexity of the client's internal and relational world, while remaining clear, strategic, and feasible (Rogers, 1957). Based on the case formulation elements outlined earlier—cognitive schemas, emotional patterns, self-states, unconscious dynamics, developmental history, existential themes, and sociocultural context—the integrative strategic psychotherapist outlines an intervention plan across three core temporal dimensions:

1. Immediate Phase (Stabilisation and Alliance Building)

This phase focuses on symptom relief, regulation, and the establishment of the therapeutic alliance. It is particularly relevant in cases involving trauma, affective dysregulation, or dissociation (Watkins & Williams, 2020). Psychoeducation, emotion regulation techniques, grounding, and mindfulness-based interventions may be employed (Ogden & Fisher, 2021). From a strategic standpoint, identifying immediate relational ruptures or resistances is also essential and can guide psychotherapist responsiveness (Korman et al., 2021). If the case formulation reveals insecure attachment or fragmented self-states, initial interventions aim to foster security, predictability, and coherence.

2. Working Phase (Deconstruction, Relearning, and Narrative Integration)

In this phase, the deeper elements of the client's difficulties are addressed. Interventions are selected based on the formulation's highlighted axes—cognitive (e.g., schema restructuring, belief testing), emotional (e.g., emotion-focused interventions, working through attachment injuries), or psychodynamic (e.g., analysis of transference, integration of unconscious material). The plastic self is particularly activated here, as change becomes possible through relational correction, internal reorganisation, and embodied experience. The psychotherapist maintains strategic flexibility, adjusting the level of confrontation, depth, or direction according to the client's evolving capacities and resistance points (Magnavita, 2020).

3. Integration and Generalisation Phase (Consolidation and Autonomy)

As therapeutic gains become stable, the treatment plan shifts toward consolidating change and supporting transfer of skills into the client's everyday life. This includes reviewing the client's progress, addressing residual schemas or self-sabotaging tendencies, and strengthening the capacity for self-reflection and self-regulation. ISP views this phase as one in which the external self becomes increasingly activated—clients begin to renegotiate their relational patterns, re-author their personal narratives, and reconnect with wider cultural and symbolic frameworks (Popescu, 2021). Techniques may include role-play, imaginal dialogue, systemic reframing, or even ritual-based meaning-making processes.

Throughout all phases, the strategic psychotherapist operates within a model that is simultaneously transdiagnostic, developmental, and integrative. There is no single "correct" treatment path. Rather, the treatment plan is a living map—revised and refined at every junction of the therapeutic journey.

Flexibility and Hypothesis Testing in Treatment Planning

A central tenet of Integrative Strategic Psychotherapy (ISP) is the understanding that case formulation is never final. It is a dynamic construct—a set of hypotheses continuously tested, refined, and adjusted throughout the therapeutic process. The formulation is not only an analytic tool but also a clinical compass that helps navigate the unfolding relational and intrapsychic landscape.

Strategic flexibility does not imply therapeutic vagueness or randomness. On the contrary, it refers to the capacity to maintain a coherent conceptual framework while being responsive to new data, emergent transference patterns, or shifts in the client's affective states (Korman et al., 2021; Erskine, 2021). As such, every intervention is both an opportunity for transformation and a moment of inquiry. How the client reacts—emotionally, cognitively, relationally—can confirm, challenge, or enrich the working formulation.

For instance, a psychotherapist may hypothesise that the client's difficulty with assertiveness is rooted in childhood relational trauma and conditioned shame. A gentle relational confrontation, offered strategically, might lead to either validation of this hypothesis (e.g., the client accesses early emotional memories) or to its revision (e.g., the client reveals current coercive relationships previously unacknowledged). The psychotherapist thus oscillates between action and observation, between targeted intervention and interpretive receptivity—a hallmark of ISP's recursive method.

Hypothesis testing is also embedded in ISP's commitment to strategic minimalism—doing just enough to catalyse change without overwhelming the client's defences or bypassing their pace of integration (Popescu & Drobot, 2012). Strategic minimalism encourages the psychotherapist to observe not only the content but also the process of the client's reaction to intervention: avoidance, resistance, alliance rupture, or spontaneous insight are all considered diagnostic signals.

In practice, this flexible attitude is operationalised through ongoing micro-formulations. After each session—or even within the session itself—the psychotherapist briefly reformulates: What do we now know about the client that we didn't know before? What assumptions were confirmed, and which were challenged? What does the client's reaction to this intervention reveal about their internal organisation? What changes might we need to make to our working hypothesis or treatment plan?

Working with Resistance and Process Diagnosis

Resistance is not merely an obstacle in psychotherapy but a valuable signal of internal conflict, unconscious fears, or relational vulnerability. ISP approaches resistance not as something to be "eliminated" but as a process to be decoded and attuned to. It provides insight into what is too painful, too shameful, or too disorganising for the client to confront directly.

From a strategic perspective, resistance may appear in many forms (Safran & Muran, 2022): 1. Narrative vagueness or abstraction (defensive intellectualisation); 2. Excessive compliance or superficial insight (false self presentation); 3. Silence or withdrawal (dissociation or avoidance); 4. Emotional flooding (disorganised affect); and 5. Symptom intensification after interventions (resistance to change).

Each manifestation invites a process diagnosis: What unconscious or systemic function is this resistance serving? What unacknowledged part of the self is being activated? Is the resistance relational (transference), structural (ego strength), or cultural (internalised norms or injunctions)?

Rather than confronting resistance directly, ISP often uses strategic relational atonement to bypass defences or provide safety for gradual deconstruction. This includes: 1. Slowing down the pace of interventions; 2. Using metaphors or imagery to access dissociated material; 3. Reflecting relational patterns in the here-and-now; 4. Exploring competing motivational systems (e.g., autonomy vs. attachment); and 5. Naming the resistance gently as a shared experience: *"It seems something in this feels hard to talk about right now. I wonder what part of you is speaking here."*

Resistance is also a mirror of the therapeutic relationship. The psychotherapist uses it to refine the case formulation: what does the emergence of resistance tell us about the client's needs, fears, or developmental stage?

3.4. Classification of Common Factors in Integrative Strategic Psychotherapy

Despite the diversity in the classification systems of common factors in psychotherapy, two elements recur with striking consistency: (1) the centrality of the therapeutic relationship, especially the therapeutic alliance, and (2) the psychotherapist's capacity to adapt technical interventions in a flexible, person-centred manner that aligns with the client's unique experience. These two domains—relational depth and technical responsiveness—intertwine in every effective therapeutic encounter, regardless of theoretical orientation. Thus, psychotherapeutic techniques are never applied in a vacuum; they are embedded in, and shaped by, the quality of the therapeutic relationship itself.

The last five years have seen a resurgence of interest in the mechanisms underlying psychotherapy effectiveness, with a growing body of literature reaffirming the centrality of common factors. Scholars such as Goldfried (2022) and Norcross & Lambert (2023) argue that common factors represent the "shared DNA" of therapeutic effectiveness across orientations. Del Re et al. (2022) confirmed that psychotherapist effects—those related to personal and relational qualities—are often more predictive of client outcomes than specific techniques.

In addition, Laska, Wampold, and Baldwin (2020) have proposed that empirically supported treatments (ESTs) should be reconceptualised in terms of common processes rather than discrete packages. Cloitre et al. (2022), working with clients with complex PTSD, demonstrated that a sequenced, relationship-based approach that prioritises alliance, affect regulation, and empowerment is often more effective than technique-driven protocols. At the neurobiological level, Siegel (2021) and Schore (2021) reiterate that the therapeutic relationship shapes neural integration and modulates emotion regulation via right-brain to right-brain communication.

Integrative Strategic Psychotherapy (ISP) proposes its own taxonomy of common factors, drawing from both classical frameworks and current research. These are classified into three strategic domains:

(1) Relational Factors

These are the heart of the therapeutic endeavour and include:

- The therapeutic relationship and the therapeutic alliance, including rupture and repair cycles, transference and countertransference management, psychological games and enactments;

- Client variables, which refer to attributes, resources, and psychological structures that the client brings into therapy. Within ISP, eleven key client variables are monitored and assessed through case formulation: 1. Stages of change (Prochaska & Norcross, 2018); 2. Resistance levels (Beutler et al., 2004); 2. Coping style – internalising vs. externalising (Luyten et al., 2020); 3. Motivation and readiness for change; 4. Self-development level; 5. Attachment style (Wallin, 2010); 6. Self-esteem and self-efficacy; 7. Capacity for insight and assimilation (Castonguay, 2000); 8. Personality traits and possible disorders; 9. Value systems, preferences, and expectations; 10. Degree of functional impairment; and 11. Sociodemographic factors – culture, religion, gender, identity, socioeconomic context. These factors serve both as prognostic indicators and strategic levers—targets for intervention or adaptation points for therapeutic technique.
- Psychotherapist variables, which underscore the psychotherapist as an active co-regulator and co-constructor of the therapeutic space. Five areas are outlined: 1. Relational qualities: Empathy, unconditional acceptance, warmth, authenticity, and interpersonal flexibility (Norcross & Goldfried, 2021; Baldwin & Imel, 2013); 2. Professional attributes: Training, orientation, theoretical coherence, strategic skilfulness; 3. Cultural atonement: Awareness of and sensitivity to the psychotherapist's and client's cultural and identity-based positioning; 4. Personality dimensions: Kindness, conscientiousness, and adaptability; and 5. Developmental capacity: Ability to self-reflect, identify countertransference, and grow within the therapeutic relationship (Rønnestad & Skovholt, 2021). Research consistently shows that psychotherapist variables may account for up to 7–9% of variance in outcomes, significantly more than specific techniques (Del Re et al., 2022).

(2) Trans-Theoretical Common Factors

These are meta-processes present in all effective psychotherapies regardless of orientation: (a) Psychoeducation and therapeutic rationale; (b) Treatment context and contracting; (c) Process monitoring and client feed-back; (d) Adaptation of interventions to personality and relational needs; (e) Hope, expectancy, and placebo mechanisms (Wampold & Imel, 2022); and (f) Extra-therapeutic factors – life events, relationships, and systems outside the therapeutic frame.

ISP considers these the glue between strategy and relationship, and ensures they are explicitly integrated in all treatment plans.

(3) Strategic Factors

This domain contains factors that are central to therapeutic interventions in most psychotherapies: (a) The therapeutic myth – a culturally resonant, emotionally engaging explanation of change; (b) Assessment and clarification – detailed diagnostic formulation that informs strategy; (c) Confrontation with reality – naming avoidance, dissociation, or projection patterns; (d) Emotional processing – facilitating regulated expression and reintegration of affect; (e) Insight development – cognitive and experiential realisation of unconscious patterns; (f) Ego strengthening – restoring boundaries, agency, and resilience; (g) Acquisition of new behaviours – rehearsal, in-vivo techniques, action experiments; (h) Consolidation of change – rituals, feedback, narrative integration; (i) Outcome attribution – helping the client internalise progress as their own doing; and (j) Strategic use of technique – rituals, timing, interventions adapted to the client.

References

Adan, A., Archer, S. N., Hidalgo, M. P., Di Milia, L., Natale, V., & Randler, C. (2012). Circadian typology: A comprehensive review. *Chronobiology International, 29*(9), 1153–1175.

American Psychological Association. (2013). *Recognition of psychotherapy effectiveness*. Psychotherapy, 50(1), 102–109. https://doi.org/10.1037/a0030276

American Psychiatric Association. (2022). *Diagnostic and statistical manual of mental disorders* (5th ed., text rev.; DSM-5-TR). American Psychiatric Publishing.

Anderson, T., Ogles, B. M., Patterson, C. L., Lambert, M. J., & Verweersch, S. (2009). Therapist effects: Facilitative interpersonal skills as a predictor of therapist success. *Journal of Clinical Psychology, 65*(7), 755–768. https://doi.org/10.1002/jclp.20583

Angus, L., & Greenberg, L. (2021). *Emotion in psychotherapy: A practice-friendly research review*. Wiley.

Antononoiu, M., & Blom, R. (2006). *Factorii comuni în psihoterapie*. Cluj-Napoca: ASCR.

Arkowitz, H. (1989). Integrative theories of therapy. In H. Arkowitz & S. Messer (Eds.), *Psychoanalytic therapy and behavior therapy: Is integration possible?* (pp. 324–356). Lawrence Erlbaum Associates.

Assay, T. P., & Lambert, M. J. (1999). The empirical case for the common factors in therapy: Quantitative findings. In M. A. Hubble, B. L. Duncan, & S. D. Miller (Eds.),

The heart and soul of change: What works in therapy (pp. 33–56). American Psychological Association.

Baillargen, M., Cote, A., & Douville, V. (2012). Alliance rupture and repair: A review of psychotherapeutic processes. *Canadian Psychology/Psychologie canadienne, 53*(2), 113–124.

Baldwin, S. A., & Imel, Z. E. (2013). Therapist effects: Findings and methods. In M. J. Lambert (Ed.), *Bergin and Garfield's handbook of psychotherapy and behavior change* (6th ed., pp. 258–297). Wiley.

Baldwin, S. A., & Imel, Z. E. (2013). Therapist effects: Findings and methods. *Psychotherapy, 50*(3), 370–377.

Barlow, D. H., SauerZavala, S., Carl, J. R., Bullis, J. R., & Ellard, K. K. (2021). The Unified Protocol for Transdiagnostic Treatment of Emotional Disorders. *Oxford University Press.*

Beck, J. S. (2021). *Cognitive behavior therapy: Basics and beyond* (3rd ed.). Guilford Press.

Berenbaum, H., Raghavan, C., Le, H. N., Vernon, L. L., & Gomez, J. J. (2003). A taxonomy of emotional disturbances. *Clinical Psychology: Science and Practice, 10*(2), 206–226. https://doi.org/10.1093/clipsy/bpg023

Beutler, L. E., Harwood, T. M., Alimohamed, S., & Malik, M. (2003). Functional impairment and coping style. *Journal of Clinical Psychology, 59*(10), 1085–1101. https://doi.org/10.1002/jclp.10210

Beutler, L. E., Harwood, T. M., Alimohamed, S., & Malik, M. (2022). *Integrative psychotherapy: A therapist's handbook* (2nd ed.). Oxford University Press.

Beutler, L. E., Harwood, T. M., Michelson, A., Song, X., & Holman, J. (2004). Resistance in psychotherapy: What conclusions are supported by research. *Journal of Clinical Psychology, 60*(2), 207–217. https://doi.org/10.1002/jclp.10243

Black, N., Hardy, G. E., Turpin, G., & Parry, G. (2005). Self-reported experiences of therapy and therapist effects in the treatment of depression. *Journal of Mental Health, 14*(3), 243–254.

Block, J. (2002). *Personality as an affect-processing system.* Lawrence Erlbaum Associates.

Blow, A. J., & Sprenkle, D. H. (2001). Common factors across theories of marriage and family therapy: A modified Delphi study. *Journal of Marital and Family Therapy, 27*(4), 385–401.

Bowlby, J. (1988). *A secure base: Parentchild attachment and healthy human development.* Basic Books.

Casement, P. J. (2014). *Learning from the patient* (2nd ed.). Routledge.

Castonguay, L. G. (2000). Predictive factors in psychotherapy: Research and clinical applications. In C. R. Snyder & R. E. Ingram (Eds.), *Handbook of psychological change* (pp. 115–137). Wiley.

Castonguay, L. G., & Beutler, L. E. (2006). Principles of therapeutic change: A task force on participants, relationships, and techniques factors. *Journal of Clinical Psychology, 62*(5), 631–638. https://doi.org/10.1002/jclp.20258

Castonguay, L. G. (2011). Psychotherapy, psychopathology, research and practice: Pathways of connections and integration. *Psychotherapy Research, 21*(2), 125–140. https://doi.org/10.1080/10503307.2011.563250

Castonguay, L. G. (2020). Integration in psychotherapy: Past, present, and future. *Psychotherapy Research, 30*(5), 501–510.

Castonguay, L. G. (1993). Common factors and the future of psychotherapy integration. *Journal of Psychotherapy Integration, 3*(3), 222–230.

Chung, M. C., & Hunt, L. J. (2021). The role of intrusive memories, trauma, and dissociation in emotional dysregulation. *Journal of Psychological Trauma*, 20(2), 153–170. https://doi.org/10.1037/tra0000987

Connor, M. (1994). *Training the counsellor: Strategies for supervision.* London: Routledge.

Constantino, M. J., Fonagy, P., Volkmar, F. R., et al. (2021). Internal experience and mental health in adolescents: Emotional awareness and dysregulation. *Journal of Adolescence, 94*, 167–176.

Coutinho, J., Ribeiro, E., Fernandes, C., Sousa, I., & Safran, J. D. (2014). Therapist interventions and patient change following a rupture in therapeutic alliance: Contrasting case studies. *Research in Psychotherapy: Psychopathology, Process and Outcome, 17*(1), 1–15.

Cuijpers, P., Karyotaki, E., Ebert, D. D., & Andersson, G. (2023). The effects of psychotherapies for adult depression: What do we know? *The Lancet Psychiatry, 10*(2), 87–96.

Davis, S. D., & Piercy, F. P. (2007). What clients of couple therapy model developers and their former students say about change, part II: Model-independent common factors and an integrative framework. *Journal of Marital and Family Therapy, 33*(3), 344–363.

DeFife, J. A., & Hilsenroth, M. J. (2011). Clinical interactions and the therapeutic alliance: Measuring mechanisms of change. *Psychotherapy, 48*(4), 344–354.

Del Re, A. C., Flückiger, C., Horvath, A. O., & Wampold, B. E. (2022). Therapist effects in psychotherapy: A meta-analytic update. *Psychotherapy Research, 32*(4), 444–459.

Dias, B. G., & Ressler, K. J. (2014). Parental olfactory experience influences behaviour and neural structure in subsequent generations. *Nature Neuroscience, 17*(1), 89–96.

Doidge, N. (2020). *The brain that heals itself: Updated stories of neuroplasticity*. Penguin.

Duarte, J. C., McWilliams, L. A., & Safran, J. D. (2020). Alliance ruptures and repair in psychotherapy: A meta-narrative review. *Psychotherapy, 57*(3), 276–288.

Duncan, B. L. (2002). The legacy of Saul Rosenzweig: The profundity of the Dodo bird. *Journal of Psychotherapy Integration, 12*(1), 32–57.

Eells, T. D. (2022). *Handbook of psychotherapy case formulation* (2nd ed.). Guilford Press.

Erskine, R. G. (2021). *Relational patterns, therapeutic presence: Concepts and practice of integrative psychotherapy*. Karnac.

Fonagy, P., Luyten, P., Allison, E., & Campbell, C. (2021). Borderline personality disorder as a limitation of resilience: What we have changed our minds about—Part I. *Borderline Personality Disorder and Emotion Dysregulation, 8*, 11.

Frank, J. D. (1973). *Persuasion and healing: A comparative study of psychotherapy*. Schocken Books.

Frank, J. D., & Frank, J. B. (1991). *Persuasion and healing: A comparative study of psychotherapy* (3rd ed.). Johns Hopkins University Press.

Flückiger, C., Del Re, A. C., Wampold, B. E., Symonds, D., & Horvath, A. O. (2020). How central is the alliance in psychotherapy? A multilevel longitudinal meta-analysis. *Journal of Counseling Psychology, 67*(2), 168–180.

Fonagy, P., Luyten, P., & Allison, E. (2021). Epistemic trust and the emergence of mentalization. *Current Opinion in Psychology*, 41, 91–95. https://doi.org/10.1016/j.copsyc.2021.04.010

Gelso, C. J., & Hayes, J. A. (2023). *Countertransference and the therapist's inner experience: Perils and possibilities* (2nd ed.). Routledge.

Geller, S. M., & Porges, S. W. (2021). Therapeutic presence and polyvagal theory: Principles and applications. *Frontiers in Psychology, 12*, 723137.

Gilbert, M. C., & Evans, K. (2003). *Psychotherapy supervision: An integrative relational approach.* Open University Press.

Gilbert, M. C., & Orlans, V. (2011). *Integrative therapy: A practitioner's guide.* Routledge.

Goldfried, M. R. (1980). Toward the delineation of therapeutic change principles. *American Psychologist, 35*(11), 991–999.

Goldfried, M. R. (2022). The future of psychotherapy integration: A return to common processes. *Journal of Psychotherapy Integration, 32*(1), 3–15.

Grawe, K. (2007). *Neuropsychotherapy: How the neurosciences inform effective psychotherapy.* Erlbaum.

Greenberg, L. S., Constantino, M. J., & Bruce, N. (2006). Are empathy, warmth, and genuineness necessary for all clients? In L. G. Castonguay & L. E. Beutler (Eds.), *Principles of therapeutic change that work* (pp. 43–56). Oxford University Press.

Greenberg, L. S., & PascualLeone, A. (2020). Emotion in psychotherapy: A practicefriendly research review. *Journal of Clinical Psychology, 76*(9), 1699–1711.

Greencavage, L. M., & Norcross, J. C. (1990). Where are the commonalities among the therapeutic common factors? *Professional Psychology: Research and Practice, 21*(5), 372–378.

Hayes, S. C., Hofmann, S. G., & Ciarrochi, J. (2020). *ProcessBased CBT: The science and core clinical competencies of cognitive behavioral therapy*. New Harbinger.

Hill, C. E., & Knox, S. (2020). *Training and supervision in psychotherapy*. APA Books.

Hofmann, S. G., & Hayes, S. C. (2021). The future of intervention science: Processbased therapy. *Clinical Psychological Science, 9*(1), 41–55.

Howe, M. L., & Lewis, M. D. (2021). Dynamic development and memory: Systems theory revisited. *Developmental Review, 60*, 100960.

Kahl, K. G., Winter, L., & Schweiger, U. (2022). The third wave of cognitive behavioral therapies: What is new and what is effective? *Current Opinion in Psychiatry*, 35(2), 125–132. https://doi.org/10.1097/YCO.0000000000000774

Karg, K., Burmeister, M., Shedden, K., & Sen, S. (2011). The serotonin transporter promoter variant (5HTTLPR), stress, and depression: A metaanalysis. *Archives of General Psychiatry, 68*(5), 444–454.

Kazdin, A. E. (2021). Research design in clinical psychology (5th ed.). Cambridge University Press.

Kernberg, O. F. (2020). The future of psychoanalysis and psychotherapy: Advances and challenges. *Journal of the American Psychoanalytic Association*, 68(4), 609–638. https://doi.org/10.1177/0003065120948586

Klengel, T., & Binder, E. B. (2020). Epigenetics of stressrelated psychiatric disorders and gene × environment interactions. *Neuron, 106*(5), 715–731.

Kim, H. S., & Sasaki, J. Y. (2022). Cultural neuroscience: Progress and challenges. *Annual Review of Psychology, 73*, 401–428.

Lambert, M. J., & Bergin, A. E. (1994). The effectiveness of psychotherapy. In A. E. Bergin & S. L. Garfield (Eds.), *Handbook of psychotherapy and behavior change* (4th ed., pp. 143–189). Wiley.

Landa, J. T., et al. (2023). Integrative approaches to psychotherapy: Synthesis and future directions. *Journal of Clinical Psychology, 79*(6), 1200–1214.

Laska, K. M., Wampold, B. E., & Baldwin, S. A. (2020). Empirically supported treatments or common factors? *Psychotherapy, 57*(4), 409–417.

Laska, K. M., Gurman, A. S., & Wampold, B. E. (2014). Expanding the lens of evidence-based practice in psychotherapy: A common factors perspective. *Psychotherapy, 51*(4), 467–481. https://doi.org/10.1037/a0034332

Lebow, J., & Jenkins, P. H. (2022). *Theory construction and model building in integrative psychotherapy.* Oxford University Press.

Lerner, R. M., et al. (2021). The development of systems theory in psychology and beyond. *American Psychologist, 76*(9), 1289–1300.

Lin, Y.-N. (2016). The classification of common factors in psychotherapy. *Counselling Psychology Quarterly, 29*(4), 386–401. https://doi.org/10.1080/09515070.2016.1166385

Luborsky, L., Rosenthal, R., Diguer, L., Andrusyna, T. P., Berman, J. S., Levitt, J. T., ... & Krause, E. D. (2002). The dodo bird verdict is alive and well – mostly. *Clinical Psychology: Science and Practice, 9*(1), 2–12.

Lundh, L.-G. (2014). The role of acceptance and mindfulness in the relation between common factors and outcome in psychotherapy. *Clinical Psychology & Psychotherapy, 21*(2), 116–126.

Luthar, S. S., Sawyer, J. A., & Brown, P. J. (2006). Conceptual issues in studies of resilience. *Annals of the New York Academy of Sciences, 1094*(1), 105–115.

Luyten, P., Campbell, C., & Fonagy, P. (2020). The psychotherapy of borderline personality disorder: Evidence, challenges and future directions. *World Psychiatry, 19*(2), 222–224.

Magnavita, J. J. (2006). *Clinical strategies for the treatment of complex psychological trauma.* American Psychological Association.

Mahoney, M. J. (1991). *Human change processes: The scientific foundations of psychotherapy.* Basic Books.

Maravita, A., & Iriki, A. (2004). Tools for the body (schema). *Trends in Cognitive Sciences, 8*(2), 79–86.

McGowan, P. O., et al. (2009). Epigenetic regulation of the glucocorticoid receptor in human brain associates with childhood abuse. *Nature Neuroscience, 12*(3), 342–348.

McWilliams, N. (2022). *Psychoanalytic case formulation* (2nd ed.). Guilford Press.

Messina, I., Grecucci, A., & Marogna, C. (2022). Therapist responsiveness and processoutcome links in psychotherapy: A metaanalysis. *Psychotherapy, 59*(2), 186–199.

Meaney, M. J. (2010). Epigenetics and the biological definition of gene × environment interactions. *Child Development, 81*(1), 41–79.

Metcalf, K., et al. (2024). Psychotherapy integration and digital mental health: Reframing the therapeutic alliance. *Clinical Psychology Review, 101*, 102198.

Norcross, J. C., & Goldfried, M. R. (2021). *Handbook of psychotherapy integration* (3rd ed.). Oxford University Press.

Norcross, J. C., & Lambert, M. J. (2023). *Psychotherapy relationships that work* (3rd ed.). Oxford University Press.

Ogden, P., & Fisher, J. (2021). *Sensorimotor psychotherapy: Interventions for trauma and attachment*. Norton.

Orlinsky, D. E., & Howard, K. I. (1987). A generic model of psychotherapy. *Journal of Integrative and Eclectic Psychotherapy, 6*(1), 6–27.

Ottens, A. J., & Klein, J. F. (2005). Common factors: Where the soul of counseling and psychotherapy resides. *Journal of Humanistic Counseling, Education and Development, 44*(1), 32–43.

Pakenham, K. I., & StaffordBrown, J. (2022). Therapist psychological flexibility and therapy outcomes: A systematic review. *Clinical Psychology Review, 92*, 102115.

Porges, S. W. (2022). *Polyvagal theory and the healing power of emotion*. Norton.

Popescu, O. M. (2021). *Psihoterapia integrativă strategică: Nivelurile sinelui și intervenția clinică*. Editura Universitară.

Popescu, O. M., & Drobot, L. (2012). *Psihoterapia integrativă strategică: Teorie și practică*. Editura Universitară.

Popescu, O. M., & Vîșcu, L. (2016). *Psihoterapia integrativă strategică: Aplicații clinice.* Editura Universitară.

Prochaska, J. O., & Norcross, J. C. (1999). *Systems of psychotherapy: A transtheoretical analysis* (4th ed.). Brooks/Cole.

Reisner, A. D. (2005). The common factors, empirically supported treatments, and recovery models of therapeutic change. *Psychological Reports, 97*(2), 417–435.

Rogers, C. (1957). The necessary and sufficient conditions of therapeutic personality change. *Journal of Consulting Psychology, 21*(2), 95–103.

Rønnestad, M. H., & Skovholt, T. M. (2021). *The developing practitioner: Growth and stagnation of therapists and counselors.* Routledge.

Rosenzweig, S. (1936). Some implicit common factors in diverse methods of psychotherapy. *American Journal of Orthopsychiatry, 6*(3), 412–415. https://doi.org/10.1111/ j.1939-0025.1936.tb05248.x

Safran, J. D., & Muran, J. C. (2022). Emotional processes in psychotherapy: Repairing the rupture in the therapeutic alliance. *Guilford Press*.

Shedler, J. (2020). Where is the evidence for "evidencebased" therapy? *Journal of Psychological Therapies, 1*(1), 11–26.

Siegel, D. J. (2021). *The developing mind: How relationships and the brain interact to shape who we are* (3rd ed.). Guilford Press.

Siegel, D. J. (2023). *Interpersonal neurobiology and the developing mind* (3rd ed.). Norton.

Smith, L., & Glass, G. V. (1977). Meta-analysis of psychotherapy outcome studies. *American Psychologist, 32*(9), 752–760.

Stewart, I., & Joines, V. (2012). *TA today: A new introduction to transactional analysis* (2nd ed.). Lifespace Publishing.

Strupp, H. H. (1978). Psychotherapy research and practice: An overview. *American Psychologist, 33*(8), 709–717.

Tallman, K., & Bohart, A. C. (1999). The client as a common factor: Clients as self-healers. In M. A. Hubble, B. L. Duncan, & S. D. Miller (Eds.), *The heart and soul of change: What works in therapy* (pp. 91–131). American Psychological Association.

Tolin, D. F. (2020). *Doing CBT: A comprehensive guide to working with behaviors, thoughts, and emotions*. Guilford Press.

Truax, C. B., & Carkhuff, R. R. (1967). *Toward effective counseling and psychotherapy: Training and practice*. Aldine Publishing Company.

Tseliou, E., & Borcsa, M. (2023). *Case-based research in psychotherapy and counselling: Integrating theory, research and practice*. Routledge.

Van der Kolk, B. (2021). *The body keeps the score: Brain, mind, and body in the healing of trauma* (Updated edition). Penguin Books.

Wachtel, P. L. (2020). *Therapeutic communication: Knowing what to say when* (2nd ed.). Guilford Press.

Wallin, D. J. (2010). *Attachment in psychotherapy*. Guilford Press.

Wampold, B. E., & Imel, Z. E. (2015). *The great psychotherapy debate: The evidence for what makes psychotherapy work* (2nd ed.). Routledge.

Wampold, B. E., & Imel, Z. E. (2022). The great psychotherapy debate: The evidence for what makes psychotherapy work. *Psychotherapy*, 57(4), 409–417.

Watkins, C. E., & Williams, E. N. (2020). The supervisory alliance: A retrospective view from the literature. *Training and Education in Professional Psychology, 14*(4), 277–283. https://doi.org/10.1037/tep0000287

World Health Organization. (2022). Intergenerational trauma and mental health: A systematic review. *WHO Reports*.

Yalom, I. D. (2020). *Existential psychotherapy*. Basic Books.

Yehuda, R., Daskalakis, N. P., Bierer, L. M., Bader, H. N., Klengel, T., & Binder, E. B. (2021). Holocaust exposure induced intergenerational effects on FKBP5 methylation. *Biological Psychiatry, 80*(5), 372–380.

Young, J. E., Klosko, J. S., & Weishaar, M. E. (2020). *Schema therapy: A practitioner's guide* (2nd ed.). Guilford Press.

Zeig, J. K. (2021). *Experiencing Erickson: An introduction to the man and his work*. Taylor & Francis.

CHAPTER 4

THE INTEGRATIVE STRATEGIC MODEL OF THE SELF

4.1. The Structure of The Self: Domains, Levels, Axes

The self is not a singular or static entity but a complex, dynamic system composed of multiple domains and organised across several levels of functioning. In the Integrative Strategic Model, the self is understood through four domains—proto-self, core self, plastic self, and external self—which interact with three levels of human existence: biological, psychological, and relational. Within the psychological level, further organisation occurs along specific axes: cognitive, emotional and psychodynamic.

The extent of impairment within these domains, levels, and axes determines the severity of difficulties and the manifestation of psychopathology. Conversely, the resilience of each domain contributes to mental health and adaptive functioning.

Despite decades of theoretical exploration, there is little consensus on the precise nature of the self. Yet, most psychotherapists agree that the sense of self is a fundamental feature of human experience (Praetorius, 2009). Zahavi (2005) argues that the self is best understood as an experiential dimension—a first-person interpretation of lived phenomena, a concept rooted in phenomenology's notion of ipseity (the self as an intrinsic feature of consciousness).

From this perspective, the self is not an object but a mode of experiencing. Present experience is always shaped by past experiences, reaching down into the proto- and core self, while simultaneously projecting into future anticipations. Each psychotherapeutic tradition captures only part of this complexity. Fall, Holden, and Marquis (2010) describe the self as a global hologram: every orientation offers a precise but incomplete representation. The strategic integrative model does not attempt to grasp the "entire hologram" but instead seeks to build a coherent and clinically usable map that integrates biological, psychological, and relational factors into a structured understanding of the self.

The Domains of the Self

The proto-self is the most basic layer of the self, formed pre-birth and in early childhood at a non-verbal, pre-reflective level. It is grounded in bodily regulation, sensory-motor patterns, and neural structures that support survival. Damasio (1999) described the proto-self as a collection of neural patterns that continuously map the state of the organism. Clinically, impairments at this level often manifest in pervasive developmental difficulties, attachment trauma, or psychosomatic symptoms. Because the proto-self is deeply embodied, psychotherapy addressing this domain must often rely on somatic, relational, and experiential techniques rather than purely verbal interventions.

The core self emerges in early childhood, integrating both verbal and non-verbal influences. It is the dimension of the self where emotional experience, memory, and identity begin to stabilise. Within ISP, the core self contains the core sets: mental schemas and neural maps governing thought, emotion, and psychodynamic functioning. The core self allows for stable emotional expression, reality-testing, and a sense of continuity. Disturbances at this level may present as mood instability, fragile identity, or difficulties with trust and relational atonement.

The plastic self represents mechanisms of adaptability and internal causality. Once core sets are established within the core self, the plastic self sustains them through feedback loops. This allows individuals to maintain identity over time, while also permitting transformation and learning. Plasticity is both a strength and a vulnerability: it enables growth but can also reinforce maladaptive schemas. For example, early trauma may produce rigid feedback loops that perpetuate maladaptive beliefs (*"I am unlovable," "The world is unsafe"*). Psychotherapy targets the plastic self to promote flexibility, reorganisation, and integration.

The external self is the interface with the social and environmental world. It is the "here-and-now" expression of the self, manifesting in behaviour, roles, cultural identity, and relational engagement. Siegel (2001) emphasises that the brain constructs an experience of a present-moment self, integrating stimuli from the inner and outer worlds. The external self is therefore both expressive and adaptive.

It mediates how inner structures are enacted in the external world, shaping how individuals are perceived by others and how they navigate societal contexts.

The Levels of the Self

The biological level provides the neurophysiological substrate of selfhood: genetics, epigenetics, brain structure, neurochemistry, and bodily regulation. Disorders at this level (e.g., genetic vulnerabilities, neurodevelopmental conditions) create foundational challenges for all domains of the self.

The psychological level encompasses cognition, emotion and psychodynamic processes. It is the arena where core sets and feedback loops play out. ISP describes this level as organised along three axes (see below).

The relational level refers to the cultural, social, and ecological contexts in which the self exists. Stressors such as poverty, migration, war, or pandemics profoundly shape self-formation. Environmental safety and supportive relationships provide resilience, while environmental chaos increases vulnerability.

The Axes of the Psychological Level

The cognitive axis involves perception, attention, memory, and meaning-making. It represents how individuals interpret the world and organise knowledge. Distortions here manifest in maladaptive beliefs and rigid thinking.

The emotional axis reflects the regulation and expression of affect. A healthy emotional axis allows individuals to experience, name, and regulate feelings. Dysregulation may manifest as mood disorders, alexithymia, or emotional numbing.

The psychodynamic axis concerns unconscious processes, conflicts, and internalised relational patterns. It shapes intrapsychic life and influences how individuals relate to others. It also highlights the importance of early attachment, intergenerational transmission, and family dynamics in shaping the self. It anchors psychological experience in real relational contexts.

Integration in Case Formulation

21st-century integrative case formulation models incorporate multiple layers of influence, from biological and medical to existential and transpersonal (Brooks-Harris, 2008; Eels, 2010; Lichner-Ingram, 2011). ISP integrates these perspectives into a structured map of selfhood:

- Depth of impairment – determines therapeutic intensity and duration (proto-self disruptions require longer-term interventions);
- Domain interplay – highlights how difficulties in one domain cascade into others (e.g., trauma at proto-self → unstable core self → rigid plastic self → maladaptive external expression);

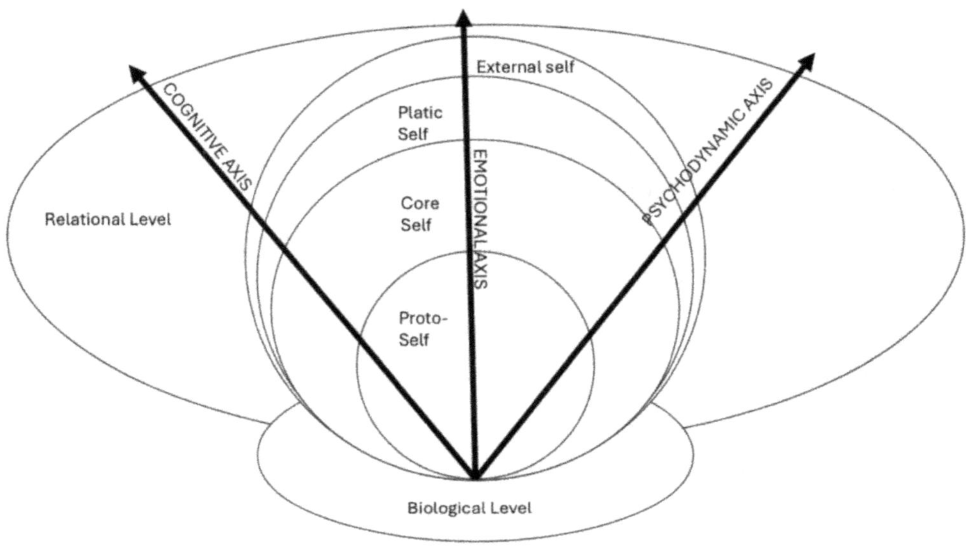

Figure 1. The Self

- Level awareness – ensures attention to biological vulnerabilities, psychological processes, and environmental stressors; and
- Axis balance – clarifies whether dysfunction is primarily cognitive, emotional or psychodynamic.

The Clinical Implications of this model in ISP are at multiple levels:

1. Assessment: Mapping symptoms onto domains, levels, and axes provides a nuanced formulation;
2. Intervention: Tailoring techniques—somatic work for proto-self, schema reorganisation for plastic self, relational interventions for external self;
3. Therapeutic alliance: Understanding where in the self difficulties arise informs how to build trust and collaboration; and
4. Prognosis: The deeper the domain affected, the longer and more intensive the therapeutic process.

4.2. The Proto-Self

The proto-self consists of neural structures and processes that take shape before and during early childhood, at a pre-verbal and pre-reflective level. It anchors human existence in the body, providing the most basic platform upon which later domains of the self—core, plastic, and external—are built. This biological level integrates genetic predispositions, neural circuits regulating physiological needs and bodily schemas, and the early formation of learning and temperamental traits. In Integrative Strategic Psychotherapy (ISP), the proto-self is understood as the biological foundation of the self-structure. It is both universal and deeply individual: universal in that all humans share these neurobiological processes, and individual in that early experiences sculpt the architecture of each person's proto-self in ways that leave a permanent mark on their development.

Every child is born with a unique genetic configuration, determined by the interaction of genome and epigenome. The genome encodes the blueprint for neural structures, body rhythms, and temperamental traits. Yet the epigenome—chemical markers that regulate gene expression—ensures that environmental influences become inscribed at the biological level (Carey, 2011).

This means that even from the prenatal stage, the proto-self is not fixed but is already being sculpted by experience. For example, maternal stress during pregnancy alters the foetus's epigenetic regulation of the hypothalamic–pituitary–adrenal (HPA) axis, increasing vulnerability to later anxiety (Oberlander et al., 2008; Klengel & Binder, 2015). Conversely, a nurturing prenatal environment promotes resilience, conferring the infant with a neurobiological template for regulation and adaptation.

Thus, the proto-self reflects a dynamic interplay between genetic inheritance and environmental inscription. It is here that vulnerability and resilience first take root.

From birth, the proto-self is organised around a set of neural circuits that regulate the most basic features of existence:

- Body schema – Early neural maps encode the position and coherence of the body in space (Maravita, Spence, & Driver, 2003);
- Chronotype and biological rhythms – Suprachiasmatic nucleus regulation aligns the infant to cycles of light and sleep–wake rhythms, gradually differentiating across the first year (Roenneberg et al., 2007);

- Physiological needs – Circuits for hunger, thirst, and elimination develop, each linked with affective states (Panksepp, 1998); and
- Affective systems – Panksepp (1998) identified primary-process emotional circuits (e.g., seeking, fear, care, play) that are operational at birth, forming the emotional ground of the proto-self.

These neural systems are not isolated: they constantly interact, creating a living map of the organism. This continuous mapping constitutes the proto-self's essence: a dynamic, embodied sense of "being alive," which precedes and supports all later forms of selfhood (Damasio, 1999).

At birth, the brain contains roughly 100 billion neurons, but relatively few synaptic connections. Development unfolds through plasticity, the ability of neurons to form, prune, and reorganise connections in response to experience. Between late gestation and the first three years, the brain undergoes a phase of overproduction of neurons and synapses (Siegel, 2001). This overproduction ensures flexibility but also requires environmental input to guide which connections are maintained. Greenough and Black (1992) termed this experience-expectant development: the brain is prepared to receive certain universal inputs (light, sound, human voices, attachment signals), and without them, key functions fail to mature. For example, infants deprived of light fail to develop normal vision. Children raised without human interaction may never fully develop language or social cognition (Perry & Szalavitz, 2017). Lack of early attachment experiences prevents the consolidation of circuits for affect regulation and trust (Schore, 2001, 2006). Thus, the proto-self is not merely a passive biological state but a readiness for experience. It anticipates relational input and sculpts itself accordingly.

Neural synapses compete for survival. Those that best encode environmental experience are strengthened; others are pruned away (Schore, 2001). This ensures that the infant's brain becomes specialised for the environment it inhabits.

If the environment is nurturing, synapses encoding safety, reciprocity, and regulation are reinforced. If the environment is neglectful or traumatic, synapses encoding hypervigilance, mistrust, or fear may dominate. In this way, the proto-self becomes the embodied archive of early experience. As Coicici and Popescu (2017) note, early experiences sculpt brain structures by either reinforcing or weakening neural connections. These imprints endure, forming the implicit templates upon which later schemas are built.

During the first year, memory exists almost entirely at the implicit level. Implicit memory includes: 1. Emotional states (e.g., fear, joy, calmness); 2. Behavioural patterns (e.g., self-soothing or distress signals); 3. Perceptual and somatosensory experiences (e.g., warmth, tone of voice, facial expression); and 4. Generalised patterns (schemas derived from repeated interactions).

These memories are not available to conscious recall, but they deeply shape later development. For example, a child who repeatedly experiences mis atonement may carry into adulthood a schema of *"others cannot be trusted,"* even if they cannot consciously recall early neglect.

Explicit memory—dependent on hippocampal maturation—emerges only in the second year of life (Siegel, 2001). Thus, the proto-self represents a silent archive of experience that cannot be narrated but is enacted in behaviour and relationship.

From late gestation through the second year, the brain passes through critical developmental windows. Each requires specific stimuli for healthy maturation:

- Attachment – Secure caregiving regulates the infant's stress systems and supports right-brain growth (Schore, 2006);
- Sensory input – Exposure to sound, touch, and visual patterns organises perceptual circuits;
- Relational synchrony – Feldman (2007) shows that face-to-face synchrony with caregivers entrains neural rhythms and builds social competence; and
- Mutual regulation – Tronick's (2007) "still-face paradigm" demonstrates how even brief relational ruptures impact infant neurobiology.

Failure to provide these inputs leads to enduring deficits. Conversely, environments rich in contingent, attuned interactions create resilience and flexibility in the proto-self.

The proto-self's biological imprint has far-reaching implications for psychotherapy:

- Attachment trauma – Experiences of neglect or abuse before language leave implicit traces that resurface as relational difficulties, anxiety, or somatic symptoms;
- Regulation strategies – Clients often "remember with their bodies," enacting implicit proto-self imprints in posture, tone, or physiological reactivity;
- Therapeutic repair – Psychotherapy can provide corrective implicit experiences, where new neural pathways of safety and trust are consolidated through relational atonement (Fonagy et al., 2002); and

- Non-verbal techniques – Because proto-self imprints are pre-verbal, interventions such as body-oriented therapy, sensorimotor work, expressive arts, or guided imagery are often necessary.

In ISP, the psychotherapist must discern whether difficulties originate at the proto-self level. Such cases often require longer and deeper interventions, targeting the body, affect regulation, and early schemas, rather than relying solely on cognitive insight.

The proto-self represents the earliest psychological structures of human development, established at a non-verbal and pre-symbolic level in early childhood (Popescu, 2021). At birth, the proto-self is the most developed layer of the self, with the core, plastic, and external selves gradually unfolding as the child matures. As the individual develops, the proto-self remains as a foundational domain upon which later layers are constructed.

Psychologically, the proto-self arises through the interaction between innate needs and early experiences. Stimuli from the environment are processed not cognitively, but affectively and bodily, creating proto-cognitions—primitive, binary evaluations of experience. These proto-cognitions form the first schemas of the world and the self, shaping the developmental trajectory of identity, resilience, and vulnerability.

Initially, the proto-self dominates. With age, the later layers gradually take precedence, but always in interaction with the proto-self, which remains the "ground floor" of the self's architecture.

What, then, are the first essential stimuli in a child's development? In the earliest months, the infant relies primarily on emerging motor and sensory abilities to explore and interact with the surrounding environment. From around the second month of life, social and emotional capacities begin to unfold, adding new dimensions to the child's relational experiences (Siegel, 2001). In other words, the earliest environmental encounters are focused on the satisfaction of basic physiological needs, later joined by needs connected to safety and self-preservation.

From the perspective of Integrative Strategic Psychotherapy, human needs can be grouped into three major categories: 1. Self-preservation needs – encompassing physiological requirements (air, food, water, reproduction) and both physical and psychological safety and security; 2. Emotional needs – including attachment, love, connection, and acceptance; and 3. Self-actualisation needs – such as competence, the capacity to transmit ideas across generations (symbolic immortality), and the drive to understand the world.

The infant is born with these needs already in place, and whether they are met or unmet becomes decisive for psychological health. Unmet needs lead to distress and compensatory strategies (Miller, 2005). Physiological and emotional needs are present from birth (Kenrick et al., 2010), and the hierarchy of needs reflects both developmental sequence and cognitive maturity. In early childhood, survival and safety take precedence, followed by the desire for affection and connection. These needs drive goal-oriented behaviour, which represents a form of psychological adaptation shaped by natural selection, enabling the infant to respond to environmental challenges and opportunities (Kenrick et al., 2010).

A distinctive feature of human beings is that when a particular need becomes dominant, it reorganises the person's outlook on life. As Maslow (1943) observed, a pressing need tends to structure behaviour and direct attention. If the need for security remains unmet, the child will be oriented primarily toward establishing safety. For psychological stability, the child requires a predictable, orderly, and trustworthy environment, one free of chaos and unmanageable threats (Coicici & Popescu, 2017). In this way, primary needs create the child's first pre-symbolic perceptions of both external and internal reality.

Needs are not merely drives but also generators of behaviour. They evoke compensatory actions, charged with affect, whose goal is satisfaction and the restoration of equilibrium (Deci & Ryan, 2000). When needs are linked with affect and goal-directed behaviour, they give rise to proto-cognitions: pre-verbal, pre-symbolic representations of the environment and the self (Coicici & Popescu, 2017). These first evaluations are simple and binary in form—good versus bad, safe versus unsafe, comfort versus discomfort.

The process by which proto-cognitions emerge can be traced through three sequential stages: 1. A need arises, producing tension and motivating the infant to seek satisfaction; 2. The infant evaluates whether and how the need is being met; and 3. From this, a generalised conclusion is formed, combining both cognitive outcome and affective tone (Coicici & Popescu, 2017).

Alongside needs, the infant is equipped with innate signalling systems. One of these is the primary affect: the automatic physiological response to stimuli that signals whether a need is satisfied. Affect includes a rudimentary appraisal—positive or negative—without requiring conscious processing. A sudden startle at a loud noise, for example, represents an affective reaction (Michael et al., 2008). For the infant, such affects are experienced as varying degrees of comfort or discomfort, tightly linked to the meeting of needs (Coicici & Popescu, 2017).

Other innate systems include: 1. Goal-directed behaviour – signalling that a need is unmet, such as crying to indicate hunger; and 2. Assimilation behaviour – the incorporation of the object that meets the need, such as breastfeeding to relieve hunger. This process can be likened to fuelling an engine: the organism integrates what it requires to continue functioning (Coicici & Popescu, 2017).

Stage I – Needs, emotions and behaviours

The first stage of proto-self functioning—when the infant strives to satisfy a need—can be represented mathematically:

$$N_p \Rightarrow Af_p$$
$$N_p \wedge Af_p \Rightarrow Beh_p$$
$$Beh_p \wedge S \Rightarrow Beh_a \wedge Em_{po}^{+}$$
$$Beh_p \wedge (-S) \Rightarrow Beh_{re} \wedge Em_{po}^{-}$$

Where:

Np = Primary need

Afp = Primary affect

Behp = Primary behaviour

S = Stimulus (object or environmental condition that satisfies the need)

Beha = Assimilation behaviour

Behre = Resignation behaviour

$Empo^{+}$ / $Empo^{-}$ = Positive or negative primary orientation emotions

This formula captures the basic architecture of proto-self functioning: needs give rise to affects, affects generate behaviours, behaviours seek stimuli, and depending on whether the stimulus is available or not, the outcome is either assimilation and comfort or resignation and discomfort.

The proto-self is equipped with primary needs from birth: hunger, thirst, warmth, safety, and attachment. Each need generates a visceral state of tension or discomfort, experienced psychologically as a primary affect (Tomkins, 1962; Panksepp, 1998). Affect here is not yet an emotion in the cognitive sense but a raw physiological signal: hunger as irritability, cold as distress, separation as panic.

This is expressed mathematically as:

$$N_p \Rightarrow Af_p$$

Without this affective signalling mechanism, orientation towards survival would be impossible. A baby who could not feel hunger would not cry, and without crying, the environment might not respond. In this sense, affect is the first language of the psyche: it translates visceral needs into signals that can elicit external responses (Siegel, 2001).

Once a need is paired with affect, the infant initiates primary behaviour (Beh_p). This is rudimentary, automatic, and universal—crying, restlessness, or reaching. These behaviours are not learned but encoded in the nervous system as survival mechanisms.

Mathematically:

$$N_p \wedge Af_p \Rightarrow Beh_p$$

Such behaviours serve two purposes: 1. Signal to the environment that assistance is required; and 2. Increase probability of satisfaction by activating caregiver responses.

In attachment theory, this corresponds to attachment behaviours—crying, clinging, or smiling—that activate parental caregiving systems (Bowlby, 1982). In affective neuroscience, these are linked to primary emotional systems (Panksepp, 1998): for example, the PANIC/GRIEF circuit is activated when the infant is separated from the caregiver, motivating crying until reunion.

The decisive turning point is the presence or absence of an appropriate stimulus (S). If the environment responds adequately (e.g., food, warmth, comfort), the infant moves into assimilation behaviour (Beha). If the environment fails to respond, the infant eventually shifts to resignation behaviour (Behre), conserving energy.

This is where the trajectory of the equation diverges:

- With stimulus:

$$Beh_p \wedge S \Rightarrow Beh_a \wedge Em_{po}^{+}$$

– Without stimulus:

$$Beh_p \wedge (-S) \Rightarrow Beh_{re} \wedge Em_{po}^-$$

Assimilation behaviours are automatic and innate. They occur when a stimulus meets the need, often through reflexes such as sucking or grasping. The presence of the satisfying stimulus initiates incorporation, reducing tension and restoring equilibrium. The outcome is a positive primary orientation emotion (Em_{po}^+). These positive states are not yet differentiated emotions but signals of comfort, safety, and relief. Baylis (2006) describes them as brain-state shifts indicating: *"Something important has just happened—equilibrium has been restored."* For example: Hunger $\wedge$ discomfort $\Rightarrow$ crying $\wedge$ presence of milk $\Rightarrow$ sucking $\wedge$ comfort.

When no adequate stimulus appears, assimilation is impossible. After prolonged signalling, the infant may shift to resignation behaviour (Behre), ceasing to cry and conserving energy. This does not represent true regulation but a withdrawal response—a survival strategy to conserve resources in the face of unresponsiveness.

The outcome is a negative primary orientation emotion (Em_{po}^-). This manifests as continued discomfort, distress, or despair. In relational terms, repeated absence of response creates proto-cognitions of *"the world is unresponsive"* or *"needs are dangerous to express."* These become the earliest building blocks of insecure attachment and maladaptive schemas (Schore, 2001; Fonagy et al., 2002).

Each cycle of need–affect–behaviour–stimulus–outcome leaves a trace in the infant's developing mind. These traces become proto-cognitions: pre-verbal, binary evaluations of reality. For example, if the need is met, then the proto-cognition might be *"The world responds; I can trust it"*, whilst if the need is unmet, the first proto-cognitions might be of the type *"The world is unresponsive; I am unsafe."*

Coicici & Popescu (2017) describe proto-cognitions as the earliest form of cognitive organisation, combining primitive appraisals with affective tone. They form the first neural maps upon which later schemas are built.

The implications for psychotherapy are profound. Many adult difficulties can be traced to unresolved proto-self experiences: 1. Binary thinking (good/bad, safe/dangerous) rooted in early proto-cognitions; 2. Attachment trauma – repeated unmet needs shaping schemas of mistrust or unworthiness; 3. Somatic distress –

embodied memories of resignation behaviours, later expressed in psychosomatic symptoms; and 4. Affect dysregulation – inability to tolerate distress due to repeated negative outcomes in infancy.

Psychotherapy thus provides an opportunity to offer new relational inputs that can re-pattern these implicit evaluations. Corrective experiences—consistent atonement, bodily-based interventions, or affect regulation in psychotherapy allow the proto-self's imprints to be integrated into a healthier self-structure.

Consider a newborn who wakes up hungry. Hunger produces discomfort ($Np \Rightarrow Afp$) and the infant starts crying (Behp). If fed promptly, sucking is initiated and the outcome is comfort ($Behp \wedge S \Rightarrow Beh_a \wedge Em_{po}^{+}$). If ignored, the infant continues crying and then withdraws, leading to distress ($Behp \wedge (-S) \Rightarrow Beh_{re} \wedge Em_{po}^{-}$). This simple cycle repeats thousands of times in early life. Over time, the balance of positive versus negative outcomes determines whether the infant develops a proto-cognition of safety and trust or one of danger and neglect.

Within the Integrative Strategic Psychotherapy model, this stage belongs primarily to the proto-self but establishes patterns that shape the core self. The balance of Em_{po}^{+} and Em_{po}^{-} experiences defines whether the child develops resilience or vulnerability. A predominance of $Empo^{+}$ outcomes supports the emergence of secure attachment, coherent schemas, and emotional regulation. A predominance of $Empo^{-}$ outcomes produces maladaptive proto-cognitions, fragile regulation, and later difficulties in the plastic and external selves.

Stage II- Assessment

Stage II represents a critical leap in the formation of the proto-self. While stage I concerns the meeting of needs and the emergence of primary orientation emotions (Em_{po}^{+} or Em_{po}^{-}), stage II involves the evaluation of those outcomes. This evaluation occurs at a pre-verbal, pre-symbolic level and is mediated by a mechanism called primary analysis (Ap).

Primary analysis serves as a rapid appraisal system: it interprets the interplay between need, affect, behaviour, and stimulus, and generates proto-cognitive conclusions that guide future orientation. In other words, stage II is the moment when the infant begins to "learn from experience"—not in a reflective way, but through embodied, implicit proto-cognitions that link emotions with actions and outcomes (Coicici & Popescu, 2017).

The proto-self operates much like a primitive monitoring and evaluation mechanism, continuously scanning: 1. The state of needs; 2. The behaviours enacted (crying, assimilation, resignation); 3. The presence or absence of environmental stimuli; and 4. The emotional outcomes of these interactions. Based on this information, the infant identifies the most effective strategies for orienting in the environment and optimising need satisfaction. This mechanism functions automatically and rapidly, ensuring that the child develops strategies of approach, avoidance, or suppression in relation to both the environment and the self. Evolutionarily, this provided a decisive advantage: the ability to quickly evaluate a behaviour or stimulus as "good" or "bad" increased chances of survival (Tronick, 1989).

The symbolic representation of Stage II is as follows:

$$Ap\ (Em_{po}^{\pm}, Beh_{p}) \Rightarrow Co_{beh}^{\pm}$$
$$Ap\ (Em_{po}^{\pm}, S^{\pm}) \Rightarrow Co_{e}^{\pm}$$
$$Ap\ (Em_{po}^{\pm}, Beh_{a}) \Rightarrow Co_{a}^{\pm}$$
$$Ap\ (Em_{po}^{\pm}, Beh_{re}) \Rightarrow Co_{re}^{\pm}$$

Where:

Ap = Primary analysis (evaluation mechanism).

$Em_{po}^{\pm}$ = Positive or negative primary orientation emotion.

Behp = Primary behaviour (need-signalling behaviour).

Beha = Assimilation behaviour.

Behre = Resignation behaviour.

$Co_{beh}^{\pm}$= Conclusion about the primary behaviour (positive/negative).

$Co_{e}^{\pm}$= Conclusion about the environment (positive/negative).

$Co_{a}^{\pm}$= Conclusion about the assimilation behaviour.

$Co_{re}^{\pm}$= Conclusion about the resignation behaviour.

This set of equations demonstrates that evaluation occurs across multiple domains: behaviour, stimulus/environment, and assimilation or resignation patterns. Each produces a proto-cognitive conclusion that will guide the infant's orientation in subsequent experiences.

The first domain of evaluation concerns the self.

$$Ap\ (Em_{po}^{\pm}, Beh_{p}) \Rightarrow Co_{beh}^{\pm}$$

Here, the infant assesses the effectiveness of their own behaviours (Behp) in securing need satisfaction. If crying (Beh_p) leads to feeding, primary analysis produces a positive conclusion ($Cobeh^+$): *"Crying works; I should cry when in discomfort"*. If crying yields no response, the result is a negative conclusion ($Cobeh^-$): *"Crying is useless; I should not waste energy"*. This pre-verbal evaluation is emotionally charged, as the polarity of the primary emotion (Em_{po}^+ or Em_{po}^-) colours the proto-cognition. Positive outcomes reinforce expression, while negative outcomes may lead to suppression. Over time, repeated negative behavioural conclusions form the basis of inhibition patterns and even emotional suppression in later development (Izard & Kobak, 1999).

The second evaluative domain concerns the external world.

$$Ap\ (Em_{po}^{\pm}, S^{\pm}) \Rightarrow Co_{e}^{\pm}$$

If a satisfying stimulus appears (e.g., mother responds) (S^+), primary analysis generates a positive conclusion about the environment (Coe^+): *"The world responds; I am safe"*. If the stimulus fails to appear, the result is a negative conclusion (Coe^-): *"The world is unreliable; I am unsafe."* These proto-cognitions form the earliest internal working models of attachment (Bowlby, 1982). Over time, repeated Co_e^+ experiences support secure attachment, while repeated Co_e^- experiences give rise to schemas of neglect, mistrust, or hostility.

The third domain of evaluation concerns the behaviours of assimilation (Beha) and resignation (Behre).

$$Ap\ (Em_{po}^{\pm}, Beh_{a}) \Rightarrow Co_{a}^{\pm}$$
$$Ap\ (Em_{po}^{\pm}, Beh_{re}) \Rightarrow Co_{re}^{\pm}$$

If assimilation leads to comfort, the conclusion is Coa^+: *"When food appears, I should take it in."* If assimilation fails (e.g., difficulty feeding), a Coa^-

proto-cognition emerges: *"Even when food is present, satisfaction is uncertain"*. If resignation preserves energy in a hostile environment, the infant may form a $Core^{+}$ conclusion: *"Stopping crying protects me"*. If resignation only leads to despair, the proto-cognition is $Core^{-}$: *"Even giving up is painful; there is no safety"*. These evaluations influence whether the child continues to signal needs or shifts towards inhibition and withdrawal. Repeated Co_{re}^{-} conclusions can predispose individuals to learned helplessness (Seligman, 1975).

Stage II is where proto-cognitions crystallise into the first mental models of the self and the environment. These are not symbolic or linguistic, but embodied and affective. They answer fundamental questions: *"Is it worth expressing my needs?"*, *"Does the world respond?"*, *"Should I persist or give up?"* Though simple, these binary proto-cognitions provide the foundational architecture of the self. They shape the later development of the core self and influence attachment patterns, self-esteem, and emotional regulation.

From a developmental perspective, Tronick's (2007) still-face paradigm demonstrates how infants rapidly evaluate caregiver responsiveness. When the caregiver withdraws responsiveness, infants initially protest (Beh_{p}), then shift to resignation (Beh_{re}), forming negative proto-cognitions. Neuroscientifically, this stage involves activation of the limbic system, particularly the amygdala and anterior cingulate cortex, which support rapid appraisal of stimuli as safe or dangerous (LeDoux, 1996). These pre-verbal evaluations are later reinforced by cortical structures as symbolic thought emerges.

For psychotherapy, stage II highlights how implicit proto-cognitions continue to shape adult experience. Clients may unconsciously carry early evaluations such as: *"Expressing needs is dangerous"*, *"The world does not respond"* or *"Giving up is safer than persisting."* These early conclusions manifest in symptoms such as: 1. Emotional inhibition and difficulty asking for help; 2. Mistrust and insecure attachment patterns; 3. Learned helplessness and depressive tendencies; and 4. Hypervigilance to environmental threats.

Psychotherapy can provide corrective experiences by creating a consistent environment where needs are recognised and responded to. Non-verbal techniques (somatic work, expressive arts, relational atonement) are often necessary to reach the implicit level of proto-cognitions, which lie beneath conscious recall.

Stage III – The conclusion

Stage III represents the culmination of the proto-self's evaluative cycle. After the satisfaction or frustration of a need (Stage I) and the evaluation of behaviours and stimuli (Stage II), the child's system integrates these micro-evaluations into a general conclusion (Cog). This is not yet a reflective judgment, but rather a global, embodied stance toward the self and the environment. It forms the earliest implicit conviction of whether life is predictable, responsive, and manageable or chaotic, unsafe, and unresponsive.

Mathematically, this synthesis can be represented as:

$$Co_{beh}^{\pm} \Rightarrow Em_{p}^{\pm}$$
$$Co_{e}^{\pm} \Rightarrow Em_{p}^{\pm}$$
$$Co_{a/re}^{\pm} \Rightarrow Em_{p}^{\pm}$$
$$A_{sec}\left((Co_{beh}^{\pm} \wedge Co_{e}^{\pm} \wedge Co_{a/re}^{\pm}), Em_{p}^{\pm}\right) \Rightarrow Co_{g}^{\pm}$$

Where:

$Em_{p}^{\pm}$ = Primary emotion (positive/negative)

$Co_{beh}^{\pm}$ = Conclusion about the primary behaviour (positive/negative)

$Co_{e}^{\pm}$ = Conclusion about the environment (positive/negative)

$Co_{a/re}^{\pm}$ = Conclusion about the assimilation or resignation behaviour (positive/negative)

A_{sec} = Secondary analysis

$Co_{g}^{\pm}$ = General conclusion

The conclusions about the self (own primary behaviour) ($Co_{beh}^{\pm}$), about the surrounding world ($Co_{e}^{\pm}$) and the assimilation or resignation behaviours ($Co_{a/re}^{\pm}$) lead to a primary emotion, either positive if the appraisal about the self, environment or the assimilation behaviour are positive, or negative if the appraisal is negative (the conclusions reached in stage II).

In this context, the secondary analysis (A_{sec}) acts as a synthesising mechanism. It receives input from these three evaluative domains identified in Stage II: conclusions about the self ($Co_{beh}^{\pm}$), conclusions about the environment ($Co_{e}^{\pm}$) and conclusions about assimilation or resignation ($Co_{a/re}^{\pm}$). To this synthesis, the primary emotion ($Em_p^{\pm}$) is attached, amplifying the energetic valence of the conclusion. The result is a general conclusion, positive or negative, that influences not only immediate behaviour but also the formation of early implicit expectations of life. This mechanism ensures efficiency: instead of endlessly re-analysing each behavioural outcome, the infant establishes generalised proto-cognitions that guide orientation in future situations.

The addition of primary emotion ($Em_p^{\pm}$) to the evaluative synthesis ensures that the general conclusion is not merely cognitive, but deeply affective. Emotions here function as motivational amplifiers, charging the conclusion with energy and making it more likely to shape behaviour and memory. For instance, a positive general conclusion (Cog^{+}), accompanied by comfort or joy, reinforces approach behaviour, trust in the environment, and persistence in signalling needs. A negative general conclusion (Cog^{-}), marked by distress or despair, strengthens avoidance tendencies, resignation, or suppression of need-expression. This illustrates how the earliest mood states emerge: the accumulation of positive or negative Co_g conclusions translates into a baseline affective climate within which the infant develops.

Stage III parallels several established developmental concepts: Erikson's psychosocial stage of trust versus mistrust (Erikson, 1963), internal working models of attachment (Bowlby, 1982) and learned helplessness versus mastery motivation (Seligman, 1975; White, 1959) and self-efficacy beliefs (Bandura, 1997). For instance, self-efficacy - the belief in one's capacity to influence outcomes—originates not in reflective thought but in the infant's proto-cognitive generalisations about whether their actions bring results. If crying consistently elicits food, the infant forms a Co_g^{+} proto-cognition: *"I can influence my world"*. If crying repeatedly yields no response, the infant develops Co_g^{-}: *"Nothing I do matters"*. These early orientation conclusions are the precursors of learned trust or helplessness (Seligman, 1975). Over time, they shape the individual's implicit sense of agency and their capacity to engage with the world confidently or withdraw in resignation. Stage III serves as the bridge between the proto-self's immediate emotional life and the emergence of stable cognitive-affective structures that support the other dimensions of the self.

Neuroscientific evidence supports the idea that repeated affective evaluations are integrated into stable neural networks. During the first three years of life, synaptic pruning and myelination sculpt circuits that consolidate frequent experiences into enduring patterns (Schore, 2001; Siegel, 2001). Positive general conclusions strengthen pathways involving dopaminergic reward systems, reinforcing approach behaviours. Negative general conclusions reinforce circuits associated with the amygdala and stress-response systems, heightening vigilance and avoidance. This consolidation explains why early emotional climates, whether responsive or neglectful, leave enduring imprints on personality and affect regulation.

In psychotherapy, many adult difficulties reflect distorted or maladaptive general conclusions formed in infancy. For example, depression may involve an implicit negative general conclusion (Cog^{-}) *"My actions cannot change anything"*, anxiety disorders may reflect negative general conclusions (Cog^{-}) about the environment: *"The world is unsafe", whilst* personality disorders may be linked to contradictory general conclusions (e.g., alternating between *"I can trust"* and *"I must never trust"*). Therapeutic interventions aim to provide corrective relational experiences that enable clients to revise these general conclusions. By consistently offering atonement, validation, and responsiveness, psychotherapy creates opportunities for general conclusions to be re-established, even at an implicit level. In ISP, this is achieved through strategic interventions that target different levels of the self: 1. Working with the proto-self through body-focused or affect-regulation techniques; 2. Addressing the core self with relational and cognitive restructuring; 3. Supporting the plastic self by reshaping sustaining mechanisms; and 4. Strengthening the external self through behavioural rehearsal and relational experiments.

4.3. The Core Self

Whereas the proto-self is largely concerned with primary needs, affects, and emotions at a pre-verbal level, the core self incorporates both verbal and non-verbal information processing, forming the first structured mental models of the self and the environment. These models, called core sets, are the fundamental schemas through which the individual interprets, anticipates, and adapts to experience.

Biologically, the development of the core self is inseparable from the processes of neural maturation, epigenetic activation, and experience-dependent plasticity. The brain provides a genetically preconfigured architecture, but the environment determines which pathways are activated, reinforced, or inhibited. Thus, the biological level of the core self can be understood as the dynamic interplay between genetic potential, neural circuitry, and experiential input.

Like the proto-self, the core self is built upon genetic foundations. Yet the decisive factor in its emergence is the activation of the epigenome in response to relational and environmental conditions. Epigenetic processes influence gene expression, regulating which neural circuits become functional and which remain silent (Meaney, 2010).

This is particularly relevant to the formation of internal working models (IWMs)—the innate, genetically preconfigured neural networks awaiting experience. The infant brain is structured with potential patterns for both secure and insecure attachment, but which map becomes active depends on the quality of early caregiving. As we have seen in the previous sub-chapter, responsive caregiving activates circuits supporting security, trust, and emotional regulation. Inconsistent or neglectful caregiving activates circuits underlying insecurity, hypervigilance, or withdrawal. This process demonstrates how biology and environment co-determine the architecture of the core self.

The core self functions as a matrix of neural maps, shaped by both inheritance and lived experience. These neural maps correspond to core sets—structured models that organise perception, emotion, and behaviour. A neural map can be defined as the pattern of neuronal activation associated with a specific kind of experience (Siegel, 1996). Over time, repeated experiences consolidate into preferred patterns, creating the core schemas that guide future orientation. For example, consistent soothing leads to the neural encoding of *"I am safe; others will help"*, whilst repeated neglect encodes *"My needs are ignored; I am alone"*. Core sets thus form the building blocks of personality, determining how information is processed and how the self interacts with the environment.

Attachment theory provides a clear framework for understanding how IWMs (internal working models) are encoded in the core self. From infancy, the child relies on the caregiver's right-brain non-verbal communication—facial expressions, tone of voice, body posture—to regulate affect and establish relational security (Schore, 2003). Secure attachment leads to positive general conclusions (Cog^{+}) (*the world is safe; my needs matter*), insecure-avoidant attachment fosters withdrawal and minimisation of need expression, insecure-ambivalent attachment reinforces hyperactivation and anxiety in signalling, and disorganised attachment creates contradictory maps, blending approach and fear. These relational experiences are mapped in the right hemisphere and integrated into the child's developing core self. Importantly, these IWMs are not fixed. Because the brain retains multiple potential pathways, corrective emotional experiences can reshape the maps, explaining the efficacy of psychotherapy (Siegel, 2006; Cozolino, 2017).

The transition from proto-self to core self highlights the importance of multisensory integration. According to Damasio (1999), the core self maps internal and external signals (e.g., interoceptive states, parental cues). These maps are then elaborated into the core self, where experiences are organised into structured schemas. The child's brain generates a multisensory image of the caregiver's non-verbal behaviour (Siegel, 2001). Smiles, gestures, and tones of voice become encoded not simply as isolated events but as patterns of safety or danger, responsiveness or neglect. These patterns are the raw material of the core sets.

The biological development of the core self occurs within sensitive periods of heightened plasticity. During early childhood, the brain is characterised by experience-expectant development (Greenough & Black, 1992): neurons overproduce connections, awaiting environmental input to stabilise relevant circuits. Positive experiences (responsive caregiving, safety, stimulation) reinforce adaptive pathways, whilst negative experiences (neglect, trauma, chronic stress) strengthen maladaptive circuits.

Because early neural networks are especially malleable, the first years of life exert a disproportionate influence on the architecture of the core self. Later psychotherapy can remodel these networks, but change is slower and requires sustained corrective experience (Popescu & Drobot, 2012).

Research suggests that the following neural processes are central to the biological level of the core self (Siegel, 2001; Schore, 2003): 1. Generation and regulation of emotions (limbic system and prefrontal cortex integration); 2. The capacity for flexible and reflective behaviour (prefrontal functioning); 3. An autobiographical sense of self and narrative continuity (hippocampal-cortical networks); 4. The theory of mind and empathy (mirror neuron systems and medial prefrontal cortex); and 5. Interpersonal communication (integration of right-hemisphere affective signalling with left-hemisphere linguistic processing). Thus, the core self is not simply a psychological construct but a biologically instantiated system of neural integration.

The transition from proto-self to core self also coincides with the development of explicit memory. Whilst the proto-self is governed by implicit, non-verbal memory, the core self incorporates explicit memory traces, enabling the consolidation of personal narrative and identity (Nelson & Fivush, 2004). Implicit memory is emotional, behavioural, somatosensory, and preverbal, and explicit memory is symbolic, verbal, and autobiographical. Past experiences are thus encoded as schemas or mental models (Johnson-Laird, 1983), which become integrated into the core self. These schemas shape expectations, interpretations, and interpersonal strategies, influencing both resilience and vulnerability.

Understanding the biological basis of the core self has profound clinical implications: 1. Attachment-focused psychotherapy targets the reactivation and reorganisation of neural pathways related to IWMs; 2. Corrective emotional experiences provide new relational inputs that can rewire established patterns; 3. Neuroplasticity-informed techniques (e.g., mindfulness, somatic regulation, expressive therapies) exploit the brain's capacity for change; and 4. ISP integrates interventions across levels: working with proto-self affect regulation, core self schemas, plastic self sustaining mechanisms, and external self behaviours. Psychotherapists thus act not only as relational partners but also as "architects of neural re-patterning"—facilitating the integration of adaptive maps and the reorganisation of maladaptive ones.

As we have already seen, the core self is the central dimension of the self that processes both verbal and non-verbal information. It emerges during early childhood and provides the organising frameworks—mental models and schemas—that structure the child's engagement with the environment. These mental structures, referred to in the ISP model as "core sets", are the first consistent systems through which the mind interprets experience and formulates strategies for adaptation (Popescu, 2021; Popescu & Vîșcu, 2016).

From a psychological perspective, the development of the core self is grounded in internal working models (IWMs)—innate cognitive-emotional structures that are activated through repeated experience. IWMs were first conceptualised by John Bowlby (1969/1982) within attachment theory, where they represent the mental representations of self and others that emerge from caregiving interactions. Integrative Strategic Psychotherapy (ISP) builds on this concept, proposing that IWMs are innate but latent, waiting for activation through the general conclusions formed in the proto-self.

According to ISP, internal working models (IWMs) appear in levels of increasing complexity, each linked to the developmental process of need satisfaction, affect, and evaluation. Primary IWMs are derived directly from general conclusions in the proto self, secondary IWMs arise when experiences are interpreted through the filter of activated primary IWMs and tertiary IWMs are formed as repeated patterns consolidate, becoming increasingly complex neural networks. This sequence explains how early proto-cognitive evaluations (proto-self) crystallise into the core psychological architecture of the individual.

Mathematically:

$$Co_g^{\pm} \Rightarrow Em_b^{\pm}$$
$$A(\Sigma Co_g^{\pm}, \Sigma Em_p^{\pm}) \Rightarrow IWM_p^{\pm}$$
$$IWM_p^{\pm} \Rightarrow Em_b^{\pm}$$
$$A(\Sigma IWM_p^{\pm}, \Sigma Em_p^{\pm}) \Rightarrow IWM_{sec}^{\pm}$$
$$IWM_{sec}^{\pm} \Rightarrow Em_b^{\pm}$$
$$A(\Sigma IWM_{sec}^{\pm}, \Sigma Em_p^{\pm}) \Rightarrow IWM_t^{\pm}$$

Where

$Co_g^{\pm}$ = General conclusion (positive or negative)

$Em_b^{\pm}$ = Basic emotion (positive or negative)

A = Analysis

$\Sigma Co_g^{\pm}$ = Sum of general conclusions (positive or negative)

$\Sigma Em_p^{\pm}$ = Sum of basic emotions (positive or negative)

$IWM_p^{\pm}$ = Primary internal working models (positive or negative)

$IWM_{sec}^{\pm}$ = Secondary internal working models (positive or negative)

$IWM_t^{\pm}$ = Tertiary internal working models (positive or negative)

The process begins when a child interprets early life events and draws primitive cognitive conclusions—unconscious, binary beliefs about the self, others, or the world. These are referred to as Cog± (positive or negative general conclusions). These are not yet complex narratives, but proto-cognitions, formed at a preverbal or early-verbal level.

These conclusions are not consciously reasoned—they are subjective and emotionally laden interpretations of relational experiences, often resulting from attachment dynamics (e.g., responsiveness or unavailability of caregivers). For example, the child may have drawn a negative general conclusion *"I'm a burden"* (Co_g^-), which induces sadness and fear (Em_b^-), or, by contrast, a positive general conclusion like *"I'm valued and safe"* (Co_g^+) which leads to joy (Em_b^+). This illustrates that conclusions (beliefs) are inherently tied to emotional states—they co-arise and reinforce each other, initiating the cognitive-emotional loop that underpins self-structure.

$$Co_g^{\pm} \Rightarrow Em_b^{\pm}$$

Over time, the child doesn't just have isolated beliefs and feelings—they accumulate, forming patterns. The symbol Σ (sigma) means "sum", referring to the aggregation of all early $Co_g^{\pm}$ and $Em_b^{\pm}$ experiences. This accumulation undergoes an unconscious analysis process (A)—a meaning-making function that is developmentally embedded. This process gives rise to Primary Internal Working Models ($IWM_p^{\pm}$)—early relational templates or self-world schemas.

$$A(\Sigma Co_g^{\pm}, \Sigma Em_p^{\pm}) \Rightarrow IWM_p^{\pm}$$

Primary IWMs are non-verbal, embodied, and pre-symbolic, rooted in attachment patterns, relational atonement or mis atonement, and often formed before age 5. Examples are: *"I am helpless when others are angry"*, *"If I cry, no one comes"* or *"Smiling makes people love me"*. These primary internal working models ($IWM_p^{\pm}$) reflect the core beliefs that shape the child's expectations about relationships and emotional safety. They are neurobiologically encoded, linked to limbic patterns and somatic memory.

Once formed, these primary internal working models ($IWM_p^{\pm}$) are activated repeatedly in everyday life, particularly in relational contexts. They predict and interpret events, often automatically and unconsciously, thereby triggering emotional states. For example, a person with a negative primary internal working model (IWM_p^-) *"People always leave"* may feel sadness or anxiety (Em_b^-) every time someone doesn't respond quickly. A person with a positive primary internal working model (IWM_p^+): *"I'm lovable as I am"* feels contentment and security (Em_b^+) even in ambiguous situations. This step shows the feedback loop: early schemas (IWM_p) shape emotion, which in turn confirms the schema.

$$IWM_p^{\pm} \Rightarrow Em_b^{\pm}$$

Through continued experiences and reflections, especially in childhood, the person unconsciously performs another integrative analysis. This time, it's not just conclusions and raw feelings, but already-formed primary IWMs, along with emotional responses to relational life. This leads to the development of secondary internal working models ($IWM_{sec}^{\pm}$), which are more articulated, symbolic, and verbal, context-sensitive (e.g., school, peer groups, performance, appearance), and often shaped by social norms, culture and family dynamics. Such examples are *"I must perform to be accepted"*, *"If I'm vulnerable, I'll be rejected"*, *"People respect me when I take charge."*"These secondary IWMs are more complex, but still unconscious. They form the basis of defensive strategies, personality traits, and relational scripts.

$$A(\Sigma IWM_p^{\pm}, \Sigma Em_p^{\pm}) \Rightarrow IWM_{sec}^{\pm}$$

In other words, primary IWMs are early, pre-verbal, emotionally encoded schemas, based on repeated relational experiences from the first years of life. They are formed through the integration of generalised cognitions (Cog±) and basic emotions (Emb±) into the child's implicit self-representation. They form at 0-3 years (pre-symbolic), are sensory-emotional, unconscious affective conclusions; not yet verbal or socially mediated, global, undifferentiated, embodied, which ensure basic survival, attachment safety and emotional orientation. Examples are: *"I am unsafe"*, *"I disappear when I'm not seen"*, *"Being sad leads to disconnection"*, *"If I cry, no one comes"*, *"I am too much / not enough"*, *"Closeness is dangerous"*, *"I don't exist unless someone reflects me"*, *"Being alone is unbearable"*. These are deeply embodied emotional templates, often tied to proto-self experiences, which later become the emotional raw material for higher symbolic elaboration.

Secondary IWMs emerge later, as the child develops symbolic language, social awareness, and contextual differentiation. These models integrate primary IWMs with external norms, family narratives, cultural expectations, and increasingly verbalised cognitive patterns. They form at 3–7 years and beyond, they are symbolic, linguistic, and socially constructed, contextualised, rule-based, generalised beliefs about self and others. Secondary IWMs are more articulated and domain-specific (e.g., school, gender, appearance) and regulate interpersonal behaviour, emotional expression, and self-presentation. Examples include: *"To be loved, I must always be good", "If I don't make people laugh, they'll ignore me", "Crying makes people uncomfortable — better to stay silent", "Smart kids don't need help", "Girls shouldn't be angry", "If I don't look perfect, I'll be made fun of", "Only weak people ask for comfort", "If I don't please others, I'll be punished or abandoned"* or *"I have to earn my place by being useful."* These models are more differentiated, domain-bound, and filtered through social-relational lenses (peers, teachers, extended family, media, etc.). They are semi-conscious or unconscious, and often mistaken for truths rather than adaptive strategies.

Secondary IWMs are symbolic reinterpretations of Primary IWMs. For example a *primary IWM may be: "I disappear when not mirrored"* and hence the *secondary IWM: "If I don't perform, people won't see me."* Secondary IWMs are often compensatory or defensive strategies built on the emotional truth of the primary ones. They form the unconscious scripts and patterns that structure roles, identity, and personality style.

As with primary IWMs, these secondary models continue to generate emotions in daily life. Because they are more abstract and symbolic, the emotions may be more nuanced or disguised (e.g., irritability, shame, guilt, envy). Someone with *"I must always be strong"* may feel intense discomfort or anger (Em_b^-) when vulnerable, even if no threat is present. This shows how later schemas regulate emotion, sometimes by suppressing or distorting it, and sometimes by facilitating self-acceptance (if IWM_{sec}^+).

$$IWM_{sec}^{\pm} \Rightarrow Em_b^{\pm}$$

The final stage of analysis in the core self represents a higher-order consolidation of the self. Over years, the accumulation of secondary schemas and the emotions associated with them are re-integrated into tertiary IWMs ($IWM_t^{\pm}$). Tertiary IWMs are deep, generalised identity models, highly resistant to change, translated into existential narratives and life scripts.

$$A(\Sigma IWM_{sec}^{\pm}, \Sigma Em_p^{\pm}) \Rightarrow IWM_t^{\pm}$$

Tertiary IWMs are the most complex, composite, and symbolically integrated relational models within the core self. They function as unconscious life scripts, identity-defining patterns, relational blueprints and self-role narratives. These are not verbal beliefs alone, but experientially encoded patterns of meaning and behaviour, reinforced across years or even decades, until they become instinctive ways of being in the world.

IWMs correspond to neural networks in the prefrontal cortex, amygdala, and hippocampus (Fonagy & Allison, 2014). Implicit memory systems encode early IWMs, while explicit systems elaborate them later (Siegel, 2001). Attachment patterns correlate with differences in right-hemisphere processing, especially in non-verbal emotional communication (Schore, 2012).

In psychotherapy, IWMs are often implicit and unconscious. They manifest as automatic relational expectations and emotional responses. Interventions may include: 1. Making IWMs explicit through interpretation, narrative, or experiential works 2. Corrective emotional experiences, which activate alternative IWMs; 3. Parts work (ego state therapy), addressing conflicting IWMs; and 4. Body-oriented techniques, targeting dissociative IWMs rooted in early affect. Through these processes, therapy enables clients to reorganise core sets, integrating adaptive IWMs and loosening maladaptive patterns.

4.4. The Plastic Self

While the proto-self provides the foundation through primary needs and affects, and the core self organises experience via internal working models and schemas, the plastic self is the dynamic maintainer of these structures. Its primary function is to preserve psychological stability by creating feedback loops that sustain core sets and maintain continuity across time.

From a biological perspective, the plastic self rests upon the principle of neuroplasticity—the brain's capacity to reorganise itself in response to experience.

It is here that we find the biological substrate of problem maintenance: maladaptive circuits are not fixed but are reinforced through repetition, creating rigid feedback patterns that shape behaviour, emotion, and cognition. At the same time, the very plasticity of the brain ensures that change is always possible: psychotherapy can stimulate the reorganisation of neural networks, creating new feedback loops that sustain healthier ways of being.

The concept of neuroplasticity is fundamental to understanding the biological level of the plastic self. Research shows that the brain is not a static organ but is constantly reshaped by experience (Kolb & Gibb, 2011). Synaptic connections strengthen or weaken depending on use—a phenomenon described by Donald Hebb's famous principle, *"neurons that fire together wire together"* (Hebb, 1949/2002).

In the context of the plastic self, neuroplasticity means that once a core set has been established in the core self, repeated activation strengthens the corresponding neural circuits. Over time, these circuits become the preferred pathways through which information is processed. This process explains why maladaptive behaviours or emotional responses persist: the brain's plasticity, which evolved to promote adaptation, can also lock individuals into dysfunctional feedback loops.

Biologically, the plastic self is therefore grounded in: 1. Synaptic plasticity – strengthening or weakening of synaptic connections based on experience (Bliss & Collingridge, 1993); 2. Structural plasticity – the growth of new dendrites, axons, and even neurons (in certain brain regions such as the hippocampus); and 3. Neurochemical modulation – changes in neurotransmitter systems (e.g., dopamine, serotonin, glutamate) that regulate mood and behaviour.

At the biological level, much of the activity of the plastic self is mediated through implicit memory systems. Unlike explicit memory, which involves conscious recall and depends on the hippocampus, implicit memory is non-conscious, procedural, and affect-laden, relying on subcortical structures such as the amygdala, basal ganglia, and cerebellum (Schacter, 1996; Siegel, 2001). When early experiences are repeated—whether secure caregiving or traumatic neglect—they create implicit templates that guide future responses. The plastic self encodes these templates biologically through the formation of preferential neural circuits. Once formed, these circuits act as feedback loops, meaning that they: 1. Filter incoming information, selecting stimuli congruent with the existing maps; 2. Generate internal stimuli that reinforce existing patterns; and 3. Bias behaviour toward maintaining internal coherence, even at the cost of maladaptation.

For example, a child repeatedly ignored when crying will develop a neural template associating need-expression with non-response. Biologically, this involves strengthened amygdala–prefrontal connections that encode vigilance and resignation. The plastic self then maintains this circuit into adulthood, filtering experiences in such a way that reinforces the belief, *"My needs will not be met."*

The biological level of the plastic self plays a critical role in emotional regulation. Schore (2003) has shown that early right-hemisphere development is shaped by affective atonement between caregiver and child. These interactions sculpt the orbitofrontal cortex and limbic circuits, establishing regulatory feedback loops.

When regulation is secure, the plastic self maintains circuits that balance arousal and restore homeostasis after stress. When regulation is insecure or disorganised, maladaptive circuits dominate:

- Hyperarousal loops (excessive sympathetic activation, as in anxiety disorders); or
- Hypoarousal loops (shutdown responses, as in depression or dissociation).

These feedback patterns are sustained biologically through repeated activation of the hypothalamic–pituitary–adrenal (HPA) axis and associated neurotransmitter systems (McEwen, 2007).

From an ISP perspective, this explains why emotional dysregulation is not simply a psychological issue but a biological expression of the plastic self. Psychotherapy must therefore provide corrective experiences that gradually rewire regulatory circuits.

The plastic self can be understood as the biological substrate of pathology maintenance. Once a maladaptive feedback loop has formed, it tends to perpetuate itself. The brain preferentially attends to stimuli that match existing schemas and activated implicit memories create internal signals that mimic or amplify external inputs. Thus, the individual behaves in ways that confirm existing expectations, strengthening the loop. Neurobiologically, this involves the repeated activation of cortico-limbic circuits, particularly those involving the amygdala, prefrontal cortex, and hippocampus. For example, in post-traumatic stress disorder (PTSD), repeated trauma sensitises the amygdala, lowering the threshold for fear responses and reinforcing hyperarousal loops (Rauch, Shin, & Phelps, 2006). In depression, dysfunctional loops between the medial prefrontal cortex and subgenual cingulate maintain negative affective bias and rumination (Disner et al., 2011).

The plastic self thus biologically embodies the principle that *"the brain is a prediction machine"*—it uses past experiences to shape future responses, often perpetuating dysfunction unless disrupted.

The same mechanisms that maintain maladaptation also allow for change. Because the brain remains plastic throughout life, corrective emotional experiences in psychotherapy can reorganise maladaptive loops (Doidge, 2007). For example, repeated therapeutic atonement strengthens prefrontal regulation of the amygdala, reducing anxiety. New relational experiences activate dormant neural maps for secure attachment, gradually replacing insecure templates. Mindfulness practices increase connectivity between the anterior cingulate cortex and insula, enhancing interoceptive awareness and emotional regulation (Farb et al., 2010).

In terms of the ISP model, psychotherapy works at the biological level of the plastic self by creating new feedback loops that override maladaptive ones. Over time, these new circuits become preferential pathways, changing the individual's behavioural repertoire.

Another essential function of the plastic self is to act as a homeostatic regulator. Biologically, the brain strives for balance across multiple systems—emotional, cognitive, physiological. The plastic self filters stimuli to maintain this balance, selecting experiences that confirm existing maps.

However, when maladaptive maps dominate, homeostasis itself becomes pathological. For example, an individual accustomed to chaos may unconsciously seek chaotic environments because these confirm internal expectations, even though they perpetuate suffering. Biologically, this reflects the plastic self's reliance on stability over accuracy: maintaining existing loops is metabolically cheaper than creating new ones. This explains why psychotherapy often requires not only insight but prolonged repetition of new experiences to overcome the biological inertia of established circuits.

Understanding the biological level of the plastic self has several implications for psychotherapy: 1. Resistance to change is not simply psychological; it reflects the biological preference for stability in neural networks; 2. Relapse often occurs because old feedback loops remain latent, ready to reactivate under stress; 3. Therapeutic techniques such as mindfulness, body-oriented approaches, and relational atonement directly target neuroplastic processes; and 4. Timing and repetition are essential: new circuits require sustained activation to become preferred pathways.

The plastic self represents one of the most dynamic aspects of the integrative strategic model of the self. Whereas the proto-self encodes the organism's initial needs and bodily-based evaluations, and the core self organises attachment and basic schemas, the plastic self refers to the internal sustaining mechanisms that preserve, stabilise, and sometimes rigidify these early structures across the lifespan.

Its function is twofold:

1. Maintenance of stability, ensuring that once core sets and internal working models are established, they remain coherent through feedback loops; and
2. Perpetuation of pathology – when maladaptive patterns dominate, the same feedback loops maintain symptoms and resist change.

In this sense, the plastic self acts both as the guardian of psychological equilibrium and as a potential obstacle to transformation. Its activity explains why many individuals repeat the same maladaptive behaviours, thoughts, and emotional cycles despite conscious awareness of their dysfunction.

All mental processes arise from the activation of neural circuits. As Siegel (1996) notes, the specific pattern of neuronal firing within a circuit generates a particular experience. Early childhood experiences repeatedly activate certain neurons, leading to preferential pathways—circuits that fire more easily and automatically than others.

This process of neural shaping means that repeated relational experiences—whether secure or traumatic—become embedded in the brain's structure. Schore (2003) emphasises that circuits responsible for emotion regulation, memory consolidation, behaviour, and interpersonal atonement are particularly sensitive in the first years of life. Once formed, these circuits become the "default settings" of the mind.

According to Siegel (2001), these early-established processes include: the generation and regulation of emotions; the capacity for flexible and reflective responses; the construction of an autobiographical sense of self; empathy and the capacity to understand other minds; and interpersonal communication. Thus, the plastic self is closely tied to implicit memory systems, which encode repeated experiences outside conscious awareness and shape future behaviour.

As Johnson-Laird (1983) proposed, human beings build mental models that represent past experiences and guide present functioning. These models are not abstract cognitive templates but are embodied, emotionally charged neural patterns. The plastic self integrates these models into stable schemas, which become the internal filters through which new information is interpreted. Popescu & Drobot (2012) argue that childhood experiences leave enduring traces in the form of preferential neural activations, which then maintain themselves through internal feedback loops.

This explains why the plastic self can maintain both adaptive and maladaptive structures. A securely attached child develops schemas of *I am lovable* and *The world is safe*. These schemas stabilise into feedback loops that support resilience. A neglected child develops schemas of *I am unworthy* or *The world is hostile*. These schemas also stabilise, but in ways that reinforce vulnerability and defensive patterns.

The plastic self sustains core sets through internal loops of self-confirmation. Once preferential neural maps exist, the self processes information in ways that match these maps, thereby ensuring stability.

This can be represented mathematically as follows:

$$IWM_a \wedge Em_b^{\pm} \Rightarrow S_{int}$$
$$S_{int} \wedge S_{ext} \Rightarrow Beh \wedge Em_c \wedge Co$$

Where:

IWM_a = Activated internal working model

$Em_b^{\pm}$ = Attached basic emotion

S_{int} = Internal stimulus

S_{ext} = External stimulus

Beh = Behavioural response

Em_c = Complex emotion

Co = Cognitive evaluation

When an internal working model is activated (e.g., *"I am not good enough," "People can't be trusted"*) and a basic emotion is attached to it (such as fear, anger, sadness, or joy), the combination triggers an internal stimulus.

$$IWM_a \wedge Em_b^{\pm} \Rightarrow S_{int}$$

In other words, the person becomes internally aroused—emotionally and cognitively—by the reactivation of this emotionally loaded relational schema (IWM). This internal stimulus could be a bodily sensation, a memory flash, an intrusive thought, or an urge, and it corresponds to the internal activation of the self in a specific relational context. This reflects the proto self and core self being engaged through primary somatic-affective reactions and core IWM structures, often early-formed, tied to attachment.

When the internal activation (from IWM + basic emotion) meets an external stimulus, a more complete psychological and behavioural response pattern is triggered. This includes: 1. Behavioural expression: a concrete action, withdrawal, verbal or non-verbal response (linked to the plastic and external self); 2. Complex emotional experience: more differentiated, often socially mediated emotions arise (like guilt, jealousy, or compassion), often shaped by secondary or tertiary IWMs; and 3. Cognitive appraisal: the person makes sense of the situation by interpreting, rationalising, or drawing conclusions (linked to tertiary IWMs or strategic processing).

$$S_{int} \wedge S_{ext} \Rightarrow Beh \wedge Em_c \wedge Co$$

This represents a full self activation process across all the domains of the self. The internal working model is activated by memory or context, a basic emotion is felt, and a situational stimulus triggers a reaction, which leads to a behavioural act, complex emotions, and a cognitive schema or narrative—which may further consolidate or rework the IWM. In other words, old emotional-relational templates (IWM) get activated inside the person in response to context (internal or external) and this activation, coupled with basic emotional energy (positive or negative), produces internal stimuli (bodily or psychological). When an external trigger is added to this already active internal state, it results in: behaviour (visible or subtle), a complex, culturally shaped emotion, and cognitive meaning-making—often reinforcing, questioning, or re-writing the internal model. Thus, behaviour and emotional responses emerge not only from the objective external situation but from the interaction between external and internal stimuli. This explains why two individuals can react so differently to the same external event: their responses are mediated by internal stimuli generated by the plastic self.

The adaptive function of the plastic self lies in its ability to maintain stability, coherence, and continuity of identity. It allows the individual to experience the world as predictable and meaningful. However, its maladaptive function arises when preferential schemas are negative or rigid. In these cases, the plastic self: filters new information in biased ways (*confirmation bias*), resists contradictory evidence, maintains pathological states, and contributes to vicious cycles of symptom maintenance. For example, in depression, the plastic self maintains *I am worthless* schemas by selectively focusing on failures and minimising successes. In trauma, it maintains hypervigilant circuits that interpret neutral stimuli as threatening. In attachment disorders, it sustains avoidance or ambivalence through repetitive relational expectations.

From a psychotherapeutic standpoint, the plastic self is crucial because it represents both the obstacle to change and the gateway for transformation. In therapy, resistance often reflects the plastic self's attempt to maintain homeostasis. The client unconsciously protects their central sets, even if maladaptive. Internal stimuli generated by the plastic self are projected into the therapeutic relationship, shaping the transference. Dysregulation often reflects rigid internal loops where maladaptive IWMs and associated affects dominate. Through therapeutic atonement, new experiences can bypass rigid loops and create alternative neural pathways. Effective interventions therefore target the plastic self's filtering mechanisms, allowing the client to integrate new experiences that modify entrenched circuits.

4.5. The External Self

The external self represents the behavioural and relational interface between the individual and the surrounding environment. It is the most visible dimension of the self, expressing the cumulative activity of the deeper domains (proto, core, and plastic selves). At the biological level, the external self is sustained by neural circuits that coordinate perception, motor control, executive functioning, and social cognition.

While the proto- and core selves encode primary needs, affects, and working models, and the plastic self maintains these through feedback loops, the external self functions as the final output system, translating inner states into observable behaviours and interactions with the world. From a biological perspective, this translation depends on the integration of multiple brain systems: sensory and motor networks, prefrontal executive regions, limbic emotional systems, and mirror neuron networks that enable interpersonal atonement.

In the ISP framework, the external self embodies the "here-and-now" dimension of the individual, mediating between internal maps and environmental demands. It is here that the individual tests strategies, expresses needs, and engages in adaptation—or maladaptation—depending on the coherence and flexibility of the deeper domains of the self.

The external self depends heavily on sensory–motor integration. The brain continuously receives information from the environment via sensory pathways (visual, auditory, tactile, olfactory, gustatory), which is then integrated with proprioceptive and interoceptive input. The posterior parietal cortex, in conjunction with premotor regions, plays a crucial role in translating perception into action (Andersen & Buneo, 2002). Biologically, this allows the external self to act as a *real-time adaptive system*: perceiving a stimulus, evaluating it against internal models, and generating motor responses.

The prefrontal cortex (PFC) provides top-down regulation of behaviour. It integrates input from limbic circuits (encoding affect and motivation) with sensory information to generate context-appropriate responses (Miller & Cohen, 2001). The dorsolateral PFC is associated with planning and problem-solving, while the ventromedial PFC is crucial for emotional regulation and social decision-making.

The external self also relies on the mirror neuron system, particularly in the premotor cortex and inferior parietal lobule (Rizzolatti & Sinigaglia, 2010). This system enables imitation, empathy, and the internal simulation of others' actions. Biologically, it grounds the interpersonal function of the external self: by mirroring others, the individual adjusts behaviour in socially adaptive ways.

The limbic system (amygdala, insula, anterior cingulate cortex) couples affective states with behavioural responses. For example, fear activates defensive motor circuits, while joy activates affiliative behaviours. Thus, the external self is not neutral; it is the embodied expression of underlying emotional and motivational states.

The external self demonstrates how behaviour, once repeated, becomes automatized. Neural pathways involving the basal ganglia and cerebellum allow frequently used behaviours to become habitual, reducing cognitive load (Graybiel, 2008). This biological efficiency, however, can also sustain maladaptive behaviours.

For example, repeated avoidance behaviour in anxiety disorders strengthens amygdala–PFC avoidance circuits. Aggressive or defensive behaviours, if reinforced in early environments, become habitual motor-emotional patterns that are difficult to unlearn. Thus, the external self is biologically predisposed to stability and repetition, even when these patterns are maladaptive.

Siegel (2001; 2012) describes the brain's capacity to create a *present-moment experience of the self*, which is mediated by integration of the medial prefrontal cortex, insula, and posterior cingulate cortex—regions involved in self-referential processing.

At the biological level, this here-and-now self enables the individual to integrate stimuli in real time and adjust behaviour dynamically. Importantly, the external self does not simply replicate past models; it continuously negotiates between past (encoded schemas), present (sensory input), and future (anticipated outcomes).

The biological functioning of the external self is highly sensitive to stress and arousal. Under acute stress, the amygdala hijacks executive circuits, producing reactive behaviours (fight, flight, freeze) that bypass reflective processing (Arnsten, 2009).

This has clear implications for psychotherapy: clients who appear resistant or impulsive may, in fact, be expressing biologically constrained external selves dominated by hyperaroused limbic circuits. Regulation strategies (e.g., grounding, mindfulness, co-regulation with therapist) are therefore essential before cognitive restructuring can occur.

At the biological level, psychotherapy modifies the external self through new relational and behavioural experiences: 1. Corrective interpersonal experiences rewire social brain circuits (mirror neurons, insula, PFC); 2. Behavioural experiments activate novel motor-emotional pathways, replacing maladaptive automatisms; and 3. Mind-body practices (movement, breathing, somatic awareness) influence vagal tone and autonomic balance, restructuring the embodied expression of the self (Porges, 2011).

In ISP, the therapist strategically engages the external self through observable behaviour while linking it back to deeper domains. For example, maladaptive avoidance may be reframed as the biological output of plastic self feedback loops, and therapeutic work will target both the visible behaviour and its underlying circuits.

Understanding the biological level of the external self has several therapeutic consequences: 1. Behavioural rigidity reflects entrenched neural circuits; flexibility requires repeated corrective experiences; 2. Conscious intention alone is insufficient; behaviour must be rehearsed until new neural patterns become automatized; 3. Resistance often reflects biological prioritisation of stability, not deliberate opposition; and 4. Integration across levels of the self (proto, core, plastic, external) is essential: change at the external level must be supported by deeper reorganisation.

At its foundation, the external self is the interface between the organism and its environment. Siegel (2001; 2012) describes how the brain generates a moment-to-moment sense of self in response to the constant flow of stimuli from both internal and external sources. This here-and-now experience is what allows us to act, speak, and respond in real time.

However, these responses are not spontaneous in the purest sense. The brain prioritises stability, relying on core sets and established neural maps to regulate behaviour. This means that, most of the time, the external self strives to maintain consistency, predictability, and coherence with pre-existing internal patterns. Change in external behaviour typically arises only when internal equilibrium is threatened or contradictions emerge between expectations and reality.

In clinical terms, this explains why clients often find it difficult to alter entrenched behaviours: the external self is not simply a reflection of present conditions, but an expression of internalised history.

Although the external self is the domain most accessible to conscious awareness, it is important to note that not all of its underlying drivers are conscious. Behavioural patterns expressed externally often stem from processes that operate outside of awareness. Information from the plastic self may sometimes become available to conscious awareness, allowing individuals to notice recurring patterns, automatic thoughts, or maladaptive cycles. By contrast, the proto-self remains largely inaccessible to consciousness because it is rooted in implicit memory systems. These systems were formed at non-verbal or pre-verbal stages of development and cannot be directly recalled. Instead, they manifest indirectly through patterns of behaviour, emotional reactions, and relational dynamics. This means that much of what appears in the external self—the visible behaviours of the individual—are not consciously chosen but are expressions of unconscious structures.

In other words, the external self functions as the behavioural channel through which the proto-self, core self, and plastic self become visible. The proto-self, with its innate needs and primary affects, manifests externally through basic signalling behaviours—crying, reaching out, or seeking comfort. The core self, with its internal working models and attachment schemas, influences patterns of relating to others: whether the person approaches relationships with trust, fear, avoidance, or ambivalence. The plastic self, with its feedback loops and selective filtering, maintains consistent patterns of behaviour that reinforce stability but can also perpetuate pathology. Thus, the external self is not merely a surface-level entity. It is the embodied expression of the deeper domains of the self. In psychotherapy, what we observe as symptoms, interpersonal styles, or maladaptive behaviours are the manifestations of these underlying processes.

Siegel (2001) describes the brain's ability to continuously generate a "here-and-now" self through the integration of sensory input, memory, and emotional states. This construction of present-moment awareness enables the individual to interact adaptively with the environment.

However, the "here-and-now" is never purely immediate. It is filtered through past experiences and internal schemas, such that present behaviour is always a blend of past and present. This blending explains why individuals may react disproportionately to present events: the external self is drawing upon unresolved implicit patterns. For example, a client may respond with intense anxiety to mild criticism because the external self is activating core self schemas of *I am not OK* and plastic self loops reinforcing past rejection. Conversely, a securely attached person may respond with confidence and resilience in the same situation, because their external self reflects positive schemas of *I am worthy* and *The world is safe*.

One of the external self's central functions is to preserve stability. It does so by maintaining behavioural patterns that are congruent with internal structures. This is adaptive in many situations: it allows for predictability, continuity, and identity coherence.

However, it also explains why resistance to change is so common in psychotherapy. Even when clients consciously desire change, the external self continues to act in accordance with older schemas, because altering behaviour threatens internal equilibrium. Change requires destabilisation of the old patterns and the creation of new feedback loops, which the system initially resists.

This insight highlights the importance of strategic intervention in psychotherapy: instead of directly confronting resistance, psychotherapists work to create corrective experiences that gradually shift the underlying schemas, making new behaviours possible.

In practice, the external self manifests through: 1. Observable behaviour – what the client does in everyday life, including coping strategies, relational styles, and symptomatic expressions; 2. Relational patterns – the ways clients interact with the therapist and others, often reflecting transference and projection; 3. Verbal expression – the narratives clients tell, which are shaped by implicit structures but expressed externally through language; and 4. Embodied expression – posture, tone of voice, facial expressions, and bodily movements, which often reveal unconscious aspects of the self.

The therapeutic encounter often begins with the external self, since it is the most visible. However, effective psychotherapy requires moving beyond surface behaviours to address the underlying domains that sustain them.

Because the external self is the most plastic and adaptable domain, it provides the clearest opportunity for intervention. Small shifts in external behaviour, such as adopting new relational patterns, experimenting with emotional expression, or engaging in corrective experiences, can gradually reshape feedback loops and activate new neural pathways. For example, a client who has always withdrawn when anxious may be encouraged to remain in connection during a moment of discomfort in psychotherapy. This small behavioural shift represents the external self opening to new possibilities, which can, over time, modify underlying schemas. Psychoeducation about implicit memory and the role of the external self can help clients understand why change feels difficult, reducing shame and increasing motivation.

4.6. The Neurobiological Model of the Self

The human self does not emerge in a vacuum of experience but is scaffolded upon the extraordinary biological machinery of the nervous system. At the heart of this machinery lies the neuron—the fundamental unit of brain structure and function. Each neuron is composed of a cell body (soma), a dense arborisation of dendrites, and a single axon. Dendrites function as the primary receivers of signals, transmitting impulses to the soma, while the axon relays information onward to other neurons. The human brain contains approximately 100 billion neurons, a number comparable to the stars of the Milky Way galaxy. Each neuron has the potential to form 1,000 to 10,000 synaptic connections with its neighbours, generating a staggering network of connections estimated at 10^{15} synapses (Kandel et al., 2013).

This dense network is not static but highly dynamic. The principle famously summarised in Hebb's rule, *"neurons that fire together wire together"*, describes the fundamental process by which connections are strengthened through co-activation (Hebb, 1949). Importantly, information is not stored in single neurons but in the patterns of interconnections and their relative strength. Memory, identity, and the building blocks of the self are thus distributed phenomena, embedded within neural maps that represent experience.

Functional connectivity studies provide critical insights into the development of neural maps during infancy and early childhood. By the age of two, increased connectivity is observed between frontal, parietal, and cingulate regions that underlie executive attention and self-regulation (Gao et al., 2009; Fair et al., 2009, 2012). In newborns, parietal regions, crucial for orienting attention, are already strongly linked to lateral and medial frontal areas. This connectivity underpins the infant's emerging capacity to orient toward relevant stimuli in the environment, such as the caregiver's face or voice. By contrast, the executive control networks—involving the anterior cingulate cortex and parietal operculum—exist in rudimentary form but only gradually assume dominance during the preschool years.

This transition has profound implications for the development of the self. In early life, behaviour is largely regulated by the orientation network, which is primarily cholinergic in modulation. From the age of three or four, control increasingly shifts toward the executive attention network, underpinned by dopaminergic modulation (Rothbart, Sheese, Rueda, & Posner, 2011). This transition marks the beginning of more intentional, goal-directed behaviour, laying the neurobiological foundation for the emergence of the core self and, later, the plastic self.

Before the age of two, children do not yet have explicit, autobiographical memory. Instead, their early experiences are encoded as implicit memory, involving emotional, sensory, behavioural, and somatosensory traces that are not available to conscious recall (Siegel, 2001). These early memory traces form the first neural maps, representing needs, affects, and the rudimentary proto-cognitions described earlier in the model of the proto-self.

Although inaccessible to conscious awareness in adulthood, these early implicit patterns exert a profound and lasting influence. They shape the way individuals relate to themselves and others, providing the raw material for internal working models that underpin attachment, emotion regulation, and interpersonal style (Schore, 2003; Bowlby, 1988). Psychotherapy often encounters these pre-symbolic traces indirectly, through patterns of affect regulation, bodily responses, or relational dynamics.

From the perspective of Integrative Strategic Psychotherapy, the proto-self, core self, plastic self, and external self can be conceptualised as layers of neural maps, each progressively more complex but all interconnected (Popescu, 2021; Popescu & Drobot, 2012; Drobot & Popescu, 2013; Vîșcu & Popescu, 2015). The proto-self is grounded in subcortical and limbic structures, it encodes basic physiological needs, primary affects, and proto-cognitions. Its neural maps are primarily implicit, reflecting the survival-oriented responses of the organism. The core self emerges from early attachment experiences, and it contains core sets—schemas that integrate both verbal and non-verbal experience. These neural maps link affective states with interpersonal contexts, giving rise to internal working models. The plastic self functions through feedback loops that maintain core sets over time. Its neural maps reflect both stability and bias, filtering environmental information in ways that sustain internal coherence. When maladaptive, these feedback loops reinforce pathological cycles of thought, affect, and behaviour. The external self represents the here-and-now interface between the individual and environment. It is expressed through observable behaviour, guided by neural maps of motor control, sensory integration, and social cognition. Mirror neurons and prefrontal systems are especially relevant here, linking inner states to interpersonal action.

This layered mapping corresponds with modern neuroscience, which shows that the brain continuously generates multisensory representations of the self—bodily, affective, and cognitive—that allow the organism to maintain coherence while adapting to change (Damasio, 1999; Siegel, 2012).

Neuroscience further demonstrates that neural processing is governed by principles of efficiency. The efficient coding hypothesis suggests that groups of neurons, or even single neurons, encode information in a compact form to optimise resource use. This means that even apparently simple firing patterns may reflect complex informational processes, depending on the activity of the surrounding network (Barlow, 1961; Olshausen & Field, 1996).

For the integrative strategic model, this highlights how neural economy underpins the stability of self-structures. Once pathways are established, the brain tends to conserve them, even if they are maladaptive. This explains why early attachment patterns or maladaptive scripts persist into adulthood: the brain has "learned" to fire in a specific way, and efficiency dictates the reuse of existing pathways rather than the costly formation of new ones.

Yet the brain remains plastic throughout life. New experiences, including corrective emotional experiences in psychotherapy, can reconfigure neural firing patterns and reshape internal working models (Doidge, 2007). This process is neither immediate nor effortless: entrenched neural maps compete with new pathways, and change requires both repetition and emotional salience.

Therapeutically, the challenge lies in creating contexts that activate maladaptive maps while simultaneously providing alternative, reparative experiences. This dual activation allows for the gradual weakening of old circuits and the strengthening of new ones. In integrative strategic psychotherapy, this principle is operationalised through the careful balance of emotional exploration, cognitive reframing, and experiential techniques that engage both implicit and explicit memory systems.

Understanding the neurobiology of the self reinforces several key clinical insights:

1. Implicit structures dominate early life: Much of psychopathology is rooted in implicit neural maps that were established before language. Psychotherapists must attend not only to narrative content but also to affective tone, bodily sensations, and relational enactments;
2. Attachment is biologically embedded: The child's early environment sculpts the architecture of the core self. Secure or insecure attachment is not merely psychological but neurobiological;
3. Plasticity is lifelong: While early experiences shape preferred neural pathways, these can be reshaped through psychotherapy, new relationships, and enriched environments;
4. The self is distributed: There is no single "centre" of the self in the brain. Instead, the proto-, core, plastic, and external selves correspond to interconnected neural maps across multiple levels of the nervous system; and

5. Therapeutic change requires multisensory engagement: Because neural maps integrate emotional, bodily, and cognitive inputs, psychotherapy must involve more than verbal dialogue—it must engage the whole person.

First-Order Neural Maps

Within the proto-self, the brain is initially characterised by an overabundance of neurons, forming what Siegel (2001) describes as a "neural network in waiting." These neurons do not yet have fixed roles; instead, they await activation and structuring through early, primarily non-verbal experiences.

In the first months of life, external stimuli that reach the proto-self are overwhelmingly non-verbal—sensations of touch, warmth, facial expressions, vocal tones, and bodily rhythms. These early stimuli guide the organisation of the neuronal excess, leading to the establishment of first-order neural maps. Such maps represent the earliest proto-cognitions and basic emotions, in effect shaping the infant's first preferences for how neurons fire electrical impulses.

When stimulation is consistent and repeated, the brain begins to form preferential neuronal pathways. One such stable configuration, termed Pathway 1, integrates early environmental, behavioural, and assimilation conclusions (Popescu, 2021; Popescu & Vîșcu, 2016). In practice, this means that the child develops an early bias toward a specific type of emotional or cognitive processing. For example, repeated experiences of comfort and atonement may establish a bias toward secure emotional processing, whereas repeated experiences of neglect or dissonance may create preferential pathways associated with anxiety, withdrawal, or hypervigilance.

From a psychotherapeutic standpoint, the age and depth of these patterns are crucial. The older and more deeply ingrained the preference for a certain neuronal firing pattern, the more resistant to change it becomes. Consequently, problems rooted in the proto-self—the level of first-order neural maps—tend to require longer, more intensive, and more complex interventions. In contrast, difficulties that primarily involve the core self or later-developed structures can often be addressed more directly, since they are shaped by pathways that are less rigidly entrenched.

Thus, first-order neural maps represent the foundational architecture of the mind, encoding the earliest implicit representations of self and environment. They provide the neurobiological scaffolding upon which later layers of the self—core, plastic, and external—will be built.

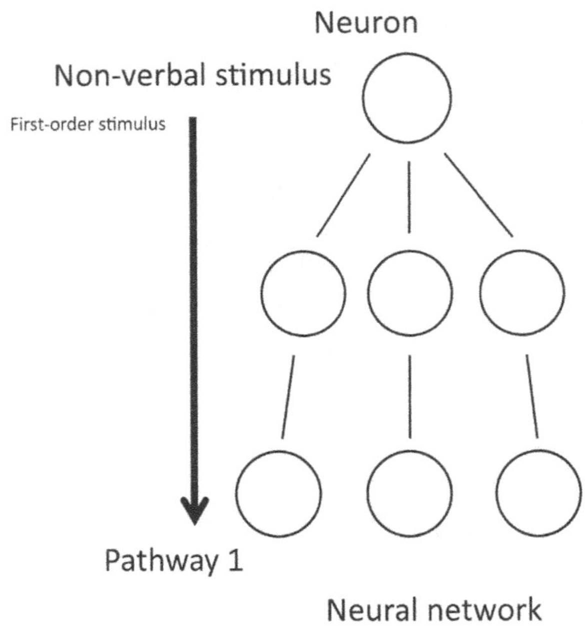

Figure 2. First-order neural maps

Second-order neural maps are located within the core self and are formed through the combined influence of both verbal and non-verbal experiences, shaping what we may call Pathway 2. When second-order stimuli are consistent with the first-order stimuli encoded in the proto-self, Pathway 1 and Pathway 2 overlap, reinforcing each other and producing a strong, stabilised preference for a particular neural map. Conversely, when the first- and second-order stimuli are inconsistent, the brain develops two divergent pathways, resulting in a weaker attachment to a specific processing pattern and preventing the consolidation of a single dominant map (Popescu, 2021; Popescu & Vîșcu, 2016).

These second-order neural maps encode the general conclusions as well as the internal working models activated through early analysis and interpretation of experience. Over time, these conclusions and working models evolve into the foundations of more complex psychodynamic patterns, shaping not only how the individual relates to the external world but also how they structure their inner world.

Through this process, the child develops core convictions about whether the world is safe or unsafe, and about their own sense of efficacy and competence. In order to preserve internal equilibrium and ensure adaptation, the system then relies on the activation of third-order neural maps within the plastic self, which further consolidate or compensate for these early conclusions.

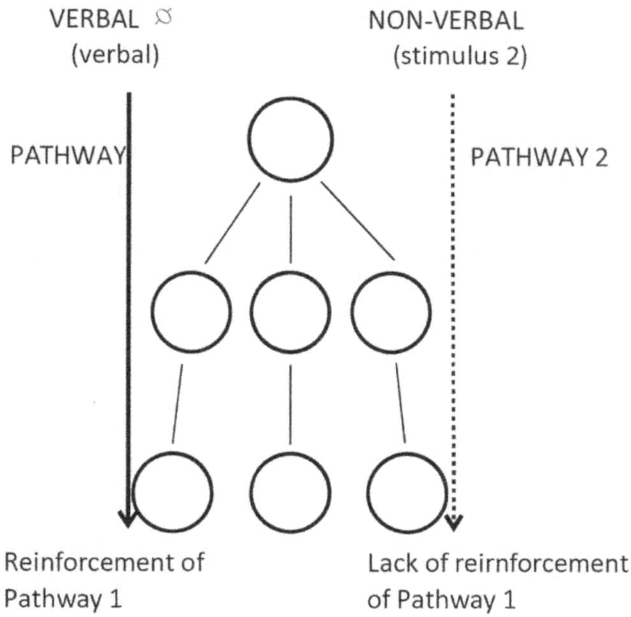

Figure 3. Second-order neural maps

Third- and fourth-order neural maps, which underpin the mechanisms of internal stability (the mental maps situated within the core self), function as maintenance systems that reinforce pre-existing neural pathways. At this stage, regulation arises through the interaction between internal feedback processes and external stimuli.

The third-order stimulus is generated internally, operating as a feedback loop that sustains systemic balance. However, this internal loop requires the presence of a fourth-order external stimulus, which acts at the level of the external self. By contrast, the third-order stimulus originates within the plastic self, drawing on the previously established first- and second-order neural maps located in the proto self and core self (Popescu, 2021; Popescu & Vîşcu, 2016).

When an external stimulus activates neuronal firing along Pathways 1 and 2, this process in turn generates an internal stimulation pathway (Pathway 3). Pathway 3 functions to reinforce Pathways 1 and 2, thereby consolidating specific neural patterns. This provides a neurobiological explanation for why different individuals respond in vastly different ways to the same external event. For instance, a relational breakup might produce only temporary sadness or anger in some individuals, but may precipitate severe psychopathology, such as schizophrenia, in others—depending on which neural pathways are reinforced and how the maintenance loops function. This mechanism resembles a binary computational process—operating on "on" and "off" positions.

In essence, people tend to select environmental cues that confirm pre-existing mental maps embedded within the core self. For example, if someone holds the unconscious belief "I am unintelligent," they will selectively perceive and attend to environmental signals that validate this belief, thereby maintaining the coherence and stability of their internal system—even when it is maladaptive.

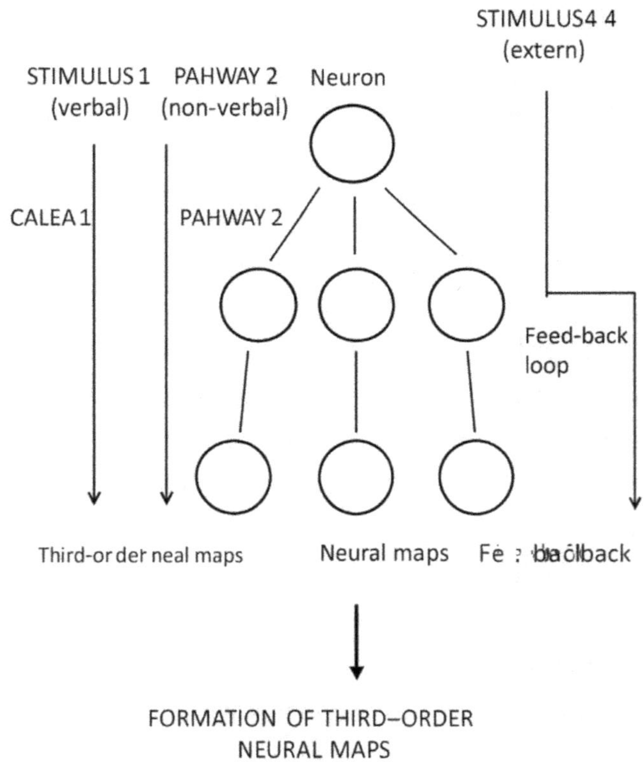

Figure 4. Third-order neural maps

4.7. The Self and The Ego

The concepts of Self and Ego occupy a central yet contested place in the history of psychology and psychotherapy. Few constructs have generated as much debate, reinterpretation, and theoretical overlap. While sometimes treated as synonymous, most traditions distinguish between them—though not always consistently (Laplanche, 2018).

The Self is generally conceived as a broader, integrative concept, representing the totality of personality and the lived sense of "who I am." It encompasses the embodied, emotional, cognitive, and relational dimensions of human existence. The Ego, by contrast, is usually understood as a functional subsystem, responsible for mediation, regulation, and adaptation. It is the executive agency of the psyche, balancing inner drives with outer demands, while the Self symbolises wholeness and identity (Miller & Cuttler, 2003).

In Integrative Strategic Psychotherapy (ISP), this distinction is both respected and transcended. ISP recognises that historical traditions have employed "Ego" and "Self" with different emphases, yet it proposes a unifying perspective: the Ego can be understood as a function within the larger construct of the Self (Popescu, 2021). At times, ISP uses the term Ego—for example, in relation to ego states or when borrowing from psychoanalytic and Gestalt traditions—but overall it privileges the term Self, defined across four components (proto, core, plastic, external) and three levels (biological, psychological, relational).

This chapter examines the theoretical landscape of Self and Ego, traces their evolution across psychoanalytic, Jungian, Gestalt, and contemporary frameworks, and integrates them into the ISP model. Clinical implications are explored, with case illustrations that highlight how working with Self and Ego dynamics enriches therapeutic practice.

In classical psychoanalysis, Freud (1923/1960) introduced the structural model of the psyche: id, ego, and superego. The Ego was seen as a regulatory agency, mediating between instinctual drives (id), internalised moral demands (superego), and the external world. It functioned through defence mechanisms, reality-testing, and executive decision-making.

Freud's use of the term Self was less systematic. At times, it referred to narcissistic investments—the way individuals perceive themselves, hope to be, or experience self-esteem (McIntosh, 1986). At other times, "self" was implicit in descriptions of ego-ideal or self-image. The asymmetry between his elaborate concept of the Ego and his vaguer use of the Self would fuel later debates.

Freud's followers, such as Anna Freud and Heinz Hartmann, expanded the concept of the Ego. In ego psychology, the Ego was not merely reactive to the id but had autonomous functions—perception, memory, motor control, and synthesis of experience (Hartmann, 1958). This shift framed the Ego as the rational, adaptive agency of the psyche, highlighting strengths rather than only conflicts.

In object relations theory, emphasis shifted from drives to relationships. The Self was foregrounded as the organising principle of experience, emerging through early interactions with caregivers. Initially undifferentiated from the object (the caregiver), the infant's Self develops by internalising and differentiating from others (Fairbairn, 1952; Winnicott, 1965). Here, the Self is fundamentally relational: it cannot be understood outside the matrix of early attachment.

The Ego, in this view, is still present but is largely a derivative of relational experience, less central than the Self as an organising construct.

For Carl Jung, the Self is one of the most important archetypes: the symbol of wholeness and integration. It represents the unity of conscious and unconscious elements, the centre and circumference of personality. The Ego, by contrast, is the centre of conscious awareness—one part of the Self, contained within it. Jung thus distinguished two centres: 1. The Self – archetypal, total, integrative; and 2. The Ego – conscious, organising, limited. The process of individuation involves the Ego's gradual recognition of, and integration with, the Self (Jung, 1953/1968).

Building on this, Michael Fordham (1947) proposed the idea of the primary Self, undifferentiated at birth, and the secondary Self, which arises through cycles of de-integration and reintegration. This anticipates modern understandings of development as dynamic and plastic (Laplanche, 2018).

Fritz Perls, in Gestalt therapy, offered a more pragmatic view: the Self is not a substantive entity but a boundary process—the dynamic distinction between "I" and "not-I." The Self is not fixed but emerges situationally, in contact with the environment (Perls, Hefferline, & Goodman, 1951). Here, the Ego as an intrapsychic structure is downplayed, while the Self is conceived as fluid and contextual. This anticipates later postmodern conceptions of identity as relationally and culturally constructed.

Contemporary theories, including self-psychology (Kohut, 1971) and interpersonal neurobiology (Siegel, 2012), highlight both the experiential sense of self and its biological underpinnings. Neuroscience demonstrates that self-related processes are distributed across brain systems integrating interoception, affect, memory, and social cognition (Damasio, 1999).

Despite differences, certain commonalities emerge: 1. The Self tends to represent wholeness, identity, and integration; 2. The Ego tends to represent mediation, regulation, and executive functions; and 3. Overlap occurs because both constructs describe aspects of organisation and agency. As Laplanche (2018) notes, much of the debate is terminological, reflecting emphases rather than fundamental contradictions. In practice, both concepts are needed: Self to capture identity and wholeness; Ego to capture functional mediation.

In Integrative Strategic Psychotherapy, the Self is the preferred overarching term, articulated into four interrelated components: 1. Proto-self – the biological ground, sustained by regulation of the nervous system and body; 2. Core self – immediate subjective awareness, affectivity, and embodied presence; 3. Plastic self – developmental adaptability, learning, and identity transformation; and 4. External self – relational, cultural, and social identity.

Within this framework, the Ego is understood as a functional subsystem of the Self. It mediates between internal impulses and external demands, organises cognition and affect, and ensures coherent action. In effect, the Ego operates across the core and plastic selves, while drawing resources from the proto-self and external self. Thus, in ISP, the Ego is a function of mediation and regulation, whilst the self is the totality of personality. However, ISP also recognises the usefulness of preserving the term Ego in contexts such as ego state therapy or parts work, where it describes sub-identities within the Self.

Modern neuroscience grounds the Ego in executive functions of the prefrontal cortex, including working memory, inhibitory control, and decision-making (Miller & Cuttler, 2003). The anterior cingulate cortex supports conflict monitoring; the orbitofrontal cortex underpins social evaluation. The Self, however, extends beyond executive functions: it includes interoceptive awareness (insula), emotional integration (limbic system), and body schema (parietal cortex). This supports the ISP distinction between Self as totality and Ego as function.

On the axes of the psychological level, the Ego is described as follows: 1. Cognitive axis – Ego as attention, reasoning, problem-solving; 2. Emotional axis – Ego as affect regulator; Self as emotional identity; and 3. Psychodynamic axis – Ego as mediator of unconscious conflict; Self as integrative wholeness.

The Ego and The Self both develop in relation to others. Secure attachment scaffolds ego strength and self-cohesion; inconsistent caregiving produces vulnerabilities. The external self depends on ego capacities to manage social roles and cultural expectations. Relational breakdowns often present clinically as ego deficits (poor regulation) or self fragmentation (loss of cohesion). ISP attends to both dimensions simultaneously.

Clinical implications for ISP are:

- Ego Deficits: Clients may lack reality-testing, impulse control, or affect regulation. ISP strengthens ego functions through structured interventions, scaffolding, and therapeutic containment;
- Ego Rigidity: Clients may over-identify with ego ideals, suppressing authentic self-expression. ISP softens rigidity, fostering plasticity through expressive and relational work;
- Self–Ego Misalignment: Confusion between ego ideals and authentic selfhood may cause distress. ISP supports integration across core and plastic selves; and
- Trauma: Trauma fragments the Self into disjointed ego states. ISP uses relational repair and somatic integration to reintegrate split parts.

In conclusion, the debate over Self and Ego reflects the richness of psychotherapeutic theory. While traditions vary—Freud's structural model, Jung's archetypes, Perls's functionalism, Winnicott's relational self—all converge on the need to account for identity and mediation, wholeness and function. In Integrative Strategic Psychotherapy, the debate is resolved by treating the Self as the encompassing totality and the Ego as one of its functional dimensions. The Ego describes mediation, regulation, and executive control; the Self describes identity, wholeness, and integration. Both are indispensable, but ISP privileges the Self as the organising framework, consistent with its focus on the biological, psychological, and relational integration of human experience.

References

Andersen, R. A., & Buneo, C. A. (2002). Intentional maps in posterior parietal cortex. *Annual Review of Neuroscience, 25*(1), 189–220. https://doi.org/10.1146/annurev.neuro.25.112701.142922

Arnsten, A. F. T. (2009). Stress signalling pathways that impair prefrontal cortex structure and function. *Nature Reviews Neuroscience, 10*(6), 410–422. https://doi.org/10.1038/nrn2648

Bandura, A. (1997). *Self-efficacy: The exercise of control.* W. H. Freeman.

Banes, G. (1998). *Neuroplasticity: The brain's capacity for change.* Oxford University Press.

Baylis, P. (2006). *Neurophysiology and emotion: Basic processes of affective orientation.* Routledge.

Bliss, T. V., & Collingridge, G. L. (1993). A synaptic model of memory: Long-term potentiation in the hippocampus. *Nature, 361*(6407), 31–39. https://doi.org/10.1038/361031a0

Bowlby, J. (1982). *Attachment and loss: Vol. 1. Attachment* (2nd ed.). Basic Books. (Original work published 1969).

Brooks-Harris, J. E. (2008). *Integrative multitheoretical psychotherapy.* Houghton Mifflin.

Carey, N. (2011). *The epigenetics revolution: How modern biology is rewriting our understanding of genetics, disease and inheritance.* Icon Books.

Coicici, V., & Popescu, O. M. (2017). Early relational trauma and implicit memory: An integrative perspective. *Romanian Journal of Psychotherapy, 19*(1), 27–42.

Cozolino, L. (2010). *The neuroscience of psychotherapy: Healing the social brain* (2nd ed.). W. W. Norton.

Damasio, A. R. (1999). *The feeling of what happens: Body and emotion in the making of consciousness.* Harcourt Brace.

Disner, S. G., Beevers, C. G., Haigh, E. A., & Beck, A. T. (2011). Neural mechanisms of the cognitive model of depression. *Nature Reviews Neuroscience, 12*(8), 467–477. https://doi.org/10.1038/nrn3027

Doidge, N. (2007). *The brain that changes itself.* Viking.

Drobot, L., & Popescu, O. M. (2013). Feedback loops in maladaptive self-organisation. *Journal of Integrative Psychotherapy, 9*(2), 45–61.

Eels, T. D. (2010). *Formulation and treatment planning in clinical practice.* Routledge.

Fair, D. A., Cohen, A. L., Dosenbach, N. U. F., Church, J. A., Miezin, F. M., Barch, D. M., ... & Petersen, S. E. (2009). The maturing architecture of the brain's default network. *Proceedings of the National Academy of Sciences, 106*(17), 6790–6795.

Fair, D. A., Dosenbach, N. U. F., Church, J. A., Cohen, A. L., Brahmbhatt, S., Miezin, F. M., ... & Schlaggar, B. L. (2012). Development of distinct control networks through segregation and integration. *Proceedings of the National Academy of Sciences, 104*(33), 13507–13512.

Fairbairn, W. R. D. (1952). *Psychoanalytic studies of the personality.* Routledge & Kegan Paul.

Fall, K. A., Holden, J. M., & Marquis, A. (2010). *Theoretical models of counseling and psychotherapy.* Routledge.

Fast, I. (2009). *The personality and its disorders.* Wiley.

Feldman, R. (2007). Parent–infant synchrony: Biological foundations and developmental outcomes. *Current Directions in Psychological Science, 16*(6), 340–345. https://doi.org/10.1111/j.1467-8721.2007.00532.x

Fonagy, P., Gergely, G., Jurist, E. L., & Target, M. (2002). *Affect regulation, mentalization, and the development of the self.* Other Press.

Fordham, M. (1947). The concept of the primary self. *Journal of Analytical Psychology, 2*(1), 5–16. https://doi.org/10.1111/j.1465-5922.1947.00005.x

Freud, S. (1960). *The ego and the id* (J. Riviere, Trans.). W. W. Norton. (Original work published 1923).

Gao, W., Zhu, H., Giovanello, K. S., Smith, J. K., Shen, D., Gilmore, J. H., & Lin, W. (2009). Evidence on the emergence of the brain's default network from 2-week-old to 2-year-old healthy pediatric subjects. *Proceedings of the National Academy of Sciences, 106*(16), 6790–6795.

Graybiel, A. M. (2008). Habits, rituals, and the evaluative brain. *Annual Review of Neuroscience, 31*(1), 359–387. https://doi.org/10.1146/annurev.neuro.29.051605.112851

Greenough, W. T., & Black, J. E. (1992). Induction of brain structure by experience: Substrates for cognitive development. In M. Gunnar & C. Nelson (Eds.), *Minnesota Symposia on Child Psychology* (Vol. 24, pp. 155–200). Lawrence Erlbaum.

Hartmann, H. (1958). *Ego psychology and the problem of adaptation.* International Universities Press.

Hebb, D. O. (2002). *The organization of behavior: A neuropsychological theory.* Psychology Press. (Original work published 1949).

Izard, C. E., & Kobak, R. (1999). Emotions system functioning and emotion regulation. In P. Salovey & D. Sluyter (Eds.), *Emotional development and emotional intelligence: Educational implications* (pp. 303–321). Basic Books.

Jung, C. G. (1968). *The archetypes and the collective unconscious* (2nd ed.). Princeton University Press. (Original work published 1953).

Kandel, E. R., Schwartz, J. H., Jessell, T. M., Siegelbaum, S. A., & Hudspeth, A. J. (2013). *Principles of neural science* (5th ed.). New York: McGraw-Hill.

Klengel, T., & Binder, E. B. (2015). Epigenetics of stress-related psychiatric disorders and gene × environment interactions. *Neuron, 86*(6), 1343–1357. https://doi.org/10.1016/j.neuron.2015.05.036

Kolb, B., & Gibb, R. (2011). Brain plasticity and behaviour in the developing brain. *Journal of the Canadian Academy of Child and Adolescent Psychiatry, 20*(4), 265–276.

Laplanche, J. (2018). *The language of psycho-analysis.* Karnac Books.

LeDoux, J. (1996). *The emotional brain: The mysterious underpinnings of emotional life.* Simon & Schuster.

Lichner-Ingram, R. (2011). Case formulation in integrative psychotherapy. *Journal of Psychotherapy Integration, 21*(3), 219–237. https://doi.org/10.1037/a0025420

Maravita, A., Spence, C., & Driver, J. (2003). Multisensory integration and the body schema: Close to hand and within reach. *Current Biology, 13*(13), R531–R539. https://doi.org/10.1016/S0960-9822(03)00449-4

McEwen, B. S. (2007). Physiology and neurobiology of stress and adaptation: Central role of the brain. *Physiological Reviews, 87*(3), 873–904. https://doi.org/10.1152/physrev.00041.2006

McIntosh, D. N. (1986). The many faces of the self in psychoanalysis. *Psychoanalytic Psychology, 3*(2), 101–116. https://doi.org/10.1037/h0079137

Meaney, M. J. (2010). Epigenetics and the biological definition of gene × environment interactions. *Child Development, 81*(1), 41–79.

Miller, E. K., & Cohen, J. D. (2001). An integrative theory of prefrontal cortex function. *Annual Review of Neuroscience, 24*(1), 167–202. https://doi.org/10.1146/annurev.neuro.24.1.167

Miller, E. K., & Cuttler, A. (2003). Prefrontal cortex and executive cognitive control. *Science, 306*(5695), 1940–1944. https://doi.org/10.1126/science.1091895

Nelson, K., & Fivush, R. (2004). The emergence of autobiographical memory: A social cultural developmental theory. *Psychological Review, 111*(2), 486–511.

Oberlander, T. F., Weinberg, J., Papsdorf, M., Grunau, R., Misri, S., & Devlin, A. M. (2008). Prenatal exposure to maternal depression, neonatal methylation of human glucocorticoid receptor gene (NR3C1) and infant cortisol stress responses. *Epigenetics, 3*(2), 97–106. https://doi.org/10.4161/epi.3.2.6034

Olshausen, B. A., & Field, D. J. (1996). Emergence of simple-cell receptive field properties by learning a sparse code for natural images. *Nature, 381*(6583), 607–609.

Panksepp, J. (1998). *Affective neuroscience: The foundations of human and animal emotions.* Oxford University Press.

Perls, F., Hefferline, R., & Goodman, P. (1951). *Gestalt therapy: Excitement and growth in the human personality.* Julian Press.

Perry, B. D., & Szalavitz, M. (2017). *The boy who was raised as a dog: And other stories from a child psychiatrist's notebook* (2nd ed.). Basic Books.

Popescu, O. M., & Drobot, L. (2012). Strategic integrative psychotherapy: Theoretical developments. *Romanian Journal of Psychotherapy, 14*(1), 15–28.

Popescu, O. M., & Drobot, L. (2012). *Psihoterapia integrativă strategică: Mecanisme interne de menținere.* Presa Universitară Clujeană.

Popescu, O. M., & Vîșcu, L. (2016). *Psihoterapia integrativă strategică: Teorie și practică.* Editura Universitară.

Porges, S. W. (2011). *The polyvagal theory: Neurophysiological foundations of emotions, attachment, communication, and self-regulation.* W. W. Norton.

Praetorius, C. (2009). Phenomenological perspectives on the self. *Journal of Consciousness Studies, 16*(1), 77–99.

Rauch, S. L., Shin, L. M., & Phelps, E. A. (2006). Neurocircuitry models of posttraumatic stress disorder and extinction: Human neuroimaging research—past, present, and future. *Biological Psychiatry, 60*(4), 376–382. https://doi.org/10.1016/j.biopsych.2006.06.004

Rizzolatti, G., & Sinigaglia, C. (2010). The functional role of the parieto-frontal mirror circuit: Interpretations and misinterpretations. *Nature Reviews Neuroscience, 11*(4), 264–274. https://doi.org/10.1038/nrn2805

Roenneberg, T., Wirz-Justice, A., & Merrow, M. (2007). Life between clocks: Daily temporal patterns of human chronotypes. *Journal of Biological Rhythms, 18*(1), 80–90. https://doi.org/10.1177/0748730402239679

Rothbart, M. K. (2011). *Becoming who we are: Temperament and personality in development.* Guilford Press.

Rothbart, M. K., Sheese, B. E., Rueda, M. R., & Posner, M. I. (2011). Developing mechanisms of self-regulation in early life. *Emotion Review, 3*(2), 207–213.

Schacter, D. L. (1996). *Searching for memory: The brain, the mind, and the past.* Basic Books.

Schacter, D. L., & Buckner, R. L. (1998). Priming and the brain. *Neuron, 20*(2), 185–195.

Schore, A. N. (2003). *Affect dysregulation and disorders of the self.* W. W. Norton.

Schore, A. N. (2001). Effects of a secure attachment relationship on right brain development, affect regulation, and infant mental health. *Infant Mental Health Journal, 22*(1–2), 7–66. https://doi.org/10.1002/1097-0355(200101/04)22:1<7::AID-IMHJ2>3.0.CO;2-N

Schore, A. N. (2006). The effects of early relational trauma on right brain development, affect regulation, and infant mental health. *Infant Mental Health Journal, 27*(6), 737–756. https://doi.org/10.1002/imhj.20124

Seligman, M. E. P. (1975). *Helplessness: On depression, development, and death.* Freeman.

Siegel, D. J. (1996). Cognition, memory, and the "self": A neurobiological view. *Developmental Review, 16*(4), 379–401.

Siegel, D. J. (2006). *An interpersonal neurobiology approach to psychotherapy: Awareness, mirror neurons, and neural plasticity in the development of well-being.* Psychiatric Annals, 36(4), 248–258.

Siegel, D. J. (2012). *The developing mind: How relationships and the brain interact to shape who we are* (2nd ed.). Guilford Press.

Siegel, D. J. (2012). *Pocket guide to interpersonal neurobiology: An integrative handbook of the mind.* W. W. Norton.

Spector, T. (2012). *Identically different: Why you can change your genes.* Orion.

Tomkins, S. S. (1962). *Affect imagery consciousness: Vol. 1. The positive affects.* Springer.

Tronick, E. (2007). *The neurobehavioral and social-emotional development of infants and children.* W. W. Norton.

Tronick, E. Z. (1989). Emotions and emotional communication in infants. *American Psychologist, 44*(2), 112–119. https://doi.org/10.1037/0003-066X.44.2.112

Vîşcu, L., Lacrămă, A., & Popescu, O. M. (2015). Neurobiological underpinnings of integrative psychotherapy. *Journal of Experiential Psychotherapy, 18*(3), 52–62.

Vîşcu, L., & Popescu, O. M. (2015). The integrative strategic model of the self: Clinical implications. *Journal of Integrative Psychotherapy, 25*(2), 43–59.

Vîşcu, L., & Popescu, O. M. (2015). Clinical applications of the integrative strategic model of the self. *Annals of the University of Oradea, Psychology Series, 17*(2), 35–52.

Vîşcu, L., & Popescu, O. M. (2015). *Self-maintenance mechanisms in integrative psychotherapy.* Presa Universitară Clujeană.

Winnicott, D. W. (1965). *The maturational processes and the facilitating environment.* Hogarth Press.

Zahavi, D. (2005). *Subjectivity and selfhood: Investigating the first-person perspective.* MIT Press.

CHAPTER 5

THE UNCONSCIOUS IN INTEGRATIVE STRATEGIC PSYCHOTHERAPY

5.1. Unconscious Processes and the Proto-Self

In the Integrative Strategic Psychotherapy (ISP) model, the proto-self represents the most archaic, pre-symbolic layer of human functioning—a neurobiological foundation upon which the rest of the self is built. Rooted in the early developmental stages of life, the proto-self is shaped by sensorimotor experiences, affective resonance, implicit relational patterns, and unconscious somatic encoding. It is primarily non-verbal, non-reflective, and operates outside conscious awareness. In this structure of the self, the unconscious is not merely a repository of repressed memories or forbidden desires, as in classical psychoanalysis, but a living, embodied process that guides perception, emotional reactivity, and physiological states.

The Neurobiological Roots of the Proto-Self

The concept of the proto-self has significant resonance with Antonio Damasio's (1999) neurobiological model. Damasio describes the proto-self as a collection of neural patterns that map the state of the organism moment by moment, serving as the bedrock for the development of core and autobiographical self. In ISP, this early structure becomes the neuro-affective substrate where unconscious processes begin to take shape—not as symbolic representations, but as *embodied tendencies* and affective reactions.

These are not accessible through verbal memory or conscious thought but are enacted through automatic physiological responses, somatic tension, affect regulation patterns, and unconscious postural habits. The proto-self is where trauma first imprints itself—not in the form of narrative, but as somatic dysregulation, vagal reactivity, or disrupted attachment synchrony (Schore, 2021; Siegel, 2021). Consequently, many of the unconscious patterns psychotherapists encounter in clients—especially those with early trauma, neglect, or attachment rupture—originate in this preverbal layer.

Unconscious Affective Schemas and Somatic Memory

The proto-self houses unconscious affective schemas that guide perception and behaviour in ways that are automatic, habitual, and deeply embodied. These schemas are rooted in implicit memory (Squire & Kandel, 1999), the type of memory that does not require conscious recall and is encoded through repeated emotional and sensorimotor experiences.

For example, a child who consistently experiences fear in the presence of an unpredictable caregiver may develop a somatic posture of collapse, muscular contraction, or freezing. Later in life, these patterns may re-emerge in situations of perceived threat, even when the conscious mind insists there is no danger. These *unconscious bodily memories* do not manifest as thoughts, but as heart rate changes, gastrointestinal tension, or dissociative responses—hallmarks of proto-self activation.

As van der Kolk (2021) notes, the body indeed "keeps the score." Early relational and emotional experiences become encoded in the right hemisphere, brainstem, and autonomic nervous system, bypassing conscious symbolic systems. ISP therapists thus pay close attention to body language, affective tone, micro-expressions, and physiological shifts, treating them as windows into proto-self dynamics and unconscious processes.

Archetypes as Proto-Cognitive Maps

Within the ISP framework, the unconscious contents of the proto-self also include what we refer to as proto-cognitions: primitive, non-verbal, affect-laden representations that organize relational experience. Some of these take the form of archetypal patterns, consistent with Jung's (1968) idea of the collective unconscious, but reconceptualized in ISP as universal affective-organizational schemas formed in the earliest relational encounters.

For instance, the "abandonment archetype" may not appear initially as a belief ("People leave me") but as a *visceral, wordless fear* triggered when relational distance is sensed. These archetypes are not symbolic narratives in their earliest form; they are embodied affective structures that take on symbolic content only later through the development of the core and plastic selves. ISP sees these archetypes as pre-linguistic, shared proto-cognitive maps that arise from interpersonal synchrony, rhythmic regulation, and cultural embedding.

Clinical Implications

The implications for psychotherapeutic work are profound. If a client's symptoms are rooted in proto-self dysfunction—such as developmental trauma, neglect, or preverbal affective disorganization—traditional cognitive or verbal techniques may not suffice. In such cases, ISP recommends bottom-up approaches, including: (1) Somatic tracking and body-oriented awareness; (2) Sensorimotor psychotherapy and movement-based integration (Ogden & Fisher, 2021); (3) Safe-touch exploration in ethically appropriate and trauma-informed settings; (4) Hypnotic and imaginal techniques targeting unconscious body memory (Zeig, 2021); and (5) Relational atonement, using tone of voice, gaze, pacing, and rhythm to co-regulate the client's nervous system (Geller & Porges, 2021).

Crucially, the therapeutic relationship itself becomes the primary instrument for restructuring the proto-self. Repeated experiences of empathic atonement, relational predictability, and neurophysiological co-regulation create new implicit memories that gradually recalibrate the unconscious structures of affect and bodily expectation (Schore, 2021).

The Proto-Self and the Emotional Axis

In ISP, the proto-self is intimately tied to the emotional axis. It is the origin point of basic affective responses—fear, joy, anger, disgust, sadness, and surprise—well before these are consciously interpreted. Emotional dysregulation, alexithymia, or somatization disorders often signal proto-self disruptions. By attending to the affective micro-moments in session, the psychotherapist decodes the non-verbal unconscious of the client and begins to work therapeutically with this foundational level of the self.

5.2. Implicit Memory and the Core Self

In the Integrative Strategic Psychotherapy (ISP) model, the core self represents the deeply embedded structures of meaning, emotion, and relational patterning that emerge from early developmental experiences. One of the key mechanisms shaping the core self is implicit memory, a form of non-declarative memory that stores procedural, emotional, and somatosensory information outside of conscious awareness (Siegel, 2021; Schore, 2021).

Implicit memory plays a crucial role in how individuals learn to anticipate, interpret, and respond to relational stimuli. These unconscious patterns—formed during the first years of life—do not rely on language or explicit recall. Instead, they manifest in affective responses, behavioural tendencies, bodily postures, and relational enactments (LeDoux, 2002; Ogden & Fisher, 2021). For example, a client who flinches when offered care or avoids eye contact during moments of emotional connection is likely expressing implicit memories of early experiences of rejection or unpredictability in attachment relationships. These responses are not chosen—they are lived.

From a neurobiological perspective, the encoding of implicit memory is primarily mediated by subcortical structures such as the amygdala, basal ganglia, and cerebellum, which develop before the hippocampus—the brain region responsible for explicit memory (McGaugh, 2004; Panksepp & Biven, 2020). This means that early relational experiences, including trauma or emotional neglect, are often stored somatically and emotionally rather than as coherent narratives. In the ISP framework, these encoded traces are seen as foundational to the development of the core self and can be observed in the unconscious choreography of posture, tone of voice, muscle tension, or somatic symptoms.

Psychotherapy becomes, in part, the reorganisation of these implicit memory systems. In this sense, healing is not merely insight-based, but experience-based: clients must not only understand their patterns but also live through new relational experiences that update their implicit maps. The psychotherapist's atonement, presence, and strategic interventions can activate neuroplastic change, gradually reshaping affective scripts and relational expectations (Doidge, 2020; Geller & Porges, 2021).

Research in infant development supports this. Stern (1985) described how early interactions with caregivers—such as the rhythm of vocalisations, touch, and gaze—create templates for "procedural knowledge" of being with others. These templates are not symbolic but embodied, and they persist into adulthood as somatically encoded expectations of self and other. ISP recognises that these expectations form the unconscious backbone of the core self and are accessible only through relational and experiential engagement.

Within the psychotherapeutic process, implicit memory often reveals itself through micro-behaviours and moment-to-moment affective shifts. A client may report feeling "nothing," but their body tells a different story—perhaps their shoulders rise subtly when discussing family, or their hands tremble when describing moments of failure. These are not theatrical displays; they are implicit memory in action. The ISP psychotherapist learns to read these signals as unconscious communications from the core self, integrating them into formulation and intervention.

One of the most powerful aspects of implicit memory is that it resists language but responds to presence. It is for this reason that many ISP interventions rely on non-verbal synchrony, rhythm, tone modulation, eye contact, somatic mirroring, and breath pacing. These elements bypass the neocortex and speak directly to the unconscious body-mind systems. In doing so, they support a new encoding of relational safety, eventually softening rigid patterns and opening space for change.

Moreover, dissociation—whether subtle or pronounced—is a common manifestation of unresolved implicit memory (van der Kolk, 2021). The psychotherapist must be alert to signs of disconnection, blankness, or affective fragmentation, not as resistance but as unconscious strategies of survival. These signal that the client's core self is still oriented around threat, unpredictability, or shame. Re-integrating dissociated states requires patient, regulated, and paced work, often through techniques like sensorimotor processing, guided imagery, or somatic tracking (Ogden & Fisher, 2021).

In Integrative Strategic Psychotherapy, the goal is not to "remember" trauma in the explicit sense, but to re-code the implicit memory by introducing relational and emotional experiences that are novel, safe, and regulated. As Siegel (2021) notes, "*what is fired together can be wired together differently*"—neural integration can occur when the psychotherapist becomes a neurobiological ally, co-regulating the client toward new implicit expectations.

Finally, ISP views implicit memory not only as a source of pathology but as a reservoir of resilience. Just as it stores early trauma, it also holds the embodied wisdom of secure moments, attuned interactions, and successful adaptations. These can be accessed, amplified, and internalised through the therapeutic process. In this way, implicit memory is both a burden and a resource—an unconscious echo of the past, and a foundation for future transformation.

5.3. The Role of Unconscious Conflict Across Axes (Cognitive, Emotional, Psychodynamic)

In Integrative Strategic Psychotherapy (ISP), the psyche is conceptualised as a multilayered and multi-axial system. Central to this model is the understanding that unconscious conflict is not confined to one isolated domain of functioning, but manifests simultaneously and dynamically across the three primary psychological axes: cognitive, emotional, and psychodynamic. These axes do not operate in parallel isolation but interpenetrate—forming a complex, interactive system of inner life that structures symptoms, defences, and potential for change.

The Nature of Unconscious Conflict in ISP

In traditional psychodynamic theory, unconscious conflict is described as the tension between instinctual drives (e.g., libido, aggression) and internalised prohibitions (e.g., the superego), leading to repression, symptom formation, and neurotic suffering (Freud, 1915/1957). ISP retains this classical insight but significantly expands the model by integrating findings from contemporary affective neuroscience, cognitive theory, developmental psychology, and trauma studies. In this enriched view, unconscious conflict arises not only from intrapsychic tension between drives and defences, but also from incompatible cognitions, affective dissonance, and unintegrated relational scripts.

In short, unconscious conflict in ISP is seen as a cross-axis disintegration, a state in which the individual's belief systems, emotions, and relational templates are in tension with each other, and with the demands of the self-system and external environment. This tension may manifest in a fragmented sense of identity, dissociative defences, maladaptive coping patterns, or somatic symptoms.

Unconscious Conflict Along the Cognitive Axis

On the cognitive axis, unconscious conflict often takes the form of contradictory beliefs or schemas—especially when early-learned beliefs become rigid, maladaptive, or incompatible with adult realities. These conflicts may exist between: (1) Core beliefs vs. intermediate beliefs (e.g., "*I am worthless*" vs. "*If I work hard, I'll be loved*"); (2) Belief systems vs. lived experience (e.g., "*The world is fair*" vs. "*I've suffered injustice*"); and (3) Unconscious logic vs. rational thought (e.g., "*I must be punished*" despite knowing one is innocent).

When such contradictions remain unexamined, they may operate as cognitive dissonance, fuelling internal tension, anxiety, avoidance, or obsessive rumination. These belief-based conflicts may become symbolically expressed through behaviour, dreams, or repetitive thought loops—particularly in clients with high levels of metacognitive avoidance or schema fusion (Young et al., 2020).

In ISP, these conflicts are not addressed solely through cognitive restructuring but through strategic clarification, symbolic exploration, and alignment with the emotional and psychodynamic axes. Insight alone is insufficient; what is needed is a systemic reorganisation of meaning across multiple levels of consciousness.

Unconscious Conflict Along the Emotional Axis

On the emotional axis, unconscious conflict typically manifests as affective contradictions and emotional suppression. A client may consciously desire closeness, yet become emotionally flooded or dismissive in intimate situations. Others may feel intense guilt for experiencing anger or shame for having needs. These are not merely problems of dysregulation but expressions of unconscious affective ambivalence, shaped by attachment history and early emotional conditioning (Schore, 2021).

Unconscious emotional conflict often emerges when an emotion is experienced as dangerous or disallowed—either due to childhood experiences (e.g., a parent rejecting displays of sadness or joy) or cultural injunctions ("*Men must not cry*," "*Anger is destructive*"). These affective contradictions create internal splits: part of the self feels, another part inhibits. This intra-emotional fragmentation is sustained by physiological arousal patterns, neurochemical imprints, and right-brain-to-right-brain imprinted fears (Porges, 2022; Geller & Porges, 2021).

Within ISP, emotional conflict is explored both verbally and non-verbally, through techniques such as emotion-focused inquiry, somatic tracking, guided imagery, and regulatory co-presence. The psychotherapist acts as a co-regulator, helping the client tolerate, name, and integrate previously dissociated or forbidden affective states. This process gradually brings unconscious emotion into conscious regulation and symbolic ownership.

Unconscious Conflict Along the Psychodynamic Axis

The psychodynamic axis captures symbolic, archetypal, and transferential conflicts that originate in early internalised relationships, life scripts, and defence structures. These tensions may remain entirely unconscious until enacted in the therapeutic relationship—often through rupture, enactment, resistance, or emotional withdrawal. The ISP psychotherapist, trained to observe non-verbal cues, affect shifts, and narrative gaps, uses these as diagnostic entry points to uncover deeper symbolic conflicts.

Unlike classical psychoanalysis, ISP does not insist on interpretation as the primary tool. Instead, it strategically combines clarification, emotional atonement, and experiential techniques to bring unconscious patterns into relational awareness. When appropriate, ISP employs symbolic language, metaphoric dialogues, or expressive techniques (e.g., drawing, dreamwork, sand-tray) to surface conflicts that words alone cannot reach.

Integrative Conflict Formulation Across Axes

A hallmark of the ISP model is its multiaxial case formulation, which allows the psychotherapist to map how unconscious conflict operates simultaneously across cognitive, emotional, and psychodynamic domains. A single presenting issue—say, procrastination—may be driven by: (1) A cognitive schema ("*If I try and fail, I'll be worthless*"), (2) An emotional conflict (anxiety about disappointment; shame about effort) and (3) A psychodynamic narrative (repetition of a childhood pattern of submission and failure to gain parental attention).

In psychotherapy, such a formulation allows the clinician to approach the problem from multiple entry points: restructuring beliefs, exploring suppressed emotions, and resolving symbolic identifications. When all three axes are engaged, transformation is not only more likely but also more sustainable—because the change occurs within the self-system as a whole, not just in one isolated part.

The Strategic Role of the Psychotherapist in Conflict Integration

In ISP, the psychotherapist does not interpret conflict from a detached expert position. Instead, the therapist becomes a strategic co-navigator, working alongside the client to identify, name, and reorganise the cross-axis conflicts at play. This requires: (1) The capacity to switch lenses (e.g., from emotion to cognition, from insight to embodiment); (2) Atonement to the client's defensive style and developmental readiness; (3) Timing and minimalism, avoiding premature confrontation of unconscious material; and (4) A relational posture that integrates containment with curiosity.

This strategic orchestration of interventions reflects the ISP principle that therapy is not about correcting the mind, but restructuring the self through multi-layered, multidimensional work.

5.4. Developmental Origins of the Unconscious

In the architecture of the Integrative Strategic Model of the Self, the unconscious is not a static repository of forgotten memories but a dynamic, developmentally sculpted system that begins long before language emerges. Nowhere is this more evident than in the domain of preverbal experience and implicit relational knowing. These early, non-verbal imprints shape the proto-self and core self long before a child can speak or consciously remember, encoding relational patterns, affective expectations, and embodied templates that structure all future interpersonal and intrapsychic functioning (Lyons-Ruth, 1999; Schore, 2021).

During the first years of life, the infant's brain is in a state of rapid neurodevelopment, marked by right-hemispheric dominance and intense synaptogenesis in areas linked to emotional processing, sensorimotor integration, and affective atonement (Schore, 2021; Siegel, 2023). At this stage, the infant cannot rely on language or symbolic cognition to understand the world. Instead, meaning is constructed through sensory-affective engagement with caregivers: tone of voice, facial expressions, rhythmic movement, and bodily synchrony. This is the bedrock of what has been termed "implicit relational knowing"—a form of procedural memory encoded through repeated interaction patterns, outside of conscious awareness (Stern, 2004).

These interactions form what Tronick (2007) called the "dyadic regulatory system," where the infant learns not just how to regulate physiological and emotional states, but also how relationships function. The child does not learn *about* safety or connection cognitively; they *become* those experiences through right-brain-to-right-brain resonance. When such resonance is consistently present, secure attachment and coherent self-organisation emerge. When it is disrupted—through neglect, misattunement, or trauma—implicit expectations of disconnection, threat, or incoherence are silently encoded (Beebe & Lachmann, 2014).

Freud famously argued that "the unconscious is the true psychic reality" (Freud, 1915/1957), but in contemporary neuropsychological terms, much of this reality is *pre-symbolic*. The child's first mappings of self and other occur in what Stern (1985) described as the "*domain of emergent relatedness*"—a preverbal field of affective micro-events and embodied relational synchrony. These events do not translate easily into words or narratives because they are stored not as stories but as sensorimotor and emotional states, procedural expectations, and relational scripts that are automatically activated in similar situations later in life.

This non-representational unconscious is particularly relevant in Integrative Strategic Psychotherapy (ISP), which distinguishes between levels of self and their corresponding modes of memory and processing. At the level of the proto-self and early core self, unconscious processes are less about repressed ideas (in the Freudian sense) and more about *undigested experience*—emotional knowledge that was never fully integrated or made explicit (Popescu, 2021). Such knowledge includes somatic reactions, orienting reflexes, affective anticipations, and relational reflexes, which are activated unconsciously in adult life, particularly in moments of stress, intimacy, or vulnerability.

The concept of implicit relational knowing was articulated by Lyons-Ruth et al. (1998) as a form of non-conscious, body-based "knowing how to be with another." This form of knowing is not logical or propositional but is enacted spontaneously in interpersonal interactions. It reflects not what the client *believes* but what they *expect*—emotionally, somatically, and relationally.

In psychotherapy, these expectations are revealed through enactments, countertransference, and moment-to-moment interaction patterns. For example, a client with early experiences of neglect may unconsciously expect the psychotherapist to fail them or ignore their needs—not because they consciously mistrust the psychotherapist, but because the implicit template of the relationship is built upon abandonment. This implicit script shapes not only how the client interprets the therapist's actions but also how they behave—perhaps by avoiding expression of needs, withdrawing emotionally, or provoking disengagement.

From an ISP perspective, the therapeutic relationship becomes the primary site of transformation for these early unconscious structures. Through repeated experiences of atonement, repair, and containment, the psychotherapist offers an opportunity for the client to encode new relational patterns—not cognitively, but somatically and emotionally. This process is gradual and often unconscious; it is not insight that leads to change, but experience that rewrites the old relational code (Wallin, 2010).

For the Integrative Strategic psychotherapist, recognising and working with preverbal unconscious processes means attuning not only to *what* the client says, but *how* they are in the room. Are they collapsing their posture? Avoiding eye contact? Speaking in a monotone voice? Alternating between hyperarousal and emotional numbing? These embodied signals are the language of the unconscious proto-self.

Interventions at this level must also be non-verbal or minimally verbal: modulation of voice, physical positioning, pacing of speech, and therapeutic silence are as important as interpretation or reflection. Techniques such as guided imagery, sensorimotor tracking, movement-based atonement, and polyvagal-informed interventions (Porges, 2022) are particularly effective for accessing and reorganising these early layers of unconscious experience.

Moreover, ISP integrates findings from developmental psychology and neuroscience to map how implicit relational knowing is shaped across contexts and over time. In cases of complex trauma or early neglect, the proto-self may be fragmented or hypervigilant, requiring careful pacing and scaffolding in therapy. The aim is not to "interpret" the unconscious, but to *co-create* new experiences that are registered and internalised at the preverbal level (Ogden & Fisher, 2021).

5.5. Attachment, Affective Encoding and Unconscious Templates

The early attachment relationship between infant and caregiver constitutes one of the most powerful developmental mechanisms through which the unconscious mind is shaped. Within the framework of Integrative Strategic Psychotherapy (ISP), the relational bond formed in early life is not merely a background context but a fundamental sculptor of unconscious templates, affective schemas, and behavioural predispositions. These deeply embedded structures influence how individuals perceive the world, regulate emotions, anticipate relationships, and construct meaning—often without conscious awareness.

From the first weeks of life, infants are attuned to the emotional rhythms and regulatory signals of their caregivers. This atonement is not based on verbal communication but on affective synchrony: tone of voice, facial expressions, touch, and prosody. According to Schore (2021), this non-verbal, right-hemispheric communication plays a central role in the development of the infant's brain, particularly in areas responsible for emotion regulation, stress reactivity, and social cognition.

Attachment patterns—secure, avoidant, ambivalent, or disorganised—are not simply relational styles but deeply encoded affective-mnemonic templates that shape unconscious expectations and relational responses (Wallin, 2010; Siegel, 2021). These templates operate beneath awareness, creating automatic predictions about self-worth, safety, vulnerability, and others' availability or danger. The attachment bond thus becomes a crucible for the formation of implicit memory and unconscious emotional rules (Fonagy et al., 2021).

Affective encoding refers to the way emotionally charged experiences are stored, especially in early life before the development of explicit memory systems. These encoded experiences, often preverbal, form the groundwork of implicit relational knowing (Stern, 2004). For example, a child who repeatedly encounters cold, intrusive, or inconsistent caregiving may develop an internalised affective expectation that closeness is dangerous or that vulnerability invites rejection. This is not consciously formulated but lives within the nervous system, body schema, and procedural memory.

Such affective encoding occurs not only through trauma but also through the accumulation of mundane emotional transactions—the "micro-affectivity" of daily caregiving interactions. Lyons-Ruth et al. (2006) demonstrated that affective misattunement in the first year of life predicts disorganised attachment and later affective dysregulation. These misattunements shape unconscious patterns that resurface in adult relationships, particularly under stress or in the context of intimacy.

Bowlby's (1988) concept of "internal working models" (IWMs) is central to understanding how attachment relationships shape the unconscious. IWMs are the cognitive-affective structures that encode beliefs about the self, others, and the world. In ISP, these models are mapped across the axes, particularly at the core self level. However, their operations remain largely unconscious—manifesting through implicit biases, automatic emotional reactions, and relationship scripts that the individual is often unaware of (Popescu, 2021).

These models are not static. Through psychotherapy and other relational experiences, they can be revised. However, without intervention, IWMs tend to be self-reinforcing: they shape perceptions in a way that confirms existing expectations, even when those expectations are maladaptive. This is why individuals may repeatedly find themselves in similar dysfunctional relationships or life situations—they are not merely acting out behaviour but enacting unconscious templates shaped by early attachment experiences (Holmes, 2014).

Attachment-based templates also give rise to what Greenberg and Pascual-Leone (2020) describe as emotional schemas: implicit rules about which emotions are acceptable, how they should be expressed, and what their meanings are. These schemas function like affective software, operating silently in the background of awareness. For example, a child raised in an environment where anger was punished may unconsciously associate assertiveness with danger, leading to chronic suppression of needs and eventual somatic complaints or depressive symptoms.

Emotional schemas are part of the unconscious affective encoding system that influences all three axes of the self in ISP—cognitive, emotional, and psychodynamic. They also shape the plastic self's development by limiting or facilitating emotional learning and interpersonal flexibility. These schemas often resist cognitive insight; they must be accessed through relational, symbolic, or body-based interventions that engage the unconscious mind (Ogden & Fisher, 2021).

In psychotherapy, unconscious templates formed through attachment can be re-enacted in the therapeutic relationship, often through transference. These enactments are not signs of resistance or pathology; they are opportunities for relational repair and neural re-patterning (Schore, 2021). The psychotherapist, acting as a "secure base" (Wallin, 2010), can provide corrective emotional experiences that gradually modify implicit memory and affective templates.

This relational process is not merely symbolic—it has neurobiological consequences. The presence of a responsive, attuned psychotherapist can activate parasympathetic regulation (via the vagus nerve), decrease amygdala reactivity, and increase the integration of subcortical affective material with cortical reflection (Geller & Porges, 2021).

Attachment-related unconscious patterns are also shaped by cultural norms and intergenerational dynamics. Affective encoding is not limited to the dyadic relationship between child and caregiver; it is embedded in larger cultural scripts about gender, emotion, power, and vulnerability. Transgenerational studies (Yehuda et al., 2021; McGowan et al., 2009) show that trauma, shame, and attachment dysregulation can be passed epigenetically and behaviourally across generations—often without conscious transmission.

In ISP, the external self houses these socio-symbolic influences, where attachment scripts are blended with cultural narratives and family myths. Psychotherapy thus becomes a space not only for personal transformation but also for intergenerational healing, allowing the client to challenge inherited affective templates and author new internal stories.

5.6. Epigenetics and Transgenerational Transmission of the Unconscious

The Integrative Strategic Psychotherapy (ISP) model acknowledges that the unconscious is not only shaped by individual experience but is also transmitted across generations—biologically, relationally, and symbolically. This recognition draws on a growing body of interdisciplinary research in epigenetics, intergenerational trauma, and attachment science, offering a deeply expanded view of unconscious processes.

Transgenerational transmission refers to the unconscious passage of affective, behavioural, and relational patterns from parents to children—patterns that are not always explicitly communicated but are internalised through repeated relational interactions, non-verbal cues, family myths, and even epigenetic markers. In other words, unconscious material can be "inherited" in ways that bypass conscious reflection or autobiographical memory, becoming embedded in the very architecture of the self.

Epigenetics refers to the study of how gene expression is regulated by environmental factors—without altering the DNA sequence itself. Epigenetic changes act as molecular switches that turn genes on or off in response to environmental stimuli, particularly in early development (Meaney, 2010; Klengel & Binder, 2015). These modifications, such as DNA methylation and histone acetylation, influence the expression of genes associated with stress regulation, emotion processing, attachment, and neurodevelopment.

Traumatic experiences—especially in early life—can induce long-lasting epigenetic changes. For example, studies show that early maternal deprivation leads to epigenetic silencing of the glucocorticoid receptor gene (NR3C1), reducing the capacity of the hypothalamic-pituitary-adrenal (HPA) axis to regulate stress (McGowan et al., 2009). Such changes affect the individual's lifelong vulnerability to anxiety, depression, dissociation, and PTSD.

Even more compelling is the evidence that epigenetic markers of trauma can be passed from parent to child. Yehuda et al. (2016) demonstrated that Holocaust survivors had distinct patterns of FKBP5 methylation—a gene involved in stress response—and that these patterns were also observed in their children, who had not directly experienced the trauma themselves. This suggests that certain unconscious predispositions are inherited not only psychologically or relationally but biologically, through molecular traces of parental experience.

While biology offers one channel, the primary mode of unconscious transmission is relational. Infants and young children absorb the affective environment of their caregivers, long before they possess symbolic or reflective capacities. Through implicit relational knowing—a concept central to both attachment theory and ISP—children internalise not only overt messages but also the caregiver's emotional style, defensive patterns, unresolved grief, and shame (Lyons-Ruth, 2006).

In families affected by trauma, dissociation, secrecy, or unresolved mourning, certain affective truths remain unspeakable, yet are powerfully communicated through tone, silence, gaze, bodily rhythms, or shifts in presence. These implicit patterns become encoded in the child's neurobiology and psyche, shaping unconscious templates of safety, trust, self-worth, and relational expectations.

ISP views these templates as proto-cognitive maps—precursors to internal working models—that influence all future development. When these unconscious maps are shaped by fear, shame, or trauma, they can generate self-states marked by hypervigilance, emotional constriction, or compulsive repair efforts.

Another layer of unconscious inheritance occurs through family myths, roles, narratives, injunctions, and cultural scripts—often transmitted through language, rituals, or silence. These elements shape the external self and may convey ancestral legacies of trauma, guilt, resilience, or identity.

For example, a child born into a family with a history of persecution may inherit unconscious messages like: "*Don't speak too loudly, it's dangerous*", "*You must be perfect to be loved*" or "*We don't talk about the past.*"

These inherited messages often operate outside of awareness, but profoundly shape identity, emotional regulation, and relational strategies. ISP clinicians are trained to decode these sociocultural archetypes, family myths, and symbolic structures during case formulation and treatment.

As Erskine (2021) notes, "*what is unspoken in the family is often what speaks most loudly in the client's unconscious.*"

In Integrative Strategic Psychotherapy, the recognition of transgenerational transmission shapes both formulation and intervention. The psychotherapist listens not only for the client's story but for the story beneath the story—those unconscious echoes of another time, another life, another voice that has shaped the self. Strategic interventions may include: (1) Genograms to map relational and emotional patterns across generations; (2) Symbolic externalisation of family roles or injunctions (e.g., writing a letter to a deceased ancestor, drawing the "legacy of silence"); (3) Imaginal dialogue with intergenerational figures (e.g., "If your grandmother could speak, what would she say to you now?"); and (4) Co-creation of new symbolic narratives, allowing the client to "carry forward" the legacy without being bound by it.

Crucially, the psychotherapist must hold space for grief, mourning, and emotional recognition—what was not seen, not said, and not processed in the family line. ISP views this work as both reparative and liberatory, enabling the client to reclaim agency over inherited unconscious material.

5.7. The Body as a Repository of the Unconscious

Within the Integrative Strategic Psychotherapy (ISP) model, the body is not viewed merely as a biological vessel or a passive recipient of psychological processes—it is considered an active, dynamic repository of unconscious experience. From preverbal memory and unprocessed trauma to dissociated self-states and archetypal symbols, the body holds and expresses what the psyche may not yet be able to articulate.

This perspective draws from numerous traditions—somatic psychotherapy, attachment neurobiology, affect regulation theory, and interpersonal neurobiology—but in ISP it is strategically integrated within a broader developmental and symbolic framework of the self. The self, as conceptualised in ISP, unfolds across domains (proto-, core, plastic, and external) and axes (cognitive, emotional, and psychodynamic). The body, in this model, is the first and most enduring medium through which unconscious material is encoded, maintained, and potentially transformed.

The earliest form of self—the proto-self—emerges through bodily sensations and regulatory interactions with caregivers. These experiences are encoded somatically and relationally before language or conscious memory develop (Damasio, 1999). The way a caregiver holds, touches, responds to, or neglects the infant contributes to implicit memory traces and visceral associations that shape the infant's affective world.

When these early interactions are attuned and regulating, the infant internalises a sense of bodily safety and emotional coherence. But when the environment is chaotic, neglectful, or traumatic, the infant may develop somatic scripts of alarm, fragmentation, or shutdown, often encoded in muscle tension, posture, or autonomic reactivity (Ogden & Fisher, 2021).

In ISP, these bodily patterns are seen as proto-symbolic forms of unconscious memory. For example, a client who tenses their shoulders whenever they speak about boundaries may be reliving an early, pre-verbal experience of helplessness or threat that was never consciously processed. The tension is not merely muscular—it is meaningful.

In cases of early trauma, especially when abuse or neglect occurred in preverbal stages, the body becomes the primary container for dissociated experience. These unintegrated fragments are often somatised—manifesting as chronic pain, gastrointestinal symptoms, migraines, or unexplained fatigue (van der Kolk, 2021). Clients may also display dissociative states such as depersonalisation, numbing, or freezing, which signal the activation of a fragmented or disembodied self-state.

In ISP, such somatic symptoms are approached not just medically, but strategically and symbolically. The clinician explores: What is the body saying that the client cannot yet say with words? What is the emotional or symbolic function of the symptom? Which self-state is holding this experience, and why?

In this way, the psychotherapist enters into a dialogue with the body, helping the client reconnect with dissociated or defended aspects of the self through embodied awareness, rather than bypassing them with interpretation.

Recent research highlights the importance of interoception—the ability to perceive internal bodily states (heartbeat, breath, gut tension)—as a foundation for emotion regulation and reflective capacity (Craig, 2002). When clients have low interoceptive awareness, they may be unable to recognise internal cues of stress, hunger, or anxiety, leading to maladaptive coping strategies (e.g., binge eating, dissociation, over-control).

ISP integrates interoceptive training into the therapeutic process through: (1) Mindful attention to bodily sensation (e.g., "Where do you feel that anger in your body?"); (2) Somatic tracking (noticing fluctuations in sensation during activation or safety); (3) Movement-based interventions (e.g., grounding, authentic movement); and (4) Right-brain atonement through the therapeutic relationship—using rhythm, tone, pacing, and presence to regulate affect via the body, not just through words (Schore, 2021).

This emphasis on right-brain processing reinforces ISP's recognition that many unconscious processes are nonverbal, nonlinear, and embodied. Thus, transformation often begins in the body—through shifts in posture, rhythm, breath, and internal resonance—before it is captured cognitively.

The body is also the site where archetypal patterns—those inherited symbolic forms described by Jung (1959)—become manifest. ISP recognises that unconscious processes carry universal themes (e.g., abandonment, betrayal, rebirth, integration) that may appear first as bodily experiences.

A client who repeatedly curls into a foetal posture during moments of emotional overwhelm may be unconsciously enacting the "wounded child" archetype. Another who finds strength and assertiveness only when standing upright with fists clenched may be invoking the "warrior" archetype. These movements are not random—they are somatic expressions of unconscious symbolic content.

In expressive or experiential components of ISP, such as guided imagery, role play, or psychodrama, the body is used as an instrument of transformation: enacting new patterns, integrating split-off states, or completing unfinished relational gestures.

Although ISP is a primarily verbal and symbolic model, it acknowledges the importance of bodily presence, proximity, and resonance within therapeutic boundaries. While physical touch is used only within ethical and cultural guidelines, relational proximity (e.g., posture, breath synchrony, silence, and tone) can create moments of implicit repair.

For clients with somatic trauma histories, the body may be a source of shame, fear, or alienation. Re-establishing safe embodiment becomes a central goal: (1) Naming and validating the body's reactions; (2) Reconnecting affective experiences to bodily cues; and (3) Re-owning the body as a legitimate site of knowing and being. When the body is reclaimed, the unconscious gains a new ally in healing.

5.8. Neuroscientific Perspectives on the Unconscious

5.8.1. Implicit Memory Systems and Emotional Brain Circuits

The unconscious, once considered a nebulous psychological construct, has increasingly gained neurobiological credibility through the study of implicit memory systems and affective circuitry. Neuroscience confirms that many of the processes which guide behaviour, perception, and affect regulation operate outside conscious awareness and are embedded in subcortical structures such as the amygdala, basal ganglia, hippocampus, and brainstem nuclei (Panksepp & Biven, 2012; LeDoux, 2015).

Implicit memory refers to the capacity to learn, store, and retrieve information without conscious recollection (Schacter, 1987). It governs skills, conditioned responses, and emotional learning—forming the core of early relational experiences and unconscious procedural knowledge. For example, a child who learns that proximity leads to rejection may unconsciously internalise avoidance strategies, long before verbal cognition can articulate these dynamics. Such relational blueprints become encoded in emotional brain circuits and expressed as unconscious relational templates, influencing adult behaviour in psychotherapy and beyond (Siegel, 2021; Schore, 2021).

The amygdala plays a central role in implicit emotional memory, particularly in processing fear, threat, and affective salience. It responds rapidly to sensory stimuli and encodes emotionally charged events, often without conscious appraisal. Its connections with the hypothalamus and autonomic nervous system facilitate immediate physiological responses—what we commonly label as "gut reactions" (LeDoux, 2015). These amygdala-driven processes bypass the neocortex, making them resistant to insight-based therapeutic interventions and necessitating body-based or relational techniques to access and re-pattern (Ogden & Fisher, 2021).

Meanwhile, the hippocampus supports contextual memory and emotional regulation but matures later than the amygdala, which explains why early affective experiences are stored in fragmented, nonverbal form. This imbalance contributes to the disorganised or unconscious nature of early trauma and attachment injuries (Perry, 2009).

In the ISP model, implicit memory systems shape the proto-self and core self, grounding the individual's unconscious emotional responses. Therapeutic interventions that access these systems—such as guided imagery, rhythmic movement, atonement-based mirroring, or psychodrama—can activate implicit memory traces and allow for their reorganisation within a secure therapeutic container (Erskine, 2021; Schore, 2021).

In short, neuroscientific findings validate the reality of the unconscious as a dynamic system operating below awareness, coded in affective neural circuits that resist declarative access but shape our deepest relational patterns.

5.8.2. Right Hemisphere Processing and the Nonverbal Unconscious

Contemporary neuroscience has increasingly validated what psychoanalytic and relational traditions have long intuited: that a vast portion of our emotional life and intersubjective experience is processed nonverbally, automatically, and primarily in the right hemisphere of the brain. Within the framework of Integrative Strategic Psychotherapy (ISP), the right hemisphere is understood as a central neural substrate of the nonverbal unconscious—housing preverbal memories, implicit relational patterns, affective templates, and embodied forms of knowing that influence the self far beyond conscious awareness.

The right hemisphere develops earlier than the left in both evolutionary and ontogenetic terms (Schore, 2021). From birth, it is dominant in processing emotional tone, facial expressions, prosody, and interpersonal cues—all foundational elements in the formation of early attachment relationships. This hemisphere becomes the primary site for the encoding of implicit relational knowing (Lyons-Ruth, 1999), the kind of unconscious, non-symbolic memory that guides our interactions, expectations, and sense of relational safety. These deeply embodied, emotionally charged experiences form a core substrate of what ISP conceptualises as proto- and core-self dynamics.

Schore (2012) argues that the right hemisphere operates as a "deep unconscious system," involved in the regulation of affect, stress responses, bodily homeostasis, and unconscious motivation. This aligns closely with ISP's understanding of the psychodynamic and emotional axes of the self—where affective dynamics, somatic patterns, and preverbal experience form the scaffolding of later symbolic and relational functioning. When early atonement is disrupted, the right hemisphere encodes dysregulated states which, in adulthood, may manifest as affect intolerance, dissociation, panic states, or inexplicable relational conflicts. These are often not accessible to left-brain, logical analysis but must be addressed via embodied, relational, and symbolic interventions.

The nonverbal unconscious also plays a critical role in psychotherapist-client resonance. Right-hemisphere-to-right-hemisphere communication between therapist and client underlies processes such as atonement, emotional synchronisation, and the co-regulation of distress (Geller & Porges, 2021; Schore, 2021). These interactions occur below the level of verbal awareness and are experienced through shifts in tone, gaze, posture, rhythm, and affective atmosphere. For the ISP psychotherapist, developing sensitivity to this level of communication is not optional but essential—it is the gateway to deeper unconscious transformation.

Moreover, the right hemisphere is responsible for the processing of metaphor, music, spatial perception, and holistic imagery—domains that are central to expressive therapies, guided imagery, and symbolic interventions commonly used within ISP. These modalities bypass verbal resistance and access deep emotional material encoded nonverbally, often from early developmental periods. Integrative Strategic Psychotherapy intentionally leverages right-brain access routes through somatic work, creative expression, voice modulation, silence, and synchronised affective presence.

A growing body of neuroimaging research supports the centrality of the right hemisphere in unconscious processing. Functional MRI studies show that emotional stimuli elicit faster and stronger responses in right-lateralised brain regions, particularly the right amygdala, insula, and orbitofrontal cortex (Gainotti, 2019). These regions are implicated in affective memory, attachment, and embodied awareness—domains that often remain unformulated in narrative but are enacted somatically or relationally.

ISP conceptualises unconscious right-hemisphere dynamics as foundational to the self's basal and core levels. These dynamics are formative not only in pathology but also in healing. Therapeutic change at these levels does not occur through insight alone but through re-atonement, embodied presence, and corrective emotional experience. Indeed, affective synchrony and dyadic regulation between therapist and client can modify right-hemisphere neural patterns, enabling implicit memory reconsolidation and the emergence of new affective meanings (Porges, 2022; Siegel, 2023).

5.8.3. Affect Regulation, the Default Mode Network and the "Hidden" Self

Affect regulation is a cornerstone of psychological health and a key therapeutic focus in Integrative Strategic Psychotherapy (ISP). At its deepest level, affect regulation is not merely a learned skill but a fundamental neurobiological process rooted in the brain's architecture, especially in the *Default Mode Network* (DMN), limbic system, and right-hemisphere functions. These systems help create the experience of the self in relation to others, in time, and in emotional continuity. Within ISP, we refer to the interweaving of these processes as the terrain of the *"Hidden Self"*—a set of unconscious, background processes that maintain internal coherence, modulate emotional salience, and govern the felt continuity of personal identity.

The DMN, first described by Raichle et al. (2001), is a network of brain regions—including the medial prefrontal cortex, posterior cingulate cortex, precuneus, and angular gyrus—that becomes active when the individual is not focused on the outside world but rather engaged in inward-focused tasks: daydreaming, imagining, autobiographical memory, and self-reflection.

In ISP, the DMN is conceptualised as a core neurobiological correlate of the internal narrative self or "background consciousness." It represents the internal narrator that weaves past, present, and imagined futures into a coherent sense of "I." This system is active even when we are not consciously aware of it, and it plays a central role in affective appraisal, meaning-making, and the management of internal states.

Disruptions in the DMN are increasingly associated with disorders of the self, such as major depression, PTSD, and dissociative identity disorder (Sheline et al., 2009; Lanius et al., 2010). In depression, for instance, DMN hyperactivity may contribute to rumination and negative self-referential thoughts, while in dissociation, hypo-connectivity may impair integration between memory, emotion, and bodily awareness (Spindler & Elklit, 2013).

The *Hidden Self*—a term we use in ISP to describe the unconscious architecture of emotional regulation—operates largely outside conscious awareness. It includes the coordinated functioning of subcortical and cortical areas involved in affect modulation: the amygdala (threat and salience detection), ventromedial prefrontal cortex (integration of emotion and cognition), anterior cingulate cortex (error detection, empathy), and insula (interoception).

This system integrates multiple inputs (internal states, external cues, past experiences, bodily sensations) and adjusts emotional responses based on perceived threat or safety. Crucially, it is deeply relational. According to Schore (2021), early caregiver-child interactions shape the right-hemisphere networks responsible for this implicit regulation. If these interactions are consistent and attuned, the Hidden Self develops a secure and flexible structure. If they are chaotic or neglectful, the resulting dysregulation becomes encoded in neural pathways as unconscious affective templates.

In psychotherapy, we often encounter the Hidden Self through affective enactments, sudden emotional shifts, or bodily responses that the client cannot explain. These phenomena reflect what is *already known*, but not *yet spoken*. ISP views the work of psyhcotherapy as facilitating the translation of implicit affect into explicit meaning.

In ISP, affect regulation is not solely a goal of therapy—it is also a process through which transformation occurs. Emotional regulation unfolds through three levels:

1. Co-regulation: The psychotherapist provides an attuned, stabilising presence. This activates the client's parasympathetic system (via the vagus nerve), calming arousal and increasing safety (Porges, 2022);
2. Symbolic Processing: Once arousal is lowered, affect can be named, visualised, or externalised. This recruits the DMN and lateral prefrontal networks, helping integrate emotion into personal narrative; and
3. Internalisation: Over time, the client develops internal models of self-soothing, reflection, and narrative identity—neural patterns formerly supported by the therapist become internal resources.

Techniques such as guided imagery, expressive writing, metaphor construction, and mentalisation activate the DMN while fostering symbolic reprocessing of affective experiences (Siegel, 2021; Fonagy & Luyten, 2020). These tools not only promote insight but also modulate unconscious emotion regulation systems.

Understanding the role of the DMN and the Hidden Self allows ISP practitioners to make strategic choices. For instance, a client who dissociates under stress may need somatic anchoring and relational co-regulation before cognitive work is introduced. Another client whose DMN is overactive (e.g., ruminative depression) may benefit from techniques that interrupt default mode patterns, such as mindfulness, active behavioural experiments, or reframing interventions.

Moreover, ISP therapists are trained to recognise moments when the client's affective regulation falters—not as pathology but as a doorway into unconscious structures that yearn for integration. The psychotherapist becomes a "translational bridge" between sub-symbolic emotion and symbolic understanding.

5.8.4. Neuroplasticity and the Transformation of Unconscious Patterns

The concept of neuroplasticity—the brain's ability to reorganise itself by forming new neural connections throughout life—has fundamentally reshaped contemporary understandings of the unconscious. Within the framework of Integrative Strategic Psychotherapy (ISP), neuroplasticity provides the biological foundation for therapeutic change, especially the restructuring of unconscious patterns encoded in early life. These patterns, often resistant to conscious effort alone, can be modified through repeated, emotionally significant relational and experiential inputs, particularly within the therapeutic encounter.

Historically, the brain was considered largely immutable after early development. However, research over the past three decades has shown that neural networks remain malleable across the lifespan, particularly in response to learning, emotion, social interaction, and trauma (Doidge, 2020). This adaptability occurs through mechanisms such as synaptogenesis (formation of new synapses), dendritic growth, neurogenesis (in limited regions), and epigenetic regulation of gene expression.

In the context of ISP, neuroplasticity is not an abstract concept but a clinical reality. Each therapeutic session holds the potential to modify dysfunctional patterns encoded in the neural architecture—whether these relate to implicit memory, attachment templates, self-states, or affect regulation strategies.

In the ISP model, unconscious patterns are often housed within the *core* and *plastic self*. These include: (1) Internal working models shaped by early attachment experiences; (2) Defensive relational patterns (e.g., withdrawal, appeasement, projection); (3) Implicit procedural memory schemas (e.g., "when I feel criticised, I freeze"); (4) Emotional reflexes conditioned by trauma (e.g., shame linked to visibility); and (5) Somatic imprints of disorganised affect (e.g., stomach tension, shallow breath).

Such patterns are not stored in the narrative cortex but in non-verbal systems: the amygdala, basal ganglia, cerebellum, and brainstem. As such, they resist change through insight alone.

Neuroplastic transformation of these patterns requires repetition, emotional salience, and relational safety—the exact conditions offered in a responsive psychotherapeutic environment.

Integrative Strategic Psychotherapy harnesses neuroplasticity through a multi-levelled intervention model that integrates symbolic, emotional, cognitive, and bodily work. Key mechanisms include:

1. Relational atonement: Secure, empathic connection activates limbic resonance, calming hypervigilant systems and enabling the reorganisation of attachment schemas (Schore, 2021; Siegel, 2023);
2. Corrective emotional experiences: These experiences disconfirm deeply held unconscious beliefs (e.g., "If I show anger, I'll be abandoned") and are encoded in new neural pathways;
3. Embodied processing: Somatic interventions such as sensorimotor tracking, breathing regulation, and movement allow procedural patterns to be accessed and transformed at subcortical levels (Ogden & Fisher, 2021);
4. Narrative integration: Transforming implicit memory into coherent autobiographical narrative recruits the medial prefrontal cortex and DMN, supporting integration across time (Fonagy & Luyten, 2020);
5. Imagination and metaphor: Guided imagery and symbolic interventions activate neurocognitive flexibility, allowing for the reshaping of entrenched cognitive-emotional schemas (Zeig, 2021); and
6. Mindfulness and interoception: Practices that enhance present-moment awareness increase insula activation and promote top-down modulation of emotional reactivity (Farb et al., 2010).

Neuroplasticity is deeply intertwined with epigenetic processes—modifications to gene expression based on environmental and relational input. As Yehuda et al. (2021) demonstrated, trauma can alter epigenetic markers across generations, especially in stress-regulation systems such as the hypothalamic-pituitary-adrenal (HPA) axis. Conversely, relational healing and psychotherapy can reverse or buffer these effects, leading to epigenetically mediated resilience (Klengel & Binder, 2020).

This reinforces the ISP view that unconscious patterns are biologically embedded but not biologically fixed. Through attuned therapeutic work, new relational and symbolic experiences become part of the client's lived body, transforming not only narrative identity but neurobiological architecture.

Understanding neuroplasticity also implies an ethical responsibility: the therapeutic relationship shapes the brain. The psychotherapist's tone, pacing, facial expressions, gaze, and responsiveness all contribute to rewiring the client's neural architecture. This amplifies the importance of psychotherapist development, supervision, and self-regulation as essential components of ethical practice (Geller & Porges, 2021).

In this light, psychotherapy is not only a narrative intervention but a neurobiological encounter—an experiential reprogramming of implicit systems through sustained co-regulation and meaning-making.

References

Adolphs, R. (2009). The social brain: Neural basis of social knowledge. *Annual Review of Psychology, 60*, 693–716. https://doi.org/10.1146/annurev.psych.60.110707.163514

Andreasen, N. C. (2011). *The creating brain: The neuroscience of genius*. Dana Press.

Aron, L. (1996). *A meeting of minds: Mutuality in psychoanalysis*. Routledge.

Barsalou, L. W. (2008). Grounded cognition. *Annual Review of Psychology*, 59, 617–645.

Beebe, B., & Lachmann, F. M. (2014). *The Origins of Attachment: Infant Research and Adult Treatment*. Routledge.

Beutel, M. E., Stern, E., & Silbersweig, D. (2003). The emerging dialogue between psychoanalysis and neuroscience: Neuroimaging perspectives. *Journal of the American Psychoanalytic Association, 51*(3), 773–801. https://doi.org/10.1177/00030651030510030301

Beutler, L. E., Harwood, T. M., & Alimohamed, S. (2022). *Integrative psychotherapy: A therapist's handbook* (2nd ed.). Oxford University Press.

Bowlby, J. (1988). *A secure base: Clinical applications of attachment theory*. Routledge.

Bucci, W. (1997). *Psychoanalysis and cognitive science: A multiple code theory*. Guilford Press.

Castonguay, L. G. (2020). Integration in psychotherapy: Past, present, and future. *Psychotherapy Research, 30*(5), 501–510.

Clark, A. (2013). Whatever next? Predictive brains, situated agents, and the future of cognitive science. *Behavioral and Brain Sciences*, 36(3), 181–204.

Craig, A. D. (2009). How do you feel—now? The anterior insula and human awareness. *Nature Reviews Neuroscience, 10*(1), 59–70. https://doi.org/10.1038/nrn2555

Damasio, A. (2010). *Self comes to mind: Constructing the conscious brain*. Pantheon.

Damasio, A. R. (1994). *Descartes' error: Emotion, reason, and the human brain*. Putnam.

Davidson, R. J., & McEwen, B. S. (2012). Social influences on neuroplasticity: Stress and interventions to promote well-being. *Nature Neuroscience, 15*(5), 689–695. https://doi.org/10.1038/nn.3093

Dehaene, S., Changeux, J. P., Naccache, L., Sackur, J., & Sergent, C. (2006). Conscious, preconscious, and subliminal processing: a testable taxonomy. *Trends in Cognitive Sciences*, 10(5), 204–211.

Doidge, N. (2020). *The brain that changes itself: Stories of personal triumph from the frontiers of brain science* (Updated ed.). Penguin Books.

Edelman, G. M. (1992). *Bright air, brilliant fire: On the matter of the mind.* Basic Books.

Erskine, R. G. (2021). *Relational patterns, therapeutic presence: Concepts and practice of integrative psychotherapy*. Karnac.

Evans, J. S. B. T., & Stanovich, K. E. (2013). Dual-process theories of higher cognition. *Perspectives on Psychological Science*, 8(3), 223–241.

Farb, N. A. S., Segal, Z. V., & Anderson, A. K. (2010). Mindfulness meditation training alters cortical representations of interoceptive attention. *Social Cognitive and Affective Neuroscience, 8*(1), 15–26. https://doi.org/10.1093/scan/nsq091

Fonagy, P., & Luyten, P. (2020). *Developmental psychopathology and psychoanalysis: New approaches to integration*. Routledge.

Fonagy, P., Luyten, P., Allison, E., & Campbell, C. (2021). Borderline personality disorder as a limitation of resilience. *Borderline Personality Disorder and Emotion Dysregulation, 8*, 11.

Fonagy, P., Luyten, P., & Allison, E. (2021). Epistemic trust and the emergence of mentalization. *Current Opinion in Psychology, 41*, 91–95. https://doi.org/10.1016/j.copsyc.2021.04.010

Freud, S. (1900/1953). *The interpretation of dreams*. In J. Strachey (Ed. & Trans.), *The standard edition of the complete psychological works of Sigmund Freud* (Vols. 4–5). Hogarth Press.

Freud, S. (1915a/1957). *The unconscious*. In J. Strachey (Ed. & Trans.), *The standard edition of the complete psychological works of Sigmund Freud* (Vol. 14, pp. 159–204). Hogarth Press.

Freud, S. (1917/1957). *Introductory lectures on psycho-analysis*. In J. Strachey (Ed. & Trans.), *The standard edition* (Vol. 16). Hogarth Press.

Freud, S. (1923/1961). *The ego and the id.* In J. Strachey (Ed. & Trans.), *The standard edition* (Vol. 19). Hogarth Press.

Friston, K. (2010). The free-energy principle: a unified brain theory? *Nature Reviews Neuroscience*, 11(2), 127–138.

Gainsburg, I. (2022). Emotional memory and the brain: Uncovering the neuroscience of feeling. *Journal of Affective Neuroscience*, 28(3), 345–359.

Gainotti, G. (2019). Emotions and the right hemisphere: Can new data clarify old models? *Neuroscience & Biobehavioral Reviews, 98*, 208–219. https://doi.org/10.1016/j.neubiorev.2019.01.002

Geller, S. M., & Porges, S. W. (2021). Therapeutic presence and polyvagal theory: Principles and applications. *Frontiers in Psychology, 12*, 723137. https://doi.org/10.3389/fpsyg.2021.723137

Goldfried, M. R. (2022). The future of psychotherapy integration: A return to common processes. *Journal of Psychotherapy Integration, 32*(1), 3–15.

Greene, J. D., Sommerville, R. B., Nystrom, L. E., Darley, J. M., & Cohen, J. D. (2001). An fMRI investigation of emotional engagement in moral judgment. *Science*, 293(5537), 2105–2108.

Greenberg, L. S., & Pascual-Leone, A. (2020). *Emotion in psychotherapy: A practice-friendly research review*. Guilford Press.

Greenwald, A. G., & Banaji, M. R. (1995). Implicit social cognition: attitudes, self-esteem, and stereotypes. *Psychological Review*, 102(1), 4–27.

Hassin, R. R. (2013). Yes it can: On the functional abilities of the human unconscious. *Perspectives on Psychological Science*, 8(2), 195–207.

Jung, C. G. (1959). *The archetypes and the collective unconscious* (R. F. C. Hull, Trans.). Princeton University Press.

Jung, C. G. (1964). *Man and his symbols*. Dell Publishing.

Jung, C. G. (1968). *The structure and dynamics of the psyche*. Princeton University Press.

Jung, C. G. (1968). *The Archetypes and the Collective Unconscious*. Princeton University Press.

Kandel, E. R. (2021). *The Disordered Mind: What Unusual Brains Tell Us About Ourselves*. Farrar, Straus and Giroux.

Kellermann, P. F. (2021). *Psychodrama: Advances in theory and practice*. Routledge.

Kernberg, O. (1976). *Object relations theory and clinical psychoanalysis*. Jason Aronson.

Kahneman, D. (2011). *Thinking, Fast and Slow*. Farrar, Straus and Giroux.

Kaplan-Solms, K., & Solms, M. (2000). *Clinical studies in neuro-psychoanalysis: Introduction to a depth neuropsychology*. Karnac Books.

Klein, M. (1946). Notes on some schizoid mechanisms. *International Journal of Psychoanalysis*, 27, 99–110.

Klengel, T., & Binder, E. B. (2020). Epigenetics of stress-related psychiatric disorders and gene × environment interactions. *Neuron, 106*(1), 134–143. https://doi.org/10.1016/j.neuron.2020.03.053

Lanius, R. A., Vermetten, E., & Pain, C. (Eds.). (2010). *The impact of early life trauma on health and disease: The hidden epidemic*. Cambridge University Press.

Laplanche, J., & Pontalis, J. B. (1973). *The language of psychoanalysis* (D. Nicholson-Smith, Trans.). W. W. Norton.

LeDoux, J. E. (2020). *The deep history of ourselves: The four-billion-year story of how we got conscious brains*. Viking.

LeDoux, J. E. (2015). *Anxious: Using the Brain to Understand and Treat Fear and Anxiety*. Viking.

LeDoux, J. (1996). *The Emotional Brain: The Mysterious Underpinnings of Emotional Life*. Simon & Schuster.

LeDoux, J. (2002). Synaptic self: How our brains become who we are. *Viking*.

LeDoux, J. E. (2015). *Anxious: Using the brain to understand and treat fear and anxiety*. Viking.

Lemma, A. (2016). *Introduction to the practice of psychoanalytic psychotherapy* (2nd ed.). Wiley-Blackwell.

Luyten, P., Campbell, C., & Fonagy, P. (2020). The psychotherapy of borderline personality disorder. *World Psychiatry, 19*(2), 222–224.

Lyons-Ruth, K. (1998). Implicit relational knowing: Its role in development and psychoanalytic treatment. *Infant Mental Health Journal*, 19(3), 282–289.

Lyons-Ruth, K. (1999). The two-person unconscious: Intersubjective dialogue, enactive relational representation, and the emergence of new forms of relational organization. *Psychoanalytic Inquiry*, 19(4), 576–617.

Lyons-Ruth, K., Bronfman, E., & Parsons, E. (1998). Maternal frightened, frightening, or atypical behavior and disorganized infant attachment patterns. *Monographs of the Society for Research in Child Development*, 67(3), 67–96.

McGaugh, J. L. (2004). The amygdala modulates the consolidation of memories of emotionally arousing experiences. *Annual Review of Neuroscience*, 27, 1–28.

McWilliams, N. (2022). *Psychoanalytic case formulation* (2nd ed.). Guilford Press.

Mitchell, S. A. (1993). *Hope and dread in psychoanalysis*. Basic Books.

Nijenhuis, E. R. S. (2017). *The trinity of trauma: Ignorance, fragmentation, and integration*. Vandenhoeck & Ruprecht.

Northoff, G., & Panksepp, J. (2008). The trans-species concept of self and the subcortical–cortical midline system. *Trends in Cognitive Sciences, 12*(7), 259–264. https://doi.org/10.1016/j.tics.2008.04.007

Nosek, B. A., Banaji, M. R., & Greenwald, A. G. (2007). The implicit association test at age 7: A methodological and conceptual review. *Social Psychology and the Unconscious: The Automaticity of Higher Mental Processes*, 265–292.

Ogden, P., & Fisher, J. (2021). *Sensorimotor psychotherapy: Interventions for trauma and attachment*. Norton.

Panksepp, J., & Biven, L. (2020). *The archaeology of mind: Neuroevolutionary origins of human emotions* (2nd ed.). W. W. Norton & Company.

Pessoa, L. (2017). *The Cognitive-Emotional Brain: From Interactions to Integration*. MIT Press.

Popescu, O. M. (2021). *Psihoterapia integrativă strategică. Vol.1: Teorie si aplicatii practice. Letras.*

Porges, S. W. (2022). *Polyvagal theory: Neurophysiological foundations of emotions, attachment, communication, and self-regulation* (2nd ed.). Norton.

Reber, A. S. (1993). *Implicit Learning and Tacit Knowledge: An Essay on the Cognitive Unconscious*. Oxford University Press.

Samuels, A. (1985). *Jung and the post-Jungians*. Routledge.

Schore, A. N. (2021). *The development of the unconscious mind.* W. W. Norton.

Schore, A. N. (2012). *The Science of the Art of Psychotherapy*. Norton.

Schore, A. N. (2021). *Right brain psychotherapy*. Norton.

Siegel, D. J. (2023). *Interpersonal neurobiology and the developing mind.* Norton.

Siegel, D. J. (2021). *The developing mind: How relationships and the brain interact to shape who we are* (3rd ed.). Guilford Press

Skinner, B. F. (1953). *Science and Human Behavior*. Macmillan.

Solms, M. (2020). *The hidden spring: A journey to the source of consciousness*. Norton.

Stern, D. N. (1985). *The interpersonal world of the infant: A view from psychoanalysis and developmental psychology*. Basic Books.

Stern, D. N. (2004). *The Present Moment in Psychotherapy and Everyday Life*. Norton.

Stewart, I., & Joines, V. (2012). *TA today: A new introduction to transactional analysis* (2nd ed.). Lifespace Publishing.

Stolorow, R. D., & Atwood, G. E. (1992). *Contexts of being: The intersubjective foundations of psychological life*. Routledge.

Squire, L. R., & Kandel, E. R. (1999). *Memory: From Mind to Molecules*. Scientific American Library.

Teicher, M. H., & Samson, J. A. (2016). Annual research review: Enduring neurobiological effects of childhood abuse and neglect. *Journal of Child Psychology and Psychiatry, 57*(3), 241–266. https://doi.org/10.1111/jcpp.12507

Tronick, E. (2007). *The Neurobehavioral and Social-Emotional Development of Infants and Children*. W. W. Norton & Company.

Tulving, E., & Schacter, D. L. (1990). Priming and human memory systems. *Science, 247(4940)*, 301–306.

Van der Kolk, B. A. (2021). *The body keeps the score: Brain, mind, and body in the healing of trauma*. Penguin.

Varela, F. J., Thompson, E., & Rosch, E. (1991). *The Embodied Mind: Cognitive Science and Human Experience*. MIT Press.

Walker, M. P., & Stickgold, R. (2010). Overnight alchemy: Sleep-dependent memory evolution. *Nature Reviews Neuroscience*, 11(3), 218.

Winnicott, D. W. (1971). *Playing and reality*. Routledge.

Wilson, T. D. (2002). *Strangers to Ourselves: Discovering the Adaptive Unconscious*. Harvard University Press.

Yehuda, R., Daskalakis, N. P., Lehrner, A., & Bierer, L. M. (2021). Epigenetic biomarkers of PTSD risk and resilience. *European Journal of Psychotraumatology, 12*(1), 1878701. https://doi.org/10.1080/20008198.2021.1878701

Young, J. E., Klosko, J. S., & Weishaar, M. E. (2020). *Schema therapy: A practitioner's guide* (2nd ed.). Guilford Press.

Zeig, J. K. (2021). *Experiencing Erickson: An introduction to the man and his work*. Taylor & Francis.

CHAPTER 6

THE BIOLOGICAL LEVEL OF THE SELF

6.1. Genetic Inheritance

6.1.1. The Genome

The formation of the self depends on the genome and the epigenome. Genes determine a wide array of traits as well as protein synthesis, but they are expressed only when activated by the epigenome, which in turn is shaped by environmental influences. This means that the self emerges from the interaction between genes, the epigenome, and the environment (Caspi et al., 2003). While the genome itself cannot be altered, and the basic structure of the epigenome is not directly modifiable, the environment can be changed. Psychotherapy, at its heart, seeks precisely this transformation: to reshape the lived environment—internal and external—so that it alters epigenetic markers and patterns of genetic expression (Popescu, 2021; Popescu & Viscu, 2016). In other words, psychotherapy works not only with thoughts, emotions, and relationships, but indirectly also with biology.

All human qualities are ultimately the result of the expression of a message contained within a single molecule: DNA (deoxyribonucleic acid). DNA is an information-containing polymer that encodes data about our mind and body, including approximately 25,000 protein-coding regions (Lander et al., 2001). Remarkably, despite its chemical simplicity, DNA encodes the developmental programme for the most complex organ in the known universe: the human brain, with its estimated 10^15 synaptic connections. The genome thus constitutes the basal layer of the self, grounding the proto-self and sustaining the biological substrate upon which more complex layers are built (Ebstein et.al., 2012).

This is consistent with the structure of the self in ISP. The proto-self—the most basic layer of human existence—is directly rooted in genetic and molecular processes. The genome defines cellular functions, neuronal wiring, and the rhythms of metabolic life. From this basal layer emerge the higher levels: the core self, which integrates bodily experience with cognition and emotion; the plastic self, which adapts and transforms through development; and the external self, which connects to others and to the cultural-symbolic world. Thus, the genome represents both the beginning of selfhood and a continuous presence throughout life.

The human genome is structured at several levels: 1. DNA – the chemical substance, a double helix of paired nucleotides (adenine, cytosine, guanine, thymine); 2. Genes – specific sequences of nucleotides carrying instructions for protein synthesis; and 3. Chromosomes – long strands of DNA bundled into 23 pairs (22 autosomes, one pair of sex chromosomes) (Meyer-Lindenberg et.al., 2006).

The genome determines how an organism develops, survives, and behaves in its environment. The genotype, representing the entirety of genetic material, forms the foundation of the proto self. It carries inherited instructions, much like an ancestral manuscript, and provides the framework for both the continuity and the uniqueness of the individual.

Disruptions in this genetic manuscript—chromosomal aberrations such as aneuploidy or deletions—may give rise to conditions such as Down syndrome, Edwards syndrome, Turner syndrome, and others (Goldman, 2012). However, these "simple transmission" diseases are only the visible part of a much larger biological iceberg. Most human variability in psychological functioning arises not from single-gene errors but from the complex interplay of thousands of genetic variants, each exerting subtle effects.

Each person inherits two sets of genes, one from each parent, resulting in a unique combination that guides both physical and psychological development. Genes influence not only visible traits (eye colour, hair type) but also the architecture of the nervous system. They determine how neurons grow, migrate, and form synapses, providing a pre-programmed yet flexible scaffold for experience-dependent brain development (Spector, 2012).

Genes therefore play two central roles (Siegel, 2012): 1. Transmission – passing information across generations; and 2. Transcription – regulating which proteins are synthesised in the organism, at what time, and under what conditions.

This dual function highlights a paradox central to ISP: the genome is both stable and responsive. It anchors the continuity of identity across generations while remaining open to modification through experience. For the developing brain, experiences directly influence how genes are expressed, how neurons connect, and which synaptic pathways are strengthened or weakened. As Doidge (2007) has shown, experience is constantly writing and rewriting neural maps—an insight that underlines psychotherapy's capacity to reshape biology.

While genes provide the instructions, the epigenome determines when and how these instructions are executed. Epigenetic mechanisms such as DNA methylation and histone modification act as switches, turning genes "on" or "off" depending on environmental conditions (Meaney, 2010). Stress, trauma, attachment relationships, and even psychotherapy can leave epigenetic marks that influence brain function and behaviour across the lifespan.

Here we see the therapeutic significance of the genome within ISP. Psychotherapy, by altering the client's lived relational environment, has the potential to modify epigenetic expression and hence to influence neural plasticity. This links the psychological level of the self (cognitive, emotional, psychodynamic axes) directly with the biological level, providing a unifying model: the genome underlies the proto-self, while psychotherapy provides corrective experiences that reverberate down to molecular levels.

The genome does not operate in isolation; it resonates with the three axes of the psychological level in ISP: 1. The cognitive axis: Genetic variation influences attention, memory, and executive functions. For instance, variants in the COMT gene affect dopamine metabolism in the prefrontal cortex, impacting working memory and cognitive flexibility (Meyer-Lindenberg et al., 2006); 2. The emotional axis: Polymorphisms in the serotonin transporter gene (5-HTTLPR) are associated with emotional reactivity and vulnerability to depression in stressful environments (Caspi et al., 2003; Karg et al., 2011); and 3. The psychodynamic axis: Genetic factors shape temperamental predispositions that influence attachment patterns, relational styles, and unconscious dynamics. For example, genes regulating oxytocin and vasopressin receptors have been linked to affiliative behaviour and bonding (Ebstein et al., 2012).

Thus, the genome provides biological scaffolding upon which psychological processes unfold, but its effects are always filtered through experience and meaning-making.

The genome also anchors individuals within a broader transgenerational narrative. Each of us embodies genetic material inherited from ancestors, transmitting it onwards to future generations. This continuity mirrors the extended external self in ISP, which situates the person in a web of historical, cultural, and familial connections. The genome is therefore not only a molecular code but also a symbolic bridge between past, present, and future.

Psychotherapeutically, engaging with the client's awareness of family history—including genetic illnesses or strengths—can open dialogues about resilience, legacy, and meaning. A family history of vulnerability may also carry hidden resources, such as creativity or adaptability, transmitted genetically or relationally (Plomin & von Stumm, 2018).

In clinical practice, understanding the genome invites psychotherapists to hold a dual awareness: 1. Respect for biological constraints – recognising that some aspects of temperament, vulnerability, or resilience are genetically influenced; and 2. Commitment to plasticity and transformation – knowing that environmental changes, including the therapeutic relationship, can modulate genetic expression through epigenetic mechanisms.

In this sense, ISP integrates acceptance (of biological givens) and agency (capacity for change). The genome provides the proto-self with its grounding, but psychotherapy enables the core, plastic, and external selves to engage with this biological script in flexible, creative, and healing ways.

6.1.2. The Epigenome

Genes exist in every cell of the human body, but they are not expressed uniformly. A liver cell, a skin cell, and a neuron all carry the same genome, yet their identities differ because of differences in gene expression. What determines these differences is not the genome itself but a set of regulatory instructions known as the epigenome (Craig & Wong, 2011). Gene expression therefore refers to the presence of genetic information for a potential trait, while the epigenome decides whether and how that trait is manifested (Carey, 2011).

The epigenome can be understood as a molecular "switchboard" that responds dynamically to environmental input. Unlike the relatively stable sequence of DNA, the epigenome is highly plastic and sensitive to both internal and external influences—including interpersonal relationships, stress, trauma, nutrition, attachment, and even psychotherapy. In Integrative Strategic Psychotherapy (ISP), the epigenome represents the most direct bridge between the biological level of the self and the psychological and relational levels, shaping how inherited dispositions are either actualised or silenced.

In ISP, the self develops through the interaction of the proto-self (biological foundation), the core self (integration of bodily, cognitive and emotional processes), the plastic self (developmental and adaptive capacities), and the external self (relational, social, and cultural dimensions).

At the proto-self level, epigenetic processes regulate basic cellular functioning, neurodevelopment, and physiological rhythms. For example, maternal stress during pregnancy can epigenetically modify foetal glucocorticoid receptor genes, influencing stress reactivity throughout life (Meaney & Szyf, 2005). At the core self level, the epigenome integrates early attachment experiences. Positive caregiving activates protective gene expression that strengthens stress resilience; neglect or abuse can silence these same genes, leaving the child more vulnerable to anxiety or depression. At the plastic self level, the epigenome allows flexibility. Adolescence, with its neurodevelopmental pruning and hormonal surges, is a prime example of epigenetic recalibration of neural circuits (Goldman, 2012). This flexibility explains why psychotherapy and other learning experiences can induce long-lasting epigenetic change. At the external self level, social interactions and cultural contexts become embodied through epigenetic regulation. Trauma transmitted across generations in communities (e.g., descendants of Holocaust survivors; Yehuda et al., 2016) illustrates how the relational environment can epigenetically programme vulnerability or resilience. In sum, the epigenome "writes" the lived environment into biology, allowing the relational and cultural matrix to shape the biological self.

For much of the 20th century, diseases were seen as either genetic or environmental in origin. Epigenetics demonstrates that these categories are deeply intertwined (Ayyanathan, 2014). Many disorders, including psychological ones, have epigenetic origins. Autism, for example, has been associated with mutations in synaptic genes, but increasing evidence shows that synaptogenesis is epigenetically regulated. Stress, infections, or toxins during pregnancy can alter gene expression without changing DNA sequence, leading to altered synaptic development (Qureshi & Mehler, 2014). Similarly, early maternal separation in rodents produces epigenetic changes in glucocorticoid receptor genes in the hippocampus. These alterations persist into adulthood, shaping stress reactivity and behavioural patterns (Meaney, 2010). Human parallels include how childhood maltreatment leads to lasting epigenetic marks on genes regulating the hypothalamic–pituitary–adrenal (HPA) axis, increasing vulnerability to depression or PTSD (McGowan et al., 2009). From an ISP perspective, this evidence underscores the strategic role of psychotherapy: interventions can create corrective relational environments that reverse maladaptive epigenetic regulation, promoting healing and resilience.

Even genetically identical twins diverge at multiple levels due to stochastic developmental processes and epigenetic variation (Goldman, 2012). These differences accumulate across the lifespan, explaining why twins often display different temperaments, personalities, and susceptibilities to illness despite identical DNA. This randomness, however, does not negate free will. On the contrary, because gene expression is epigenetically regulated by environment and experience, individuals retain capacity for agency (Spector, 2012). ISP emphasises this paradox: the self is simultaneously rooted in biological givens and open to transformation through relational and symbolic environments. The proto-self provides the groundwork, but the central and plastic selves are continuously sculpted by epigenetic processes.

On the cognitive axis, learning alters gene expression. Studies show that memory consolidation requires epigenetic modifications (Day & Sweatt, 2011). For instance, histone acetylation is necessary for long-term memory formation. This means that every cognitive act leaves a biological trace.

On the emotional axis, emotional experiences, particularly attachment and trauma, exert epigenetic influence on genes regulating oxytocin, serotonin, and stress hormones. Such epigenetic regulation explains why early emotional deprivation may predispose to affective disorders later in life.

On the psychodynamic axis: Epigenetics provides a biological correlate for unconscious processes. Repressed trauma, for example, may remain encoded not only in procedural memory but also in epigenetic patterns, influencing behaviour and transference dynamics in therapy.

In ISP, integrating these axes into an epigenetic framework reinforces the idea that psychotherapy reshapes not only narratives and emotions but also the underlying biological machinery that sustains them.

Epigenetics also reveals that behaviour itself shapes biology. Howe & Lewis (2005) argue that mind development is recursive: what we present to the world influences what the world presents back to us. For example, a child who cries frequently may elicit soothing responses, reinforcing both the behaviour and its underlying neural pathways. Conversely, if the environment responds with neglect, different epigenetic pathways may be strengthened, predisposing to dysregulation. Thus, behaviour modifies gene expression, which in turn shapes neural connections and behaviour—a circular process at the heart of ISP. The plastic self is where this recursive loop is most visible: therapy aims to break maladaptive cycles and initiate new, healthier epigenetic trajectories.

Adolescence is a period of intense synaptic pruning and neural reorganisation. During this window, the brain is highly plastic but also vulnerable. Epigenetic regulation determines which synapses are retained or eliminated, potentially unmasking latent vulnerabilities (Goldman, 2012). This explains why many psychiatric disorders, from schizophrenia to bipolar disorder, emerge during adolescence: the pruning process interacts with inherited vulnerabilities and epigenetic regulation. Therapeutically, this highlights adolescence as a critical period for intervention. ISP interventions targeting relational patterns, stress regulation, and identity formation can alter epigenetic trajectories before vulnerabilities crystallise into pathology.

But one of the most profound findings in modern biology is that epigenetic markers can be inherited. Contrary to the long-held belief that acquired traits cannot be transmitted, we now know that stress, trauma, and even nutritional deprivation can leave epigenetic marks passed to subsequent generations (Ayyanathan, 2014; Heard & Martienssen, 2014). For example, studies of Holocaust survivors' children show altered cortisol regulation linked to inherited epigenetic changes (Yehuda et al., 2016). Similarly, famine exposure during the Dutch Hunger Winter of 1944–1945 produced epigenetic alterations detectable in descendants decades later (Heijmans et al., 2008). This has significant implications for ISP: transgenerational trauma is not only a psychological narrative but also a biological legacy. Yet, because epigenetic modifications are reversible, psychotherapy can play a reparative role, interrupting cycles of inherited vulnerability and enabling new narratives and new biology.

If our genes and epigenome shape who we are, do we still have free will? ISP responds affirmatively, grounding its optimism in the plasticity of the epigenome. Experiences, especially corrective relational experiences in therapy, can re-programme gene expression. Thus, while the proto-self is anchored in biology, the plastic and external selves offer genuine avenues for freedom. Psychotherapy becomes an act of strategic rewriting—helping clients re-author not only their stories but also their biology. This dual transformation exemplifies the integrative essence of ISP: biology and meaning, gene and narrative, intertwined in the self's unfolding.

6.1.3. The Phenotype

The phenotype represents the "external" expression of the genotype, the observable set of characteristics shaped by the interaction of the genome, the epigenome, and environmental factors. It encompasses everything from physical features such as eye colour, height, or susceptibility to certain illnesses, to complex psychological traits and even the likelihood of developing mental health conditions (Popescu, 2021; Popescu & Vîşcu, 2016).

In other words, what occurs at the unseen molecular level—in DNA sequences and epigenetic regulation—emerges at the level of the self as phenotype. For psychotherapists, the phenotype is significant because it provides observable signs from which inferences can be made about the individual's biological predispositions, vulnerabilities, and resources.

The phenotype is more than an outcome of genetic instructions; it is an active interface between biology and environment. For instance, a child may inherit genes associated with heightened emotional reactivity. Whether this becomes a trait of resilience (sensitivity to positive environments) or a vulnerability (risk for anxiety disorders) depends on the epigenetic regulation of those genes and the relational context in which the child develops (Belsky & Pluess, 2009).

Thus, the phenotype reflects not only inherited potential but also the lived history of the self. This aligns with ISP's model of the proto-self (biological grounding), core self (emotional and cognitive integration), plastic self (adaptive development), and external self (relational expression). The phenotype is visible at all these levels: 1. Proto-self: motor reflexes, physiological reactivity, and temperament; 2. Core self: emotional expression, regulation capacity, embodied gestures; 3. Plastic self: adaptive behaviours, developmental achievements, and vulnerabilities; and 4. External self: relational patterns, attachment behaviours, symbolic self-presentation.

In this sense, the phenotype functions as the embodied biography of the self: a record of the genome's script, epigenetic regulation, and relational experiences.

At the biological level, the phenotype includes visible traits such as facial morphology, skin tone, and metabolic tendencies, as well as less obvious physiological characteristics like immune system functioning or hormonal profiles. In medicine, phenotypic markers help identify syndromes or predispositions to disease. In psychotherapy, somatic presentations—such as chronic tension, posture, voice tone, or psychosomatic symptoms—can also be understood as part of the phenotypic expression of the self. For example, genetic variations in the dopamine system may predispose individuals to impulsivity, but it is through their phenotypic manifestation—behaviours such as risk-taking or attentional instability—that clinicians can recognise these predispositions (Montag & Reuter, 2014).

The phenotype extends to psychological traits, encompassing personality, cognitive capacities, and affective styles. These observable patterns arise from the interplay of genetic predispositions, epigenetic regulation, and lived experience.

At the level of cognitive axis, phenotypic expression can be seen in intellectual functioning, attentional patterns, or memory styles. For example, individuals with the APOE ε4 allele show phenotypic differences in memory performance decades before the onset of Alzheimer's disease (Caselli et al., 2009). On the emotional axis, emotional reactivity, regulation, and resilience are part of the phenotypic profile. A child who consistently displays withdrawal or hypervigilance in response to stress may be expressing an underlying genetic vulnerability combined with environmental reinforcement. On the level of psychodynamic axis, defence mechanisms, relational patterns, and unconscious enactments are all visible expressions of deeper genetic–epigenetic–environmental dynamics. For instance, avoidant attachment behaviours can be seen as phenotypic strategies arising from both inherited temperament and early relational epigenetic programming. Phenotype thus offers psychotherapy a visible window into otherwise hidden processes.

At the relational level, the phenotype is expressed in interpersonal styles, communication patterns, and cultural participation. This includes: 1. Attachment behaviours: proximity seeking, avoidance, ambivalence—patterns observable in psychotherapy; 2. Social traits: introversion vs. extraversion, empathy, aggressiveness; and 3. Cultural expression: language, rituals, symbolic self-presentation. For ISP, the phenotype is not simply an individual characteristic but part of a dialogical field: it interacts with others, evoking responses that further reinforce or transform the individual's developmental trajectory.

In psychotherapy, clinicians continuously "read" the phenotype: body language, affective tone, cognitive style, and relational patterns. These observable expressions provide clues about underlying vulnerabilities and resources. For instance, a rigid posture and flattened affect may suggest epigenetically reinforced stress regulation difficulties. High emotional sensitivity, though sometimes a vulnerability, may also indicate potential for deep empathy and creativity. Thus, the phenotype is not only a diagnostic clue but also a psychotherapeutic resource. ISP emphasises working with the whole visible self—embracing vulnerabilities as entry points for transformation.

Phenotypic traits are not static. They evolve over time as epigenetic regulation responds to experience. Adolescence, for instance, often reveals latent vulnerabilities (e.g., schizophrenia, mood disorders) through phenotypic changes in behaviour and cognition. Conversely, protective environments can redirect trajectories, allowing initially vulnerable phenotypes to flourish. In this sense, the phenotype is dynamic: a moving picture of the ongoing dialogue between genes, environment, and self.

Phenotypes carry transgenerational echoes. A family may "recognise" inherited traits—eye colour, temperament, or even relational patterns—as part of a lineage. Epigenetic inheritance reinforces this, as trauma, stress, or resilience can be passed down phenotypically (Yehuda et al., 2016). For ISP, this resonates with the extended self: the individual is not an isolated organism but part of a generational chain. Phenotypic patterns become part of family narratives and life scripts, shaping identity and relational dynamics.

Although the phenotype reflects genetic and epigenetic influences, it is not destiny. The visible traits of the self can change. Psychotherapy, new relationships, or cultural shifts can reconfigure phenotypic expression, especially at the psychological and relational levels. This reflects ISP's core principle: strategic intervention at the environmental level can re-shape biology's expression in the self.

Strategic clinical applications include: 1. Observation as diagnosis: Therapists attend closely to observable phenotypic markers—posture, tone, affect, relational style—as indicators of deeper processes; 2. Phenotype as narrative: Clients often describe themselves in phenotypic terms ("I've always been shy," "I have my father's temper"). Psychotherapy helps integrate these traits into a coherent identity; and 3. Phenotypic flexibility: By reshaping relational environments, therapy can alter phenotypic expression (e.g., anxiety manifesting as avoidance can, over time, become expressed as assertiveness).

In sum, the phenotype is the visible theatre of the self. It is where the unseen molecular dramas of the genome and epigenome take form, where relational histories become embodied, and where therapeutic transformation can be witnessed.

6.1.4. Genetic Vulnerability and Resilience

Vulnerability refers to the predisposition or susceptibility of individuals to illness or maladaptive development when faced with adverse experiences. Resilience refers to positive adaptation demonstrated in response to negative or threatening experiences (Popescu, 2021; Popescu & Vîşcu, 2016).

Both vulnerability and resilience arise at the intersection of the genome, the epigenome, the environment, and the lived experience of the self. Some vulnerabilities are apparent from birth, rooted in genetic mutations or inherited predispositions, while others emerge over time, shaped by developmental experiences, attachment histories, and environmental exposures (Lander et.al., 2001). Crucially, vulnerability is probabilistic, not deterministic: having a genetic susceptibility does not guarantee pathology, but rather increases the likelihood of difficulties if risk factors are present. Resilience, on the other hand, represents the consistent demonstration of adaptive capacity under stress, often supported by protective relationships and environments (Karg et.al., 2011).

From an ISP perspective, vulnerability and resilience are not merely medical categories but dimensions of the self's developmental pathways. The proto-self encodes genetic vulnerabilities, the core self integrates resilience through emotional atonement, the plastic self adapts or falters depending on developmental support, and the external self either amplifies or mitigates vulnerability through relational environments.

Some vulnerabilities are hardwired from birth, reflecting specific genetic variations. A classic example is phenylketonuria (PKU), caused by a defect in a recessive gene responsible for breaking down phenylalanine. Without dietary intervention, exposure to phenylalanine leads to intellectual disability. However, by altering the environment—removing phenylalanine from the diet—the genetic vulnerability does not manifest in pathological form (McCartney & Phillips, 2008). This illustrates a central ISP principle: while the genome cannot be altered, the expression of vulnerability is profoundly shaped by environment.

Other vulnerabilities are more subtle, involving polygenic influences. For example, variations in genes regulating serotonin and dopamine function are associated with increased sensitivity to stress and risk of mood disorders (Caspi et al., 2003). Yet, these vulnerabilities do not guarantee illness. They highlight conditional probabilities: under negative environments, they increase risk, but under supportive environments, they may confer advantages such as greater empathy or creativity.

Vulnerability is not fixed across the lifespan. Certain developmental windows—such as early childhood, school entry, or puberty—are periods of heightened susceptibility. During these times, the brain undergoes rapid reorganisation, making it more responsive to environmental input but also more fragile (Andersen & Teicher, 2008).

In early childhood, the child-parent system determines vulnerability. Because infants and toddlers cannot fully self-regulate, they depend on caregivers for co-regulation. If caregivers are inconsistent, fearful, or chaotic, children develop increased vulnerability to stress (Sroufe, Carlson, Levy, & Egeland, 1999). During school entry, peer dynamics and academic challenges create new vulnerabilities. Children with insecure attachment histories may struggle to adapt, leading to phenotypic expressions of anxiety or withdrawal. Adolescence introduces biological vulnerabilities via hormonal surges and neural pruning. Latent genetic risks, such as those associated with schizophrenia, may manifest during this period (Goldman, 2012).

From an ISP standpoint, these windows correspond to moments when the plastic self is under greatest tension—pulled between inherited vulnerabilities and relational scaffolding.

But not all vulnerabilities originate in genes. Experiential vulnerabilities emerge from adverse relational environments. For example, chronic neglect can epigenetically dysregulate the HPA axis, creating life-long vulnerability to stress (McGowan et al., 2009). Exposure to parental depression or anxiety can increase children's vulnerability, both biologically (through prenatal stress effects) and relationally (through modelling maladaptive regulation). Social marginalisation, poverty, or cultural discrimination also contribute to vulnerability, underscoring that the external self is always embedded in broader systems.

On the other hand, resilience is more than the absence of vulnerability. It is an active, adaptive capacity to respond positively to adversity. Unlike vulnerability, which is probabilistic, resilience tends to manifest consistently when protective factors are present (Masten, 2014). The foundations of resilience lie in: 1. Secure attachment: Children rely on parental signals to evaluate safety. Facial expressions, tone of voice, and responsiveness provide regulatory cues (Hornik & Gunnar, 1988). Secure attachment equips children with emotional tools to withstand stress; 2. Supportive environments: Warm, predictable family relationships serve as protective mechanisms, enhancing resilience across the lifespan (Graber, 2015); 3. Cognitive flexibility and problem-solving skills: These are phenotypic expressions of resilience, supported by both genetic and environmental factors (Luthar, Sawyer, & Brown, 2006); and 4. Community and cultural resources: Social belonging, cultural narratives, and collective rituals foster resilience, demonstrating that the external self plays a crucial role.

In Integrative Strategic Psychotherapy, vulnerability and resilience are viewed not as fixed traits but as dynamic potentials. The psychotherapist's task is to identify vulnerabilities—biological, psychological, or relational—while simultaneously mobilising resilience. At the biological level, psychotherapy acknowledges genetic predispositions but focuses on modifiable pathways (diet, stress regulation, epigenetic plasticity). At the psychological level, interventions target the three axes: cognitive (challenging maladaptive beliefs), emotional (enhancing regulation), and psychodynamic (resolving unconscious patterns). At the relational level, psychotherapy strengthens the external self through corrective attachment experiences and supportive social connections. This strategic integration ensures that vulnerabilities are not seen as deterministic flaws but as areas where resilience can be activated.

A child diagnosed with PKU exemplifies biological vulnerability. Through environmental modification (diet), the vulnerability does not manifest pathologically. Psychotherapy echoes this principle by reshaping environments to prevent maladaptive trajectories. A child raised with inconsistent caregiving develops vulnerability to anxiety. In psychotherapy, the provision of a secure therapeutic relationship acts as a corrective environment, fostering resilience. An adolescent genetically predisposed to schizophrenia may show early phenotypic markers (withdrawal, odd thinking). Strategic interventions at the plastic self level—fostering support, reducing stress, enhancing regulation—may delay or even prevent full manifestation.

Vulnerability and resilience across the self's components are as follows:

- Proto-self: Encodes vulnerabilities at the genetic and biological level;
- Core self: Expresses resilience through early emotional regulation and atonement;
- Plastic self: Balances vulnerability and resilience across developmental transitions; and
- External self: Embodies resilience or exacerbates vulnerability through relational and cultural environments.

Thus, the dialectic between vulnerability and resilience is woven throughout the structure of the self. Vulnerability and resilience represent two sides of the same developmental coin. Both are shaped by the genome, epigenome, environment, and lived experience. Vulnerability is probabilistic, requiring triggers to manifest, while resilience is an active, adaptive response. From an ISP perspective, psychotherapy functions as a protective environment, capable of reducing vulnerability, enhancing resilience, and reshaping developmental trajectories at every level of the self.

6.2. The Role of Genetics in Psychotherapy Practice

Brain development depends on multiple layers of interaction: between genes themselves, between the genome and the epigenome, and between the epigenome and the environment. These interactions shape the connectivity of more than 100 billion neurons. Each neuron forms thousands of synaptic connections, and collectively the human brain contains over 100 trillion neural links. Moreover, neuronal communication is highly complex, as each neuron employs around 100 neurotransmitters, and each neurotransmitter can interact with several receptor subtypes. For example, serotonin is known to act through at least 14 receptor subtypes (Hyman, 2000).

Neurotransmitter receptors initiate the transmission of electrical impulses within neurons, and each synapse is embedded within broader neural circuits. The mental patterns discussed in the previous chapter are activated through these circuits. Importantly, the configuration of these circuits is influenced by genetic heritage, and modifications in their organisation result in behavioural changes. The pathogenesis of conditions such as addictive disorders or post-traumatic stress disorder (PTSD), for instance, stems from alterations in normal learning processes within circuits responsible for encoding fear and reward (Berke, 2000).

Understanding complex pathologies such as schizophrenia requires an appreciation of both their genetic configuration and the epigenetic processes that may be disrupted or altered. Genetic factors contribute to the emergence of all mental disorders, shaping either resilience or vulnerability. Research consistently shows that many psychiatric conditions—including schizophrenia, autism spectrum disorder, bipolar disorder, major depression, ADHD, and panic disorder—demonstrate familial aggregation, suggesting a genetic contribution to risk (Hyman, 2000).

Genes play a central role in the development and stabilisation of synaptic structures in the brain. Variations in DNA sequences can result in altered protein expression, which may be either adaptive or harmful to neuronal function. However, genetic risk is inherently complex and non-linear. As Barondes (1999) points out, interactions between genes are not simply additive. The activity of one gene may depend on the activity of another—a phenomenon referred to as epistasis. Moreover, genes never act in isolation; they must interact with environmental inputs for a disorder to manifest.

This has important clinical implications. Novice psychotherapists may prematurely assume that if a client has a family history of schizophrenia, then they must also carry the same diagnosis—even when the client's presentation does not meet DSM-5 criteria. The presence of a genetically linked disorder within a family does not guarantee transmission, and the specific symptoms of the client must always be carefully evaluated.

Indeed, no mental disorder shows 100% concordance in monozygotic twins, underscoring the complexity of transmission. Most psychiatric disorders involve polygenic risk factors and environmental contributions rather than single-gene inheritance. Monogenic disorders with psychiatric features are extremely rare, though examples include Rett syndrome, which presents with autism-like symptoms, and early-onset Alzheimer's disease (Hyman, 2000).

Nevertheless, knowledge of a client's family and personal history remains clinically valuable. Patterns of comorbidity—such as the frequent co-occurrence of depression and anxiety, or tics and obsessive-compulsive disorder—can guide therapeutic exploration. However, the predictive value of genetic tests is limited, because environmental influences mediated by the epigenome play a dominant role in determining whether genetic risks are expressed.

Stressful environments, particularly in early childhood, can induce lasting epigenetic programming of the stress response system. Such programming may heighten vulnerability by producing exaggerated physiological reactions even to mild stressors (Klengel & Binder, 2015). Through these mechanisms, stress reshapes gene regulation over the long term. For example, post-traumatic stress disorder (PTSD) appears predominantly in individuals with elevated methylation of the enzyme DNMT3B, a process influenced by genetic patterns that are themselves activated by early traumatic experiences (Klengel & Binder, 2015).

Maternal care is one of the most influential factors in shaping epigenetic regulation, with significant consequences for stress reactivity and development. Research shows that the quality of maternal caregiving alters the expression of messenger RNA and the functioning of the hypothalamic–pituitary–adrenal (HPA) axis. Activation of specific mRNA pathways influences gene regulation, thereby modifying both endocrine and behavioural responses to stress. For example, early maternal separation has been shown to trigger genetic responses in newborns and young children. Current evidence suggests that such effects may be mitigated if compensatory "over-caring" occurs before epigenetic memory becomes fully established (Klengel & Binder, 2015).

The impact of early stress depends on several factors: the intensity of stress, the timing of exposure, and the type of stress encountered. Epigenetic responses are not static across the lifespan. Separation from the mother may have profound consequences for an infant but may register only as a minor inconvenience—or even as a positive experience—for an adult (Klengel & Binder, 2015). From the prenatal period through adolescence, individuals construct neural circuits that underlie complex behaviours, as well as pathways governing immune and hormonal regulation. These systems are epigenetically tuned during development and shape stress reactivity in adulthood.

Socioeconomic conditions during childhood also exert powerful influences on the epigenome. Children raised in environments of poverty or chronic social stress show altered epigenetic profiles, which in turn affect both health and psychological outcomes (Lam et al., 2012).

Moreover, maternal stress during pregnancy has been demonstrated to epigenetically programme the foetus, creating long-term vulnerability to stress regulation difficulties (Oberlander et al., 2008). Intriguingly, stress experienced by parents even prior to conception can also be transmitted to offspring via epigenetic pathways, as shown in studies of intergenerational trauma (Dias & Ressler, 2014).

From a psychotherapeutic perspective, this evidence suggests that when evaluating the biological level of the self in case formulation, traumatic experiences of the child may be more significant than a family history of illness. Clinicians should ask: What was the mother's health and stress level during pregnancy? Did parents experience major trauma or chronic stress before conception? What stressful events marked the client's early years? What was the family's socioeconomic status during childhood?

The answers to such questions provide critical insights into a client's vulnerability to stress and guide intervention strategies. Importantly, cognitive or emotional processing alone may be insufficient when addressing early or transgenerational trauma. In these cases, non-verbal therapeutic approaches—such as body-focused techniques, attention to somatic sensations, or guided imagery—may provide more direct access to the proto self, where these early imprints are held.

6.3. Body Schema

The body schema is an innate and fundamental component of human development, existing alongside genetic inheritance and emerging early in life. It relies on information processing across both the central and peripheral nervous systems (Botvinik & Cohen, 1998). Although infants in the first months of life do not yet differentiate clearly between self and environment, the body schema is present from birth, as body movements occur without requiring explicit cognitive processing. This innate capacity enables the child to gradually build a sense of embodiment and agency (Carlson et. Al., 2010).

Perception of one's own body is essential for interaction with the environment. In everyday life, it seems effortless to know where our limbs are in space and to control them fluidly. Yet this "normal" capacity is the result of highly complex processes in which specialised neurons integrate visual, tactile, and proprioceptive information (Maravita, Spence, & Driver, 2003).

In conceptual terms, the body schema is a representation of the spatial properties of the body, encompassing limb size and arrangement, the configuration of body segments, and the shape of the body's surface (Popescu, 2021; Popescu & Vîșcu, 2016). As a postural model, the body schema tracks the positions of limbs and guides the planning and execution of action. This model is typically unconscious, continuously updated, and indispensable for spatial organisation and motor control (Carlson et al., 2010).

Holmes and Spence (2004) identified seven fundamental properties of the body schema. These offer a useful framework for connecting neuroscience with ISP:

1. Spatial coding – The body schema encodes the body's position and three-dimensional configuration. This capacity results from integrating sensory signals, especially tactile and visual inputs. Spatial coding provides the biological substrate for the proto-self, allowing the infant to orient within space. Clinically, deficits in spatial coding (e.g., body neglect in stroke patients) disrupt self-experience, illustrating the deep link between embodiment and psychological identity;

2. Modularity – The body schema is distributed across different brain regions. For example, the cortical maps for the hands and legs are distinct, and even individual fingers are represented in separate somatosensory areas. This modularity resonates with ISP's axes of the self, suggesting that specific vulnerabilities or strengths in embodiment can influence particular cognitive, emotional, or psychodynamic processes. For instance, fine motor coordination deficits may affect self-confidence (cognitive axis), while distortions in bodily self-perception (as in eating disorders) can destabilise emotional regulation;

3. Adaptability – The body schema changes dynamically throughout life, accommodating growth, injury, or the use of tools. This adaptability provides the neurobiological foundation of the plastic self in ISP. Just as a child's schema expands to incorporate longer limbs, so psychotherapy can help reshape embodied experience to accommodate new psychological realities. Tool use research demonstrates this adaptability: holding a tennis racket or driving a car temporarily expands the body schema to include external objects (Maravita & Iriki, 2004);

4. Supra-modality – The body schema integrates information across sensory modalities. Proprioceptive, tactile, and visual inputs converge into a unified representation, creating an abstract, amodal sense of body position. This supra-modality echoes the integrative principle of ISP, where multiple levels of self (biological, psychological, relational) are synthesised into a coherent whole. Clinically, disruptions of supra-modality are seen in depersonalisation, where patients report a fragmented sense of embodiment;

5. Coherence – The body schema must resolve conflicts between sensory inputs to maintain a stable representation. For instance, in the "rubber hand illusion," incongruent visual and tactile inputs are reconciled by temporarily incorporating

the rubber hand into the schema (Botvinick & Cohen, 1998). Coherence thus underpins the core self, maintaining continuity of bodily identity despite environmental fluctuations. In psychotherapy, restoring coherence between bodily sensations and cognitive narratives can be central in trauma recovery;

6. Interpersonal dimension – The body schema not only represents one's own body but also enables the perception of others' bodies. Mirror neurons contribute to this interpersonal projection, allowing imitation and empathy (Rizzolatti & Sinigaglia, 2010). The interpersonal body schema is vital for the external self, enabling relational atonement and embodied resonance with others. In ISP, working with bodily synchrony in the therapeutic relationship (e.g., matching breathing rhythms) can activate this interpersonal schema, deepening atonement; and

7. Dynamic modification during movement – The body schema is not static; it constantly updates during action. It monitors and predicts the trajectory of movements, correcting deviations in real time. This dynamic updating allows intentionality and goal-directed behaviour, linking embodiment with the cognitive axis (anticipation), the emotional axis (regulation during action), and the psychodynamic axis (expression of unconscious impulses through movement).

At a biological level, the body schema provides neural architecture, integrating multisensory input and motor control. At a psychological level, it shapes self-awareness, agency, and identity. Distortions of the schema (e.g., in phantom limb syndrome or body dysmorphic disorder) impact all three psychological axes. At a relational level, it allows embodied interaction with others. Non-verbal communication, imitation, and empathy rely on the interpersonal extension of the body schema.

The body schema has correlates in each of the components of the self. The proto-self represents the biological ground of human existence, encompassing innate physiological processes and the basic sense of bodily existence. The body schema is a direct manifestation of the proto-self because it is innate, pre-reflective, and embodied. From the first days of life, infants can move, orient, and coordinate limbs without conscious awareness, guided by an underlying bodily map. This sensorimotor representation anchors the individual in space and provides the biological platform on which higher aspects of selfhood can emerge. When the proto-self is disrupted—for example, in neurological damage or developmental disorders—the body schema may fragment, leading to disturbances in the most fundamental sense of being.

The core self emerges as the proto-self interacts with emotional and perceptual experience, giving rise to a subjective sense of continuity. The body schema contributes by supporting embodied self-awareness: it integrates proprioceptive and interoceptive signals into a stable sense of "this is my body." Emotional experiences—joy, fear, shame—are felt in the body, and their meaning is partially mediated through bodily posture, gesture, and expression. A coherent body schema allows the person to recognise emotions as "mine" and to regulate them effectively. Conversely, disruptions in the body schema (as seen in depersonalisation or trauma) may cause a detachment between bodily sensation and self-awareness, weakening the cohesion of the core self.

The plastic self is the adaptive, developmental dimension that evolves through learning and change. The body schema's adaptability mirrors this plasticity: as the body grows or engages in new tasks (from walking to playing an instrument), the schema reorganises itself to accommodate new dimensions. Similarly, psychotherapy can help recalibrate distorted or rigid body schemas—such as those found in body dysmorphic disorder or anorexia—by reshaping the individual's embodied experience of themselves. The flexibility of the body schema thus parallels the capacity of the plastic self to modify patterns of thought, emotion, and behaviour in response to new relational and symbolic contexts.

The external self is expressed through relationships, social interactions, and cultural embodiment. The interpersonal nature of the body schema—mediated by mirror neurons and non-verbal resonance—supports imitation, empathy, and synchronisation with others. Through posture, gesture, and embodied communication, the body schema extends outward, enabling individuals to "read" others' bodies and project their own bodily states into interpersonal space. In psychotherapy, this is reflected in subtle phenomena such as postural mirroring, shared rhythms, and embodied atonement between therapist and client. Thus, the body schema becomes a relational tool, bridging the inner sense of embodiment with external social worlds.

Clinical implications of body schema in ISP are:

1. Embodiment in psychotherapy – ISP emphasises the body as a gateway to deeper layers of the self. Attending to posture, gestures, and bodily rhythms provides access to the proto-self and core self;
2. Trauma and body schema – Trauma often disrupts coherence in the body schema. Survivors may feel alienated from their bodies or experience

somatic flashbacks. ISP can help reintegrate body perception with emotional and cognitive processing;

3. Developmental disorders – Children with autism spectrum conditions often show atypical body schema functioning (e.g., difficulties with imitation or interpersonal atonement). Interventions that enhance bodily synchrony can strengthen both plastic and external selves; and
4. Expressive therapies – Movement, dance, and art therapies explicitly engage the body schema, using its adaptability to promote psychological integration.

In conclusion, the body schema is a foundational, dynamic representation of the body in space, crucial for action, identity, and relationship. It bridges biology and psychology, supporting both the individual's embodied sense of self and their relational atonement to others. In ISP, understanding and working with the body schema allows therapists to address vulnerabilities and mobilise resilience at the most fundamental level of the self.

6.4. Biological Clocks and Chronotypes

6.4.1. Biological Clocks

Biological clocks are internal mechanisms that regulate rhythms of physiology and behaviour across all living organisms. They enable humans and animals to measure time and organise bodily activities such as sleeping, waking, feeding, resting, becoming active, and reproducing. These rhythms are not merely reactive to the environment; they are endogenously generated and genetically encoded, though they remain sensitive to external cues such as light, temperature, and seasonal change (Roenneberg et al., 2007).

Biological clocks allow us to orient ourselves in time, adjusting our internal states to daily, monthly, and annual cycles. They are responsible for aligning our physiology with both immediate needs and broader environmental contexts. Importantly, they begin functioning before birth and develop progressively during infancy and childhood. By around seven months, infants begin to establish sleep–wake patterns independent of sunrise and sunset. Other rhythms, such as bladder control, consolidate around ages three to four. By young adulthood (approximately age 20), most individuals fully adapt to the 24-hour circadian cycle.

The suprachiasmatic nucleus (SCN) of the hypothalamus serves as the master clock of the brain, synchronising body rhythms with the Earth's rotation. Located above the optic chiasm, the SCN receives direct input from the retina, making light the most powerful zeitgeber (time-giver). This system ensures that circadian rhythms—such as core body temperature, cortisol secretion, and sleep–wake cycles—remain synchronised with the 24-hour day (Moore, 2013).

However, the suprachiasmatic nucleus does not function in isolation. Peripheral clocks exist in virtually every organ, from the liver to the heart, each contributing to local timing of metabolic or physiological processes (Partch, Green, & Takahashi, 2014). These clocks are orchestrated by genetic regulatory networks, involving so-called clock genes (e.g., PER, CRY, CLOCK, BMAL1) that generate rhythmic transcription and translation cycles. Alterations in clock genes have been linked to sleep disorders, metabolic conditions, and mood disturbances.

The ontogeny of biological clocks is central for understanding the proto-self. Even before birth, foetal rhythms are influenced by maternal hormonal and metabolic cycles. For example, maternal cortisol fluctuations cross the placenta, shaping foetal circadian organisation (Mirmiran, Maas, & Ariagno, 2003). As the child grows, biological rhythms provide the foundation for psychological stability. Sleep patterns, feeding schedules, and hormonal cycles all contribute to the formation of regulatory capacities in the core self. Misalignment or disruption of these rhythms during critical developmental periods may contribute to long-term vulnerabilities. For instance, irregular sleep in early childhood has been associated with attentional difficulties and emotional dysregulation later in life (Mindell & Owens, 2015).

At a biological level, circadian rhythms regulate endocrine cycles, sleep architecture, and metabolic processes—foundational elements of the proto-self. At a psychological level, cognitive performance, emotional regulation, and psychodynamic processes are all modulated by circadian variation. For example, depressive symptoms often worsen in the evening, while anxiety may peak in the morning. At a relational level, chronotypes influence social functioning. Partners with mismatched chronotypes may experience relational strain, while families synchronise daily rhythms to maintain cohesion.

Circadian rhythms are intimately linked with stress regulation. Disruptions in biological clocks—for example, through shift work, jetlag, or chronic insomnia—affect the hypothalamic–pituitary–adrenal axis and immune functioning, increasing vulnerability to depression, anxiety, and physical illness (Walker, 2017).

Recent evidence shows that circadian rhythm disruptions can induce epigenetic changes in clock gene expression, thereby perpetuating maladaptive cycles (Azzi et al., 2014). From an ISP perspective, this highlights how external factors (e.g., lifestyle, relational stress) can alter biological time at the epigenetic level, influencing both vulnerability and resilience.

In the proto-self, biological clocks sustain physiological regularity, ensuring survival functions such as sleep, feeding, and reproduction remain coherent. The proto-self thus depends on rhythmic biological cycles for stability. In the core self, regular rhythms provide predictability, which supports emotional regulation. Irregular cycles—such as disrupted sleep—are strongly associated with emotional dysregulation and psychiatric vulnerability. In the plastic self, adaptability to new time zones, developmental changes, or altered life routines demonstrates the flexibility of the plastic self. Adolescents, for instance, experience a natural shift towards later chronotypes, which must be integrated into identity and daily functioning. At the level of external self, synchronisation with social and cultural rhythms allows participation in communal life. Chronotype mismatches (e.g., night-shift workers) may lead to isolation or relational difficulties, showing how the external self is intimately tied to temporal regulation.

Biological clocks have clinical implications for ISP:

- Case formulation should include assessment of biological rhythms: sleep quality, energy fluctuations, daily mood cycles;
- Interventions may target circadian hygiene (regular sleep schedules, light exposure, reduced evening screen use);
- Expressive therapies can re-establish rhythm through music, movement, or breathing exercises, engaging both body and psyche;
- The therapeutic relationship benefits from rhythm atonement: regular session times and pacing contribute to stability and predictability, reinforcing resilience; and
- Trauma work may address how disrupted rhythms (e.g., hypervigilance at night) perpetuate stress and fragmentation of the self.

Biological clocks and chronotypes are far more than biological curiosities: they are foundational regulators of selfhood. They ensure continuity at the proto-self level, coherence at the core self, adaptability at the plastic self, and synchrony at the external self. Integrative Strategic Psychotherapy acknowledges that aligning clients' psychological rhythms with their biological timing enhances resilience, reduces vulnerability, and promotes holistic well-being.

6.4.2. The Chronotype

Although humans share a broadly similar circadian structure, individuals differ in their chronotype—their preferred timing of sleep and activity. The chronotype refers to the individual preference for the timing of daily activities, particularly sleeping and waking patterns, as well as the optimal period for cognitive and physical performance. The chronotype has a genetic basis, shaped by variations in circadian clock genes, and influences the temporal organisation of physiological functions and behaviours. Consequently, it exerts a profound effect on cognitive performance, emotional regulation, and personality traits throughout the day (Popescu, 2021; Popescu & Vîșcu, 2016).

Human circadian rhythmicity is a complex phenotype, the product of genetic predispositions interacting with environmental and social factors. Research identifies three primary circadian typologies: 1. Morning type (larks) – individuals who prefer early bedtimes and wake early, achieving peak performance in the morning; 2. Evening type (owls) – individuals who go to bed late and achieve peak performance later in the day; and 3. Intermediate type – individuals who fall somewhere between the two extremes, representing the majority of the population (Roenneberg et al., 2007; Montaruli et al., 2021).

Morning-type individuals are typically 2–4 hours "ahead" of evening types regarding circadian variables such as subjective alertness, core body temperature, and melatonin secretion. Most people (approximately 60%) belong to the intermediate category, while strong morning or evening chronotypes represent the minority. These differences have both genetic and environmental bases. Variations in clock genes influence circadian phase preference, while social demands (e.g., school start times, work schedules) can exacerbate or suppress natural chronotypes. Evening types often experience "social jetlag", a chronic misalignment between biological rhythms and societal schedules, leading to sleep deprivation, decreased performance, and greater vulnerability to mood disorders (Roenneberg, Allebrandt, Merrow, & Vetter, 2012).

The chronotype is largely determined by variations in clock genes (e.g., PER3, CLOCK, BMAL1). These genes regulate the timing of melatonin secretion, core body temperature cycles, and other circadian rhythms (Takahashi, 2017). Melatonin, produced by the pineal gland, acts as an internal synchroniser: it promotes sleep by lowering core body temperature through vasodilation, while simultaneously influencing mood and metabolism. Morning chronotypes exhibit earlier melatonin onset and peak, leading to earlier sleep times and greater alertness in the morning. Evening chronotypes show delayed melatonin secretion, which shifts their sleep–wake cycle later into the night. These biological rhythms are not only intrinsic but also shaped by environmental factors such as light exposure, lifestyle, and social schedules.

A key concept in chronotype research is the synchrony effect, which refers to the alignment between an individual's chronotype and the time of day of performance. Morning types tend to excel in the morning, while evening types perform better later in the day (Lera, Madrid, & Correa, 2014). Performance differences include:

- Response speed and accuracy: Morning types peak early, evening types later;
- Fluid intelligence: Problem-solving and creativity often align with chronotype-specific peaks; and
- Cognitive control: Evening types may be disadvantaged in early school or work schedules.

From an ISP perspective, the synchrony effect highlights the importance of temporal context in psychotherapy. Scheduling sessions at times congruent with a client's chronotype can optimise engagement and emotional openness.

The chronotype influences not only performance but also attitudes, lifestyle, and personality traits. Research suggests that morning types tend to be more conscientious, organised, and risk-averse. Evening types often score higher on openness, novelty seeking, and creativity but are also more prone to impulsivity and mood vulnerability (Katzenberg et al., 1998; Randler, 2008). These traits demonstrate how the proto-self (biological rhythms) shapes the plastic self (adaptive traits) and influences the external self (social expression).

The chronotype shifts naturally across the lifespan. Children tend to be morning types, while adolescents gravitate towards eveningness, reflecting developmental changes in melatonin secretion and circadian phase delay (Hagenauer & Lee, 2013). With ageing, individuals generally shift back towards morningness.

Gender differences are also reported: men are more likely than women to exhibit evening chronotypes, particularly in young adulthood (Montaruli et al., 2021). These differences may arise from hormonal influences, social roles, and environmental expectations.

A major challenge for evening chronotypes arises from social constraints such as early school start times or fixed work schedules. This mismatch between biological rhythms and societal demands leads to circadian desynchronisation, reduced sleep quality, and chronic fatigue (Wittmann, 2008). Evening types forced into early routines experience "social jetlag," resembling the fatigue of time-zone shifts. They often accumulate a weekly sleep debt, compensating with extended weekend sleep. Morning types generally adapt more easily to social schedules, but extreme chronotypes (morning or evening) suffer greater strain under imposed schedules.

From an ISP viewpoint, such desynchronisation illustrates how external self pressures (social schedules, cultural expectations) conflict with the biological foundations of the proto-self. This dissonance may contribute to vulnerability in mood and anxiety disorders.

The chronotype is a significant predictor of mental health outcomes. Eveningness is consistently associated with: higher rates of depression and anxiety (Au & Reece, 2017); increased risk for substance use disorders (Hasler et al., 2010); and greater impulsivity and emotional instability. Conversely, morning types often benefit from closer alignment between internal rhythms and societal norms, conferring resilience. However, this does not imply superiority; evening types often display strengths in creativity, adaptability, and divergent thinking.

In ISP, recognising a client's chronotype provides valuable insight into both vulnerability and resilience factors, shaping interventions accordingly. At the proto-self level, the chronotype originates in genetic and biological timing systems, regulating basic rhythms of sleep and energy. In the core self the chronotype influences affect regulation: misalignment often contributes to emotional dysregulation and fatigue. In the plastic self, adaptation to life's demands may require shifting rhythms, but this often comes with psychological costs. Psychotherapy can help balance adaptation with self-care. At the level of external self, the chronotype plays a role in social participation and relational atonement. Mismatches between partners' or family members' chronotypes can affect relational harmony.

Clinical implications for ISP are:

- Assessment: Exploring a client's chronotype provides insight into daily patterns of vulnerability and resilience;

- Psychoeducation: Explaining chronotype helps clients and families normalise differences and reduce guilt or conflict (e.g., parents misunderstanding adolescents' eveningness);
- Intervention: Strategies may include light therapy, sleep hygiene, or lifestyle adjustments aligned with chronotype;
- Therapeutic timing: Psychotherapists may adapt session scheduling to optimise engagement and processing; and
- Trauma and rhythm: Eveningness may interact with trauma by increasing vulnerability to intrusive memories at night. Addressing rhythm disruptions can support integration.

The chronotype represents a vital intersection of genetics, biology, psychology, and culture. It exemplifies how the proto-self sets biological rhythms, how the core self regulates energy and emotion, how the plastic self adapts across life stages, and how the external self negotiates social and cultural demands. In Integrative Strategic Psychotherapy, acknowledging chronotype enables a more nuanced, embodied, and compassionate approach to clients' struggles and strengths.

References

Adan, A., Archer, S. N., Hidalgo, M. P., Di Milia, L., Natale, V., & Randler, C. (2012). Circadian typology: A comprehensive review. *Chronobiology International, 29*(9), 1153–1175. https://doi.org/10.3109/07420528.2012.719971

Andersen, S. L., & Teicher, M. H. (2008). Stress, sensitive periods and maturational events in adolescent depression. *Trends in Neurosciences, 31*(4), 183–191. https://doi.org/10.1016/j.tins.2008.01.004

Au, J., & Reece, J. (2017). The relationship between chronotype and depressive symptoms: A meta-analysis. *Journal of Affective Disorders, 218*, 93–104. https://doi.org/10.1016/j.jad.2017.04.021

Ayyanathan, K. (2014). Epigenetic codes in development and disease. *Epigenetics, 9*(1), 7–10. https://doi.org/10.4161/epi.27089

Azzi, A., Dallmann, R., Casserly, A., Rehrauer, H., Patrignani, A., Maier, B., ... & Brown, S. A. (2014). Circadian behavior is light-reprogrammed by plastic DNA methylation. *Nature Neuroscience, 17*(3), 377–382. https://doi.org/10.1038/nn.3651

Barondes, S. H. (1999). *Mood genes: Hunting for origins of mania and depression.* Oxford University Press.

Belsky, J., & Pluess, M. (2009). The nature (and nurture?) of plasticity in early human development. *Perspectives on Psychological Science, 4*(4), 345–351. https://doi.org/10.1111/j.1745-6924.2009.01136.x

Berke, J. D. (2000). Learning and memory mechanisms involved in compulsive drug use and relapse. *Biological Psychiatry, 47*(9), 768–779. https://doi.org/10.1016/S0006-3223(00)00897-6

Botvinick, M., & Cohen, J. (1998). Rubber hands 'feel' touch that eyes see. *Nature, 391*(6669), 756. https://doi.org/10.1038/35784

Carey, N. (2011). *The epigenetics revolution: How modern biology is rewriting our understanding of genetics, disease, and inheritance.* Icon Books.

Carlson, N. R., Miller, H., Heth, D. C., Donahoe, J., & Martin, G. N. (2010). *Psychology: The science of behaviour.* Pearson.

Caspi, A., Sugden, K., Moffitt, T. E., Taylor, A., Craig, I. W., Harrington, H., ... & Poulton, R. (2003). Influence of life stress on depression: Moderation by a polymorphism in the 5-HTT gene. *Science, 301*(5631), 386–389. https://doi.org/10.1126/science.1083968

Caselli, R. J., Dueck, A. C., Osborne, D., Sabbagh, M. N., Connor, D. J., Ahern, G. L., ... & Reiman, E. M. (2009). Longitudinal modeling of age-related memory decline and the APOE ε4 effect. *New England Journal of Medicine, 361*(3), 255–263. https://doi.org/10.1056/NEJMoa0809437

Craig, J. M., & Wong, N. C. (2011). *Epigenetics: A reference manual.* Caister Academic Press.

Day, J. J., & Sweatt, J. D. (2011). Epigenetic mechanisms in cognition. *Neuron, 70*(5), 813–829. https://doi.org/10.1016/j.neuron.2011.05.019

Dias, B. G., & Ressler, K. J. (2014). Parental olfactory experience influences behaviour and neural structure in subsequent generations. *Nature Neuroscience, 17*(1), 89–96. https://doi.org/10.1038/nn.3594

Doidge, N. (2007). *The brain that changes itself: Stories of personal triumph from the frontiers of brain science.* Viking.

Ebstein, R. P., Israel, S., Chew, S. H., Zhong, S., & Knafo, A. (2012). Genetics of human social behaviour. *Neuron, 65*(6), 831–844. https://doi.org/10.1016/j.neuron.2010.02.020

Goldman, D. (2012). *Our genes, our choices: How genotype and gene interactions affect behavior.* Academic Press.

Graber, R. (2015). Protective processes in child and adolescent development. *Journal of Youth Studies, 18*(3), 355–373. https://doi.org/10.1080/13676261.2014.963539

Hasler, B. P., Sitnick, S. L., Shaw, D. S., & Forbes, E. E. (2010). Eveningness among late adolescent males predicts substance use development: A longitudinal study. *Drug and Alcohol Dependence, 111*(3), 157–162. https://doi.org/10.1016/j.drugalcdep.2010.04.008

Hagenauer, M. H., & Lee, T. M. (2013). Adolescent sleep patterns in humans and laboratory animals. *Hormones and Behavior, 64*(2), 270–279. https://doi.org/10.1016/j.yhbeh.2013.01.011

Heard, E., & Martienssen, R. A. (2014). Transgenerational epigenetic inheritance: Myths and mechanisms. *Cell, 157*(1), 95–109. https://doi.org/10.1016/j.cell.2014.02.045

Heijmans, B. T., Tobi, E. W., Stein, A. D., Putter, H., Blauw, G. J., Susser, E. S., ... & Lumey, L. H. (2008). Persistent epigenetic differences associated with prenatal exposure to famine in humans. *Proceedings of the National Academy of Sciences, 105*(44), 17046–17049. https://doi.org/10.1073/pnas.0806560105

Holmes, N. P., & Spence, C. (2004). The body schema and multisensory representation(s) of peripersonal space. *Cognitive Processing, 5*(2), 94–105. https://doi.org/10.1007/s10339-004-0013-3

Hornik, R., & Gunnar, M. (1988). A descriptive analysis of infant social referencing. *Child Development, 59*(3), 626–634. https://doi.org/10.2307/1130565

Howe, M. L., & Lewis, M. D. (2005). The importance of dynamic systems approaches for understanding development. *Developmental Review, 25*(3–4), 247–251. https://doi.org/10.1016/j.dr.2005.09.005

Hyman, S. E. (2000). The molecular foundations of psychiatry. *American Journal of Psychiatry, 157*(5), 655–672. https://doi.org/10.1176/appi.ajp.157.5.655

Karg, K., Burmeister, M., Shedden, K., & Sen, S. (2011). The serotonin transporter promoter variant (5-HTTLPR), stress, and depression meta-analysis revisited: Evidence of genetic moderation. *Archives of General Psychiatry, 68*(5), 444–454. https://doi.org/10.1001/archgenpsychiatry.2010.189

Katzenberg, D., Young, T., Finn, L., Lin, L., King, D. P., Takahashi, J. S., & Mignot, E. (1998). A CLOCK polymorphism associated with human diurnal preference. *Sleep, 21*(6), 569–576. https://doi.org/10.1093/sleep/21.6.569

Klengel, T., & Binder, E. B. (2015). Epigenetics of stress-related psychiatric disorders and gene × environment interactions. *Neuron, 86*(6), 1343–1357. https://doi.org/10.1016/j.neuron.2015.05.036

Lam, L. L., Emberly, E., Fraser, H. B., Neumann, S. M., Chen, E., Miller, G. E., & Kobor, M. S. (2012). Factors underlying variable DNA methylation in a human community cohort. *Proceedings of the National Academy of Sciences, 109*(Suppl. 2), 17253–17260. https://doi.org/10.1073/pnas.1121249109

Lander, E. S., Linton, L. M., Birren, B., Nusbaum, C., Zody, M. C., Baldwin, J., ... & Collins, F. S. (2001). Initial sequencing and analysis of the human genome. *Nature, 409*(6822), 860–921. https://doi.org/10.1038/35057062

Lera, F., Madrid, J. A., & Correa, Á. (2014). Performance on morningness–eveningness tests depends on chronotype and time of day. *Chronobiology International, 31*(8), 947–956. https://doi.org/10.3109/07420528.2014.940087

Luthar, S. S., Sawyer, J. A., & Brown, P. J. (2006). Conceptual issues in studies of resilience. *Annals of the New York Academy of Sciences, 1094*(1), 105–115. https://doi.org/10.1196/annals.1376.009

Maravita, A., & Iriki, A. (2004). Tools for the body (schema). *Trends in Cognitive Sciences, 8*(2), 79–86. https://doi.org/10.1016/j.tics.2003.12.008

Maravita, A., Spence, C., & Driver, J. (2003). Multisensory integration and the body schema: Close to hand and within reach. *Current Biology, 13*(13), R531–R539. https://doi.org/10.1016/S0960-9822(03)00449-4

Masten, A. S. (2014). Global perspectives on resilience in children and youth. *Child Development, 85*(1), 6–20. https://doi.org/10.1111/cdev.12205

McCartney, K., & Phillips, D. (2008). *Blackwell handbook of early childhood development.* Blackwell Publishing.

McGowan, P. O., Sasaki, A., D'Alessio, A. C., Dymov, S., Labonté, B., Szyf, M., ... & Meaney, M. J. (2009). Epigenetic regulation of the glucocorticoid receptor in human brain associates with childhood abuse. *Nature Neuroscience, 12*(3), 342–348. https://doi.org/10.1038/nn.2270

Meaney, M. J. (2010). Epigenetics and the biological definition of gene × environment interactions. *Child Development, 81*(1), 41–79. https://doi.org/10.1111/j.1467-8624.2009.01381.x

Meaney, M. J., & Szyf, M. (2005). Environmental programming of stress responses through DNA methylation: Life at the interface between a dynamic environment and a fixed genome. *Dialogues in Clinical Neuroscience, 7*(2), 103–123. https://doi.org/10.31887/DCNS.2005.7.2/mmeaney

Meyer-Lindenberg, A., Nichols, T., Callicott, J. H., Ding, J., Kolachana, B., Buckholtz, J., ... & Weinberger, D. R. (2006). Impact of complex genetic variation in COMT on human brain function. *Molecular Psychiatry, 11*(9), 867–877. https://doi.org/10.1038/sj.mp.4001861

Mindell, J. A., & Owens, J. A. (2015). *A clinical guide to pediatric sleep: Diagnosis and management of sleep problems.* Lippincott Williams & Wilkins.

Mirmiran, M., Maas, Y. G., & Ariagno, R. L. (2003). Development of fetal and neonatal sleep and circadian rhythms. *Sleep Medicine Reviews, 7*(4), 321–334. https://doi.org/10.1053/smrv.2002.0228

Montag, C., & Reuter, M. (2014). *Neuroeconomics: The neuroscience of decision making.* Springer.

Montaruli, A., Castelli, L., Mulè, A., Scurati, R., Esposito, F., Galasso, L., & Roveda, E. (2021). Biological rhythm and chronotype: New perspectives in health. *Frontiers in Psychology, 12*, 700600. https://doi.org/10.3389/fpsyg.2021.700600

Moore, R. Y. (2013). The suprachiasmatic nucleus and the circadian timing system. *Progress in Molecular Biology and Translational Science, 119*, 1–28. https://doi.org/10.1016/B978-0-12-396971-2.00001-4

Oberlander, T. F., Weinberg, J., Papsdorf, M., Grunau, R., Misri, S., & Devlin, A. M. (2008). Prenatal exposure to maternal depression, neonatal methylation of human glucocorticoid receptor gene (NR3C1) and infant cortisol stress responses. *Epigenetics, 3*(2), 97–106. https://doi.org/10.4161/epi.3.2.6034

Partch, C. L., Green, C. B., & Takahashi, J. S. (2014). Molecular architecture of the mammalian circadian clock. *Trends in Cell Biology, 24*(2), 90–99. https://doi.org/10.1016/j.tcb.2013.07.002

Plomin, R., & von Stumm, S. (2018). The new genetics of intelligence. *Nature Reviews Genetics, 19*(3), 148–159. https://doi.org/10.1038/nrg.2017.104

Popescu, O. M., & Vîşcu, L. (2016). *Psihoterapia integrativă strategică: Teorie și practică.* Editura Universitară.

Qureshi, I. A., & Mehler, M. F. (2014). Advances in epigenetics and epigenomics for neurodegenerative diseases. *Current Neurology and Neuroscience Reports, 14*(8), 1–10. https://doi.org/10.1007/s11910-014-0461-3

Randler, C. (2008). Morningness–eveningness comparison in adolescents from different countries around the world. *Chronobiology International, 25*(6), 1017–1028. https://doi.org/10.1080/07420520802551519

Rizzolatti, G., & Sinigaglia, C. (2010). The functional role of the parieto-frontal mirror circuit: Interpretations and misinterpretations. *Nature Reviews Neuroscience, 11*(4), 264–274. https://doi.org/10.1038/nrn2805

Roenneberg, T., Allebrandt, K. V., Merrow, M., & Vetter, C. (2012). Social jetlag and obesity. *Current Biology, 22*(10), 939–943. https://doi.org/10.1016/j.cub.2012.03.038

Roenneberg, T., Kuehnle, T., Pramstaller, P. P., Ricken, J., Havel, M., Guth, A., & Merrow, M. (2007). A marker for the end of adolescence. *Current Biology, 17*(24), R1038–R1039. https://doi.org/10.1016/j.cub.2007.11.068

Shonkoff, J. P., & Phillips, D. A. (2000). *From neurons to neighborhoods: The science of early childhood development.* National Academies Press.

Spector, T. (2012). *Identically different: Why you can change your genes.* Weidenfeld & Nicolson.

Sroufe, L. A., Carlson, E., Levy, A., & Egeland, B. (1999). Implications of attachment theory for developmental psychopathology. *Development and Psychopathology, 11*(1), 1–13. https://doi.org/10.1017/S0954579499001923

Takahashi, J. S. (2017). Transcriptional architecture of the mammalian circadian clock. *Nature Reviews Genetics, 18*(3), 164–179. https://doi.org/10.1038/nrg.2016.150

Triandis, H. C., & Suh, E. M. (2002). Cultural influences on personality. *Annual Review of Psychology, 53*(1), 133–160. https://doi.org/10.1146/annurev.psych.53.100901.135200

Walker, M. (2017). *Why we sleep: Unlocking the power of sleep and dreams.* Penguin.

Wittmann, M. (2008). Time and behaviour: Biological clocks and the timing of human behaviour. *Philosophical Transactions of the Royal Society B: Biological Sciences, 363*(1505), 2061–2071. https://doi.org/10.1098/rstb.2008.0017

Yehuda, R., Daskalakis, N. P., Bierer, L. M., Bader, H. N., Klengel, T., Holsboer, F., & Binder, E. B. (2016). Holocaust exposure induced intergenerational effects on FKBP5 methylation. *Biological Psychiatry, 80*(5), 372–380. https://doi.org/10.1016/j.biopsych.2015.08.005

CHAPTER 7

THE COGNITIVE AXIS

7.1. Cognitive Maps

7.1.1. Proto-Cognitions

One of the fundamental assumptions of Integrative Strategic Psychotherapy is that the roots of human cognition and subjective experience can be traced back to proto-cognitions—pre-symbolic, non-verbal mental representations that emerge in the earliest stages of development. Before the child acquires language, conceptual thinking, or even a stable sense of self, the mind is already constructing meaning from sensory inputs, emotional states, and embodied interactions. These proto-cognitions represent the raw material from which later cognitive, emotional, and relational structures are built. They are, in effect, the first drafts of reality, woven from the interplay of sensation, affect, and primitive self-organization.

Proto-cognitions are non-verbal, pre-symbolic representations formed through sensory experiences. The infant's world is not yet organized through concepts or words; it is felt and perceived in fragments of sensory impressions, rhythms, and affective tones. A proto-cognition is closer to the stimulus itself than to its symbolic representation. It precedes categorization, generalization, and the interpretative filters imposed later by language and culture.

Daniel Siegel (2012) describes sensory representations as basic symbols—units of information that point beyond themselves but do not yet carry the layered meanings of language-based concepts. For instance, the feeling of warmth in a parent's arms, the rhythmic rocking of the body, or the sudden absence of sound when a caregiver leaves the room are proto-cognitive experiences that form the bedrock of the child's representational system. They are encoded not as explicit memories, but as implicit sensory-affective patterns that will influence the organisation of self and the formation of later beliefs.

Allan Schore (2002, 2009, 2012) emphasises that these early pre-verbal experiences are stored in right-brain systems, deeply embedded in implicit memory networks. They shape not only subjective experience but also the neurobiological architecture of self-regulation and relational capacities. Proto-cognitions thus stand at the intersection of neurobiology and lived experience.

The child's initial representations emerge from three primary sources of sensory input: 1. The external world – visual, auditory, tactile, olfactory, and gustatory stimuli provide the raw material for perception; 2. The body – proprioceptive and interoceptive signals communicate states of balance, tension, hunger, comfort, or pain; and 3. The brain itself – internally generated patterns of arousal, rhythms, and regulatory signals contribute to the experience of self.

These streams of information converge to create pre-symbolic representations. A baby who repeatedly experiences soothing when held forms a proto-cognitive representation of safety, while a baby who is met with inconsistent care may internalise a diffuse sense of uncertainty or threat. Importantly, these are not yet beliefs in the cognitive sense, but *felt patterns*—emotional imprints that will later crystallise into expectations, intentions, and beliefs.

Mesquita et al. (2010) demonstrate that emotions act as organizing principles in this early meaning-making process. The child does not merely register sensory input; it is immediately coloured by affect. Thus, proto-cognitions are both perceptual and emotional: they encode not only *what* is happening, but *how it feels*.

Proto-cognitions are foundational for the process of self-organization. The self is not given at birth but emerges gradually as the brain integrates sensory, affective, and relational experiences. Schore (2009) highlights that right-brain mediated implicit processes underpin this self-construction, which depends heavily on the atonement and responsiveness of caregivers. Proto-cognitions are the "silent architects" of selfhood, guiding the infant's construction of coherence, continuity, and stability.

These representations also form the proto-narratives of experience. Long before the child can speak, the body and brain are telling stories: of comfort and distress, of presence and absence, of safety and danger. Proto-cognitions are the earliest drafts of these narratives, laying the groundwork for later symbolic meaning-making. Popescu & Vîșcu (2016) describe them as the foundations of cognitive maps, orienting the individual toward the world even in the absence of verbal or explicit representations.

Understanding proto-cognitions has profound implications for integrative strategic psychotherapy. Because these representations are non-verbal and implicit, they are not easily accessible through traditional verbal approaches. Instead, they surface in the therapeutic space through:

- Affective resonance: The client's emotional responses to the therapist often reveal early proto-cognitive patterns. For example, the sudden sense of abandonment when a session is rescheduled may reflect proto-cognitions of relational instability;
- Embodied memory: Sensations, postures, and gestures often carry traces of proto-cognitive experiences. Working somatically can bring these representations into awareness;
- Relational dynamics: Proto-cognitions are enacted in the therapeutic relationship. Clients may unconsciously recreate early relational scenarios, inviting the therapist into a reenactment of proto-cognitive scripts;
- Symbolic play and expressive techniques: Since proto-cognitions are pre-verbal, methods such as art, sandplay, movement, or guided imagery can provide pathways to access and reorganize them.

Therapy thus involves not only *interpreting* explicit narratives but also *revisiting and reshaping* these pre-symbolic foundations. By offering new sensory-affective experiences—of safety, resonance, and atonement—the therapist can help clients transform maladaptive proto-cognitions into more adaptive ones.

Proto-cognitions are not static; they evolve as the child interacts with the world. Repeated experiences transform them into beliefs, intentions, and explicit memories. For example:

- A proto-cognition of safety in the caregiver's arms may evolve into a belief that "others can be trusted";
- A proto-cognition of inconsistency may evolve into a belief that "people are unreliable";
- A proto-cognition of rejection may evolve into an intention to withdraw or avoid closeness.

Thus, proto-cognitions form the *seeds* of cognitive schemas, attachment styles, and personality structures. They are the unseen architects of both resilience and vulnerability.

When maladaptive proto-cognitions dominate—such as those formed in contexts of trauma, neglect, or mis atonement—they predispose individuals to later difficulties, including anxiety, depression, relational instability, and impaired self-regulation. Conversely, proto-cognitions grounded in consistent care and emotional resonance foster adaptive functioning, secure attachment, and psychological flexibility.

Within integrative strategic psychotherapy, proto-cognitions are conceptualised as the strategic starting point for intervention. Rather than beginning with the client's explicit narrative or belief system, the therapist attends to the pre-symbolic layers of experience. These are accessed through: 1. Sensory awareness – inviting clients to notice bodily sensations and affective tones that may link back to proto-cognitive experiences; 2. Emotional exploration – recognising the emotional colouring of early representations; 3. Relational repair – providing corrective experiences in the therapeutic alliance; and 4. Symbolic expression – facilitating expression through metaphors, stories, images, or creative modalities.

The therapist's task is to help the client identify and update maladaptive proto-cognitions, integrating them into a coherent narrative that supports adaptive self-organisation. This is a process of both integration (connecting implicit and explicit domains) and transformation (reshaping early representations through new experience).

In conclusion, proto-cognitions represent the pre-verbal foundations of the mind. They are the earliest representations through which the child organizes reality, grounded in sensory experience and shaped by emotion. Though silent and implicit, they continue to influence the formation of beliefs, intentions, and relational patterns throughout life.

Integrative strategic psychotherapy acknowledges their central role, offering pathways to access and transform them through relational atonement, embodied exploration, and expressive methods. In doing so, psychotherapy does not merely address cognitive distortions or explicit memories, but reaches back to the origins of subjectivity, reshaping the very foundations of the self.

7.1.2. Core Beliefs

As we have seen in the previous chapters, within integrative strategic psychotherapy (ISP), the self is conceptualised as a dynamic, multi-layered construct consisting of the proto-self, core self, plastic self, and external self. These layers represent developmental stages of organisation and adaptation, beginning with pre-symbolic sensory impressions and extending to the complex, socially mediated narratives of adult life. Each level of the self is shaped by the interaction between the individual's embodied experience, their environment, and their relational context.

The core self represents a crucial phase in this continuum. Emerging alongside the acquisition of language and symbolic thought, the core self crystallises from early proto-cognitions into enduring cognitive maps. These maps structure the individual's sense of identity, orientation in the world, and relational patterns. They contain core beliefs, intermediate beliefs, and automatic or irrational thoughts (Popescu & Vîşcu, 2016), which together form the blueprint of subjective experience and guide behaviour throughout life.

The proto-self consists of early, pre-verbal representations—proto-cognitions—that arise from sensory, affective, and embodied experience (Schore, 2009; Siegel, 2012). These proto-cognitions serve as the foundation for later symbolic thinking. They are, in essence, the child's first conclusions about the world: the basic feeling-tones of safety, fear, satisfaction, or deprivation that emerge from interactions with caregivers and the environment.

As the child acquires language and symbolic capacities, these proto-cognitions begin to organise into more stable structures within the core self. It is at this level that cognitive maps emerge: representations of reality that combine both verbal and non-verbal data into coherent internal models.

Thus, the transition from proto-self to core self is marked by a qualitative shift—from felt experience to structured belief. While proto-cognitions are fluid and pre-symbolic, core beliefs are crystallised, language-based structures that shape how the individual perceives and interprets events.

Cognitive maps within the core self consist of three interrelated levels: 1. Core Beliefs – deeply held convictions about oneself, others, and the world. These are typically formed in childhood and internalised as absolute truths. Resistant to change, they function as organising principles for perception and behaviour; 2. Intermediate Beliefs – conditional assumptions and rules derived from core beliefs. For example, the core belief *"I am not good enough"* may generate the intermediate belief *"If I try hard to please others, I will be accepted"*; and 3. Automatic or Irrational Thoughts – moment-to-moment cognitions that arise spontaneously in response to situations. These thoughts are surface-level manifestations of deeper structures. They often reflect distortions consistent with the individual's core beliefs (Beck, 2000).

These levels interact dynamically. Core beliefs generate intermediate rules, which in turn produce automatic thoughts when triggered by daily events. Over time, these interactions reinforce the stability of cognitive maps, ensuring continuity of the self but also perpetuating maladaptive patterns when core beliefs are dysfunctional.

Core beliefs are absolute, global statements about the self, others, and the world (Popescu & Vîşcu, 2016). They are not usually experienced as beliefs but as truths. Hoffmann (2012) notes that individuals often do not question their core beliefs, instead treating them as self-evident realities. For example: *"I am unlovable"*, *"People cannot be trusted"* or *"The world is unsafe."*

Such beliefs are maintained through selective attention and confirmation bias. Once activated, they filter perception, allowing only confirmatory evidence while disregarding disconfirming data. This explains why dysfunctional core beliefs can persist even in the face of contradictory experiences.

Beck (2000) provides the classic illustration: an individual holding the belief "I am stupid" interprets difficulty with a complex text as proof of stupidity, ignoring alternative explanations such as fatigue, poor presentation, or the inherent difficulty of the material.

Core beliefs evolve from proto-cognitions, integrating non-verbal and verbal experiences across development. This process can be understood through the following developmental sequence: 1. Proto-cognitive conclusion (pre-verbal): A baby cries when hungry but is inconsistently fed. The implicit proto-cognition may be *"Something is wrong with me; I am not effective"*; 2. Verbal reinforcement: Parents begin labelling the child negatively: *"You're clumsy," "You never get it right," "Stop asking questions."* These verbal inputs anchor the emerging cognitive map; 3. Social comparison: At school, the child receives lower grades than peers and is negatively compared: *"Why can't you be more like George?"* This reinforces the negative core belief; and 4. Confirmation bias: The child filters information in line with the belief. When laughed at in class, the laughter is interpreted as evidence of stupidity, regardless of the actual cause. Through this sequence, a proto-cognition develops into a rigid core belief. Importantly, these beliefs are not merely cognitive errors; they are emotional truths, rooted in the lived experiences of the child.

The core self is distinct yet interconnected with the other layers of the self in ISP:

- Proto-self: Provides the raw, pre-verbal sensory-affective material from which the core self develops;
- Core self: Structures this material into enduring cognitive maps, dominated by core beliefs;
- Plastic self: Represents the adaptive and flexible capacity to re-interpret core beliefs and develop new cognitive-emotional strategies in response to changing contexts; and
- External self: Refers to the socially constructed self, the narrative identity shaped by cultural, familial, and social discourses.

Thus, the core self functions as a bridge: it anchors the felt immediacy of the proto-self within symbolic structures, while also influencing the adaptability of the plastic self and the narratives of the external self.

In psychotherapy, working with the core self involves identifying and reshaping maladaptive core beliefs. This requires: 1. Accessing proto-cognitive origins – exploring the pre-verbal experiences that underlie the crystallisation of dysfunctional beliefs; 2. Identifying core beliefs – bringing implicit convictions into conscious awareness; 3. Challenging selective attention – helping clients notice disconfirming evidence that contradicts maladaptive beliefs; 4. Developing alternative beliefs – facilitating the construction of more adaptive cognitive maps; and 5. Strengthening the plastic self – supporting clients in experimenting with new perspectives, behaviours, and relational patterns.

Expressive and experiential techniques are particularly effective in accessing the proto-cognitive level, while cognitive restructuring methods support transformation at the level of the core self. The therapist thus engages in a dual strategy: addressing both the origins of beliefs and their current manifestations.

Consider Anna, a 32-year-old teacher who enters therapy with symptoms of anxiety and low self-esteem. Through exploration, it becomes clear that Anna carries the core belief *"I am worthless."*

- Proto-self origins: As an infant, Anna's cries were often ignored. The proto-cognitive conclusion: *"My needs do not matter";*
- Verbal reinforcement: As a child, Anna was told, *"Stop being a burden,"* and *"Why are you so difficult?"*;

- Social comparison: At school, she was frequently compared unfavourably with her younger sister; and
- Crystallisation: These experiences solidified the belief "I am worthless."

In therapy, Anna begins to identify this belief and notice its influence on her daily thoughts (automatic self-criticism when making mistakes). The therapeutic process involves both experiential techniques (guided imagery to revisit early experiences) and cognitive restructuring (challenging the assumption that mistakes equal worthlessness). Through corrective relational experiences with the therapist and the strengthening of her plastic self, Anna gradually develops alternative beliefs such as *"I am valuable even when I make mistakes."*

In other words, the core self is the site where proto-cognitions crystallise into cognitive maps, containing core beliefs, intermediate assumptions, and automatic thoughts. These beliefs are deeply resistant to change because they are rooted in pre-verbal emotional truths. However, within integrative strategic psychotherapy, the recognition of the layered self allows for targeted interventions. By working simultaneously with the proto-self, core self, plastic self, and external self, the psychotherapist supports a holistic reorganisation of the individual's cognitive-emotional system.

The transformation of maladaptive core beliefs is thus not a purely cognitive process but a deeply integrative one, requiring the integration of early experience, relational atonement, and strategic therapeutic methods.

Injunctions

Transactional Analysis (TA) introduced the concept of injunctions to describe early, often unconscious, prohibitive messages received from caregivers that become central to the child's life script (Berne, 1996; Fowlie & Sills, 2011). These injunctions shape behaviour, emotional responses, and relational dynamics throughout life. In Integrative Strategic Psychotherapy (ISP), injunctions are reinterpreted within the framework of the multi-layered self (proto-self, core self, plastic self, and external self) as a type of core belief—deeply embedded cognitive-emotional convictions that crystallise from early proto-cognitions and become resistant to change.

By viewing injunctions as maladaptive core beliefs, ISP provides both a theoretical bridge and a therapeutic strategy: injunctions are not merely unconscious prohibitions but can be understood as strategic survival decisions made by the child in response to relational and environmental conditions.

Injunctions function as fundamental organising principles of the core self. Like other core beliefs, they are experienced not as choices or assumptions but as absolute truths: ways the world "is" and ways the self "must be" in order to survive. At the proto-self level, the child receives repeated sensory-emotional experiences (e.g., neglect, mis atonement, rejection). At the core self level, these proto-cognitions crystallise into injunctions: prohibitive beliefs about existence, identity, behaviour, and belonging. At the level of the plastic self, the individual develops conditional strategies to navigate these injunctions ("If I try hard, I will be accepted"). At the level of the external self, injunctions are woven into life scripts, social roles, and narratives of identity. Thus, injunctions are both internalised parental messages and strategic survival responses to developmental environments.

Berne (1996) and later Fowlie and Sills (2011) described twelve central injunctions, which ISP reframes as twelve maladaptive core beliefs of the life script. Each injunction originates in relational dynamics with caregivers, reinforced by verbal and non-verbal messages, and later consolidated through selective attention and self-confirmation.

1. Don't Exist

The injunction *"Don't Exist"* represents one of the most devastating prohibitive life messages, as it targets the very foundation of being. At its core, it communicates that one's existence is unwanted, dangerous, or harmful to others. This injunction is most commonly rooted in early environments marked by neglect, rejection, or explicit hostility from caregivers. A parent who repeatedly communicates verbal or non-verbal messages such as *"I wish I'd never had you,"* or *"If it weren't for you, my life would be better,"* sows the seeds of a child's proto-cognitive conclusion that their very being is an error. In some cases, the parental stance is less direct but equally damaging—for example, a chronically depressed caregiver who consistently withdraws from contact, implicitly signalling to the infant that their presence is burdensome.

At the proto-self level, this injunction originates from the experience of unmet basic needs and the absence of attuned caregiving. When an infant's cries are not answered, when hunger or discomfort is not alleviated, or when the caregiver's gaze is persistently absent, the proto-cognitive conclusion emerges: *"My presence has no impact,"* or more painfully, *"My existence is too much."*

As the child develops into the core self, these implicit experiences crystallise into the core belief *"I should not exist."* This belief becomes encoded as an absolute truth, colouring all future interpretations of self and world. The child begins to anticipate rejection, interprets neutral signals as hostility, and filters out experiences that might contradict the core conviction of unworthiness. In adolescence and adulthood, this injunction often manifests through suicidal ideation, self-harm, chronic feelings of worthlessness, and psychosomatic expressions of erasure (e.g., fainting, withdrawal, eating disorders that diminish bodily presence). These are not merely symptoms but enactments of the injunction: unconscious attempts to obey the parental command not to exist.

Within the plastic self, survival requires finding a strategy to negotiate the impossible injunction. Common decisions include: *"I can exist only if I am useful,"* leading to compulsive caregiving; *"I can exist only if I am invisible,"* resulting in withdrawal, social avoidance, or self-effacement; or *"I can exist only if I am perfect,"* producing relentless striving to justify existence. These conditional strategies allow the individual to stay alive while remaining loyal to the injunction, but they do so at the cost of spontaneity, authenticity, and inner freedom.

At the level of the external self, the injunction "Don't Exist" is woven into the individual's life script, appearing in relationships where they tolerate neglect, abuse, or invisibility. Socially, they may present as self-deprecating, avoidant, or excessively compliant, often unconsciously inviting others to confirm their belief of non-worth.

From a clinical perspective, working with this injunction in ISP requires attending to all four layers of the self. At the proto-self level, psychotherapy must provide corrective experiences of atonement, safety, and recognition, often through the therapist's presence and emotional resonance. At the core self level, maladaptive core beliefs must be named, externalised, and gradually challenged. At the plastic self level, the psychotherapist supports the client in developing new survival strategies not based on invisibility or perfection but on acceptance and authenticity. Finally, at the external self level, clients are encouraged to rewrite their life narratives, transforming *"I should not exist"* into *"I am worthy of life, presence, and love."*

The injunction *"Don't Exist"* thus illustrates both the destructive power of early relational trauma and the transformative potential of psychotherapy: to offer a reparative context where existence is affirmed, validated, and celebrated.

2. Don't Be You

The injunction *"Don't Be You"* strikes at the heart of identity, conveying the message that one's authentic self is unacceptable, disappointing, or fundamentally wrong. It typically arises when a parent or caregiver cannot fully accept the child as they are. This rejection may be explicit—through statements such as *"We wanted a boy, but we got you,"*—or implicit, through subtle but persistent disappointment, comparison with siblings, or conditional love based on performance or conformity. The child internalises the belief that their true self is defective or unworthy, and survival requires abandoning or reshaping their identity to gain acceptance.

At the proto-self level, the child's earliest sensory-emotional experiences involve a mismatch between expression and reception. For instance, when the infant's spontaneous joy, anger, or sadness is consistently ignored or punished, the proto-cognitive conclusion emerges: "Something is wrong with me as I am." This pre-verbal impression lays the groundwork for a sense of shame tied not to behaviour but to being.

As development progresses, the core self crystallises these impressions into the core belief: *"It is wrong to be who I am."* This belief is not held as an opinion but as an unquestioned truth. It fuels chronic shame and identity confusion. The child may attempt to suppress traits associated with rejection—gender identity, temperament, talents—or may over-identify with roles imposed by others. Over time, these adaptations obscure the authentic self and create a fragile sense of identity, vulnerable to collapse when external approval is withdrawn.

The plastic self responds to this injunction with survival strategies such as self-abandonment, over-conformity, and role-taking. The individual may strive to become the "ideal child" that the parents desired, or later, the "ideal partner," "ideal student," or "ideal worker" demanded by society. While these strategies provide temporary belonging, they perpetuate an inner division: the authentic self remains hidden, and the externalised role-self becomes dominant.

At the external self level, this injunction manifests in the person's life script. Socially, the individual may appear adaptable, compliant, or excessively pleasing, but beneath this lies a pervasive fear of rejection. They may enter relationships where they are valued only for fulfilling roles (e.g., caretaker, achiever, entertainer), further reinforcing the belief that their true self is unworthy. Others may sense inauthenticity, which paradoxically deepens the individual's isolation.

Clinically, the *"Don't Be You"* injunction is associated with a wide range of difficulties: chronic shame, depression, anxiety, gender or identity struggles, difficulties with intimacy, and even somatic symptoms linked to disconnection from embodied experience. In some cases, the injunction contributes to dissociation or fragmented identity, as parts of the self are "banished" in order to comply with external expectations.

In psychotherapy, the task is to create a relational environment where the client's authentic self is invited, welcomed, and validated. At the proto-self level, the therapist's atonement counters early mis atonement, offering a lived experience of acceptance. At the core self level, the maladaptive belief *"It is wrong to be who I am"* must be named, externalised, and gently challenged. At the plastic self level, the psychotherapist helps the client experiment with new strategies that privilege authenticity over compliance. Finally, at the external self level, the life script is gradually rewritten to include narratives of self-acceptance and belonging.

The injunction *"Don't Be You"* reveals the profound psychological cost of conditional love. Yet it also demonstrates the reparative power of psychotherapy: when the authentic self is consistently met with recognition and acceptance, the individual can recover a sense of dignity, coherence, and freedom to live in accordance with who they truly are.

3. Don't Be a Child

The injunction *"Don't Be a Child"* emerges when a child receives the message—often implicitly—that expressions of playfulness, vulnerability, or dependency are unacceptable. Instead of being allowed to inhabit the natural developmental stage of childhood, the child is required to function prematurely as a "little adult." This injunction is common in families where the parents are overwhelmed, emotionally immature, or in conflict, and the child is subtly or explicitly drawn into adult roles such as caretaker, mediator, or confidant. The message is that childish spontaneity is dangerous or shameful, and that only seriousness and responsibility guarantee acceptance.

At the proto-self level, this injunction originates when early expressions of need, joy, or curiosity are consistently met with irritation, neglect, or punishment. A toddler's playful laughter might be dismissed with coldness, or a child's tears may be met with *"Stop crying, you're too old for that."* The proto-cognitive conclusion becomes: *"My natural state of being a child is wrong."*

At the level of the core self, these impressions crystallise into the core belief: *"It is wrong to play, depend, or need."* This belief distorts the child's orientation to life by replacing spontaneity with inhibition and dependency with premature self-reliance. Vulnerability is reinterpreted as weakness, and joy as frivolity.

The child develops a rigid self-image, believing they must act older than their years in order to be tolerated or valued.

The plastic self responds by developing survival strategies such as hyper-maturity, suppression of joy, and avoidance of vulnerability. The child might become the "responsible one," caring for younger siblings, managing household tasks, or even consoling a parent. While these strategies allow survival in a dysfunctional environment, they do so at a cost: the natural developmental experiences of play, exploration, and trust are sacrificed.

At the external self level, this injunction is woven into the life script. As adults, such individuals often manifest rigidity, difficulty relaxing, and discomfort in playful or spontaneous contexts. They may feel anxious in situations that demand creativity or silliness, perceiving them as unsafe or shameful. Many take on caregiving roles in relationships, feeling compelled to look after others while struggling to allow themselves to be nurtured. Their relational pattern often includes hiding vulnerability, which in turn limits intimacy.

Clinically, this injunction is associated with presentations of chronic tension, perfectionism, relational difficulties, and even somatic complaints linked to suppressed spontaneity. Depression or burnout may also develop when the weight of hyper-responsibility becomes overwhelming. Importantly, beneath these manifestations lies grief for a lost childhood: the absence of playful freedom and safe dependency.

In psychotherapy, the *"Don't Be a Child"* injunction requires a reparative process across all levels of the self. At the proto-self level, the therapist's atonement allows the client to safely re-experience the spontaneous expressions once inhibited. At the core self level, the belief "It is wrong to play, depend, or need" must be externalised and reframed, often through exploration of childhood dynamics. At the plastic self level, the psychotherapist encourages new adaptive strategies that integrate responsibility with playfulness, competence with vulnerability. Finally, at the external self level, the client is supported in rewriting their life script, reclaiming the right to play, depend, and need without shame.

The injunction *"Don't Be a Child"* illustrates the paradox of survival adaptations: the child forfeits spontaneity to secure belonging, yet this adaptation later prevents them from experiencing life fully. Psychotherapy thus becomes a process of permission-giving—helping clients rediscover their right to be playful, spontaneous, and vulnerable, not as regression but as a necessary integration of the full self.

4. Don't Grow Up

The injunction *"Don't Grow Up"* arises in families where a child, most often the youngest, receives the explicit or implicit message that maturity, autonomy, or independence will result in the loss of parental love. Parents who are anxious about separation, emotionally dependent on their child, or fearful of ageing may discourage growth by keeping the child in a dependent role. The injunction conveys: *"If you grow up, you will hurt me, leave me, or no longer be mine."* For the child, the cost of maturation is framed as unbearable guilt or abandonment, leading to a developmental arrest where adulthood itself feels unsafe.

At the proto-self level, the origins lie in repeated experiences where natural steps toward autonomy—such as walking away, going to school, or asserting independence—are met with parental withdrawal, sadness, or anger. The infant or toddler, sensitive to these emotional cues, draws the proto-cognitive conclusion: *"If I separate, something bad happens to my parent."* This lays the groundwork for the belief that growth is inherently harmful.

At the level of the core self, these impressions crystallise into the core belief: *"If I grow up, I will hurt or lose my parents."* This belief is deeply resistant to change because it is bound not only to fear but also to loyalty and love. The child does not experience the injunction as oppression but as a moral obligation: staying small or dependent becomes an act of protection.

The plastic self responds by developing survival strategies that maintain closeness at the expense of growth. These include remaining dependent, adopting childlike mannerisms, or avoiding responsibility. Such strategies are paradoxical: they allow continued attachment but at the cost of developmental potential. Many individuals later seek relationships with controlling or parental partners, unconsciously recreating the dynamic of dependency.

At the external self level, this injunction results in difficulties with adult tasks such as career progression, financial independence, or establishing mature partnerships. On the surface, these individuals may appear compliant, innocent, or "sweet," but beneath this lies a pervasive anxiety about separation and autonomy. Growth is experienced not as expansion but as danger.

In adulthood, the *"Don't Grow Up"* injunction manifests in a variety of ways: avoidance of responsibility, struggles with commitment, procrastination in life decisions, or overwhelming feelings under stress. Some adults oscillate between bursts of competence and regression into helplessness. Others sabotage opportunities for advancement, fearing that success will distance them from loved ones.

Clinically, this injunction is often associated with patterns of dependency, relationship difficulties, and blocked individuation. The client may present with anxiety, depression, or identity struggles, yet at the core lies the unspoken belief that growing up equals betrayal.

In psychotherapy, addressing the *"Don't Grow Up"* injunction requires careful exploration of both fear and loyalty. At the proto-self level, the psychotherapist provides experiences of safe separation—times where the client expresses autonomy and the therapeutic relationship remains intact. At the core self level, the maladaptive belief *"If I grow up, I will hurt or lose my parents"* is named and externalised, often revealing the client's deep sense of guilt. At the plastic self level, the psychotherapist supports experimentation with new strategies of autonomy that coexist with connection. Finally, at the external self level, the client is encouraged to rewrite their life script, constructing narratives in which growth enriches rather than threatens relationships.

The injunction *"Don't Grow Up"* highlights the paradox of loyalty: the child sacrifices their own development in order to protect parental attachment. In psychotherapy, the healing task is to release this false responsibility, affirming that true loyalty does not mean remaining small, but rather allowing both self and relationships to evolve.

5. Don't Succeed

The injunction *"Don't Succeed"* emerges when a child internalises prohibitive messages about achievement, excellence, or visibility. It typically arises in families where parental envy, fear, or insecurity is unconsciously projected onto the child's potential. Parents who feel threatened by their child's growth, or who never fulfilled their own ambitions, may discourage success in subtle or overt ways. The message communicated is: *"If you succeed, you will hurt me, surpass me, or lose my love."* Thus, success becomes equated with danger, betrayal, or rejection.

At the proto-self level, the roots of this injunction lie in early sensory-affective experiences where the child's displays of competence—such as learning to walk, speaking, or excelling at school—are met with withdrawal, ridicule, or punishment rather than celebration. The proto-cognitive conclusion becomes: *"My achievements make others upset; my growth causes harm."*

As development progresses, the core self crystallises these impressions into the core belief: *"Success is dangerous or forbidden."* The child learns that striving forward may bring not praise, but loss of connection. Success becomes associated not with pride or expansion, but with guilt, anxiety, or shame. Consequently, the individual may unconsciously sabotage opportunities or interpret achievements as unsafe, all the while longing for approval that remains conditional.

The plastic self negotiates this paradox by oscillating between contradictory strategies: *"trying hard"* in order to gain love and recognition, while simultaneously ensuring failure in order to remain loyal and safe. This oscillation creates chronic ambivalence, as efforts are undermined just before fruition. The individual may present as highly motivated and talented, yet unable to cross the threshold into sustained success.

At the external self level, the injunction becomes scripted into life patterns of underachievement, stagnation, or repetitive failure. These individuals may start projects with enthusiasm but abandon them prematurely, enter relationships where their talents are minimised, or avoid opportunities that would bring recognition. In professional settings, they may feel anxious when promoted, uncomfortable when praised, or even provoke failure to maintain alignment with the injunction.

In adulthood, manifestations of this injunction often include self-sabotage, abandoning goals, difficulty tolerating recognition, and anxiety when on the verge of achievement. These patterns are not simply weaknesses of will but expressions of loyalty to the early relational contract: "I must not outshine those I love." In some cases, success is pursued but immediately followed by collapse, illness, or burnout—unconscious ways of neutralising the perceived danger of achievement.

Clinically, the *"Don't Succeed"* injunction is associated with low self-esteem, chronic frustration, anxiety disorders, and depressive states rooted in repeated self-defeat. It may also be accompanied by perfectionism, where relentless striving masks a deeper fear of actual success. The double bind of "try hard but don't succeed" often leaves the client exhausted, resentful, and confused.

In psychotherapy, working with this injunction requires careful exploration of both the fear of success and the underlying loyalty to caregivers. At the proto-self level, the therapist offers attuned responses that affirm achievement without withdrawal, providing new sensory-emotional experiences of safety in success. At the core self level, the belief *"Success is dangerous or forbidden"* is brought into awareness and re-examined in the light of adult reality. At the plastic self level, the client is supported to develop alternative strategies that allow striving and achievement without self-sabotage. Finally, at the external self level, the psychotherapist encourages the rewriting of the life script so that success is integrated as a natural, relationally safe, and meaningful aspect of the self.

The injunction *"Don't Succeed"* illustrates how love and loyalty can become bound to self-limitation. The healing process involves disentangling achievement from guilt, allowing clients to discover that they can succeed without betraying those they love, and that true loyalty is not expressed through failure but through living fully into one's potential.

6. Don't Do Anything

The injunction *"Don't Do Anything"* arises when a child receives the implicit or explicit message that initiative, action, or exploration is unsafe or unwelcome. Parents may communicate this prohibition by overprotecting the child, warning them constantly about potential dangers, or by punishing initiative, criticising attempts to act independently. The child gradually learns that action itself carries risk—risk of rejection, punishment, ridicule, or even harm. The implicit conclusion becomes: *"It is safer to do nothing than to risk doing something wrong."*

At the proto-self level, this injunction originates in sensory-affective experiences where curiosity and spontaneous action are met with negative or anxious responses. A toddler reaching for an object might be scolded harshly, or an energetic child's play may be dismissed as reckless or irritating. The proto-cognitive conclusion emerges: *"My impulses to act are dangerous; stillness keeps me safe."* This bodily-felt association between action and danger lays the foundation for a passive stance toward life.

At the level of the core self, these experiences crystallise into the core belief: *"It is safer to do nothing."* The child learns to suppress initiative, avoid risk, and retreat from situations requiring choice or effort. This belief becomes self-reinforcing, as inaction prevents mistakes but also prevents learning and growth. Over time, the child internalises a worldview in which agency itself is suspect.

The plastic self develops survival strategies such as procrastination, passivity, and indecision. These strategies allow the individual to avoid criticism and protect themselves from perceived danger. However, they also lead to paralysis when faced with challenges, as the avoidance of risk becomes a habitual pattern. The oscillation between desire to act and fear of consequences creates chronic inner conflict: *"If I do something, I may fail or be hurt; if I do nothing, I remain stuck but safe."*

At the external self level, the injunction manifests in underachievement, dependency, or avoidance of responsibility. These individuals may appear indecisive, passive, or "stuck" in repetitive patterns of inaction. In relationships, they may rely on others to make decisions, while in professional contexts they may struggle to take initiative or to complete projects. Although often experienced as frustrating by others, this passivity is, at its core, a loyal enactment of the early injunction not to act.

In adulthood, the *"Don't Do Anything"* injunction is frequently expressed through procrastination, paralysis in decision-making, and chronic passivity. Many individuals describe feeling immobilised when confronted with new opportunities or challenges, accompanied by anxiety, guilt, or shame for "not doing enough." This can contribute to depression, low self-esteem, or feelings of futility, reinforcing the belief that action is pointless or dangerous.

Clinically, this injunction often presents as an underlying dynamic in clients struggling with anxiety disorders, depression, or motivational difficulties. In ISP, psychotherapy focuses on addressing both the fear of action and the adaptive function of inaction. At the proto-self level, the psychotherapist provides corrective experiences where action and expression are met with safety and validation. At the core self level, the belief *"It is safer to do nothing"* is identified, externalised, and reframed. At the plastic self level, the psychotherapist encourages experimentation with small, safe actions that challenge the paralysis of the injunction. Finally, at the external self level, clients are supported in rewriting their life script, integrating narratives of agency, competence, and resilience.

The injunction *"Don't Do Anything"* highlights the paradox of safety achieved through paralysis. While inactivity may have protected the child in a threatening environment, it later becomes a prison that limits growth and fulfilment. Psychotherapy thus becomes a process of restoring agency—helping clients reclaim the freedom to act, risk, and create, without fear of annihilation or rejection.

7. Don't Be Important

The injunction *"Don't Be Important"* arises when a child grows up in an environment where their visibility, achievements, or needs threaten the parent's fragile sense of self. This dynamic is often rooted in parental narcissism, competition, or insecurity. A parent who experiences their child's growth as rivalry, or who cannot tolerate sharing attention, may convey—verbally or non-verbally—that the child must remain small, quiet, or insignificant. The implicit message is: *"If you shine, you will hurt me,"* or *"If you take space, I will withdraw."* The result is that importance itself becomes associated with danger, guilt, or rejection.

At the proto-self level, the child's earliest experiences of seeking attention or asserting needs are met not with atonement but with withdrawal, irritation, or shaming. A toddler proudly showing a drawing may be ignored, or an older child asking for help may be ridiculed. The proto-cognitive conclusion emerges: *"When I seek recognition, I cause pain or lose love."* Over time, this felt sense of risk becomes embodied as inhibition in taking space.

As development progresses, the core self crystallises these impressions into the core belief: *"I am insignificant."* This belief is experienced as an unquestioned truth and becomes a lens through which the child interprets interactions. When others fail to notice or affirm them, the belief is reinforced; when others offer attention, the child may feel anxious or undeserving, dismissing the recognition before it can be integrated.

The plastic self responds by developing strategies of being invisible, pleasing others, and minimising one's presence. These adaptive manoeuvres reduce the risk of parental retaliation or rejection by ensuring that the child does not appear threatening. Many individuals become adept at blending in, avoiding leadership, and deflecting praise. While these strategies maintain attachment and safety, they also stifle growth, confidence, and authentic expression.

At the external self level, the injunction *"Don't Be Important"* is scripted into adult life patterns. Such individuals often struggle to assert their needs in relationships, fearing that doing so will burden or alienate others. Professionally, they may avoid leadership roles, even when competent, or sabotage opportunities that would bring them recognition. In groups, they may take the background role, ensuring that others shine while they remain unseen. This invisibility can paradoxically attract exploitation, as others may take advantage of their reluctance to claim space.

In adulthood, the manifestations include low self-esteem, fear of visibility, difficulty asserting needs, and avoidance of leadership. Social anxiety, imposter syndrome, and patterns of over-pleasing often trace back to this injunction. Some individuals alternate between invisibility and sudden bursts of assertion, which are then followed by guilt and retreat, reinforcing the sense of insignificance.

Clinically, the *"Don't Be Important"* injunction is associated with depression, chronic self-doubt, and difficulties in relationships where the individual feels unseen or undervalued. In ISP, therapy involves addressing the injunction across all four layers of the self. At the proto-self level, the therapist's consistent recognition provides corrective experiences that validate presence and significance. At the core self level, the maladaptive belief *"I am insignificant"* is externalised and challenged. At the plastic self level, the therapist encourages experimentation with new strategies such as speaking up, taking space, and tolerating recognition. At the external self level, the client is supported in rewriting their life script to include narratives of importance, value, and contribution.

The injunction *"Don't Be Important"* demonstrates how a child's natural desire for recognition can be distorted into lifelong invisibility. Psychotherapy offers a pathway to reclaim significance—not through competition or grandiosity, but through the authentic recognition that every self has inherent worth and the right to take space in the world.

8. Don't Belong

The injunction *"Don't Belong"* communicates to the child that they are fundamentally an outsider, unwelcome in their family, peer group, or community. Unlike other injunctions that may be conveyed through explicit parental statements, this one is often transmitted intergenerationally—passed down in families where exclusion, marginalisation, or social disconnection has been the norm. Parents who themselves feel they do not belong may unconsciously transmit this belief to their children, who then internalise the conviction that connection is unsafe or impossible.

At the proto-self level, this injunction originates in repeated sensory-emotional experiences of being ignored, excluded, or left out of family dynamics. For example, a child whose attempts at joining group activities are met with rejection or whose presence is consistently overlooked develops a proto-cognitive conclusion: *"I am not part of this."* Over time, the embodied sense of exclusion becomes a defining feature of their felt self.

At the core self level, these impressions crystallise into the core belief: *"I do not belong anywhere."* This belief becomes global, extending beyond the family into school, friendships, and later workplaces or communities. Belonging is experienced not as a natural right but as an elusive, unattainable goal. Even when included, the individual may feel like an imposter, anticipating eventual rejection.

The plastic self responds with survival strategies such as self-exclusion before rejection can occur. This adaptation protects against the pain of being actively excluded by pre-emptively withdrawing or minimising participation. Some individuals become observers rather than participants, blending into the background. Others oscillate between attempts to belong and retreat when closeness feels unsafe. While these strategies minimise hurt, they reinforce the conviction of not belonging by preventing genuine engagement.

At the external self level, the injunction is scripted into life narratives of alienation and isolation. Such individuals often describe themselves as "different" or "out of place" regardless of context. They may move frequently between jobs, groups, or even countries in search of belonging, only to repeat the pattern of exclusion. In relationships, they may feel disconnected even in the presence of intimacy, struggling to trust that they are truly part of a "we."

In adulthood, the manifestations include chronic loneliness, difficulty integrating into groups, and feelings of alienation. Many individuals report standing on the margins of social or professional life, unable to step fully into membership. The injunction may also contribute to identity struggles, where the person questions not only their place in a group but their fundamental right to exist within human community.

Clinically, the *"Don't Belong"* injunction is often associated with depressive states, social anxiety, and relational difficulties. It can also underpin experiences of cultural alienation in families with migration histories, where belonging itself is fractured across generations. In ISP, therapy must address the injunction across multiple layers of the self. At the proto-self level, the therapist offers atonement and inclusion, counteracting early experiences of exclusion. At the core self level, the belief *"I do not belong anywhere"* is brought into awareness and reframed as a learned conviction rather than truth. At the plastic self level, the therapist encourages experimentation with safe forms of group participation and closeness. Finally, at the external self level, the client is supported in rewriting their life script, constructing narratives of inclusion, connection, and community.

The injunction *"Don't Belong"* illustrates how deeply the human need for connection can be distorted into a lifelong expectation of rejection. The therapeutic task is to help clients reclaim their inherent right to belong—not by conforming or erasing themselves, but by discovering communities and relationships where authenticity and inclusion coexist.

9. Don't Get Close

The injunction *"Don't Get Close"* develops when a child repeatedly learns that closeness—whether physical or emotional—is unsafe. This may arise in environments where affection is inconsistent (sometimes warm, sometimes rejecting), or where proximity is linked to danger, betrayal, or abandonment. For example, a caregiver might hug the child one moment and push them away the next, or a parent may be affectionate only when the child performs or submits. The mixed messages create confusion: closeness becomes simultaneously longed for and feared.

At the proto-self level, this injunction originates from embodied experiences of approaching a caregiver and receiving unpredictable responses. The infant or young child, whose nervous system depends on consistent atonement, learns through repeated mismatches that touch, gaze, or proximity may bring rejection, anger, or withdrawal. The proto-cognitive conclusion emerges: *"When I reach out, I get hurt—therefore closeness is unsafe."* This embodied sense of risk around intimacy is stored implicitly, long before language can name it.

At the core self level, these experiences crystallise into the core belief: *"Closeness is unsafe."* This belief colours the individual's perception of relationships, leading them to expect betrayal, rejection, or engulfment when intimacy arises. Even when others behave kindly, the person may interpret their actions with suspicion or anticipate eventual harm. The longing for closeness is continually at war with the fear of it, creating inner conflict and relational ambivalence.

The plastic self develops survival strategies such as defensive distance and maintaining superficial relationships. Some individuals manage relationships by remaining friendly but never fully vulnerable; others engage intensely but withdraw when intimacy deepens. These strategies provide protection against potential harm but also prevent the nourishment of genuine closeness.

At the external self level, this injunction shapes the life script through recurring patterns of relational instability. Such individuals may cycle through relationships, alternating between pursuit and withdrawal, or may remain in long-term partnerships where emotional distance is maintained. Friendships may stay at a superficial level, and professional relationships are often carefully managed to avoid vulnerability.

In adulthood, manifestations of the *"Don't Get Close"* injunction include avoidance of intimacy, fear of touch, mistrust, and relational ambivalence. Some individuals present as highly independent, priding themselves on self-sufficiency, while others feel lonely and frustrated, aware of their longing for closeness but unable to tolerate it. This injunction often underpins attachment difficulties, ranging from avoidant patterns (dismissing closeness) to disorganised ones (approach–withdraw cycles).

Clinically, this injunction is associated with anxiety in relationships, mistrust, relational trauma, and sometimes psychosomatic symptoms linked to the suppression of physical or emotional closeness. In ISP, psychotherapy must carefully address the injunction across layers of the self. At the proto-self level, the therapist provides consistent, attuned presence that allows the client to experience closeness as safe. At the core self level, the belief *"Closeness is unsafe"* is named, externalised, and gradually challenged. At the plastic self level, clients are encouraged to experiment with tolerating small increments of intimacy, first within the therapeutic alliance and later in their external relationships. Finally, at the external self level, the life script is re-authored to include narratives of connection, trust, and safe closeness.

The injunction *"Don't Get Close"* captures the paradox of human attachment: the very connections that are essential for survival may become coded as dangerous. The psychotherapeutic task is to disentangle closeness from threat, enabling clients to discover that intimacy need not equal betrayal, and that they can exist safely in relationships marked by mutual trust and authenticity.

10. Don't Be Healthy (Physically or Mentally)

The injunction *"Don't Be Healthy"* emerges in family systems where illness—whether physical or psychological—is unconsciously idealised, rewarded, or used as a vehicle for receiving attention, love, or control. In such families, health is subtly devalued, while sickness becomes a pathway to intimacy, recognition, or significance. The implicit message communicated to the child is: *"If you are well, you will be ignored or abandoned; if you are unwell, you will be loved and cared for."*

At the proto-self level, this injunction originates in early sensory-affective experiences where states of illness or fragility are consistently met with warmth and atonement, while states of vitality or independence are neglected. For example, a baby who receives extra affection when unwell but minimal attention when active and playful may draw the proto-cognitive conclusion: *"Illness ensures closeness; health leads to disconnection."* This embodied association between care and unwellness becomes the foundation of a distorted survival strategy.

At the core self level, these experiences crystallise into the core belief: *"Being healthy means being abandoned."* This belief creates a paradox in which wellness becomes threatening, while illness feels safe. Over time, the individual may unconsciously sabotage their own physical or mental health in order to maintain attachment. They may develop patterns of psychosomatic illness, recurrent health issues, or a vulnerability to depression and anxiety that maintains a sense of closeness with family members.

The plastic self adapts by developing strategies such as maintaining illness, fragility, or dependency as a way of preserving love and loyalty. The child learns that by being unwell—either physically, emotionally, or behaviourally—they secure a role in the family system. This may manifest as the "sick child," the "fragile one," or the "dependent one." Although this role ensures connection, it prevents the development of autonomy, resilience, and authentic self-expression.

At the external self level, the injunction is scripted into adult life through recurring patterns of vulnerability, illness, or psychological distress. Such individuals may unconsciously identify with family members who were chronically unwell, carrying forward the intergenerational loyalty to suffering. They may struggle to sustain wellness, feeling uneasy when things are going well, as if waiting for illness or breakdown to restore a sense of belonging. Relationships may be shaped by the dynamic of "being cared for," which can limit mutuality and equality.

In adulthood, the manifestations of this injunction include psychosomatic symptoms, recurrent illnesses, vulnerability to depression, and unconscious identification with unwell family members. Some clients report a lifetime of "mysterious" ailments, frequent fatigue, or cycles of wellness and relapse that coincide with relational needs. Others experience difficulty sustaining psychological health, feeling compelled to collapse into helplessness when independence or strength threatens relational bonds.

Clinically, the *"Don't Be Healthy"* injunction is associated with psychosomatic disorders, health anxiety, chronic depression, and relational patterns of dependency. In ISP, therapeutic work addresses this injunction across all levels of the self. At the proto-self level, the psychotherapist offers consistent care regardless of the client's state, affirming that connection is not contingent upon illness. At the core self level, the maladaptive belief *"Being healthy means being abandoned"* is externalised and reframed. At the plastic self level, clients are supported in developing new strategies for maintaining closeness while also embracing vitality and independence. At the external self level, the life script is re-authored so that wellness is integrated into narratives of belonging, not exclusion.

The injunction *"Don't Be Healthy"* demonstrates how even the most fundamental aspect of human flourishing—health—can become entangled in early relational contracts of love and loyalty. The psychotherapeutic task is to release health from guilt, allowing clients to live fully, vibrantly, and independently, while discovering that connection and love are not dependent on suffering.

11. Don't Think

The injunction *"Don't Think"* takes shape in developmental environments where a child's attempts at reasoning, questioning, or problem-solving are repeatedly dismissed, ridiculed, or punished. Parents who feel threatened by a child's curiosity or independence may undermine their intellectual efforts, sending explicit messages such as *"Stop asking questions,"* or implicit ones through mockery, withdrawal, or hostility when the child tries to think for themselves. Over time, the child learns that thinking is not only unvalued but dangerous, leading to the core belief: *"My thoughts are invalid or dangerous."*

At the proto-self level, this injunction originates when the child's early signals of curiosity—pointing, questioning with gestures, exploring objects—are consistently misatoned. If the child's exploratory impulses are met with scolding or disinterest, the proto-cognitive conclusion emerges: *"Exploring with my mind brings disconnection or danger."* These embodied impressions form a pre-symbolic association between thought and relational threat.

At the core self level, these experiences consolidate into the rigid belief *"My thoughts are invalid or dangerous."* The child begins to distrust their cognitive processes, deferring instead to parental or external authority. Thinking independently becomes equated with risk—risk of rejection, humiliation, or conflict. In many cases, the injunction coexists with conditional counter-messages such as *"Do as I say"* or *"Obey without question,"* which reinforce dependence on others for decisions.

The plastic self develops adaptive strategies such as emotional reactivity and dependence on authority figures. When faced with decisions, the individual may bypass reasoning altogether, relying instead on emotional impulses or deferring to someone "stronger" or "smarter." These strategies reduce the risk of being wrong or criticised but prevent the development of genuine intellectual autonomy.

At the external self level, the injunction *"Don't Think"* scripts itself into adult life patterns marked by avoidance of problem-solving, indecision, or reliance on others in personal and professional contexts. In groups, these individuals may remain silent, fearing that voicing their ideas will expose them to ridicule. In relationships, they may adopt dependent roles, relying on partners, colleagues, or authority figures to do the "thinking" for them. Over time, this reinforces both the belief of inadequacy and the behavioural avoidance of independent thought.

In adulthood, manifestations include confusion under pressure, avoidance of analytical tasks, reliance on others for decision-making, and difficulties trusting one's own judgement. Many individuals describe their mind as "going blank" in stressful situations, reflecting the internalised prohibition against thinking. In some cases, overreliance on emotions or impulsive reactions replaces reflective reasoning, leading to cycles of instability and regret.

Clinically, the *"Don't Think"* injunction is often associated with anxiety, low self-confidence, imposter syndrome, and difficulties in academic or professional development. In some cases, it contributes to relational dysfunction, as individuals become overly dependent on partners or authority figures, fearing the consequences of independent thought.

In ISP, therapeutic work with this injunction involves creating a safe relational environment where thinking is not only permitted but valued. At the proto-self level, the psychotherapist's attuned responses to the client's curiosity provide corrective experiences of safety in exploration. At the core self level, the maladaptive belief *"My thoughts are invalid or dangerous"* is externalised and reframed as an internalised parental message rather than truth. At the plastic self level, clients are encouraged to experiment with decision-making and problem-solving in small, supportive contexts. At the external self level, the life script is rewritten to include narratives of competence, autonomy, and intellectual agency.

The injunction *"Don't Think"* highlights how intellectual development can be stifled not by lack of capacity but by relational prohibitions against autonomy. Psychotherapy offers a space where clients can reclaim the right to think, to question, and to trust their cognitive processes—transforming thinking from a source of danger into a foundation of selfhood.

12. Don't Feel

The injunction *"Don't Feel"* emerges when a child is repeatedly discouraged, punished, or shamed for expressing their emotions. Parents who are uncomfortable with their own affect, or who hold rigid cultural or familial beliefs about emotional expression, may send explicit messages such as *"Stop crying, there's nothing to be sad about"* or *"Big boys don't cry."* More subtle forms of dismissal—ignoring tears, ridiculing anger, or rewarding emotional suppression—equally communicate that feelings are unwelcome. The child gradually internalises the belief: *"Feelings are dangerous or forbidden."*

At the proto-self level, this injunction originates in the child's earliest embodied experiences of affective expression being met with misattunement. An infant who cries and is ignored, or whose anger is met with aggression, learns at a bodily level that expressing emotions brings disconnection or danger. The proto-cognitive conclusion becomes: *"When I show what I feel, I am not safe."* This pre-verbal imprint sets the stage for emotional inhibition.

At the core self level, these experiences crystallise into the core belief: *"Feelings are dangerous or forbidden."* This belief becomes a filter through which the child interprets their own inner states, often disconnecting from or suppressing them. Emotions are reframed as weakness, risk, or even moral failure. Over time, the capacity to recognise and integrate feelings becomes compromised, leading to difficulties in self-awareness, regulation, and relational intimacy.

The plastic self adapts by developing strategies such as intellectualisation, emotional withdrawal, and the use of compulsive or addictive behaviours to mask emotion. The child learns to prioritise cognition over affect, hiding behind rationalisation or detachment. Others may turn to food, substances, or compulsive activities as substitutes for forbidden feelings, using behaviour to manage what cannot be expressed. While these strategies protect against rejection, they perpetuate emotional disconnection.

At the external self level, the injunction *"Don't Feel"* is woven into life narratives of detachment and disconnection. Adults shaped by this injunction often present as emotionally numb, detached, or overly controlled. They may struggle with alexithymia—the inability to identify or describe feelings—or with relational patterns where intimacy is blocked by their emotional inaccessibility. Outwardly successful, they may nevertheless feel a profound emptiness, as if something vital is missing from their sense of self.

In adulthood, manifestations include emotional numbness, compulsive behaviours that distract from affect, relational detachment, and difficulties with vulnerability. These individuals may describe themselves as "numb," "cold," or "robotic," often accompanied by an underlying depression or anxiety that surfaces when defences falter. In relationships, partners may complain of emotional distance, while the individual themselves may feel bewildered by their incapacity to feel or express emotion.

Clinically, the *"Don't Feel"* injunction is associated with alexithymia, affective disorders, addictions, and relational dysfunction. In ISP, therapy aims to restore the client's connection to affect across all four levels of the self. At the proto-self level, the psychotherapist provides attuned responses to emotional expression, offering corrective experiences where feelings are welcomed rather than rejected. At the core self level, the maladaptive belief *"Feelings are dangerous or forbidden"* is named and reframed as an inherited injunction rather than reality. At the plastic self level, the psychotherapist supports the client in experimenting with safe forms of emotional expression—through imagery, movement, art, or language. Finally, at the external self level, the life script is re-authored to include narratives in which emotions are experienced as sources of connection, vitality, and authenticity.

The injunction *"Don't Feel"* illustrates how emotional suppression, initially a survival adaptation to misattuned environments, becomes a lifelong prison that severs the individual from the richness of their inner world. Psychotherapy offers a space where clients can rediscover the right to feel, reclaiming affect as a central dimension of the self and restoring the possibility of authentic relationships marked by empathy, vulnerability, and resonance.

By reframing injunctions as core beliefs, ISP highlights their role in shaping the core self and influencing the plastic and external selves. This creates a therapeutic model where: 1. The Proto-self provides the emotional ground from which injunctions emerge; 2. The Core self crystallises injunctions as absolute truths, integrated into cognitive maps; 3. The Plastic self creates compensatory strategies (e.g., "Try hard," "Please others") to manage injunctions; and 4. The External self expresses these beliefs in relational scripts, roles, and identity narratives.

This layered perspective emphasises that injunctions are not simply passive internalisations but strategic responses designed to ensure attachment and survival in the child's developmental context.

Working with injunctions in ISP involves a multi-layered strategy:

- Accessing proto-cognitive origins through embodied, affective, and sensory methods (e.g., guided imagery, expressive arts);
- Identifying injunctions as maladaptive core beliefs within the client's narrative;
- Exploring compensatory strategies in the plastic self (e.g., "If I try hard, I will be accepted");
- Transforming injunctions by developing new beliefs and experiences of self-worth, belonging, safety, and competence; and
- Integrating change at the level of the external self, rewriting life scripts into adaptive narratives.

Mark, a 40-year-old engineer, repeatedly sabotages career opportunities. Exploration reveals the injunction "Don't Succeed," reinforced by a father who belittled achievements and compared him unfavourably to siblings.

- Proto-self: repeated emotional withdrawal when he displayed initiative;
- Core self: crystallised belief "Success will make me lose love";
- Plastic self: strategy of "Trying hard but never finishing"; and
- External self: narrative of being "the one who almost makes it."

In therapy, Mark reconnects with the proto-cognitive sense of fear when showing competence, reframes his father's envy as parental limitation rather than personal flaw, and experiments with new plastic self strategies that allow achievement without self-sabotage. Over time, he constructs an external self narrative that integrates success with secure relationships.

Injunctions, as conceptualised in TA, find a natural home within ISP as maladaptive core beliefs of the core self. They represent the crystallisation of early proto-cognitions into prohibitive messages that shape the life script. By situating injunctions within the four-layer model of the self, ISP provides both a theoretical integration and a practical roadmap: psychotherapy must address injunctions not only cognitively but also somatically, emotionally, relationally, and narratively.

Transformation occurs when the client reclaims the freedom to exist, to be themselves, to feel, to think, to succeed, to belong, and ultimately to live without the constraints of early prohibitive beliefs.

7.1.3. Intermediate Beliefs

Intermediate beliefs derive from an individual's core beliefs and constitute a set of *rules for living.* While core beliefs form the deepest, most rigid layers of cognition—global and overgeneralised convictions about the self, others, and the world—intermediate beliefs are more accessible, flexible, and situational. They take the form of attitudes, rules, and assumptions, functioning as cognitive mechanisms that maintain and reinforce the underlying core beliefs.

In cognitive psychotherapy, intermediate beliefs are understood as the organising principles that mediate between core beliefs and automatic thoughts (Beck, 2000; Fall, Holden & Marquis, 2011). Within Integrative Strategic Psychotherapy (ISP), they are conceptualised as the strategic rules an individual adopts in order to survive within the constraints imposed by their core beliefs. In other words, intermediate beliefs serve as *protective adaptations* that enable the individual to navigate life while remaining loyal to their underlying convictions, however dysfunctional these may be.

Core beliefs are deeply entrenched, often unconscious convictions—such as *"I am stupid," "I am unlovable,"* or *"The world is unsafe."* These beliefs, once crystallised, shape how reality is experienced. Yet, because they are often intolerable in their raw form, individuals develop intermediate beliefs that soften, disguise, or compensate for the harshness of the core belief. For example, if the core belief is *"I am stupid,"* intermediate beliefs may unfold as follows (Fall, Holden & Marquis, 2011): 1. Attitude: *"It's awful to be stupid"; 2.* Rule/ Expectation: *"I must always work hard"; and 3.* Assumption: *"If I work hard, then perhaps I can manage tasks others find easy."*

Thus, while the individual carries the unspoken conviction *"I am stupid,"* this is managed and partially hidden beneath layers of rules and assumptions that organise behaviour. In practice, the child believes that their value lies not in intelligence but in effort, which becomes the compensatory strategy for coping with the shame and fear associated with perceived inadequacy.

Within ISP's model of the Cognitive Axis, proto-cognitions give rise to core beliefs, which in turn generate intermediate beliefs and, finally, automatic thoughts. This hierarchy represents a continuum from deep, rigid convictions to fleeting cognitive expressions. Intermediate beliefs act as a bridge in this structure, translating global convictions into specific behavioural rules:

- Core Beliefs: Absolute truths (e.g., *"I am worthless"*);
- Intermediate Beliefs: Rules for living (e.g., *"If I please others, I will be accepted"*); and
- Automatic Thoughts: Immediate interpretations of situations (e.g., *"They didn't smile—I must have annoyed them."*)

From an ISP perspective, intermediate beliefs are not simply cognitive structures but strategic adaptations. They represent attempts by the plastic self to maintain coherence and ensure survival while still aligning with the rigid convictions of the core self.

Intermediate beliefs function as implicit life rules that dictate behaviour. They often take the form of *"If... then..."* statements or conditional assumptions. For example: *"If I work hard, then I will be safe from criticism", "If I never show anger, then people will love me", or "If I always take care of others, then I will not be abandoned."*

These beliefs are compensatory in nature: they attempt to mitigate the painful implications of core beliefs while also reinforcing them. For instance, the belief *"If I work hard, I will be accepted"* may temporarily protect against the shame of *"I am inadequate,"* but it also implicitly validates the assumption that the person is indeed inadequate without extraordinary effort. Thus, intermediate beliefs maintain a paradox: they protect the individual from the raw pain of core beliefs while simultaneously perpetuating their influence.

From childhood, individuals strive to organise their experiences into coherent patterns that make sense of the world (Hoffmann, 2012). Because children are dependent on caregivers for survival, their interpretations of experience are strongly shaped by parental feedback, cultural messages, and environmental conditions. For example: A child raised in a critical family may develop the core belief *"I am inadequate."* To cope with this, they adopt the intermediate belief *"If I achieve enough, I will finally be accepted."* At school, they may work tirelessly, interpreting every mark or comment as evidence of adequacy or inadequacy.

Robertson (2010) notes that intermediate beliefs profoundly influence how individuals perceive and interpret situations. Because they function as filters, they determine not only how events are understood but also which aspects of reality are noticed in the first place.

Intermediate beliefs shape everyday cognition, behaviour, and emotion. Some common manifestations include: 1. Perfectionism – derived from the belief

"If I do everything perfectly, then I will avoid criticism"; 2. People-pleasing – based on the assumption *"If I always please others, then I will not be rejected"; 3.* Overachievement – linked to the rule *"If I constantly succeed, then I will prove my worth"; 4.* Avoidance – shaped by beliefs such as *"If I avoid risks, then I will not fail"; and 5.* Control-seeking – rooted in *"If I control everything, then I will be safe."*

While these strategies often help the child survive difficult environments, in adulthood they become rigid and dysfunctional, restricting spontaneity, authenticity, and resilience.

Consider Maria, a 35-year-old lawyer who presents with burnout and anxiety. Exploration reveals a core belief: *"I am not good enough",* intermediate attitude: *"It is shameful to fail",* rule: *"I must always be the best" and* assumption: *"If I overwork, then others will respect me"*

These intermediate beliefs drive Maria to overcommit, neglect self-care, and interpret any criticism as devastating. Though they protect her from directly confronting the pain of inadequacy, they also reinforce it by creating conditions for chronic exhaustion and further failure.

In psychotherapy, identifying and reframing these intermediate beliefs allows Maria to challenge the assumption that her worth is contingent upon overwork. This opens the possibility of constructing new rules for living based on balance, authenticity, and self-acceptance.

In ISP, intermediate beliefs are situated within the Cognitive Axis but interact dynamically with the other axes and levels:

- Emotional Axis: Intermediate beliefs regulate emotional expression (e.g., *"If I show anger, I will be rejected"* leads to suppression of emotion);
- Psychodynamic Axis: They guide patterns of action or inaction (e.g., *"If I avoid risks, I will stay safe"* produces avoidance); and
- Relational Axis: They shape how individuals approach others (e.g., *"If I always please, then I will be loved"* structures relationships around compliance).

This multidimensional interplay shows that intermediate beliefs are not purely cognitive—they are woven into the fabric of experience across domains of selfhood.

In ISP, therapeutic engagement with intermediate beliefs involves: 1. Identification – helping the client articulate attitudes, rules, and assumptions that organise their behaviour; 2. Linking to Core Beliefs – uncovering how these intermediate beliefs protect or reinforce deeper convictions; 3. Challenging and Testing – encouraging clients to question the validity and utility of their rules for living; 4. Developing Alternatives – supporting the creation of new, flexible, and adaptive beliefs that enable authenticity and resilience; and 5. Integration across Axes – ensuring that new beliefs are embodied (emotional axis), enacted (behavioural axis), and relationally validated (relational axis).

Corrective relational experiences in psychotherapy play a crucial role. When a psychotherapist validates the client's worth independently of performance or compliance, the implicit assumption *"If I don't perform, I will be rejected"* can be gradually disconfirmed.

Intermediate beliefs represent the strategic layer of the cognitive system: adaptive rules that protect against the raw pain of core beliefs while simultaneously perpetuating them. They are central to the Cognitive Axis of the self in Integrative Strategic Psychotherapy, acting as the hinge between deep convictions and surface-level automatic thoughts.

Understanding intermediate beliefs is vital because they are often more accessible than core beliefs in therapy, yet they hold the key to uncovering deeper convictions. By working with these rules for living, psychotherapists can help clients move from rigid, compensatory strategies toward more authentic, flexible, and adaptive patterns of thought and behaviour.

Drivers as Intermediate Beliefs

Within Transactional Analysis (TA), the concept of drivers refers to unconscious motivational pressures that shape an individual's behaviour and decision-making. Taibi Kahler (1975) identified five central drivers: *Be Perfect, Be Strong, Please Others, Hurry Up,* and *Try Hard.* These drivers function as internalised imperatives, pushing individuals toward particular behavioural patterns in order to maintain acceptance, avoid punishment, and survive within their family systems.

In Integrative Strategic Psychotherapy (ISP), drivers are reinterpreted as a specific form of intermediate beliefs—cognitive "rules for living" that develop from core beliefs. If core beliefs are the rigid, global convictions that shape identity (e.g., *"I am inadequate," "I am unlovable"*), then intermediate beliefs are the conditional rules derived from these convictions (e.g., *"If I always work hard, then perhaps others will accept me"*). Drivers fit precisely into this intermediate layer, representing powerful adaptive strategies that seek to protect the individual from the raw pain of their core beliefs.

Thus, drivers can be understood as strategic adaptations of the plastic self: conditional imperatives that both shield the core self and perpetuate its beliefs. Drivers operate according to a logic of conditional acceptance: *"If I follow this rule, I will be safe, accepted, or valued."* They are compensatory strategies, designed to manage the vulnerability created by early injunctions and core beliefs. For example: A child who internalises the injunction *"Don't Be Important"* may develop the driver *"Please Others"* as a way of gaining conditional approval, whilst a child who believes *"I am stupid"* may rely on the driver *"Be Perfect"* in an effort to avoid exposure and criticism.

In this sense, drivers represent the bridge between injunctions (as core beliefs) and automatic thoughts. They transform global prohibitions into daily behavioural rules. While they may provide temporary safety, they do so at the expense of spontaneity, authenticity, and flexibility.

In Integrative Strategic Psychotherapy (ISP), drivers are reframed as a particular form of intermediate beliefs within the Cognitive Axis of the self. They are not free-floating tendencies but conditional rules of living that originate in core beliefs and function across all three levels of the self:

- Biological level: Drivers regulate arousal, affect, and behavioural activation/inhibition;
- Psychological level: Drivers organise cognitions, rules, and assumptions that protect the self from the raw pain of core beliefs; and
- Relational level: Drivers structure interactions, determining how individuals seek attachment, recognition, and safety in their relationships.

Thus, drivers are best understood in ISP as strategic survival rules: conditional imperatives that help the child negotiate the tension between prohibitive injunctions (core beliefs) and the need for attachment.

Within the Cognitive Axis, the hierarchy is as follows:

- Core Beliefs – deep convictions about the self, others, and the world (e.g., *"I am inadequate"*);
- Intermediate Beliefs – rules for living that compensate for or disguise the core belief (e.g., *"If I am perfect, then I will be safe"*); and
- Automatic Thoughts – surface-level cognitions arising in specific situations (e.g., *"I made a mistake, they'll think I'm incompetent."*).

Drivers fall squarely within the intermediate level, as they embody rigid *"if–then"* assumptions that govern behaviour and perception. They operate as bridges between the deep rigidity of core beliefs and the fleeting immediacy of automatic thoughts.

At a biological level, drivers influence the organism's physiological regulation. For instance, *Hurry Up* creates heightened arousal and restlessness, while *Be Strong* suppresses autonomic expressions of distress (e.g., tears, trembling). Over time, these biological adaptations can lead to stress-related disorders, psychosomatic symptoms, or emotional numbing.

At a psychological level, drivers manifest as conditional rules: *"If I am perfect, then I will not be criticised,"* or *"If I never show weakness, I will be respected."* They are internalised as part of the individual's self-structure and influence cognition, emotion, and motivation.

Last but not least, at a relational level, drivers guide interpersonal behaviour and relational strategies. *Please Others* leads to chronic compliance, *Be Perfect* drives performance-based worth, and *Be Strong* prevents intimacy by blocking vulnerability. Drivers thus sustain relational patterns that reinforce the original injunctions.

Although drivers belong primarily to the Cognitive Axis, they exert influence across all three axes:

- Cognitive Axis – Drivers shape rules for thinking, assumptions about self and world, and patterns of decision-making;
- Emotional Axis – Drivers regulate the expression or suppression of affect (*Be Strong* suppresses sadness; *Please Others* suppresses anger); and
- Psychodynamic Axis – Drivers interact with unconscious material, defences, and life scripts. For example, *Be Perfect* may represent an internalised parental ego ideal, while *Try Hard* reflects a child's unresolved struggle with parental expectations.

This multidimensional influence explains why drivers are persistent and resistant to change: they are deeply integrated across levels and axes of the self.

1. Be Perfect

The driver *"Be Perfect"* usually arises from early core beliefs such as *"I am inadequate," "I am stupid,"* or *"Mistakes mean rejection."* These convictions typically form in contexts where the child's performance, behaviour, or achievements were consistently evaluated, compared, or criticised. When parents or caregivers respond to mistakes with harshness, ridicule, or withdrawal of affection, the child internalises the message that error equals unworthiness. Related injunctions are *Don't Be You* (authenticity is not acceptable, so worth must be "earned" by flawlessness), *Don't Be a Child* or *Don't Succeed, which imply not to make mistakes, and mistakes equal rejection. The logic is:* If being myself or being fallible is unsafe, I must compensate by being perfect.

At the biological level, this often manifests as a heightened stress response to failure—physiological arousal, muscle tension, or rapid heart rate when errors occur. At the psychological level, it crystallises into the belief that adequacy is conditional upon perfection. At the relational level, the child learns that love, acceptance, and belonging are granted only when they excel, reinforcing the injunction *"Don't Make Mistakes."*

Thus, *Be Perfect* becomes a survival adaptation: if the child can eliminate mistakes, they may secure safety and attachment.

The driver *"Be Perfect"* functions as an intermediate belief—a conditional rule for living: *"If I am perfect, I will be acceptable."* This belief protects the individual from directly experiencing the unbearable pain of the core conviction *"I am inadequate."* Instead, the person channels energy into flawlessness, believing that perfection will mask or neutralise inadequacy. Yet, the very existence of the rule presupposes the core belief: by striving to be perfect, the individual confirms the assumption that they are fundamentally deficient without perfection.

Manifestations Across the Three Levels of the Self are: 1. Biological Level: Chronic physiological arousal when under pressure; Psychosomatic symptoms linked to tension: headaches, digestive issues, sleep disturbances, and Fatigue and burnout due to relentless striving. 2. Psychological Level: Cognitive Axis: Perfectionistic standards, intolerance of mistakes, overgeneralisation ("If I am not the best, I am a failure"); Emotional Axis: Anxiety, shame, guilt, fear of exposure; emotional flatness when spontaneity is suppressed; and Psychodynamic Axis: Internalised parental voices demanding flawlessness; unconscious loyalty to critical or perfectionistic caregivers. 3. Relational Level: Relationships become conditional: love is earned by performance; The person may criticise others harshly, projecting their own perfectionism outward; and Fear of vulnerability and intimacy, since revealing flaws risks rejection.

Be Perfect is a compensatory strategy: it provides temporary safety by shielding the self from the accusation of inadequacy. If the individual can achieve flawless performance, criticism may be avoided and belonging preserved. Yet, the strategy is self-defeating. It maintains the core belief, because worth is always conditional on performance. It creates paralysis, as the fear of imperfection leads to procrastination or avoidance. It blocks authenticity, since spontaneity and experimentation inevitably involve mistakes.

In adulthood, the *Be Perfect* driver manifests as: 1. Perfectionism – endless striving without satisfaction; 2. Fear of mistakes – avoidance of new or risky situations; 3. Procrastination – postponing tasks until perfection seems achievable; 4. Chronic anxiety – hypervigilance about errors and judgement; and 5. Relational strain – imposing perfectionistic standards on others, or avoiding closeness out of fear of exposure.

Often, clients with this driver present in therapy with burnout, depression, or relational difficulties. They describe themselves as "never good enough," regardless of actual competence or success.

In ISP, therapy with *Be Perfect* involves interventions across all levels and axes:

- Biological level: Helping clients notice physiological signs of perfectionistic stress and practising regulation strategies (breathing, relaxation, embodied awareness);
- Psychological level: 1. Cognitive Axis: Identifying the conditional rule *"If I am perfect, I am acceptable,"* linking it to the core belief *"I am inadequate,"* and challenging its validity; 2. Emotional Axis: Allowing the client to experience shame and fear of imperfection safely within the therapeutic relationship; and 3. Psychodynamic Axis: Exploring the origins of the driver in parental or cultural expectations; addressing unconscious loyalties to critical caregivers; and
- Relational level: Offering unconditional acceptance within psychotherapy, so the client can test the hypothesis that worth is independent of flawlessness.

The ultimate therapeutic aim is to help the client replace conditional self-worth with intrinsic self-acceptance, transforming the driver *Be Perfect* into a healthier flexibility: striving for excellence when appropriate, but tolerating and even embracing imperfection as part of authentic human experience.

The driver *Be Perfect* exemplifies how intermediate beliefs function as strategic adaptations within ISP. Rooted in the core conviction of inadequacy, it seeks to mask vulnerability by striving for flawlessness. Yet, this adaptation traps the individual in a cycle of anxiety, shame, and relational disconnection.

In psychotherapy, addressing *Be Perfect* requires integrating work across the biological, psychological, and relational levels, and across all three psychological axes. Only then can the client experience that worth is not contingent on flawlessness, but on the deeper reality of being human—imperfect, vulnerable, and yet inherently valuable.

2. *Be Strong*

The driver *"Be Strong"* often develops in children who have received injunctions such as *"Don't Be a Child"* or *"Don't Feel."* In these environments, vulnerability, dependence, or emotional expression are met not with care but with rejection, punishment, or neglect. The child quickly learns that expressing sadness, fear, or need will lead to shame, criticism, or abandonment. Related injunctions are *Don't Feel* (emotions are dangerous or shameful) and *Don't Be a Child* (vulnerability and dependence are forbidden). The logic is: If feelings and needs are not allowed, I must always be strong, invulnerable, and self-reliant.

At the biological level, the child suppresses natural physiological responses to distress (e.g., tears, trembling) in order to avoid negative parental reactions. At the psychological level, the child internalises the conviction that safety is contingent upon strength and emotional control. At the relational level, attachment becomes conditional on invulnerability: being cared for is replaced by being valued for "coping alone."

Thus, the core belief emerges: *"Vulnerability is dangerous; I must not need others."*

The driver functions as the intermediate belief: *"If I am strong, I will be safe and acceptable."*

This rule becomes the organising principle of the person's inner world. By hiding weakness, the child avoids punishment or ridicule and earns recognition for their apparent maturity. However, the rule also presupposes the conviction that weakness is unacceptable, reinforcing the deeper belief that dependency or vulnerability equals danger.

Manifestations Across the Three Levels of the Self are: 1. Biological Level: Inhibition of natural emotional expression: tears suppressed, facial expressions minimised; Chronic tension in the body, leading to somatic issues such as headaches, back pain, or digestive problems; and Physiological over-activation when vulnerability threatens to surface. 2. Psychological Level: Cognitive Axis: Beliefs such as *"I must always cope alone," "Needing others is weakness"*; Emotional Axis: Restricted access to sadness, fear, or tenderness; emotional flatness or premature detachment; and Psychodynamic Axis: Unconscious identification with powerful figures (e.g., a stoic parent) or defensive splitting, where weakness is projected onto others. 3. Relational Level: Difficulty seeking help or comfort; relationships structured around self-reliance; Others may perceive the person as distant, unapproachable, or overly independent; and Intimacy is compromised, as true closeness requires showing need and vulnerability.

The *Be Strong* driver is a strategic survival rule: it enables the child to endure environments where emotional expression was unsafe. By suppressing feelings, the child avoids shaming, punishment, or the disappointment of unresponsive caregivers. In the short term, this adaptation preserves attachment and dignity. However, over time it becomes self-defeating. It restricts emotional intimacy, as vulnerability is essential for closeness. It leads to over-responsibility, where the person takes on too much without seeking support. It contributes to burnout and isolation, since no one can sustain invulnerability indefinitely.

In adulthood, the *Be Strong* driver appears as: 1. Reluctance to ask for help, even when overwhelmed; 2. Emotional suppression or minimisation of distress ("It's fine," "I can handle it"); 3. Over-responsibility in family or professional roles, often leading to exhaustion; 4. Relational distance, with partners feeling shut out emotionally; and 5. Somatic symptoms linked to unprocessed affect.

While such individuals are often admired for their resilience, underneath lies unacknowledged pain, loneliness, and fear of rejection should weakness be revealed.

Addressing *Be Strong* in psychotherapy requires interventions across all levels and axes:

- Biological level: Helping clients notice physiological markers of suppression (tightness in chest, clenched jaw) and safely release held tension;
- Psychological level: 1. Cognitive Axis: Identifying the intermediate rule *"I must always be strong"* and linking it to the core belief *"Vulnerability is dangerous."*; 2. Emotional Axis: Facilitating safe expression of sadness, fear, and tenderness in the therapeutic space; and 3. Psychodynamic Axis:

Exploring unconscious identifications (e.g., with a stoic parent) and mourning the absence of attuned caregiving; and

- Relational level: Creating a therapeutic relationship where vulnerability is met with acceptance rather than rejection. Over time, this corrects the expectation that weakness will lead to loss or shame.

The goal is not to eliminate strength but to integrate it with vulnerability—allowing resilience to coexist with authentic dependence and emotional expression.

The *Be Strong* driver exemplifies how children transform prohibitions into survival rules. It shields against the pain of rejection by suppressing vulnerability, but in adulthood it limits emotional intimacy, authenticity, and balance.

Within ISP, *Be Strong* is understood as an intermediate belief that bridges core convictions (*"Vulnerability is unsafe"*) and surface-level behaviour (emotional distance, over-responsibility). Addressing it requires work across biological, psychological, and relational levels, and across the cognitive, emotional, and psychodynamic axes.

Psychotherapy helps clients discover that true strength does not mean invulnerability but the capacity to integrate both resilience and vulnerability in authentic human connection.

3. *Please Others*

The driver *"Please Others"* typically develops in environments where a child internalises the injunctions *"Don't Be You"*, *"Don't Be Important"* or *"Don't Belong"*. When a child's authentic needs or expressions are consistently dismissed, criticised, or punished, they may develop the conviction: *"I am unlovable,"* or *"I don't matter unless I comply."* In these families, love and attention are conditional—granted only when the child meets parental expectations or prioritises the needs of others over their own.

Thus, the child learns that to maintain attachment, they must suppress authenticity and orient themselves towards the desires of others. Over time, this crystallises into the driver *Please Others*: *"If I please others, then I will be accepted."*

As an intermediate belief, *Please Others* functions as a rule for living: *"I must give up my voice and needs in order to earn love."* This strategy protects the child from the raw pain of rejection or abandonment. However, it also sustains the deeper conviction that they are unworthy of love in their own right. The rule maintains attachment, but at the cost of authenticity and autonomy.

Manifestations Across the Three Levels of the Self are: 1. Biological Level: Heightened physiological stress in situations of potential conflict or rejection; Somatic symptoms (tension headaches, gastrointestinal issues) linked to chronic self-suppression; and Activation of the stress response when asserting needs, often leading to withdrawal or collapse. 2. Psychological Level: Cognitive Axis: Beliefs such as *"My needs are less important," "If I assert myself, I'll be rejected."*; Emotional Axis: Chronic guilt when expressing anger or desire; fear and anxiety when authenticity surfaces; and Psychodynamic Axis: Unconscious identification with a self-sacrificing parent, or unresolved attachment dynamics where compliance ensured conditional love. 3. Relational Level: Relationships dominated by compliance and self-sacrifice; Partners or colleagues may exploit the individual's inability to say no; Intimacy is fragile, as authenticity is hidden behind a mask of agreeableness; and Resentment accumulates, as the individual feels unseen or unappreciated despite sacrifices.

The *Please Others* driver is a strategic survival rule. It ensures safety in childhood by maintaining parental approval and avoiding conflict. For many children, pleasing becomes the only way to secure minimal attachment. However, this strategy has high long-term costs. It erodes the authentic voice, as the individual loses touch with their own desires and boundaries. It creates dependency, since self-worth is always tied to others' approval. It generates resentment, as suppressed needs and desires inevitably surface in indirect or destructive ways.

In adulthood, *Please Others* manifests as: 1. People-pleasing behaviours and difficulty saying no; 2. Chronic guilt when prioritising self over others; 3. Anxiety in conflict situations; 4. Vulnerability to exploitation in relationships; and 5. Hidden anger or resentment that undermines relational stability.

Such individuals often present in therapy feeling "burned out" by others' demands, yet paralysed by guilt when trying to establish boundaries. They may describe themselves as "invisible" or "walking on eggshells," living lives shaped by others' expectations rather than their own values.

Interventions must address *Please Others* across the three levels and axes:

- Biological level: Supporting clients to notice bodily responses to self-suppression and to regulate anxiety when asserting boundaries;
- Psychological level: 1. Cognitive Axis: Identifying the belief *"If I please others, I will be accepted"* and linking it to the core conviction *"I am*

unlovable as I am"; 2. Emotional Axis: Facilitating the safe expression of anger, frustration, and desire—emotions often repressed under this driver; and 3. Psychodynamic Axis: Exploring unconscious patterns of loyalty to parents or family roles where pleasing was essential for survival; and

– Relational level: The therapeutic relationship becomes a laboratory where the client tests authenticity. The psychotherapist's acceptance of the client's voice and boundaries corrects the early relational message that love is conditional on compliance.

The therapeutic task is twofold: to mourn the grief of a childhood where love had to be earned, and to learn that authenticity does not equal abandonment.

The *Please Others* driver exemplifies how survival strategies emerge in response to conditional attachment. It shields the child from rejection by ensuring compliance, but in adulthood it perpetuates self-suppression, guilt, and exploitation.

Within ISP, *Please Others* is understood as an intermediate belief at the cognitive axis, expressed through the emotional and psychodynamic axes, and enacted across biological, psychological, and relational levels. Psychotherapy aims to help clients reclaim their authentic voice, to experience that love and acceptance are possible without self-abandonment, and to establish relationships based on mutual recognition rather than compliance.

4. *Hurry Up*

The driver *"Hurry Up"* often develops in environments where the child internalises core convictions such as *"I am not enough,"* or *"My worth depends on productivity."* Sometimes this arises in families where urgency dominates daily life: parents constantly rushing, emphasising speed and efficiency over presence and connection. At other times, the child receives subtle or explicit messages that time is scarce and value is measured by how much is accomplished. Related injunctions are: *Don't Succeed* (achievement may be sabotaged, but frantic activity proves effort), *Don't Be Important* (my worth lies not in presence, but in constant productivity) and *Don't Do Anything* (action feels dangerous, so rushing provides the illusion of effectiveness without sustained presence). The logic is: If I am not inherently enough, maybe I can make up for it by rushing to keep up.

When affection and recognition are linked to achievement, the child comes to equate speed and productivity with love. Slowness, rest, or play may be perceived as laziness, incompetence, or grounds for criticism. Over time, this crystallises into the driver *Hurry Up*: *"If I hurry, then I will keep up and avoid failure."*

At the level of intermediate beliefs, *Hurry Up* functions as a conditional rule for survival: *"If I move quickly, I can avoid criticism and prove my worth."*

This compensates for the painful conviction *"I am not enough,"* but at the same time maintains it. By rushing, the person hopes to escape failure; yet the haste often leads to mistakes, reinforcing the belief of inadequacy. Thus, the driver creates a self-perpetuating cycle: the faster one goes, the more one fears falling behind.

Manifestations Across the Three Levels of the Self are: 1. Biological Level: Chronic hyperarousal: restlessness, racing heart, shallow breathing; Somatic consequences of sustained stress: hypertension, digestive problems, insomnia; and Difficulty relaxing or tolerating stillness, as the body has become conditioned to urgency. 2.Psychological Level: Cognitive Axis: Beliefs such as *"If I don't rush, I'll be left behind,"* or *"Slowness means failure"*; Emotional Axis: Anxiety, frustration, and irritability when delayed; inability to savour success or enjoy the present moment; and Psychodynamic Axis: Identification with hurried caregivers; unconscious replay of family scripts where worth was tied to efficiency and speed; and

- Relational Level: Impatience in relationships; pressure on others to move faster; Lack of atonement, as the person is preoccupied with speed rather than presence; Difficulty in intimacy, where slowness and lingering are essential; and Conflicts in professional and personal life, as urgency can alienate others.

The *Hurry Up* driver is a strategic survival rule: it allows the child to avoid criticism, gain recognition, and secure conditional acceptance in environments that equate productivity with worth. Yet the costs are high: 1. Inefficiency despite speed – rushing leads to errors that require more correction; 2. Exhaustion – constant urgency depletes energy and undermines health; 3. Alienation – relationships suffer when others feel pressured or unheard; and 4. Self-fulfilling prophecy – the frantic pace often proves the very belief of inadequacy the child is trying to escape.

In adulthood, *Hurry Up* may manifest as: 1. Workaholism, multitasking, or constant busyness; 2. Difficulty resting or engaging in leisure without guilt; 3. Chronic anxiety linked to time management; 4. Somatic complaints tied to stress (headaches, insomnia, cardiovascular problems); and 5. Relational strain due to impatience, irritability, or emotional absence.

Clients often present in therapy describing themselves as “always on edge” or “never having enough time.” Beneath the urgency lies the deeper pain of inadequacy and the fear of being left behind.

Psychotherapy must address *Hurry Up* across the levels and axes:

- Biological level: Helping clients notice bodily states of urgency and cultivate relaxation. Breathing, grounding, and mindfulness practices can restore balance;
- Psychological level: 1. Cognitive Axis: Identifying the intermediate rule *“If I hurry, I will avoid failure”* and linking it to the core belief *“I am not enough.”* Challenging the false equation between speed and worth; 2. Emotional Axis: Exploring the fear and shame that emerge when slowing down; allowing the client to tolerate feelings of “not enoughness”; and 3. Psychodynamic Axis: Working through unconscious identifications with hurried caregivers or cultural/familial scripts that equated value with speed; and
- Relational level: The therapeutic relationship offers a space of slowness, where presence and atonement are modelled. The therapist’s calm pacing helps the client experience that connection is not lost when time is not rushed. The ultimate aim is not to eliminate urgency altogether, but to help the client develop a flexible relationship with time: to distinguish contexts where efficiency is appropriate from those where presence, reflection, and stillness are more valuable.

The *Hurry Up* driver reflects a child’s strategic attempt to cope with the fear of inadequacy by equating speed with safety. It allows survival in environments that reward urgency, but in adulthood it becomes a source of stress, inefficiency, and relational strain.

In ISP, *Hurry Up* is recognised as an intermediate belief that operates across biological, psychological, and relational levels, shaping the cognitive, emotional, and psychodynamic axes. Psychotherapy helps clients dismantle the false link between speed and worth, reclaim the capacity for presence, and discover that authenticity and value are not measured in urgency but in the quality of being.

5. *Try Hard / Work Hard*

The driver *“Try Hard / Work Hard”* usually arises from early internalisations of injunctions such as *“Don’t Succeed”*, *“Don’t Be You”* or *“Don’t Be Important”*. In such contexts, the child is repeatedly exposed to critical or contradictory parental expectations: achievement may be demanded, but success is never quite enough, or is immediately devalued. As a result, the child absorbs the conviction: *"I am incompetent,"* or *"I must constantly prove myself to be acceptable."*

This creates a relational paradox: the child is recognised for effort but rarely for actual accomplishment or intrinsic value. To survive, they form the rule: *"If I try hard enough, maybe I will succeed or be accepted."* Effort becomes a substitute for worth.

As an intermediate belief, *Try Hard* functions as a compensatory strategy against the core conviction of incompetence. By exerting relentless effort, the child seeks to disprove the inner belief of inadequacy. However, because the focus is on trying rather than achieving, the driver ensures that success remains elusive. Each effort, no matter how great, confirms the assumption that more effort is required.

Thus, *Try Hard* maintains a perpetual loop: effort leads to temporary relief, collapse follows exhaustion, and shame reinforces the cycle.

Manifestations Across the Three Levels of the Self are: 1. Biological Level: Chronic fatigue and cycles of overexertion followed by burnout; Somatic symptoms: tension, headaches, digestive issues, lowered immunity due to constant stress; and Dysregulated energy patterns, oscillating between hyperactivation ("trying harder") and depletion. 2. Psychological Level: Cognitive Axis: Rigid beliefs such as *"I must never stop trying"* or *"If I don't push myself, I will fail"*; Emotional Axis: Shame when effort does not yield results; guilt when resting; anxiety when performance is questioned; and Psychodynamic Axis: Internalised parental voices demanding effort without satisfaction; unconscious loyalty to parents who themselves lived in cycles of effort and disappointment. 3. Relational Level: Relationships framed around effort and sacrifice: giving more than receiving; Difficulty tolerating ease, support, or success—leading to unconscious sabotage; Partners, colleagues, or friends may perceive the individual as overcommitted but never content; and Chronic resentment when unrecognised for effort, despite striving.

The *Try Hard / Work Hard* driver is a survival strategy: it offers the child a way to secure recognition, however minimal, in environments where unconditional love was absent. By demonstrating relentless effort, the child avoids rejection and earns some semblance of value. Yet this adaptation has inherent costs: 1. Exhaustion – sustained effort drains energy without delivering fulfilment; 2. Perpetual dissatisfaction – success is never enough; effort is valued over outcomes; 3. Self-sabotage – overcommitment leads to collapse, reinforcing beliefs of incompetence; and 4. Loss of authenticity – the individual equates identity with struggle, leaving little space for joy, creativity, or rest.

In adulthood, *Try Hard* may manifest as: 1. Overworking, often beyond what is required, without feeling satisfaction; 2. Difficulty resting or engaging in leisure activities without guilt; 3. Cycles of high productivity followed by collapse and shame; 4. Perfectionistic procrastination: investing immense effort but avoiding completion for fear of inadequacy; and 5. Vulnerability to burnout, depression, and relational breakdowns.

Such individuals may present in therapy exhausted, describing themselves as "always running but never arriving." They often believe they are only valued for effort, never for who they are.

Interventions with *Try Hard* require a multi-layered approach:

- Biological level: Helping clients regulate cycles of overactivation and collapse, through pacing, grounding, and restorative practices;
- Psychological level: 1. Cognitive Axis: Identifying the rule *"If I try hard enough, maybe I will be accepted"* and linking it to the core belief *"I am incompetent"*; 2. Emotional Axis: Exploring the shame and grief that drive the endless striving; working through guilt associated with rest and play; and 3. Psychodynamic Axis: Addressing unconscious loyalty to parental or cultural scripts that equated worth with effort, and mourning the absence of unconditional acceptance; and
- Relational level: The therapeutic relationship becomes a corrective experience where the client is valued for presence rather than performance. Through consistent acceptance, the psychotherapist models a reality where worth is not dependent on effort.

The goal is to transform the *Try Hard* driver into a more balanced orientation: valuing effort when appropriate, but no longer equating it with survival or identity. Clients are supported to discover intrinsic worth, joy in achievement, and the possibility of rest without guilt.

The *Try Hard / Work Hard* driver exemplifies how children adapt to environments that deny unconditional love. It offers survival through effort but perpetuates exhaustion, shame, and dissatisfaction.

In ISP, this driver is understood as an intermediate belief that links core convictions of incompetence to surface behaviours of relentless striving. It operates across all three levels—biological, psychological, relational—and expresses itself through the cognitive, emotional, and psychodynamic axes.

Psychotherapy dismantles the false equation between effort and worth, enabling clients to experience value beyond struggle, and to embrace rest, authenticity, and self-acceptance.

All five drivers illustrate the paradox of intermediate beliefs: they are designed to protect the self from the pain of core convictions, yet they simultaneously reinforce them: *Be Perfect* confirms *"I am inadequate unless flawless"*; *Be Strong* confirms *"Vulnerability is dangerous"*; *Please Others* confirms *"I am unlovable unless compliant"*; *Hurry Up* confirms *"I am insufficient unless fast"*; and *Try Hard* confirms *"I am incompetent unless I exhaust myself."*

In this way, drivers can be seen as the operational face of core beliefs: they translate deep prohibitions into daily behavioural rules, ensuring the continuity of the life script.

From an ISP perspective, drivers can be seen as the linking mechanisms between injunctions (core prohibitions) and life scripts (externalised patterns): Injunction (core belief): *"Don't Be Important"*; Driver (intermediate belief): *"Please Others"*; and Life script (external self): Chronic invisibility, difficulty asserting needs, exploitation in relationships.

Thus, drivers translate the child's early prohibitions into workable but costly strategies for navigating life. While they may serve a protective function in childhood, in adulthood they perpetuate patterns of rigidity, exhaustion, and relational disconnection. Therapeutic work with drivers therefore represents a central task of the Cognitive Axis, but it also necessarily engages the emotional and psychodynamic axes, as well as all three levels of the self: biological, psychological, and relational.

Working with drivers typically involves several interconnected steps:

- Identification – Helping clients recognise their internal imperatives and the "rules for living" they unconsciously follow. For example, noticing repeated phrases such as *"I must always try harder"* or *"I cannot show weakness"*;
- Linking to Core Beliefs – Demonstrating how drivers serve as protective adaptations rooted in deeper convictions. A *Be Perfect* driver may mask the core belief *"I am inadequate"*;

- Exploration of Costs and Benefits – Understanding the protective role of the driver in childhood (securing safety, recognition, or belonging), while also highlighting its limitations in adulthood (burnout, alienation, emotional suppression);
- Challenging and Reframing – Encouraging clients to question the validity of drivers, testing new beliefs and behaviours in a safe therapeutic context; and
- Integration across Axes – Supporting clients in embodying new patterns not only cognitively, but also emotionally, behaviourally, and relationally.

For example, a client driven by *Be Perfect* may first need to experience in therapy that making mistakes does not lead to rejection. Such relational correction allows for the gradual replacement of perfectionistic rules with more flexible, compassionate beliefs.

Psychotherapy with drivers in ISP is most effective when it addresses them across all three levels of the self and within each of the psychological axes:

- Biological level – Helping clients become aware of the physiological signatures of driver activation, such as tension, restlessness, shallow breathing, or chronic fatigue. Developing body-based regulation strategies can loosen the grip of drivers on the nervous system;
- Psychological level: 1. Cognitive Axis: Identifying drivers as intermediate beliefs, linking them to core beliefs, and testing their validity; 2. Emotional Axis: Reconnecting with suppressed affects (e.g., sadness hidden under *Be Strong*, anger under *Please Others*); and 3. Psychodynamic Axis: Exploring unconscious loyalties to parental figures or family narratives that continue to sustain driver rules; and
- Relational level – Investigating how drivers shape interpersonal dynamics, particularly within the therapeutic relationship, where early patterns of compliance, perfectionism, or distance are often replayed.

Across these dimensions, psychotherapy provides the client with opportunities to experience that worth and safety are not conditional upon following driver imperatives.

True change emerges when clients encounter new embodied, emotional, and relational experiences that directly contradict the old rules. For instance, a *Be Strong* client may discover that showing vulnerability in therapy leads to deeper connection rather than rejection. A *Please Others* client may experience that asserting their needs does not result in abandonment but in respect and recognition. A *Hurry Up* client may come to realise that slowing down does not lead to failure, but to greater presence and effectiveness. Such corrective experiences gradually loosen the hold of drivers, enabling clients to live with greater authenticity, balance, and resilience.

Drivers, as described in Transactional Analysis, find a natural theoretical home in Integrative Strategic Psychotherapy as intermediate beliefs within the Cognitive Axis. They represent conditional survival strategies that shield individuals from the raw pain of core beliefs but simultaneously perpetuate them.

By addressing drivers as strategic rules for living, ISP provides a comprehensive approach: identifying the driver, linking it to its core belief origin, exploring its protective function, and fostering new adaptive beliefs and behaviours. In this way, clients can move beyond the compulsions of perfection, strength, compliance, speed, or endless effort, toward lives marked by authenticity, balance, and relational freedom.

7.1.4. Automatic Thoughts

In Integrative Strategic Psychotherapy (ISP), automatic thoughts are seen as rapid, often unconscious, cognitive evaluations that arise in specific situations. They are shaped by core beliefs (rigid convictions about the self, others, and the world) and intermediate beliefs (conditional rules for living, such as drivers). Automatic thoughts are considered "automatic" because they appear almost instantaneously, without deliberate reflection, and strongly influence emotional and behavioural reactions.

As Hoffmann (2012) notes, automatic thoughts occur with such speed that individuals often perceive them as objective truths rather than as subjective interpretations. Robertson (2010) highlights several common patterns of automatic thoughts, such as black-and-white thinking, personalization, negative filtering, disqualifying the positive, jumping to conclusions, overgeneralization, catastrophizing, and emotional reasoning.

From the perspective of ISP, automatic thoughts represent the surface-level expression of deeper structures within the self. They are the most accessible layer of the cognitive process for therapeutic exploration, but they are never isolated. Instead, they are the tip of the iceberg, rooted in the proto-self, crystallised in the core self, organised strategically in the plastic self, and enacted behaviourally and relationally through the external self.

At the proto-self level, the foundation for automatic thoughts is laid in early sensory-affective experiences. These pre-symbolic impressions shape how the child interprets stimuli long before language develops. For instance, an infant repeatedly met with parental criticism or lack of atonement may embody a proto-cognition such as *"Something is wrong with me."*

Later, when encountering minor mistakes, this embodied conclusion can quickly trigger automatic thoughts like *"I am stupid"* or *"I always mess things up."* Thus, even though automatic thoughts appear "cognitive," they are rooted in early affective-somatic experiences.

At the core self level, proto-cognitions crystallise into rigid core beliefs (e.g., *"I am inadequate," "I am unlovable"*). Automatic thoughts are the immediate, situation-specific echoes of these global convictions. When a student does not greet their teacher, the teacher may automatically think: *"She must be upset with me,"* reflecting the core belief *"I am unworthy of respect."* Automatic thoughts at this level demonstrate the link between the unconscious stability of core beliefs and the conscious fluidity of daily cognition.

At the level of the plastic self, automatic thoughts are shaped by intermediate beliefs (drivers) and serve as moment-to-moment strategies for navigating life. For example: a *Be Perfect* driver produces automatic thoughts like: *"If I don't perform flawlessly, I will be rejected."* A *Please Others* driver fuels thoughts like: *"If I say no, they will leave me."* A *Be Strong* driver generates thoughts such as: *"If I cry, I will look weak."*

Here, automatic thoughts operate as micro-adaptations: rapid cognitive tools designed to maintain attachment and avoid shame. They are less stable than core beliefs but more flexible, which makes them particularly amenable to therapeutic intervention.

At the external self level, automatic thoughts manifest in observable behaviour and relational dynamics. For example, a manager who catastrophises (*"If my team misses this deadline, I'll be fired"*) may overwork employees, damaging relationships. A person who disqualifies positives (*"They praised me only because they felt sorry for me"*) may appear dismissive of compliments, creating distance in friendships.

Thus, automatic thoughts are not purely intrapsychic—they shape scripts of action, interaction, and identity in the external world.

Following Robertson (2010), common categories of automatic thoughts can be reinterpreted within the ISP framework:

1. Black-and-White Thinking. Example: *"If I don't study perfectly, I'm stupid"*. ISP View: Reflects rigid core beliefs (*"I am inadequate"*) and perfectionistic drivers (*Be Perfect*). Rooted in proto-self experiences where only flawless behaviour elicited approval;
2. Personalisation. Example: *"If a student laughs, it's because they're mocking me."* ISP View: The external self interprets ambiguous relational cues through the lens of inadequacy or unlovability. Often connected with *Please Others* or *Don't Be Important* injunctions;
3. Negative Filtering. Example: Ignoring positive feedback while focusing on one criticism. ISP View: Cognitive strategy of the plastic self to confirm core beliefs (*"I am not good enough"*), even when reality offers disconfirming evidence;
4. Disqualifying the Positive. Example: *"Even though students said they enjoyed the presentation, one person laughed—so clearly, I'm stupid."* ISP View: A self-sabotaging mechanism that sustains shame-based beliefs by dismissing corrective relational feedback;
5. Jumping to Conclusions. Example: *"If my friend didn't text me, she must be upset with me."* ISP View: A rapid attachment-based evaluation rooted in fear of rejection (*"I don't matter"*). At the relational level, this often produces defensive or clingy behaviours;
6. Overgeneralisation. Example: *"If I have the flu, it means I am sickly and will always be ill."* ISP View: Expansion of specific events into global identities, reflecting the stability of core beliefs over transient experiences;
7. Catastrophising. Example: *"If my son was stopped by the police, he'll lose his licence, drive without one, and end up in jail."* ISP View: Reflects hyperactivation of threat responses at the biological level, amplified by core beliefs of helplessness or danger; and
8. Emotional Reasoning. Example: *"I feel worthless, so I must be worthless."* ISP View: Collapse of cognitive and emotional axes; affect is misinterpreted as evidence. Originates in proto-self experiences where strong emotions were unmediated by attuned caregivers.

Because automatic thoughts are the most accessible entry point into the deeper layers of cognition, they are often the starting place for therapeutic work:

- Cognitive Axis: Clients are encouraged to identify automatic thoughts, trace them back to intermediate and core beliefs, and reframe them into more adaptive cognitions;
- Emotional Axis: Psychotherapists invite exploration of the affect underlying the thought (e.g., shame, fear), providing corrective emotional experiences where these feelings are validated; and
- Psychodynamic Axis: Automatic thoughts are analysed in the context of transference and life scripts, uncovering unconscious loyalties to parental figures or family narratives.

At the biological level, attention to physiological correlates (e.g., racing heart during catastrophising) helps clients recognise the embodied nature of these thoughts. At the relational level, the therapeutic alliance itself becomes the context for testing alternative interpretations: clients discover that expressing fear, shame, or anger does not inevitably lead to rejection.

A client with the core belief *"I am unlovable"* and the driver *Please Others* might automatically think during a minor disagreement: *"If I assert my opinion, she will leave me"*:

- Proto-Self: Embodied fear of abandonment when expressing needs as a child;
- Core Self: Conviction *"I don't matter"*;
- Plastic Self: Rule *"If I comply, I will be accepted"*; and
- External Self: Behaviour of self-silencing in relationships, leading to resentment.

In psychotherapy, identifying this automatic thought opens the path to deeper exploration of the core belief and the relational scripts that perpetuate it.

In conclusion, automatic thoughts in ISP are not isolated cognitive errors but surface expressions of a layered self-system. They arise from embodied proto-cognitions, crystallised core beliefs, strategic rules of the plastic self, and are enacted in relational scripts through the external self.

Understanding and working with automatic thoughts therefore requires an integrative approach: identifying the thought itself, linking it to deeper structures, exploring its emotional and embodied correlates, and transforming relational scripts through corrective experiences.

Therapeutic change occurs when clients come to see automatic thoughts not as truths, but as signals—reminders of old survival strategies that can now be replaced with flexible, authentic, and life-enhancing ways of thinking, feeling, and relating.

7.2. Perfectionism

Perfectionism has long been recognised as a multidimensional construct with both adaptive and maladaptive aspects. On the one hand, striving for excellence can promote achievement, conscientiousness, and resilience; on the other, excessive perfectionism can generate debilitating anxiety, depression, obsessive-compulsive traits, and relational dysfunction. In the context of Integrative Strategic Psychotherapy (ISP), perfectionism is understood as more than a personality style or cognitive pattern: it represents a complex survival strategy rooted in early relational experiences, sustained by core beliefs, and enacted through rigid intermediate beliefs, such as the *Be Perfect* driver.

Flatt and Hewitt (2002) identify six dimensions of perfectionism:

1. Excessive concern over mistakes;
2. Excessively high personal standards (e.g., *"I must be the best"*);
3. High parental expectations (the belief that parental approval is unattainable);
4. Parental criticism;
5. Exaggerated emphasis on precision, order, and organisation; and
6. Doubts about actions.

Of these, excessive concern over mistakes and doubts about actions are most strongly associated with psychopathology, often linked to obsessive-compulsive tendencies (Stoeber & Childs, 2010).

Perfectionism can manifest in self-oriented forms (the individual demands flawlessness from themselves) or other-oriented forms (the individual imposes excessively high standards on others) (Hewitt & Flett, 1991). In both cases, perfectionism reflects a deeper struggle with self-worth, attachment, and identity.

While some perfectionist behaviours may appear adaptive—ambition, conscientiousness, efficiency—maladaptive perfectionism carries heavy psychological costs. Individuals may live under a rigid internal rule that *"nothing can go wrong."* Delays or minor mistakes are experienced catastrophically, leading to feelings of incompetence and despair.

Perfectionists often adopt maladaptive coping strategies when confronted with stressors. For example, they may interpret failure as evidence of helplessness or incompetence, which leads to avoidance rather than problem-solving. In this way, perfectionism paradoxically undermines performance (Stoeber & Childs, 2010).

Social relationships are also affected. Perfectionists frequently perceive others as unaccepting, which mirrors their own lack of self-acceptance (Shafran & Mansell, 2001). They may believe they do not deserve affection unless flawless, leading to withdrawal, hostility, or chronic disappointment. While non-perfectionists can endure setbacks while maintaining self-confidence, perfectionists link failure with unworthiness.

Cognitively, perfectionism is sustained by rumination: repeated revisiting of perceived mistakes or failures. Rumination functions as an attempt to regain control, yet it traps the individual in cycles of shame and self-criticism (Flatt & Hewitt, 2002).

In ISP, perfectionism is not seen as a fixed personality trait, but as a multilevel adaptation shaped by early relational contexts and organised across the layers of the self. Perfectionism originates in the proto-self through early sensory-affective impressions. Infants who encounter critical or inconsistent caregiving may embody pre-symbolic conclusions such as *"Something is wrong with me when I fail"*. These proto-cognitions are not verbal but are stored somatically as tension, hypervigilance, or states of anxiety. At the core self level, these embodied impressions crystallise into rigid beliefs: *"I am inadequate," "I am only loved when perfect," "Mistakes mean rejection."* Such beliefs form the foundation of perfectionism. They are global, rigid, and often unconscious. At the plastic self level, perfectionism manifests through intermediate beliefs, specifically the *Be Perfect* driver: *"If I am flawless, then I will be safe and accepted."* Here, perfectionism functions as a survival strategy: it protects the individual from shame and rejection by maintaining the illusion of control. However, it also sustains the very core belief it seeks to mask, as worth remains conditional on flawless performance.

Automatic thoughts at this level illustrate perfectionist patterns: Black-and-white thinking (*"If I don't succeed completely, I have failed"*); Catastrophising (*"If I make a mistake, I will be humiliated"*); and Disqualifying the positive (*"They praised me, but they didn't mean it"*).

At the external self level, perfectionism is enacted in behaviour, identity, and relationships. The perfectionist may overwork, avoid risks, procrastinate when perfection is unattainable, or become critical of others. Relationally, perfectionists may distance themselves to avoid exposure of flaws, or impose impossible standards on partners and children. In professional contexts, they may oscillate between overachievement and burnout.

The *Be Perfect* driver epitomises perfectionism in ISP. Originating from injunctions such as *"Don't Exist"* or *"Don't Be You"*, this driver operates as an intermediate belief: *"If I am perfect, I will be acceptable."* While this driver protects against the core conviction of inadequacy, it also maintains the wound. Perfectionism becomes the self's armour—useful for survival in childhood, but restrictive and self-defeating in adulthood.

Clinically, the *Be Perfect* driver is often associated with: 1. Chronic anxiety and fear of criticism; 2. Procrastination, when flawlessness cannot be guaranteed; 3. Shame when imperfection is revealed, and 4. Rigid relational patterns, where vulnerability and authenticity are avoided.

Neuroscientific research supports the ISP view that perfectionism is not merely cognitive but also embodied. Repeated exposure to critical or inconsistent parenting sensitises the stress response system (HPA axis), leading to hyperactivation when mistakes or failures occur (Shields et al., 2016). The right hemisphere, associated with affect regulation and social-emotional processing (Schore, 2009), becomes primed for shame responses, while prefrontal networks over-engage in control and rumination.

Thus, perfectionism can be understood as a neuropsychological adaptation: a chronic state of vigilance designed to avoid relational rejection.

Perfectionism profoundly affects relationships. The perfectionist often fears intimacy, equating vulnerability with exposure of flaws. Alternatively, they may project their perfectionism outward, imposing high standards on others. In both cases, relationships are strained: partners may feel criticised, children pressured, or colleagues alienated.

At the external self level, perfectionism becomes a script:

- In families, the perfectionist child becomes the "responsible one," striving to meet parental expectations while suppressing their own needs;
- In work contexts, the perfectionist employee over-delivers but is never satisfied, perpetuating cycles of burnout; and

- In psychotherapy, perfectionism can manifest as performance in the therapeutic relationship: clients may seek to "do therapy perfectly" to avoid criticism.

Therapeutic work with perfectionism involves interventions across all levels and axes:

- Biological Level: Helping clients recognise physiological correlates of perfectionism (tension, restlessness) and practise regulation strategies;
- Cognitive Axis: Identifying perfectionistic automatic thoughts, linking them to the Be Perfect driver and core beliefs, and reframing them (e.g., *"Mistakes are part of learning"*);
- Emotional Axis: Creating a safe space for clients to experience and process shame, fear of rejection, and grief for the absence of unconditional acceptance;
- Psychodynamic Axis: Exploring unconscious loyalties to perfectionistic parents or family scripts. Addressing transference when perfectionism plays out in therapy; and
- Relational Level: Modelling acceptance in the therapeutic alliance, demonstrating that worth is not conditional upon flawless performance.

The psychotherapeutic aim is to help clients transform conditional worth into intrinsic self-acceptance. Perfectionism can then shift from rigid survival rule to flexible striving for excellence, balanced with compassion and tolerance for imperfection.

In conclusion, perfectionism in ISP is best understood as a multilevel, multi-axial adaptation. Rooted in proto-self impressions of inadequacy, crystallised as core self convictions, organised through the *Be Perfect* driver in the plastic self, and enacted in external scripts, perfectionism is both a protective strategy and a source of suffering.

While adaptive forms of striving may coexist with perfectionism, maladaptive forms perpetuate anxiety, shame, and relational strain. Integrative psychotherapy must therefore address perfectionism not only cognitively but also emotionally, somatically, psychodynamically, and relationally.

Healing occurs when clients discover that worth is not contingent on flawlessness but on the inherent value of being human.

7.3. The Explanatory Style

The explanatory style refers to the habitual way in which people interpret the causes of life events—why things happen to them, both positive and negative. It is not simply a matter of optimism versus pessimism but represents a more nuanced pattern of cognitive processing that reflects the individual's deepest core beliefs and their strategic adaptations for managing uncertainty, success, or failure.

According to Hoffmann (2012), the explanatory style is shaped by three dimensions: 1. Personalisation – whether the individual attributes the cause of events internally (*"It's my fault"*) or externally (*"It was bad luck, poor design, or someone else's responsibility"*); 2. Permanence – whether the person perceives causes as stable (*"This will never change")* or temporary (*"This was a one-time mistake"*); and 3. Pervasiveness – whether the explanation is seen as global, affecting all areas of life (*"I can't do anything right"*), or specific, limited to one domain (*"I am not good at maths, but I am good at art"*).

Robertson (2010) notes that a pessimistic explanatory style tends to personalise negative events, view them as permanent, and generalise them across life domains. Conversely, an optimistic explanatory style externalises or contextualises negative events, sees them as temporary, and limits their scope.

A pessimistic explanatory style is strongly associated with depression, anxiety, and even physical illnesses, as it colours the individual's ability to recover from setbacks. Optimism, on the other hand, supports resilience, persistence, and improved health outcomes. Importantly, the explanatory style is not static; individuals may show different explanatory styles in different areas of their lives (e.g., optimistic about career, pessimistic about relationships).

Within the framework of Integrative Strategic Psychotherapy (ISP), the explanatory style is understood as the cognitive interface between early self-organisation and present-day meaning-making. It reflects how proto-cognitions, core beliefs, and drivers are activated in daily life and translated into habitual interpretations of events.

At the proto-self level, the explanatory style has its roots in pre-symbolic representations. If an infant's cries are consistently met with frustration or indifference, the embodied proto-cognition may be: *"Something is wrong with me."* This is not yet a conscious attribution but a somatic-affective conclusion encoded into the nervous system. Later in life, such embodied impressions predispose the individual to personalise negative events (*"It must be my fault"*).

At the core self level, proto-cognitions crystallise into rigid core beliefs (e.g., *"I am inadequate," "I am unlovable"*). These core convictions heavily determine explanatory style. For example, a belief of *"I am incompetent"* produces explanations that emphasise permanence and pervasiveness (*"I always fail; I fail at everything"*). A belief of *"Others cannot be trusted"* generates external attributions, blaming others or circumstances for failures. Thus, the explanatory style is the cognitive echo of core beliefs in everyday life.

At the level of the plastic self, the explanatory style is shaped by drivers (intermediate beliefs), which function as conditional rules. For example, the *Be Perfect* driver leads to excessive personalisation of mistakes (*"I should have prevented this; I must always be flawless"*). The *Be Strong* driver minimises vulnerability and externalises blame (*"This isn't about me; I just need to endure"*). The *Please Others* driver generates pervasiveness: failures in one domain are generalised (*"If I can't please my boss, I can't please anyone"*). Here, the explanatory style becomes a strategic adaptation: a way to preserve attachment and protect against shame.

At the external self level, the explanatory style shapes identity, relationships, and social interactions. For instance, an employee with a pessimistic explanatory style may interpret a negative performance review as proof of global incompetence, leading to withdrawal from colleagues and diminished career growth. Conversely, someone with an optimistic explanatory style may see the same review as temporary and specific, using it as motivation for improvement.

The explanatory style thus becomes a script for navigating the world, influencing not only how the individual thinks about events but also how they act, relate, and position themselves socially.

A pessimistic explanatory style is strongly correlated with: 1. Depression – The individual attributes failures internally, permanently, and globally, creating a sense of hopelessness (Abramson, Seligman, & Teasdale, 1978); 2. Anxiety – Catastrophic interpretations of events amplify fear and avoidance; and 3. Physical illness – Research indicates that pessimism is associated with poorer immune function and higher morbidity (Peterson & Steen, 2002).

Conversely, an optimistic explanatory style supports resilience, problem-solving, and persistence in the face of adversity. Yet, extreme optimism may also be maladaptive if it fosters denial of responsibility or minimisation of risks.

Examples of explanatory style in practice are:

- Personalisation: A client says, *"The relationship ended because I wasn't good enough,"* reflecting internalisation of blame;
- Permanence: After a failure, a student concludes, *"I'll never succeed in life,"* seeing the cause as unchangeable; and
- Pervasiveness: Following a single rejection, a client states, *"Nobody will ever love me,"* extending the event to all domains.

Optimistic counterparts include: *"This exam went badly, but it doesn't mean I'm unintelligent"* (external, temporary, specific) or *"This conflict with my partner is difficult, but it's limited to this situation, and we can work through it".*

Psychotherapy in ISP targets the explanatory style across all axes and levels:

- Biological level: Helping clients notice physiological arousal when confronted with setbacks (tightness, racing heart) and regulate stress responses, preventing over-personalisation or catastrophising;

- Cognitive Axis: Identifying explanatory patterns, linking them to drivers and core beliefs, and reframing attributions into more balanced forms;
- Emotional Axis: Exploring the shame, fear, or grief underlying pessimistic attributions, and creating space for corrective emotional experiences;
- Psychodynamic Axis: Addressing unconscious identifications with pessimistic or critical parental figures who modelled negative explanatory styles; and
- Relational level: Within the therapeutic alliance, the client experiences acceptance that is not contingent on flawless explanations. The psychotherapist models more flexible, contextualised interpretations of events. For example, a *Be Perfect* client who blames themselves for every error may, in therapy, test new interpretations: *"Perhaps the situation was complex, and not everything depended on me."* Over time, these new experiences reconfigure the explanatory style from pessimistic and rigid to more adaptive and flexible.

In other words, the explanatory style in ISP is conceptualised as the bridge between deep self-structures and surface cognitive habits. It is rooted in proto-self impressions of safety or danger, crystallised as core beliefs, shaped by drivers in the plastic self, and enacted relationally through the external self. A pessimistic explanatory style perpetuates depression, anxiety, and relational withdrawal, while an optimistic explanatory style supports resilience and growth. Therapeutic change requires not just cognitive reframing but also embodied, emotional, psychodynamic, and relational corrections, enabling the client to experience events in ways that no longer confirm the old wounds of inadequacy or rejection.

In this way, ISP reframes the explanatory style as not simply a cognitive bias but as a strategic narrative of survival, one that can be revised and healed through integrative therapeutic work.

7.4. Self-Efficacy

Self-efficacy, as defined by Bandura (1977), refers to the belief or expectation that one is capable of executing behaviours necessary to manage future situations. It represents not an objective measure of skill, but a subjective evaluation of one's own capacity to mobilise resources, take action, and persist despite obstacles.

In practical terms, self-efficacy is the confidence in one's ability to exert control over one's functioning and environment (Bandura, 1989). An individual's judgment of self-efficacy influences whether they attempt a behaviour, how much effort they put into it, and how long they persist when confronted with difficulty (Themanson et al., 2011).

Research shows that higher self-efficacy predicts greater resilience, achievement, and psychological well-being, whereas lower self-efficacy is associated with avoidance, hopelessness, and vulnerability to relapse in maladaptive behaviours (Candiotte & Lichtenstein, 1981; Green, 2003).

In ISP, self-efficacy is not treated as a mere "trait," but as a dynamic interplay between early representations of the self, cognitive rules for living, and relational scripts. It reflects how the different layers of the self (proto, core, plastic, external) organise expectations about the future, and how injunctions, drivers, and automatic thoughts converge to shape motivation.

At the proto-self level, self-efficacy is rooted in early sensory-affective experiences of agency. When infants' signals (crying, reaching, moving) are consistently met with attuned caregiving, they embody a proto-cognition: *"My actions bring predictable results."* This is the first building block of self-efficacy. In contrast, inconsistent or neglectful responses produce a proto-cognition of inefficacy: *"What I do has no effect."* This embodied impression can later resurface as passivity, avoidance, or a pessimistic explanatory style.

At the core self level, proto-cognitions crystallise into core beliefs such as: *"I can influence my environment"* (high self-efficacy) or *"I am powerless; nothing I do matters"* (low self-efficacy). These core beliefs then determine global expectations about success, resilience, and the ability to cope with stress. For instance, the core belief *"I am incompetent"* will colour self-efficacy judgments across life domains, leading the individual to underestimate their ability even in areas where they may in fact be competent.

At the plastic self level, self-efficacy is mediated by drivers and intermediate beliefs. For example, the *Be Perfect* driver sustains conditional self-efficacy: *"I am effective only if I never make mistakes."* The *Be Strong* driver fosters a rigid self-efficacy: *"I must always cope alone; seeking help means failure."* The *Please Others* driver leads to relationally dependent self-efficacy: *"I can manage only if others approve of me."* Here, self-efficacy is less about actual capacity and more about conditional rules derived from injunctions (*Don't Be You*, *Don't Feel*, *Don't Succeed*). The result is often fragile or domain-specific self-efficacy, easily undermined by criticism or failure.

At the external self level, self-efficacy is expressed in behaviours, identity, and relational patterns. A person with high self-efficacy demonstrates initiative, persistence, and flexible problem-solving. Someone with low self-efficacy may procrastinate, avoid challenges, or give up quickly.

In relationships, low self-efficacy manifests as dependency, avoidance of conflict, or over-reliance on others for decision-making. In professional life, it may appear as reluctance to take responsibility, fear of leadership roles, or chronic self-doubt despite competence.

In ISP, self-efficacy cannot be understood without considering injunctions (prohibitions) and drivers (conditional rules). Injunctions such as *Don't Succeed*, *Don't Be You*, and *Don't Do Anything* directly undermine self-efficacy by prohibiting agency, autonomy, and success. Drivers then attempt to compensate: *Be Perfect* - "If I am flawless, then I will be effective"; *Try Hard* - "If I keep struggling, maybe I will succeed"; *Be Strong* → "I must cope without help to prove my capacity"; and *Please Others* → "I am effective only when approved by others."

This dynamic explains why many clients present with a paradox: they appear competent externally but remain plagued by chronic self-doubt internally. Their self-efficacy is conditional, fragile, and dependent on external validation.

Self-efficacy is closely linked to the explanatory style (Seligman, 1991). Individuals with high self-efficacy tend to interpret setbacks as temporary, specific, and surmountable. Those with low self-efficacy interpret failures as permanent, pervasive, and personal. For example, an individual with high self-efficacy might say: *"This presentation went badly, but I can improve next time"*, whilst someone with low self-efficacy may think: *"I always fail; I can't do anything right."* Thus, the explanatory style serves as the cognitive pathway through which self-efficacy shapes resilience or vulnerability.

Clinical Implications of Self-Efficacy in ISP are considered at multiple levels: 1. Cognitive Axis: Identify core beliefs undermining self-efficacy (e.g., *"I am powerless"*); Trace conditional drivers (*Be Perfect*, *Try Hard*) that create fragile efficacy; and Reframe automatic thoughts: *"I failed once"* → *"This is an opportunity to learn"*; 2. Emotional Axis: Address shame and fear of failure underpinning low self-efficacy; and Provide corrective emotional experiences where vulnerability is met with acceptance; 3. Psychodynamic Axis: Explore unconscious loyalties to parents with pessimistic or critical explanatory styles; and Work through transference where the therapist is experienced as a critical evaluator; 4. Biological Level: Regulate physiological states (stress, hyperarousal) that reinforce learned helplessness; and 5. Relational Level: Within the therapeutic alliance, model collaborative problem-solving and persistence; and help clients test new behaviours in safe relational contexts.

Prochaska and DiClemente's (2005) stages of change model shows that self-efficacy is essential for progression through pre-contemplation, contemplation, preparation, action, and maintenance. In early stages, temptations (impulses to relapse) are high, self-efficacy is low. In later stages, temptations decrease, and self-efficacy strengthens. Successful change requires building belief in one's capacity to act, not only reducing risk factors.

Maria, a 35-year-old lawyer, sought psychotherapy for anxiety and burnout. Despite professional success, she felt "incompetent" and dreaded making mistakes. Her explanatory style was pessimistic: setbacks were seen as permanent and personal:

- Proto-self: Early experiences of parental criticism left her with the embodied proto-cognition *"My actions are never enough"*;
- Core self: She carried the belief *"I am inadequate"*;

- Plastic self: She adopted the *Be Perfect* driver: *"If I am flawless, I will be safe"*; and
- External self: At work, she over-prepared, avoided risk, and collapsed into exhaustion.

In therapy, Maria identified her automatic perfectionist thoughts, explored the shame underlying them, and gradually tested new relational experiences with her therapist where mistakes were tolerated. Over time, her self-efficacy increased: she began to attempt new strategies, delegate tasks, and interpret setbacks as opportunities for growth.

As a conclusion, self-efficacy in ISP is not just a trait but a multi-layered construct that reflects how the self organises expectations of agency and control. It originates in early proto-cognitions of efficacy or helplessness, crystallises into core beliefs of competence or incompetence, is shaped by conditional drivers such as *Be Perfect* or *Be Strong*, and manifests in external scripts of avoidance, persistence, or overcompensation. Therapeutic work in ISP aims to strengthen self-efficacy by: uncovering the injunctions and core beliefs that undermine it, challenging conditional drivers that make efficacy fragile, reframing the explanatory style toward optimism, offering corrective emotional and relational experiences, and helping clients embody new patterns of agency across life domains.

When self-efficacy is rebuilt, clients not only change specific behaviours but also transform their orientation to the future: from helplessness and avoidance to initiative, persistence, and authentic engagement with life.

7.5. Learned Helplessness

Learned helplessness is a phenomenon first described by Seligman and colleagues, whereby a person, despite having all the opportunities to help themselves avoid unpleasant circumstances or obtain rewards, fails to act. This passivity arises from the expectation that future events are uncontrollable, leading to profound disruptions in motivation, learning, and emotional regulation (Bauer et al., 2003; Cemalcilar et al., 2003).

In essence, learned helplessness represents a generalised conclusion of inefficacy: *"No matter what I do, it will not matter."* While initially tied to specific adverse experiences, this conclusion often generalises across life domains, undermining self-efficacy, the explanatory style, and ultimately the capacity for autonomous action.

Neurobiologically, research suggests that the anterior cingulate cortex (ACC), responsible for conflict monitoring and goal-directed processing, plays a crucial role. In situations of repeated failure or uncontrollability, ACC activity is inhibited by hyperactivation of the amygdala (associated with fear and learned threat), resulting in diminished goal-directed behaviour and the passivity characteristic of helplessness (Bauer et al., 2003).

The relationship between learned helplessness and the explanatory style is critical. As Hagger et al. (2010) emphasise, two individuals may encounter the same adverse situation, yet their interpretations of the event—whether framed as temporary/specific or permanent/pervasive—determine whether helplessness develops. A pessimistic explanatory style (personal, permanent, pervasive attributions) makes the individual have high vulnerability to helplessness and depression. An optimistic explanatory style (external, unstable, specific attributions) leads to protection against helplessness. Thus, the explanatory style functions as the cognitive pathway through which past uncontrollability becomes future passivity.

From the perspective of Integrative Strategic Psychotherapy, learned helplessness is not merely a behavioural deficit, but a multi-layered self-organisation phenomenon. It must be understood across the four levels of the self.

At the proto-self level, helplessness arises from early sensory-affective experiences of uncontrollability. If the infant's cries are repeatedly ignored, or their attempts at self-expression punished, the proto-cognition emerges: *"What I do has no effect."* This pre-verbal conclusion becomes embedded in the nervous system, priming the child to expect futility in later life.

At the core self level, proto-cognitions crystallise into rigid core beliefs such as: *"I am powerless"*, *"Nothing I do matters"* and *"I am incapable of change."* These beliefs serve as the foundation for learned helplessness, colouring the individual's global perception of agency.

At the plastic self level, helplessness interacts with drivers and conditional rules: *Be Perfect*: "If I can't do it perfectly, there's no point in trying"; *Please Others*: "If they won't approve, I cannot act"; *Be Strong*: "If I can't endure, I have failed—so better not to act"; and *Try Hard*: paradoxically reinforces helplessness by sustaining futile effort in contexts perceived as uncontrollable. Here, helplessness becomes codified into rules of living, shaping strategic adaptations that protect the individual from anticipated shame, rejection, or failure.

At the external self level, learned helplessness manifests in behaviours and relationships: 1. Passivity in the face of opportunities; 2. Withdrawal from social interaction; 3. Reluctance to initiate change or assume responsibility; and 4. Scripts of dependency or chronic victimhood. In this sense, helplessness is not only an internal cognitive style but a relational script, enacted in social, professional, and therapeutic contexts.

Learned helplessness is closely linked with injunctions such as: *Don't Succeed,* which blocks initiative and fosters withdrawal; *Don't Do Anything* that reinforces passivity; and *Don't Be Important,* which supports the belief that one's actions have no value. Drivers then form compensatory but ultimately fragile strategies: *Try Hard* masks helplessness with over-effort, often ending in collapse, *Be Perfect* creates paralysis: if perfection is unattainable, inaction follows; and *Please Other* shifts control externally, reinforcing dependence.

Thus, helplessness represents the endpoint of unresolved injunction-driver dynamics, where the proto-self's embodied futility crystallises into a lived script of passivity.

Learned helplessness may appear as: 1. Behavioural deficits: passivity, procrastination, failure to act even in solvable situations; 2. Motivational deficits: lack of initiative, diminished persistence, rapid giving up; 3. Cognitive deficits: difficulty generating problem-solving strategies, rigid thinking, overgeneralisation of failure; and 4. Emotional deficits: low self-esteem, frustration, dysphoria, depressive affect. In psychotherapy, clients may present with statements like: *"What's the point? It won't change"*, *"I've tried before; it never works"* or *"I can't do anything right."*

The anterior cingulate cortex (ACC) plays a key role in conflict monitoring and initiating adaptive responses. In learned helplessness, the ACC fails to sustain adaptive engagement, likely due to inhibitory influence from the amygdala—the neural hub of fear and threat (Bauer et al., 2003). This neurobiological pattern explains why helplessness is not simply a choice but a conditioned neural state, requiring therapeutic intervention to re-establish a sense of agency.

Self-efficacy and learned helplessness are two poles of agency. Where self-efficacy reflects belief in one's capacity to influence events, helplessness reflects the conviction of uncontrollability. High self-efficacy leads to persistence, resilience, optimism, whilst learned helplessness leads to passivity, withdrawal, depression.

In depression, helplessness manifests as global hopelessness, sustained by a pessimistic explanatory style. Rebuilding self-efficacy is therefore central to therapeutic recovery.

Therapeutic intervention must occur across levels and axes: 1. Cognitive Axis: Identify pessimistic explanatory styles; Challenge core beliefs of powerlessness; and Reframe helpless thoughts into specific, temporary, external attributions; 2. Emotional Axis: Address the shame and grief underlying helplessness; and Provide experiences where vulnerability leads to support, not rejection; 3. Psychodynamic Axis: Explore unconscious identifications with helpless caregivers or family narratives of futility; and Analyse transference dynamics where the therapist is positioned as rescuer or controller; 4. Biological Level: Teach regulation strategies to manage amygdala-driven hyperarousal; and Use body-based interventions to reconnect action with outcome; and 5. Relational Level: Support clients in testing new actions within therapy; and Provide corrective relational experiences where agency is acknowledged and reinforced.

Andrei, a 42-year-old teacher, entered psychotherapy reporting chronic depression and hopelessness. He described himself as "stuck" and repeatedly said, *"It doesn't matter what I do, nothing changes"*:

- Proto-self: Early neglect (parents absent, needs ignored) left him with the embodied conclusion *"My actions have no effect"*;
- Core self: This crystallised into the belief *"I am powerless"*;
- Plastic self: He adopted the *Try Hard* driver, working excessively, but collapsed into passivity when efforts felt futile; and
- External self: He withdrew socially and avoided new projects, reinforcing a script of helplessness.

In psychotherapy, the clinician linked his explanatory style (personal, permanent, pervasive) with his early proto-self experiences. Through small behavioural experiments, relational support, and cognitive reframing, Andrei began to test new possibilities. Over time, his self-efficacy increased, and the helplessness script weakened.

Thus, in ISP, learned helplessness is conceptualised as the embodied outcome of early uncontrollability, sustained by a pessimistic explanatory styles, core beliefs of powerlessness, and driver-based compensations. It is both a cognitive phenomenon and a relational script, enacted at all four levels of the self. Psychotherapy focuses on re-establishing agency: challenging pessimistic beliefs, providing corrective relational experiences, addressing embodied helplessness, and rebuilding self-efficacy.

When clients begin to experience that their actions matter—and that agency is not conditional upon perfection or approval—the cycle of helplessness is broken. They move from passivity to participation, from futility to possibility, reclaiming their place as active agents in their own lives.

7.6. Mentalization

Mentalization, also known as theory of mind, refers to the human capacity to understand one's own and others' mental states—thoughts, feelings, intentions, and beliefs—as representations of reality rather than reality itself (Fonagy & Target, 2002; Popescu, 2021). It is the ability to grasp that behaviour is driven not only by external stimuli but also by internal, subjective experiences.

Mentalization requires the construction of secondary representations of the world—models of past, desired, or hypothetical states—that allow individuals to predict and interpret their own behaviour and that of others. This capacity evolves developmentally and is central to self-organisation, emotional regulation, and relational functioning.

Children begin life with only primary representations: direct, sensory-based impressions of their environment. A baby perceives hunger, warmth, or the presence of a caregiver but cannot conceptualise these experiences.

By the second year of life, children begin forming secondary representations, allowing them to imagine scenarios not immediately present—such as a toy being in another room or anticipating their caregiver's return. This capacity underlies pretend play and the ability to distinguish between reality and imagination (Doherty, 2009).

Around the age of four, children achieve a critical milestone: they understand that their own mental models may differ from external reality and from the perspectives of others. This marks the emergence of theory of mind—the recognition that other people have independent mental states. Classic developmental examples illustrate this process. A two-year-old who hides by covering their eyes assumes that if they cannot see others, they themselves cannot be seen. By three to four years of age, the child realises that others can still see them, and that perception is subjective and differentiated. Thus, mentalization evolves from egocentric perception to a more flexible recognition of multiple perspectives.

In ISP, mentalization is not merely a cognitive milestone but a multi-level process embedded in the self. At the foundational level of the proto-self, proto-cognitions (pre-symbolic impressions) determine whether the child experiences the world as contingent and responsive or unpredictable and chaotic. If early caregiving is attuned, the proto-self encodes a sense of coherence: *"When I signal, something happens."* This is the rudimentary basis for later mentalization: the recognition that behaviour links to intention. If early experiences are neglectful, the proto-self encodes *"What I feel does not matter,"* undermining the development of reflective awareness of mental states.

At the level of core self, proto-impressions crystallise into core beliefs: either positive: *"I have an inner world that can be understood"* or negative: *"My inner world is irrelevant or incomprehensible."* Children with supportive caregivers develop core beliefs that mental states are meaningful and shareable. Those with inconsistent caregivers may develop injunctions such as *Don't Feel* or *Don't Think*, impeding reflective functioning.

At the level of plastic self, drivers and conditional rules structure mentalization. For example, *Be Perfect* restricts mentalization by equating worth with flawless external behaviour, suppressing awareness of doubt or uncertainty. *Be Strong* inhibits emotional reflection, discouraging awareness of vulnerability. *Please Others* fosters hyper-mentalization of others' states while neglecting one's own. Thus, mentalization is skewed by conditional rules, leading to imbalance: either excessive concern with others' minds at the cost of one's own (externalising style), or preoccupation with one's own perspective without recognition of others (egocentric style).

At an external self level, in adulthood, mentalization is enacted relationally. Individuals with healthy reflective capacity can negotiate conflicts, empathise, and integrate multiple perspectives. Those with impaired mentalization may misinterpret others' intentions, project their own fears, or oscillate between mind-blindness and hyper-mentalization (over-reading into others' states).

Mentalization also directly shapes how core beliefs and the explanatory style operate. A person who can mentalize flexibly is able to distinguish between subjective beliefs and external reality, softening the rigidity of core convictions. For example: without mentalization the individual might think: *"I am stupid; this is the truth"*, whilst with mentalization the thought might change into: *"I think I am stupid right now, but that is just a thought, not reality."*

Deficits in mentalization sustain pessimistic explanatory styles. When individuals fail to differentiate between their interpretation and reality, they generalise negative conclusions (e.g., *"I can't do anything right"*).

Mentalization also interacts with self-efficacy and helplessness. High self-efficacy requires recognising mental states as representations—understanding that failure is not permanent but situational. Learned helplessness is sustained by impaired mentalization: the inability to reframe events as temporary, external, or specific. Thus, mentalization acts as a buffer against helplessness by enabling flexible reinterpretation of events.

Neuroscientific studies identify a mentalization network involving: 1. The medial prefrontal cortex (mPFC) – self-referential thinking; 2. The temporo-parietal junction (TPJ) – distinguishing self from others; 3. The anterior cingulate cortex (ACC) – conflict monitoring and reflective processing; and 4. The mirror neuron system – simulating others' actions and intentions. When stress, trauma, or attachment insecurity overwhelm these systems, mentalization collapses, leading to pre-mentalistic modes of functioning (Fonagy et al., 2002): 1. Psychic equivalence (thoughts = reality); 2. Pretend mode (thoughts disconnected from reality); and 3. Teleological stance (only observable actions count).

Clients with impaired mentalization may show: 1. Difficulty distinguishing thoughts from facts; 2. Misinterpretation of others' intentions; 3. Emotional dysregulation (because feelings are not seen as transient mental states but as overwhelming truths); 4. Projection and paranoia; and 5. Relational ruptures driven by misattributions.

For example, a client may believe: *"The psychotherapist looked away—she must hate me."* Without reflective capacity, this thought is experienced as reality rather than a hypothesis.

Therapeutic interventions in ISP aim to strengthen mentalization across axes: 1. Cognitive Axis: Help clients distinguish between thoughts, beliefs, and reality; and Develop metacognitive awareness: *"This is a thought I am having, not necessarily the truth"*; 2. Emotional Axis: Support recognition of emotions as transient mental states rather than overwhelming facts; and Facilitate naming, reflecting, and tolerating emotions; 3. Psychodynamic Axis: Explore how transference-countertransference dynamics involve misattributions of mental states; and Interpret unconscious projections and support differentiation of self and other; and 4. Relational Level: Use the therapeutic relationship as a "mentalization laboratory," where misinterpretations can be safely explored; and Model curiosity about the client's mind, demonstrating that mental states can be understood and valued.

Ana, a 29-year-old client with borderline personality traits, often misinterpreted her partner's behaviour. When he came home late, she concluded: *"He doesn't love me anymore":*

- Proto-self: Early neglect had embedded *"When others disappear, I cease to exist"*;
- Core self: She believed *"I am unlovable"*;
- Plastic self: The *Please Others* driver dominated, making her hyper-attuned to her partner's moods while ignoring her own; and
- External self: She engaged in relational protests (accusations, withdrawal) that reinforced conflict.

In therapy, Ana learned to mentalize: to recognise that her thought (*"He doesn't love me"*) was a mental state, not an objective fact. With practice, she could generate alternative interpretations (*"He may be late due to work"*). Over time, this reflective stance reduced her reactivity, stabilised her relationships, and enhanced her sense of agency.

In ISP, mentalization is seen as a cornerstone of cognitive development and therapeutic change. It allows individuals to move from pre-symbolic proto-cognitions to flexible, reflective engagement with the world. When impaired, it sustains rigid core beliefs, pessimistic explanatory styles, low self-efficacy, and helplessness.

Psychotherapy restores mentalization by offering new relational experiences where mental states are recognised, valued, and explored. Clients learn to see their thoughts and feelings as representations, not realities, opening space for flexibility, resilience, and authentic connection.

7.7. Archetypes as Universal Proto-Cognitive Maps

Archetypes, as described by Carl Gustav Jung, are among the most fascinating and contested concepts in psychology. They are patterns of thought and behaviour that appear universally across human cultures, reflected in myths, dreams, symbols, and collective narratives. Jung proposed that archetypes belong to the collective unconscious, a layer of the psyche deeper than the personal unconscious, where shared human experiences and predispositions reside (Jung, 1959/1990). Archetypes are not inherited images or concrete representations, but organising structures—potentials for imagery and behaviour—that manifest through universal symbols such as the Mother, the Hero, the Shadow, or the Trickster.

In Integrative Strategic Psychotherapy (ISP), these Jungian insights can be reframed in developmental and neurobiological terms. From the ISP perspective, archetypes are understood as universal proto-cognitive maps: pre-verbal and unconscious structures that take shape in all individuals as a result of early childhood interactions with the environment. A proto-cognition in ISP refers to a primitive cognitive-emotional map, formed at the proto-self level, prior to the development of language or symbolic thought (Popescu & Vîşcu, 2016). These proto-cognitions are born from the intersection of a primary need, the affect linked to that need, the behaviours enacted to signal or satisfy the need, and the environmental response. Because every child in every culture faces similar developmental tasks—feeding, attachment, boundary-setting, exploration, individuation—the resulting proto-cognitions are universal. Archetypes, in this sense, are a particular category of proto-cognitions: universal pre-symbolic maps that organise human experience across cultures, unconscious in nature, formed early, and carried forward throughout life.

What Jung described as the collective unconscious can thus be understood as the universality of early human experience. The need for nurturance and safety, the reality of limits and authority, the inevitability of separation, and the striving for autonomy are common to all infants. These universal conditions generate universal proto-cognitions, which crystallise into what Jung called archetypes. The Mother archetype, for example, is the proto-cognitive imprint of the caregiving figure who regulates the infant's physiological and emotional needs. The Shadow archetype arises as the imprint of rejected or punished impulses, experienced pre-verbally as parts of the self that cannot be expressed. The Hero archetype encodes the experience of struggling against obstacles in order to grow, first represented in preverbal struggles such as standing up, crawling, or learning to walk.

From the perspective of ISP, archetypes are encoded at the proto-self level, through implicit memory. They remain unconscious and inaccessible to explicit recollection, but they shape emotional dispositions, schemas, and behaviours throughout life. They are then elaborated at the level of the core self into internal working models, maintained in the plastic self through feedback loops, and enacted in the external self in relation to the surrounding world. They are expressed across the cognitive, emotional, and psychodynamic axes: archetypes provide primitive symbolic categories for perception (cognitive), affective orientations for experience (emotional), and organising templates for unconscious dynamics (psychodynamic). In short, archetypes can be understood as the earliest symbolic skeleton of the human self, bridging Jung's vision of collective forms with ISP's vision of developmental proto-cognitions.

The Mother archetype is perhaps the most central of all. It represents the pre-symbolic imprint of caregiving, safety, and nurturance. In every culture, infants are born entirely dependent on a caregiver for survival. Their earliest proto-cognitions are formed around the satisfaction of physiological needs—hunger, thirst, warmth—accompanied by affective signals of comfort or discomfort. When these needs are met consistently, the resulting proto-cognition links the image of the caregiver with safety, warmth, and continuity. When inconsistently or harshly met, the same archetypal imprint forms, but coloured by fear, unpredictability, or abandonment. As a proto-cognitive map, the Mother archetype encodes not only the literal mother but the universal template of nurturance itself. Later in life, this map organises expectations of care, intimacy, and relational security, and is projected onto partners, leaders, or even symbolic figures such as the earth or the divine.

If the Mother represents nurturance, the Father archetype represents structure, protection, and authority. Infants not only need comfort but also encounter boundaries and external regulation. The proto-cognition here is formed through experiences of limit-setting: the hand that holds back, the presence that provides external safety, the voice that stimulates exploration. A consistent and reliable father figure imprints the archetype with strength and guidance; an absent or harsh father imprints it with fear and insecurity. From an ISP perspective, the Father archetype begins in the proto-self through affective encounters with strength and limitation, grows into schemas of support or rejection in the core self, and later becomes enacted in adult relationships to authority. Like the Mother, it is universal because all infants must confront the reality of protection, limit, and external order.

The Shadow archetype represents the repository of rejected impulses and affects. Every child experiences desires or behaviours that are met with prohibition: anger, aggression, envy, or even needs considered excessive. When these impulses are punished or ignored, a proto-cognitive imprint forms: "this part of me is not allowed." The affect is experienced as shame, fear, or internal rejection. The Shadow is therefore a universal proto-cognition, because every child must learn that some impulses are unacceptable to caregivers or culture. If integrated with guidance, the Shadow remains available to consciousness; if harshly rejected, it becomes split off, projected outward, or expressed indirectly. In ISP terms, the Shadow begins with proto-self level codings of "good/bad" linked to needs, grows into core schemas of self-acceptability, and is maintained in the plastic self as loops of suppression. It manifests in the external self as avoidance or projection, and becomes a critical target in therapy, where re-owning Shadow elements is part of integration.

The archetypes of anima and animus represent the encoding of gender polarities. Every child perceives differences between caregivers and internalises them pre-verbally, long before acquiring symbolic notions of gender. The receptive, nurturing, or relational qualities of one caregiver are contrasted with the active, assertive, or protective qualities of another. These differences form proto-cognitive maps of polarities—archetypal templates of masculine and feminine energy. When both polarities are available, the child's proto-cognitions carry balance and flexibility; when rigid or absent, distortions occur. In ISP terms, the anima and animus are proto-cognitions of relational and gendered polarities, elaborated into schemas of gender roles and enacted later in intimate relationships. They are universal because all children observe differences between caregivers, encoded pre-verbally as categories of human relating.

The Persona archetype is the mask worn to adapt to the social world. Infants quickly learn that some behaviours elicit approval while others do not. The proto-cognitive imprint is formed around the affective message: "I am loved when I smile," or "I am rejected when I cry." These pre-symbolic maps evolve into strategies of showing only certain aspects of the self to ensure belonging. The Persona is thus a proto-cognition of adaptation, universal because every child must "perform" in order to be accepted by family and later by society. In ISP, the Persona begins at the proto-self with preverbal signals, becomes schemas in the core self about conditional acceptance, is reinforced in the plastic self as stable feedback loops, and is enacted in the external self as roles and identities.

The Hero archetype emerges from the universal human need to overcome obstacles. At a preverbal level, this is encoded through the infant's struggles—rolling over, crawling, standing, or walking. Each struggle creates a proto-cognition of challenge and mastery: "I can struggle and succeed." If supported, this map encodes resilience; if undermined, it encodes helplessness. As development continues, the Hero archetype organises narratives of overcoming adversity and striving for autonomy. In ISP, this begins with bodily proto-cognitions of effort, evolves into schemas of competence or incompetence in the core self, is maintained through feedback loops of approach or avoidance, and is enacted in adult pursuits of autonomy and success.

The Wise Old Man or Wise Woman archetype represents the experience of guidance and knowledge. Every infant perceives caregivers as "the ones who know," who anticipate needs and provide direction. The proto-cognitive map is the preverbal imprint of a guiding presence, a source of meaning and orientation. When this guidance is consistent, the archetype encodes trust in inner wisdom; when absent or punitive, mistrust. In ISP, this archetype is formed at the proto-self through sensory recognition of guidance, elaborated into schemas of wisdom availability in the core self, and enacted through seeking or rejecting mentors in adulthood.

The Child archetype is perhaps the most obvious, since each of us begins life as a child. It represents vulnerability, dependence, and potential. The proto-cognition here is the preverbal experience of being small, in need, and open to the future. When supported, the archetype carries hope, creativity, and innocence. When shamed or neglected, it carries fragility and fear. In ISP terms, the Child archetype encodes the earliest bodily proto-cognitions of dependence, evolves into schemas of worth or unworthiness in the core self, is maintained in the plastic self through feedback loops of helplessness or playfulness, and is expressed in adulthood through creativity, regression, or the search for safety.

The Trickster archetype arises from the universal behaviour of boundary-testing. Infants and children explore rules, break patterns, and play with limits. These preverbal acts of play and mischief form a proto-cognitive map of disruption and creativity. When play is allowed, the Trickster encodes adaptability; when harshly punished, it rigidifies into rebellion or destructiveness. In ISP, the Trickster is formed at the proto-self level through proto-cognitions of play, elaborated into schemas of exploration or punishment in the core self, reinforced as loops of compliance or rebellion in the plastic self, and enacted in adult creativity, humour, or destructiveness.

Across all these archetypes, we see the same pattern. Each represents a universal proto-cognitive map, formed at a pre-verbal, pre-symbolic level in early childhood, as a result of needs, affects, and environmental responses. They are universal because all children encounter the same developmental tasks, regardless of culture. They remain unconscious, encoded in implicit memory, yet they organise later schemas, feedback loops, and behaviours. In ISP, archetypes correspond to proto-cognitions in the proto-self, elaborated into internal working models in the core self, reinforced in the plastic self, and enacted in the external self. They operate across the cognitive axis as symbolic maps of reality, across the emotional axis as affective dispositions, and across the psychodynamic axis as unconscious templates of conflict and integration.

In this way, Jung's archetypes and ISP's proto-cognitions meet. Jung's vision of timeless symbolic patterns finds a developmental and neurobiological explanation in ISP: archetypes are the universal proto-cognitions formed in every human child, at a pre-verbal and unconscious level, through early relational experience. They are not just mythical motifs, but lived pre-symbolic maps that shape the structure of the self.

References

Abramson, L. Y., Seligman, M. E. P., & Teasdale, J. D. (1978). Learned helplessness in humans: Critique and reformulation. *Journal of Abnormal Psychology, 87*(1), 49–74.

Bandura, A. (1977). Self-efficacy: Toward a unifying theory of behavioural change. *Psychological Review, 84*(2), 191–215.

Bandura, A. (1989). Human agency in social cognitive theory. *American Psychologist, 44*(9), 1175–1184.

Bauer, R. M., Furedy, J. J., & Crawford, H. J. (2003). Learned helplessness, stress, and the anterior cingulate cortex. *Biological Psychology, 63*(1), 87–103.

Beck, A. T. (2000). *Cognitive therapy of depression.* New York: Guilford Press.

Beck, A. T. (2000). *Prisoners of hate: The cognitive basis of anger, hostility, and violence.* HarperCollins.

Beck, A.T. (2000). The Evolution of the Cognitive Model of Depression and Its Neurobiological Correlates. *American Journal of Psychiatry, 165,* 969-977.

Beck, J. S. (1995). *Cognitive Therapy: Basics and Beyond.* New York: The Guilford Press.

Beitman, B. D. (2002). Why do good things happen to good people? *Journal of Psychotherapy Integration, 12*(3), 241–253.

Berne, E. (1996). *What Do You Say After You Say Hello?* London: Corgi.

Berne, E. (1996). *Games people play: the psychology of human relationships. 40th aniversary edition.* New York: Ballantine Books.

Berne, E (2006): *Ce spui după bună ziua?* Bucureşti: Trei.

Boszormenyi-Nagy, I., & Spark, G. M. (1973). *Invisible loyalties: Reciprocity in intergenerational family therapy*. Harper & Row.

Bowen, M. (1978). *Family therapy in clinical practice*. Aronson.

Buller, D. (2005). *Adapting minds: Evolutionary psychology and the persistent guess for human nature.* Cambridge, M.A.: Bradford/MIT.

Candiotte, K., & Lichtenstein, E. (1981). Self-efficacy and relapse in smoking cessation programs. *Journal of Consulting and Clinical Psychology, 49*(5), 648–658.

Cemalcilar, Z., Canbeyli, R., & Sunar, D. (2003). Learned helplessness, therapy, and the role of attribution style. *Journal of Personality and Clinical Studies, 19*(1), 63–78.

Clarkson, P. (1992). *Transactional Analysis psychotherapy. An integrated approach.* London: Routledge.

Damasio, A. (1999). *The feeling of what happens: Body and emotion in the making of consciousness*. Harcourt Brace.

Damasio, A. (2010). *Self comes to mind: Constructing the conscious brain*. Pantheon.

Doherty, M.J. (2009). *Theory of Mind. How Children Understand Others' Thoughts and Feelings.* New York: Psychology Press.

Fall, K. A., Holden, J. M., & Marquis, A. (2011). *Theoretical Models of Counseling and Psychotherapy*. New York: Routledge.

Flatt, A. E., & Hewitt, P. L. (2002). Perfectionism: Theory, research, and treatment. In G. Flett & P. L. Hewitt (Eds.), *Perfectionism: Theory, research, and treatment* (pp. 5–31). American Psychological Association.

Fonagy, P., & Target, M. (2002). Early intervention and the development of self-regulation. *Psychoanalytic Inquiry, 22*(3), 307–335.

Fonagy, P., Gergely, G., Jurist, E. L., & Target, M. (2002). *Affect regulation, mentalization, and the development of the self.* Other Press.

Fowlie, H., & Sills, C. (2011). *Relational Transactional Analysis: Principles in Practice.* London: Karnac.

Green, J. (2003). The role of self-efficacy in psychotherapy. *Journal of Clinical Psychology, 59*(9), 947–960.

Hagger, M. S., Koch, S., & Chatzisarantis, N. L. (2010). The influence of causality orientations and locus of control on learned helplessness. *Motivation and Emotion, 34*(2), 107–121.

Happaney, K., Zeloro, P.D. & Stuss, D.T. (2004). Development of orbitofrontal function: current themes and future directions. *Brain and Cognition, 55(1),* 1-10.

Hersen, M. (2005). *Encyclopedia of Behaviour Modification and Cognitive Behaviour Therapy.* New York: Sage Publications

Hewitt, P. L., & Flett, G. L. (1991). Perfectionism in the self and social contexts: Conceptualization, assessment, and association with psychopathology. *Journal of Personality and Social Psychology, 60*(3), 456–470.

Hoffmann, L. (2012). *Introduction to cognitive-behavioural approaches.* London: Sage.

Hoffman, S. (2012). *An Introduction to Modern CBT. Psychological Solutions to Mental Health Problems.* Chichester: John Wiley & Sons.

Hoffmann, S. G. (2012). Cognitive processes during emotional disorders: A review of attention, memory, and executive function. *Clinical Psychology Review, 32*(3), 362–381. https://doi.org/10.1016/j.cpr.2012.01.003

Johnson-Laird, P. N. (1983). *Mental models: Towards a cognitive science of language, inference and consciousness.* Cambridge: Harvard University Press.

Jung, C. G. (1951). *Aion: Researches into the phenomenology of the self.* Princeton University Press.

Jung, C. G. (1959/1990). *The archetypes and the collective unconscious.* Princeton University Press.

Kahler, T. (1975). Drivers: The Key to the Process Script. *Transactional Analysis Journal,* 5(3), 280–284.

Kelly, G. A. (1955). *The psychology of personal constructs.* Norton.

Kinsella, P. & Garland, A. (2008). *Cognitive Behavioral Interventions for Mental Health Practitioners: A Beginner's Guide.* New York: Taylor and Francis.

Lewis, E. & Lloyd, D.M. (2010). Embodied experience: A first-person investigation of the rubber hand illusion. *Phenomenology and the Cognitive Sciences, 9(3),* 317-339.

Madsen, W. C. (1999). Collaborative therapy with multi-stressed families. *Guilford Press.*

Megler, C. (1982). Locus of control and therapeutic outcome. *Psychotherapy: Theory, Research & Practice, 19*(2), 174–180.

Messer, S.B. (1992). A critical examination of belief structures in integrative and eclectic psychotherapy. In J.C. Norcross & M.R. Goldfried (Eds.) *Handbook of psychotherapy integration.* (pp. 130-165). New York: Basic Books.

Mesquita, B., Barrett, L. F., & Smith, E. R. (2010). The cultural context of emotion. *Psychological Science in the Public Interest*, 10(2), 1–40.

Mesquita, B., Barrett, L. F., & Smith, E. R. (2010). The cultural regulation of emotions. In M. Lewis, J. M. Haviland-Jones, & L. F. Barrett (Eds.), *Handbook of emotions* (3rd ed., pp. 486–503). Guilford Press.

Minuchin, S. (1974). *Families and family therapy*. Harvard University Press.

Nichols, M., & Davis, S. (2020). *Family therapy: Concepts and methods* (12th ed.). Pearson.

Peterson, C., & Steen, T. A. (2002). Optimistic explanatory style. In C. R. Snyder & S. J. Lopez (Eds.), *Handbook of positive psychology* (pp. 244–256). Oxford University Press

Popescu, O. M., & Vîşcu, L. (2016). *Psihoterapie integrativă strategică. Teorie şi practică.* Timişoara: Eurostampa.

Prochaska, J. O., & DiClemente, C. C. (2005). The transtheoretical approach. In J. C. Norcross & M. R. Goldfried (Eds.), *Handbook of psychotherapy integration* (2nd ed., pp. 147–171). Oxford University Press.

Prochaska, J. O., & Norcross, J. C. (2007). *Systems of psychotherapy: A transtheoretical analysis*. Brooks/Cole.

Robertson, D. (2010). *The Philosophy of Cognitive-Behavioural Therapy (CBT): Stoic Philosophy as Rational and Cognitive Psychotherapy*. London: Karnac.

Sarno, J. (2006). *The Divided Mind.* New York: Regan Books

Schick, B., De Villiers, P., De Villiers, J. & Hoffmeister, R. (2007). Language and theory of mind. A study of deaf children. *Child Development, 78(2),* 376-396.

Schore, A. N. (2002). *Affect regulation and the repair of the self.* New York: Norton.

Schore, A. N. (2002). Dysregulation of the right brain: A fundamental mechanism of traumatic attachment and the psychopathogenesis of posttraumatic stress disorder. *Australian and New Zealand Journal of Psychiatry, 36*(1), 9–30. https://doi.org/10.1046/j.1440-1614.2002.00996.x

Schore, A. N. (2009). Relational trauma and the developing right brain. *Annals of the New York Academy of Sciences*, 1159(1), 189–203.

Schore, A. N. (2009). Right-brain affect regulation: An essential mechanism of development, trauma, dissociation, and psychotherapy. In D. Fosha, D. J. Siegel, & M. F. Solomon (Eds.), *The healing power of emotion: Affective neuroscience, development & clinical practice* (pp. 112–144). Norton.

Schore, A. N. (2012). *The science of the art of psychotherapy*. New York: Norton.

Seligman, M. E. P. (1991). *Learned optimism: How to change your mind and your life.* Knopf.

Shafran, R., & Mansell, W. (2001). Perfectionism and psychopathology: A review of research and treatment. *Clinical Psychology Review, 21*(6), 879–906.

Shields, G. S., Sazma, M. A., & Yonelinas, A. P. (2016). The effects of acute stress on core executive functions: A meta-analysis and comparison with cortisol. *Neuroscience & Biobehavioral Reviews, 68*, 651–668.

Siegel, D. J. (2012). *The developing mind: How relationships and the brain interact to shape who we are* (2nd ed.). New York: Guilford Press

Sticker, L. J., & Gold, M. S. (1993). Drug abuse and self-efficacy: A psychological perspective. *International Journal of the Addictions, 28*(9), 877–893.

Stoeber, J., & Childs, J. H. (2010). The assessment of self-oriented and socially prescribed perfectionism: Subscales make a difference. *Journal of Personality Assessment, 92*(6), 577–585.

Themanson, J. R., Pontifex, M. B., & Hillman, C. H. (2011). Self-efficacy and executive function: Examining the effects of exercise. *Journal of Sport & Exercise Psychology, 33*(5), 684–707.

Vancouver, J. B., More, K. M., & Yoder, R. J. (2008). Self-efficacy and resource allocation: Support for a nonmonotonic, discontinuous model. *Journal of Applied Psychology, 93*(1), 35–47.

CHAPTER 8

THE EMOTIONAL AXIS

8.1. Affect, Emotions and Feelings

In integrative strategic psychotherapy (ISP), the understanding and modulation of emotional experience represent core therapeutic goals. Emotional phenomena—ranging from pre-reflective affective responses to complex social feelings—are embedded within the dynamic architecture of the self, which is conceptualised in ISP through four interrelated domains: the proto-self, core self, plastic self, and external self (Popescu, 2021). Each of these domains processes affective information differently, and therapeutic interventions must be tailored to the specific domain at which emotional disruptions occur.

Emotion is not simply a psychological construct—it is a neurobiological, intersubjective, and phenomenological event that shapes identity and behaviour. It informs perception, decision-making, and interpersonal connection. In the context of psychotherapy, emotional experience often brings individuals into treatment and becomes the primary terrain for transformation.

While the terms "emotion," "feeling," and "affect" are often used interchangeably in everyday discourse, their meanings diverge significantly in neuroscientific and psychotherapeutic frameworks. According to contemporary emotion theory, these terms can be differentiated both structurally and developmentally (Barrett, 2017):

- Affect is considered the most primitive form of response: an immediate, automatic, and often unconscious physiological evaluation of stimuli as positive or negative. It arises in the proto-self, the most basic level of the self, which maintains homeostasis and registers core bodily states (Damasio, 1999);
- Emotion is a more elaborated construct that incorporates physiological arousal, subjective experience, and behavioural expression. It often emerges

from the core self, where bodily signals are integrated with early interpersonal meaning and relational patterns; and

– Feeling refers to the conscious perception and labelling of an emotional state—what one becomes aware of, reflects upon, and articulates through language. This process is more characteristic of the plastic self, which constructs narrative coherence and emotional insight.

Popescu and Vîşcu (2016) define *feeling* as the quality of subjective awareness situated along a pleasure–displeasure continuum, often influenced by the interpretation of bodily states. This distinction allows clinicians to better differentiate between unconscious emotional reactions (affect), emerging but unarticulated emotional responses (emotion), and fully formulated emotional awareness (feeling).

The proto-self is the evolutionary foundation of the self-system. It comprises automatic, sensorimotor, and interoceptive processes that enable the organism to maintain biological integrity. Affect, in this context, serves a homeostatic function—detecting deviations in internal states and prompting regulatory responses (Damasio, 1999).

For instance, a sudden loud noise may evoke an affective response of startle or alarm, accompanied by an increased heart rate and muscle tension. This response does not require cognitive appraisal or conscious thought. As such, affective reactions are not mediated by narrative meaning but by survival-based evaluative mechanisms (Panksepp, 2011).

These bodily responses are often the first layer of emotional experience encountered in psychotherapy, especially in clients with trauma, anxiety disorders, or dissociation. In such cases, emotional dysregulation may stem from dysregulated proto-self functioning, leading to exaggerated or blunted affective responses.

As affective reactions become integrated into interpersonal experience and symbolic meaning, they are elaborated into primary emotions within the proto self and core self. This level involves early attachment patterns, nonverbal relational experiences, and implicit memory (Schore, 2021).

Primary emotions—such as fear, sadness, joy, anger, and disgust—are considered evolutionarily conserved and universal across cultures (Ekman, 1992). These emotions serve adaptive functions, mobilising the body for action in response to environmental demands. For example, fear facilitates avoidance of danger, while anger can assert boundaries.

These emotions emerge reflexively but are modulated by early relational experiences. For instance, a child raised in an emotionally validating environment may learn to differentiate between sadness and anger, while another child, raised in an emotionally avoidant family, may suppress both feelings. This leads to maladaptive emotional schemas stored within the core self and enacted in adulthood (Siegel, 2020).

From a neurobiological perspective, primary emotions are rooted in subcortical structures, such as the amygdala, hypothalamus, and brainstem. They involve autonomic arousal, hormonal activation, and rapid behavioural impulses (Davidson & Begley, 2012). However, they are also shaped by early caregiving, emotional resonance, and mirroring—processes that encode attachment-based patterns into the affective core of the self (Fonagy et al., 2002).

With the development of reflective capacities, language, and social identity, emotional experience becomes increasingly differentiated and nuanced. This transformation occurs in the core self and plastic self, where emotions are integrated into autobiographical narratives, self-concepts, and interpersonal roles.

At this level, individuals begin to make meaning of their emotional states: *Why do I feel this way? What does it remind me of? Is this feeling acceptable or shameful?* The plastic self thus encompasses the capacity for emotional insight, regulation, and reorganisation.

However, many clients enter psychotherapy with distorted emotional narratives—e.g., interpreting anger as dangerous, sadness as weakness, or anxiety as evidence of failure. These distortions often originate from early prohibitions or invalidations of emotional expression. Therapeutic work involves reconstructing these narratives, expanding emotional vocabulary, and fostering tolerance for emotional ambiguity. In ISP, interventions at this level include expressive techniques, emotional awareness training, metaphorical dialogue, and schema restructuring. This enables the client to integrate previously dissociated or repressed emotions into a coherent self-narrative.

The external self refers to the outward expression of the self in social, cultural, and performative contexts. It is the interface between inner emotional states and external behavioural roles. Here, emotions become performances, regulated by social expectations, norms, and scripts.

For example, a client may feel intense grief (core self), reframe it through personal meaning (plastic self), but display composure and detachment in social situations (external self), due to cultural norms around emotional suppression.

Psychotherapeutically, this level addresses the discrepancy between felt emotion and displayed emotion. Many clients learn to suppress or fake emotional states for acceptance or survival, leading to internal fragmentation and loss of authenticity. ISP helps clients reclaim congruence between inner emotional truth and outer expression.

Emotions and the Therapeutic Process

Emotions play a central role in therapeutic change. According to Greenberg (2015), transformation occurs through accessing maladaptive emotional schemes, activating adaptive emotions, and facilitating emotional processing. This sequence requires the psychotherapist to work across all domains of the self, matching interventions to the client's emotional development and needs.

In ISP, therapeutic work with emotions involves: biological regulation of affect (proto-self), attachment-informed emotional exploration (core self), narrative restructuring and emotional meaning-making (plastic self) and authentic expression and relational congruence (external self). Moreover, therapeutic atonement—nonverbal synchrony, facial mirroring, and voice modulation—serves to co-regulate the client's emotional state and foster emotional safety, particularly in dysregulated or traumatised clients (Schore, 2021).

From a clinical perspective, basic emotions such as fear, anger, sadness, and shame are transdiagnostic—they appear across a wide range of disorders, from depression to borderline personality disorder. Often, these emotions are unregulated, misunderstood, or avoided.

For example, in clients with anxiety disorders, fear is overgeneralised and linked to catastrophic cognitions. In depressive states, sadness is internalised as worthlessness. In personality disorders, anger is suppressed or explosively expressed due to unresolved developmental trauma.

ISP aims to uncover the emotional templates that underlie these maladaptive responses. By tracing emotional experience back to its origin in the self, clinicians can identify the point at which dysregulation occurs and tailor their interventions accordingly.

Emotional Development and Internal Working Models

Emotional development is a dynamic process that begins in early infancy and is closely intertwined with attachment experiences. In the ISP model, the core self serves as the foundational arena for affective learning, where the infant's spontaneous emotional expressions are mirrored, modulated, or inhibited by caregivers (Fonagy & Target, 2003).

Secure attachment fosters emotional atonement, helping the child learn that emotions are tolerable, meaningful, and manageable. Conversely, disorganised or avoidant attachment can disrupt emotional development, leading to patterns of suppression, hyperactivation, or dissociation (Schore, 2021). These early interactions form the blueprint for internal working models—unconscious templates that guide expectations about emotion in self–other relationships.

These models can become rigid and maladaptive, especially when emotional responses are chronically invalidated or punished. For example, a child whose anger is met with rejection may internalise the belief that assertiveness is dangerous, leading to chronic self-silencing. Such beliefs may be stored implicitly and remain inaccessible to language, yet shape emotional expression in adulthood. Therapeutic work in ISP involves identifying these implicit emotional rules and transforming them through relational, embodied, and narrative interventions.

The Integration of Emotion and Cognition

While emotion and cognition are often treated as separate domains, contemporary neuroscience underscores their mutual interdependence (Pessoa, 2021). Emotional arousal enhances attention and memory encoding, while cognitive appraisals influence the valence and intensity of emotional responses (Gross, 2015).

This interplay is particularly relevant in the plastic self, where clients develop complex emotional schemas that combine thought, feeling, and meaning. For example, a client may appraise a minor interpersonal conflict as abandonment, triggering a disproportionate emotional response rooted in earlier experiences of neglect.

In integrative strategic psychotherapy, cognitive and emotional integration is achieved by facilitating meta-cognition, narrative elaboration, and self-reflection. Clients learn to observe, label, and reframe their emotional states, thereby increasing their capacity for emotional literacy and self-regulation.

A central ISP technique for this purpose is the "emotional tracing" method—inviting the client to trace an emotion backward to its origin in early memory, bodily sensation, or interpersonal schema. This technique promotes coherence across the levels of the self, enabling the individual to reconstruct fragmented emotional experiences into a unified narrative.

8.2. Emotion Regulation

Emotion regulation refers to the capacity to manage, modulate, and integrate one's emotional experience so that it supports adaptive, coherent, and goal-directed behaviour—even in the face of high stress or inner turbulence (Popescu & Vîşcu, 2016). It is a cornerstone of psychological resilience and is closely tied to self-organisation, the ability to remain flexible, emotionally stable, and behaviourally coherent under conditions of change or threat.

This capacity becomes a central therapeutic focus in Integrative Strategic Psychotherapy (ISP), where emotional dysregulation is often understood as both a symptom and a developmental blockage within one or more levels of the self. While the proto-self reacts to affective arousal at a physiological level, the core self holds implicit affective memory and attachment-based templates. The plastic self gives meaning to emotional experience, and the external self negotiates emotional expression through the lens of social context and performance.

Thus, emotion regulation is never a monolithic skill—it is a multi-level process that emerges developmentally and is mediated by a confluence of biological, relational, and cognitive factors. Emotion regulation is shaped by both internal and external sources (Davidson & Begley, 2012). Internal sources encompass constitutional and neuroregulatory systems, such as: the neuroendocrine system (involving cortisol, oxytocin, and stress-related hormones), the autonomic nervous system (e.g., heart rate variability, vagal tone), and the frontal lobes of the brain, especially the prefrontal cortex, which is instrumental in top-down control of emotional reactivity.

These systems constitute the biological substrate of the proto-self, which sets the threshold for arousal, tolerance for novelty, and baseline affective responsiveness. Children born with heightened reactivity, for instance, may exhibit elevated stress responses to even minimal social stimuli, often interpreted as behavioural inhibition or shyness (Silke et al., 2006).

Over time, these reactivities are shaped by external factors, particularly caregiving dynamics. Responsive, attuned caregivers model emotional containment and repair, co-regulating the infant's affect and gradually internalising these regulatory strategies. Insecure or disorganised attachments, however, can lead to chronic dysregulation, emotional overmodulation (e.g., dissociation), or under-modulation (e.g., emotional flooding) (Schore, 2021).

From the perspective of the plastic self, emotion regulation involves a set of learned cognitive and behavioural strategies, including awareness and labelling of emotional states, capacity for meta-cognitive reflection, appraisal and reappraisal of emotionally charged situations, and the intentional modulation of emotional expression.

These regulatory capacities depend on emotional literacy, belief systems about emotions, and previous experiences of emotional safety or rupture. For instance, an individual raised in an environment where anger was taboo may suppress this emotion automatically, often without conscious awareness, creating internal tension and relational incongruence.

In such cases, emotional dysregulation reflects not only a failure to manage arousal but also deficits in the symbolic representation of emotion, meaning that the plastic self cannot properly encode and integrate the emotional signal. In psychotherapy, this often presents as clients struggling to "find the words" for what they feel or reporting a sense of emotional numbness.

A range of psychological disorders are underpinned by difficulties in emotion regulation (Gross, 2012; Vanderkerckhove et al., 2008): (1) Major depressive disorder: Dysregulated sadness, low mood, and emotional blunting; impairments in reward sensitivity; (2) Generalised anxiety disorder: Hypervigilance and persistent arousal; distorted threat appraisals; (3) Panic disorder: Sudden affective surges, often misinterpreted as catastrophic (e.g., impending death); (4) Attachment-related disorders: Disconnection from affect, lack of awareness of emotional states, or inconsistent affective responses; (5) Dissociative disorders: Detachment from affective experience, with splitting between parts of the self; (6) Borderline and narcissistic personality disorders: Impulsive affective reactions, unstable identity structures, and difficulty in sustaining affective equilibrium, etc.

In these cases, emotion–behaviour sequences become maladaptive. For example, anger might lead to destructive outbursts, or shame might trigger withdrawal and suicidal ideation. A hallmark of dysregulation is context-inappropriate emotionality, or emotional reactions that are disproportionate to the triggering event.

Neurodevelopmental research confirms that the brain's regulatory capacity is shaped by interactive experiences—particularly the degree to which caregivers scaffold, mirror, and name emotional states for the child (Gross, 2012; Porges, 2021). This interaction not only facilitates the child's capacity to feel certain emotions but also activates and strengthens the neural circuits involved in managing them.

Children raised in emotionally flat or chaotic environments may fail to develop these circuits adequately. For example, children of chronically depressed mothers often exhibit blunted affect, poor stress recovery, and diminished capacity for joy (Silke et al., 2006). In contrast, emotionally supportive environments promote flexibility and resilience.

Over time, emotional regulation becomes partially automatised, encoded through procedural memory and embodied responses. Thus, regulatory deficits in adulthood may not always be conscious or intentional—they are often pre-reflective adaptations to early relational climates, held within the body and implicit systems of the self.

According to Vanderkerckhove et al. (2008), signs of impaired emotional regulation include: (1) Emotional responses that are inappropriate to the situation; (2) Sequences in which emotions are followed by maladaptive behaviours; (3) Prolonged and intense episodes of negative emotions without effective regulation strategies; and (4) Difficulty recovering from emotional distress, resulting in rumination or avoidance.

Emotional regulation is both a developmental achievement and a relationally mediated skill. It reflects the integration of affective, cognitive, and behavioural processes across the multiple layers of the self. In ISP, emotional dysregulation is not merely a symptom—it is a portal into unresolved developmental challenges, unmet needs, and dissociated emotional truths.

By facilitating the client's capacity to *experience*, *name*, *tolerate*, and *express* emotions in a coherent and meaningful way, the psychotherapist becomes not only a witness to the client's emotional life but a co-regulator of their evolving selfhood.

Psychotherapy offers a structured and emotionally attuned relational context in which emotion regulation can be relearned, re-experienced, and reintegrated across the domains of the self.

Key therapeutic objectives include: (1) Creating emotional safety (especially for the core self); (2) Enhancing emotional awareness and labelling (plastic self); (3) Building tolerance for distress without avoidance or impulsivity (proto- and core self); and (4) Rewriting emotional narratives and relational scripts (plastic and external self). Specific ISP interventions include: (1) Relaxation and imagery to regulate arousal at the biological level; (2) Mentalisation and reflective dialogue to develop narrative coherence; (3) Expressive techniques and metaphorical exploration to access repressed affect; and (4) Cognitive restructuring to challenge distorted appraisals and facilitate reappraisal.

When clients learn that emotions are neither dangerous nor permanent—and that they can be understood, expressed, and survived—emotion regulation becomes a pathway to empowerment.

8.3. Emotional Expression

The expression of emotion is a vital mechanism through which the inner world becomes visible and communicable. In psychotherapy, the way clients express – or fail to express – their emotions provides important diagnostic information and therapeutic entry points. Emotional expression includes facial movements, vocal inflections, posture, gestures, and subtle shifts in tone or bodily activation (Izard, 1999). It is through these channels that affective states become perceivable to others and, often, to the self.

In the framework of Integrative Strategic Psychotherapy (ISP), emotional expression is not viewed as a singular act but as a layered and developmentally embedded process. It reflects and interacts with the structure of the self across the four interconnected domains: the proto-self, which mediates automatic physiological responses; the core self, where early relational patterns and attachment-based emotional responses take shape; the plastic self, which assigns meaning and narrative to emotional experiences; and the external self, which negotiates the social expression and suppression of emotion in accordance with interpersonal dynamics and cultural norms.

From infancy, the human organism is equipped to express basic affective states. Infants cry, coo, smile, or grimace in ways that signal emotional needs long before words become available. These early expressions arise from the proto-self and are mediated by autonomic processes that function to maintain internal regulation and elicit external support (Michael et.al., 2008). Yet it is only through the caregiver's attuned response to these expressions that a deeper level of emotional integration begins to emerge. When a caregiver accurately mirrors and names the infant's emotional states, a crucial process of dyadic regulation is established (Kinsella & Garland, 2008). The child not only experiences emotional relief but begins to internalise the idea that their emotional experience is real, shareable, and tolerable.

Daniel Siegel's concept of "feeling felt" (Siegel, 2001) illustrates this well: when the caregiver resonates with and gives meaning to the infant's affective state, the child develops a foundational sense of self-coherence. Emotional expression becomes not only a signal but a relational act—a way of being known. This foundational process contributes to the formation of the core self and underpins the ability to later identify, name, and modulate emotions.

As development progresses, emotional expression becomes increasingly shaped by family scripts, social norms, and personal adaptations (Kinsella & Garland, 2008). While some children are encouraged to express sadness or fear openly, others may learn that such emotions are unwelcome, weak, or even dangerous. The way emotional expression is received—whether it is met with validation, neglect, ridicule, or punishment—fundamentally shapes the internal working models that govern emotional life. These models are not purely cognitive but encoded somatically and relationally. In adulthood, the individual may find themselves expressing emotions only in certain relational contexts, or not at all, often without awareness of the original shaping experiences (Parker et.al., 2001).

Over time, discrete emotional reactions such as anger, joy, fear, or sadness tend to blend into more stable emotional patterns known as mood. Mood is best understood as a general affective leaning of the psyche. It colours perception, memory, and thought (Schore, 2021). For example, a person in a low mood is likely to interpret ambiguous events negatively, anticipate unfavourable outcomes, and selectively recall emotionally congruent memories. In depressive states, the mood becomes so dominant that it limits emotional variability; the person feels unable to access alternative emotional states, remaining emotionally stuck or "flattened".

Mood, therefore, plays a significant role in emotional expression. Someone in a persistently anxious mood may speak quickly, with tension in their voice and posture, while someone in a melancholic mood may move slowly, speak softly, or avoid eye contact (Siegel, 2001). These expressive patterns can become habitual, reinforcing the underlying mood state and creating self-perpetuating cycles. In clinical work, shifting mood tone—through the psychotherapist's affective presence, the rhythm of the session, or symbolic interventions—can open space for more flexible and authentic emotional expression.

The external self, a concept particularly relevant in ISP, is the aspect of the self that learns to adapt emotional expression to social expectations. It governs the performed self—the one that participates in professional roles, family dynamics, and cultural narratives. Here, emotion may be managed strategically: masked, exaggerated, withheld, or feigned depending on perceived consequences. This social regulation of emotional expression is not inherently pathological; it is often necessary for survival or relational harmony (Jones et. al., 2004). However, when the external self becomes dissociated from the core emotional experience, incongruence and psychological strain may result.

Many clients enter psychotherapy having learned to suppress or distort their emotional expressions. A woman who smiles while describing traumatic experiences may be unaware that her smile functions as a defence against vulnerability. A man who never raises his voice may have internalised a belief that anger is unacceptable or dangerous. These expressions—or lack thereof—are shaped by both external demands and internalised prohibitions. They may serve adaptive purposes but often become rigid, limiting the individual's capacity for authentic relational contact and emotional integration.

One of the more severe disruptions in emotional expression is found in alexithymia, a construct that literally means "no words for emotions" (Izard & Kobak, 1999). Individuals with alexithymia struggle to identify and describe their emotions, confuse emotional states with physical sensations, and often have difficulty engaging in imaginative or symbolic thought. Their thinking tends to focus on external events, with limited access to the inner emotional world. From a neurological perspective, alexithymia has been associated with reduced connectivity between the brain's left and right hemispheres—specifically, the left hemisphere's role in verbal expression and the right hemisphere's role in emotional processing. When these systems are poorly integrated, the result is a diminished capacity to translate bodily affect into words (Kinsella & Garland, 2008).

In terms of the ISP model, alexithymia may be understood as a developmental arrest or fragmentation at the level of the plastic self. The individual may possess strong affective responses at the proto-self and core self levels, but without symbolic processing and reflective function, these emotional energies remain unarticulated. This often leads to somatisation, interpersonal confusion, and chronic feelings of emptiness or detachment.

Such clients often do not respond well to insight-oriented approaches that rely on verbalisation and introspection. Instead, interventions that engage other expressive channels—such as body-based work, art therapy, or structured cognitive-behavioural tasks—may be more effective in gradually building emotional vocabulary and tolerance. Psychoeducation, group formats, and emotional awareness training can also facilitate movement toward a more integrated emotional expression (Michael et. Al., 2008).

Within the therapeutic process, the expression of emotion serves both a diagnostic and a healing function. The psychotherapist pays close attention to what is said, how it is said, and what remains unsaid. A change in voice tone, a gesture, or a moment of silence may signal emerging affect. These signals offer an opportunity for intervention—either by mirroring, naming, or deepening the emotional experience (Jones et. Al., 2004).

For the client, the experience of expressing emotion and being met with atonement rather than judgment can be transformative. It can restore a sense of coherence, reconnect dissociated emotional states, and foster new relational templates. Gradually, the client begins to inhabit their emotions more fully, express them more congruently, and use them as sources of information rather than threats to be avoided.

In this way, emotional expression in psychotherapy is not simply about catharsis or disclosure. It is a process of reorganising the self, allowing for greater authenticity, flexibility, and integration. It reconnects the various layers of the self—physiological, relational, symbolic, and performative—and restores the capacity to move fluidly between them (Jones et. al., 2004).

In clinical settings, difficulties with emotional expression are commonly encountered across a wide range of psychopathological presentations. Clients may exhibit emotional expressions that are exaggerated, blunted, contextually inappropriate, or entirely absent (Parker et. al., 2001). These patterns are rarely incidental; rather, they reflect adaptations to developmental, relational, or neurobiological constraints that have shaped the person's expressive repertoire.

For example, in depressive disorders, individuals often show a diminished capacity to express a range of emotions. Facial affect may be flat or restricted, voice may become monotonous, and gestures subdued. This reduction in expressive vitality reflects both the low-energy state of depression and the internal experience of hopelessness or shame. In contrast, individuals with anxiety disorders may display heightened emotional expression, particularly of fear or apprehension, often through rapid speech, fidgeting, or hyper-alert gaze. Yet even in these cases, certain emotions—such as anger or sadness—may remain under-expressed or entirely inaccessible (Kinsella & Garland, 2008).

In disorders involving emotional dysregulation, such as borderline personality disorder, expression may appear intense, unstable, and disproportionate to context (Parker et. al., 2001). Clients may oscillate between emotional flooding and emotional numbing, with little capacity to modulate intensity or duration. In such cases, the external self may become overwhelmed, unable to contain the affective overflow, while the plastic self struggles to make sense of the experience. Similarly, in dissociative disorders, emotional expression may be disconnected from the internal state altogether. Clients might describe terrifying experiences in a flat tone or show no affective response to distressing narratives (Izard & Kobak, 1999). This kind of expressive disconnect often signals fragmentation across levels of the self.

In ISP, the therapeutic task is not simply to encourage more emotional expression, but to understand the history, meaning, and structure of the client's expressive patterns. This involves careful assessment of when, how, and in what contexts expression becomes inhibited, exaggerated, dissociated, or performative. Through this lens, emotional expression becomes a map of the client's relational history and internal world.

Intervention strategies are selected based on the level of the self that appears most implicated in the client's difficulties. At the level of the proto-self, body-based interventions such as breathwork, grounding techniques, and sensory awareness can support clients in reconnecting with the physiological foundations of emotion. At the level of the core self, the therapeutic relationship itself becomes the primary instrument of change. The therapist's atonement, facial mirroring, voice modulation, and empathic presence provide a new relational experience that helps recalibrate the client's capacity to express emotion safely and congruently.

When working with the plastic self, techniques such as narrative therapy, metaphor exploration, journaling, and imagery can facilitate the client's capacity to assign meaning and language to previously inexpressible emotional states. Finally, interventions targeting the external self may include role-play, assertiveness training, or expressive arts approaches that explore how emotions are performed and suppressed in social settings.

Across all levels, the psychotherapist supports the client in moving toward a more authentic and integrated mode of emotional expression—one that aligns inner affective experience with outer communication, without sacrificing either safety or spontaneity. It is through this alignment that emotional truth emerges, and with it, the potential for self-reorganisation.

Emotional expression, therefore, is not merely a behavioural output; it is a fundamental organiser of human experience (Michael et. al., 2008). It mediates between the internal and external worlds, reflects the history of attachment and affect regulation, and signals the current state of the self in relation to others. When expression becomes flexible, coherent, and responsive to context, it reflects an underlying integration across the levels of the self. When it is fragmented, distorted, or absent, it points to ruptures that psychotherapy can begin to address.

In integrative strategic psychotherapy, emotional expression is not treated as an isolated skill to be trained or corrected. It is approached as a dynamic and relational phenomenon that reveals the architecture of the self and offers a pathway toward deeper healing. By attending to how emotions are expressed—and just as importantly, how they are not—the therapist invites the client into a process of rediscovery, connection, and ultimately, integration.

8.4. Neurotic Guilt and Repression of Emotions

Repression of emotional experience remains one of the most pervasive and subtle dynamics contributing to psychological distress. Within the integrative strategic framework, emotional repression is understood as a complex defensive pattern that manifests when authentic affective responses are consistently invalidated, punished, or rendered unsafe within the interpersonal and developmental environment. Although often invisible on the surface, this defensive structure can underpin a broad spectrum of clinical presentations, including depression, anxiety, psychosomatic complaints, dissociative symptoms, passive-aggressive behaviour, and unresolved neurotic guilt (Silke, Evans, & Michael, 2006; Reevy, 2010).

From the earliest stages of life, emotions serve as vital signals, connecting the organism to its internal needs and external environment. These emotions emerge from the level of the proto-self as somatic responses to pleasure, pain, threat, or comfort (Popescu & Vîșcu, 2016). As development progresses, emotions become embedded in the core self—encoded through early relational experiences, attachment patterns, and affective communication with caregivers. When these experiences provide adequate mirroring, containment, and validation, the individual develops an internal sense of emotional safety and competence. However, when the caregiving environment consistently punishes, invalidates, or ignores emotional states—particularly so-called "negative" emotions such as anger, sadness, or fear—the child is forced to suppress their emotional signals in order to preserve attachment bonds or avoid punishment (Moursund & Erskine, 2003).

A child who is punished for expressing anger—whether through overt discipline or subtle emotional withdrawal—quickly learns that expressing certain feelings jeopardises safety or love. Responses such as "*Don't talk back,*" "*Go to your room until you're calm,*" or "*You should be ashamed of yourself*" convey powerful messages that one's emotional state is unacceptable or shameful (Reevy, 2010). These early experiences often result in the repression of emotion at the level of the core self. The child begins to disconnect from their own inner reality in order to conform to the demands of their attachment environment. Over time, this repression becomes internalised as part of the core self, shaping one's beliefs about emotions, self-worth, and interpersonal expression (Popescu & Vîşcu, 2016).

Importantly, children do not learn solely from what is said to them; they also learn by observing the emotional strategies of adults around them. If a parent consistently numbs their own emotional states through alcohol, medication, dissociation, or compulsive behaviours, the child receives a powerful, albeit implicit, lesson: strong feelings are dangerous and must be anaesthetised (Block, 2012). Later in life, when confronted with emotional distress, the individual may repeat these patterns of avoidance—reaching for substances, distractions, or dissociative strategies rather than turning toward the feeling itself.

The repression of emotion is often gendered and culturally patterned. In many family and societal systems, boys are discouraged from expressing sadness or vulnerability, while girls are punished for showing anger or assertiveness. As a result, many men struggle to access or express grief, while many women experience guilt or self-doubt when they feel angry or set boundaries (Moursund & Erskine, 2003). These culturally enforced emotional restrictions further constrain the development of emotional fluency and contribute to patterns of chronic dysregulation and self-alienation.

When emotional expression is consistently blocked, the emotional energy does not disappear. Rather, it becomes displaced, somatised, or redirected into indirect forms of expression. Passive-aggressive behaviour is one common manifestation of repressed anger—anger that cannot be expressed directly may instead emerge through sarcasm, chronic lateness, stonewalling, or subtle sabotage (Reevy, 2010). The emotional signal is preserved but stripped of clarity, making it more difficult to recognise, own, or transform.

One of the most insidious consequences of emotional repression is the development of neurotic guilt. This form of guilt is often not linked to actual wrongdoing but emerges from unconscious conflicts involving forbidden feelings—particularly anger, resentment, or the wish for autonomy (Erskine & Moursund, 2011). Neurotic guilt frequently develops in families where children are held responsible for their parents' emotional wellbeing. Phrases such as "*You'll be the death of me,*" "*I gave up everything for you,*" or "*After all I've done, this is how you repay me?*" impose a tremendous emotional burden. The child, even in adulthood, becomes convinced that any expression of anger or boundary-setting will cause irreparable harm to the parent.

This dynamic represents a collapse in the emotional differentiation of the plastic self. The individual internalises the idea that their emotions, particularly anger or assertiveness, are dangerous or morally wrong. When such feelings do arise—as they inevitably do—they are accompanied by intense guilt, anxiety, or shame (Silke et al., 2006). This prevents the full integration of the emotional experience and reinforces the original pattern of repression.

At the same time, the external self becomes caught in a double bind: outward compliance is maintained in order to avoid guilt and conflict, while the inner self grows increasingly fragmented and resentful. This can give rise to relational patterns marked by dependency, martyrdom, or sudden eruptions of anger after prolonged suppression. In some cases, these dynamics also underlie depressive states, where repressed anger is turned inward and experienced as hopelessness, worthlessness, or chronic self-criticism (Popescu, 2021).

From a therapeutic perspective, the clinician must be attuned to both the content and the absence of emotion in the client's narrative. Repression is not always immediately evident; it is often revealed through silences, evasions, forced smiles, or bodily signs of discomfort. A client may speak at length about traumatic events in a flat tone or smile when recalling painful memories. In such moments, the psychotherapist's task is not to confront the repression directly but to gently invite awareness and safety into the emotional space. Questions such as "What would it be like to allow yourself to feel something here?" or "Do you notice anything in your body as you talk about this?" can help bring the client into contact with their underlying affective states.

Working with neurotic guilt involves a careful unpacking of internalised messages, distorted responsibility, and loyalty binds. Clients must come to understand that having feelings—particularly anger or disappointment—does not equate to being harmful or disloyal (Erskine & Moursund, 2011). This process often requires reprocessing developmental experiences, grieving unmet needs, and redefining one's identity beyond the role of the "good child" or "emotional caretaker".

The integrative strategic psychotherapist will tailor interventions to the level of the self where repression is most active. At the proto-self level, the focus may be on reawakening bodily awareness through somatic tracking and breathwork. At the core self level, the emphasis is on restoring emotional contact through relational atonement, validation, and empathic presence. Work at the level of the plastic self involves constructing new internal narratives that permit the full range of affective experience. Finally, at the level of the external self, clients may practise new forms of expression, assertiveness, or boundary-setting in therapeutic enactments or through expressive modalities such as writing, art, or voice work (Popescu & Vîşcu, 2016).

Ultimately, the therapeutic aim is not merely to uncover repressed emotion, but to support the client in safely experiencing, expressing, and integrating these feelings within a coherent and compassionate view of the self. In doing so, the once-feared emotions become accessible, meaningful, and usable in the service of healing, autonomy, and authentic connection.

References

Barrett, L. F. (2017). *How emotions are made: The secret life of the brain*. Pan Macmillan.

Baylis, P. (2006). *Emergence of emotions and development of affect regulation*. Auckland: New Zealand Psychologists' Board.

Block, J. (2012). *Paths toward self-insight and emotional healing*. New York: Insight Books.

Clark, A. (2013). Whatever next? Predictive brains, situated agents, and the future of cognitive science. *Behavioural and Brain Sciences, 36*(3), 181–204. https://doi.org/10.1017/S0140525X12000477

Damasio, A. (1999). *The feeling of what happens: Body and emotion in the making of consciousness*. Harcourt Brace.

Davidson, R. J., & Begley, S. (2012). *The emotional life of your brain*. Hudson Street Press.

Ekman, P. (1992). An argument for basic emotions. *Cognition & Emotion, 6*(3–4), 169–200.

Erskine, R. G., & Moursund, J. P. (2011). *Beyond empathy: A therapy of contact-in-relationship* (2nd ed.). Routledge.

Fonagy, P., & Target, M. (2003). *Psychoanalytic theories: Perspectives from developmental psychopathology*. Whurr Publishers.

Fonagy, P., Gergely, G., Jurist, E., & Target, M. (2002). *Affect regulation, mentalization, and the development of the self.* Karnac Books.

Greenberg, L. (2015). *Emotion-focused therapy: Coaching clients to work through their feelings*. American Psychological Association.

Gross, J. J. (2012). Emotion regulation: Affective, cognitive, and social consequences. *Psychophysiology, 39*(3), 281–291.

Gross, J. J. (2015). Emotion regulation: Current status and future prospects. *Psychological Inquiry, 26*(1), 1–26.

Griffiths, R. (1997). The neurobiology of affect. *Journal of Affective Disorders, 43*(2), 103–113.

Izard, C. E., & Kobak, R. R. (1999). Emotion system functioning and emotion regulation. *Development and Psychopathology, 11*(4), 803–809. https://doi.org/10.1017/S0954579499002363

Jones, N. A., Ward, A., & Parker, J. D. A. (2004). Alexithymia and the processing of emotional stimuli: Theory, research, and clinical implications. *Journal of Psychosomatic Research, 56*(4), 341–350. https://doi.org/10.1016/j.jpsychores.2004.01.003

Kinsella, M. T., & Garland, A. (2008). Affect regulation and depressive symptoms in young adults: Roles of cognitive appraisals, coping strategies, and mood. *Behaviour Research and Therapy, 46*(9), 1142–1150. https://doi.org/10.1016/j.brat.2008.06.002

Lepannen, J. M. (2006). Emotional information processing in mood disorders: A review of behavioural and neuroimaging findings. *Current Opinion in Psychiatry, 19*(1), 34–39. https://doi.org/10.1097/01.yco.0000191500.46411.00

Michael, R., Silke, K., & Evans, C. (2008). *Emotional systems and the brain: The neurobiology of affect*. Cambridge University Press.

Moursund, J. P., & Erskine, R. G. (2003). *The healing relationship: Integrative psychotherapy at work*. Crown House Publishing.

Pessoa, L. (2021). *The entangled brain: How perception, cognition, and emotion are woven together*. MIT Press.

Popescu, O. M., & Vîșcu, L. (2016). *Fundamentele psihoterapiei integrative strategice.* Timișoara: Eurobit.

Panksepp, J. (2011). Cross-species affective neuroscience decoding of the primal affective experiences of humans and related animals. *PLOS ONE, 6*(12), e21236.

Parker, J. D. A., Taylor, G. J., & Bagby, R. M. (2001). The alexithymia construct: Relationship with sociodemographic variables and intelligence. *Comprehensive Psychiatry, 42*(6), 471–478. https://doi.org/10.1053/comp.2001.27893

Popescu, O.M. (2021). Psihoterapie integrative strategică. Vol.1. Teorie și aplicații practice. Snagov: Letras.

Porges, S. W. (2021). *Polyvagal theory: Neurophysiological foundations of emotions, attachment, communication, and self-regulation* (2nd ed.). W. W. Norton & Company.

Reevy, G. M. (Ed.). (2010). *Encyclopedia of emotion* (Vol. 1–2). ABC-CLIO.

Scherer, K. R., & Ekman, P. (Eds.). (2014). *Approaches to emotion*. Psychology Press.

Schore, A. N. (2021). *Right brain psychotherapy*. W. W. Norton & Company.

Siegel, D. J. (2020). *The developing mind: How relationships and the brain interact to shape who we are* (3rd ed.). The Guilford Press.

Silke, K., Evans, C., & Michael, R. (2006). Emotion, cognition, and the human brain. *Psychological Science, 17*(5), 421–428. https://doi.org/10.1111/j.1467-9280.2006.01724.x

Tronick, E. (1989). Emotions and emotional communication in infants. *American Psychologist, 44*(2), 112–119.

Vanderkerckhove, M., Gross, J. J., & Braet, C. (2008). Emotion regulation and psychopathology: A transdiagnostic perspective. In A. M. Kring & D. M. Sloan (Eds.), *Emotion regulation and psychopathology: A transdiagnostic approach to etiology and treatment* (pp. 179–202). Guilford Press.

CHAPTER 9

COMPLEX PSYCHODYNAMIC PATTERNS

9.1. Conditions of Worth

Human beings have an intrinsic need to be loved, valued, and accepted—not merely for what they do, but for who they are. This form of love, often referred to as *unconditional positive regard,* represents an ideal relational environment in which the individual is embraced fully, without demands for compliance, performance, or perfection (Mearns & Thorne, 2000). However, in real-world relationships—especially in early childhood—such unconditional acceptance is often compromised. More commonly, children experience *conditional acceptance*, where love, attention, and approval are made contingent on behaviour that conforms to the expectations of caregivers or other significant figures.

From the earliest stages of development, the child's sense of worth and identity is shaped by the feedback they receive from attachment figures. If parents consistently communicate that love is earned—rather than freely given—the child internalises the belief that their value is dependent on external performance. For instance, a parent may withhold affection after a disappointing school result and express affection only when the child excels. A message such as "*I love you when you succeed, but not when you fail*" does not need to be spoken explicitly to have a profound effect. The child quickly learns to suppress, hide, or deny aspects of the self that may elicit criticism or rejection.

In such an environment, the developing self becomes fragmented. The child's core self—which naturally contains a wide spectrum of emotions, impulses, and spontaneous expressions—is forced to adapt in order to secure attachment. As a result, a false or compliant self begins to dominate, particularly within the external self, where expression becomes tailored to perceived expectations. These internal compromises may appear adaptive in the short term, but over time they contribute to emotional disconnection, anxiety, perfectionism, and chronic insecurity.

A key consequence of conditional acceptance is the shift from an *internal* to an *external locus of evaluation* (Wilkins, 2010). Ideally, the child should develop an internal reference point for making sense of experiences, making decisions, and evaluating their own worth. This requires trust in one's own perceptions, feelings, and judgments. However, when conditional love dominates early experience, the child begins to defer to others' evaluations instead. They learn that the approval of significant others takes precedence over their own internal cues—a relational adaptation that, while ensuring attachment, erodes self-trust.

In adulthood, this external orientation can manifest as people-pleasing, chronic self-monitoring, or a compulsive need for validation. The individual may find themselves working excessively to meet expectations, fearful of disappointing others, or plagued by perfectionistic standards. These patterns are often driven by an internalised voice that equates failure with rejection and approval with safety.

Clinical examples of these dynamics are readily observable. A client may report feeling deeply ashamed of making a mistake at work—not simply because of the error itself, but because it threatens their sense of lovability. Others may describe an inability to relax or feel satisfaction after accomplishments, as their self-worth remains tethered to the next achievement, the next compliment, the next metric of approval.

In the integrative strategic psychotherapy model, such dynamics are understood as rooted in disruptions across multiple levels of the self. At the level of the proto-self, chronic stress responses may become activated whenever there is perceived rejection, triggering physiological anxiety. At the level of the core self, the original injury resides—the unmet need for secure, unconditional love and mirrored emotional presence. The plastic self is often saturated with intermediary beliefs such as "*I am only lovable if I succeed*," or "*Making mistakes means I am bad*." These beliefs, though adaptive at the time of acquisition, now drive self-sabotage and emotional exhaustion. Meanwhile, the external self often presents as competent, agreeable, or successful—masking deep vulnerabilities and an absence of authentic self-worth.

Therapeutic work with such individuals involves a gradual reorganisation of these internal structures. At the heart of the process is the therapeutic relationship itself, which becomes a new emotional experience in which acceptance is not contingent upon performance. The psychotherapist offers a consistent, attuned, and non-judgmental presence that counters earlier conditional dynamics.

Over time, clients begin to risk revealing aspects of themselves that were previously hidden or devalued, and with that, a more integrated and resilient self begins to emerge.

Interventions may include exploring the origins of conditional self-worth, challenging internalised narratives, and cultivating emotional awareness beyond the approval-seeking reflex. Clients are supported in re-establishing an internal locus of evaluation—learning to check in with their own needs, values, and emotional states, rather than deferring to others' judgments.

Ultimately, the restoration of unconditional self-acceptance is not a return to naivety, but a return to wholeness. It is a psychological and relational process in which the fragmented self is welcomed home—not for what it produces, but for what it truly is.

9.2. Self-Esteem

9.2.1. Definitions and Functions of Self-Esteem

Self-esteem is a central construct in psychological theory and practice, one that exerts a significant influence on human behaviour, emotional regulation, interpersonal relationships, and long-term adaptation. It is often defined as the evaluative aspect of the self-concept—that is, the degree to which an individual experiences themselves as worthy, competent, and valuable (van Zyl et al., 2006). Self-esteem informs not only how one feels about oneself but also how one anticipates future outcomes, engages with challenges, and maintains or avoids relationships. In psychotherapy, it is frequently one of the most distorted internal experiences, underlying or contributing to a wide array of psychological symptoms.

Although many conceptualisations of self-esteem exist, they generally converge on the idea that it encompasses both cognitive and affective components. Cognitively, it involves the individual's perception of their personal strengths, efficacy, and ability to meet the demands of life. Affectively, it reflects one's emotional tone toward the self—feelings of pride, shame, guilt, satisfaction, or self-loathing. Mruk (2013) synthesises these elements by identifying two primary dimensions: *competence*, or the belief in one's effectiveness, and *worth*, or the sense that one is intrinsically valuable.

From the perspective of integrative strategic psychotherapy (ISP), self-esteem is not merely a cognitive appraisal or emotional state; it is a multi-layered phenomenon embedded in the structure of the self. It is encoded at every level—from the somatic-emotional reactions of the proto-self to the internalised relational scripts of the core self, the belief systems of the plastic self, and the performative adaptations of the external self. As such, self-esteem is not static but evolves in relation to early attachment experiences, social environments, cultural messaging, and internal narratives.

A key psychological function of self-esteem is to serve as a regulatory system that influences motivation, decision-making, and coping strategies. High self-esteem enables individuals to take risks, recover from failure, and engage in authentic self-expression. In contrast, low self-esteem is associated with avoidance, defensive posturing, and chronic emotional dysregulation. Baumeister and colleagues (2003) describe self-esteem as serving both *self-protection*—avoiding damage to the self—and *self-enhancement*—promoting growth, mastery, and expansion. Individuals with fragile or unstable self-esteem tend to over-invest in self-protection at the expense of growth, often developing self-sabotaging behaviours or "self-handicapping" strategies (Guindon, 2010).

Self-handicapping occurs when individuals, consciously or unconsciously, create obstacles to success in order to protect their sense of self-worth. For example, a person who fears failure in a romantic relationship may sabotage emotional intimacy to avoid the perceived humiliation of being rejected. Another may avoid taking on a new professional opportunity to pre-emptively escape the possibility of not performing well. In these cases, self-esteem acts as a psychological barometer—if perceived worth is too fragile, the individual retreats into inaction or defensiveness rather than tolerate the emotional consequences of perceived failure.

In psychodynamic traditions, self-esteem has long been linked to the internal tension between the "real self" and the "ideal self"—a discrepancy that generates discomfort, shame, or self-criticism. When the individual feels distant from their internalised standards or aspirations, self-esteem declines (Mruk, 2013). This discrepancy is often deeply rooted in childhood, where ideals are shaped by parental expectations, cultural ideals, or unattainable perfectionism. The therapeutic process often involves identifying and interrogating these unrealistic standards, as well as healing the emotional wounds that accompany chronic self-criticism.

From a cognitive perspective, self-esteem is closely related to self-efficacy—Bandura's (1977) construct describing an individual's belief in their capacity to successfully engage in specific tasks or challenges. While self-efficacy pertains to domain-specific competence (e.g., "*I can give this presentation*"), self-esteem is more global and emotionally laden (e.g., "I am worthy even if I fail"). Nevertheless, low self-efficacy in repeated domains can erode global self-esteem over time, especially when the individual's internal critic is harsh or when external feedback is consistently negative.

ISP integrates these perspectives by viewing self-esteem not as a fixed trait, but as an emergent property of internal and relational processes across the lifespan. For example, at the level of the proto-self, early embodied experiences of comfort or distress shape a baseline of emotional safety that influences later feelings of worthiness. At the level of the core self, repeated relational patterns—particularly those involving acceptance, rejection, praise, or punishment—are internalised into attachment schemas that govern self-appraisal. The plastic self transforms these early experiences into more elaborate cognitive frameworks and beliefs, often laden with culturally inherited narratives of success, morality, or gendered worth. Finally, the external self manages the expression or concealment of self-esteem-related vulnerability in social situations, often through impression management, perfectionism, or submission.

Global self-esteem, as Baumeister (1998) points out, refers to one's general evaluation of self-worth across domains and time. It is not specific to a task or role but reflects an overall attitude toward the self. Selective or domain-specific self-esteem, on the other hand, refers to one's self-evaluation in particular areas such as academic competence, social desirability, physical appearance, or emotional intelligence. Importantly, a person may feel confident and capable in one domain while still experiencing pervasive low self-esteem due to unresolved issues in another. For example, a client may present as professionally successful while suffering from deep emotional insecurity in intimate relationships.

This nuanced understanding of self-esteem allows for more targeted therapeutic interventions. Rather than assuming a global deficit, the psychotherapist explores with the client which aspects of the self feel intact and which feel shame-bound, invisible, or unworthy. In ISP, this mapping is further guided by identifying the level of the self where the rupture in self-esteem originates. A sense of incompetence may stem from early embodied experiences of helplessness (proto-self), from relational neglect (core self), from internalised narratives of failure (plastic self), or from chronic performative overcompensation (external self).

Ultimately, self-esteem is neither fragile nor rigid—it is plastic. It can be damaged by developmental trauma, distorted by rigid social norms, or inflated through defensive grandiosity. But it can also be repaired through relational atonement, corrective experiences, emotional integration, and the construction of new meaning. The psychotherapeutic task is not to artificially inflate self-esteem, but to support clients in developing a more grounded, coherent, and compassionate relationship with themselves. In doing so, self-esteem becomes a quiet inner certainty—a sense that one is fundamentally acceptable, even in the face of imperfection, failure, or vulnerability.

9.2.2. Factors Contributing to The Development of Self-Esteem

Self-esteem, while often treated as a relatively stable trait, is in fact the dynamic outcome of a complex interplay between biological predispositions, early attachment experiences, family environment, social learning, cultural context, and internal value systems. In integrative strategic psychotherapy, these influences are understood as shaping the developmental trajectory of the self across multiple levels—biological, relational, cognitive, and social—each corresponding to a domain of the self (proto-self, core self, plastic self, and external self).

One of the foundational frameworks for understanding the multifactorial nature of self-esteem comes from the work of Mruk (2006), who identifies a range of interrelated contributors that explain why individuals, even within the same family, can develop vastly different self-evaluative frameworks.

Genetic predispositions are a significant but not deterministic factor. Research suggests that heritable traits such as temperament, energy levels, and cognitive abilities account for approximately 30–40% of the variability in self-esteem among siblings (Kendler et al., 1998; Mruk, 2006). These temperamental factors—rooted in the proto-self—may predispose some individuals to higher emotional resilience, while others may be more vulnerable to criticism, social rejection, or internalised shame. Yet these inborn traits interact constantly with the child's environment, especially the relational field in which the core self is formed.

Parental support plays a pivotal role in shaping the emerging sense of worth. Studies indicate that maternal support is more strongly associated with the development of self-worth, while paternal support often correlates with a child's emerging sense of competence (Mruk, 2006; Guindon, 2010). However, this distinction is not absolute and may vary depending on attachment configurations and gender dynamics within the family. What remains consistent is that children internalise the emotional tone of the caregiving system—whether nurturing, critical, responsive, or dismissive—and this tone becomes embedded in the relational matrix of the core self.

Parental warmth and unconditional acceptance are perhaps the most critical determinants of healthy self-esteem. Acceptance in this context refers to the parent's capacity to see and reflect the whole child—not just their achievements or compliance, but also their vulnerabilities, limitations, and emotional states. A child who is allowed to explore their emotional world safely, without being shamed or dismissed, develops a robust internal sense of legitimacy: "*I am allowed to exist as I am*." In the absence of such acceptance, children often grow up relying on extrinsic sources of validation, becoming overly sensitive to the approval of others or dependent on external achievements to feel worthy.

Parental expectations and the consistency with which these are communicated also shape self-esteem in critical ways. When expectations are clearly articulated and boundaries are maintained in a stable, emotionally regulated manner, the child learns both self-discipline and the sense that their actions have meaning. In contrast, erratic or excessively rigid parenting—often associated with authoritarian or permissive styles—can lead to confusion, insecurity, or feelings of inadequacy. Children need limits not as constraints, but as structures within which the self can differentiate and grow.

Parenting style is one of the most widely studied variables associated with self-esteem development. Authoritative parenting—characterised by warmth, structure, and responsiveness—has consistently been associated with higher levels of self-esteem (Baumrind, 1991; Mruk, 2006). In contrast, authoritarian (harsh and controlling) or permissive (lacking boundaries) styles have been linked to poorer emotional regulation, higher impulsivity, and a fragile or inflated sense of self.

Birth order may also exert subtle influences. First-born children and only children, due to receiving undivided attention during early developmental stages, are more likely to experience enhanced self-worth (Mruk, 2006). However, this is not universally true and may be moderated by sibling dynamics, parental stress, or other environmental variables. What seems to matter most is not the order per se, but the quality of early attention and emotional availability during sensitive periods of development.

Modelling is another critical factor. Children absorb not only direct messages about their worth but also the unspoken attitudes their caregivers hold toward themselves. A parent who consistently demonstrates self-respect, healthy boundaries, and resilience models these qualities implicitly. Studies suggest a positive correlation between a mother's level of self-esteem and that of her child (Guindon, 2010). Through everyday observation, children learn how to process failure, accept compliments, express vulnerability, and manage frustration—all of which contribute to the development of internalised self-worth.

Social and cultural values also influence the formation of self-esteem. While the association between social class and self-esteem is relatively weak, it is consistent. Individuals raised in environments that emphasise achievement, autonomy, or conformity may adopt these values into their own self-evaluative framework—particularly if they remain connected to their family or community of origin. This contributes to the development of the plastic self, where value systems and internal beliefs are shaped and refined.

The individual's own self-values—deeply held beliefs about what is desirable, admirable, or shameful—also evolve in response to life events and relational ruptures. According to Mruk (2006), these values serve as the lens through which the person evaluates their own behaviour, achievements, and character. Significant life transitions, such as the loss of a loved one or a radical change in social environment, can trigger a re-evaluation of these internal standards, leading to sudden fluctuations in self-esteem.

Gender, while accounting for only minor differences, is relevant in the context of societal expectations and emotional socialisation. Men, in many cultures, tend to derive self-esteem more from competence and achievement, whereas women's self-esteem is more strongly linked to relational acceptance and social inclusion (Kling et al., 1999). These gendered dynamics can exacerbate vulnerability to low self-esteem when individuals deviate from culturally idealised roles.

Racial, ethnic, and economic factors further complicate the picture. Experiences of marginalisation, discrimination, or internalised stigma can erode self-esteem over time. At the same time, some individuals from minority groups demonstrate higher self-esteem when they cultivate a strong positive racial or cultural identity—a phenomenon described as *the racial identity hypothesis* (Crocker & Major, 1989). Self-protective mechanisms such as selective comparison (e.g., minimising the importance of domains in which one's group is disadvantaged) can also buffer against the erosion of self-worth in the face of structural inequality.

Cultural orientation plays a significant role in how self-esteem is defined, expressed, and reinforced. In individualistic cultures, where autonomy and self-expression are prioritised, self-esteem is often tied to personal achievement and independence. In collectivistic cultures, by contrast, self-worth may derive more from harmony, group affiliation, and social responsibility (Heine et al., 1999). Psychotherapists must remain culturally sensitive to these frameworks, particularly when working with clients whose internalised values may not align with the dominant norms of the society in which they currently live.

Taken together, these influences often culminate in the formation of internal labels—statements about the self that become internalised during childhood and continue to shape emotional and behavioural patterns in adulthood. These labels are often inherited from parental messages, repeated criticisms, comparisons, or shaming experiences. "*You are lazy*," "*You never get it right*," or "*You always need attention*" are not just remembered phrases—they become embedded as core beliefs within the plastic self, often manifesting as an inner critic or punitive internal dialogue.

Different psychotherapeutic traditions describe this phenomenon through their own conceptual lenses: irrational beliefs in cognitive-behavioural therapy (Beck, 1976), the internal Parent in transactional analysis (Berne, 1964), the internalised critical object in psychodynamic psychotherapy, or contact boundary disturbances in gestalt therapy (Perls et al., 1951). Regardless of the terminology, these internalised evaluations are activated in moments of stress, failure, or relational tension, often resulting in emotional distress, self-sabotage, or behavioural avoidance.

In integrative strategic psychotherapy, identifying the origin, structure, and domain of the self in which these negative evaluations are encoded becomes a core therapeutic task. This enables the clinician to develop targeted interventions—whether somatic, relational, cognitive, or expressive—that restore internal coherence and self-worth across all levels of the self.

9.2.3. Self-Esteem Assessed According to Competence and Worth

Within the literature on self-esteem, a particularly useful distinction—especially for clinical formulation—lies in the differentiation between *competence* and *worth* as two fundamental evaluative dimensions of the self. Christopher Mruk (2013) describes these as the twin pillars of self-esteem: the individual's *cognitive evaluation* of their capacity to cope with life's demands (competence) and their *emotional sense* of being intrinsically valuable (worth). Both components are required for self-esteem to be experienced as stable, resilient, and authentic. When one dimension is underdeveloped or overcompensated, the resulting self-esteem may appear functional on the surface but is often fragile, defensive, or vulnerable to collapse under pressure.

Competence, in this context, refers to a person's belief in their ability to act effectively in the world—to plan, make decisions, solve problems, and achieve goals. This is closely related to the construct of *self-efficacy* as proposed by Bandura (1977), which involves the belief that one can successfully organise and execute actions required to deal with prospective situations. The competence dimension of self-esteem is thus fundamentally cognitive in nature, structured around perceived agency, performance, and control.

Worth, on the other hand, refers to the affective dimension of self-esteem: the degree to which an individual *feels lovable*, acceptable, and worthy of belonging, regardless of achievement or success. It is rooted in early relational experiences of being seen, valued, and accepted for who one is—not simply for what one does. This dimension is typically shaped within the core self, through the internalisation of attachment dynamics and relational mirroring.

According to Mruk's (2006) typology, self-esteem can be categorised into four distinct types, based on the interaction of these two dimensions:

(1) High competence, high worth – This reflects *genuine high self-esteem*, in which individuals feel both effective and intrinsically valuable. Such individuals tend to be resilient, adaptable, and relatively free from chronic anxiety about approval or performance. They are capable of handling failure without catastrophic self-doubt, and of seeking connection without losing their sense of identity. This integrated self-esteem is rooted in all levels of the self: the proto-self contributes physiological coherence and affective stability; the core self houses secure attachment and internalised acceptance; the plastic self supports realistic narratives of identity and success; and the external self reflects authenticity in social expression;

(2) High worth, low competence – Individuals in this category *feel loved* or believe themselves to be inherently valuable, but doubt their ability to succeed, act independently, or meet challenges. Their self-esteem is *emotionally positive* but

cognitively undermined by learned helplessness, self-doubt, or fear of failure. In therapy, such clients may show dependency or difficulty taking initiative, and may interpret challenges as threats to safety rather than opportunities for growth. Their plastic self may contain internalised narratives such as "I'm a good person, but I can't do anything right," while the external self may seek protection through avoidance, submissiveness, or appeasement;

(3) High competence, low worth – Here we find clients who appear outwardly confident, driven, or successful, but whose *sense of worth is contingent* on achievement, recognition, or external validation. Their high performance masks a deeper fear of inadequacy or rejection. Such self-esteem is typically rigid and defensive—an identity constructed to prevent others from seeing the underlying vulnerability. When success falters, criticism arises, or abandonment is perceived, the fragile inner structure becomes exposed, often resulting in anxiety, depression, or shame. This is a common presentation in therapy, particularly among clients with perfectionistic, narcissistic, or compulsive tendencies. Therapeutically, the work involves supporting the client in cultivating *unconditional self-acceptance* and decoupling their identity from performance; and

(4) Low competence, low worth – This represents the state of *low self-esteem in its most global form*. Individuals in this quadrant tend to feel both ineffective and unlovable, often experiencing chronic shame, hopelessness, or internalised failure. They may struggle to engage in life's demands, take initiative, or form secure attachments. In such cases, therapeutic work must often begin with establishing safety at the level of the proto-self (e.g., affect regulation, grounding), rebuilding emotional trust at the core self level, and gradually reconstructing more realistic and compassionate self-narratives in the plastic self. The external self in such individuals is frequently marked by withdrawal, passivity, or self-effacing behaviours.

While types two and three may present as forms of high self-esteem on the surface, they are inherently unstable, as the underlying imbalance between competence and worth creates vulnerability to emotional disintegration when the dominant dimension is threatened. An individual with high worth but low competence may fear rejection in situations that demand autonomy or skill, while one with high competence but low worth may collapse under emotional strain such as abandonment, perceived failure, or personal criticism.

Mruk (2006, p. 161) notes that self-esteem based primarily on worth often manifests as a relentless attempt to meet external ideals—such as a parent's perfectionistic expectations or a partner's emotional standards. These individuals may adopt religious, social, or cultural ideals that are incongruent with their personal values in order to gain approval or avoid rejection. The external self becomes a mask—a carefully crafted persona designed to please, seduce, or serve. In such cases, self-worth is maintained not through authentic inner experience, but through social performance, sexualisation, or conformity.

In contrast, those who rely heavily on competence may appear confident and self-sufficient, yet find themselves devastated by any failure that threatens their self-image. They may become addicted to success or chronically anxious about performance, perceiving any setback as confirmation of their unworthiness. Their emotional world is often narrowed, as vulnerability is equated with weakness. In psychotherapy, such clients may resist emotional exploration and instead seek to "solve" their problems cognitively or behaviourally, avoiding contact with the underlying affective injury.

In integrative strategic psychotherapy, understanding where a client's self-esteem is anchored—competence, worth, or both—provides a valuable foundation for therapeutic direction. Treatment may involve helping clients rebalance these dimensions, integrating affective validation with cognitive agency, and developing a self-structure that is resilient, coherent, and adaptable across life domains.

Rather than pathologizing imbalances, the therapist views them as adaptive responses to developmental experiences. The aim is not to force symmetry between competence and worth, but to foster internal dialogue, relational safety, and meaning-making processes that can restore self-esteem to a grounded and integrated state.

9.2.4. Additional Dimensions of Self-Esteem

While self-esteem is often conceptualised as a global evaluation of the self, recent psychological literature has delineated several subtypes or dimensions of self-esteem that offer a more nuanced understanding of how self-worth operates in individuals. These aspects have significant clinical relevance, as they reflect the ways in which self-esteem is shaped by group identity, internal stability, and unconscious processes. Guindon (2010) identifies three key dimensions: collective self-esteem, contingent versus non-contingent self-esteem, and implicit versus explicit self-esteem. These forms of self-esteem not only enrich theoretical understanding but offer valuable tools for assessment and intervention in integrative psychotherapy.

Collective self-esteem refers to the aspect of self-worth that arises from one's identification with a particular social, cultural, or identity group. It reflects how positively individuals view themselves as members of a group and how they believe others evaluate that group (Crocker & Luhtanen, 1990). This form of self-esteem is especially relevant in multicultural, marginalised, or identity-diverse contexts. A client may experience high self-esteem not because of individual accomplishments, but because they derive strength and affirmation from belonging to a particular ethnic, religious, professional, or social group.

Within the ISP model, collective self-esteem is often anchored in the external self, as it connects with socially constructed roles and identities. However, it can also influence the core self, particularly when early relational experiences are mediated through cultural or group narratives. In therapy, strengthening collective self-esteem may involve exploring cultural pride, addressing internalised oppression, or reconnecting with community values and histories. A secure sense of belonging, especially for clients who have experienced marginalisation, can serve as a stabilising force in the therapeutic process and a protective buffer against individual self-esteem threats (Phinney & Ong, 2007).

Contingent self-esteem refers to self-worth that is dependent on external validation, performance, or adherence to perceived standards. Individuals with contingent self-esteem derive their value from the approval of others, success in specific domains (e.g., academic, physical appearance, popularity), or conformity to moral, social, or relational ideals. This type of self-esteem is often unstable, as it fluctuates with life circumstances and is highly sensitive to criticism, rejection, or failure (Deci & Ryan, 1995).

Clinically, contingent self-esteem manifests in perfectionism, people-pleasing, social anxiety, and identity diffusion. Such individuals often over-identify with the expectations of others and may struggle to maintain a coherent sense of self in the absence of external affirmation. In integrative strategic psychotherapy, this dynamic often reflects a split between the core self (which longs for authentic expression) and the external self (which performs in accordance with social demands). Clients with contingent self-esteem often struggle with boundaries, assertiveness, and emotional resilience, as their self-concept lacks internal anchoring.

For example, a client who reports feeling "worthless" after receiving a negative evaluation at work is demonstrating a fragile, externally-based self-esteem structure. Therapeutic work involves exploring the origins of this contingency—often found in early conditional acceptance by caregivers—and supporting the development of a non-contingent sense of worth, which does not rely on continuous success or approval.

Non-contingent self-esteem, by contrast, is stable and enduring. It reflects a deep internalised belief that one is fundamentally worthy, regardless of achievement, failure, or relational approval. It is not inflated, nor is it defensive—it emerges from early experiences of unconditional positive regard and secure attachment. In the ISP framework, non-contingent self-esteem is a marker of integration across the core and plastic selves. It implies that the client has developed an internal source of validation and can withstand external pressures or failures without collapsing into shame, anxiety, or overcompensation.

Therapeutically, the aim is often to help clients move from contingent to non-contingent self-esteem through processes such as emotional validation, deconstructing internalised standards, and reinforcing authentic self-expression. The therapeutic relationship itself can provide the consistent, accepting presence that was missing or conditional in early development (Rogers, 1961).

Implicit versus ***explicit self-esteem*** represents another important distinction. Explicit self-esteem refers to the conscious and deliberate evaluations that individuals make about their own worth. This is often measured through self-report questionnaires and may be influenced by social desirability, self-presentation strategies, or denial of underlying issues. For instance, a client may insist that they feel confident and successful, even while displaying symptoms of anxiety, avoidance, or emotional detachment.

Implicit self-esteem, in contrast, refers to unconscious, automatic evaluations of the self that are not readily accessible through introspection. These may be formed early in development and influenced by non-verbal, affective, and preverbal experiences. Measures such as the Implicit Association Test (Greenwald & Farnham, 2000) attempt to access these unconscious self-attitudes.

In clinical practice, discrepancies between implicit and explicit self-esteem can be particularly telling. A client who verbally expresses high self-worth but exhibits intense self-criticism, emotional fragility, or hypervigilance may be harbouring low implicit self-esteem. Conversely, a client with low explicit self-esteem may nonetheless demonstrate resilience, curiosity, and self-regulation that suggests more robust implicit foundations.

In the ISP model, these two dimensions can be mapped onto the plastic self (explicit narrative beliefs) and the core self (nonverbal, relationally encoded emotional truths). Helping clients reconcile these dimensions—so that their conscious self-narratives align with their felt, embodied experience—is a core therapeutic goal. When this alignment is achieved, self-esteem becomes more integrated, authentic, and sustainable.

Taken together, these dimensions—collective, contingent, non-contingent, implicit, and explicit—highlight the complexity and layered structure of self-esteem. Each dimension offers insight into how self-worth is constructed, maintained, and expressed across the levels of the self. By attending to these nuances, integrative strategic psychotherapy offers a flexible and personalised approach to understanding and restoring a client's self-esteem in both depth and breadth.

9.2.5. States of Self-Esteem

While self-esteem is frequently understood as a stable trait or enduring evaluation of the self, it also manifests in moment-to-moment psychological states—shifting, dynamic expressions of how an individual feels about themselves in response to particular events, relationships, or internal experiences. These fluctuating self-evaluations may not always align with the person's global or narrative self-esteem, revealing important discrepancies between what a person believes about themselves and what they actually feel in the here and now.

Ross (2013) proposed a clinically valuable classification of self-esteem into three states: fragmented, vulnerable, and strong. Each of these states is distinguished not only by the content of the self-evaluation but by the *stability*, *depth*, and *emotional regulation* associated with it. This classification is particularly useful in psychotherapy, as clients may move fluidly between these states across different contexts, relationships, or life stages.

Fragmented self-esteem is the most unstable and distressing of the three states. Individuals who experience this state tend to perceive themselves as *deeply inadequate, unworthy, or fundamentally unlovable.* Their inner dialogue is often dominated by self-criticism, shame, and helplessness. Rather than being episodic, these experiences may feel constant or pervasive, especially when the individual lacks protective relational factors or is navigating unresolved trauma. This form of self-esteem is associated with high levels of affective dysregulation, dissociation, and passivity. Typical behaviours include self-blame, withdrawal, rumination, and emotional paralysis.

From the perspective of the ISP model, fragmented self-esteem reflects disruptions across multiple levels of the self. At the level of the proto-self, chronic emotional dysregulation and physiological hyperarousal often emerge. At the core self, relational wounds from childhood—such as neglect, rejection, or inconsistent atonement—undermine any basic sense of being lovable or "held" in relationship. The plastic self tends to be dominated by rigid internalised beliefs such as "I am a failure," "I ruin everything," or "No one could love someone like me." The external self, in turn, may manifest learned helplessness, shame-based behaviours, or a performative compliance that masks despair. Therapeutic work with such clients must begin with establishing safety, emotional stabilisation, and the reconstruction of basic self-worth through relational repair.

Vulnerable self-esteem represents a more nuanced and common clinical presentation. Individuals in this state often *appear confident and competent on the surface*, but their self-esteem is fragile and easily disrupted by criticism, failure, or social rejection. This vulnerability may not be visible in ordinary interactions; rather, it becomes apparent in situations involving performance, competition, intimacy, or public evaluation. Despite projecting self-assurance, these individuals often feel unworthy, anxious, or defensive beneath the surface.

Clinically, vulnerable self-esteem is frequently maintained through a variety of defence mechanisms, including projection, rationalisation, avoidance, and minimisation. For example, a client may pre-emptively "lose" a game or competition so that failure can be attributed to lack of effort rather than lack of ability. Others may act indifferent to social feedback, all the while craving validation and fearing exclusion. This is particularly prevalent in individuals with perfectionistic traits, narcissistic adaptations, or high-functioning depression. The fear of being "found out" as inadequate or unlovable is a dominant internal experience, often masked by competence or humour.

In the ISP framework, this state reflects a discrepancy between the external and internal self, where the external self presents an image of competence or detachment, while the core and plastic selves remain unintegrated or wounded. The plastic self is often shaped by conditional love or performance-based validation, creating internal narratives like "*I'm only valuable if I'm perfect*" or "I must not show weakness." The core self, however, houses the original longing for unconditional acceptance. Therapeutic work focuses on softening the external façade, allowing the client to access and explore the more vulnerable core, and rebuilding a more integrated sense of self.

Strong self-esteem, by contrast, is characterised by an enduring sense of inner worth and emotional stability. Individuals with strong self-esteem are not immune to failure, criticism, or rejection; rather, they are able to navigate these experiences without becoming emotionally overwhelmed or destabilised. They possess the capacity to acknowledge their mistakes, learn from setbacks, and accept both their strengths and limitations. Their sense of self is anchored in an internalised belief that they are fundamentally acceptable—even in imperfection.

Interestingly, individuals with strong self-esteem may come across as modest or understated. This is not because they lack confidence, but because they do not *need* to defend or assert their worth. Their self-esteem is non-contingent—it does not rise and fall with external success, social approval, or relational dynamics. They can enter and maintain intimate relationships without being consumed by fears of abandonment or inferiority, and they tend to be more resilient in the face of life's uncertainties.

In integrative strategic psychotherapy, strong self-esteem represents a state of integration across all levels of the self. The proto-self supports baseline affective regulation and resilience. The core self holds secure attachment representations and emotional coherence. The plastic self contains flexible, self-compassionate narratives. And the external self aligns with the internal world rather than masking or distorting it. In this state, the individual can respond authentically to life, engage in meaningful relationships, and pursue personal growth without being dominated by fear, shame, or self-judgment.

It is important to note that individuals may not reside in one of these states permanently. Rather, they may move between them depending on stress, developmental stage, life transitions, or relational context. A person may experience strong self-esteem in professional life but fragmented self-esteem in romantic relationships, or may oscillate between vulnerability and strength depending on emotional triggers. In psychotherapy, recognising these fluctuations is key to developing a treatment plan that is both empathic and strategic.

By helping clients become aware of their current state of self-esteem, name it, and understand its origins and manifestations, therapists can co-construct pathways toward greater integration, self-acceptance, and psychological freedom.

9.2.6. High and low self-esteem: Clinical features and functional implications

Self-esteem, while a broad construct, has clear clinical implications when considered in terms of *functionality, stability*, and *psychosocial expression*. People with either high or low self-esteem exhibit consistent patterns of cognitive, emotional, and behavioural functioning that significantly affect their relationships, decision-making processes, and overall psychological health. However, it is essential to distinguish between *secure high self-esteem*, which is integrated and resilient, and *defensive high self-esteem*, which appears strong but is, in fact, vulnerable and reactive to external threats.

Baumeister (2003) provides a detailed profile of individuals with genuinely high self-esteem—not inflated or narcissistically constructed, but grounded in realistic self-perception and secure internal regulation. These individuals tend to exhibit the following characteristics:

1. They maintain and defend their core values and beliefs while remaining open to new perspectives based on lived experience. This balance of conviction and flexibility indicates cognitive maturity and psychological autonomy;
2. They make choices based on their own judgement and moral compass, and do not become paralysed by guilt or shame if those choices are criticised;
3. Their temporal orientation is adaptive—they learn from the past, anticipate the future, but live consciously in the present;
4. They demonstrate confidence in their problem-solving abilities and resilience in the face of setbacks. They are not afraid to seek support when needed, which reflects both internal strength and relational maturity;
5. They perceive themselves as equal in dignity to others, neither superior nor inferior, and are able to recognise differences without devaluing themselves or others;
6. They are aware of their value and presence in others' lives—not through arrogance, but through a secure sense of interpersonal resonance;

7. They are resistant to manipulation, and enter cooperative relationships voluntarily and selectively;
8. They experience and regulate a wide range of internal states without compulsively disclosing or suppressing them;
9. They enjoy a diverse set of interests and can engage fully with life, without obsessive goal-orientation or compulsive behaviour;
10. They show empathy, observe appropriate social norms, and do not derive satisfaction from exploiting or dominating others; and
11. They are capable of confronting conflict constructively, expressing disagreement without collapsing into blame, shame, or aggression.

Defensive self-esteem, on the other hand (Baumeister, 2003) may present as confidence, assertiveness, or even dominance, but is in fact built on fragile internal structures. Individuals with defensive self-esteem may be hypersensitive to criticism, highly reactive to perceived slights, and dependent on external validation to maintain their self-concept. Because their internal self-worth is unstable, they require continual reinforcement and may react with hostility, arrogance, or grandiosity when that reinforcement is threatened.

In the ISP model, defensive self-esteem is understood as a disconnection between the plastic and core selves. The external self is over-developed to perform a narrative of confidence, while the core self remains insecure, unprocessed, or wounded. Such individuals may perform well professionally, appear socially successful, or express strong opinions, yet find themselves destabilised by minor failures or interpersonal rejection. Psychotherapy with these clients often requires gradual deconstruction of the defensive structure while affirming the existential right to self-worth beneath it.

In contrast, individuals with low self-esteem often present with a pervasive sense of inadequacy, shame, and self-doubt. As Baumeister (2003) outlines, common features include:

1. Chronic dissatisfaction and habitual self-criticism;
2. Heightened sensitivity to feedback, especially negative criticism, often followed by rumination, withdrawal, or resentment;
3. Indecisiveness and a debilitating fear of making mistakes, rooted in the belief that failure confirms worthlessness;
4. An excessive need to please others, often at the cost of authenticity or personal boundaries;

5. Perfectionism—driven not by ambition but by the fear of disapproval or rejection;
6. Neurotic guilt and disproportionate self-blame for past events;
7. Hostile or defensive behaviour that emerges in the absence of clear provocation;
8. Pessimistic worldview and anticipatory helplessness;
9. Envy or generalised resentment toward those perceived as more confident or successful; and
10. Tendency to interpret temporary failures as permanent, personal, and intolerable.

Such clients often experience self-esteem as a fixed, internal verdict: "*I am not good enough.*" In ISP terms, this experience may reflect early core self injury—emotional neglect, criticism, or inconsistency in attachment—alongside plastic self narratives that reinforce helplessness or internalised rejection. The external self of such individuals is often marked by withdrawal, submission, avoidance, or self-erasure in relationships.

Importantly, low self-esteem is dimensional, not categorical. Not all individuals with low self-esteem meet clinical thresholds for psychopathology (Mruk, 2006). Some may experience neutral self-esteem, a moderate, ambivalent relationship to the self in which self-worth is inconsistent but not distorted. This concept is useful in cases where individuals may function adequately in daily life but still struggle with chronic self-doubt, diminished motivation, or a sense of internal flatness.

Low self-esteem also impacts cognitive processing and interpersonal behaviour. Individuals with poor self-worth tend to filter information through a negative cognitive schema: they personalise criticism, downplay or reject positive feedback, and interpret ambiguous situations as rejection. Berk (2003) notes that they often lack the capacity for perspective-taking, becoming trapped in an egocentric or self-punitive internal world.

In relationships, these individuals tend to struggle with assertiveness, over-accommodate others, and pre-emptively withdraw due to the fear of being seen and subsequently rejected. According to van Zyl et al. (2006), this often results in interpersonal isolation, loneliness, and a deepening of their self-perception as unwanted or defective.

From a psychotherapeutic perspective, the aim is not merely to "increase" self-esteem as if it were a measurable unit, but to foster a reorganisation of the self across levels: healing the attachment wounds of the core self, challenging the internalised narratives of the plastic self, and reshaping the performative strategies of the external self to align with emerging authenticity. Only then can self-esteem become not just high—but whole.

9.3. Motivation

9.3.1 Conceptual Foundations of Motivation

Motivation represents one of the fundamental psychological forces that bridge biology, cognition, emotion, and relational experience. It is both an activating and organising principle of behaviour, directing the organism toward goals that hold meaning or value (Ryan & Deci, 2008). From the earliest psychodynamic formulations to contemporary neuropsychological theories, motivation has been regarded as the dynamic link between internal needs and external action, shaping both the conscious and unconscious processes that sustain personal development. Sifneos (cited in Simon & Siwiak-Kobayashi, 2008) defined motivation as a problem-solving process aimed at controlling uncomfortable feelings and obtaining gratification. In this sense, motivation serves not only as a drive toward fulfilment but also as a regulatory system that manages discomfort and internal conflict. The motivational dimension profoundly influences the course and outcome of psychotherapy, as numerous studies have shown significant correlations between a client's initial motivation and final therapeutic results (Simon & Siwiak-Kobayashi, 2008; Rosengren, 2009; Zuroff et al., 2020).

Motivation is not static; rather, it is a dynamic process evolving throughout the psychotherapeutic journey. The degree of engagement, openness to change, and willingness to explore internal experiences often fluctuate across phases of therapy. The client's motivational structure can therefore be understood as a mirror of the underlying self-organisation. In Integrative Strategic Psychotherapy (ISP), motivation is conceptualised as a core functional process that mediates between the organism's biological energy, emotional meaning, cognitive purpose, and relational field. Symptom improvement is closely related to shifts in motivational dynamics, as these shifts reflect deeper changes in the client's capacity for self-regulation, integration, and agency.

A continuum of motivational states can be identified, ranging from amotivation to active personal engagement. In a state of amotivation, the individual lacks the intention to act, and the sense of personal causality is absent. Amotivation arises from perceiving little value in an activity, a lack of competence, or a belief that actions will not lead to desired results (Seligman, 1975). This condition resonates with the phenomenon of learned helplessness, where agency collapses under repeated experiences of failure or uncontrollable outcomes. From an integrative perspective, amotivation may indicate a dissociation between the biological and relational levels of the self, where affective energy is cut off from cognitive meaning and intentional direction. Thus, to be motivated means not only to do something, but also to feel the self as an agent capable of directing experience toward purpose and value.

9.3.2 Intrinsic and Extrinsic Dynamics of Motivation

Human motivation can be understood as existing along a continuum from intrinsic to extrinsic forms, reflecting both the degree of autonomy and the level of internalisation of behavioural regulation (Ryan & Deci, 2000). These two motivational orientations—intrinsic and extrinsic—are not opposites but complementary poles within a dynamic system. They interact continuously throughout life, shaping how individuals engage with the environment, pursue goals, and experience self-determination.

Intrinsic motivation represents the purest form of self-regulated behaviour. It arises from the inherent satisfaction of engaging in an activity for its own sake—out of curiosity, mastery, creativity, or a sense of challenge (Deci & Ryan, 1985). From infancy, humans display a spontaneous drive to explore and learn, even in the absence of external rewards. White (1959) referred to this tendency as the "effectance motive," the innate desire to feel effective in interaction with the environment. In the neuropsychological domain, intrinsic motivation is associated with activation of dopaminergic pathways in the mesolimbic system, which reinforce exploratory behaviour and pleasure derived from learning (Murayama et al., 2022).

Within psychotherapy, intrinsic motivation is visible when clients engage in the process of self-exploration out of genuine interest or the wish to understand themselves more deeply. For example, a client who keeps a reflective journal after sessions, experimenting with new emotional expressions simply to know themselves better, demonstrates intrinsic motivation. Another example is the client who continues practising mindfulness or expressive writing not because the therapist insists, but because they have discovered its internal reward—a sense of peace, clarity, or coherence.

Intrinsic motivation satisfies three fundamental psychological needs: autonomy, competence, and relatedness (Deci & Ryan, 2008). Autonomy refers to the experience of self-direction, competence to the sense of mastery and effectiveness, and relatedness to the feeling of belonging and emotional connection. In the Integrative Strategic Psychotherapy model, these needs correspond to distinct but interrelated levels of the self. Autonomy reflects the integrative function of the plastic self, capable of aligning inner desire with outer expression. Competence arises from the integration of cognitive and biological levels, where mastery is experienced as both mental clarity and embodied efficacy. Relatedness corresponds to the relational and emotional axes of the self, grounding personal motivation in connection and attunement. When these needs are fulfilled, motivation flows naturally and behaviour feels authentic and self-endorsed.

However, intrinsic motivation can be easily undermined by external contingencies. Cognitive evaluation theory (Deci & Ryan, 1985) demonstrated that external rewards, controlling feedback, or rigid expectations can shift the locus of control from internal to external, diminishing intrinsic engagement. This dynamic is frequently observed in clinical contexts. For example, a client initially motivated by genuine curiosity about personal growth may begin to focus excessively on meeting the therapist's approval or achieving a "perfect" outcome, thereby losing spontaneous engagement. The shift from intrinsic to externally controlled motivation often reflects an underlying attachment dynamic—where approval or safety is sought at the expense of authentic self-expression. In ISP terms, such a shift indicates a dominance of the external self and a weakening of the core and plastic selves.

Extrinsic motivation, by contrast, refers to engaging in behaviour to achieve an outcome that is separable from the activity itself. It encompasses a wide range of behaviours that differ in the degree of internalisation—from externally imposed compliance to self-endorsed values that have become integrated into one's identity (Ryan & Deci, 2000). The four main forms of extrinsic motivation—external regulation, introjected regulation, regulation through identification, and integrated regulation—represent progressive stages along the continuum from external control to internal autonomy.

The most controlled form, external regulation, is driven by external rewards or punishments. The behaviour occurs solely to satisfy external demands or to avoid negative consequences. A typical example is a client who attends psychotherapy only because their spouse insists or because it is required by an employer after a disciplinary issue. The individual does not yet perceive therapy as personally meaningful; their motivation lies outside the self. While such motivation can initiate participation, it is rarely sufficient for sustained change. In ISP, this reflects functioning dominated by the external self, where compliance and adaptation replace authentic engagement. The therapeutic strategy in such cases involves creating a relational context that supports gradual internalisation—transforming external compliance into self-directed exploration.

Introjected regulation represents a partial internalisation of external demands. The individual has absorbed the rule but experiences it as internal pressure, driven by guilt, shame, or pride. Behaviour is maintained to avoid self-reproach or to maintain self-esteem. For instance, a client who feels compelled to "be good" or "work hard" in therapy to avoid disappointing the therapist or to preserve a sense of worth exemplifies introjected regulation. The client acts not from genuine desire but from internalised control, reflecting a critical or perfectionistic superego dynamic. Psychodynamically, this often corresponds to internalised parental figures whose conditional love has been introjected into the self-structure. Therapeutic work here focuses on recognising and externalising the internal critic, cultivating a compassionate, autonomous stance, and strengthening the core self's capacity to regulate motivation through self-acceptance rather than coercion.

Regulation through identification represents a more autonomous form of extrinsic motivation. Here, the person consciously identifies with the importance or personal value of a behaviour, even if it is not inherently enjoyable. For example, a client in recovery from an eating disorder may not find therapy pleasurable but recognises it as vital to their health and emotional growth. The behaviour becomes self-endorsed because it aligns with personally meaningful values. Within the ISP model, this marks the involvement of the plastic self—the capacity to integrate external goals into a coherent sense of self. Cognitive processes of meaning-making and emotional resonance are essential in this phase, as the client begins to experience congruence between inner values and outer action.

The most autonomous form of extrinsic motivation is integrated regulation, where the identified values and goals have been fully assimilated into the self-system. The behaviour, while still extrinsically motivated, becomes congruent with one's core sense of identity. A recovering alcoholic, for instance, might initially engage in therapy to satisfy family expectations but gradually internalises sobriety as an authentic aspect of self-care, freedom, and self-respect. The act of maintaining recovery no longer feels imposed but becomes a natural expression of who they are. Integrated regulation thus bridges extrinsic and intrinsic motivation, reflecting a mature, coherent motivational structure. Within ISP, this stage represents full alignment of the core and external selves, with motivation flowing freely across levels of the self and axes of functioning.

Social context plays a crucial role in facilitating this internalisation process. Environments characterised by empathy, non-judgement, and autonomy support foster the transformation of controlled motivation into self-determined motivation (Ng et al., 2021). In psychotherapy, this means that the therapist's relational stance—attuned, non-controlling, and collaborative—serves as a catalyst for motivational integration. The therapeutic relationship thus becomes both the field and the instrument through which motivation evolves.

Intrinsic and extrinsic motivations are therefore not static categories but dynamic processes that can transform one into the other. In the course of psychotherapy, clients often begin with externally driven motives—relief from suffering, social approval, avoidance of guilt—but through relational atonement and insight, these motives become internalised and self-endorsed. The process mirrors the broader developmental trajectory of the human self, moving from external dependency to internal coherence. This transformation is both a psychological and neurobiological process, involving the gradual integration of affective, cognitive, and motivational networks within the brain (Di Domenico & Ryan, 2017).

In ISP, this evolution of motivation is seen as a central indicator of therapeutic progress. The client's ability to shift from externally imposed goals to intrinsically meaningful ones reflects deep structural change within the self-system. It signifies the movement from heteronomy to autonomy, from defensive adaptation to authentic living. Motivation, therefore, is not merely an energy that drives behaviour; it is a measure of integration itself—the degree to which life energy, emotional truth, and cognitive intention converge toward coherence.

9.3.3 Psychodynamic and Relational Dimensions of Motivation

In psychodynamic thought, motivation has historically been linked to instinctual drives and unconscious wishes. Freud's early drive theory framed motivation as the pressure of biological impulses seeking discharge (Freud, 1915/1957), while later developments by object relations and self-psychology introduced more relational and developmental nuances. Motivation, from this perspective, is not merely about achieving pleasure or avoiding pain but about maintaining self-coherence and connection with significant others. Kohut (1971) described self-object needs as motivational systems oriented toward the preservation of self-esteem and cohesion, whereas Bowlby (1988) conceptualised attachment as a motivational system aimed at maintaining proximity and safety.

Integrative Strategic Psychotherapy views motivation as a multilevel construct. At the biological level, motivational processes reflect the organism's homeostatic regulation and energetic activation. At the emotional level, motivation is intertwined with affective meaning, reflecting the dynamic tension between desire, fear, and need. At the cognitive level, motivation is shaped by values, goals, and anticipatory representations of outcomes. At the relational and psychodynamic levels, motivation involves the unconscious templates and internalised relational patterns that guide desire and attachment. These multiple layers interact dynamically within the self-system. Motivation thus becomes a bridge between the proto-self's biological impulses, the core self's emotional authenticity, the plastic self's capacity for creative adaptation, and the external self's socially mediated goals.

Recent integrative research has demonstrated that motivational processes operate across both explicit and implicit levels of consciousness (Bargh et al., 2021). Implicit motivation—unconscious tendencies toward competence, affiliation, or power—often manifests through nonverbal cues, affective resonance, and transference dynamics in psychotherapy. The therapist's task is to recognise and mirror these implicit motivational signals while fostering awareness and ownership. Within the therapeutic relationship, motivational transference often reproduces early attachment patterns: clients may seek approval, control, or merging as a means of securing belonging or self-worth. Recognising these patterns allows the therapist to help clients differentiate authentic desire from defensive compliance.

Motivation is therefore a field phenomenon, co-constructed within the relational matrix. ISP conceptualises motivation as both intrapsychic and intersubjective—a force that is at once self-generated and relationally modulated. The therapist's attuned presence provides a secure base from which the client's motivational energy can reorganise itself. Empirical findings in neuro-psychotherapy support this relational model: motivational activation is linked to oxytocinergic and dopaminergic systems that are responsive to social bonding and trust (Quirin et al., 2022). Consequently, the relational field in psychotherapy serves as a neurobiological as well as psychological catalyst for motivational transformation.

9.3.4 Motivation and The Integrative Strategic Model of the Sself

Within the ISP model, motivation reflects the dynamic interplay of the self's levels. At the biological level, motivation emerges as an energetic impulse—an innate drive for survival, exploration, and pleasure. At the core self level, motivation becomes affectively encoded as desire, fear, or longing, reflecting the individual's attachment history and affective representations. The plastic self integrates motivation into coherent goals, using symbolic and cognitive processing to align impulses with meaning and context. Finally, the external self expresses these motivations through socially adaptive behaviours and roles.

Dysregulation or fragmentation at any of these levels leads to motivational pathology. For instance, chronic amotivation may indicate disconnection between the proto-self and core self—when the bodily sense of vitality is not integrated into conscious emotion. Conversely, compulsive goal pursuit without emotional depth may reflect dominance of the external self, where behaviour is driven by compliance and social approval rather than authentic desire. The task of psychotherapy is therefore to restore vertical integration of motivational processes across the levels of the self, allowing energy, emotion, and intention to align coherently.

ISP also emphasises the importance of motivational alignment across the five therapeutic levels: biological, emotional, cognitive, psychodynamic, and relational. At the biological level, motivation is supported through regulation of arousal and somatic vitality. On the emotional axis, the psychotherapist facilitates access to authentic feeling states that energise behaviour. On the cognitive axis, motivational clarity is strengthened through goal setting, meaning-making, and the restructuring of irrational beliefs. On the psychodynamic axis, unconscious conflicts and ambivalences are explored to free motivational energy previously bound in defence. At the relational level, motivational patterns are re-enacted and transformed within the therapeutic alliance. When these axes are synchronised, motivation becomes an integrated self-regulatory force, guiding the client toward congruence and agency.

9.3.5 Motivation, Goals, and Agency in Psychotherapy

Motivation is closely linked to goal-setting and agency, both of which are central to behavioural change. Goal setting provides direction to motivational energy, transforming diffuse desire into structured intentionality. Deci and Ryan (2008) distinguish between intrinsic aspirations (e.g., personal growth, relatedness) and extrinsic aspirations (e.g., wealth, fame). Empirical studies confirm that intrinsic goals are associated with higher wellbeing and therapeutic progress, whereas extrinsic goals often correlate with external validation needs and fragile self-esteem (Kasser & Ryan, 2001; Martela & Ryan, 2021). In the therapeutic context, aligning goals with intrinsic values increases adherence, engagement, and resilience during difficult phases of change.

Motivational processes also operate at both conscious and unconscious levels, influenced by three causality orientations—autonomous, controlled, and impersonal (Deci & Ryan, 2008). These orientations parallel the functional organisation of the self within ISP. Autonomous orientation corresponds to integrated self-regulation across all levels of the self; controlled orientation reflects partial satisfaction of competence and relatedness but reduced autonomy; and impersonal orientation reflects global disengagement and fragmentation. The therapist's role is to facilitate the client's movement toward autonomous orientation, supporting both self-determination and connection.

Motivational energy derives from basic psychological needs. Controlled regulation tends to deplete psychological energy, producing fatigue and defensive compliance, whereas autonomous regulation increases vitality and engagement (Ryan & Deci, 2017; Reeve & Cheon, 2021). This distinction parallels the ISP understanding of vitality as the biological correlate of meaning integration. When motivation is autonomous and coherent, clients experience a sense of aliveness and forward movement. When motivation is externally controlled or split, stagnation and symptoms often emerge.

Autonomous motivation for treatment—the sense of engaging in psychotherapy as a freely chosen, self-endorsed activity—is a strong predictor of positive outcomes (McBride et al., 2010; Ryan et al., 2021). Clients with higher autonomous motivation show greater adherence, emotional openness, and reflective capacity. Conversely, controlled motivation—driven by guilt, obligation, or external pressure—correlates with premature dropout and superficial compliance. Thus, assessing motivational orientation is essential for case formulation in ISP, as it provides insight into the functional integrity of the self-system and the likely trajectory of change.

9.3.6 Contemporary Research and Integrative Implications

Recent advances in neuroscience and psychotherapy research have deepened our understanding of motivational systems. Neuroimaging studies have identified overlapping neural networks for intrinsic motivation, reward anticipation, and self-related processing, involving regions such as the ventral striatum, medial prefrontal cortex, and insula (Murayama et al., 2022). These networks are modulated by interpersonal context and emotional resonance, supporting the integrative view that motivation is inherently relational and embodied.

Furthermore, the integration of self-determination theory with attachment and emotion regulation frameworks has given rise to new models of motivational health (Weinstein et al., 2021; Di Domenico & Ryan, 2017). These studies highlight that autonomy and relatedness are not opposing forces but complementary dimensions of human flourishing. The ISP model, by uniting motivational theory with a developmental and systemic understanding of the self, provides a framework for translating these findings into clinical practice.

In psychotherapy, motivational interventions include enhancing self-reflection, identifying authentic desires, re-evaluating introjected goals, and reconstructing meaning. Techniques drawn from motivational interviewing (Miller & Rollnick, 2013) can be integrated within the ISP framework, not as stand-alone strategies but as relational processes that respect the client's autonomy while gently evoking change. Motivation becomes not a tool for compliance but an unfolding process of self-organisation, guided by relational atonement and strategic timing.

Motivation is a multidimensional process that unites biological energy, emotional significance, cognitive meaning, and relational orientation. It represents the dynamic capacity of the self to move toward integration, authenticity, and growth. Within Integrative Strategic Psychotherapy, understanding motivation is essential for assessing readiness for change, designing interventions, and facilitating long-term transformation. The therapeutic relationship itself functions as a motivational field, where implicit drives toward autonomy, competence, and relatedness are reactivated and reorganised. Ultimately, psychotherapy succeeds when clients reclaim motivation as an inner resource—when behaviour is no longer governed by external control or unconscious compulsion, but by an internally integrated sense of purpose and vitality.

9.4. Body Image

9.4.1 Conceptual Foundations of Body Image

Body image refers to the internalised perception, cognition, and emotional evaluation of one's own physical appearance. It is both a subjective construct—based on individual feelings, beliefs, and bodily awareness—and a social construct, influenced by cultural norms and interpersonal feedback. Popescu (2021) describes body image as encompassing a person's feelings regarding the aesthetics and sexual attractiveness of their own body, shaped by the interaction between personal experience, personality, and social context. In its essence, body image is a dynamic and relational phenomenon: the body is both the object of perception and the medium through which the self is experienced in the world.

The individual's perception of their appearance is seldom objective. It is filtered through personal meaning systems, emotional states, and developmental experiences. As Ferguson et al. (2011) noted, one's perception of their own appearance often diverges substantially from how others perceive them. This discrepancy between internal image and external reality can lead to significant psychological distress, especially when self-perception becomes rigid, distorted, or shame-based.

Within the framework of Integrative Strategic Psychotherapy (ISP), body image is not viewed merely as a cognitive construct or an aesthetic judgment but as an *embodied representation of the self.* The body serves as both container and expression of internal experience, embodying implicit relational memories, affective states, and developmental patterns. Consequently, disturbances in body image are interpreted in ISP as indicators of fragmentation or imbalance across the levels and axes of the self, often reflecting unresolved conflicts between authenticity and adaptation.

9.4.2 Developmental and Sociocultural Formation of Body Image

The formation of body image begins early in life and evolves across developmental stages. Infants experience their bodies initially through sensation and movement – the proto-self's direct engagement with the world. Through interactions with caregivers, bodily sensations become associated with affective meaning: warmth, safety, tension or rejection. These early experiences lay the foundation for a pre-reflective sense of bodily self (Trevarthen, 2011). The core self later integrates this sensory-emotional awareness into more stable representations of identity, while the plastic and external selves shape socially mediated interpretations of attractiveness, competence, and worth.

Family environment plays a significant role in the development of body image. Parental attitudes toward food, appearance, and self-discipline can either promote bodily acceptance or instil shame and control. Children whose parents frequently comment on their weight or appearance may internalise critical voices that later manifest as self-judgment or perfectionism. In adolescence, when identity consolidation intensifies, body image becomes central to self-concept. Peer comparison, romantic interest, and social media exposure further amplify vulnerability to external validation.

Sociocultural pressures are among the most pervasive influences on body image. Salk and Engeln-Maddox (2011) demonstrated that the media's portrayal of the "thin ideal" exerts powerful psychological effects, especially on women and adolescent girls. Constant exposure to images of flawless, digitally altered bodies creates unrealistic standards and fosters chronic dissatisfaction. The internalisation of such ideals correlates strongly with depressive symptoms, anxiety, and disordered eating behaviours. Recent studies indicate that these effects have intensified with the rise of visual-based social media platforms such as Instagram and TikTok, where appearance-based feedback loops reinforce objectification and comparison (Fardouly et al., 2020; Holland & Tiggemann, 2021).

The cultural imperative to be thin or muscular is not limited to one gender. Men increasingly face pressure to achieve the "fit" or "athletic" ideal, leading to rising rates of muscle dysmorphia and compulsive exercise (Griffiths et al., 2021). In both genders, the idealised body becomes a moral symbol of control, productivity, and social success. This cultural narrative reduces the body to an object of evaluation, severing it from lived experience. ISP conceptualises this as a dominance of the external self: a socially adapted façade that disconnects from the body's authentic sensations and emotions.

Economic and political forces also shape body ideals. Advertising, fashion, and wellness industries profit from body dissatisfaction, sustaining cycles of consumption through promises of transformation. In response to growing concern, some countries have begun implementing regulations aimed at mitigating these harmful effects. For instance, Israel's legislation banning underweight models from fashion shows requires a minimum body mass index of 18.5 and medical certification of healthy weight (Esanola et al., 2010). More recently, France and Norway introduced regulations mandating disclosure of digitally altered images in advertising campaigns (Perloff, 2022). These policy efforts reflect an emerging recognition that body image is not a private concern but a public health issue linked to self-esteem, depression, and eating disorders.

9.4.3 Psychodynamic and Relational Dimensions of Body Image

From a psychodynamic perspective, the body is the first locus of identity. Freud (1923/1961) referred to the ego as "first and foremost a bodily ego," suggesting that self-awareness originates from bodily boundaries and sensations. Early experiences of touch, gaze, and care create internalised representations of the body as safe or dangerous, lovable or shameful. Winnicott (1965) emphasised the "holding environment" provided by the caregiver, through which the infant's bodily experiences are mirrored and contained. Failure of this empathic mirroring can result in fragmented body image and difficulties in self-cohesion.

In adolescence and adulthood, body image continues to serve as a mediator of relational meaning. The body becomes a canvas for unconscious communication—expressing vulnerability, seduction, control, or rebellion. In disorders such as anorexia nervosa, the body symbolises mastery and self-sufficiency; in contrast, obesity may express unmet relational needs or protective withdrawal. McDougall (1989) described such phenomena as "psychosomatic equivalents," where the body speaks when the psyche cannot.

Within the ISP model, disturbances in body image are understood as manifestations of disconnection between levels of the self. For instance, when the biological level (bodily sensations and instincts) is dissociated from the psychological level, the person may lose the capacity to feel hunger, pleasure, or bodily comfort. When the external self dominates, the body becomes an object of control or display, valued only for its social approval. Conversely, when the core and plastic selves are integrated, the body is experienced as an expressive and trustworthy dimension of being.

In psychotherapy, relational dynamics often mirror the client's body image conflicts. A client who perceives their body as "too much" or "unacceptable" may project these feelings into the therapeutic relationship, fearing judgment or rejection. The therapist's task is to provide a non-objectifying, attuned presence that allows the client to reclaim ownership of their bodily experience.

This relational re-embodiment can repair early deficits in affective mirroring and restore trust in one's sensory self.

9.4.4 Embodiment, the Self, and the Integrative Strategic Model

In contrast to reductionist perspectives that treat body image as a cognitive distortion, the ISP model conceptualises it as an *embodied narrative*—a synthesis of sensory, emotional, cognitive, and relational meanings. The body is not merely the container of the self but an active participant in psychological organisation. Damasio's (2010) theory of the self underscores this view, describing how interoceptive signals from the body underpin consciousness and emotion. In ISP, the proto-self corresponds to this somatic foundation: the biological homeostasis from which selfhood arises. The core self adds affective colouring, giving meaning to bodily sensations through emotion. The plastic self translates these experiences into symbolic representations, and the external self expresses them socially.

When body image is coherent, information flows freely between these levels. The individual feels present, grounded, and capable of authentic expression. When the connection is disrupted—by trauma, shame, or cultural alienation—the self becomes divided. The body may feel foreign, or conversely, hyper-controlled. Such fragmentation underlies both the rigidity of eating disorders and the dissociation of trauma survivors who "leave" the body as a defence against overwhelming affect (Van der Kolk, 2014).

Embodiment is thus both a developmental achievement and a therapeutic goal. In ISP, restoring embodiment means re-establishing communication between the biological and symbolic dimensions of self. Techniques that integrate awareness of posture, breathing, and gesture with verbal exploration help clients reinhabit their bodies. Expressive methods—drawing, movement, or guided imagery—support this reconnection by allowing implicit memory and affect to surface in nonverbal form.

Psychotherapy offers a corrective relational experience through which distorted body image can be transformed. The therapeutic process involves both *deconstruction*—challenging internalised ideals and critical self-talk—and *reconstruction*—developing a compassionate, embodied sense of self.

At the biological level, somatic regulation techniques (such as breathing, grounding, and mindfulness) help clients reconnect with bodily sensations and modulate arousal. On the emotional axis, the psychotherapist facilitates access to feelings of shame, disgust, or grief associated with body rejection. Processing these affects allows reintegration of split-off parts of the self. On the cognitive axis, distorted beliefs about attractiveness, control, or worth are examined and reframed. On the psychodynamic axis, underlying conflicts related to autonomy, dependency, or sexuality are explored, often through transference manifestations in the therapeutic relationship. Finally, at the relational level, the psychotherapist's attuned, non-judgemental presence serves as a corrective mirror that enables the client to internalise acceptance and empathy.

Consider, for example, a young dancer struggling with anorexia who perceives her body as "too large" and "unworthy." From an ISP perspective, this symptom expresses a collapsed relationship between the biological and relational levels of the self. Her body becomes the battleground for unresolved early experiences of conditional love and control. Psychotherapy might begin with stabilising the biological level—reconnecting her with hunger cues and energy regulation—while simultaneously working on the emotional axis to access shame and fear of rejection. Cognitive restructuring would address perfectionistic beliefs, while psychodynamic exploration would uncover the relational meaning of self-denial. As integration progresses, the client learns to experience her body not as an enemy but as an ally—a living expression of her inner truth.

Recent research supports such integrative approaches. Studies show that combining cognitive-behavioural methods with body-based and relational interventions yields stronger improvements in body image and self-esteem than purely cognitive treatments (Alleva et al., 2020; Cox & Olatunji, 2023). Moreover, neurobiological findings reveal that interventions enhancing interoceptive awareness lead to measurable changes in brain connectivity within the insula and anterior cingulate cortex—areas implicated in body awareness and emotional regulation (Khalsa et al., 2020). These results confirm that body image change is not purely psychological but involves reorganisation of embodied neural networks.

ISP's emphasis on strategic integration allows psychotherapists to adapt interventions dynamically according to the client's level of self-organisation. For clients dominated by the external self, work focuses on reducing self-objectification and promoting authenticity. For those with trauma-related dissociation, the priority is safe reconnection with bodily experience before exploring cognitive or relational meanings. The psychotherapist functions as both witness and co-regulator, facilitating the client's gradual re-embodiment.

9.5. Mental Schemas About Illness and Health

9.5.1 Conceptual Foundations: Health Beliefs and Behaviour

Beliefs about health and illness form a core dimension of an individual's psychological and behavioural functioning. They shape the ways in which people interpret bodily sensations, assess risks, seek medical care, and engage in preventive behaviours. Popescu (2021) emphasised that health beliefs are expressed through behaviours related to disease and wellbeing, reflecting underlying schemas about control, vulnerability, and survival. These schemas are not purely cognitive; they are deeply affective, relational, and symbolic, integrating the person's history, family narratives, and cultural context.

At the cognitive level, health beliefs represent interpretative frameworks—mental maps that help individuals make sense of illness, symptoms, and recovery. At the emotional level, they express fundamental anxieties about mortality, dependency, and loss of control. At the relational level, they reveal how the person negotiates care, autonomy, and trust. Within the model of Integrative Strategic Psychotherapy (ISP), health beliefs are understood as manifestations of the self's dynamic organisation across its multiple levels: biological, psychological, and relational. The body, the mind, and the social field interact continuously, shaping a person's approach to health maintenance, illness prevention, and recovery.

People's beliefs about health, perceived benefits and barriers to action, and sense of self-efficacy are powerful predictors of their engagement in health-promoting behaviours (Conner & Norman, 1996). These beliefs are often implicit, arising from early attachment patterns and family models of care. They influence not only medical adherence and treatment outcomes but also the individual's capacity for resilience and self-regulation. In this sense, health belief systems function as motivational structures that can either support or obstruct the organism's natural healing tendencies.

9.5.2 The Health Belief Model and Its Components

One of the most influential frameworks for understanding health-related beliefs is the Health Belief Model (HBM), developed in the 1950s and refined over subsequent decades (Glanz, Rimer, & Lewis, 2002). The model proposes that a person's health behaviour is determined by their perceptions of susceptibility, severity, benefits, and barriers, combined with cues to action and self-efficacy.

These constructs form a cognitive-emotional map that guides responses to health threats.

Perceived severity refers to an individual's assessment of the seriousness of an illness and its potential consequences. This includes both physical implications (such as pain or disability) and secondary effects such as financial costs or social stigma. For example, while one person might view influenza as a minor inconvenience, another may regard it as a severe threat due to potential disruption of work or family obligations. Perceived severity often correlates with personal experience or exposure to illness in significant others.

Perceived susceptibility involves the subjective evaluation of one's likelihood of developing a particular condition. Some individuals experience exaggerated vulnerability, leading to hypervigilance or health anxiety, while others exhibit unrealistic optimism or denial. Personality factors, such as neuroticism or locus of control, and early attachment experiences influence how risk is appraised (Norman, Boer, & Seydel, 2021).

Perceived benefits refer to the individual's belief in the efficacy of preventive or corrective actions. When people believe that a behaviour will protect them from harm or improve their wellbeing, they are more likely to engage in it. Conversely, perceived barriers represent the costs—financial, emotional, or practical—associated with these actions. A person might, for instance, believe that regular dental check-ups are valuable but avoid them due to fear of pain, embarrassment, or financial strain.

In ISP terms, these four constructs mirror the cognitive and emotional axes of the self. Perceived severity and susceptibility relate to the emotional axis, where affective encoding of fear and vulnerability determines behavioural readiness. Perceived benefits and barriers correspond more to the cognitive axis, where beliefs, rationalisations, and meaning-making shape conscious decision-making. Integration across these axes leads to coherent health behaviour; disintegration results in inconsistency, avoidance, or denial.

The HBM also emphasises the role of cues to action—external or internal triggers that activate behaviour. Symptoms, medical advice, or social messages can serve as such cues. These triggers interact with motivational and emotional readiness, aligning closely with ISP's view of the self as a dynamic system responsive to environmental signals. Finally, self-efficacy, introduced by Bandura (1997), represents the belief in one's ability to execute the necessary actions for achieving a goal. It forms the motivational backbone of health behaviour, directly linked to the plastic self's capacity for self-regulation and adaptive problem-solving.

9.5.3 Family, Culture, and the Social Learning of Health Attitudes

Beliefs about health and illness are acquired through social learning. Family patterns of care, illness narratives, and cultural scripts transmit implicit rules about vulnerability and control. In some families, illness is met with excessive anxiety and caregiving—where even mild symptoms elicit alarm and collective attention. In others, stoicism or denial prevails, and even serious conditions are minimised. These familial prototypes form the foundation of what the ISP model terms relational schemas of health—internal working models that guide the individual's later responses to bodily signals and medical advice.

Cultural context adds another layer of influence. Societies differ in how they conceptualise health, balance individual responsibility and fate, and interpret suffering. In Western biomedical paradigms, health is often framed as a personal achievement, rooted in self-discipline and control. In contrast, collectivist cultures may view health as relational equilibrium or spiritual harmony (Ma-Kellams & Fessler, 2020). These cultural narratives shape both perception and behaviour, determining what is considered normal, shameful, or heroic in the face of illness.

Within the relational field of psychotherapy, such schemas become evident in how clients communicate somatic experiences, seek help, or resist medical recommendations. A client who grew up in a family that idealised stoicism may find it difficult to express pain or vulnerability. Another, raised in a context of excessive medical attention, may develop somatisation or illness anxiety. The therapeutic task involves identifying and reinterpreting these implicit health narratives, linking them to early attachment experiences and current patterns of self-regulation.

9.5.4 Anxiety, Control, and Psychodynamic Patterns in Health Beliefs

Anxiety is a central force in shaping health beliefs and behaviours. It reflects the existential tension between the wish for control and the inevitability of vulnerability. The onset of illness activates archaic fears—of dependency, abandonment, and mortality—that resonate at the level of the core and proto-self.

According to psychodynamic theory, the body can become the stage for the expression of unconscious conflict (McDougall, 1989). Illness may symbolise guilt, punishment, or a defence against psychic pain.

The COVID-19 pandemic that began in 2019 offered a striking illustration of how anxiety shapes collective and individual health beliefs. Populations oscillated between hypervigilance, panic, and denial, reflecting deep-seated psychodynamic patterns. For some, the virus represented uncontrollable chaos, leading to obsessive sanitising and fear of contamination. For others, it evoked defiance and denial, expressed through conspiracy beliefs and resistance to vaccination. Both extremes reflect the psyche's attempt to manage overwhelming anxiety—either through exaggerated control or dissociation from reality (Taylor, 2021; Schimmenti et al., 2020).

In ISP, such reactions are interpreted as manifestations of defensive fragmentation across levels of the self. Excessive control represents the dominance of the external and cognitive selves, which suppress biological and emotional spontaneity. Denial, on the other hand, reflects disconnection between the cognitive axis and the biological level, where the mind defends against anxiety by negating somatic evidence. Psychotherapy aims to restore integrative dialogue between these levels, helping the client tolerate uncertainty and reclaim agency.

9.5.5 Illness, Denial, and the Dynamics of Meaning

The way individuals interpret illness reveals the symbolic structure of their internal world. Illness can be experienced as threat, punishment, failure, or even opportunity for renewal. Frank (1995) described illness narratives as meaning-making processes through which individuals reconstruct identity in the face of bodily disruption. These narratives reveal the tension between helplessness and coherence—the drive to transform suffering into story.

Denial serves as one of the most common defences against illness-related anxiety. It allows temporary psychological stability when facing existential threat. However, when rigid, denial can prevent timely medical intervention or emotional processing. Psychodynamic research shows that denial operates not only cognitively but at the level of affect regulation: bodily sensations of fear or pain are split off from consciousness (Grecucci et al., 2020). In ISP, denial is seen as an adaptive but partial form of self-protection. It indicates that the biological and emotional levels are overwhelmed, and the cognitive self has taken over regulation by excluding distressing material.

Conspiracy beliefs, particularly evident during global health crises, represent a collective form of denial. They offer a substitute narrative that restores a sense of control and belonging. From an integrative perspective, these beliefs emerge when the relational need for security merges with cognitive distortion. The person defends against anxiety by aligning with a perceived community of "truth," thereby regaining coherence and significance (Douglas et al., 2021).

9.5.6 Integrating Health Beliefs in the Framework of Integrative Strategic Psychotherapy

Within the ISP framework, mental schemas about illness and health are approached as multilevel constructs shaped by developmental history, relational context, and neurobiological regulation. Each level of the self contributes distinct components to health-related meaning-making.

At the biological level, genetic predispositions and neurophysiological responses influence sensitivity to stress and illness perception. For example, heightened autonomic reactivity can amplify interoceptive sensations, predisposing individuals to health anxiety (Khalsa et al., 2020). On the emotional axis, affective templates derived from early caregiving experiences shape how vulnerability and dependency are experienced. The cognitive axis organises beliefs and explanatory models about illness, integrating information from culture, family, and media. At the relational level, interpersonal dynamics determine how help-seeking, trust in authority, and autonomy are negotiated.

ISP posits that health behaviours reflect the degree of integration among these levels. A coherent self-system allows the individual to perceive bodily sensations accurately, interpret them flexibly, and take adaptive action. Fragmentation—such as dominance of the cognitive self detached from the body—leads to rigid or avoidant patterns. Clients with health anxiety, for example, may overinterpret minor symptoms due to disconnection between emotional and cognitive regulation. Conversely, individuals who neglect health issues may exhibit dissociation between biological and cognitive awareness.

Therapeutically, the ISP approach involves working along all three levels: biological, psychological (emotional, cognitive, psychodynamic), and relational. At the biological level, interventions address somatic awareness and regulation—helping clients interpret bodily signals without catastrophising. On the emotional axis, anxiety and fear of illness are explored and normalised. On the cognitive axis, maladaptive beliefs are examined, linking them to early experiences and societal messages. On the psychodynamic axis, unconscious meanings of illness—such as guilt, control, or dependency—are identified and recontextualised. Finally, at the relational level, the therapeutic relationship itself becomes a model for secure care and trust, correcting internalised expectations of neglect or intrusion.

Motivation for health behaviour is also considered through the lens of self-determination. Autonomous motivation—acting from an internalised sense of value—leads to sustained health-promoting behaviour, while controlled motivation—acting out of guilt or fear—produces compliance without integration (Ryan & Deci, 2017). The goal of psychotherapy is not simply to correct false beliefs but to facilitate the client's intrinsic motivation for self-care and embodiment.

9.6. Psychosomatic Mechanisms

9.6.1. Developmental Foundations of Psychosomatic Regulation

Psychosomatic functioning represents one of the most intricate areas in the study of human development, standing at the intersection between affect regulation, attachment, neurobiology, and the immune system. The early regulation of physiological and emotional states is an inherently interpersonal process. During the initial stages of life, the infant's immature nervous and immune systems depend heavily on the caregiver for external modulation. This dependency has led several authors to conceptualise the infant as an "external foetus," whose psychobiological homeostasis continues to rely on the mother after birth (Schore, 2012).

The mother provides essential life-sustaining functions by regulating arousal, feeding, and physiological stability. Her regulatory role extends to the immune system: in the neonatal period, the infant cannot yet synthesise antibodies and immunoglobulins independently, relying instead on maternal transfer through breast milk. This biological interdependence has long-term consequences for resilience and vulnerability to illness. Studies have demonstrated that early secure attachment and maternal responsiveness predict stronger immune function and stress resilience in adulthood, whereas maternal deprivation is associated with reduced immunoglobulin levels and impaired immune recovery (Micchaut et al., 1981; Schore, 2012; Hostinar & Gunnar, 2020).

From the perspective of Integrative Strategic Psychotherapy (ISP), this primary stage of external regulation corresponds to the developmental activity of the *proto-self*. The proto-self, formed through embodied interactions with the caregiver, is responsible for the early integration of interoceptive and exteroceptive information. When maternal care provides consistent atonement, the proto-self internalises a template of safety and predictability. When maternal care is inconsistent or neglectful, early disorganisation emerges, resulting in dysregulated autonomic and immune responses that become somatically encoded.

9.6.2 Neurobiological Integration of Emotion and Immunity

The relationship between the nervous, endocrine, and immune systems is characterised by continuous bidirectional communication. These systems utilise shared biochemical messengers—hormones, lymphokines, and cytokines—that mediate mutual regulation (Schore, 2012). Pathogenic agents activate lymphocytes, which release lymphokines that, in turn, influence the hypothalamic–pituitary–adrenal (HPA) axis and the sympathetic–adrenal–medullary axis. These neuroendocrine changes subsequently affect mood, behaviour, and cognitive functioning. Emotional changes in response to infection—such as fatigue, irritability, or social withdrawal—are not merely psychological but represent integrated physiological adaptations known as "sickness behaviour" (Dantzer & Kelley, 2007; Irwin, 2019).

Conversely, cognitive and emotional stimuli can directly modulate immune function. Emotional stress activates the HPA axis, leading to cortisol secretion, which alters T-cell activity and inflammatory responses. The right hemisphere, particularly its fronto-limbic regions, plays a central role in these processes. It is responsible for socio-affective processing and modulates cortisol secretion during emotionally charged situations (Neven, 1992). This integration highlights the inseparability of emotion and immune regulation: our affective world continuously sculpts physiological responses to internal and external challenges.

In ISP, this interaction exemplifies the reciprocal communication between the biological level and emotional axis of the self. Emotions arise not only from psychological appraisals but from embodied neurophysiological feedback loops. Therefore, emotional dysregulation inevitably affects somatic homeostasis, and chronic physiological imbalance manifests as psychosomatic vulnerability. The client's body becomes the mirror of their affective history—a physical expression of the unintegrated emotional self.

9.6.3 Attachment, Affect Regulation, and Somatic Vulnerability

Attachment theory provides a crucial bridge between psychodynamic understanding and psychobiological findings. Schore's (2012) extensive work demonstrated that the developing right hemisphere is shaped through early attachment interactions and serves as the regulatory centre for autonomic and emotional integration. The mother's face, tone of voice, and responsiveness function as primary affective regulators. Through repeated experiences of comfort and co-regulation, neural connections between the orbitofrontal cortex and hypothalamus are strengthened, forming the structural basis for later self-regulation.

Attachment disruptions, however, interfere with this process. When the caregiver fails to provide consistent regulation, the child's stress-response systems become hyperactivated or blunted. Chronic activation of the HPA axis during sensitive developmental periods can lead to altered cortisol rhythms, impaired immune function, and vulnerability to both affective and somatic disorders in adulthood (Reite & Capitanio, 1985; Beebe & Lachmann, 1998). Early deprivation has been linked to reduced density of opioid and oxytocin receptors, including those on immunocytes (Bonnet et al., 1976), highlighting a neurochemical pathway through which social pain translates into physiological dysregulation.

Within ISP, attachment regulation is conceptualised as the foundation for the *core self*, where affective coherence and bodily atonement emerge. When early caregiving fails, the integration between the proto-self and core self is compromised. The individual may grow into adulthood with fragmented regulatory capacities—capable of cognitive reflection but unable to restore physiological equilibrium under stress. Such fragmentation manifests clinically as anxiety, fatigue, pain syndromes, or immune-related conditions, often without identifiable medical causes.

9.6.4 The Psychobiology of Early Deprivation and Illness Formation

Deficits in maternal psychobiological regulation predispose the developing child to psychosomatic disorders later in life. When the attachment environment is marked by neglect, rejection, or chronic stress, inhibitory patterns form within the limbic–hypothalamic circuitry. The child's body learns to downregulate vitality and expression to maintain attachment bonds, leading to long-term autonomic constriction. Schore (2012) demonstrated that early regulatory failure affects the orbitofrontal cortex—an area central to emotional homeostasis—and disrupts cortisol secretion patterns.

The structural substrate for many psychosomatic illnesses appears to reside within this fronto-limbic system, which governs autonomic nervous system functioning (Pribram, 1981; Kolb, 1984). Dysfunctions here are linked to gastrointestinal disorders, weight dysregulation, and disorders such as bulimia and chronic fatigue syndrome (Popescu, 2021; Thayer & Lane, 2020). For example, gastric ulcers may be associated with hyperactivation of the orbital cortex, while hypoactivation of prefrontal regions is related to compulsive eating behaviours.

The concept of "learned bodily helplessness" describes the mechanism through which chronic emotional neglect shapes somatic reactivity. When repeated experiences of helplessness occur during development, the autonomic system adapts by maintaining low arousal and limited variability in heart rate and vagal tone (Porges, 2017). This defensive immobilisation, initially adaptive, later manifests as alexithymia, chronic pain, or immunosuppression. In ISP, this represents a state of frozen integration between the biological and emotional levels—where the organism's vitality is inhibited to maintain psychological survival.

9.6.5 Psychosomatic Expression and the Dynamics of the Self

The bidirectional relationship between mind and body implies that psychological states can both precipitate and maintain physical symptoms. Medically unexplained symptoms—headaches, gastrointestinal discomfort, palpitations, or chronic pain—account for a significant proportion of medical consultations, ranging from 15% to 66% (Levenson, 2006). While some of these symptoms stem from undetected medical causes, many are expressions of dysregulated affect.

Sarno (2006) proposed that repressed emotions, particularly anger, can manifest through physical symptoms such as ulcers or musculoskeletal pain. Although this hypothesis was initially controversial, subsequent neuroimaging and psychophysiological studies have confirmed that emotional suppression is associated with increased activation in limbic and insular regions, areas involved in pain perception and autonomic regulation (Wager et al., 2021). Individuals with histories of trauma or chronic emotional inhibition show increased prevalence of conditions such as fibromyalgia, chronic fatigue syndrome, and irritable bowel syndrome (Afari & Buchwald, 2003; Luyten et al., 2021).

From an integrative standpoint, these disorders can be viewed as failures of symbolic transformation: when the psyche cannot express distress verbally or relationally, the body becomes its language. In ISP, psychosomatic expression is interpreted as communication from the fragmented self. The *external self* often dominates, maintaining social compliance and cognitive control, while the *core self* remains silenced. The unprocessed affect, residing within the body's implicit memory, manifests through somatic symptoms as a call for integration.

People with multiple adverse childhood experiences are particularly vulnerable to psychosomatic patterns. Studies have shown that childhood trauma correlates with a higher prevalence of chronic pain, pelvic discomfort, and unexplained fainting spells (Felitti et al., 1998; Popescu, 2021). In such individuals, severe dissociation impairs awareness of emotion; physical symptoms become the only remaining avenue for expressing internal distress.

9.6.6 Integrative Strategic Psychotherapy Perspective on Psychosomatic Disorders

Integrative Strategic Psychotherapy approaches psychosomatic mechanisms as expressions of disrupted integration across the levels of the self and the five therapeutic axes. The *biological level* involves dysregulation of the autonomic and immune systems; the *emotional axis* reflects affective disorganisation or inhibition; the *cognitive axis* encompasses distorted beliefs about control, danger, or worthiness; the *psychodynamic axis* reveals unconscious conflicts and defensive structures; and the *relational level* captures the interpersonal patterns that sustain or relieve psychosomatic tension.

At the biological level, ISP interventions focus on restoring body–mind communication through somatic awareness, breathwork, and interoceptive grounding. These methods aim to re-establish connection with the proto-self and increase vagal tone, supporting autonomic balance. At the emotional level, therapy helps clients recognise and express repressed affects—especially anger, fear, or grief—through safe relational containment. The psychotherapist's attuned presence enables emotional states to be experienced without overwhelming the system, facilitating re-regulation.

On the cognitive axis, ISP examines health-related schemas and meaning structures. Clients often hold unconscious beliefs such as *"I am only cared for when I am ill"* or *"Being strong means never feeling pain."* These beliefs sustain psychosomatic cycles and are gradually restructured through insight and corrective experience. The psychodynamic axis involves exploring transference dynamics that replicate early attachment failures—such as dependency, control, or rejection. The therapeutic relationship itself becomes a reparative field in which new modes of regulation are internalised.

Relationally, the psychotherapist functions as a co-regulator of the client's autonomic state, mirroring the early maternal function but within the boundaries of professional containment. The psychotherapist's empathic atonement activates right-hemispheric resonance (Schore & Schore, 2021), re-establishing a secure attachment context that promotes physiological and psychological healing. Over time, the client develops the capacity for *self-regulation*—the hallmark of integration across the self's levels.

9.7. Parts of the Self

9.7.1 Conceptual Foundations of Parts of the Self

The concept of *parts of the self*—also referred to as subpersonalities, ego-states, or self-states—describes the dynamic, multilayered structure of human consciousness and personality. Each part represents a relatively autonomous configuration of affect, cognition, bodily sensation, and behavioural tendency, organised around particular needs, experiences, or defences. Popescu and Vîşcu (2016) define subpersonalities as emotional and informational modules or neural pathways formed through intense use, constituting an "internal family" that serves adaptive or defensive purposes. These parts emerge through both external interactions and internal processes of introjection, gradually shaping the individual's subjective sense of continuity and multiplicity.

Within the framework of *Integrative Strategic Psychotherapy (ISP)*, the notion of parts of the self aligns with the model's multi-level conception of human organisation. The self is not a monolithic entity but a dynamic system comprising multiple states that emerge, interact, and integrate across the biological, emotional, cognitive, and relational axes. Parts of the self represent operational subsystems of this complex network—temporary yet meaningful configurations of the *proto-self* (bodily sensations and instincts), *core self* (affective coherence), *plastic self* (adaptive cognition), and *external self* (social expression).

Subpersonalities are not inherently pathological. They are the natural by-products of human differentiation and adaptation. In healthy functioning, these parts maintain permeable boundaries and cooperate fluidly, giving rise to flexibility and creativity. Problems arise when differentiation becomes rigid, integration fails, or specific parts assume dominance to the detriment of the whole. In such cases, the personality's internal harmony is disrupted, leading to dissociative experiences, emotional volatility, or psychosomatic manifestations.

9.7.2 Neurobiological and Developmental Basis

The formation of subpersonalities corresponds with the brain's natural tendency toward modular organisation. As the brain develops, distinct neural networks consolidate through repeated activation, creating emotional and informational "clusters" that later manifest as parts of the self (Siegel, 1996). These clusters integrate sensory input, emotional meaning, and behavioural responses into coherent, experience-based patterns. When a neural pathway is repeatedly activated in response to specific relational or environmental conditions, it becomes reinforced through synaptic plasticity—a principle often summarised as "neurons that fire together wire together" (Hebb, 1949; Siegel, 2012).

In early development, nonverbal experiences lay the foundation for subpersonalities within the *core self*. Preverbal states of distress, joy, fear, or shame are encoded as implicit memory—networks of affect and bodily response that remain accessible throughout life (Schore, 2012). These implicit patterns later re-emerge as emotional states or self-parts, especially under stress. Thus, what appears in adulthood as a "child part" is often a neurobiological reactivation of early implicit memory structures that were once adaptive within the caregiving context.

From the perspective of interpersonal neurobiology, subpersonalities correspond to state-dependent neural patterns linking the limbic system, prefrontal cortex, and right-hemispheric integrative networks. The right hemisphere—dominant in processing emotion, attachment, and bodily awareness—houses the neural substrates of self-states that arise during interpersonal exchanges (Schore & Schore, 2021). These self-states are not merely symbolic representations but embodied neural events that bridge affect, cognition, and interpersonal regulation.

9.7.3 The Function and Organisation of Subpersonalities

Each part of the self develops with a purpose: to solve a problem, manage a conflict, or protect the organism from emotional overwhelm. Initially, these functions are adaptive responses to developmental challenges. Over time, however, they may become fixed defensive structures, continuing to operate beyond their original context. Emmerson (2007) and Frederick (2005) describe subpersonalities as forming an "internal family" that mirrors the external environment. Some parts carry pain, others defend, and still others manage or criticise.

In ISP, these intrapsychic structures are understood as emergent patterns within the system of the self—each part expressing specific constellations of needs and defensive strategies across levels of functioning. A "protector" part, for instance, may engage cognitive defences (rationalisation), emotional suppression (affective inhibition), and somatic rigidity (muscle tension). A "vulnerable child" part, by contrast, may manifest through physiological collapse, helplessness, or tears, reflecting the activation of early attachment memories.

Emmerson (2007) noted that subpersonalities possess distinct identities, ages, feelings, and internal logic. They may hide, change, or assume new names. While parts cannot be eliminated, they can be transformed through relational integration. Their developmental age corresponds to the period when the original adaptation occurred. Hence, child parts think concretely and respond emotionally rather than abstractly, whereas adolescent parts may express autonomy, defiance, or mistrust toward authority (Stewart, 2007).

This developmental logic resonates with the ISP model's understanding of vertical integration. Parts that operate primarily at the emotional or biological level may lack access to the cognitive and relational resources of the mature self. Therapeutic work, therefore, involves strengthening inter-level communication—linking emotion with reflection, body with mind, and experience with meaning.

9.7.4 Introjection, Mirror Neurons, and Embodied Simulation

The process of introjection plays a central role in the formation of subpersonalities. Erskine and Moursund (2011) define introjection as the unconscious internalisation of another person's attitudes, behaviours, or values, leading to the creation of internal representations that influence self-organisation. Through introjection, aspects of caregivers, siblings, teachers, or significant others become embodied within the personality as distinct voices, expectations, or relational templates. These internalised "others" may become either supportive or critical parts of the self.

Neuroscientific research provides an embodied basis for introjection through the discovery of mirror neurons—cells that activate both during the execution of an action and during the observation of that action in others. Located in the premotor and inferior parietal cortices, mirror neurons are considered key mechanisms for empathy, imitation, and understanding intentions (Gallese, Eagle, & Migone, 2003). When a child observes the emotional expressions or gestures of a caregiver, similar neural circuits activate in the child's brain, creating a shared bodily representation of the experience.

This *shared activation* constitutes the foundation for *embodied simulation*, through which individuals implicitly internalise others' emotional states. Gallese et al. (2003) argued that this process occurs automatically and unconsciously, forming a neural basis for empathy and attachment. In ISP, embodied simulation represents a biological correlate of the *relational level* of the self. It explains how early affective resonance between child and caregiver becomes encoded as enduring internal parts.

While mirror neuron theory has faced critique (Schore, 2002; Hickok, 2014), more recent studies confirm that similar mechanisms of embodied resonance operate across sensory and affective domains (Keysers & Gazzola, 2021). These findings align with the integrative understanding of subpersonalities as emergent from both interpersonal experience and neural plasticity.

9.7.5. Parent, Adult and Child as Parts of the Self

The conceptual triad of Parent, Adult, and Child (P–A–C) originates in Transactional Analysis (TA), developed by Eric Berne in the late 1950s. Berne (1961) proposed that human personality is structured into three Ego States—each representing a coherent system of feelings, thoughts, and behaviours derived from different periods of experience. These are the Parent, which reproduces parental attitudes and norms; the Adult, which processes information in the present; and the Child, which expresses early emotional and experiential patterns.

In classical TA, these Ego States serve as both intrapsychic structures and interpersonal communication modes. Every interaction can be analysed according to which state is dominant, forming the basis of "transactions" between individuals

(Berne, 1964). However, beyond its communicative application, the P–A–C model offers a rich metaphorical framework for understanding internal multiplicity, self-regulation, and the interplay between autonomy and introjection.

Within the framework of Integrative Strategic Psychotherapy (ISP), the Parent, Adult, and Child are reinterpreted as *parts of the self*, corresponding to specific constellations of neural, emotional, and cognitive functioning. Rather than fixed compartments, they are viewed as dynamic self-states operating across the domains of the self (proto-self, core self, plastic self, and external self) and across the therapeutic levels and axes (biological, emotional, cognitive, psychodynamic, and relational). This reinterpretation allows the P–A–C model to be integrated with contemporary neuroscience, attachment theory, and affect regulation.

The Parent represents the internalisation of authority, care, and regulation. It is composed of thoughts, feelings, and behaviours assimilated from caregivers and significant figures during development. Clarkson (1992) described it as a "recording" of early experiences with those who provided nurture and protection. In this sense, the Parent is both the echo of external authority and the prototype of internal moral and regulatory systems.

In ISP, the Parent corresponds primarily to introjected representations within the *plastic self*—the level where learned values, beliefs, and relational scripts are stored and integrated. It functions as a mediator between the *core self* (emotional experience) and the *external self* (social adaptation), translating internal affect into socially sanctioned behaviour. The Parent embodies both supportive and restrictive dimensions, which can be distinguished as the *Nurturing Parent* and the *Controlling Parent* (Stewart, 2007).

The Nurturing Parent represents the internalised capacity for care and empathy. Its adaptive functions include offering reassurance, promoting safety, and supporting the self's cohesion under stress. When balanced, this aspect facilitates self-compassion and prosocial motivation. However, when exaggerated, it can lead to overprotection, intrusive caregiving, or emotional enmeshment. Neurobiologically, these dynamics correspond to the activation of oxytocinergic systems and right-hemispheric networks associated with caregiving and empathy (Schore, 2012).

The Controlling Parent, by contrast, represents the internalised dimension of authority and discipline. In its positive form, it provides structure, boundaries, and consistency, supporting the organism's capacity for self-regulation. In its negative form, it manifests as the *Critical Parent*—a harsh, punitive, and perfectionistic voice that induces shame and guilt. This pattern reflects the activation of defensive neural circuits within the anterior cingulate cortex and amygdala, associated with moral evaluation and fear conditioning (Porges, 2017).

From an integrative standpoint, the Parent thus represents the introjected regulatory system—adaptive when flexible, pathological when rigid. The task of psychotherapy is not to dismantle the Parent but to *differentiate* and *update* it, transforming archaic introjects into mature, empathic internal guides.

The Adult embodies the self's capacity for reflection, rationality, and reality testing. It corresponds to cognitive and metacognitive processes that integrate information from the environment and the internal world. Berne (1961) described it as the "data-processing centre" of the personality—objective, logical, and capable of distinguishing past conditioning from present reality.

In the ISP model, the Adult represents the functional expression of the *plastic self* in its integrative capacity. It coordinates input from the core and proto-self (emotional and somatic signals) with the relational and cognitive systems that guide behaviour. Neurobiologically, this function corresponds to the activation of the prefrontal cortex, particularly the medial and dorsolateral regions responsible for executive control, perspective-taking, and emotion regulation (Siegel, 2012).

The Adult is essential for maintaining equilibrium between the other two parts. It acts as the internal "mediator," assessing the needs of the Child and the rules of the Parent, and enabling adaptive responses. When underdeveloped, individuals may oscillate between impulsive emotional expression (Child) and rigid self-criticism (Parent). Strengthening the Adult involves enhancing reflective functioning and self-awareness—capacities linked to the *plastic self's* integrative processing and the *external self's* coherent communication.

Clinically, the Adult corresponds to what contemporary neuroscience calls the "integrative network of self-regulation" (Qin et al., 2020). This network dynamically balances the salience of emotional stimuli with rational assessment. In psychotherapy, activating the Adult means cultivating mindful presence—an awareness that neither suppresses emotion nor collapses into reactivity but observes and integrates.

The Child contains the individual's early experiences, needs, and emotional memories. It includes behaviours, feelings, and attitudes acquired in childhood—essentially, the recordings of the person's emotional past.

Stewart (2007) differentiated between the *Free Child* and the *Adapted Child*, each reflecting distinct developmental responses.

The Free Child expresses spontaneity, curiosity, playfulness, and creativity. It embodies the vitality of the *proto-self*, where emotion, movement, and imagination intertwine. When balanced, this part contributes to authenticity and joy. When unintegrated, however, it may become impulsive, self-centred, or emotionally labile.

The Adapted Child, on the other hand, reflects compliance with external expectations and adaptation to relational contingencies. It learns to please, obey, or rebel, depending on the emotional climate of early caregiving. Its positive aspects include social cooperation and empathy; its maladaptive forms involve passivity, guilt, rebellion, or emotional manipulation. These patterns correspond to learned relational strategies encoded during attachment interactions and mediated by right-hemispheric limbic networks (Schore & Schore, 2021).

In ISP, the Child represents the *core self's* emotional and motivational core. It carries the implicit memory of affective states that organise the sense of aliveness. The Free Child corresponds to the unconditioned expression of this vitality; the Adapted Child to the constrained form shaped by early relational contingencies. Healing involves re-establishing communication between these parts and the Adult, allowing emotional spontaneity to coexist with reflective awareness.

In the integrative perspective, the P–A–C system can be conceptualised as a regulatory triangle within the dynamic architecture of the self. Each element corresponds to a particular function within the broader hierarchy of integration.

The Parent represents *top-down regulation*—the inherited norms, beliefs, and moral frameworks that shape behaviour. The Child represents *bottom-up affective processes*—the raw emotional impulses and needs arising from the body and the limbic system. The Adult mediates between the two, providing *horizontal integration* that harmonises cognition and emotion.

When this triadic balance is functional, the personality operates cohesively: emotional energy from the Child fuels vitality, moral guidance from the Parent provides containment, and the Adult ensures realistic adaptation. When the system becomes unbalanced, pathology emerges. For instance, an overactive Parent suppresses emotion and spontaneity, leading to perfectionism or somatisation. A dominant Child without sufficient Adult mediation leads to impulsivity, dependency, or chaos. A weak Parent results in boundary issues and poor impulse control.

From the standpoint of ISP, therapeutic change involves *recalibrating* this system through strategic interventions at the relevant levels. Work on the emotional axis strengthens the connection to the Child; cognitive restructuring modifies internalised Parent scripts; and relational atonement supports the Adult's integrative role. Over time, this process results in a flexible and self-reflective system where each part contributes adaptively to overall coherence.

Integrating the P–A–C model within ISP allows psychotherapists to conceptualise client dynamics in terms of self-regulatory patterns rather than static traits. For instance, a client who continually self-criticises may be dominated by a harsh Controlling Parent, while their suppressed Child manifests through somatic symptoms or passive resistance. An ISP formulation would address this by engaging both axes: cognitively exploring the origins of the internal critic and emotionally validating the Child's unmet needs.

Therapeutic techniques include *dialogue between parts*, where the psychotherapist facilitates communication between the internal voices, helping the Adult mediate. Expressive and experiential approaches—such as empty-chair dialogues, guided imagery, and role-play—help externalise these parts, enabling observation and integration. Somatic awareness and mindfulness practices re-establish connection with the embodied Child, while cognitive reframing supports the restructuring of Parent beliefs.

Recent research supports the effectiveness of integrative parts-based work. Studies in affective neuroscience demonstrate that relational and emotional integration modifies the brain's default mode and salience networks, enhancing self-coherence (Messina et al., 2023). Furthermore, models like Internal Family Systems (Schwartz & Sweezy, 2020) echo the ISP principle that all parts possess positive intentions, even when expressed maladaptively. In both frameworks, the goal is not elimination but transformation through compassion and relational resonance.

9.7.6. The ISP Perspective: The Dynamic System of Selves

Integrative Strategic Psychotherapy conceptualises the self as a stratified and interactive system composed of multiple dynamic parts. Each part embodies a distinct configuration of the five components—biological, emotional, cognitive, psychodynamic, and relational—operating within one or more levels of the self. For instance, a *caretaker* part may represent relational compliance (relational level), hypervigilance (biological level), and self-sacrificial cognition (cognitive axis). Conversely, a *rebellious* part may express suppressed anger (emotional axis) and individuation conflict (psychodynamic axis).

The ISP model proposes that therapeutic progress occurs through the alignment of parts around a central integrative structure. The psychotherapist facilitates this alignment by supporting awareness, differentiation, and empathy among self-states. Rather than eliminating parts, the goal is to bring them into dialogue, transforming defensive isolation into cooperative regulation.

Neuroscientific findings from the past decade support this integrative approach. Resting-state fMRI studies show that self-related processing involves dynamic coordination among large-scale networks such as the default mode, salience, and executive systems (Qin et al., 2020). Disruptions in this integration correlate with dissociative disorders and identity fragmentation.

Psychotherapy, by fostering narrative coherence and affective regulation, enhances connectivity within these networks, reinforcing a stable sense of self.

Working with parts of the self in ISP requires a relational stance characterised by empathy, curiosity, and respect for each part's protective intention. The psychotherapist serves as a *mediator of integration*, facilitating dialogue between dissociated or conflicting self-states. Drawing upon methods from ego-state therapy, internal family systems, and affective neuroscience, the process involves recognising the adaptive origin of each part and helping it update its function in the present.

Therapeutic interventions progress through several stages: recognition, differentiation, negotiation, and integration. Recognition involves identifying and naming self-parts as distinct yet legitimate aspects of the person. Differentiation clarifies their emotional needs and historical origins. Negotiation supports cooperation between parts with conflicting agendas—such as a perfectionistic protector and an exhausted vulnerable child. Integration involves linking the part's experience across the self's levels, allowing emotional, cognitive, and somatic coherence to emerge.

ISP also emphasises the role of the therapeutic relationship in re-regulating dissociated states. Through empathic atonement, the psychotherapist becomes a co-regulator of the client's nervous system, promoting right-hemispheric synchronisation and facilitating integration (Schore & Schore, 2021). Expressive methods—such as guided imagery, movement, or drawing—can support this process by giving non-verbal form to implicit self-states.

9.8. Dissociative Processes and Structural Fragmentation of the Self

9.8.1 Conceptual Foundations of Dissociation

The concept of dissociation has evolved considerably since its early formulations in nineteenth-century psychology. Originally described by Pierre Janet as a *disaggregation of consciousness* (Janet, 1889/1973), dissociation referred to the mind's capacity to separate incompatible experiences, memories, or affects from ordinary awareness. Freud's early writings (1894) similarly described hysterical conversion as a splitting of psychic processes—defensive operations designed to exclude painful affects from consciousness.

Over time, the concept has shifted from an exclusively intrapsychic to an integrative biopsychosocial perspective. Dissociation is now understood as a complex neuropsychological phenomenon that arises when an individual's integrative capacities are overwhelmed by trauma, chronic stress, or attachment insecurity (van der Kolk et al., 1996; Schore, 2012). Rather than a purely defensive act of repression, dissociation involves a breakdown in communication between systems of self-representation, resulting in fragmentation across cognitive, affective, somatic, and relational levels of functioning.

In contemporary understanding, dissociation lies on a continuum that ranges from adaptive compartmentalisation—useful in maintaining function under stress—to severe structural fragmentation, as seen in dissociative identity disorder (Brown, 2006). Mild forms of dissociation appear in everyday life (daydreaming, absorption, transient detachment), while pathological dissociation involves persistent disruptions in memory, identity, affect, or perception.

From the perspective of Integrative Strategic Psychotherapy (ISP), dissociation represents the failure of communication between the domains of the self. When the system is exposed to intolerable affect or contradictory experiences, the natural flow between proto-self (biological regulation), core self (affect and motivation), plastic self (cognition and meaning), and external self (social adaptation) becomes interrupted. The individual may continue to function outwardly, but the inner system remains fragmented and asynchronous.

9.8.2 Structural Dissociation and the Continuum of Fragmentation

The theory of structural dissociation, formulated by van der Hart, Nijenhuis, and Steele (2006), offers a contemporary framework for understanding how traumatic experiences divide the personality. They distinguish between the *apparently normal part* (ANP), which manages daily functioning, and the *emotional part* (EP), which remains fixated on traumatic memories. This division may range from simple (one ANP and one EP) to complex (multiple parts), depending on the chronicity and severity of trauma.

Emmerson (2007) described differentiation and dissociation as existing on a continuum. At one pole lies *healthy differentiation*—the ability to hold multiple aspects of experience while maintaining internal communication; at the other lies *pathological dissociation*—a rigid fragmentation that prevents integration. Watkins and Watkins (1997) defined an ego-state as an organised system of behaviour, thought, and feeling linked by a unifying principle. When one ego-state is invested with "ego energy," it takes executive control of consciousness while the others recede.

In trauma-related dissociation, defensive parts (e.g., protectors, controllers, avoiders) dominate awareness, while vulnerable or wounded parts (e.g., frightened child, ashamed self) remain exiled. This structural pattern mirrors neurobiological mechanisms of survival: under threat, the brain's integrative networks (especially prefrontal and hippocampal regions) deactivate, allowing subcortical defence systems to assume control (Schore & Schore, 2021). Dissociation therefore represents both a protective adaptation and a disruption of integrative functioning.

Two main forms of dissociation are typically observed (Brown, 2006; Gilbert & Orlans, 2013):

(1) Primary dissociation (detachment) – the sensory and emotional components of an experience fail to integrate into personal narrative, producing intrusive memories, flashbacks, or depersonalisation. This form characterises post-traumatic stress disorder (PTSD); and

(2) Secondary dissociation (compartmentalisation) – a more profound separation between observing and experiencing selves, in which the person perceives the event as happening to someone else. This split can evolve into distinct identities with separate emotional, cognitive, and behavioural patterns, as seen in dissociative identity disorder (DID).

9.8.3 The Developmental Origins of Fragmentation

Dissociation originates in early developmental environments where the child's need for safety and atonement is unmet. Disorganised attachment, abuse, neglect, or emotional unavailability disrupt the infant's capacity to integrate affective experience. In secure attachment, the caregiver's regulation of the child's arousal fosters the formation of a cohesive self. In contrast, inconsistent or frightening caregiving generates paradoxical messages: the source of comfort is also a source of fear (Lyons-Ruth & Jacobvitz, 2016). The child's mind resolves this paradox by splitting self-states—some oriented toward connection, others toward defence.

Schore (2012) demonstrated that early trauma interferes with right-hemispheric development—the neural substrate for emotional regulation and autobiographical memory. Chronic misattunement impairs connectivity between limbic and prefrontal regions, resulting in an unstable affective system. The body learns to survive by dissociating: by shutting down overwhelming emotional and somatic signals.

From an ISP perspective, early fragmentation represents a breakdown in the synchronisation of the domains of the self. The proto-self (autonomic and sensory regulation) may remain hyper- or hypo-aroused; the core self (emotional experience) becomes suppressed; the plastic self (cognitive interpretation) constructs defensive narratives that deny vulnerability; and the external self (social presentation) adapts through compliance or false self-behaviour. Such fragmentation becomes embedded as a relational template, reproduced in adult relationships and psychotherapeutic encounters.

9.8.4. Dissociation Across the Domains of The Self (ISP Framework)

Integrative Strategic Psychotherapy conceptualises the self as a multi-layered, dynamic system. Dissociative phenomena can therefore be mapped across the four domains:

1. Proto-self: Dissociation manifests as disruptions in autonomic regulation—somatic numbness, derealisation, fainting, or alterations in body temperature and pain perception. These physiological states correspond to immobilisation responses mediated by the dorsal vagal complex (Porges, 2017);
2. Core self: Emotional disconnection, alexithymia, and affective blunting reflect the severing of links between emotion and awareness. The individual may "know" they are sad or afraid but feel nothing;
3. Plastic self: Cognitive fragmentation occurs through denial, splitting, or contradictory beliefs. The person may hold conflicting narratives ("*It didn't*

happen" versus "*It ruined my life*"), each associated with a distinct part of the self; and

4. External self: The dissociative system adapts socially by developing a false or compliant persona. Outward functionality masks internal chaos. Such individuals may appear successful, empathic, and composed while experiencing profound internal alienation.

Therapeutic work within ISP addresses dissociation through *vertical integration*—reconnecting bodily, emotional, cognitive, and relational processes. The psychotherapist facilitates safe oscillation between connection and separation, gradually restoring the synchrony among levels of the self.

9.8.5 The Body, Memory, and Implicit Dissociation

Dissociation is not limited to cognition but is inscribed in the body. The body "remembers" what the mind cannot (van der Kolk, 2014). Implicit memory systems—mediated by subcortical and sensorimotor networks—store unprocessed fragments of experience. These manifest as chronic tension, somatic symptoms, or postural adaptations. Research in embodied cognition confirms that emotional and procedural memories are encoded through bodily states and can be accessed non-verbally through movement, breath, or sensory awareness (Payne et al., 2023).

Implicit dissociation occurs when sensorimotor patterns remain disconnected from explicit narrative memory. For example, a client may intellectually recall a trauma but experience sudden bodily immobilisation when discussing it. Therapeutic engagement must therefore include somatic atonement and grounding techniques that re-link bodily sensations with affective meaning.

ISP emphasises *bottom-up regulation*: beginning with the body and progressing toward cognitive integration. Interventions on the biological and emotional axes—breath regulation, posture work, guided imagery, expressive movement—activate implicit memories in a contained environment. Gradually, these experiences are symbolised at the plastic level (language, meaning-making) and integrated into the narrative self.

9.8.6 Therapeutic Reconstruction and Integration

The goal of psychotherapy is not to "remove" dissociation but to transform it from a rigid defence into a flexible adaptive capacity. Integration involves re-establishing communication among parts of the self and restoring coherence between self-levels.

In ISP, this process unfolds through several stages:

1. Stabilisation and Safety: Establishing physiological and relational safety. The psychotherapist's attuned presence helps regulate the client's autonomic system, counteracting hyper- or hypo-arousal;
2. Recognition of Parts and States: Through mindful observation, the client learns to identify internal states without judgement. Dialogue between parts (e.g., protective and vulnerable selves) is encouraged in a compassionate, non-confrontational manner;
3. Emotional Processing: Once safety is established, suppressed affect is accessed and processed through emotional, expressive, or somatic work. The therapist supports titrated exposure—"pendulation" between distress and safety (Levine, 2010);
4. Narrative Reconstruction: The fragmented story of the trauma is reorganised within the broader life narrative. This process re-engages the hippocampus and medial prefrontal cortex, allowing implicit memories to be explicitly contextualised (Brewin et al., 2021); and
5. Integration and Reconnection: The final phase involves strengthening the connections between self-levels. Clients experience themselves as coherent agents capable of regulating emotion, making meaning, and engaging relationally.

Therapeutic integration also includes re-establishing a *relational self.* The therapist's empathic atonement functions as an external regulator, providing the corrective experience of being safely mirrored and held. This interpersonal synchrony activates neural circuits associated with right-hemispheric integration and oxytocin release (Schore & Schore, 2021), gradually internalising the capacity for self-soothing and empathy.

9.9. The Life Script

9.9.1 Origins and Theoretical Context

The concept of the life script originates from Transactional Analysis (TA), formulated by Eric Berne (1961, 1972), who proposed that each person develops an unconscious life plan early in childhood. This script, like a dramatic narrative, directs thoughts, feelings, and behaviours throughout life. It answers the implicit question: *"What does someone like me do in a world like this?"*

In TA, the life script is viewed as a scenario written through early interactions with caregivers, particularly through the parental injunctions and permissions that shape identity, autonomy, and relational expectations. The script is sustained by introjected messages—some verbal, others non-verbal—communicated through tone, gesture, and emotional resonance. It represents the synthesis of experience, defence, and meaning-making that the child constructs to survive within their emotional environment (Clarkson, 1992; Erskine & Moursund, 2011).

Within Integrative Strategic Psychotherapy (ISP), the life script is understood as a multi-level regulatory structure that originates in early affective experience and extends into cognitive and relational patterns. The script begins in the core self, where emotional experiences and attachment patterns are encoded; it develops through the plastic self, where cognition and meaning are elaborated; and it manifests in the external self, through behavioural and relational strategies. This perspective integrates TA with neurobiological and attachment-based insights, emphasising that scripts are embodied and affectively encoded before they are conceptualised as beliefs.

9.9.2 Early Encoding: From Proto-Self to Core Self

Life scripts are not purely psychological constructs; they begin as physiological patterns of regulation and adaptation. From birth, and possibly prenatally, the infant's experiences of safety, atonement, and distress regulation are recorded in the body's neural and biochemical systems (Schore & Schore, 2021). These implicit memories form the proto-script—patterns of autonomic response and affective expectation that shape how the individual perceives the world's safety and predictability.

The core self integrates these embodied responses with early emotions and relational templates. Here, the child begins to internalise affective meanings: *"When I cry, someone comes,"* or *"When I need, I am ignored."* Such experiences gradually crystallise into implicit assumptions about worth, love, and agency. Over time, these affective maps become the foundation for the later cognitive life script.

Erskine and Moursund (2011) describe this process as the layering of experience—first physiological, then emotional, and finally cognitive. Each layer builds upon the previous one, creating continuity between body, feeling, and belief. In ISP terms, the life script is the cumulative result of this progressive encoding across levels of the self.

9.9.3 The Formation of the Script

Life scripts form through two primary mechanisms: introjection and protective decision-making.

Introjection involves the internalisation of parental attitudes, emotions, and prohibitions. The child adopts the voice of the parent—both nurturing and critical—as an internal regulatory system. For example, a child repeatedly told "Don't cry" or "Be strong" may internalise a prohibition against vulnerability, which later manifests as emotional suppression. Such introjects function as early attempts to maintain attachment security by aligning with the caregiver's expectations (Fowlie & Sills, 2011).

Protective decisions, in contrast, arise from the child's own adaptive efforts to manage distress. Faced with neglect or rejection, the child unconsciously decides how to survive: by becoming compliant, competent, invisible, or rebellious. These early solutions solidify into enduring behavioural and relational patterns. A child with an alcoholic mother, for instance, may decide "I must take care of everything," and grow into a perfectionistic adult driven by control.

These decisions are often reinforced by both internal (emotional relief) and external (parental approval) feedback loops, gradually forming a self-reinforcing belief system. Over time, they become self-fulfilling prophecies that confirm the individual's expectations of self and world (James & Jongeward, 1978).

Parents communicate script messages in both direct and indirect ways (Clarkson, 1992; Moursund & Erskine, 2003). Some messages define what the child must *do* ("Be perfect," "Hurry up," "Be strong"), while others define who the child *is* ("You're a disappointment," "You're the good one"). When these messages are internalised, they become the organising grammar of the script.

The child interprets such injunctions literally. "You don't need anything," told to a neglected child, may become an enduring life position of self-denial and emotional detachment. Even the most subtle parental cues—tone of voice, facial expression, withdrawal of attention—communicate powerful messages about the child's right to exist, feel, or belong. In extreme cases, implicit injunctions such as "Don't exist" or "Don't feel" become incorporated into the script and may later manifest as self-sabotage, chronic depression, or suicidal ideation (Berne, 2006).

In the ISP framework, these injunctions are imprinted within the core self as emotional memories and belief structures. They are maintained through repetitive neural pathways and reinforced by the relational environment.

9.9.4. Script Maintenance and Re-Enactment

The life script persists because it fulfils two psychological functions (Fowlie & Sills, 2011): (1) It protects the individual from re-experiencing the original pain of unmet needs; and (2) It provides predictability and coherence, even if maladaptive.

The illusion of predictability gives the individual a sense of control in an uncertain world. Deviation from the script evokes anxiety because it threatens to reawaken the original vulnerability. Consequently, people unconsciously organise perceptions, relationships, and behaviours to confirm their script beliefs. This process mirrors what contemporary neuroscience describes as predictive processing—the brain's tendency to minimise surprise by maintaining internal models, even when they are inaccurate (Friston, 2010; Wilkinson, 2023).

Scripts are therefore self-reinforcing systems. Behaviour, language, tone, and body posture all express the underlying narrative. For example, a person whose script belief is "I am unworthy" may either behave submissively to elicit rejection or overcompensate through achievement to conceal shame. In both cases, the script's central theme is confirmed.

Recent advances in affective neuroscience show that early relational experiences shape brain architecture in ways that sustain life scripts. Emotional neglect or critical parenting alters the connectivity between limbic and prefrontal regions, reinforcing self-critical or avoidant patterns (Schore & Schore, 2021). The orbitofrontal cortex, which mediates social meaning and self-evaluation, becomes the neurobiological seat of the internalised parent. The anterior cingulate processes conflict between competing self-states, reflecting the inner dialogue between the adaptive and rebellious parts of the self.

From an ISP standpoint, this neurobiological understanding supports a unified model: the life script is simultaneously a narrative, a neural pattern, and a relational structure. It is maintained through synchronised feedback between cognition, emotion, body, and interpersonal environment.

9.9.5 Life Script Types and Existential Patterns

Berne (1996) described the life script as a dramatic narrative with predictable settings, characters, and outcomes. Depending on early decisions and reinforcements, scripts may be categorised as winner, loser, or non-winner (neutral) (Fowlie & Sills, 2011). Each script carries implicit conclusions about success, love, and meaning.

Steiner (1994) identified three pathological life scripts leading to self-destruction: (1) *Life without love* – lived by individuals who believe they are unlovable and seek relationships destined to fail; (2) *Life without mind* – marked by confusion, passivity, and loss of agency; and (3) *Life without joy* – characterised by chronic suppression of pleasure, vitality, and spontaneity.

These existential scripts mirror the dysregulation of the domains of the self in ISP: emotional deprivation (*core self*), cognitive confusion (*plastic self*), and somatic inhibition (*proto-self*). Thus, the script's theme reflects which domain of the self has been most constrained during development.

9.9.6. Transformation of the Life Script in Psychotherapy

Therapeutic change involves bringing implicit script patterns into awareness and rewriting the internal narrative. Within ISP, this occurs through the coordinated activation of all levels and axes:

1. Biological level: Restoring somatic regulation through breath, movement, and sensory awareness helps release the embodied dimension of the script;
2. Emotional axis: Accessing suppressed affect allows the client to reconnect with unmet needs frozen in the core self;
3. Cognitive axis: Identifying and reframing script beliefs transforms introjected parental voices into self-directed reflection;
4. Psychodynamic axis: Exploring unconscious motivations and transferential patterns reveals the repetition compulsion that sustains the script; and
5. Relational level: The therapeutic relationship provides a reparative experience in which the client can experiment with new ways of being seen and validated.

Through this multi-axial work, the client learns to differentiate between past and present, and between parental voices and authentic self-experience. Integration replaces repetition, and agency replaces determinism.

Narrative approaches within psychotherapy affirm that meaning-making is central to identity transformation. The client's autobiographical narrative evolves from a deterministic story ("*I must fail*") to an agentic narrative ("*I once learned that I would fail, but I can now choose differently").* Research on narrative identity shows that individuals who reframe their life stories with themes of growth and redemption demonstrate greater psychological well-being and coherence (Adler et al., 2021).

In ISP, narrative reconstruction is not merely verbal but experiential—it involves emotional re-symbolisation, bodily regulation, and relational atonement. By engaging the *plastic self* (reflective awareness) while grounding in the *core and proto-self* (embodied affect), the psychotherapist helps the client to write a new, coherent "chapter" that integrates the once-fragmented self.

9.10. The Perception of Time

9.10.1. Time Perspectives

Time is one of the most fundamental yet elusive dimensions of human experience. While it cannot be seen or touched, it permeates every aspect of perception, memory, and identity. Psychological time refers to the subjective sense of duration, sequence, and flow that allows us to perceive ourselves as continuous beings. Unlike physical time, which is measurable and uniform, psychological time is malleable, shaped by emotion, attention, memory, and consciousness (Cohen et al., 1999).

From the standpoint of Integrative Strategic Psychotherapy (ISP), the perception of time is deeply linked to the dynamic functioning of the self. Each level and axis of the self—biological, emotional, cognitive, psychodynamic and relational—contributes to the experience of temporal flow. Disruptions at any level may lead to temporal distortions that are clinically relevant in trauma, anxiety, depression, and dissociative disorders. The way we inhabit time—whether we live trapped in the past, suspended in the present, or anxiously anticipating the future—reveals the structure of our inner world and the state of our integration.

The accumulation of memories creates a mental direction of time, defined by the transition from the known (past) to the unknown (future). The anticipation of the unknown forms the *psychological future*, while memory constructs the *psychological past*. Together, these produce the subjective sense of temporal continuity—what William James called the "stream of consciousness."

Cohen et al. (1999) note that this sense of temporal flow is a product of neural integration, emerging as the brain continuously correlates current sensory input with memory traces. Saniga (2003) argued that this correlation parallels the second law of thermodynamics: as entropy increases, new memories are formed, linking the arrow of time in physics with the directionality of psychological experience. Thus, while physical time may be reversible, psychological time is inherently unidirectional—rooted in memory and expectation.

From a phenomenological perspective, we live in three temporal modes simultaneously: the remembered past, the experienced present, and the anticipated future (Husserl, 1991). Yet only the present is directly accessible. The past exists as memory, the future as imagination. Our capacity to bridge these temporal domains—through reflection and anticipation—defines the coherence of selfhood.

Time is a *tacit dimension* of experience because it cannot be perceived directly. We perceive time only through change—the movement of bodies, the unfolding of sound, or the progression of thought. Conway (2004) observed that time perception depends on the dynamic integration of neural and psychological processes that encode the order and duration of events.

Neuroscientific research supports the idea that multiple brain regions collaborate to create temporal awareness. The prefrontal cortex and hippocampus are responsible for sequencing and planning, while the basal ganglia and cerebellum regulate rhythm and duration (Wittmann, 2013). Emotionally charged events recruit the amygdala, which enhances memory consolidation and subjective elongation of time—explaining why traumatic moments seem to last "forever."

In ISP terms, temporal perception emerges from the synchronisation of levels of the self. The proto-self organises biological rhythms (circadian cycles, heartbeat); the core self experiences affective duration ("*time slows when I am afraid*"); the plastic self interprets and conceptualises time ("*I have wasted years*"); and the external self expresses time socially, through narratives and routines. The cohesion among these layers gives rise to a stable sense of continuity.

Zimbardo and Boyd (2008) identified six major time perspectives in Western cultures: (1) Past-negative – dominated by regret or trauma; (2) Past-positive – characterised by nostalgia and gratitude; (3) Present-fatalistic – a sense that life is beyond control; (4) Present-hedonistic – focus on pleasure and immediacy; (5) Future-oriented – driven by goals and planning; and (6) Transcendental-future – belief in existence beyond death.

An adaptive temporal orientation requires flexibility across these perspectives. Mental well-being arises from the ability to integrate past, present, and future into a coherent whole (Vogeley & Kupke, 2007). Overemphasis on any one perspective leads to imbalance: the trauma survivor relives the past, the depressive is trapped in timeless despair, and the anxious individual lives in perpetual anticipation.

Clinical psychology increasingly recognises the link between temporal orientation and ego strength. A balanced time perspective correlates with self-regulation, resilience, and optimism (Stolarski et al., 2020). Conversely, disturbed temporal experience—such as the timelessness of dissociation or the accelerated urgency of mania—signals fragmentation across the self-system.

Trauma profoundly alters the perception of time. During overwhelming events, the brain's integrative functions collapse, and the present moment expands into an "eternal now" of helplessness (van der Kolk, 2014). The hippocampus, responsible for contextualising memory, becomes inhibited by stress hormones, while the amygdala hyperactivates, encoding sensory fragments without temporal sequence. As a result, traumatic memories remain "frozen in time"—relived as if happening in the present.

This disruption illustrates the collapse of communication between the core and plastic selves. The emotional system (core self) remains trapped in the original affective state, while the cognitive system (plastic self) continues forward in chronological time. In ISP, such fragmentation explains why traumatised clients oscillate between emotional re-experiencing and intellectual detachment. Therapy seeks to re-establish the temporal bridge, allowing emotional experiences to be placed within narrative and meaning.

Dissociation represents another distortion of time. In depersonalisation, time slows or stops entirely; in fugue states, whole periods disappear from memory. For individuals with dissociative identity structures, each self-part may live in a different temporal frame—one anchored in childhood, another in the present. Integration involves synchronising these temporalities into a shared internal clock.

Children initially live in a *present-centred world*. Their sense of time is bodily and affective rather than conceptual. The proto-self organises rhythms of feeding and sleep; the core self experiences anticipation and delay. Through interaction with caregivers, the child begins to internalise sequences—first emotionally ("*Mum always comes back*"), then symbolically ("*after sleep comes breakfast*").

Attachment relationships play a decisive role in temporal development. Secure attachment fosters a stable sense of continuity: the child learns that time unfolds predictably, with return and repair. In contrast, inconsistent caregiving produces disorganised temporal schemas—waiting becomes endless, or comfort arrives unpredictably. Such experiences may later manifest as impatience, anxiety, or hopelessness.

Neuroscientific studies show that temporal awareness depends on the maturation of prefrontal-limbic networks. Adolescents, whose prefrontal cortex is still developing, tend to overvalue short-term rewards and underestimate long-term consequences—a neurobiological explanation for impulsivity (Steinberg et al., 2018). Thus, the capacity to "think in time" is both a cognitive and emotional achievement.

Different cultures shape temporal experience through language, ritual, and worldview. Western societies, dominated by linear time, emphasise progress and efficiency. Many Eastern and Indigenous traditions perceive time cyclically, as renewal and return (Tse et al., 2020). These cultural models influence identity: linear cultures foster goal orientation and anxiety about the future, while cyclical cultures encourage acceptance and presence.

Existential psychology views time as the horizon within which meaning is created. Awareness of mortality transforms time into urgency—the recognition that life is finite gives depth to existence. Frankl (1946/2017) argued that human freedom lies in how we relate to time: we cannot change the past, but we can choose the meaning we assign to it. Integrative psychotherapy embraces this existential dimension, helping clients move from fatalism to authorship.

Psychotherapeutic work often involves re-establishing temporal coherence helping clients locate themselves within a continuous narrative. In ISP, temporal integration is both a goal and a process. Each level and axis contributes uniquely:

1. Biological level: Grounding and breathwork anchor the client in the present moment, recalibrating the body's temporal rhythm;
2. Emotional axis: Processing affective memories reopens frozen temporal zones, allowing repressed emotions to find resolution;
3. Cognitive axis: Reframing and narrative reconstruction restore chronological order to fragmented experiences;
4. Psychodynamic axis: Interpretation of transferential cycles reveals repetitive temporal loops—unconscious reliving of early dramas; and

5. Relational axis: The therapist's attuned presence provides temporal containment—an experience of "safe time" that contrasts with the timelessness of trauma.

Through this integrative process, clients regain the ability to move freely across temporal dimensions: to remember without reliving, to anticipate without anxiety, and to inhabit the present with awareness.

Not all alterations of time are pathological. States of *flow*, as described by Csikszentmihalyi (1990), involve a temporary suspension of ordinary time perception. During deep engagement, the self becomes fully absorbed in the activity; past and future dissolve into an expanded present. This "positive timelessness" contrasts sharply with the traumatic "frozen time." Both, however, involve heightened synchrony across brain networks.

In ISP, flow represents the optimal alignment of the domains of the self—the proto-self's rhythm, the core self's emotion, the plastic self's focus, and the external self's purpose converge. It is the experiential opposite of dissociation, demonstrating that the self's temporal dynamics can support creativity and healing.

9.10.2. Neurobiology of Time Perception

Human timing is distributed rather than localised: circadian rhythms are governed primarily by the suprachiasmatic nuclei, ultradian cycles are coordinated by other hypothalamic and brainstem generators, while prospective timing on the scale of milliseconds to seconds depends on cortico-striato-thalamo-cerebellar loops. In Integrative Strategic Psychotherapy (ISP), these strata of timing map onto the levels of the self. Oscillatory and autonomic pacemakers belong to the proto-self; affects stretch or compress subjective duration in the core self; symbolic and prospective timing (planning, sequencing) are plastic-self functions; and the external self translates temporal organisation into routines, deadlines, and social time.

A long tradition in cognitive neuroscience models interval timing via an internal clock or pacemaker–accumulator: pulses emitted by a pacemaker are gated into an accumulator, and the counted pulses index perceived duration. Heightened attention and physiological arousal open the gate or increase pacemaker rate, thereby increasing the number of accumulated "ticks" and lengthening subjective time (Kyu Kim & Zauberman, 2009). This framework aligns with clinical observations that boredom, depression, and anxiety slow time, whereas high engagement or flow compresses it.

Mellor (2008) proposed that the brain represents time using time itself: the very sequence of neural events encodes temporal order. Dennett (1992) challenged clock-like models, suggesting content-dependent timing in which temporal order is inferred from causal coherence among representations rather than read off a dedicated clock. Within ISP, these are complementary lenses on the same phenomenon: bottom-up embodied timing in the proto/core self and top-down inferential timing in the plastic/external self.

A distinct family of accounts replaces a central clock with state-dependent dynamics. On this view, time is encoded in evolving activity patterns of neuronal networks whose transient trajectories carry temporal information; the system "knows" elapsed time by its current state (Aizzizudin et al., 2006). This dovetails with ISP's emphasis on patterned self-states: the organism's internal milieu flows through recurrent configurations, and duration is read from the trajectory of the whole system rather than a single metronome.

Short-term distortions show how attention modulates temporal experience. Time appears dilated during saccades and after adaptation to flicker or motion (Kanai & Verstraten, 2005). When a rare or behaviourally salient item occurs in a rapid sequence, it seems to last longer than equiprobable items—the "oddball" effect—consistent across auditory and visual modalities. Tse and colleagues (2004) proposed that the brain misattributes changes in the rate of internal information processing to changes in external time; a sudden increase in processing rate makes the world appear to slow down. Karmakar and Buonomano (2007) questioned a single global mechanism, favouring locally tuned circuits whose coding properties depend on recent history. For ISP, these findings show why emotional salience, vigilance, and threat appraisal on the emotional axis so powerfully reshape the lived tempo of experience.

Convergent evidence assigns sub-second timing to cerebellar and sensory cortices and supra-second timing to fronto-striatal circuits, with strong dopaminergic modulation. Fronto-striatal networks provide prospective timing, sequencing, and working-memory support; lesions or developmental alterations in these regions impair interval estimation and produce greater temporal variability. Functional imaging typically implicates the right inferior frontal cortex, supplementary motor area, basal ganglia, and cerebellum in duration judgements, with context-dependent recruitment of hippocampus and parietal cortex for temporal order and episodic placement. In ISP language, reliable supra-second timing is a plastic-self competence that scaffolds the external self's planning; cerebellar and sensory timing provide the proto-self's fine-grained temporal resolution for action and perception.

Dopamine is especially relevant for clinical work: increased dopaminergic tone tends to speed the pacemaker (subjective time lengthens for a given objective interval), whereas reduced tone slows it. This helps explain time distortions in disorders with dopamine dysregulation and why psychostimulants can normalise interval timing in some populations.

Temporal experience is not only about duration but about when events occurred relative to action. People judge the effects of their own actions as occurring slightly earlier than identical effects produced externally, an illusion interpreted as an ongoing temporal calibration of agency (Conway, 2004). The nervous system must continually retune expected delays between motor commands and sensory consequences to overcome neural latencies; otherwise agency would feel fractured (Popescu & Vîșcu, 2016). In therapy this is more than a curiosity: traumatised clients often report a dislocated sense of "when" in relation to their own actions. Recalibrating agency in the session—through paced enactment, tracking of intention, and interoceptive timing—can restore coherence between initiating and experiencing, strengthening the Adult's integrative role within ISP.

Affect reshapes time. Threat, pain, and high anxiety typically dilate duration; sadness and boredom lengthen perceived intervals; high engagement compresses them. Depressed individuals often describe a sticky, slowed time; anxious clients overestimate waiting intervals; cancer patients with high anxiety commonly report prolonged subjective time. These patterns reflect coordinated shifts across axes: autonomic arousal (biological), vigilance and salience (emotional), expectancy and prediction error (cognitive), and attachment-based anticipation of help or abandonment (relational). In trauma, stress hormones suppress hippocampal context binding while amygdala-centred salience dominates, leaving unsequenced fragments that feel perpetually present; hence traumatic memories are "now" rather than "then."

Temporal valuation links timing to choice. When delayed outcomes are discounted steeply, immediate, smaller rewards are preferred over larger, later ones. Impulsive individuals typically perceive delays as longer and less tolerable, pushing them toward sooner outcomes (Wittmann & Paulus, 2007, 2009). From a pacemaker–accumulator perspective, heightened arousal and attention to delay increase accumulated "ticks," lengthening perceived waiting time and devaluing delayed rewards (Kyu Kim & Zauberman, 2009; Zauberman et al., 2009). Neurobiologically, fronto-striatal and limbic systems jointly compute temporal discounting; when the Adult's prefrontal control is compromised, the Child's present-hedonic tendencies dominate. Within ISP, strengthening temporal skills—prospection, episodic future thinking, and present-moment regulation—reduces discounting by bringing the future emotionally closer and the present physiologically quieter.

Clinical implications for ISP

First, assess temporal style explicitly: Does the client routinely overestimate waits, live in rushed urgency, or report timeless emptiness? These are not only cognitive habits but signatures of arousal set-points and attachment expectancies. Second, intervene bottom-up to retune the proto-self's timing: breath pacing, rhythmic movement, and sensorimotor synchrony stabilise internal tempo. Third, work on the emotional axis to reduce salience-driven dilation (fear, hypervigilance) and increase capacity for grounded activation; mindfulness of feeling-tone changes the gate on the pacemaker. Fourth, on the cognitive axis, train prospection and episodic future thinking, converting abstract future rewards into vivid scenes, which reduces delay discounting and supports strategic behaviour. Fifth, use the relational level to provide a reliable temporal container: consistent session rhythms, clear time boundaries, and repair after ruptures re-write expectations about how time is held with another. Finally, integrate agency calibration exercises—slow motion intention–action–outcome tracking—to rebuild the felt continuity between "I intend," "I act," and "I experience," reinforcing the Adult's executive integration of Parent rules and Child vitality.

9.10.3. Urgency and Time Perspective

Time, in psychological experience, is not a neutral continuum but a deeply personal construction that reflects temperament, attachment, culture, and developmental history. Each individual inhabits a unique relationship with time an inner rhythm shaped by both biological clocks and subjective narratives. Within the framework of *Integrative Strategic Psychotherapy* (ISP), the perception and management of time are seen as dynamic expressions of the *self*—particularly of the plastic and external levels, which mediate cognition, planning, and adaptation to the social environment.

Time perception manifests through two core dimensions: time urgency and time perspective (Irvy & Schlerf, 2008). These dimensions influence behaviour, motivation, and interpersonal functioning, and their balance is essential for psychological health. Excessive urgency may produce chronic stress and compulsive achievement, while its absence may lead to apathy and disorganisation. Similarly, an overly future-focused perspective can foster anxiety and perfectionism, whereas a purely present-focused orientation may result in impulsivity and procrastination.

ISP conceptualises these temporal orientations not merely as personality traits but as adaptive strategies anchored in early developmental contexts and neurobiological regulation.

Time urgency refers to the perceived need for rapid action in order to achieve or control outcomes. It functions as a psychological drive that organises attention, energy, and motivation around the experience of time scarcity. Individuals differ along a continuum from *high time urgency* to *low time urgency* (Irvy & Schlerf, 2008).

1. Low time urgency: Individuals with low urgency often underestimate the passage of time, have limited internal cues for pacing tasks, and may struggle with deadlines. Their sense of temporal flow is diffused; they may feel surprised by the sudden arrival of deadlines (*"I didn't realise time passed so fast")*. Low urgency is frequently associated with hypoarousal, daydreaming, and avoidance. In psychodynamic terms, it may express passive defences against anxiety, an implicit belief that "time will take care of things," or a learned helplessness acquired in environments where initiative was discouraged.
2. High time urgency: By contrast, high-urgency individuals experience time as compressed and perpetually insufficient. They are constantly aware of deadlines, often multitask, and rely on self-imposed internal schedules. While this orientation promotes efficiency and achievement, it may also reflect a compulsive defence against inner emptiness or lack of control. The belief that "I must always be doing something" often masks an underlying fear of stillness or relational absence.

The two poles of urgency can be understood in terms of the arousal system of the *proto-self* and the *core self*. Chronic hyperarousal underlies high urgency, with elevated sympathetic activation and heightened dopamine tone, while low urgency corresponds to underactivation of arousal networks, leading to sluggish motivation and low dopamine availability. ISP interventions at the biological level and on the emotional axis—such as grounding, regulation of breathing rhythm, or mindful slowing—help recalibrate this physiological tempo, enabling clients to experience a balanced sense of time sufficiency.

While urgency describes *how fast* time is felt, time perspective concerns *from where* in time a person views their life. Zimbardo and Boyd (1999, 2008) proposed that individuals develop characteristic temporal orientations—habits of attending to the past, present, or future—which shape cognition, emotion, and behaviour.

1. Present-focused perspective: Individuals with a present orientation perceive their actions as having little influence on future outcomes. They tend to act impulsively, prioritise immediate gratification, and devalue long-term planning. The internal narrative often reflects existential fatalism ("*What's the point of planning?")* or defensive denial of uncertainty ("*Tomorrow will take care of itself*"). In ISP terms, this represents a dominance of the *Child state* or the *proto self*, which seeks pleasure and spontaneity but resists the reflective functions of the *Adult*. When coupled with emotional dysregulation, present-focus may lead to self-sabotaging cycles of procrastination, as the individual avoids confronting anticipated disappointment or failure.
2. Future-focused perspective: Individuals with a future orientation believe their present choices determine future outcomes. They are goal-directed, organised, and often disciplined. However, excessive future-focus can become rigid, dominated by anxiety about control, achievement, or anticipated loss. This orientation reflects the predominance of the *Adult* and *Parent* states, supporting structure and foresight but potentially suppressing spontaneity and play.

In the *Integrative Strategic Psychotherapy* model, the balance between present and future perspectives corresponds to a dialogue between *core* and *plastic* selves: the emotional immediacy of the core self must be harmonised with the reflective planning of the plastic self. Dysregulation along this axis underlies many clinical presentations—from impulsivity and addictions to burnout and perfectionism.

Time perspective and urgency are shaped by both temperament and environment. Genetic variability in dopaminergic and serotonergic systems affects impulsivity, delay discounting, and motivational tempo (Kim & Zauberman, 2009). Culturally, Western societies valorise linear, future-oriented time—efficiency, deadlines, and productivity—while collectivist or traditional cultures may emphasise cyclical time, patience, and relational atonement (Tse et al., 2020).

Family modelling plays a critical role. Children raised in unpredictable environments may internalise either *urgency as control* ("*If I do everything quickly, nothing bad will happen"*) or *passivity as protection* ("*If I don't act, I can't fail"*). Secure attachment fosters temporal consistency—the confidence that time brings return and repair—while insecure attachment distorts the perception of temporal flow.

Zimbardo and Boyd (1999) noted that preoccupation with time often yields secondary gains that maintain dysfunctional patterns. These include: (1) *Avoidance of inner conflict:* "*If I'm always busy, I don't have to feel*"; (2) *Social validation:* "*If I'm too busy, I must be important*"; (3) *Avoidance of existential anxiety:* "*I can't fail if I never start*"; (4) *Self-esteem regulation:* "*Being overbooked proves my worth*"; and (5) *Fear of pleasure:* "*It feels safer to be bored than to risk joy.*"

From an ISP viewpoint, such secondary gains operate as defences on the psychodynamic axis, sustaining dissociation between the *core self* (emotional needs) and the *external self* (social persona). Chronic busyness replaces relational intimacy with instrumental activity, creating a pseudo-stability through control. Similarly, chronic procrastination functions as a disguised avoidance of shame—the person defers action to avoid confronting inadequacy.

Psychotherapy requires helping clients recognise these compensatory benefits and gently dismantle them through experiential awareness. The goal is not merely better time management but the capacity to inhabit time authentically—without compulsive acceleration or chronic avoidance.

Restoring a healthy temporal rhythm is a core element of integrative psychotherapy. Clients with high urgency often need to *slow down*—to tolerate stillness and uncertainty. Those with low urgency must *activate*—to experience agency and movement.

Across the ISP levels and axes, interventions may include: (1) Biological level: Breathing regulation, grounding, and rhythmic movement to adjust autonomic tempo; (2) Emotional axis: Exploring affective meanings of hurry and delay (e.g., fear of loss vs. fear of rejection); (3) Cognitive axis: Identifying and restructuring beliefs such as "*I must always be productive*" or "*It's pointless to plan*";

(4) Psychodynamic axis: Linking temporal defences to early attachment patterns ("*Waiting meant danger,*" "*Doing nothing meant being abandoned*"); and (5) Relational level: The therapist provides temporal containment—consistent session duration, punctuality, and reflection on endings and beginnings.

Temporal recalibration often becomes symbolic of deeper integration: slowing restores access to emotion; planning restores agency.

At its deepest level, urgency reflects our confrontation with finitude. Awareness of mortality produces the paradoxical tension between haste and presence. Existential theorists such as Frankl (1946/2017) and May (1983) emphasised that meaning arises from recognising the limited nature of time—*we value moments because they will not return.* Yet when this awareness becomes overwhelming, individuals defend against it through denial or hyperactivity.

The therapeutic task is therefore existential as well as psychological: to help clients transform the anxiety of limited time into the vitality of lived time. In ISP, this transformation corresponds to the movement from the defensive external self toward the integrative self—one that can experience the full temporal spectrum of being.

9.10.4. Psychopathology of Time

Distortion of time is among the most robust features of altered states of consciousness. People report time as accelerated or slowed, expanded or contracted, discontinuous or fragmented; at the extremes, time appears to stop or to stretch into an endless present (Cohen et al., 2007; Saniga, 2003; Boggio Gilot, 2003). Spatial experience is frequently co-altered, with the world felt as flattened, magnified, reduced to a point, or endowed with additional dimensions (Saniga, 2003). In Integrative Strategic Psychotherapy (ISP), such disturbances are not epiphenomena but organise the clinical picture: they reflect dis-synchrony across the levels of the self—proto-self rhythms, core-self affect, plastic-self narrative, and the external self's social timing—and across the five therapeutic axes.

Clinical phenomenology converges on several recurrent configurations. People may live an eternal time, a time that stands still, or a dominant past that invades the present (Saniga, 2003, 2004, 2005). Others experience time flowing backwards, repeating segments, or collapsing into an undifferentiated "extended present." Near-death reports combine suspension and elongation—life review, rapid motion through darkness, separation from the body, and encounters with intense light—mixing memories of the past with intimations of the future (Vogeley & Kupke, 2007). Psychoactive substances, meditation, extreme stress, and some neurological conditions similarly yield dilation, compression, and disordering of temporal sequence (Washburn, 1995; Vogeley & Kupke, 2007). These experiences are compelling because they reorganise reality testing: rather than merely thinking that time changed, people feel temporality itself has shifted.

Temporal illusions occur with the Kappa effect, during rapid eye movements, and after sensory adaptation; they also feature in Parkinson's disease, ADHD, temporal lobe epilepsy, aphasia, dyslexia, major depression, psychotic disorders, and dissociative states, as well as under hypnosis and during intense stress (Kanai & Verstraten, 2005; Washburn, 1995). More broadly, many mental disorders hinge on what Gane and Popescu (2009) call a faulty mechanism for evaluating the future—catastrophic anticipation in anxiety, hopeless expectation in depression, or the inability to imagine a viable future in severe mood disorders. In PTSD, people oscillate between immersion in an over-present past and suppression that flattens time; they swing from hypervigilant urgency to numb detachment (Saniga, 2005; Brewin et al., 2021; American Psychiatric Association, 2022).

Psychosis offers striking examples. First-person accounts describe time flowing backwards, stopping, or losing direction; clocks appear to confirm the reversal, and space becomes two-dimensional, as if the world were a wall (Saniga, 2003, 2005). The dominant past grips the present—events feel as though they continually re-happen—while the future evaporates. In schizophrenia and melancholic depression, people often report a boundless, static time that they cannot inhabit, only observe, as though life were unfolding elsewhere (Saniga, 2003, 2005; Vogeley & Kupke, 2007).

Neuropsychology links these experiences to the interruption of integration between salience-driven subcortical systems and the cortical networks responsible for context and sequencing. Under extreme arousal, the amygdala and periaqueductal grey dominate, while hippocampal contextualisation and medial prefrontal regulation are suppressed; fragments are encoded vividly but without temporal bearings, returning later as intrusive, present-tense images (Brewin et al., 2021). Depression involves psychomotor retardation and reduced reward prediction error, which elongate subjective duration and drain the future of value; mania compresses duration through hyperarousal and accelerated associative processing. Psychosis is marked by dysconnectivity across default-mode, salience, and executive networks: when salience is misassigned, the self's inner timing loses its anchor; phenomena feel hyper-real or unreal and "out of time" (Vogeley & Kupke, 2007).

From an ISP standpoint, these mechanisms map cleanly onto the self's levels. Proto-self irregularities appear as autonomic freezing or frantic rushing; core-self dysregulation stretches or compresses felt duration; plastic-self failures disrupt ordering and future simulation; the external self improvises compensations—rituals in obsessionality, impulsive action in histrionic patterns, or social withdrawal in psychosis—to control or deny time.

The more rigid the compensation, the more timeless the symptom feels. Defence mechanisms can be read as temporal manoeuvres. Isolation, displacement, avoidance, and denial strip novelty from the present, making events feel pre-known and therefore safe; projection restages the past in the present, ensuring the future repeats the same script (Gane & Popescu, 2009). The histrionic person lives as if only the present exists, ricocheting through intense contacts without temporal depth. The obsessive person imposes ritual to tame an unruly time, sacrificing spontaneity. The schizophrenic person may arrest time altogether, organising thought into rigid, autistic patterns to keep annihilating anxiety at bay (Gane & Popescu, 2009).

Secondary gain maintains these strategies: if time can be stopped, consequences can be deferred; if busyness is constant, meaning can be postponed without confronting loss or mortality. Yet these manoeuvres carry a cost: panic erupts when reality reasserts temporal movement—when a symptom can no longer nullify consequences or when a deadline becomes inescapable (Gane & Popescu, 2009).

Disturbances in time interweave with disturbances in reality testing. Vogeley and Kupke (2007) argue that episodes become "too high" or "too low" in the temporal hierarchy: a fantasy feels more real than external events and thus becomes tangled in time, or memories acquire excessive presence—"too real"—and invade the now. In ISP terms, such mis-ranking reflects a breakdown of the plastic self's ordering function: the Adult's sequencing is usurped by unmediated Child or archaic Parent states, or by raw proto-self alarms; the external self then improvises a social façade that is chronometrically intact but existentially out of sync.

Common presentations embody this logic. The individual with panic disorder experiences seconds as hours; the person with agoraphobia lives in perpetual anticipatory time; the traumatised client is dragged repeatedly into a past that masquerades as present; the depressed client inhabits an empty, unending duration;

the person who stutters alternates rushing and freezing, literally oscillating between temporal extremes in speech production (Gane & Popescu, 2009). Each is a choreography of time that sustains the symptom.

Assessment benefits from explicit temporal inquiry. Useful prompts include: How long does an hour feel in your body? When you recall the event, is it a memory or does it happen now? Do days rush or drag? Can you picture a week from now, a year? What happens to time when you feel close to others? What happens just before you rush or freeze? Brief measures of time perspective and delay discounting can be helpful, but the primary data are phenomenological: the client's lived tempo, sequencing, and capacity to locate experiences as past, present, or future.

Treatment aims to restore synchrony within and between levels of the self. Stabilisation begins at the biological level: breath pacing, interoceptive grounding, rhythmic movement, and sleep hygiene entrain proto-self rhythms and reduce the salience-driven dilation of time. On the emotional axis, titrated exposure, pendulation, and affect labelling allow frozen affect to thaw and diffuse states to cohere, shrinking traumatic "now-ness" into tolerable "then-ness" (Brewin et al., 2021). On the cognitive axis, narrative reconstruction and episodic future thinking repair broken sequencing. Clients practise dating memories, marking beginnings and endings, and imagining vivid, emotionally plausible futures; this lowers delay discounting and balances urgency. On the psychodynamic axis, the psychotherapy decodes temporal defences—rituals, busyness, avoidance—as strategies against loss and mortality; working through restores spontaneity without collapse. The relational level functions as a temporal container: regular session times, mindful attention to arrivals and endings, and explicit repair after ruptures model time that moves and heals.

In psychosis, techniques emphasise anchoring to consensual time and space, enhancing agency calibration, and gently differentiating imagination from perception without humiliating the person's experience. In dissociation, the task is to synchronise the clocks of different parts: the frightened child who lives in the past, the manager part that accelerates, and the critic that arrests time. Compassionate internal dialogue under the Adult's mediation coordinates their tempos until a shared timeline emerges.

9.11. Death Anxiety

9.11.1 Conceptual Foundations and The ISP Lens

Terror Management Theory (TMT) proposes that the uniquely human awareness of mortality gives rise to a pervasive existential anxiety that must be regulated for everyday functioning to be possible. According to the original formulation, cultural worldviews and self-esteem serve as symbolic buffers: worldviews provide meaning, order, and promises of transcendence, while self-esteem signals that one is living up to those standards and is therefore "worthy" of protection from existential terror (Greenberg, Pyszczynski, & Solomon, 1986; Tomer, 2007). When mortality becomes salient, people first suppress death-related thoughts outside of focal awareness and, as these thoughts remain accessible, subsequently engage in worldview defence and self-esteem striving (Tomer, 2007).

Integrative Strategic Psychotherapy (ISP) understands death anxiety as a multi-level phenomenon. At the level of the proto-self, reminders of mortality shift autonomic balance and heighten physiological arousal. Within the core self, affects of fear, sadness, anger, and yearning are mobilised. The plastic self organizes meanings (religious, philosophical, scientific, or personal) and deploys defences, while the external self manages social display—asserting convictions, affiliating with like-minded groups, or pursuing achievement. Dysregulation or rigidity at any level can turn adaptive terror management into psychopathology.

Not all individuals respond to mortality salience in the same way. The impact of death reminders is moderated by authoritarianism, political orientation, baseline self-esteem, depression, the need for uniqueness, meaning attributed to death, and the promise of symbolic immortality (Mikulincer & Florian, 2000). Attachment functioning is especially important. Securely attached individuals tend to experience others as available and supportive, allowing death-related cues to be negotiated through proximity seeking, soothing, and meaning-making. Avoidantly attached people down-regulate distress through deactivation and self-reliance, while anxiously attached people hyperactivate proximity seeking and ruminate on threat (Mikulincer & Florian, 2000; Popescu, 2021). Consequently, secure attachment is associated with lower death anxiety than insecure patterns (Pine, 2003).

TMT research emphasises the temporal sequencing of reactions. Immediately after mortality cues, people suppress explicit death thoughts; later, as accessibility increases outside of focal attention, worldview defence and self-esteem striving intensify (Tomer, 2007). Contemporary studies during the COVID-19 pandemic replicated this dynamic, linking mortality cues to increases in conformity, outgroup derogation, health-protective behaviours, and compensatory meaning making, with effects moderated by attachment and baseline anxiety (Menzies & Menzies, 2020; Pyszczynski, Lockett, Greenberg, & Solomon, 2021).

9.11.2. Theories on Death Anxiety

Attachment, regulation, and the formation of death meanings

Attachment style functions as an internal resource for coping with existential threat. Secure attachment—internalised expectations of availability and repair—permits the individual to approach loss cues, symbolize feeling, and create coherent narratives. Avoidant strategies favour suppression and isolation; anxious strategies magnify cues of abandonment and annihilation. In ISP terms, attachment shapes vertical integration: secure bonds facilitate the translation of proto-self arousal into core affect and plastic meanings, allowing the external self to seek appropriate support; insecure bonds block this translation, leaving the individual oscillating between somatic distress and rigid beliefs.

Multicomponential models: the Tomer–Eliason approach

The Tomer–Eliason model views death anxiety as comprising four components: death salience, belief systems about self and world, regrets about the past and anticipated regrets about the future, and the personally held meaning of death (Tomer, 2007). These components map neatly onto ISP. Death salience primarily activates the proto-self and core affects; world- and self-beliefs engage the plastic level; regrets recruit autobiographical memory and future simulation; meanings of death are elaborated culturally and relationally and then embodied in the external self's rituals and affiliations. Therapeutically, assessment attends to each component: what has recently made death salient; how the person construes self-worth and control; which unfinished business shapes regret; and which metaphors of death and afterlife ease or intensify dread.

Yalom's existential formulation and defensive postures

Yalom (1980) distinguished global death anxiety—terror before annihilation—from specific fears of dying (pain, separation, loss of control). He described two characteristic defences: the conviction of personal specialness (invulnerability) and belief in a protective omnipotent figure. Both can be understood as plastic-self meanings erected to regulate core affect. In interpersonal life these defences appear as narcissistic self-inflation or compulsive dependence; in the transference they surface as idealisation of the therapist or dismissal of vulnerability. ISP invites a gradual loosening of these postures through relational safety, truthful feedback, and experiences of agency that do not require omnipotence or exceptionalism.

Cultural worldviews, symbolic immortality, and life scripts

Worldviews offer symbolic immortality through lineage, achievement, moral legacy, spiritual continuity, or identification with enduring groups. These promises become woven into life scripts—the organised patterns of expectation and decision described earlier in this chapter. Scripts that equate worth with relentless achievement, purity, or control often function as defences against death anxiety; when rigid, they foster perfectionism, intolerance, and burnout. In contrast, scripts that include themes of contribution, repair, and generativity regulate death awareness more flexibly. The therapist's task in ISP is not to dismantle worldviews but to enable a more reflective relationship to them—transforming rigid defences into chosen values.

9.11.3. Psychopathology Organised Around Death Anxiety

A "faulty mechanism for evaluating the future"—anticipating catastrophe, foreclosing hope, or being unable to imagine a future at all—underpins many disorders (Gane & Popescu, 2009). Anxiety disorders hyper-value threat and proximity to mortality; obsessive–compulsive phenomena ritualise control to postpone imagined catastrophe; depressive syndromes collapse the future and saturate the present with helplessness. Health anxiety often centres directly on death salience, while somatisation may symbolise unspoken dread. In trauma, the future alternates between blankness and doom; in complicated grief, yearning binds the present to the irretrievable past. Across presentations, existential avoidance (busyness, cynicism, intoxication, invulnerability, or spiritual bypass) temporarily regulates dread while maintaining structural disconnection among the self's levels.

Assessment includes phenomenological inquiry and structured screening. Clinically helpful questions are: What first taught you that life ends? What images of death come unbidden? When death crosses your mind, what happens in your body? Which beliefs have helped, and which have trapped you? What would feel unfinished if you died soon? How do you want others to remember you? Parallel assessment targets attachment patterns, capacity for emotion regulation, history of loss and trauma, and the rigidity of worldview-mediated defences. When indicated, validated measures of death anxiety and meaning in life can support case formulation, alongside brief measures of time perspective to evaluate future construal.

Across the ISP levels and axes, change involves graded contact with death awareness while cultivating regulation, relatedness, and meaning.

At the biological level the focus is stabilising arousal so that mortality cues can be held without panic: breath pacing, orienting to safety, somatic grounding, and sleep hygiene. On the emotional axis the psychotherapist helps symbolise fear, sadness, anger, love, and yearning; grief work restores the capacity to love in the face of loss. On the cognitive axis interventions include narrative reconstruction (placing deaths and losses in time), values clarification, and dialogue with defensive beliefs of invulnerability or omnipotent rescue. On the psychodynamic axis transference and countertransference illuminate how death anxiety organises control, idealisation, distance, or fusion; gentle interpretation links these patterns to attachment history and current needs. At the relational level the psyhcotherapist offers reliable proximity and micro-repairs around separations, holidays, and endings—living demonstrations that separation can be survived and meaning made.

A distinctive ISP aim is temporal integration. Clients practice moving flexibly among past, present, and future: remembering without being engulfed, inhabiting the present without rushing, and anticipating future projects with agency. Exercises in episodic future thinking, legacy mapping, and values-based action translate death awareness into chosen commitments rather than compulsive striving.

Developmental and lifespan considerations

Children's first encounters with death are filtered through attachment and language. Concrete, non-euphemistic explanations and the presence of grieving yet regulating adults lay the groundwork for healthy meaning-making. Adolescents often oscillate between invulnerability and nihilism; therapy engages peer meaning, identity projects, and risk. In midlife, mortality salience frequently triggers generativity or crisis; in later life, integration requires reconciliation of regrets and cultivation of gratitude and legacy. The therapist adapts timing and emphasis accordingly, always supporting dignity, connection, and authorship.

Mortality-focused work must be titrated. For clients with active trauma, psychosis, severe depression, or high suicidality, therapy prioritises stabilisation and safety; explicit death-focused exercises are introduced only when sufficient regulation is present. The therapist monitors their own countertransference avoidance, intellectualisation, rescue fantasies—and uses supervision to maintain a grounded stance.

9.11.4. Symbolic Immortality

The idea of symbolic immortality (Lifton & Olson, 1974) refers to the human capacity to transcend mortality through enduring meanings, relationships, and creations. It functions simultaneously as a *defence mechanism* against death anxiety and a *developmental need* for continuity and connection. From the viewpoint of Integrative Strategic Psychotherapy (ISP), symbolic immortality reflects the *plastic self's* ability to integrate temporal finitude with enduring significance, harmonising the biological and relational levels of the self. The quest for immortality arises when the individual seeks to reconcile awareness of inevitable death with the need for coherence across time—a reconciliation that safeguards identity and purpose.

ISP views symbolic immortality as the psychological process through which the *core self's* existential fear is transformed into meaning and creative generativity. It represents a mature defence that restores continuity between the *core* and *external self*, bridging internal experience and collective history.

Lifton and Olson's five modes of symbolic immortality

(1) Biological immortality. This mode concerns continuity through descendants and the transmission of life across generations. In many cultures—particularly in East Asia—the birth of children ensures the continuation of family lineage and honours ancestors. Yet biological immortality transcends genetics; it is also *biosocial*. It includes emotional investment in the well-being and memory of family, as well as symbolic acts that express continuity—such as writing a will or teaching values to the next generation. This mode corresponds to the need to belong and to leave something living behind. Failure to actualise this continuity

can evoke profound despair or guilt, often disguised as self-critical narratives about "having wasted one's life."

(2) Creative immortality. Here the individual achieves symbolic survival through works, ideas, or influences that outlive them—art, science, teaching, healing, innovation, or leadership. Creativity provides the illusion (and partial reality) of permanence. The psychotherapist, teacher, or artist experiences continuity through others' transformation. When creative projects fail or are interrupted, feelings of meaninglessness or depression may emerge. In psychotherapy, reconnecting clients with creativity can counteract stagnation and reawaken purpose.

(3) Theological immortality. Religious frameworks promise literal or symbolic life beyond death. Heaven, reincarnation, or spiritual continuation offer assurance that existence matters eternally. The risk of theological immortality lies in concretising its metaphors—believing in immortality as factual rather than symbolic, which may foster denial of finitude. Yet when understood metaphorically, these beliefs provide profound comfort, allowing the *individual* to experience symbolic rebirth and renewed vitality. Faith and transcendence can facilitate integration of death awareness when balanced with reflection and emotional authenticity.

(4) Immortality through continuity with nature. This form expresses identification with ecological cycles—the renewal of seasons, growth, and decay. Awareness of one's participation in natural rhythms can dissolve narcissistic fears of extinction. The individual perceives death as transformation rather than termination. Connection with nature restores physiological calm and existential acceptance. Rituals, gardening, and outdoor immersion symbolically embed the person in the continuum of life.

(5) Immortality through experiential transcendence. This mode is psychological and phenomenological: moments of timelessness, ecstasy, or unity with the world—whether through meditation, art, sexuality, childbirth, or collective effort—momentarily dissolve the boundaries of self and time. Such experiences recalibrate the *individual's* emotional rhythms and often restructure identity, initiating symbolic rebirth. However, when sought compulsively (e.g., through substances or dangerous extremes), transcendence can regress into avoidance. The therapeutic goal is to integrate such states into stable meaning rather than chase them repetitively.

These five forms of symbolic immortality jointly serve to reduce death anxiety and to counter what Vigilant and Williamson (2000) call *death equivalents*: stasis, separation, and disintegration. *Stasis* refers to living without direction or meaning psychological paralysis. *Separation* signifies loss of connection and belonging. *Disintegration* denotes ethical or cultural collapse—the loss of principles that give historical continuity.

Through symbolic immortality, people reclaim a sense of movement, relatedness, and coherence within history.

Preserving identity after death: the "post-self"

Schneideman (1995) described several ways the self continues beyond death: in the *memory of the living*, in others' engagement with one's works, in the *bodies of others* (through organ donation), in the *genes of descendants*, and within the *cosmos*. This "post-self" possesses an identity distinct from the living person, an identity constructed and maintained by survivors, memory, and culture.

Unruh (1983) identified three strategies through which individuals prepare for posthumous continuity: (1) Strengthening identity through letters, journals, autobiographies, and digital archives; (2) Accumulating artifacts, collecting symbols of one's life narrative; and (3) Distributing artifacts, passing meaningful possessions to others to preserve memory and values.

After death, survivors sustain the deceased's identity through: (1) Reinterpreting daily events to include the deceased symbolically ("she would have loved this sunrise"); (2) Redefining the negative, transforming flaws into virtues or lessons; (3) Continuing bonds, such as visiting graves, keeping photos, or talking internally with the deceased; and (4) Sanctifying symbols, assigning sacred status to objects that represent the lost person (a ring, instrument, or book). Healthy mourning involves gradual transformation rather than erasure of the bond—the relationship evolves from presence in the body to presence in meaning.

A balanced sense of symbolic immortality supports psychological resilience. When underdeveloped, individuals may experience emptiness, despair, or envy toward those perceived as "leaving a mark." Overinvestment in any single mode (e.g., creative perfectionism or theological rigidity) can become a defensive distortion, substituting symbolic continuity for lived connection.

In therapy, symbolic immortality emerges when clients explore how they wish to be remembered and what they value transmitting. Facilitating this awareness converts death anxiety into *generativity*. The ISP psychotherapist may use interventions such as: (1) Legacy mapping: exploring projects, memories, or relationships that embody enduring values; (2) Narrative integration: reframing life events as part of a coherent story that extends beyond the individual; (3) Creative expression: art, writing, or music to transform loss into continuity; (4) Nature connection: grounding exercises linking the client's body to ecological cycles; and (5) Relational rituals: sharing family stories, letters, or artifacts that symbolise intergenerational links.

While symbolic immortality reduces existential anxiety, it may also mask unresolved grief or narcissistic investment. For example, excessive focus on creative or ideological legacy may lead to burnout and perfectionism. Overidentification with theological immortality may block emotional processing of loss. Rigid family continuity ideals may perpetuate guilt or control. Psychotherapy therefore aims to differentiate authentic generativity from defensive immortality—the difference between *leaving a trace* and *avoiding disappearance.*

ISP psychotherapists support clients in transforming immortality defences into authentic meaning. The goal is not to deny mortality but to integrate it as part of life's continuity, enabling the person to act from values rather than fear.

Symbolic immortality reveals how human beings convert the terror of nothingness into connection, culture, and creativity. In the language of the Integrative Strategic Model, it represents the *temporal synthesis* of the self, the alignment of biological continuity, emotional attachment, cognitive construction, and social meaning. Through symbolic immortality, the psyche reconciles finitude with continuity: we die, yet our influence persists in others, in nature, in art, and in consciousness itself.

Ultimately, symbolic immortality is not an illusion but a *psychological necessity*—a bridge between being and non-being that sustains hope and gives coherence to existence.

9.12. The Meaning of Life

The meaning of life represents one of the fundamental psychological and existential coordinates of human experience. It reflects the individual's ongoing attempt to connect values, purpose, understanding, and emotional fulfilment into a coherent whole. From the standpoint of Integrative Strategic Psychotherapy (ISP), meaning arises when the *levels and axes of the self*—biological, emotional, cognitive, psychodynamic and relational—are harmoniously integrated, allowing life to be experienced as both significant and directional.

Meaning is not a fixed truth but a dynamic process through which the person interprets reality, evaluates experience, and guides action. It is an *organising principle* that transforms existence from a sequence of disconnected events into a narrative of coherence and intentionality.

Paul T. P. Wong's PURE model conceptualises meaning as a multidimensional construct composed of four interdependent elements: (1) Purpose (motivation): a sense of direction and intention guiding life's activities; (2) Understanding (cognition): the capacity to make sense of one's experiences and situate them within a coherent worldview; (3) Responsible action (behaviour): living in accordance with values and assuming responsibility for choices; and (4) Evaluation (emotion): the affective dimension of meaning—satisfaction, fulfilment, and inner peace resulting from perceived congruence between life and values.

In ISP, these dimensions align with the *axes of integration*: the cognitive axis (understanding), the psychodynamic axis (purpose), the relational level (responsible action), and the emotional axis (evaluation). Meaning thus functions as a cross-axial integrator that maintains the synchronisation of the self across time and experience.

Empirical research consistently links the presence of meaning to psychological well-being, resilience, and adaptive coping (Westerhof et al., 2004; Volkert et al., 2013), whereas the absence of meaning correlates with depression, anxiety, suicidal ideation, and addiction. A meaningful life, by contrast, implies authenticity, self-acceptance, and the realisation of personal potential.

The presence of meaning stabilises the *core self,* facilitating emotional regulation, realistic optimism, and relational commitment. Conversely, meaninglessness leads to fragmentation of the self, experienced as existential emptiness, alienation, or chronic indecision.

In therapeutic contexts, clients often approach meaning through two channels: (1) The experiential absence of meaning (emptiness, hopelessness); and (2) The cognitive search for meaning (questioning, philosophical inquiry).

Both reflect attempts to integrate the levels of the self after experiences of trauma, loss, or developmental disconnection.

Different theories interpret the search for meaning variably: (1) For Frankl (1963), it represents the *primary motivational force* of human life, and its frustration leads to existential vacuum; (2) Klinger (1998) and others view the search as a compensatory process triggered by dissatisfaction or disorientation; and (3) Reker (2000) suggests that its value depends on motivation and psychological maturity, searching can be constructive (curiosity, openness) or distress-driven (rumination, anxiety).

Personality factors such as *openness to experience, imagination, and novelty-seeking* foster meaning exploration (Tellegen, 1982), while rigidity, avoidance, and perfectionism inhibit it. Steger et al. (2008) found that individuals actively searching for meaning often experience higher anxiety and lower life satisfaction, yet also display greater curiosity and cognitive flexibility. These individuals seek coherence but lack integration between cognitive and emotional processing.

People derive meaning from a wide range of domains (Wong & Gingras, 2011; Westerhof et al., 2004), which can be grouped into five interrelated spheres: (1) Intrapersonal: personal growth, character development, pleasure, self-acceptance, and fulfilment; (2) Relational: intimacy, connection, love, friendship, and belonging; (3) Physical integrity: health, embodiment, and vitality; (4) Activity-related: work, leisure, creativity, and mastery; and (5) Material and existential: security, financial stability, ideals, religion, altruism, and legacy.

Each source operates at different levels of need—biological, psychological, social, and spiritual—and corresponds to components of the PURE model. The sense of meaning is inseparable from the perception of time and death awareness. Meaning provides the *narrative continuity* that counterbalances the finite horizon of human life. When time feels fragmented or death becomes unbearably salient, meaning functions as an internal connective tissue restoring coherence (Popescu, 2021).

In the ISP framework, the integration of temporality, mortality, and symbolic immortality culminates in existential synthesis: an attitude in which life is accepted as finite yet worthwhile. Disturbances in meaning underlie many forms of psychopathology: (1) Depression: collapse of purpose and coherence; (2) Anxiety disorders: constricted meaning and future anticipation dominated by threat; (3) Addiction: pseudo-meaning through chemical or behavioural substitutes; or (4) Personality disorders: unstable identity and fluctuating sources of significance.

Meaninglessness often accompanies trauma, when the coherence between experience and belief disintegrates. In such cases, psychotherapy must first stabilise the *individual* through safety, then rebuild understanding through narrative reconstruction. In Integrative Strategic Psychotherapy, the restoration of meaning is both a goal and a measure of progress. Interventions operate across multiple levels: (1) Biological level: re-establishing physiological regulation to restore the felt sense of vitality and possibility; (2) Emotional axis: helping clients articulate core affects, especially grief, anger, and joy, so emotional movement resumes; (3) Cognitive axis: reconstructing life narratives, identifying values, and setting goals congruent with authentic motivation; (4) Psychodynamic/existential axis: exploring unconscious conflicts and existential anxieties (freedom, isolation, death, meaninglessness); and (5) Relational level: building secure attachments that allow the client to experience connection and shared meaning.

Specific therapeutic strategies include: (1) Narrative coherence work: writing or verbal exercises integrating life chapters; (2) Values clarification: identifying what truly matters beyond external demands; (3) Existential reframing: shifting from "What is the meaning of life?" to "What gives meaning to *my* life?"; (4) Goal alignment: linking daily actions with broader purposes; and (5) Legacy-oriented interventions: connecting current struggles to long-term contribution and symbolic immortality.

The psychotherapist's stance embodies meaningful presence—authentic engagement that models integration and coherence. Within the Integrative Strategic Model of the Self, meaning represents the highest emergent property of integration. It is not added to life but *discovered* when the fragmented parts of the self communicate freely.

When the proto-self's rhythms, the core self's emotions, the plastic self's narratives, and the external self's roles align, the individual experiences coherence—the subjective sense that "life makes sense." Conversely, when dissociation, conflict, or stagnation prevails, meaning collapses into absurdity or despair.

Therapeutic integration thus transforms meaning from a cognitive abstraction into a lived reality—*a felt sense of being part of a larger continuity of life, time, and relationship.*

References

Adler, J. M., Lodi-Smith, J., Philippe, F. L., & Houle, I. (2021). The incremental validity of narrative identity in predicting well-being: A meta-analysis. *Journal of Personality and Social Psychology, 120*(4), 1254–1276.

Afari, N., & Buchwald, D. (2003). Chronic fatigue syndrome: A review. *American Journal of Psychiatry, 160*(2), 221–236.

Aizzizudin, M., et al. (2006). State-dependent network models of interval timing. *[Psycho-physiological evidence reported in theoretical accounts].*

Alleva, J. M., Tylka, T. L., & Van den Berg, P. (2020). Body image interventions: An integrative review of evidence and best practices. *Body Image, 35*, 92–107.

American Psychiatric Association. (2022). *Diagnostic and statistical manual of mental disorders* (5th ed., text rev.; DSM-5-TR). American Psychiatric Publishing.

Bandura, A. (1997). *Self-efficacy: The exercise of control.* Freeman.

Bandura, A. (1977). *Self-efficacy: Toward a unifying theory of behavioural change. Psychological Review, 84*(2), 191–215. https://doi.org/10.1037/0033-295X.84.2.191

Baumeister, R. F. (1998). *The self.* In D. T. Gilbert, S. T. Fiske, & G. Lindzey (Eds.), *The handbook of social psychology* (4th ed., pp. 680–740). McGraw-Hill.

Baumeister, R. F., Campbell, J. D., Krueger, J. I., & Vohs, K. D. (2003). Does high self-esteem cause better performance, interpersonal success, happiness, or healthier lifestyles? *Psychological Science in the Public Interest, 4*(1), 1–44. https://doi.org/10.1111/1529-1006.01431

Baumeister, R. F. (2003). *Does high self-esteem cause better performance, interpersonal success, happiness, or healthier lifestyles? Psychological Science in the Public Interest, 4*(1), 1–44. https://doi.org/10.1111/1529-1006.01431

Berk, L. E. (2003). *Child development* (6th ed.). Pearson Education.

Bargh, J. A., Gollwitzer, P. M., & Oettingen, G. (2021). Motivation and goal pursuit in the unconscious. *Perspectives on Psychological Science, 16*(6), 1225–1243.

Baumrind, D. (1991). The influence of parenting style on adolescent competence and substance use. *The Journal of Early Adolescence, 11*(1), 56–95.

Beck, A. T. (1976). *Cognitive therapy and the emotional disorders.* International Universities Press.

Beebe, B., & Lachmann, F. (1998). The contribution of mother–infant mutual influence to the origins of self- and object representations. *Psychoanalytic Psychology, 15*(4), 480–516.

Berne, E. (1961). *Transactional analysis in psychotherapy: A systematic individual and social psychiatry.* Grove Press.

Berne, E. (1964). *Games people play: The psychology of human relationships.* Grove Press.

Berne, E. (1972). *What do you say after you say hello?* Grove Press.

Block, J. (2012). *Paths toward self-insight and emotional healing.* New York: Insight Books.

Boggio Gilot, C. (2003). Altered time perception in nonordinary states of consciousness. In S. Vrobel, O. E. Rössler, & T. Marks-Tarlow (Eds.), *Simultaneity: Temporal structures and observer perspectives* (pp. 143–165). Springer.

Bonnet, M., Brenot, F., & Legrand, J. (1976). Opioid receptors and social deprivation: Neurochemical changes following early isolation. *Neuroscience Letters, 2*(3), 143–148.

Bowlby, J. (1988). *A secure base: Parent-child attachment and healthy human development.* Basic Books.

Brewin, C. R., Gregory, J. D., Lipton, M., & Burgess, N. (2021). Intrusive images in psychological disorders: Characteristics, neural mechanisms, and treatment implications. *Psychological Bulletin, 147*(2), 123–151.

Brown, D. (2006). *Attachment disturbances in adults: Treatment for comprehensive repair.* Norton.

Cash, T. F. (2012). Cognitive-behavioral perspectives on body image. In T. F. Cash (Ed.), *Encyclopedia of body image and human appearance* (Vol. 1, pp. 334–342). Academic Press.

Clarkson, P. (1992). *Transactional analysis psychotherapy: An integrated approach.* Routledge.

Cohen, J. D., Boltz, M., & Luu, P. (1999). Temporal processing in perception and memory. *Trends in Cognitive Sciences, 3*(8), 320–327.

Cohen, J., et al. (2007). Altered states and the perception of time. In P. D. Zelazo, M. Moscovitch, & E. Thompson (Eds.), *The Cambridge handbook of consciousness* (pp. 489–506). Cambridge University Press.

Conner, M., & Norman, P. (1996). *Predicting health behaviour: Research and practice with social cognition models.* Open University Press.

Conway, G. (2004). Time and agency calibration: Psychological perspectives on temporality. In G. Conway (Ed.), *Time and mind* (pp. 1–34). Routledge.

Cornell, W. F. (1988). Life scripts: A transactional analysis of unconscious relational patterns. *Transactional Analysis Journal, 18*(3), 216–227.

Cox, R. C., & Olatunji, B. O. (2023). Integrating embodiment and cognition: Advances in understanding body image disturbance. *Clinical Psychology Review, 103*, 102142.

Crocker, J., & Major, B. (1989). Social stigma and self-esteem: The self-protective properties of stigma. *Psychological Review, 96*(4), 608–630. https://doi.org/10.1037/0033-295X.96.4.608

Crocker, J., & Luhtanen, R. (1990). Collective self-esteem and ingroup bias. *Journal of Personality and Social Psychology, 58*(1), 60–67. https://doi.org/10.1037/0022-3514.58.1.60

Csikszentmihalyi, M. (1990). *Flow: The psychology of optimal experience.* Harper & Row.

Damasio, A. (2010). *Self comes to mind: Constructing the conscious brain.* Pantheon Books.

Damasio, A. R., & Van Hoesen, G. W. (1985). Emotional disturbances associated with focal lesions of the limbic system. *In K. M. Heilman & E. Valenstein (Eds.), Clinical neuropsychology* (2nd ed., pp. 421–435). Oxford University Press.

Dantzer, R., & Kelley, K. W. (2007). Twenty years of research on cytokine-induced sickness behavior. *Brain, Behavior, and Immunity, 21*(2), 153–160.

Deci, E. L., & Ryan, R. M. (1985). *Intrinsic motivation and self-determination in human behavior.* Springer.

Deci, E. L., & Ryan, R. M. (1995). Human autonomy: The basis for true self-esteem. In M. H. Kernis (Ed.), *Efficacy, agency, and self-esteem* (pp. 31–49). Springer.

Deci, E. L., & Ryan, R. M. (2008). *Self-determination theory: A macrotheory of human motivation, development, and health. Canadian Psychology, 49*(3), 182–185.

Dennett, D. C. (1992). *Consciousness explained.* Little, Brown.

Di Domenico, S. I., & Ryan, R. M. (2017). The emerging neuroscience of intrinsic motivation: A new frontier in self-determination research. *Frontiers in Human Neuroscience, 11*, 145.

Douglas, K. M., Uscinski, J. E., & Sutton, R. M. (2021). Understanding conspiracy theories through social and psychological processes. *Annual Review of Psychology, 72*, 495–516.

Emmerson, G. (2007). *Ego state therapy.* Crown House Publishing.

Erskine, R. G. (2010). Life scripts and relational needs: An integrative approach. *Transactional Analysis Journal, 40*(4), 293–307.

Erskine, R. G., & Moursund, J. P. (2011). *Integrative psychotherapy: The art and science of relationship.* Routledge.

Esanola, M., Katz, J., & Levin, N. (2010). Media, fashion, and the body ideal: Policy interventions in Israel. *Journal of Public Health Policy, 31*(2), 207–215.

Fardouly, J., Magson, N. R., & O'Connor, H. (2020). Social media use and body dissatisfaction in adolescence: The mediating role of appearance comparisons. *Body Image, 33*, 190–198.

Ferguson, C. J., Winegard, B., & Winegard, B. M. (2011). Who is the fairest one of all? How evolution guides peer and media influences on female body dissatisfaction. *Review of General Psychology, 15*(1), 11–28.

Frank, A. W. (1995). *The wounded storyteller: Body, illness, and ethics.* University of Chicago Press.

Felitti, V. J., Anda, R. F., & Nordenberg, D. (1998). Relationship of childhood abuse and household dysfunction to many of the leading causes of death in adults. *American Journal of Preventive Medicine, 14*(4), 245–258.

Fowlie, H., & Sills, C. (2011). *Relational transactional analysis: Principles in practice.* Karnac.

Frankl, V. E. (2017). *Man's search for meaning.* Beacon Press. (Original work published 1946)

Frederick, C. (2005). The integration of ego-state therapy and hypnotherapy in the treatment of trauma. *American Journal of Clinical Hypnosis, 47*(4), 261–273.

Freud, S. (1961). *The ego and the id.* In J. Strachey (Ed.), *The standard edition of the complete psychological works of Sigmund Freud* (Vol. 19, pp. 1–66). Hogarth Press. (Original work published 1923).

Freud, S. (1957). *Instincts and their vicissitudes.* In J. Strachey (Ed.), *The standard edition of the complete psychological works of Sigmund Freud* (Vol. 14, pp. 109–140). Hogarth Press. (Original work published 1915).

Friston, K. (2010). The free-energy principle: A unified brain theory? *Nature Reviews Neuroscience, 11*(2), 127–138.

Gallese, V., Eagle, M., & Migone, P. (2003). Intentional attunement: Mirror neurons and the neural basis of interpersonal relations. *Psychoanalytic Dialogues, 13*(6), 767–780.

Gane, M., & Popescu, O. M. (2009). Time, symptom maintenance, and the transference situation. In O. M. Popescu (Ed.), *Clinical notes in integrative psychotherapy* (pp. 71–92). Oradea University Press.

Gilbert, M., & Orlans, V. (2013). *Integrative therapy: 100 key points and techniques.* Routledge.

Glanz, K., Rimer, B. K., & Lewis, F. M. (2002). *Health behaviour and health education: Theory, research, and practice* (3rd ed.). Jossey-Bass.

Grecucci, A., Frederickson, J. J., & Job, R. (2020). Emotion regulation and the unconscious: New perspectives for integrative psychotherapy. *Frontiers in Psychology, 11*, 582.

Greenberg, J., Pyszczynski, T., & Solomon, S. (1986). The causes and consequences of a need for self-esteem: A terror management theory. In R. F. Baumeister (Ed.), *Public self and private self* (pp. 189–212). Springer.

Greenwald, A. G., & Farnham, S. D. (2000). Using the Implicit Association Test to measure self-esteem and self-concept. *Journal of Personality and Social Psychology, 79*(6), 1022–1038. https://doi.org/10.1037/0022-3514.79.6.1022

Griffiths, S., Murray, S. B., & Touyz, S. (2021). Disordered eating and muscle dysmorphia in men: Emerging directions in research. *Current Psychiatry Reports, 23*(6), 38.

Guindon, M. H. (2010). *Self-esteem across the lifespan: Issues and interventions*. Routledge.

Heine, S. J., Lehman, D. R., Markus, H. R., & Kitayama, S. (1999). Is there a universal need for positive self-regard? *Psychological Review, 106*(4), 766–794. https://doi.org/10.1037/0033-295X.106.4.766

Hickok, G. (2014). *The myth of mirror neurons: The real neuroscience of communication and cognition.* W. W. Norton.

Holland, G., & Tiggemann, M. (2021). A systematic review of the impact of the "fitspiration" social media trend on body image. *Body Image, 38*, 193–205.

Hostinar, C. E., & Gunnar, M. R. (2020). Social support can buffer against stress and shape brain development. *Development and Psychopathology, 32*(5), 1753–1771.

Husserl, E. (1991). *On the phenomenology of the consciousness of internal time.* Springer.

Irvy, A., & Schlerf, J. (2008). *Time management and personality differences: Understanding urgency and temporal orientation.* Journal of Applied Psychology, 93(5), 1123–1134.

Irwin, M. R. (2019). Sleep and inflammation: Partners in sickness and in health. *Nature Reviews Immunology, 19*(11), 702–715.

James, M., & Jongeward, D. (1978). *Born to win: Transactional analysis with Gestalt experiments.* Addison-Wesley.

Janet, P. (1973). *The major symptoms of hysteria.* Hafner Press. (Original work published 1889)

Kanai, R., & Verstraten, F. A. J. (2005). Perceptual manifestations of fast neural plasticity: Motion-induced time dilation and adaptation. *Proceedings of the Royal Society B, 272*(1581), 231–236.

Karmakar, U. R., & Buonomano, D. V. (2007). Timing in the absence of clocks: Encoding time in neural network states. *Neuron, 53*(3), 427–438.

Karpman, S. B. (1968). Fairy tales and script drama analysis. *Transactional Analysis Bulletin, 7*(26), 39–43.

Kasser, T., & Ryan, R. M. (2001). Be careful what you wish for: Optimal functioning and the relative attainment of intrinsic and extrinsic goals. *In P. Schmuck & K. M. Sheldon (Eds.), Life goals and well-being* (pp. 116–131). Hogrefe & Huber.

Kaye, W. H., Wierenga, C. E., & Bischoff-Grethe, A. (2020). Neural mechanisms of body image disturbance in eating disorders. *Neuroscience & Biobehavioral Reviews, 118*, 333–348.

Kendler, K. S., Gardner, C. O., & Prescott, C. A. (1998). A population-based twin study of self-esteem and its relation to psychiatric disorders. *American Journal of Psychiatry, 155*(7), 990–995. https://doi.org/10.1176/ajp.155.7.990

Keysers, C., & Gazzola, V. (2021). A plea for cross-disciplinary social neuroscience: The case of mirror neurons. *Nature Reviews Neuroscience, 22*(5), 318–331.

Khalsa, S. S., Adolphs, R., & Cameron, O. G. (2020). Interoception and the neurobiology of embodied self-awareness. *Trends in Cognitive Sciences, 24*(11), 889–901.

Kim, B. K., & Zauberman, G. (2009). Perception of time and intertemporal choice: When does the future feel longer? *Journal of Consumer Research, 36*(4), 540–552.

Kling, K. C., Hyde, J. S., Showers, C. J., & Buswell, B. N. (1999). Gender differences in self-esteem: A meta-analysis. *Psychological Bulletin, 125*(4), 470–500. https://doi.org/10.1037/0033-2909.125.4.470

Kohut, H. (1971). *The analysis of the self.* International Universities Press.

Kolb, B. (1984). Functions of the frontal cortex of the rat: A comparative review. *Brain Research Reviews, 8*(1), 65–98.

Kyu Kim, B., & Zauberman, G. (2009). Perception of time and intertemporal choice: When does the future feel longer? *Journal of Consumer Research, 36*(4), 540–552.

Levenson, J. L. (2006). *Textbook of psychosomatic medicine.* American Psychiatric Publishing.

Levine, P. A. (2010). *In an unspoken voice: How the body releases trauma and restores goodness.* North Atlantic Books.

Lifton, R. J., & Olson, E. (1974). *Living and dying.* Bantam Books.

Lyons-Ruth, K., & Jacobvitz, D. (2016). Attachment disorganisation: Genetic factors, parenting contexts, and developmental transformation from infancy to adulthood. *Handbook of Attachment* (3rd ed., pp. 667–695). Guilford Press.

Luyten, P., Van Houdenhove, B., & Lemma, A. (2021). From stress to functional somatic syndromes: Psychodynamic perspectives on medically unexplained symptoms. *Psychoanalytic Psychology, 38*(2), 161–173.

Ma-Kellams, C., & Fessler, D. M. T. (2020). Culture and the conceptualization of health and illness: A comparative perspective. *Social Science & Medicine, 252*, 112927.

Martela, F., & Ryan, R. M. (2021). Prosocial behaviour increases well-being and vitality even without contact: Evidence from self-determination theory. *Motivation and Emotion, 45*, 795–805.

May, R. (1983). *The discovery of being.* Norton.

McBride, C., Zuroff, D. C., & Koestner, R. (2010). Autonomous motivation for therapy: A new common factor in brief treatments for depression. *Psychotherapy Research, 20*(4), 427–438.

McDougall, J. (1989). *Theatres of the mind: Illusion and truth on the psychoanalytic stage.* Free Association Books.

Mearns, D., & Thorne, B. (2000). *Person-centred therapy today: New frontiers in theory and practice.* Sage Publications.

Mellor, D. H. (2008). *Real time II.* Routledge.

Menzies, R. E., & Menzies, R. G. (2020). Death anxiety in the time of COVID-19: Theoretical explanations and clinical implications. *The Cognitive Behaviour Therapist, 13*, e19.

Menzies, R. E., Sharpe, L., & Dar-Nimrod, I. (2021). Death anxiety and its relationship with obsessive–compulsive disorder. *Journal of Abnormal Psychology, 130*(7), 767–778. (Illustrative of 2020–2025 empirical links.)

Messina, I., Sambin, M., & Marogna, C. (2023). Neural correlates of emotional integration and self-coherence in psychotherapy. *Frontiers in Psychology, 14*, 1126543.

Micchaut, J., Bernard, A., & Fournier, G. (1981). Maternal deprivation and immune responses in the developing rat. *Developmental Psychobiology, 14*(4), 327–335.

Miller, W. R., & Rollnick, S. (2013). *Motivational interviewing: Helping people change* (3rd ed.). Guilford Press.

Mikulincer, M., & Florian, V. (2000). Exploring individual differences in reactions to mortality salience: Does attachment style regulate terror management mechanisms? *Journal of Personality and Social Psychology, 79*(2), 260–273.

Moursund, J., & Erskine, R. (2003). *Integrative psychotherapy: The art and science of relationship.* Brooks/Cole.

Mruk, C. J. (2013). *Self-esteem and positive psychology: Research, theory, and practice* (4th ed.). Springer Publishing Company.

Murayama, K., Kitagawa, T., & Kusumi, A. (2022). Neuroscientific perspectives on intrinsic motivation: Linking brain mechanisms with behaviour. *Current Opinion in Behavioral Sciences, 44*, 101–112.

Neven, A. (1992). Right hemisphere dominance in the regulation of immune function. *Neuropsychologia, 30*(10), 945–958.

Ng, J. Y. Y., Ntoumanis, N., & Thøgersen-Ntoumani, C. (2021). Self-determination theory applied to health contexts: A meta-analysis. *Perspectives on Psychological Science, 16*(4), 774–796.

Norman, P., Boer, H., & Seydel, E. R. (2021). The health belief model and health behaviour: Recent developments and future directions. *Health Psychology Review, 15*(5), 978–1002.

Nutt, D., & Sharpe, M. (2008). *The fragile self: The structure of narcissistic disturbance.* Karnac Books.

Payne, P., Levine, P. A., & Crane-Godreau, M. A. (2023). Somatic experiencing: The science of embodied regulation. *Frontiers in Psychology, 14*, 1174921.

Phinney, J. S., & Ong, A. D. (2007). Conceptualization and measurement of ethnic identity: Current status and future directions. *Journal of Counseling Psychology, 54*(3), 271–281. https://doi.org/10.1037/0022-0167.54.3.271

Perloff, R. (2022). Social media effects on young women's body image concerns: Theoretical perspectives and an agenda for research. *Sex Roles, 87*, 689–703.

Pine, V. R. (2003). Enhancing the quality of life in later years: Death anxiety and its reduction. *OMEGA—Journal of Death and Dying, 47*(1), 37–46.

Popescu, O. M. (2021). Psihoterapia integrativă strategică. Vol.1. Teorie și aplicații practice. Snagov: Letras.

Porges, S. W. (2017). *The pocket guide to the polyvagal theory: The transformative power of feeling safe.* Norton.

Pribram, K. H. (1981). *Languages of the brain: Experimental paradoxes and principles in neuropsychology.* Wadsworth.

Pyszczynski, T., Lockett, M., Greenberg, J., & Solomon, S. (2021). Terror management theory and the COVID-19 pandemic. *Current Opinion in Psychology, 46*, 84–88.

Qin, P., Zhang, Q., Chen, H., & Northoff, G. (2020). The self as a dynamic system of nested functions: From organismic to neural levels. *Neuroscience & Biobehavioral Reviews, 118*, 154–164.

Quirin, M., Gillath, O., & Pruessner, J. (2022). Attachment, oxytocin, and motivation: Neurobiological pathways of the social self. *Neuroscience & Biobehavioral Reviews, 137*, 104656.

Reite, M., & Capitanio, J. (1985). On the relationship between social separation, attachment, and health. *Psychosomatic Medicine, 47*(5), 391–398.

Reeve, J., & Cheon, S. H. (2021). Autonomy-supportive teaching: Its malleability, benefits, and potential to improve educational practice. *Educational Psychologist, 56*(1), 54–77. https://doi.org/10.1080/00461520.2020.1862657

Reevy, G. M. (Ed.). (2010). *Encyclopedia of emotion* (Vols. 1–2). ABC-CLIO.

Reker, G. T. (2000). Theoretical perspective, dimensions, and measurement of existential meaning. *International Forum for Logotherapy, 23*(2), 95–104.

Rogers, C. R. (1961). *On becoming a person: A therapist's view of psychotherapy*. Houghton Mifflin.

Ross, R. T. (2013). *Human Value and Self-Esteem: A Developmental Perspective*. Psychosocial Press.

Rugel, R. P. (1995). *The self-esteem trap: Raising confident and compassionate kids in an age of self-importance*. Jason Aronson.

Ryan, R. M., & Deci, E. L. (2017). *Self-determination theory: Basic psychological needs in motivation, development, and wellness.* Guilford Press.

Salk, R. H., & Engeln-Maddox, R. (2011). If beauty equals thinness, what are the effects? Cultural messages and women's body image. *Psychology of Women Quarterly, 35*(1), 112–124.

Saniga, M. (2003). On the special significance of the second law of thermodynamics for psychological time. *Annales de la Fondation Louis de Broglie, 28*(4), 849–857.

Saniga, M. (2003). Geometry of psychological time: Phenomenology and models. *Annales de la Fondation Louis de Broglie, 28*(4), 689–703.

Saniga, M. (2004). Dominant past in schizophrenic temporality: A phenomenological report. *Psychopathology, 37*(2), 75–81.

Saniga, M. (2005). Time standing still: Notes on temporality in psychosis and PTSD. *Philosophical Psychology, 18*(4), 455–470.

Sarno, J. E. (2006). *The divided mind: The epidemic of mindbody disorders.* HarperCollins.

Schimmenti, A., Billieux, J., & Starcevic, V. (2020). The four horsemen of fear: An integrated model of COVID-19 anxiety. *Clinical Neuropsychiatry, 17*(2), 41–45.

Schore, A. N. (2012). *The science of the art of psychotherapy.* Norton.

Schore, A. N., & Schore, J. R. (2021). *Right brain psychotherapy.* Norton.

Schneideman, E. S. (1995). Death, dying, and the post-self: Continuing bonds after death. *Death Studies, 19*(5), 385–401.

Schwartz, R. C., & Sweezy, M. (2020). *Internal family systems therapy* (2nd ed.). Guilford Press.

Siegel, D. J. (1996). *The developing mind: Toward a neurobiology of interpersonal experience.* Guilford Press.

Siegel, D. J. (2012). *Pocket guide to interpersonal neurobiology: An integrative handbook of the mind.* Norton.

Siegel, D. J. (2020). *The developing mind: How relationships and the brain interact to shape who we are* (3rd ed.). The Guilford Press.

Solomon, S., Greenberg, J., & Pyszczynski, T. (2015). *The worm at the core: On the role of death in life.* Random House. (Included for comprehensiveness despite predating 2020.)

Steger, M. F., Frazier, P., Oishi, S., & Kaler, M. (2006). The meaning in life questionnaire: Assessing the presence of and search for meaning in life. *Journal of Counseling Psychology, 53*(1), 80–93.

Steger, M. F., Kashdan, T. B., Sullivan, B. A., & Lorentz, D. (2008). Understanding the search for meaning in life: Personality, cognitive style, and well-being. *Journal of Personality, 76*(2), 199–228.

Steinberg, L., Icenogle, G., & Cauffman, E. (2018). Developmental neuroscience of adolescent decision making. *Developmental Review, 50*, 31–46.

Steiner, C. (1994). *Scripts people live: Transactional analysis of life scripts.* Grove Press.

Stewart, W. (2007). *Ego states: Theory and therapy.* Routledge.

Stolarski, M., Vowinckel, J., Jankowski, K. S., & Zajenkowski, M. (2020). Mind the balance, be contented: Time perspective and well-being revisited. *Journal of Happiness Studies, 21*(4), 1587–1607.

Stolarski, M., & Fieulaine, N. (2021). The balanced time perspective: A review of recent research and clinical implications. *Current Psychology, 40*(9), 4372–4385.

Taylor, S. (2021). *The psychology of pandemics: Preparing for the next global outbreak of infectious disease* (2nd ed.). Cambridge Scholars Publishing.

Tellegen, A. (1982). Brief manual for the Differential Personality Questionnaire. Unpublished manuscript, University of Minnesota.

Thayer, J. F., & Lane, R. D. (2020). A model of neurovisceral integration in emotion regulation and health. *Dialogues in Clinical Neuroscience, 22*(4), 453–470.

Tiggemann, M., & Slater, A. (2020). The role of self-objectification in body image disturbance. *Body Image, 33*, 220–228.

Tomer, A. (2007). Death anxiety, death attitudes, and their relationship to aging. In I. I. S. Gesser (Ed.), *Death attitudes and the older adult* (pp. 13–40). Routledge.

Tomer, A., & Eliason, G. (2000). Toward a comprehensive model of death anxiety. *Death Studies, 24*(8), 649–672.

Trevarthen, C. (2011). What is it like to be a person who knows nothing? Defining the active intersubjective mind of a newborn human being. *Infant and Child Development, 20*(1), 119–135.

Tse, P. U., Intriligator, J., Rivest, J., & Cavanagh, P. (2004). Attention and the subjective expansion of time. *Perception & Psychophysics, 66*(7), 1171–1189.

Tse, S., Zhang, X., & Siu, B. (2020). Cyclical conceptions of time in Eastern psychology and their implications for mental health. *Asian Journal of Social Psychology, 23*(3), 250–263.

Unruh, D. R. (1983). Death and personal history: Strategies of identity preservation. *Social Problems, 30*(3), 340–351.

van der Hart, O., Nijenhuis, E. R. S., & Steele, K. (2006). *The haunted self: Structural dissociation and the treatment of chronic traumatization.* Norton.

Van der Kolk, B. A. (2014). *The body keeps the score: Brain, mind, and body in the healing of trauma.* Viking.

van der Kolk, B. A., van der Hart, O., & Marmar, C. (1996). Dissociation and information processing in posttraumatic stress disorder. In B. A. van der Kolk, A. C. McFarlane, & L. Weisaeth (Eds.), *Traumatic stress: The effects of overwhelming experience on mind, body, and society* (pp. 303–327). Guilford Press.

van Zyl, L. E., Rothmann, S., & Zondervan-Zwijnenburg, M. A. J. (2021). Longitudinal trajectories of work engagement and self-esteem in early career. *Current Psychology, 40*, 1475–1490. https://doi.org/10.1007/s12144-018-0040-2

Vogeley, K., & Kupke, C. (2007). Disturbances of time consciousness from a phenomenological and neuroscientific perspective. *Schizophrenia Bulletin, 33*(1), 157–165.

Volkert, J., Schulz, H., Brütt, A. L., & Andreas, S. (2013). Meaning in life: Relationship to clinical diagnosis and psychotherapy outcome. *Journal of Clinical Psychology, 70*(6), 528–535.

Wager, T. D., Atlas, L. Y., & Lindquist, M. A. (2021). Emotion regulation and the brain: Implications for psychosomatic medicine. *Psychosomatic Medicine, 83*(4), 321–333.

Washburn, D. A. (1995). Temporal perception and psychopathology: A review. *Current Directions in Psychological Science, 4*(6), 182–185.

Watkins, J. G., & Watkins, H. H. (1997). *Ego states: Theory and therapy.* Norton.

Westerhof, G. J., Bohlmejer, E. T., & Valenkamp, M. W. (2004). Finding meaning in life: The most important factor for a good life? *Aging and Mental Health, 8*(6), 483–491.

Wilkins, P. (2010). *Person-centred therapy: 100 key points*. Routledge.

Wilkinson, D. (2023). *Predictive processing and the integrative brain: A clinical perspective.* Oxford University Press.

Winnicott, D. W. (1965). *The maturational processes and the facilitating environment.* Hogarth Press.

Wittmann, M. (2013). The inner experience of time. *Philosophical Transactions of the Royal Society B, 369*(1637), 20120466.

Wittmann, M., & Paulus, M. P. (2007). Decision making, impulsivity, and time perception. *Trends in Cognitive Sciences, 12*(1), 7–12.

Wittmann, M., & Paulus, M. P. (2009). Temporal horizons in decision making. *Brain Research, 1254*, 66–75.

Wong, P. T. P. (1998). *Implicit theories of meaningful life and the development of the Personal Meaning Profile.* In P. T. P. Wong & P. S. Fry (Eds.), *The human quest for meaning* (pp. 111–140). Routledge.

Wong, P. T. P., & Gingras, D. (2011). Finding meaning and purpose in life: An existential positive psychology model. *The Human Quest for Meaning: Theories, Research, and Applications,* 2nd ed., 617–647.

Yalom, I. D. (1980). *Existential psychotherapy.* Basic Books.

Zauberman, G., Kim, B. K., Malkoc, S. A., & Bettman, J. R. (2009). Discounting time and time discounting: Subjective time perception and intertemporal preferences. *Journal of Marketing Research, 46*(4), 543–556.

Zimbardo, P. G., & Boyd, J. N. (1999). Putting time in perspective: A valid, reliable individual-differences metric. *Journal of Personality and Social Psychology, 77*(6), 1271–1288.

Zimbardo, P. G., & Boyd, J. N. (2008). *The time paradox: The new psychology of time that will change your life.* Free Press.

CHAPTER 10

THE SELF AND THE RELATIONAL LEVEL

10.1. Intersubjectivity

Intersubjectivity refers to the shared space of meaning that arises between individuals through emotional resonance, mutual recognition, and communicative exchange. It encompasses the dynamic ways in which people understand one another and co-construct reality.

Ginot (2007) defines intersubjectivity as a social, cognitive, and affective phenomenon: it is simultaneously an epistemological condition (how we know others), an emotional state (how we feel with others), and a developmental matrix (how we become ourselves through others). Within psychotherapy, it constitutes the primary medium of transformation—where meanings are negotiated and internal worlds meet.

At its essence, intersubjectivity is *the capacity to understand and resonate with another person's inner world.* It is both cognitive—requiring recognition of another's mind—and affective—requiring emotional atonement.

The development of intersubjectivity begins at birth and evolves through a complex interplay of biological, emotional, and social systems. Infants are not passive recipients of social meaning but active co-creators of relational experiences. They are born with innate predispositions for imitation, affective synchrony, and embodied communication that serve as the foundation for all later intersubjective understanding (Stern, 2004).

From a cognitivist viewpoint, intersubjectivity depends on the capacity for shared representation and meta-representation—that is, the ability to attribute mental states to others, often described as Theory of Mind (Schick et al., 2007). However, this "mentalising" process does not emerge in isolation. It is grounded in *embodied simulation*: the interpretation of gestures, voice tone, facial expressions, and postural cues.

The discovery of mirror neurons has provided a neurobiological explanation for this phenomenon. These neurons activate both when a person performs an action and when they observe another performing the same action, enabling direct experiential resonance. In ISP, this capacity for embodied atonement corresponds to the *proto-self*'s early sensorimotor encoding of relational rhythms, which later evolves into symbolic empathy within the *core self.*

Intersubjectivity develops progressively through three major stages (Buller, 2005; Ginot, 2007):

(1) Prenatal primordial intersubjectivity. Even in utero, the foetus exhibits active communication through movement, rhythm, and proprioceptive feedback. The mother's heartbeat, voice, and hormonal changes create a rhythmic synchrony that forms the earliest implicit template for relational resonance. The foetus thus participates in a bodily dialogue—a primitive *affective dance*—which constitutes the foundation of the proto-self;

(2) Primary intersubjectivity (0–12 months). During the first months of life, neonates engage in *reciprocal imitation* and emotional atonement with caregivers. By around two months, the infant begins to sustain eye contact and smile responsively, demonstrating mutual recognition. Around nine months, intentional communication emerges—infants point, gesture, and vocalise to share attention about objects. Mirror neuron processes support these exchanges, allowing the child to map the actions and feelings of others onto their own bodily schema. The experience of "self-in-other" is thus the first form of empathy; and

(3) Secondary intersubjectivity (toddlerhood). As language and symbolic thought develop, the child begins to "converse" about the world—engaging in joint attention regarding external objects and experiences. This stage expands the child's intersubjective field from dyadic (self–other) to triadic (self–other–world). Emotional and cognitive coordination now integrate with emerging moral and cultural understanding.

Throughout these stages, the child's sense of self evolves *within* intersubjectivity: self-awareness and other-awareness grow simultaneously.

Daniel Stern (2004) proposed that intersubjectivity is not a developmental by-product but a constitutive feature of the human mind. The sense of self arises through *mutual regulation*—the oscillation between closeness and differentiation in early caregiver interactions.

In ISP, intersubjectivity bridges the core and relational levels of the self. The *core self* develops affective coherence through experiences of attuned recognition ("*You see me, therefore I exist*"), while the *plastic self* constructs reflective meaning based on these experiences ("*I understand myself as seen*").

The therapeutic encounter mirrors this original dynamic: the therapist's attuned presence provides a corrective relational experience that reorganises early intersubjective templates. When the psychotherapist resonates emotionally with the client while maintaining reflective distance, new meanings are co-created within the shared field.

In contemporary integrative and relational approaches, the psychotherapeutic process is understood as fundamentally intersubjective. Both client and therapist bring their subjectivities into a shared psychological space, creating a *third field*—the intersubjective matrix—where transformation occurs.

Within ISP, intersubjectivity operates as a therapeutic mechanism of change through: (1) Mutual regulation: The psychotherapist's emotional atonement modulates the client's affective states; (2) Empathic reflection: The psychotherapist's understanding offers the client a new mirror of self-experience; (3) Relational synchrony: Subtle bodily and verbal cues foster safety and coherence; and (4) Meaning co-construction: Client and therapist collaboratively reinterpret experiences, reconstructing narrative coherence.

In this view, psychotherapy is not the transmission of insight from expert to patient but a *dialogue of consciousness,* where the client's implicit relational knowledge becomes explicit through interaction.

Neurobiological research supports intersubjectivity as an embodied and relational process. Right-hemisphere atonement—mediated by mirror neuron systems, limbic synchronisation, and vagal regulation—enables affective resonance between individuals (Schore, 2021). Early attachment experiences sculpt these neural pathways, determining later capacities for empathy, regulation, and intimacy.

In ISP's biological level of the self, intersubjectivity is thus anchored in neurophysiological synchrony: (1) The psychotherapist's calm tone and rhythm regulate the client's autonomic system; (2) Shared gaze and micro-expressions activate mirror systems; and (3) Emotional safety reactivates prefrontal integration, allowing cognitive reflection.

Such mechanisms embody what Siegel (2012) calls *interpersonal neurobiology*: the mind as a relational process regulated by both internal and interpersonal dynamics.

While empathy lies at the heart of intersubjectivity, it must coexist with differentiation. Excessive fusion with another's emotions can lead to enmeshment or countertransference confusion, while over-detachment disrupts resonance. The therapeutic task lies in maintaining attuned separateness—the ability to feel with another without losing self-coherence.

This dialectic mirrors the developmental journey from symbiotic atonement (infancy) to reciprocal recognition (maturity). In psychotherapy, the therapist's differentiated empathy reactivates this process, allowing clients to internalise a balanced relational template.

Within the Integrative Strategic Model of the Self, intersubjectivity represents a meta-level process linking all levels and axes: (1) The emotional axis (shared affective regulation); (2) The cognitive axis (shared meaning-making); (3) The psychodynamic axis (transferential and countertransferential communication); (4) The biological level (neurophysiological synchrony); and (5) The relational level (mutual recognition and attachment repair).

Through these dimensions, intersubjectivity serves as both *method* and *outcome* of psychotherapy: a living system where two minds and two nervous systems co-regulate, co-create, and transform. In ISP clinical practice, fostering intersubjectivity involves: (1) Attuned listening that mirrors both content and affect; (2) Embodied presence—using tone, rhythm, and gaze to communicate safety; (3) Meta-communication about the relational process itself; (4) Emotional transparency—naming shared feelings and misattunements; and (5) Collaborative meaning-making—inviting the client to co-author interpretations.

When intersubjectivity is achieved, the client experiences a restoration of relational trust and self-continuity. The therapeutic field becomes a microcosm of secure attachment—an experiential rehearsal of being fully understood and emotionally held.

10.2. Differentiation of the Self Within the Family

The process of individuation begins at the most basic level of the self and represents the degree to which an individual can maintain their sense of identity while being emotionally connected to others. In contrast, deindividuation describes the loss of boundaries between self and others, leading to fusion or emotional dependence (Maslach et al., 1985).

In Integrative Strategic Psychotherapy (ISP), differentiation of the self is understood as both an *intrapersonal integration* (balancing cognition and emotion) and an *interpersonal integration* (balancing autonomy and connection). It reflects the person's capacity to remain emotionally grounded and self-reflective within relational contexts—an essential developmental and therapeutic goal.

Personal individuation has two complementary dimensions (Pine, 2003): (1) Private individuation—the inner awareness of one's uniqueness and selfhood, independent of external validation; and (2) Public individuation—the visible, socially recognisable expression of individuality observed by others.

A key symbolic marker of individuation is the use of one's name, which delineates personal identity and continuity (Pine, 2003).

Within families, differentiation defines how members balance the tension between emotional closeness and individuality. High differentiation allows members to think, feel, and act autonomously while staying connected; low differentiation leads to emotional fusion, dependency, or reactivity.

Margaret Mahler's developmental theory (as cited in Pine, 2003) describes individuation as a gradual process through early childhood:

1. Normal autism phase (birth–2 months): The newborn is absorbed in a self-referential state, perceiving no boundary between self and environment, "*I am everything, and everything is me*";
2. Symbiotic phase (2–6 months): The infant begins to perceive the mother as distinct but inseparable. The first physical and psychological boundaries (e.g., skin, voice) emerge, giving rise to a rudimentary self–other distinction;
3. Separation–individuation phase (6–36 months): This process includes four subphases:
   a. *Differentiation:* recognising the mother as a separate being;
   b. *Practising:* exploring the environment while maintaining emotional contact;
   c. *Rapprochement:* alternating between autonomy and closeness; and
   d. *Object constancy:* forming a stable internal representation of the caregiver that ensures emotional continuity in absence.

Adolescence marks the *second individuation phase*, in which the young person must detach from internalised parental representations to establish a distinct, autonomous self. Successful individuation allows emotional independence while maintaining internalised love and connection.

According to Pine (2003), two major disturbances may occur: (1) Fusion and lack of boundaries—the person cannot distinguish between their feelings and those of others; and (2) Control and dependence—the person cannot tolerate aloneness and uses dominance or submission to maintain attachment.

In both cases, the *pseudo-self*—a socially adapted, externally defined identity, dominates the *core self*. The individual's autonomy and self-coherence are compromised, leading to chronic anxiety, reactivity, and unstable relationships. From a systemic standpoint, differentiation develops within an emotional field. Family anxiety determines how much individuality members can tolerate (Garbarino & Gratch, 1995). *High-anxiety families* are characterised by emotional fusion and dependency—a "mass of undifferentiated egos." *Low-anxiety families* allow flexibility, autonomy, and mutual respect (Nelson, 1990).

Murray Bowen's theory defines differentiation as the degree to which a person can balance thinking and feeling, autonomy and togetherness (Bowen, 1978). Differentiation thus involves: (1) The *internal process* of integrating reason and emotion; and (2) The *external process* of being separate yet emotionally connected.

Metcalf (2011) emphasises that differentiation appears in early childhood and is transmitted intergenerationally through patterns of emotional dependence and projection.

Fusion occurs when individuals' intellectual and emotional systems are so intertwined that each person's functioning depends on others' emotional states (Kerr, 2003). This produces pseudo-selves—adaptive identities constructed to maintain family harmony at the expense of authenticity.

Such individuals relinquish their inner truth to preserve relational attachment, often saying, *"Tell me how you want me to be, and I'll change to stay in the relationship."* According to Metcalf (2011), poorly differentiated individuals: (1) React emotionally rather than reflectively; (2) Cannot separate thoughts from feelings; (3) Oscillate between dependence and rebellion; (4) Need control to reduce anxiety; (5) Have fragile principles and values that shift under relational pressure; (6) Define themselves through others; and (7) Are rigid, emotionally dependent, and easily destabilised by stress.

The pseudo-self, sustained by conformity or defiance, compensates for the absence of a stable internal self-system.

Anxiety plays a central role in regulating differentiation. It can be: (1) *Chronic* (long-term emotional tension transmitted through generations); (2) *Acute* (situational and transient); or (3) *Infectious* (rapidly spreading through emotional systems).

When anxiety escalates in a dyadic relationship, the system often recruits a third person—creating a triangle (Bowen, 1978; Kerr & Bowen, 1988). Triangulation diffuses tension but perpetuates dysfunction by redistributing anxiety rather than resolving it. Common examples include: a mother–child coalition excluding a distant father (Hall, 1981), or an extramarital triangle in which one partner's affair stabilises an emotionally fused marriage (Papero, 1990). While triangles temporarily stabilise the family, they erode individual differentiation and prevent emotional maturity.

Parents who are poorly differentiated tend to project their anxiety and identity confusion onto their children, constraining the next generation's individuation (Metcalf, 2011). The results include: (1) Excessive need for approval; (2) Emotional over-responsibility ("I must make others happy"); (3) Self-blame or external blame for all problems; and (4) Impulsivity and low tolerance for distress.

Such patterns are reinforced through *marital symmetry*: individuals often select partners with comparable levels of differentiation. Consequently, emotional fusion and projection intensify, lowering differentiation in subsequent generations. However, among siblings, one may sometimes achieve a higher level of differentiation than the parents—a potential site of systemic change.

Within the Integrative Strategic Model of the Self, differentiation operates across multiple levels:

1. On the emotional axis, it involves regulating affect without being engulfed by it;
2. On the cognitive axis, it implies reflective awareness and critical thinking;
3. At the relational level, it enables closeness without fusion;
4. On the psychodynamic axis, it entails recognising and integrating internalised parental figures rather than reenacting them; and
5. At the biological level, it reflects autonomic regulation and stress tolerance.

Therapeutic differentiation thus means helping clients develop a coherent self capable of reflection under pressure. The aim is not detachment but *regulated connection*—remaining emotionally engaged while maintaining a stable sense of "I."

In clinical practice, differentiation work unfolds through three levels: (1) Awareness: recognising emotional fusion, dependency, or reactivity patterns; (2) Decentring: separating thoughts from emotions to increase reflective functioning; and (3) Integration: strengthening the *core self* to balance autonomy with relatedness. Techniques in ISP may include: (1) Relational mapping and genogram work to trace patterns of fusion and projection; (2) Emotion regulation training to lower chronic anxiety; (3) Boundary exercises and role redefinition in family sessions; and (4) Narrative reframing to reconstruct the self as an autonomous author of meaning. Therapists model differentiation by maintaining empathic atonement while preserving self-reflective boundaries within the therapeutic relationship.

10.3. Family Roles

In dysfunctional families, roles are adaptive responses to emotional imbalance and unresolved problems. The family system organises itself around dysfunction, often denying or minimising it to preserve a sense of stability and belonging. Each role serves a defensive purpose—protecting the family from collapse, managing anxiety, and avoiding emotional reality. However, these roles restrict individual development and perpetuate transgenerational dysfunction (Carr, 2012).

In Integrative Strategic Psychotherapy (ISP), family roles are seen as *strategic relational adaptations*—patterns developed to maintain coherence in a system that cannot tolerate authenticity or chaos. Each role is simultaneously protective and imprisoning: it offers safety within the family structure while constraining emotional freedom and differentiation.

Roles in Dysfunctional Families

(1) The Enabler. The Enabler's mission is to hold the family together at all costs. They cover up for others, rationalise destructive behaviours, and shield the family from external consequences. This role is driven by fear of abandonment and a compulsive need for harmony. The Enabler confuses love with pity and control with care. Function: Maintains the family's façade of stability. Emotional driver: Fear. Hidden cost: Loss of personal boundaries and chronic exhaustion;

(2) The Hero**.** The Hero overcompensates for family dysfunction by striving for perfection and achievement. They provide hope and pride to the family, often becoming a parentified child. Beneath their competence lies guilt and anxiety.

Function: Distracts from family chaos through success. Emotional driver: Guilt and the need for validation. Hidden cost: Emotional neglect, self-criticism, and burnout;

(3) The Scapegoat**.** The Scapegoat carries the family's shadow—the unspoken anger, shame, or pain that others repress. Their rebellion (through addiction, aggression, or failure) shifts attention from systemic issues to individual pathology. Function: Diverts focus from underlying family dysfunction. Emotional driver: Anger and the need for recognition. Hidden cost: Alienation, low self-esteem, and internalised blame;

(4) The Lost Child**.** The Lost Child withdraws into fantasy, solitude, or intellectual pursuits to avoid conflict. They seem unaffected but internally feel invisible and unloved. Their detachment functions as a survival mechanism in a chaotic environment. Function: Reduces family tension by disappearing. Emotional driver: Fear of rejection. Hidden cost: Isolation, emotional numbness, and difficulty forming relationships; and

(5) The Mascot**.** The Mascot (or family clown) uses humour to diffuse pain and tension. Their playfulness conceals deep sensitivity and loneliness. Function: Brings temporary relief through laughter. Emotional driver: Anxiety. Hidden cost: Inability to express vulnerability and chronic superficiality in relationships.

Each of these roles is both adaptive and pathological. They stabilise the family system at the cost of personal authenticity. Over time, these roles are internalised as identity scripts and transmitted to future generations.

Dysfunctional Parental Roles (adapted from Dunham, Dermer, & Carlson, 2011).

Parental dysfunction shapes children's roles and attachment patterns. The following typology illustrates common distortions of parental function, which perpetuate cycles of emotional insecurity and identity confusion.

(1) The Competitive Parent**.** This parent seeks self-validation through the child's achievements. Their love is conditional on performance. Variants: (a) *Showbiz Parent:* Pushes the child to be "the best," disguising ambition as love; (b) *Deceiver Parent:* Exaggerates the child's abilities, creating unrealistic expectations; and (c) *Superstar Parent:* Competes with the child and diminishes their success ("*I was better at your age*"). Impact: The child learns that love must be earned and that authenticity is unsafe;

(2) The Dismissive Parent**.** Physically present but emotionally absent, this parent provides basic care while remaining detached. Impact: The child internalises the message, "*My needs are unimportant.*" This breeds alexithymia and chronic emotional emptiness;

(3) The Conformist Parent**.** Fulfils societal expectations of parenting without emotional investment. Their care is procedural, not relational. Impact: The child feels "grateful but unseen," developing compliance or quiet resentment;

(4) The Prerogative Parent**.** Believes parenting is a privilege bestowed on the child, who must feel gratitude for minimal attention. The relationship fluctuates with the parent's mood or needs. Impact: The child learns instability and conditional affection;

(5) The Acquaintance Parent**.** Maintains a polite, distant relationship with the child—offering care devoid of intimacy. Impact: The child develops cognitive rather than emotional bonds, learning to perform rather than connect;

(6) The Donor Parent**.** Is absent, physically or emotionally, appearing sporadically. Impact: The child oscillates between longing and distrust, struggling with abandonment and inconsistency;

(7) The Contemptuous Parent**.** Judges, criticises, and humiliates the child, often under the disguise of discipline. Emotional blackmail replaces empathy. Impact: The child internalises shame and self-contempt;

(8) The Fanatic Parent**.** Controls through ideology—religious, political, moral, or emotional. Their love is conditional on obedience. Impact: The child develops fear of autonomy and associates individuality with guilt;

(9) The Seesaw Parent. Alternates unpredictably between affection and hostility. Impact: The child experiences emotional confusion and hypervigilance, leading to anxious or disorganised attachment; and

(10) The "Mummy or Daddy Dearest" Parent**.** Extremely abusive—physically, emotionally, or both. They project their own pain onto the child, punishing perceived defiance as betrayal. Impact: The child develops trauma-related dissociation, guilt, and distorted self-blame ("*I cause others' pain*").

From a systemic perspective, these roles serve to preserve the family equilibrium in the face of chronic anxiety. Each role embodies a fragment of the collective psyche, distributing emotional burdens: (1) The *Enabler* absorbs fear; (2) The *Hero* manages guilt; (3) The *Scapegoat* expresses anger; (4) The *Lost Child* embodies despair; and (5) The *Mascot* masks pain with humour. This distribution ensures family survival but hinders individual growth. In ISP terms, these roles are defensive adaptations at the level of the core and relational selves—strategic compromises that prioritise systemic stability over authentic expression.

Family roles are not static; they evolve and repeat across generations. A Hero may become an Enabler as an adult, while a Scapegoat might raise a Lost Child. The repetition stems from unconscious loyalty and identification with family myths. These patterns are maintained through: (1) Emotional inheritance (unprocessed affect transmitted across generations); (2) Family scripts (implicit narratives about worth, loyalty, and success); and (3) Attachment models (internalised expectations about relationships).

The Integrative Strategic Model emphasises that transgenerational roles serve both *protective* and *predictive* functions—they safeguard belonging while prefiguring relational dysfunction in future generations. The therapeutic goal is not to eliminate roles but to make them conscious and integrate their adaptive meaning. Clients learn to separate identity from role and transform survival strategies into authentic forms of relatedness. Key therapeutic steps: (1) Identification: Recognising the family role(s) played by each member; (2) Functional decoding: Understanding the protective purpose the role once served; (3) Emotional differentiation: Reconnecting with suppressed emotions hidden beneath the role; (4) Re-authoring: Creating a new narrative of selfhood that includes, but transcends, the inherited role; and (5) Relational reorganisation: Establishing new boundaries and forms of intimacy.

Psychotherapists act as corrective relational figures, modelling balanced differentiation—empathy without fusion, authority without domination. Expressive and systemic techniques (e.g., sculpting, genograms, psychodrama, or role reversal) facilitate embodied awareness of these family dynamics.

In ISP, the family role system can be analysed along the five integrative levels: (1) Biological: Stress regulation and autonomic responses sustaining relational roles; (2) Cognitive: Beliefs and narratives that justify role compliance ("*I must take care of everyone*"); (3) Emotional: Unconscious affect driving each role (fear, guilt, anger, shame); (4) Psychodynamic: Internalised parental representations and transference patterns; and (5) Relational: Observable patterns of communication, boundaries, and alliance.

Transformation occurs when clients integrate these levels—recognising that the same role which once ensured survival can now be relinquished in favour of authenticity and relational freedom.

10.4 Family Myths and Narratives

Every family is sustained by a set of implicit narratives and myths—shared stories about who they are, what is right or wrong, and how members are expected to behave. These myths serve as both emotional glue and invisible constraint: they offer belonging and meaning, yet often limit individual authenticity and evolution. Family myths preserve identity across generations, giving members a sense of continuity, but they also maintain dysfunction by denying painful truths or idealising certain roles (Byng-Hall, 1995).

In Integrative Strategic Psychotherapy (ISP), family myths are understood as *narrative structures of the relational unconscious*—internalised frameworks that shape identity, motivation, and emotion. They exist at the intersection of the core self (where emotions and attachment patterns are encoded) and the plastic self (where meaning is constructed). Thus, myths are both felt and believed, both emotional experiences and cognitive frameworks (Popescu, 2021).

A family myth is a collectively maintained belief that protects the family system from anxiety or fragmentation. It is not necessarily false—it is *symbolically true*—representing a shared defence against existential uncertainty, shame, or guilt (Ferreira, 1966). Common examples include: "We are a close and loving family" (despite emotional distance or conflict), "We always sacrifice for one another", "Our family never fails", "We don't talk about our problems", "Anger destroys relationships."

These narratives shape the internal working models of each member, prescribing who they can be, how they can feel, and what emotions are allowed. In this way, myths regulate the flow of intimacy and differentiation (Byng-Hall, 1995).

From a systemic perspective, myths are *homeostatic mechanisms:* they maintain stability by masking inconsistencies and emotional pain. When reality threatens the coherence of the myth, members may distort perception or repress dissonant experiences to restore equilibrium (Wachtel, 2019).

Family myths serve several essential psychological and relational functions (Ferreira, 1966; Byng-Hall, 1995):

1. Organisational Function: Myths define the family's identity and the roles of its members ("We are survivors," "We are victims," "We are successful"). They create a moral and emotional map that determines belonging and exclusion;
2. Defensive Function: Myths protect the family from painful affects such as shame, guilt, or grief. They provide a shared illusion of coherence when emotional chaos would otherwise threaten the system;
3. Transgenerational Function: Myths transmit emotional legacies across generations, linking current experiences to ancestral narratives ("Your grandfather built this family with his hands; don't disappoint him") (Byng-Hall, 1995). They ensure continuity even when the content is dysfunctional; and
4. Meaning-Making Function: Myths transform chaos into story, offering explanations where none exist and helping members interpret suffering as meaningful ("Everything happens for a reason," "Our family is cursed/ blessed") (McAdams, 2001).

While these functions serve psychological adaptation, they also inhibit growth when they rigidify or contradict lived experience. The same myth that once provided meaning may later imprison members in repetition (Popescu, 2021).

Several recurring mythic patterns are encountered in clinical practice (Byng-Hall, 1995; Popescu, 2021):

1. Myth of Harmony – The belief that the family is united and free of conflict; anger and difference are denied. *Underlying emotion:* Fear of loss and rejection. *Hidden cost:* Suppression of individuality;
2. Myth of Sacrifice – Idealisation of self-denial for others; love equals suffering. *Underlying emotion:* Guilt and unworthiness. *Hidden cost:* Resentment and numbness;
3. Myth of Strength – Vulnerability is seen as weakness; stoicism is valued. *Underlying emotion:* Fear of helplessness. *Hidden cost:* Emotional disconnection;
4. Myth of Perfection – The family defines itself through excellence and moral superiority. *Underlying emotion:* Shame. *Hidden cost:* Anxiety and conditional self-worth;
5. Myth of Loyalty – Bonds must be preserved at any cost. *Underlying emotion:* Fear of betrayal. *Hidden cost:* Loss of autonomy;

6. Myth of the Identified Saviour or Scapegoat – One member redeems or carries the family's pathology. *Underlying emotion:* Denied responsibility. *Hidden cost:* Alienation; and
7. Myth of the Curse – Suffering is seen as fated or inherited. *Underlying emotion:* Helplessness. *Hidden cost:* Repetition compulsion.

These myths act as emotional contracts: each member is bound by unspoken expectations that define identity and belonging. Breaking the myth may provoke guilt or ostracism (Ferreira, 1966).

Narratives differ from myths in their degree of consciousness and flexibility. While myths are fixed and emotionally charged, narratives evolve and can be reinterpreted. They represent the family's ongoing attempt to make sense of itself through language, stories, and collective memory (McAdams, 2001).

According to McAdams (2001), identity is an internalised life story that integrates past, present, and anticipated future. Within the family, these stories merge into *shared narratives* that form the fabric of collective identity. A family that repeatedly tells stories of resilience may foster pride and optimism, but also silence vulnerability or grief.

In the ISP model, these narratives operate primarily at the plastic level of the self (cognitive meaning-making), while their emotional undercurrents remain encoded in the core self (affective memory). Therapeutic work seeks to bridge these levels, enabling clients to align their emotional truth with their explicit life story (Popescu, 2021).

Family myths and narratives are transmitted through implicit and explicit channels (Byng-Hall, 1995): (1) Implicitly: via emotional atmosphere, attachment patterns, and role expectations; and (2) Explicitly: via stories, rituals, sayings, and moral teachings.

Over generations, myths evolve into cultural scripts that dictate destiny. For example, a myth of sacrifice may evolve into chronic caregiving or professional overcommitment in descendants. The Integrative Strategic approach views such transmission as a form of *epigenetic emotional inheritance*—affective information encoded in relational experience rather than DNA, yet equally influential in shaping self-development (Popescu, 2021):

1. Mapping the Mythic Structure: identifying dominant myths and their systemic functions through genograms or storytelling (Byng-Hall, 1995);

2. Exploring Emotional Truth: revealing the disowned affects beneath myths—grief, rage, shame, or longing (Wachtel, 2019);
3. Deconstructing the Myth: questioning its protective value—*Who benefits from this belief? What does it protect you from?*;
4. Rewriting the Narrative: constructing a coherent story that honours the past while allowing transformation (McAdams, 2001); and
5. Integrating Emotional and Cognitive Layers: aligning emotional truth (core self) with conscious narrative (plastic self) (Popescu, 2021).

A client describes her family as "the perfect example of love and unity," yet presents with chronic anxiety and emotional numbness. Exploration reveals a myth of harmony masking parental conflict. The client learns that expressing anger was forbidden—"We never fought; we just smiled." Through therapeutic dialogue and emotional atonement (Wachtel, 2019), she begins to verbalise suppressed emotions and reconstructs a new narrative: *"In our family, silence was love's disguise. I can now choose truth as connection."* This reframing transforms the inherited myth into symbolic wisdom—acknowledging both its function and limitation (Byng-Hall, 1995).

The psychotherapist's task is to *de-mythologise without desecrating*—to honour the symbolic value of myths while freeing the client from their literal authority (Byng-Hall, 1995; Wachtel, 2019).

10.5. Family Patterns and Structures

Every family is an organised system, defined by its interactional patterns, relational boundaries, and hierarchies that determine the functioning and psychological development of its members. The family's internal structure governs how individuals relate to one another, how they adapt to stress, and how symptoms emerge or are maintained. When these patterns become rigid or dysfunctional, they can perpetuate distress across generations (Metcalf, 2011; Carr, 2012).

The family system not only shapes emotional regulation and attachment patterns but also influences meaning-making processes, self-concept, and behavioural responses. Dysfunctional patterns thus affect multiple levels of the self—biological (stress reactivity), emotional (anxiety and fusion), cognitive (rigid beliefs), psychodynamic (internalised roles), and relational (interactional cycles).

The family functions as a system of interdependent *subsystems*—smaller relational units with specific tasks and rules of interaction (Carr, 2012). These include: (1) The marital subsystem, which provides companionship, intimacy, and mutual support; (2) The parental subsystem, responsible for caregiving, nurturing, and establishing family leadership; and (3) The sibling subsystem, which offers a context for learning cooperation, competition, and social negotiation.

Each individual is both a subsystem in themselves and part of multiple overlapping subsystems (Kerr, 2003). In turn, the family operates within broader systems such as the extended family, community, and culture—a concept known as *holon*, meaning a subsystem that is simultaneously a whole and a part (Kerr & Bowen, 1988).

Subsystems interact through implicit rules that determine inclusion, exclusion, and proximity. These rules, known as *boundaries*, shape the permeability between members and subsystems. Boundaries may be clear, diffuse, or disengaged, and their configuration profoundly affects both the individual's differentiation and the family's flexibility (Kets de Vries, Carlock, & Florent-Treacy, 2007).

10.5.1. Boundaries and Family Functioning

Clear boundaries represent the optimal balance between autonomy and connectedness. Family members are emotionally involved yet maintain personal identity and independence. The system allows for open communication, emotional expression, and negotiated leadership. Families with clear boundaries are characterised by mutual respect, emotional safety, and a capacity to repair conflicts (Carr, 2012). Typical features include: (1) Emotional openness combined with respect for individuality; (2) Acceptance of all feelings as valid and discussable; (3) Recognition and forgiveness of mistakes; (4) Shared leadership within generations; and (5) Unconditional love despite conflict or error.

From an ISP perspective, clear boundaries correspond to a *balanced self-structure,* where the individual integrates both emotional resonance (core self) and reflective function (plastic self). Such environments support secure attachment, resilience, and self-differentiation.

In contrast, *diffuse boundaries* emerge in families characterised by excessive emotional enmeshment. The self becomes blurred within relationships—members are overly involved in one another's lives and find it difficult to separate personal emotions from collective affect. There is a chronic lack of privacy, independence, and internal boundaries. Parents in such families often intrude in the children's lives under the guise of protection or care (Metcalf, 2011).

These families are typically dominated by anxiety, hypervigilance, and over-responsibility. Members call each other multiple times a day, catastrophise minor issues, and interpret distance as rejection. Though the intention is connection, the outcome is dependency and fusion (Carr, 2012). Rigid or over-involved families often show the following characteristics: (1) Control of emotional expression through shame or fear; (2) Emphasis on compliance, obedience, and loyalty; (3) Punitive or moralising responses to mistakes; (4) Transgenerational repetition of rules and rituals; and (5) A family identity based on duty rather than authenticity.

Such systems maintain equilibrium through emotional control rather than differentiation. Within the ISP model, this corresponds to *fusion at the core level*—the inability to distinguish one's affective experience from that of significant others. The pseudo-self develops as an adaptation to relational anxiety, leading to internal conflicts between the need for autonomy and the fear of rejection.

At the opposite extreme are *disengaged families*, in which boundaries are rigid, impermeable, and isolating. Members are emotionally detached and often disconnected from one another's experiences. Parents may consider this detachment a form of respect for autonomy, but it frequently reflects avoidance of intimacy and emotional neglect (Carr, 2012). Disengaged–chaotic systems exhibit: (1) Minimal emotional connection and lack of leadership; (2) Poorly defined rules and inconsistent boundaries; (3) Absence of shared meaning or emotional support; (4) Parental unawareness of children's inner worlds; and (5) Repetition of emotional detachment across generations.

In ISP terms, disengagement reflects a *split between the core and external self:* emotions are dissociated from interpersonal functioning, leading to relational avoidance, existential loneliness, and difficulties forming secure attachments.

Boundaries also manifest through hierarchies that define authority, responsibility, and caregiving roles. A well-functioning hierarchy ensures parental leadership, generational boundaries, and protection for the child's developmental needs (Carr, 2012).

However, dysfunctional hierarchies distort these roles:

(1) Diffuse Parent–Child Hierarchy: Parents fear asserting authority or discipline due to guilt or the desire to be the child's friend. The child thus gains disproportionate power, often leading to anxiety or behavioural acting out;

(2) Disengaged Parent–Child Hierarchy: Parents are unaware of or indifferent to the child's emotional and behavioural life. While rules may exist formally, they are inconsistently applied, leading to insecurity and lack of containment; and

(3) Child–Parent Hierarchy (Parentification): The parent abdicates the caregiving role, and the child assumes responsibility for emotional or practical needs within the family. This reversal of roles constitutes a major risk factor for anxiety, perfectionism, and identity diffusion in adulthood.

In all three cases, hierarchical confusion compromises the development of a coherent self.

10.5.2. Alliances, Coalitions and Triangles

Alliances form when family members unite to achieve a goal or maintain emotional stability. These can be adaptive—such as cooperation between parents, or maladaptive when based on exclusion or manipulation (Metcalf, 2011).

Coalitions occur when two or more members align *against* another member. For example, one parent and a child may form a coalition against the other parent. These coalitions serve defensive purposes, managing anxiety by redirecting attention from underlying conflict toward an external "problem person."

A *triangle* is a specific form of coalition involving three people, where tension between two members is stabilised by involving a third (Kerr & Bowen, 1988). When anxiety increases between two members, the third is unconsciously drawn in to diffuse emotional tension. For instance, in a marital conflict, the parents might focus on a child's behaviour, turning the child into the symptom-bearer of the family's anxiety.

Triangles can also be *transgenerational*, such as when a child allies with a grandparent against a parent. This pattern emerges when one member seeks external support to balance power disparities within the immediate dyad (Metcalf, 2011).

Deflection, or *detouring*, is another variant of this mechanism: parents shift their focus onto the child to avoid confronting their own marital issues. The child then becomes the container for unresolved parental affect—a process often misinterpreted as individual pathology but more accurately understood as *systemic symptom formation.*

The individual's identity is shaped through participation in relational triads, often replaying early attachment patterns. Therapeutic intervention seeks to restore direct emotional communication and disentangle the client from unconscious loyalty dynamics.

Structural patterns are rarely confined to one generation. Families tend to replicate boundary styles, hierarchies, and relational alliances across time. A disengaged parental system often produces emotionally distant adults, while diffuse families tend to create enmeshed couples in the next generation (Metcalf, 2011; Carr, 2012).

From the perspective of Integrative Strategic Psychotherapy, such repetition reflects the *transmission of unconscious relational templates*—internal working models that determine how the individual navigates proximity, autonomy, and power. These templates operate implicitly, guiding emotional expectations and behavioural choices long after the original family system is left behind.

Transgenerational structures are therefore both relational and symbolic: they sustain invisible contracts of loyalty and belief. For instance, a family that values sacrifice over autonomy may unconsciously perpetuate dependency and guilt across generations, despite overt aspirations for freedom.

10.6. Intergenerational and Transgenerational Patterns

Human behaviour, emotion, and identity are shaped not only by personal experience but also by the inherited legacies of one's family system. Patterns of thought, emotion, and relationship are transmitted across generations through both explicit and implicit channels—genetic, epigenetic, emotional, and symbolic. These patterns influence how individuals perceive themselves, their families, and the world. In Integrative Strategic Psychotherapy (ISP), such transgenerational dynamics are viewed as expressions of continuity between the proto-self, core self, and plastic self, connecting the individual's internal organisation with ancestral narratives and systemic loyalties that span time.

10.6.1. Intergenerational Transmission and Its Mechanisms

Intergenerational transmission refers to the process by which beliefs, attitudes, and behaviours are passed directly from one generation to another through conscious or unconscious modelling, reinforcement, and identification (Jones, 2012). Families are living systems that store and communicate memory across generations, and children inevitably absorb the emotional atmosphere, coping styles, and relational scripts of their parents.

Research has consistently demonstrated that various forms of psychopathology in children—such as anxiety, depression, and behavioural difficulties—often emerge within the relational and emotional architecture of the family system (Ende, 2009). While a genetic component may contribute to vulnerability—for instance, certain genetic polymorphisms influence susceptibility to stress, temperament, and emotional reactivity (Van de Rakt et al., 2009)—environmental and relational factors exert a far more substantial impact on the persistence and expression of maladaptive patterns.

Parental practices are central in shaping this process. Bailey et al. (2009) emphasise that parental warmth, discipline, and emotional availability are crucial mediators of intergenerational behavioural transmission. Children learn through both direct instruction and *modelling*, internalising their caregivers' ways of handling conflict, expressing emotion, and coping with distress. When caregivers display destructive coping mechanisms—such as substance misuse, violence, or avoidance—these behaviours may be replicated by children, establishing what sociologists have termed the "cycle of deprivation." This concept describes patterns of deprivation, neglect, or abuse that repeat across generations, manifesting as early school dropout, domestic violence, teenage pregnancy, or addictions.

In ISP, intergenerational learning occurs along multiple levels of the self. The proto-self internalises the somatic rhythms of caregiving (soothing, synchrony, or neglect); the core self encodes emotional patterns of safety, threat, or attachment; and the plastic self perpetuates these relational experiences. Thus, intergenerational patterns form not only through behavioural imitation but through the integration of bodily, emotional, and symbolic memories.

10.6.2. Transgenerational Transmission and The Unconscious

While intergenerational transmission refers to direct behavioural continuity, transgenerational transmission encompasses the unconscious processes by which unprocessed emotions, traumas, and relational dynamics are carried beyond direct experience. This form of inheritance often bypasses awareness, operating through implicit emotional fields, silences, myths, and family secrets (Nichols, 2010).

From an ISP perspective, transgenerational transmission represents a form of *intersubjective inheritance*—an ongoing dialogue between the living and their ancestors, through which unconscious content is maintained within family systems.

It links individual self-organisation to the collective emotional field, transmitting implicit patterns of attachment, loss, and loyalty.

Carr (2012) suggests that such unconscious legacies frequently arise through projection processes: parents attribute disowned or unresolved parts of themselves onto their children, who become the "carriers" of unintegrated emotional material. The child who bears such projections often becomes the least differentiated member of the family, functioning as an emotional regulator for others. As adults, these individuals may repeat similar relational configurations by choosing partners who mirror the emotional structure of their family of origin, perpetuating unresolved dynamics across generations.

Within ISP, this can be conceptualised as a relational homeostasis between *fusion* and *differentiation*: the inherited tension between belonging to the system (the ancestral "we") and defining the self as a separate entity.

Nelson (1990) described family life as composed of four interrelated dimensions: facts, psychology, transactions, and ethics. *Facts* refer to observable realities such as family structure, socioeconomic conditions, or birth order. *Psychology* includes the emotional and cognitive patterns shared by family members—the internal family climate. *Transactions* encompass habitual interactional patterns, including communication, boundaries, and alliances. *Ethics* represents the moral equilibrium of giving and receiving—the sense of justice within family relationships.

When ethical balance is disrupted, invisible loyalties arise: unspoken obligations binding individuals to their family's emotional history (Boszormenyi-Nagy & Spark, 1973; Nelson, 1990). A neglected child, for instance, may unconsciously reproduce neglect toward their own offspring, interpreting self-care as betrayal of their parents. This *intergenerational justice* preserves systemic equilibrium at the cost of individual well-being.

In ISP terms, such dynamics represent distortions within the *relational level*: empathy becomes entangled with guilt, and autonomy is sacrificed to maintain ancestral belonging. Therapeutic work thus involves identifying these hidden loyalties and transforming them into conscious, balanced commitments.

Each person carries within them *internalised relational maps*—implicit blueprints of how relationships function, formed through early attachment and repeated across adulthood (Carr, 2012). These maps shape expectations of intimacy, trust, and conflict. When unexamined, these maps compel the individual to recreate familiar emotional climates. The psychotherapist's task is to help the client *disidentify* from these inherited templates, facilitating new patterns of perception and connection that honour both the past and the present.

Families sustain coherence through *scripts*—recurring storylines that define roles, motivations, and relational expectations (Nelson, 1990). These scripts may serve adaptive or defensive purposes, providing continuity but also perpetuating rigidity. Nelson identified four principal types: (1) Replicative scripts, in which individuals replay experiences from their family of origin; (2) Corrective scripts, which attempt to invert past experiences ("I will never be like my parents"); (3) Improvised scripts, spontaneously created to meet new relational demands; and (4) Underlying scripts, the deeper narrative structures binding the visible ones together.

Therapeutic work helps the client uncover these patterns, distinguish between authentic and inherited motives, and construct a more flexible life narrative aligned with the integrated self.

Symptoms within families often serve *systemic* rather than merely individual functions. Nelson (1990) and Carr (2012) suggest that symptomatic behaviour performs two complementary roles: (1) It continues the dynamic of the family of origin, maintaining the family's emotional equilibrium; and (2) It supports the partner's unconscious repetition of their own familial role, thereby preserving couple homeostasis.

In this view, the symptom is both a message and a compromise—an attempt by the core self to resolve a loyalty conflict between individuation and belonging. ISP interprets symptoms as meaningful communications embedded in relational fields rather than isolated pathologies. Healing occurs when the client can recognise the *function* of the symptom and consciously renegotiate its purpose.

Belief systems organise the family's sense of identity, coherence, and meaning (Feltham & Horton, 2009). However, when these systems become overly rigid, they inhibit emotional flexibility and adaptation to life-cycle transitions. Families may cling to outdated myths of sacrifice, success, or silence that once ensured survival but now constrain growth.

The genogram—a multigenerational map of family relationships and patterns—is a cornerstone of transgenerational assessment (Lieberman, 1979). By charting at least three generations, therapists can identify recurrent motifs such as: (1) Repeating relational roles (rescuer, victim, scapegoat, or outsider); (2) Cycles of loss, migration, or illness; (3) Birth-order parallels (e.g., middle children consistently assuming caretaker roles); and (4) Symbolic prohibitions or "family rules" (e.g., "only one artist per generation").

Such findings illuminate unconscious loyalties and conflicts, allowing clients to understand how their current life fits within the family's larger narrative. Interestingly, transgenerational repetitions sometimes *skip* a generation, re-emerging as if awaiting resolution. These dormant emotional patterns can be reactivated by similar life circumstances, signifying the unfinished business of the family's emotional system.

The ISP approach addresses transgenerational material through a four-phase process:

1. Mapping: The psychotherapist and client co-construct the multigenerational narrative through genograms, timelines, and symbolic representations. This phase fosters curiosity rather than blame, inviting recognition of the system's coherence;
2. Decoding: The emotional meaning of repeated patterns is explored. For instance, a client may realise that their perfectionism is a loyalty to a parent's unfulfilled ambition;
3. Differentiation: The client learns to distinguish between inherited emotions and personal affect, developing boundaries between past and present. This stage strengthens the plastic self's integrative function; and
4. Integration: The client transforms unconscious repetition into conscious connection—honouring ancestors without reliving their suffering. Expressive methods such as letter writing, art therapy, or guided dialogues with symbolic ancestors support this transformation.

The psychotherapist's stance is empathic, non-pathologising, and systemic, acknowledging the client's embeddedness in a multigenerational network while fostering autonomy and creative renewal.

Transgenerational patterns do not merely preserve the past—they shape the family's *expectations* of the future. Lieberman (1979) observed that families often "predict" outcomes through repetition: a lineage of teachers produces another teacher, or a family marked by abandonment anticipates further loss. Such anticipatory structures act as self-fulfilling prophecies.

In ISP, this predictive function represents the plastic self's temporal integration, the way inherited narratives frame the individual's perception of possibility.

When clients internalise ancestral limitations ("no one in our family is successful in love"), they unconsciously constrain their future scripts.

Therapeutic awareness transforms *fate into authorship.* By recognising and reframing inherited meanings, clients reclaim agency and construct new trajectories that integrate their familial past without being bound by it.

10.7. The Individual and Spirituality

Spirituality represents a fundamental dimension of human experience, encompassing the search for meaning, connection, and transcendence beyond the immediate boundaries of the self. It manifests both as a cognitive construction, linked to symbolic and existential meaning—and as an embodied, affective process, arising from deep neurobiological and relational roots.

The neuroscientific study of spirituality has revealed that spiritual and mystical experiences correlate with specific patterns of brain activity, particularly within subcortical and limbic regions responsible for emotion, attention, and sensory integration.

Borg et al. (2003) found that inhibition of serotonin secretion in subcortical structures—regions associated with sensory processing and emotional modulation—correlates with materialistic or rational worldviews, while higher serotonergic activity corresponds with greater openness to spiritual experience and self-transcendence. Similarly, Kurup and Kurup (2003) observed that variations in dopaminergic and serotonergic functioning may underlie differences in spiritual inclination, suggesting that neurochemical diversity partly explains the range of spiritual experiences among individuals.

From this perspective, spirituality emerges from neurobiological systems that mediate affective atonement and perceptual integration—the same systems fundamental to attachment and emotional regulation. Early emotional experiences, especially preverbal forms of resonance such as gaze, rhythm, touch, and tone, shape the neural maps that later facilitate or inhibit access to spiritual states (Nelson, 2009).

Neuroendocrine systems also play a significant role. Endorphins, oxytocin, and melatonin—hormones deeply involved in attachment, circadian rhythm, and affect regulation—are associated with states of mystical absorption and transcendence (Hill & Persinger, 2003). These biochemical mediators link early relational safety with the later capacity for spiritual surrender and awe.

Genetic research supports the hypothesis that spiritual orientation is partly heritable. Waller et al. (1990) demonstrated that while religious affiliation is predominantly influenced by cultural and familial factors, spiritual *tendencies,* such as openness, intuition, and transcendent sensitivity—show moderate heritability. Later twin studies confirmed that genetic variance accounts for approximately 25–35% of individual differences in spiritual or religious interests (Koenig et al., 2005; Kapogiannis et al., 2009).

These findings suggest that spiritual propensity results from complex polygenic interactions influencing neurotransmitter systems (particularly dopamine and serotonin), limbic regulation, and temperament traits such as absorption, empathy, and novelty seeking. However, genetic potential only becomes expressed within supportive relational and cultural contexts—again highlighting the relational roots of spiritual development.

Neuroimaging research (Newberg & Newberg, 2005; D'Aquili & Newberg, 1999; Nelson, 2009) identifies specific neural correlates of religious and spiritual experience: (1) Right frontal and temporal lobes – implicated in emotion, empathy, and self-other integration; (2) Cingulate gyrus – mediating attention, empathy, and moral cognition; (3) Parietal lobes – responsible for spatial orientation and self-boundaries; and (4) Limbic system (amygdala, hippocampus, hypothalamus), regulating affect, memory, and autonomic arousal.

During meditation, prayer, or ecstatic experience, activity in these networks changes significantly. The right parietal lobe—associated with self–world differentiation—often shows *deactivation*, corresponding to the reported loss of boundaries and the sense of unity characteristic of mystical states (Newberg et al., 2001). Simultaneously, the limbic and frontal regions display *synchronous activation*, integrating emotion and awareness into a coherent, unitive state.

D'Aquili and Newberg (1999) describe five categories of excitatory events that give rise to such experiences: (1) Tropotrophic activation, producing relaxed vigilance (e.g., meditation, contemplation); (2) Ergotropic activation, generating alert focus and flow; (3) Tropotrophic with ergotropic co-activation, yielding a state of oceanic bliss; (4) Ergotropic with tropotrophic co-activation, producing ecstatic arousal; and (5) Maximal stimulation of both systems, resulting in profound mystical absorption.

These patterns mirror the oscillation between the parasympathetic and sympathetic branches of the autonomic nervous system, demonstrating how deep spiritual experience reflects a unique neurophysiological synchrony rather than dissociation or pathology.

From a cognitive neuroscience perspective, spiritual ideas and experiences are structured by what D'Aquili and Newberg (1999) called cognitive operators, fundamental mental functions through which the brain organises perception and meaning. Among these, the holistic operator plays a central role in religious and mythic cognition.

The holistic operator, located primarily in the right parietal lobe, enables the brain to perceive patterns and gestalts that connect disparate elements into a unified whole. When activated—through ritual, meditation, myth, or aesthetic experience, it allows individuals to integrate paradoxical realities (life and death, finite and infinite) into a coherent symbolic field.

Thus, myths and religious symbols are not arbitrary cultural constructs but *neurocognitive expressions* of the human tendency toward integration and coherence. They allow the individual to face existential anxieties through structured meaning systems (Nelson, 2009; Buss, 2002).

Attachment theory provides a bridge between emotional regulation and spiritual experience. Siegel (2012) and Pargament (2013) note that early secure attachment fosters the neurobiological foundation for trust, surrender, and openness—qualities mirrored in spiritual experience. Conversely, insecure attachment may predispose individuals either to rigid religiosity (seeking control and certainty) or to spiritual avoidance (fear of dependence or surrender).

Nelson (2009) and Hill & Persinger (2003) suggest that the *transpersonal capacity* for unity and transcendence develops from early non-verbal synchrony—eye contact, mirroring, shared rhythms. These experiences sculpt neural circuits linking the limbic system and prefrontal cortex, supporting both affect regulation and symbolic meaning-making.

Working with spirituality in psychotherapy requires sensitivity, humility, and reflexivity. The psychotherapist's role is not to promote a particular belief system but to facilitate the client's exploration of personal meaning, connection, and transcendence.

Key therapeutic principles in ISP include: (1) Respect for diversity – Spirituality manifests in secular, religious, aesthetic, or existential forms; each is valid; (2) Dialogical neutrality – The therapist remains curious and empathic, not directive, about the client's beliefs; (3) Integration, not conversion – The aim is to harmonise spiritual experiences with emotional and cognitive systems, preventing dissociation or inflation; (4) Symbolic exploration – Dreams, rituals, metaphors, and creative expression provide access to the transpersonal field; and (5) Embodied awareness – Breath, rhythm, and sensory grounding connect spiritual insight with the body, preventing dissociative spirituality.

For individuals with trauma histories, spiritual experiences may sometimes trigger anxiety or fragmentation. In such cases, the psychotherapist helps the client regulate arousal, integrate meaning, and differentiate authentic transcendence from defensive dissociation (Pargament, 2013; Siegel, 2012).

In integrative practice, spirituality also carries an ethical dimension—it informs how individuals relate to others and to life itself. Compassion, gratitude, forgiveness, and humility are seen as expressions of spiritual maturity and indicators of a differentiated self.

10.8. Multiculturality

According to Aasnani and Hoffmann (2012), several principles must guide the activity of psychotherapists, principles present in all existing cross-cultural psychotherapeutic models. These themes and common features are:

(1) Culturally informed and accurate assessment of the presenting problem. As psychotherapists, we must be aware of the connection between a client's presenting problem and the cultural environment from which they come. All of our clients are unique individuals, and regardless of their cultural affiliation, we must remember that any group is heterogeneous. On the other hand, we must inform ourselves about the client's beliefs that might interfere with certain techniques or interventions;

(2) Education regarding specific cultural norms and consulting specialized literature about culturally specific treatment techniques. Clients benefit most from treatment techniques adapted to the culture they belong to. Furthermore, psychotherapists must be aware of the cultural norms of the community their client belongs to, in order to reduce communication barriers as much as possible;

(3) Training psychotherapists in cultural competence. Depending on the cultural competence of the psychotherapist, the therapeutic alliance will be more or less effective. To be culturally competent, a psychotherapist must first be aware of their own cultural and racial identity and how this may impact the way they work with clients;

(4) Exploring the client's perspective regarding psychotherapy and the nature of the therapeutic relationship. Some cultural minorities consider it a social stigma to seek psychotherapy. As a result, it may be necessary to address this stigma as a first step in treatment. Another aspect to consider is how the client perceives their relationship with the psychotherapist. Most psychotherapeutic approaches in the U.S. and Western Europe emphasize collaboration in the therapeutic relationship, but for members of certain cultures, such an approach may create confusion, as individuals from Eastern cultures may prefer a more directive and authoritative approach from the psychotherapist. Moreover, psychotherapy often involves direct questioning, which in some cultures may be perceived as disrespectful;

(5) Granting respect. It is important to let the client fully express their story and explain how their cultural affiliation has influenced the problem they are facing. In this context, it is important to validate the client's experience, including experiences related to racial or cultural discrimination, or oppression;

(6) Identifying and incorporating the client's strengths as resources in treatment. Identifying the client's resources is common in psychotherapy, but we can take this further by identifying those culturally influenced strengths or culture itself as a resource for the client. Additionally, culture influences certain individual abilities (such as cooking, fishing, animal raising, etc.) as well as their coping mechanisms. On the other hand, modesty regarding one's own qualities may be a norm in some cultures; and

(7) Using culturally specific techniques. While it is natural to use treatment techniques that have proven effective, we must be prepared to modify these techniques in a culturally sensitive manner. For example, we may confront the client's core beliefs, but we must be careful not to attack the client's cultural belief system, especially if the psychotherapist belongs to a different culture.

References

Abraham, N., & Torok, M. (1994). *The shell and the kernel: Renewals of psychoanalysis.* University of Chicago Press.

Bailey, J. A., Hill, K. G., Oesterle, S., Hawkins, J. D., & Kosterman, R. (2009). Parenting practices and intergenerational continuity in substance use. *Journal of Adolescent Health, 45*(2), 123–129.

Borg, J., Andrée, B., Soderstrom, H., & Farde, L. (2003). The serotonin system and spiritual experiences. *American Journal of Psychiatry, 160*(11), 1965–1969.

Boszormenyi-Nagy, I., & Spark, G. M. (1973). *Invisible loyalties: Reciprocity in intergenerational family therapy.* Harper & Row.

Bowen, M. (1978). *Family therapy in clinical practice.* Jason Aronson.

Buller, D. (2005). *Adapting minds: Evolutionary psychology and the persistent quest for human nature.* MIT Press.

Buss, D. (2002). *The evolution of desire: Strategies of human mating.* Basic Books.

Byng-Hall, J. (1995). *Rewriting family scripts: Improvisation and systems change.* Guilford Press.

Carr, A. (2012). *Family therapy: Concepts, process and practice* (3rd ed.). Wiley-Blackwell.

D'Aquili, E. G., & Newberg, A. B. (1999). *The mystical mind: Probing the biology of religious experience.* Fortress Press.

Dunham, S. M., Dermer, S. B., & Carlson, J. (2011). Dysfunctional family roles and the family projection process: Reconsidered and redefined. *The Family Journal, 19*(3), 269–273.

Ende, J. (2009). Family systems and child psychopathology: Transmission and context. *Journal of Family Psychology, 23*(4), 515–523.

Feltham, C., & Horton, I. (Eds.). (2009). *The Sage handbook of counselling and psychotherapy* (2nd ed.). Sage Publications.

Ferreira, A. J. (1966). Family myths: A framework for family therapy. *Archives of General Psychiatry, 15*(4), 333–347.

Garbarino, J., & Gratch, L. (1995). *Psychological maltreatment of children and youth.* Jossey-Bass.

Ginot, E. (2007). Intersubjectivity and neuroscience: Understanding enactments and their therapeutic significance. *Psychoanalytic Psychology, 24*(2), 317–332.

Hall, C. S. (1981). *A primer of Freudian psychology.* Penguin.

Hill, P. W., & Persinger, M. A. (2003). The neuropsychological basis of religious and spiritual experience. *Journal of Consciousness Studies, 10*(6–7), 51–68.

Jones, R. A. (2012). Intergenerational transmission of behaviour and family functioning. *Family Relations, 61*(3), 315–329.

Kapogiannis, D., Barbey, A. K., Su, M., Krueger, F., & Grafman, J. (2009). Neurocognitive and genetic correlates of religious belief. *Proceedings of the National Academy of Sciences, 106*(12), 4876–4881.

Kerr, M. E. (2003). *Family evaluation: An approach based on Bowen theory.* Norton.

Kerr, M. (2003). *One family's story: A primer on Bowen theory.* Bowen Center for the Study of the Family.

Kerr, M., & Bowen, M. (1988). *Family evaluation: An approach based on Bowen theory.* Norton.

Kets de Vries, M. F. R., Carlock, R. S., & Florent-Treacy, E. (2007). *Family business on the couch: A psychological perspective.* Wiley.

Koenig, L. B., McGue, M., & Iacono, W. G. (2005). Genetic and environmental influences on religiousness. *Journal of Personality, 73*(2), 471–488.

Kurup, R. K., & Kurup, P. A. (2003). Hypothalamic digoxin, hemispheric chemical dominance, and spirituality. *International Journal of Neuroscience, 113*(4), 479–493.

Lieberman, M. A. (1979). Family therapy: An overview and critique. *Annual Review of Psychology, 30*, 591–608.

Lieberman, M. (1979). *The family life cycle: A conceptual framework for family therapy.* Gardner Press.

Maslach, C., Stapp, J., & Santee, R. T. (1985). Individuation: Conceptual analysis and assessment. *Journal of Personality and Social Psychology, 49*(3), 729–738.

McAdams, D. P. (2001). The psychology of life stories. *Review of General Psychology, 5*(2), 100–122.

Metcalf, L. (2011). *Marriage and family therapy: A practice-oriented approach.* Springer Publishing.

Nelson, P. (2009). *The spiritual door: Neuropsychology of transcendent experience.* Palgrave Macmillan.

Nelson, T. (1990). *The intimacy paradox: Personal authority in the family system.* Brunner/Mazel.

Nelson, T. (1990). *Family systems and ethical balance.* Guilford Press.

Newberg, A. B., & Newberg, D. (2005). *Why God won't go away: Brain science and the biology of belief.* Ballantine Books.

Nichols, M. (2010). *Family therapy: Concepts and methods* (9th ed.). Pearson.

Papero, D. (1990). *Bowen family systems theory.* Allyn & Bacon.

Pargament, K. I. (2013). *Spiritually integrated psychotherapy: Understanding and addressing the sacred.* Guilford Press.

Pine, F. (2003). *Developmental theory and clinical process.* Yale University Press.

Popescu, O. M. (2021). *Psihoterapie integrativă strategică. Vol.1. Teorie și aplicații practice. Snagov: Letras.*

Schick, B., de Villiers, P., de Villiers, J., & Hoffmeister, R. (2007). Language and Theory of Mind: A study of deaf children. *Child Development, 78*(2), 376–396.

Schore, A. N. (2021). *Right brain psychotherapy.* Norton.

Siegel, D. J. (2012). *The developing mind: How relationships and the brain interact to shape who we are* (2nd ed.). Guilford Press.

Stern, D. N. (2004). *The present moment in psychotherapy and everyday life.* Norton.

Thomas, L., & Malone, T. (1979). *Theories of psychotherapy.* Lippincott.

Van de Rakt, M., Nieuwbeerta, P., & de Graaf, N. D. (2009). Genetic and environmental influences on intergenerational transmission. *American Journal of Sociology, 114*(3), 801–830.

Wachtel, E. F. (2019). *Therapeutic communication: Knowing what to say when.* Guilford Press.

Waller, N. G., Kojetin, B. A., Bouchard, T. J., Lykken, D. T., & Tellegen, A. (1990). Genetic and environmental influences on religious interests. *Journal of Personality, 58*(1), 163–173.

www.ingramcontent.com/pod-product-compliance
Lightning Source LLC
Chambersburg PA
CBHW061352240926
51846CB00007B/1378
9786303126326